R

RABELAIS

M. A. SCREECH

Fielden Professor of French
Language and Literature
University College London

CORNELL UNIVERSITY PRESS
Ithaca, New York

First published 1979 by Cornell University Press.

Library of Congress Cataloging in Publication Data

Screech, Michael Andrew.
   Rabelais.

   Bibliography: p.
   Includes index.
   1. Rabelais, François, 1490 (ca.)–1553?–Criticism
and interpretation. I. Title.
PQ1694.S36   843'.3   79–2448
ISBN 0–8014–1268–4

Printed in Great Britain

FOR ANNE
AND FOR MATT, TIM AND TOBY

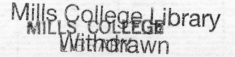

Contents

Contents

x   *Contents*

Preface

The reader of Rabelais does not always have an easy time. The past, as Sir Ernst Gombrich has soberly pointed out, is going away from us at a frightening pace.[1] So much of Rabelais which was no doubt fairly clear a hundred years ago has now become remote from a public which shares less and less of his assumptions and which has less and less contact with the erudition, the commonplace knowledge and accepted wisdom which he could take for granted. At the same time some scholarly studies of Rabelais have made quite remarkable progress in the last fifty years, while others have raised fresh questions or spread new fogs. The problem is how to make the fruits of scholarship accessible to the reader who wants to read Rabelais with that peculiarly satisfying pleasure which comes from understanding. An intelligent and charming American student once confessed to me that she had given up all attempts to understand Rabelais himself, but still hoped to understand some of the footnotes. . . .

The aim of this book is to make Rabelais more accessible to a wider public, without drowning readers in a mass of polyglot annotations. There still are a few footnotes, but they can be ignored by anyone prepared to take on trust what is said in the text or who simply does not want to pursue his inquiries any further. I have tried to reduce the footnotes as far as possible to chapter-and-verse reference to Rabelais's writings or to similar matters. To refer regularly to modern studies on Rabelais would not infrequently lead to that peculiarly unpleasing necessity of referring to books, editions or articles written by myself. No amount of modest protestation can make that other than distasteful to all concerned. I have normally left scholarly controversy aside. Such things should be found, if anywhere, in the learned reviews. The ideas expressed in this book have not all come unaided out of my own head. Some of the studies which have helped me are mentioned in the suggestions for further reading found at the end. But many other excellent studies are not: they all appear in the standard bibliographies to which the Renaissance scholar is soon led by his reading.

One of the difficulties placed in the way of an understanding of Rabelais

[1] Ernst Gombrich, *In Search of Cultural History*, London 1969, p.45.

is the mass of preconceptions attached to the adjective *Rabelaisian*, which often means little more than lavatory humour leading to gigantic guffawing. Insofar as Rabelais the man is known at all, he is primarily thought of as an ex-monk turned doctor. Many readers naturally find it hard to square this simplified picture with the widespread assumption among cultured men and women that Rabelais is an author to be placed beside Homer and Shakespeare as one of those geniuses who seem to breast-feed all the others. Excellent studies in French, English, German and Italian have charted at least some of the ways in which Rabelais has influenced European literature. Others have striven to explain his meaning or his art. Studies of Rabelais have come from Russia and Japan, as well as from more obvious places. Many of them throw great light on Rabelais's literary and philosophical achievement. But lurking in the background is another less flattering judgment, summed up by Dr Gervase Fen who placed Rabelais and James Joyce firmly in the category of unreadable books. Not everybody on first reading finds Rabelais, in the words of the poet, 'irresistible'. But everyone soon finds that Rabelais will not fit into easy categories. An admirer of Trollope who has accepted Rabelais as fit reading for Archdeacon Grantly, because he secretly enjoyed his merry jests when he should have been preparing his sermons, may then have troubling glimpses of what Rabelais can mean today for men struggling under tyranny, when he reads his Solzhenitsyn.[2]

To understand Rabelais, to pass from easy and trivial popular conceptions to an understanding of the text itself, requires quite a lot of effort. Most readers who manage to persevere beyond the early difficulties and discouragements do indeed find in Rabelais a breadth, a depth and a scope of comedy which is strictly *sui generis*, amply justifying their efforts. The rewards, in sheer delight, can last a lifetime. Rabelais can also claim to be a vehicle for a peculiar kind of wisdom.

Yet it is true that almost everything conspires to put the casual reader off. The French of Rabelais is sometimes very difficult indeed. Scholarly and literary Frenchmen have been known to classify Rabelais as the most difficult author of any period writing in French. It may be a comfort to remember that an English speaker who knows French well may find Rabelais's language less of a problem than many Frenchmen do: so many of his words, lost to French, linger on in English. And Rabelais's assumptions about this world and the next are much closer to Shakespeare's than they are to, say, Racine's or Molière's.

[2] Cf. Chateaubriand, *Essai sur la littérature anglaise*, Paris 1836, 1, p.192f. E. Crispin, *The Moving Toyshop*, London (1946) 1971, p.83. G. Barker, 'To my Mother', in *The Penguin Book of Contemporary Verse*, ed. K. Arlott, Harmondsworth 1959, p.219: 'Sitting as huge as Asia, seismic with laughter, Gin and chicken helpless in her Irish hand, Irresistible as Rabelais....' A. Solzenitsyn, *Cancer Ward*, Harmondsworth (1971) 1974, p.311.

Translations are of only limited value where Rabelais's art is concerned. If a modern reader turns for help to the standard English version of Urquhart and Motteux – which is a monument in its way – he will often find himself baffled when he tries to place the English text beside the French original. Urquhart especially is a good example of the traitor translator; Scottish puritan that he was, he can rarely restrain himself from expanding the dirty bits. More modern translations may be less disloyal in one sense, but the genius fails to come through. And, with the sole exception of W. F. Smith's unobtainable version, none have enough notes (when they have any at all) to help the reader to understand what Rabelais is talking about. Rabelais should really be tackled in the original, unless that is quite impossible. If elementary help is required, it is best to turn to Demerson's readable modern French version, printed in parallel columns with an uncritical text. The best way of all is to read Rabelais in the scholarly editions of the various works published by Droz of Geneva, making at least occasional reference to the incomplete and obsolescent *Edition Critique*, especially in the case of *Pantagruel*.

For readers with little or no French I have taken care to give fairly literal translations of passages quoted from Rabelais or other French and Latin writers. (I claim no literary value for them: they are designed to elucidate the originals; no more.) I shall not assume – as Rabelais often did – that his readers all have a sound knowledge of Latin, an aspiring knowledge of Greek, a smattering of Hebrew, a genuine knowledge of Roman law, an acquaintance with Renaissance medical or philosophical commonplaces and, indeed, a grasp of the whole encyclopaedia of Renaissance learning. I hope, naturally, that this book will be of interest to specialist scholars; but the reader I most want to help towards a fuller enjoyment of Rabelais is not the specialist as such, but that Gentle Reader who would like to get to know Rabelais for his laughing wisdom and for the aesthetic experience he has to offer – not forgetting today's undergraduate who suddenly finds that this 'unreadable author' of genius occupies a large place in his syllabus. It might strengthen the resolve of Rabelais's captive audience in the second group to know that a knowledgeable Rabelais scholar whom I taught found Rabelais on his first reading to be so osbcure, so gratuitously and unfunnily obscene, that he felt a resentment against him, and against me, which lasted until he had broken through the barrier of understanding into the joy of comedy at its best and most profound.

In all the collected editions of Rabelais's works, including all trans-lations, we are invited to read the first two novels (*Pantagruel* and *Gargantua*) the wrong way round. *Gargantua*, published some two years after *Pantagruel*, is always printed first. This is because the chronology of the stories (insofar as it has any validity at all) naturally places the events related about Gargantua, the father of Pantagruel, before those related in *Pantagruel*.

Up to a point Rabelais does adhere to the fictional chronology of his Chronicles, despite the fact that *Gargantua* pokes fun at events which had not even happened when *Pantagruel* was first printed. This can cause a great deal of confusion, but the confusion is at least partly intended. Rabelais encouraged it by publishing collected editions in which *Gargantua* precedes *Pantagruel*. But to study them in this order thwarts any serious attempt to understand the development of Rabelais's art and thought. One jumps from *Gargantua*, 1534, or perhaps even 1535, back to *Pantagruel*, probably 1532. As if this were not enough, the collected editions lead straight on from *Pantagruel* to the *Tiers Livre de Pantagruel*, 1546. This results in some writers referring to Rabelais's first book as his second one, his second one as his first. Then, ignoring the version of the *Quart Livre de Pantagruel* published in 1548 – and the *Sciomachie* published in 1549 – we are presented with the full revised *Quart Livre* of 1552. Then follows the so-called *Cinquiesme Livre de Pantagruel*, which first saw the light in 1564, some eleven years after Rabelais's death, and which itself was preceded in 1562 by a partial and significantly different version entitled *l'Isle Sonante, par M. Françoys Rabelays, qui n'a point encores esté imprimée ne mise en lumière*. . . . Having reached 1564 in the collected editions, the reader then finds he is presented with a job-lot of *opuscules*: the *Pantagrueline Prognostication* for 1533, but never in the first version, always in the very different versions published in 1542 or even 1553. Then follow two incomplete *Almanachs* for 1533 and 1535, as well as letters in French, and in elegant Latin with copious Greek interpolations, Latin prefaces to erudite medical and legal works in Greek and Latin dating from 1532, a Latin preface to Marliani's *Topography of Rome* dated 1534, a Greek epigram, a French poem, and so on. The most important of Rabelais's Latin letters, the one he wrote to Erasmus in 1532, may follow, headed (as it is for example in Marty-Laveaux's and Plattard's editions), not *To Erasmus* but *To Bernard Sallignac* – often without a word of explanation.

The useful *Edition Critique* of the *Oeuvres de Rabelais* shares all these defects – or would do so if it were complete. The first volume, *Gargantua*, appeared in 1913. We have now reached the *Quart Livre*, for the second fascicule of it was published in 1955, though we still await not only the third fascicule but the first. A worrying rumour would have it that a World War is required between each volume. This critical edition is now in the charge of M. Robert Marichal, whose work on Rabelais is worth reading for its historical precision, even though the little of the *Quart Livre* that has been published so far suggests some weaknesses where theology is concerned. But earlier volumes are not always as accurate as they should be. Moreover the *Edition Critique* takes as its base-text of *Pantagruel* and *Gargantua* the revised and partially expurgated versions of 1542; the principal earlier versions, though not all of them, are relegated to the footnotes; others are discarded without a trace. This method of editing, current on the Continent, has the looking-glass effect of suggesting that something added in 1542 was 'lacking' in (say) 1534. To reconstitute the original text from the *Edition Critique* alone is a veritable jigsaw-puzzle, complicated by some of the pieces being wrongly cut. Nevertheless, when the full text of the *Quart Livre* is published it will constitute a major contribution to the understanding of what was the last book to appear in Rabelais's lifetime and probably his very last work of all.

The disadvantages of such a chaotic presentation of these writings are in part obvious: we are clearly hindered in our attempts to follow Rabelais from the comparatively modest *Pantagruel* of 1532 to the full comic and epic grandeur of the *Quart Livre* of 1552; moreover, works which date from the same period – *Pantagruel*, say, and the *Pantagrueline Prognostication* – are widely separated and so rarely read together. There are other and more treacherous disadvantages. The reader starts with *Gargantua*; he has barely opened the book before he has to tackle the long enigmatic poem *Les Fanfreluches antidotées*, which literally nobody today begins to understand; then, after the puzzling mixture of theology, medicine and law in chapter three, he is plunged into a serio-comic diatribe on the meaning of colours, of Egypto-Hellenic hieroglyphic emblems, and so on, as a prelude to the scatology of chapter twelve. This at least he expected to find funny; it probably leaves him vaguely disappointed or even bored. He may be tempted to give up. If he perseveres, it is to be hoped that he does not chance to fall upon the type of study which claims to help him through this maze but in fact ends up in the pit reserved for the blind led by the blind.

In this book I usually treat Rabelais's works in the order in which he published them. In the case of each book except *Pantagruel* I start, as a rule, at the beginning and go right on to the end. But there are times when the matter of widely separated chapters is best considered together. Since Rabelais does not expose some of his more complex ideas all at one go in the earlier books, it has sometimes been necessary to take more than one bite at the apple – explaining his linguistic ideas, for example, more than once, first in outline, eventually in appropriate detail. Not to do this would involve the risk of antedating ideas which are found in embryo in 1532 or 1534-5, only being fully developed much later.

The method adopted in this book is a version of the one which scholars of the French Renaissance often associate with the Warburg Institute, and with the Renaissance as studied in the Department of French Language and Literature at University College London since the time that Professor D. P. Walker was a young lecturer there in the late 1940s and early 50s. The method consists in trying to place a work of art back into its fullest intellectual, historical and aesthetic context. The goal is authenticity, however tempting passing fads and fancies may be. The aim is to understand the *Tiers Livre*, say, as a book published in 1546 by a legally trained, medical and Evangelical humanist (steeped in the assumptions and stimulated by the aspirations of his day), and seeking a learned public. Whether or not the text read that way happens to flatter current fads, or the adherents of later theories, later political systems, later and greyer conceptions of man and his world, is a matter of complete indifference. Great works of art read in context have a human richness which nothing else can replace.

Rabelais did not call his stories *romans* (novels) but Chronicles. They are fictional histories. The term is a happy choice and I use it in this study. By and large the account of the Chronicles of Gargantua and Pantagruel given here is one that has emerged and developed during some thirty years of my interest in them, including over a quarter of a century spent helping University undergraduates and postgraduates to understand and appreciate them. Such an interpretation primarily arose out of long and repeated readings of Renaissance books in the British Museum, the Bodleian, University College London, the Warburg Institute, the Bibliothèque Nationale and elsewhere. I have rarely read even the most routine classical author in a modern edition, when a Renaissance one was accessible. Nevertheless, nobody lives, works or reads in a vacuum; I owe a debt to modern scholars, both to those who have established new truths or projected new insights and to those who planted seeds which germinated in other minds. It was Professor Walker who, in the late 1940s, led me to think of Rabelais and some other Renaissance authors as men engaged in a desperate game; as *homines ludentes* whose propaganda purposes were not blunt, hate-ridden explosions of prejudice but gay, balanced, harmonious forays leading to the righting of wrongs, the establishment of harmonies, the restoration of sanity. The greatest debt of all I owe to the interest, keenness and questioning of those students at home and abroad whom it has been my privilege and pleasure to try to teach.

In my own reading of Rabelais I normally use the sixteenth-century originals or photocopies of them. But to refer to them in this way in this book would be confusing, since most readers cannot have access to them. References are given to both the chapter and line number in the various texts as published by Droz of Geneva, in the series *Textes Littéraires Français*; immediately after, is normally given the corresponding reference in the *Edition Critique* when it has reached that far. This should enable quotations and allusions to be easily traced in other editions as well. Naturally, the spelling and punctuation will vary from edition to edition. I sometimes use French accents where Rabelais has none, if it seems helpful or if it avoids confusion.

A sustained attempt is made not to burden the reader with unnecessary technicalities. Long partisan excursions into areas of controversy are avoided when possible.

There is more than one side to many questions in Rabelaisian scholarship. I have nevertheless gone through my text crossing out most of the *perhapses, maybes, probablys* and *possiblys*. Such words are irritating to the reader and do not even successfully convey the feeling of scepticism any scholar must feel before the efforts of himself and others to discover the fuller truth, in the case of an author as profound and as well-read as Rabelais.

Having finished this book the reader may like to find out more about some of the questions raised, if he has not already done so. On the other hand, he may prefer to by-pass the lot and jump into his Rabelais again off the deep end.

One aspect of this book I should explain and justify at the outset. I have omitted all study of the *Isle Sonante* of 1562 and the so-called *Cinquiesme Livre* of 1564. This omission is deliberate. With another colleague I am at present working on an edition of these texts: it will be some time before the work is finished. The main arguments against their authenticity have been recently passed in review. On the other hand claims have been made to have resolved the whole question in favour of authenticity by number and computer. But the mathematically based analysis we require is not one which can show what we all know already, that Rabelais or Pseudo-Rabelais has a style different from, say, Margaret of Navarre's, but one which can differentiate, by its own criteria alone, between, say, the so-called prologue to the *Cinquiesme Livre*, a palpable fake, and other parts of that tardy Chronicle which good and sensitive critics have sometimes felt to be possibly by Rabelais.

Those who do accept the authenticity of the *Isle Sonante* or of the complete *Cinquiesme Livre* interpret Rabelais differently, especially those who read back into the four undoubtedly authentic Chronicles attitudes which they see, or which they think they see, in the volume which brings us at last to the Dive Bouteille and then back to Rabelais's homeland of Touraine, ten years or more after Rabelais himself had run his long course here on earth and had left his body to be honourably buried in Paris.

The aim of this study is to try and make sense out of the four Chronicles of Gargantua and Pantagruel which Rabelais published in the course of a busy, eventful and itinerant life. The fullest meaning of these writings can only be appreciated by the sensitive reader who is on the look-out for his plays on words and who savours them when he finds them, and by the reader who appreciates his allusive and elusive subtleties. Personally I do not enjoy studies which explain the obvious or which explain too much: to deal adequately with the detail of such matters, in addition to those I have treated in these many pages, would have made this book far, far longer, unreadable, and rightly unpublishable. I hope the picture presented here will help more readers to see the wood despite the trees: indeed, I hope they will be able, in their own reading of Rabelais, to concentrate more on the trees – to appreciate more fully the comic or philosophical detail of Rabelais's writing – precisely because the wood has been firmly sketched in for them.

My published contributions to the study of Rabelais over several years have been technical and partial. In this book I try to leave the technicalities aside and to treat Rabelais as a whole. Essentially I present Rabelais's Chronicles here as I regularly read him with students, both postgraduate and undergraduate, at University College London, and frequently with D. P. Walker's students at the Warburg Institute. For a good many years now I have felt that the insights into Rabelais which I try to get across in tutorials and so on are as interesting – and certainly as valid – as those which I have already committed to print, and so to the judgment of a wider public. This book is an attempt to make these insights more generally available.

I owe special thanks to Professor D. P. Walker, Dr Margaret Mann Phillips and Mr Colin Haycraft, who all read my typescript and made helpful suggestions which I have tried to meet. Mrs Sonia Wakely did miracles of typing from a manuscript which sometimes looked like Balzac's corrected galleys. In this she was helped by Mrs Pamela King. Mrs Sally North and Miss Anne Reeve, research assistants at University College London, helped me with their usual efficiency and unfailing, cheerful courtesy.

I owe a great debt to the Institute for Research in the Humanities of the University of Wisconsin (Madison). Although the text of this book was completed almost a year before I took up residence there as the Johnson Visiting Professor for the session 1978–9, the generous salary granted me was partly spent in advance on important visits to continental libraries. The page proofs were corrected and the index drawn up during the first semester of my stay in that elegant and friendly seat of learning. The index was kindly typed for me, with exemplary efficiency, by my colleague at Wisconsin, Mrs Loretta Freiling.

November 1978   M. A. S.

1
Humanist Comedy

The works of a comic writer of genius who lived four and a half centuries ago pose special difficulties of interpretation. These problems are more acute than those we face when we try to appreciate the tragedies of former ages. Tragedy, insofar as it is dealing with the fear of death, the destructive nature of much sexual passion, or the feeling of pity which the suffering of mankind evokes, is treating subjects which seem fairly constant pre-occupations among civilised men and women. But the comedy, the laughter, the sense of humour of differing countries and differing ages, seem to arise out of circumstances and conventions which even a sympathetic reader cannot always recognise, let alone share spon-taneously. Perhaps this is partly because comedy and humour are often linked with religious or philosophical beliefs, with ethical norms, with social morals and conventions, which are by their nature less stable and less permanent elements in human culture. There are, of course, actions, jests and plays on words, which do leap easily from country to country and across the centuries; but one only has to think of the puzzled or embarrassed silence with which an audience may greet some of Shake-speare's comics, and to compare that with the readier response the same audience may make to the anguish of Hamlet or the sufferings of King Lear, to realise that comedy is often circumscribed by time and place in a way that tragedy is not.

Many of the obscurities in Rabelais's comedy can be cleared up by patient scholarship. A jest may depend on a learned pun; on the recovery of a lost meaning for an apparently well-known word; on the identification of an historical allusion. There will remain things which defy our efforts, but scholarship has been surprisingly effective in recapturing the quality and the detail of Rabelais's humour. Not that erudition, in itself, is enough; but without the guidance which scholarship may provide, much of Rabelais has become too obscure for laughter to be spontaneously aroused.

More difficult to pin down are the basic assumptions of a comic writer. These too, in Rabelais's case, are largely recoverable, since he was a bookish man. The books he read are still available, even though one does have to travel from library to library to find them.

It is best to come to Rabelais with the minimum of preconceptions, letting his text guide us to the books which the scholar must read, if he is to be of use to those who turn to him for help and elucidation, and if he is to make Rabelais's comedy come more fully back to life. Such sources range from Plato's *Philebus*, to Lucian, Plutarch, Homer and Virgil among the ancients, to dry works of legal, medical and linguistic erudition, dating from his own and earlier times.

To these classical sources must be added Christian ones, especially the Bible and the writings of admired contemporaries such as Erasmus. These classical and Christian authorities are not merely placed side by side: they are interwoven. Rabelais, like so many of his contemporaries, is a 'syncretist' making one complex whole out of his ancient learning and his dominant evangelical religion. Rabelais is a Christian for whom Plato, Plutarch, the sceptics, the cynics, the stoics, are not totally discredited rivals; they are, with Lucian, welcome allies in the laughing battle against ignorance, error, superstition, ugliness, and wickedness. Together, they enrich Rabelais's philosophy, without attacking the normative uniqueness of the Christian revelation.

Rabelais was a humanist with widely catholic tastes. This is already true of his first two Chronicles. It is even truer of the *Tiers Livre* and the *Quart Livre*. In varying degrees Rabelais's writings are aimed, in whole or in part, at an educated readership. In the case of the *Tiers Livre*, the royal *Privilège* specifically states that it was 'the learned and the studious' who eagerly awaited the continuation of the tales of Gargantua and Pantagruel. Such studious admirers included Margaret of Navarre, the sister of Francis I. Among his less studious but powerful admirers he counted Francis I and Henry II.

Theodore Beza (later, as a Calvinist, an enemy of Rabelais) wondered what Rabelais must be like when he was serious, if he was so profound when he was jesting (Lazare Sainéan cites this, and other judgments, in his *Influence . . . de Rabelais*, 1930). It is precisely this learned, bookish quality of the *Tiers Livre* which makes it in some ways the most understandable of the Chronicles. The books Rabelais read are still available to us – provided we can read Latin and have some Greek; the authoritative classical and Christian commonplaces around which his thought revolves are those which can be found in many of the writers of the Renaissance; his legal and medical erudition may seem strange to us, but its import can be gauged with reasonable certainty from a reading of the numerous legal and medical books of the time. Yet this very recoverability of Rabelais's thought can, in another sense, be an obstacle. To recognise, to trace, and to study the books which Rabelais and his contemporaries knew requires time, trouble and patient industry. There is always a temptation to push aside the scholarship and leap in to explain what Rabelais must 'obviously' mean in the light of our temporally parochial prejudices. Such a method is disastrous: Rabelais moves in an intellectual world whose common-place wisdom is now hard-won knowledge; almost all the terms of reference of ordinarily educated humanists have been abandoned by modern European culture, some very recently. To understand Rabelais's wisdom and to appreciate his comic vision means going back in time to a period whose doubts and whose certainties were not our doubts or our certainties: at least, they do not seem to be so at first. Yet within the dusty encyclopaedic erudition of the Renaissance can be found a system of comic wisdom and moral insight which cannot be lightly dismissed as being of only historical interest.

For Rabelais, the syncretistic learning of evangelical humanists is fre-quently normative. He seems to have often set himself the task of showing that departures from the norms of evangelical humanist Christianity are not merely wrong, but laughably so. The man who worships the wrong God; does not love his neighbour as himself; worships his belly or his backside; prefers ugliness to beauty; believes he can go against the wisdom of classical adage, proverb or apophthegm, is wrong, certainly, but more than wrong – stupid.

In this book I try to be as clear and precise as possible about these norms. Where they derive from the New Testament, they still partly linger on in general culture; but those deriving from classical times, from philosophical Christianity, from Renaissance legal precepts or Renaissance mythology, have ceased to do so. Not everybody can trot out in order the four cardinal virtues, the seven deadly sins, the three injunctions inscribed on the temple at Delphi . . . And the awe that Rabelais felt for Socrates, Plato, Plutarch or Virgil, has largely evaporated.

The ancient authors whom Rabelais cites are not simply 'sources'. In the ancient authors, sages, apophthegms and myths, Rabelais sought 'authori-ties'. For Rabelais, as for many of his contemporaries, authority was the key to knowledge. The hieroglyphs of Egypt, the philosophy of Plato, the myths of Greece and Rome, were not simply sources of stylistic ornament or of elaboration: they were examples of a partially veiled revelation of truth to mankind, needing only clarification, unveiling and slight adaptation, to bring them into line with Christianity, itself the greatest revealed authority of them all. As for myth, it is not only used to explain, say, Rabelais's beliefs about the rôle of revelation in the life of men; it supplies a rollicking Bacchus, to place beside more obviously Christian figures, as a source of enlightenment and inspiration.

English readers who know their Chaucer and their Shakespeare are not normally puzzled by Rabelais's juxtaposition of the serious and the comic; the exalted and the trivial; the erudite and the obvious. It was part of the balance and elasticity of an entire culture. To read *Romeo and Juliet* is to realise that the play is bawdy not in spite of the high exalted love of Romeo and Juliet but because of it; to read *Twelfth Night* is to be reminded of licensed revels. These truths dawn upon literate English children from about the age of fourteen, as they prepare their school examinations. But in French-speaking cultures this is not so. Rabelais seems very odd indeed when read in isolation by a young man or woman battling backwards in time through the veil of the Silver Age of seventeenth-century French classicism. Rabelais is an author of balance, of harmony, of light-hearted laughter and joy, which is in easy harness with a contrasting seriousness and sobriety about humanity – which finds its expression in laughter of another stamp. The importance of this aspect of Renaissance culture in the works of Rabelais has only recently been widely appreciated outside English-speaking countries. It has tended to be both over-emphasised and over-codified. Yet it is a very necessary rectification of the balance, in cases where this basic truth had been lost sight of or underplayed. There is much in Rabelais to remind us of the juxtaposition of tragedy and comedy in Shakespeare, who delighted to make the dishonoured Falstaff play the fool and counterfeit death while the heroic Hotspur dies before our eyes; much to remind us that a chaste Romeo may be balanced by a bawdy Mercutio, to our considerable enrichment, just as there is much that is redolent of the Twelfth-night revel, the pre-Lenten Carnival, the under-graduate farce. Critics who have helped to increase an awareness of this have done something important that needed doing. In my undergraduate days it was the lecturer or professor who was not taken off in the Christmas play who was unhappy, not the ones we laughed at. That is in the true spirit of licensed revels, which led mediaeval scribes to copy out scurrilous Goliardic verses and to keep them in the same manuscript as their religious verse. To bear this in mind is to stop every joke in Rabelais from being interpreted in grey earnest as a blow for this or a call for that. Many of Rabelais's jesting passages are balanced by passages of great seriousness. He knew how to laugh at what he loved and admired.

But there is a danger in going too far, as it is fashionable to do. Some of the plays which delighted the university audiences and the denizens of La Basoche (that company of lawyers' clerks in Paris who traditionally indulged themselves in revels presided over by a Lord of Misrule, the *Roy de la Basoche*) were biting and bold. In the early 1530s such plays had openly caricatured Queen Margaret of Navarre and her evangelical priest Girard Roussel. Students of a more evangelical persuasion had put a harsh parody of Noël Béda (the Syndic of the Sorbonne) on the trestles, asserting that the university was ruled by a monster. (Béda was hunchbacked and lame.) Both the king and the university were inclined to crack down hard. In an age of stakes, dungeons, torturings and persecutions, Rabelais naturally hides some of his propaganda beneath the cloak of traditional fun-and-games. I would be less inclined now than I was thirty years ago to accept at its face-value Huizinga's classifying of Rabelais as the 'play-spirit incarnate'.[1] There is some truth in that judgment, but the playful Rabelais was allied with a half-hidden earnest Rabelais, the occasional hater.

Rabelais was a good hater, it seems, but this fact does not dominate his works as a whole. Hatred finds its outlets in scathing satire and diatribe more easily than in comedy. Rabelais has his diatribes, but his Chronicles are satirical in ways which subordinate satire to laughter and rarely divorce it from a sense of humour. The hatred, if hatred there be, is evaporated in the process and the mind left more open and purer, whereas hatred leaves it narrower and venomous.

Rabelais knew his Roman satirists and frequently draws upon them. Yet he has little enough in common with Juvenal, Horace or even Persius, where hatred is concerned. A satirist working in the Roman tradition of moral indignation and hatred of wickedness stirs up his reader to just such indignation and hatred, emphasising all that favours these unlovely passions. Where he does make us laugh, such a satirist (as Joachim du Bellay points out in his *Regrets*) exploits not true laughter but that 'bastard laughter' caused by pain and suffering: sardonic laughter. There are passages of that sort in Rabelais's writings, but they are rare. A comic satirist has both a more difficult and a more attractive task. His artistic challenge is to turn evil and error, even at their most frightful and terrible, into sources of amusement and laughter. This is Rabelais's special genius, one not to be found again in French literature until Molière.

Certain kinds of parody are not in the least unkind or destructive. Many examples of indulgent laughter are to be found in his pages. But when we laugh at an idea or a person in another way, we reject them far more satisfactorily than when we increase their stature by dignifying them, and diminishing ourselves, through our sharpened hatred. Rabelais can make his readers laugh at a bloodthirsty bishop who yearns to torture and to kill his enemies as a prologue to boiling them in Hell. And in the end, we do not find ourselves loathing the prelate; we find ourselves laughing his ideas out of court. Faced with a censuring Sorbonne, Rabelais writes pages of sheer delight, which not only make us laugh at the cruel old diehards of that citadel of anti-humanist, anti-evangelical reaction, but make us laugh in such a way that it is impossible to hate them, however totally we dismiss everything they stand for.

Rabelais knew how humane laughter can drive out fear at its most acute.

What makes his Chronicles sometimes difficult for us to disentangle, is that this kind of laughter which leads to mocking rejection is interwoven

---

[1] English translation used here: J Huizinga, *Homo Ludens: A Study of the Play-element in Culture*, Boston (Mass.) 1950, p.181.

with the attractive indulgent laughter we reserve, in moments of relaxation, for our innermost beliefs or for objects of awe and veneration.

The sense of balance which Rabelais achieves in his Chronicles is one more at ease with the golden mean conceived as a resolution of Heraclitean tensions than as a wishy-washy compromise; more at ease with a religion that hates the sin and not the sinner, than with the hate-ridden political philosophies of other times or with the hate-ridden rival orthodoxies of his own.

This equilibrium can lead us to the core of Rabelais's comedy.

There is a sense in which *Gargantua* and *Pantagruel* show us a humanist at play. But the stakes Rabelais played for included truth herself and hope of eternal life. The risks he took in this desperate game included poverty, exile and precipitous flight – and might have included, had he not been lucky, torture and prolonged, painful death.

Without powerful and effective patronage these risks would have been certainties. So, naturally, his laughter is not all balance and harmony. The ideas he succeeds in laughing off the stage were not infrequently ones which his enemies held so dear that they would have killed him if they could. He knew from hard experience the risks he was taking. Sensible men do not take such risks lightly.

Rabelais combined wide erudition with acute comic awareness: even his moments of laughing relaxation are likely to be unexpectedly profound. When he turns the light of his comic vision on to the darker or obscurer parts of the human condition, he finds a way to wisdom which leaves the mere theorists of comedy and laughter standing still in their traces.

I must declare a fundamental prejudice in Rabelais's favour. The more I read him the more I enjoy him, and the more I find there is to learn from him.

Nevertheless, when emphasising the high humanist and evangelical aspects of Rabelais's comedy there is a risk that other aspects may be underplayed. Unlike many of the humanists, Rabelais delighted in the more accessible literary and sub-literary writings of his day. He knew and admired the French farces, citing, several times, the *Farce de Maistre Pathelin*, and basing some of his most successful episodes of philosophical comedy on the techniques which the farces had made familiar. He delighted in the French and Italian *conteurs*, retelling some of their tales and telling others in the same spirit. Even bad Latin did not put him off, when the effect was to heighten the comedy. Teofilo Folengo wrote – in 'macaronic' Latin, which drew heavily on Italian words and constructions – a mock-heroic epic, telling the story of Baldus and of Cingar. Rabelais not only borrowed from this *Opus macaronicorum*, but may have been fundamentally influenced by it in the conception of his own Chronicles. He similarly rejoiced in the grotesquely funny Latin of the *Letters of Obscure Men*, which reduced the enemies of Reuchlin and of humanist Hebrew studies to the status of clowns.

And one can never forget that *Pantagruel* and *Gargantua*, when they first appeared, invited comparisons with a work of no literary merit whatso- ever: *Les grandes et inestimables Cronicques: du grant et enorme geant Gargantua*, which derive their laughter from gross and simple parodies of mediaeval tales of King Arthur and his Court.

Laughter was, for Rabelais, a very human activity: it was indeed the exclusive property of man. As such it could well be the duty of a Christian doctor to encourage it, relieving in this way the pain attendant on physical and spiritual illnesses.

To catalogue all Rabelais's sources and to list all the influences to which he and his art were subjected would need a very large book. It cannot be done here, though many will be touched upon in the studies on each of his Chronicles. But one author stands out above the others, repaying from the outset special attention from the student of Rabelais: Lucian of Samosata. This second-century comic and sceptical Greek really was 'born again' in the Renaissance. Lucian had delighted in mocking the gods of the pagan pantheon, in making his readers laugh at the confused theology of late paganism and in reducing by laughter the fear that his contemporaries felt for the fate that awaited them after death. He is irreverent, and devastatingly effective in his use of laughter to deflate pomposity and pretentiousness. No person, human or divine, in this world or the next, was automatically exempt from his laughter, though in practice he avoided politics and did not laugh at the Emperor. No event, doctrine or fact was too holy or too august to be held up to mockery, when Lucian turned his sceptically laughing gaze upon them.

That Rabelais was an enthusiastic student of Greek his Chronicles show. But long before he wrote his masterpieces he had translated two works from Greek into Latin, works which strangely prefigure his own: the second book of the History of Herodotus (whom Cicero called the 'Father of History' and others called the 'Father of Lies') and some work or works of Lucian. For many Frenchmen of his day, both those favourably disposed to him and those who hated him, Rabelais was to be the French Lucian. And it may be with an eye on Herodotus that Rabelais chose to call his comic tales by the name of Chronicles. (His interest in Herodotus has long been common knowledge; his translation of Lucian is a recent discovery of M. Secret: *Colloque International de Tours* XIV, 1973, p.222, note 27.)

The importance of Rabelais's taste for Lucian can hardly be over- emphasised. That his translation has been lost is a source of real regret. All four of Rabelais's definitely authentic Chronicles are evidently influenced by Lucian. The comparative easiness of Lucian's Greek made him one of the most accessible of classical writers; the lightness and happiness of his style was greatly appreciated by readers who were not over-supplied with lighter literature. Those who could not read him in Greek turned eagerly to the Latin translations, or else enjoyed him at second-hand, as transmuted into the pure gold of the *Colloquies*, in which Erasmus uses Lucianesque techniques of witty dialogue to deflate those errors in contemporary Christianity which seem to him to correspond to the pagan objects of Lucian's mockery. Lucian's influence on Rabelais's *forma mentis* was so profound that one can postulate that there was a natural sympathy between the two authors, just as there was between Lucian and Erasmus.

But did Rabelais already aspire to become the French Lucian, when he translated part of his works in those early days as a Franciscan? Nothing really makes such a conclusion inevitable. He may have been testing out his knowledge of Greek! And he translated Lucian into Latin not French. His earliest known French work, a poetic epistle to Jean Bouchet the chronicler-poet, does not suggest very high ambitions as a French author. Its very title as supplied by Bouchet suggests otherwise: '*Epistre de Maistre François Rabellays, homme de grans lettres Grecques et Latines*' (Bouchet, *Epistres morales et familieres*, ed. J. Beard; Ep. fam. no. 48).

But from the very outset of his first Chronicle, Lucian is to the forefront, the first chapter of *Pantagruel* actually ending with his name. Erasmus and Rabelais were not the only humanist evangelicals to be attracted to Lucian. By partly translating him, Rabelais joined a select group of Christian humanists comprising not only Erasmus but Thomas More and Melanchthon. That men such as these translated Lucian, edited him, imitated him, were influenced by him, really ought to have scotched the belief that to admire and imitate Lucian's *True History*, the *Dialogues of the Gods* or the *Dialogues of the Dead*, was to have moved half-way down the road to atheism! But it has not done so entirely, not least because the word *athée* was so freely tossed about in Renaissance controversy. When Rabelais was accused of Lucianism, some at least of his opponents *were* accusing him of atheism. But as Lucien Febvre remarked: in the sixteenth century one was always an atheist for someone or other. Rabelais was no exception to that rule, both calling men atheists when he disagreed with them and being called an atheist in his turn.

Lucian, despite his essentially classical Greek, was late enough to know Christianity and to loose a couple of his mocking shafts against it. But this did not put Christian humanists off him: he was too funny, and too valuable a teacher of methods of mocking error and pomposity, for that to happen. Erasmus, More, Melanchthon, Rabelais – men sure within their faith – did not expect their classical authors all to be proto-Christians such as Socrates and Plato. If all the great classical authors had been veiled Christians living before their time, there would have been no special place for the unique Christian revelation. Lucian's occasional anti-Christian moments could be understood and regretted by those who took him as a model. Renaissance humanists were, by conviction and temperament, inclined to see the religious errors of Lucian – or indeed of Cicero, Seneca or Plutarch – as their misfortune, not as their fault. The sober-sided defenders of power and hyperorthodoxy whom Rabelais dubbed *agelastes* (non-laughers) were only too ready to cry heresy, as soon as they smelled the influence of Lucian in the writings of their opponents. But men like Erasmus, Thomas More, Melanchthon and Rabelais could both delight in Lucian's debunking of the religious errors of his time and use him as a model for mocking 'mediaeval' superstition or non-evangelical accretions to Christian truth in their own.

It was a real advance – an advance for which Lucian deserves post-humous credit – when even a few theologians began to laugh at their opponents, rather than to thunder against them, while they oiled their thumbscrews and gathered the wood for public burnings.

Rabelais exploits Lucian in many ways. He takes him as a guide when telling us of the odd events which attended the birth of Pantagruel, for example, or when mocking Picrochole's schemes for world conquest. More fundamentally, he uses Lucian to justify his marrying of laughter to dialogue in the *Tiers Livre*. The *Quart Livre* both expounds positive evangelical ideas and explodes 'papist' error with the help of Lucian and his comic techniques.

Great Renaissance authors who strove to emulate classical models did not do so slavishly. In choosing and emulating their models, authors of importance did not sacrifice their originality. Their approach to imitation is admirably summed up by Petrarch: 'An imitator,' he says, 'must take care to see that what he writes should be similar to his model, not identical with it.' He goes on to state that a successful imitator is not like a portrait painter, in whose case, the more a work resembles its model, the better it is. The similarity true artists should aim at is different, being that of a son's resemblance to his father. There will be many differences of detail. 'So too we should take care to see that, while something should be similar, many things should be dissimilar. Even the similarity should be so hidden as not to be detected except by silent investigation.' The best imitation is one where the similarity can be 'perceived rather than put into words'.[2]

That even a writer of genius should be prepared to imitate classical models was one of the fundamental axioms of Renaissance aesthetics. Rabelais's striving to be the French Lucian is no different in kind from Ronsard's desire to be the French Pindar or Joachim du Bellay's aim of being the French Horace. Imitation of classical or Italian models was believed to be the way in which literature in the vulgar tongues could

---

[2] Petrarch, *Le Familiari*, ed. V. Rossi, IV, Florence 1942, XXIII, 19, p.206. Cited, with useful discussion, by M. Baxendall, *Giotto and the Orators*, Oxford 1971, p.33.

aspire to be placed beside those Greek and Latin works which were so universally admired.

Rabelais is a good example of Petrarch's ideal imitator. His imitation of Lucian is never slavish; it is never exclusive. He does not strive to recreate, in all its detail, for Christian France, an irreverent philosophy only applicable as a whole to paganism in its decline. But a father-son resemblance between Lucian and Rabelais can be 'perceived', even though it cannot always be 'put into words'. Since the same father-son resemblance can be perceived in Lucian and Erasmus too, that may help to explain why Rabelais thought of Erasmus as the 'father and mother' of his own mature self.

Lucian provided a model, a stimulus, a mental attitude. But he did not provide the matter for much of Rabelais's constructive philosophy. For that Rabelais turned to the gospel, to the sages of Greece and Rome, and to Christian contemporaries such as Erasmus. High on the list of classical authors contributing to his religious syncretism was Plato. For Rabelais Socrates is a divinely inspired authority; Plato, that venerated author whom Renaissance scholars readily called 'divine'. Another author whose influence grew and grew until he provided Rabelais with the matter of whole chapters at a time, was Plutarch. Plutarch was especially open to veneration from Renaissance syncretists, since his works, long unknown in the Latin West, were believed to contain a veiled but historical account of Christ's victories over Satan and perhaps, even, of the Crucifixion. Rabelais refers to it in the *Quart Livre* (see below, pp.354ff.).

Rabelais read authors such as Plutarch mainly in the original Greek. Others, including Plato, he read sometimes in Latin, sometimes in the original. When tracing the influence of classical authors on Rabelais, especially the poets, it is wise to remember that he normally read them in heavily annotated editions. More often than not the scholarly footnotes were at least as important to him as the classical texts themselves. In other words, Rabelais often interpreted his classical authorities in the light of what Renaissance scholarship made of them. Such editions frequently sought the 'purer' – that is the more Christian – meanings of Aristotle; they often emphasised those aspects of Plato, Ovid or Virgil, among others, which most resembled their own interpretation of the Christian religion. Socrates, Plato, Aristotle, Plutarch, Virgil, Ovid (in the *Fasti*), and many others, were not thought of as hoary old authors from another age, but as broad and spacious bridges, linking the classical and Christian worlds together, enriching them both and partly reconciling them to each other. In ways such as these, the classical writers could be treated not only as authors, but authorities.

'Authority' is a concept to which students of the Renaissance have constantly to return. Rabelais's comedy works within a context of

certainties, based upon the New Testament and on a Christian interpretation of the Old but also embracing large elements of classical wisdom. It
is here that Erasmus plays so great a rôle in Rabelais's art and thought.
Rabelais constantly turns to his great contemporary's works as a guide to
Christian and classical wisdom, as well as a ready source of condensed
classical knowledge. When Rabelais quotes his New Testament to make a
serious point, as he often does, he frequently accepts Erasmus's interpretation of disputed doctrines. Works such as the *Antibarbari* which Erasmus
published in 1520 influenced his life as well as his art. But the book of
Erasmus which has constantly to be cited in this study of Rabelais is the
Adagia, a work now accessible to English readers thanks to the sensitive
scholarship of Dr Margaret Mann Phillips.

The *Adagia* consist of a great collection of classical sayings, explained in
elegant essays, some short, some long. Many are controversial, seeking to
advance the peaceful 'philosophy of Christ' which formed the essence of
Erasmus's religion. When Rabelais cites the *Adagia* to make us laugh, say, at
Panurge's departures from the good and the true, he is citing a source
which can be almost as normative as Holy Writ.

In form and conception the *Adages* of Erasmus seem simple enough. In
fact these *Adages* are one of the most original and seminal books of the
Renaissance. Rabelais drew upon them again and again. They were so
widely read that Rabelais could be sure that points made with their
help would be widely understood by his own readers. In this way he can
establish his certainties with ease and clarity. When he wishes to condemn
that love of self which leads to moral and spiritual blindness, Erasmus
provided the classical proverbs and supporting authority. What Rabelais
supplied was the art and the laughter. When he wishes to show that this
world is dominated by the fear of hunger, Erasmus again is the major
source of authority, but not, of course, of the paradoxical humour and
comedy.

Rabelais sought his authority from a wide range of classical thinkers and
from a multitude of contemporary writers. Whenever possible he seems to
have selected his material from those aspects of his authors which had
entered into the popularising compendia of the time: in this way he ensured
that even moderately educated men could follow much of what he had to
say. When such authors are mentioned in this study they should often be
thought of as *auctoritates*, 'authorities'. They are not presented as infallible
in themselves, but are often considered as the vehicles of authoritative
wisdom.

Since this is so, it follows that Rabelais's Chronicles are only 'popular'
on the surface. They are the works of a highly-placed professional man
considered unusually learned in a century outstanding for its scholarship
and erudition. Behind the protection of powerful statesmen connected

with his native Touraine and Anjou he turned his comic vision on to the follies and errors of his time, and addressed himself to readers of some real culture, while avoiding the error of only amusing the specialists.

Rabelais was never a popular author, if by 'popular' one means 'understanded of the people'. Uneducated contemporaries, whether dwelling in hall or hovel, could never have understood a tithe of what he wrote in the *Tiers Livre*. Even *Pantagruel* and *Gargantua* assume knowledge available exclusively to the Latin-educated who were sympathetic to Hebrew and Greek culture. What seems popular in Rabelais is as often as not a reading back into the Renaissance of Victorian ideas of vulgarity. This is a pure anachronism, wrongly dividing up the society of the day. Society at this time, despite its vast gulf between rich and poor, was curiously homogeneous, in the sense that one might meet the same moral commonplace in popular sermon or obscure intellectual treatise. Popular songs were known to the ladies at court: while a song sung at court might also be sung in town and village, after due delay. A society in which the well-being of its leaders depends on hosts of servants is not entirely cut off from relationships with ordinary people. But even in his most popular moments Rabelais often calls upon knowledge which was the exclusive reserve of the educated minority, a class which excluded most of the nobility and most of the people. The only partial exceptions to this are perhaps *Gargantua* in some of its chapters – for *Gargantua* appears to be aimed, much of the time, at an enlightened court audience – and the *Quart Livre*, in the chapters given over to religious satire.

We do a disservice to Rabelais if we try and turn him into a popular author, especially if the overt or covert motivation for this is political. We do an equal disservice if we think of Rabelais primarily as a monk or as a doctor. He was never confined within the traditional horizons of such professions. At the times of writing his Chronicles his Christian humanism was widely based and growing wider still. Together with many of the best minds of his day in a score of European kingdoms and principalities he was convinced that the way to truth lay in a return to the sources. Vital truths, it was widely believed, could only be re-acquired by studying ancient texts in the original tongues. Where this concerns Rabelais, it includes a yearning to know one's New Testament in Greek – and if possible one's Old Testament in Hebrew, or at least in versions based on the *veritas Hebraica*, the true Hebrew text. *Mutatis mutandis*, in all areas of knowledge, the same applied.

For all but the richest men, the acquisition of humanist culture was impossible without patronage.

When, as Rabelais did, humanist scholars enjoyed the patronage and protection of powerful statesmen, noblemen or princes of the Church who were themselves humanists, their joy and gratitude often knew no bounds.

Patron and scholar should not be thought of in terms of uncouth moneybags and compromised intellectual. Rabelais seems to have been so wedded to the interests of the du Bellays, of his monarchs, of Cardinal Odet de Châtillon, that it would be a bold man who would suggest that his works were not joyfully but slavishly designed to further their interests. Rabelais's Chronicles are, in part, works of propaganda; it is the twentieth century which has debased both the concept and the practice of propagating ideas one believes to be true.

Pantagruel is in part the relaxation of an erudite humanist, not perhaps his main concern; not perhaps at first, in his own eyes, his prime claim to the attention of his contemporaries and of posterity. *Gargantua*, like the *Pantagrueline Prognostication* which preceded it, is more closely allied to propaganda aims; the *Tiers Livre* combines almost timeless wisdom with acute political and religious propaganda of immediate relevance to his day; it is clearly a work of considerable self-conscious artistry; the *Tiers Livre* and the *Quart Livre* in its final form may claim to be among the profoundest statements of philosophical comedy ever conceived.

Rabelais's concern to propagate certain ideas and attitudes is not in any way at variance with his sense of relaxed amusement. But it often led him into areas of knowledge now closed books for most of us.

His sense of the potential comedy of word and gesture was sharpened by lawyer's learning and lawyer's jokes. With the aid of law and of classical and post-classical linguistic theories, we are brought to laugh at some of the ways in which men interpret the signals they make to each other with word and gesture. Unexpectedly, this eventually leads Rabelais, towards the end of his life, to expound through myth and laughter his belief in divine inspiration. Laughter does not exist in a watertight compartment in these surprising Chronicles. The ways of laughter can lead directly to the ways of Rabelais's God and to the words and signs through which he reveals his truth to enlightened men throughout the ages.

Humanist Frenchmen of Rabelais's generation had received a thorough grounding in rhetoric and dialectic as codified by the scholastic philosophers. They mostly rebelled against it. Classical rhetoric aimed at enhancing the elegance of oratory; dialectic claimed to sharpen argumentative and logical skills. Ideally, both disciplines were concerned with truth: dialectic led towards a knowledge of the truth, sifting the true from the false; rhetoric made truth, once acquired, more readily understandable, more widely known, more persuasive in its force. But the codification of such skills by mediaeval scholastic theologians, lawyers, philosophers and preachers had led to barren battles of words. So the old scholastic methods were under attack, largely in the light of a renewed appreciation of classical rhetoricians such as Aphthónius and Quintilian. As for dialectic, Rabelais, like many others, was suspicious of chop-logic when divorced from the guidance of revered authorities and revealed truth. A word from Socrates or from Christ is worth volumes of *logomachia*. Rabelais achieves many of his comic effects by using rhetorical and dialectical techniques which his public was schooled to appreciate, having suffered an old-fashioned education themselves, and having also accepted new approaches to education, not least in these domains. When, in *Pantagruel* and *Gargantua*, Rabelais laughs at the gods of scholastic dialectic – at Peter of Spain, say, and his *Parva Logicalia* – his readers knew where he stood in the renewed controversies. When he bases the structure of part of the *Tiers Livre* on ideas drawn from Aphthonius and Quintilian, they were surer still.

Even without the technical knowledge which Rabelais took for granted, a modern reader sensitive to both elegant and comic oratory and to the use and abuse of argument will find his enjoyment of Rabelais greatly enhanced. But his enjoyment will lack an important dimension if it is not based upon a sensitive appreciation of what passed for authorities amongst the humanists.

With such knowledge, and such sensitivity, Rabelais's laughter can blossom into what at best it is: philosophical comedy of lasting value.

One final word. Rabelais's comic philosophy is firmly based on the twin pillars of classical and Christian verities. The student of Rabelais will find that even some of the best-known scholars are weak on theology – yet it was for theological *nuances* that people like Rabelais suffered, died, fled into exile, or inflicted the same anguish on others. As for the Bible, it is a major source of Rabelais's jests and wisdom. The effect of ignoring the theological dimension is to knock away one of the pillars on which Rabelais's intellectual achievement stands.

2
Rabelais before Pantagruel

Rabelais's life spanned the last decade of the fifteenth century and the first half of the sixteenth.[1] He saw the establishment of the Renaissance in France. He witnessed the end of mediaeval Catholicism and its replacemen by the complex patchwork which Western Christendom presented after the Reformers and others had done their work. Echoes of these great events abound in his Chronicles; the names of men such as Luther and Calvin, as well as eirenic Catholics like Erasmus or eirenic schismatics like Melanchthon, will be found again and again in this study. For Rabelais was not a private man, quietly writing his works from a country retreat, removed from the storms and stresses of the age in which he lived. He lived a life which, in personal terms, took him out of his Franciscan habit into the retinue of great and powerful diplomatists, who were closely concerned with Church and State affairs in England, Germany and Italy, as well as in their native France. Both Jean du Bellay and Guillaume his brother had been on embassies to England, remaining staunch supporters of the divorce of Henry VIII.

The poverty, celibate chastity and obedience which he had once espoused he abandoned for a public life in high places. The life he led as a doctor – married enough to have children who bore, not their mother's name, but (with papal indulgence) the name of their father – seemed to many men of his time to be more in accord with evangelical religion than the widely discredited ideals of the friars and the monks.

This book attempts to make aesthetic, historical and philosophical sense out of the four great books of comic Chronicles which Rabelais published during his lifetime as well as of his shorter works. Although this is not a 'Life of Rabelais' some knowledge of the kind of life he led, the men he lived among and the times he lived in does help us to understand his writings more fully.

Rabelais published *Pantagruel* in Lyons before autumn 1532. His printer

---

[1] Bibliographical details have been reduced to the minimum. Some suggestions for further reading are given at the end of this book. Details to be found in the notes of the *Edition Critique* (*EC*) or the *Textes Littéraires Français* (*TLF*) are only repeated here when essential to the argument.

apparently, and his publisher certainly, was the good but ailing Claude
Nourry, who was surnamed *Le Prince* after a carved wooden figure above
his stationery shop. At this time Rabelais was not a young man. There is
some hesitation about the date of his birth, but he was probably born about
1483 – the same year as Martin Luther, that is, some fifteen years after the
birth of Erasmus, and some sixteen years before the birth of Calvin. This
would have made him nearly fifty years old when *Pantagruel* appeared – an
advanced age in those days. (Montaigne retired to his tower at the age of
forty, but he was a nobleman and did not need to work.) An alternative
date for Rabelais's birth, 1494, is based on slender evidence; even that
would have brought him to the threshold of his forties before his first
Chronicle was thumped off the press.

Rabelais was not a nobleman by birth, nor was he a poor man; he
belonged to the professional, property-owning classes, the *noblesse de robe*.
His father, Antoine Rabelais, was a leading lawyer in Chinon, a gentleman
owning lands and houses scattered fairly widely over the surrounding
countryside. Rabelais had a particular affection for La Devinière, a
farmstead which can still be visited. In all likelihood he was born there. He
certainly spent part of his childhood there and knew the area inside out. La
Devinière and several other family properties are mentioned affection-
ately in the Chronicles, some of them more than once. I am not much given
to literary or religious pilgrimages, but it is well worth making a visit to
Rabelais's old haunts. La Devinière, especially, is a complete antithesis to
commercialised Stratford-upon-Avon, being so unspoiled as to be fairly
hard to find. Once there, you can see the miniature terrain of the
Picrocholine War in *Gargantua* stretched out before you.

Rabelais's first serious studies were probably concerned with the law, a
major interest of many educated Renaissance men. This may have entailed
his visiting several different universities, but need not have done so. Where
he or his father learned their law we have no real means of knowing; it may
have been at Bourges. By 1521 Guillaume Budé (the brilliant legal scholar
whom contemporaries saw as the glory of France, a man to rank with
Erasmus, say, or Thomas More), could refer flatteringly in a letter to
Rabelais's legal studies, as well as to his outstanding skill in 'both the
languages' – classical Greek and Latin. This great and fastidious jurisconsult not only attributed to Rabelais a serious knowledge of the law but –
final accolade for an erudite Renaissance scholar – a thorough knowledge
of sound and elegant Latin, as well as of the heady revolutionary tongue of
Plato and the New Testament. Such knowledge marks out Rabelais as a
humanist, a term which is used in Renaissance studies to mean a man –
normally of course a convinced Christian – who was prepared to devote
great time and effort to mastering the classical languages, enriching his art
and his thought in the process, as he pondered over the meanings of the

ancient classical and Christian texts, seeking erudition, wisdom, moral insights and aesthetic challenge.

Humanist Latin, as distinct from the work-a-day Latin of the common run of scholars, writers and teachers, was an accomplishment treasured by Rabelais. As for Greek, it opened up a new world of thought. The possession of that subtle tongue was still not an easy thing to acquire in the France of Rabelais's youth. It marked Rabelais out as a member of an intellectual élite, who had access to truer and surer texts of the great authorities, theological, moral, legal, medical, scientific, philosophical, mythological. . . .

Of at least equal importance is Budé's aside to Rabelais, made when alluding to a legal point: 'As you know, you who have studied the law' (*Opera*, 1557, I, p.325B; cf. 435D). Since this was in a letter addressed to 'Rabelais the Franciscan friar', it is virtually certain that a taste for jurisprudence preceded his religious vocation. He retained close contacts with legal specialists during his Franciscan years. The law remained in many ways the most formative of all the influences on his mind. His writings bear witness to this. He was later a doctor and is above all remembered as such. But it was the law that seems to have had the more profound and lasting effect on his way of thinking and writing.

This letter of Budé's is the first dateable information we have about Rabelais the man. Other letters were written, but most are lost.

Some time before Budé's letter – perhaps as early as 1510 – Rabelais entered the Observantine Franciscans as a novice. After this date, but doubtless well before Budé's letter, Rabelais was priested, possibly at La Baumette. He was later translated to the Franciscan house of Puy-Saint-Martin at Fontenay-le-Comte. In 1520 Rabelais's scholarly fellow Franciscan Pierre Amy was complaining to Budé of having no ally in this convent. That was in February. This may mean tht Rabelais only arrived at Fontenay-le-Comte after February 1520.

Today Fontenay-le-Comte is an unpretentious little place. Then it was quite an important centre for that part of Poitou. Rabelais did not lack stimulating intellectual company there. Apart from Pierre Amy – a man of great learning, who was to die soon after fleeing from his convent – there was a group of legal humanists, including André Tiraqueau and Amaury Bouchard. These two men were destined for great things in their profession.

Memories of these early days in Poitou are scattered throughout *Gargantua* and *Pantagruel*. Most of them are pleasant ones, evoking happy recollections of childhood freedoms, youthful friendships and valued professional relationships. Yet it is during these years spent at La Baumette and Fontenay-le-Comte that Rabelais's belief in the religious life was undermined. He was not the only Christian man of his time to find this way of life and worship dry, stultifying, ignorant and often venally self-interested. It is a mistake to think that only bad monks left their cloisters in the sixteenth century. By and large bad monks were quite happy, as long as they remained outside the power of reforming superiors. The good men who abandoned their vocation were not all reformers such as Luther. They included Catholics like Erasmus.

Both Luther and Erasmus dominate the times in which Rabelais lived. Luther's influence on Frenchmen was very great, not least among those liberal Catholics known as Evangelicals, who shared with Luther a respect for the text of the New Testament studied in the original Greek and who yearned for the establishment of a purer church, closer to the early days of the Christian religion and stripped of mediaeval accretions. Neither Luther's condemnation by the pope in 1520 nor the censuring of his works by the universities of Louvain and Paris put a stop to his influence in France. Many Catholics felt great sympathy for his religious ideas – accepting that the clergy ought to be able to marry; sharing in his hostility to monasticism in its decline; believing, like him, that the doctrine of purgatory, and the theology which led to a fervent search for religious merit through works of penitence, undermined the uniqueness of Christ's gratuitous redemption of sinful men in a sinful world. They also thought that the search for a certain kind of ecclesiastically based merit led to the triumph of superstition and the undervaluing of personal and social morality.

Rabelais's writings show that he was open to Lutheran influences. But even more important is the influence of Erasmus. Much of what Luther stood for in stormy public debate, Erasmus advanced with a studied moderation which in no wise compromised his basic integrity. Possibly it was Erasmus's thought which enabled Rabelais to remain a Catholic even after leaving his monastery. On the vital question of free will, Rabelais remained much closer to Erasmus than to Luther. Luther denied that man can do anything whatsoever of his own free will to further his own salvation, which is entirely the fruit of God's grace, freely bestowed. Erasmus is more prudently concerned with *nuances*, leaving room for a small but vital area of human freedom, which both permitted and required man to contribute something of his own to the scheme of salvation operated by Christ in all his uniqueness.

In the fifteenth and sixteenth centuries many young men entered upon the religious life for a variety of reasons, not all strikingly religious-seeming to us. But Rabelais was no lazy, ignorant, permanent lay-brother. We do not know when he took orders, but the very fact that he did so within the Observantine Franciscans, as distinct from the slacker Conventuals, implies commitment as well as presupposing a serious study of scholastic theology, partly centred upon the writings of Duns Scotus and St

Bonaventura. His Chronicles show that he was at home with scholastic concepts, even though he rejected those which clashed with the ones he found in his Greek New Testament.

The sixteenth-century Franciscans do not have the reputation of being a very learned order. This judgment has been influentially challenged. Anyway, Rabelais was in no ways a typical friar. He was certainly learned.

His friend Amaury Bouchard alluded to him in 1522 as 'the most erudite of the Franciscans'. He does this in a book written in Latin (despite its partly Greek title) called, *Of the Female Sex, against André Tiraqueau*. It is a partly platonising defence of women, in reply to an originally slender volume of André Tiraqueau's called *The Laws of Marriage*. This was a long commentary on the matrimonial laws of Poitou; it grew in the course of several re-editions into a massive work of legal scholarship.[2]

Bouchard became an influential man, among other things a *maître des requêtes*. Tiraqueau ended up as one of the great legal humanists of his day; his many volumes are dense, scholarly and authoritative, but of extraordinary difficulty for us to read today. Rabelais was inevitably drawn into the quarrel between Bouchard and Tiraqueau over the dignity of women – a long-established theme of scholarly controversy. His support was clearly worth having. He seems to have remained on reasonable terms with both parties. In 1532 he dedicated a learned book to each of them.

Reading *Of the Female Sex* or *The Laws of Marriage*, especially in its original version, is a useful exercise for those who have access to them. It shows us what a wide range of authors was being discussed and read by these touchy friends. It also serves to emphasise that it was not only groups of schismatics who believed the Western Church to be traditionally anti-feminist and unjustifiably sour about Christian marriage. The fact that Rabelais touches on these subjects marks him out as an intelligent man of his time. This was an age when married laymen such as More and Budé were moving into the forefront, showing by their example that one did not have to be a celibate priest in order to attain to the rarest heights of scholarship or virtue.

The correspondence with Budé is interesting, since it shows us that in studying Greek Rabelais was doing something deeply displeasing to his religious superiors. Greek was feared by many men of power and influence, not so much because of possibly pagan influences – Socrates and Plato were being yet again adapted to Christianity – but because it placed all exclusively Latin-based culture hopelessly at risk. For example, medicine was, after a millennium and a half, still based on Greek

[2] Almaricus Bouchardus, *Tēs gunaikeias phutlēs adversus Andream Tiraquellum*, Paris 1522; a reply to A. Tiraqueau's *Ex Commentariis in Pictonum Consuetudines Sectio de Legibus Connubialibus*, Paris 1513: expanded editions 1524, 1546, 1554. (The 1546 text drops all mention of Rabelais.)

authorities, principally Hippocrates and Galen, or on Arabic doctors who were themselves indebted to them, such as Avicenna. A doctor who could read Hippocrates or Galen in the original could correct another, however venerable, who only knew his Greek authors in Latin re-translations from the Arabic.

The same applied, with even greater force, to theology. An undergraduate who knew Greek could correct the most venerable professors of Paris, theologians included: these were men who had power of life or death over many of their fellows, when they gained the ear of their monarch or established a hold on the Paris Parlement.

In theology a knowledge of Greek was potentially shattering. The Latin Vulgate could be by-passed, criticised, corrected; Fathers like Augustine or theologians like Aquinas could be shaken on their thrones, when what they wrote proved incompatible with the Greek originals of the New Testament. In addition, Eastern Greek theology provided a rich alternative to the Western Latin variety; many thought, like Thomas More, that it was superior. Some of the dearest dogmas of the Roman West were shown to be doubtful, even untenable, in the light of Renaissance theological studies based upon Greek originals.

When Rabelais joined Pierre Amy in the Franciscan house at Fontenay-le-Comte, there must have been mutual rejoicing. But Rabelais's Greek studies, and Pierre Amy's too, got them both into serious difficulties in 1524. Their superiors confiscated their books, perhaps even going so far as to imprison the offending scholars within their convent. That they owed the restoration of their books and their liberty of movement to the direct influence of Budé is unlikely; but Budé was informed about their troubles and deeply disturbed by them. This is proved by the letter he sent to Pierre Amy after he had illegally left his convent – a letter written prudently in Greek and containing a very favourable allusion to Rabelais.

We do not know exactly when Pierre Amy fled his convent in fear or disgust, but he seems to have made up his mind by consulting Homeric lots. Rabelais's Chronicles show a similar respect for divination and for the use of lots in reaching decisions. For an evangelical humanist, lots had the greatest of authority behind them. There are many examples which Rabelais can cite of classical generals or statesmen who had recourse to lots. As for Christian authority, the fact that, in the *Acts of the Apostles*, the disciples chose the successor to Judas Iscariot by casting lots, gave to this method of decision a virtually unchallengeable dignity. Roman law and its Renaissance interpreters were, in the main, as favourably disposed towards deciding certain problems by lots as Rabelais and Pierre Amy were. Tiraqueau's works, among many others, confirm this.

When Pierre Amy broke from his convent, Rabelais did *not* flee. He got himself duly transferred to the superior Benedictine order. For the first time he was now a monk – Franciscan friars not being monks in the stricter sense of the word. He did not go far, moving ten miles or so from the Franciscan house at Fontenay-le-Comte to the Benedictine priory of Saint-Pierre-de-Maillezais. There he came under the close protection and patronage of bishop Geoffroy d'Estissac. This protection was no mere formality. We can confidently assume that Geoffroy d'Estissac's influence and protection smoothed the way for this switching of orders. The bishop took Rabelais with him on his travels and acted as his Maecenas, encouraging his study of medicine – probably paying for it. When Rabelais cast his frock to the stinging-nettles and finally left his priory we do not know. But it was apparently with the connivance of his patron.

These earlier events are worth remembering for the light they throw on Rabelais's state of mind in 1531 or 1532, when he prepared *Pantagruel* for publication and then had it printed in Lyons. In 1532 he also published three other works, two medical, one legal. The first of these books, a supplementary volume of Manardi's *Medical Letters*, he dedicated to André Tiraqueau; the second, a bilingual Greek-Latin edition of Hippocrates's *Aphorisms* and Galen's *Ars Parva*, he dedicated to Bishop Geoffroy d'Estissac; the third work, an edition of Lucius Cuspidius's supposititious *Will*, was dedicated to Amaury Bouchard. The desire to mend fences by dedicating books to both Bouchard and Tiraqueau was there for all to see. The fulsome public dedication of his edition of *Some Works of Hippocrates and Galen* to the bishop shows that there was nothing hugger-mugger about his leaving the Benedictine order, however irregular his action may have been. (Texts and translations of Rabelais's learned prefaces are given in most editions of the *Œuvres*, towards the end of the final volume.)

If Geoffroy d'Estissac did pay for Rabelais's medical studies, then his money was well spent.

In 1530 Rabelais acquired his medical degree at Montpellier after a few weeks' formal study – proof that he had done the bulk of the work already. From now on he was Dr Rabelais – medical graduates then as now quietly turning their bachelor's degrees into a doctorate. He lectured on the Greek text of Hippocrates as part of his qualifying examination and, in November 1532, was appointed physician to one of the most important hospitals of France, the Hôtel-Dieu in Lyons, after spending a period practising in the provinces, including a period at Narbonne. He was living very irregularly for a professed monk, but that seems to have worried nobody. He had clearly arrived. His little son Théodule, 'Slave of God', was (we are told) dandled on the knees of 'roman pontiffs'.[3] Did this beloved child, destined to die young, date from this period?

From now onwards Rabelais's name figures increasingly in the

[3] For Latin verse of Boysonné, see Plattard, *Vie de Rabelais*, Paris/Brussels 1928, p.164f.

marginalia of the great persons of his day. In 1532 he wrote a letter to Erasmus, pouring out his gratitude for all that that humanist had done for him, without even knowing that he existed. This letter shows that he was on familiar terms in Lyons with Hilaire Bertolph, an intimate friend of Erasmus, who had once entrusted him with a mission to Francis I. He and his entire family soon died of the plague: something to remember when Rabelais alludes to this dread scourge in *Gargantua*, for it had come close to him and to those he most admired. His letter to Erasmus also shows (as the first words of the carefully written letter eye-catchingly emphasise) that he had connexions with the entourage of Georges d'Armagnac, a learned, powerful diplomatist and churchman, who belonged to the family of the counts of Armagnac.[4] Georges d'Armagnac's evangelical sympathies during the 1530s led him to be favoured by Margaret of Navarre, the sister of Francis I, a poet and novelist of some real value, who exerted great influence on her royal brother, encouraging him to support evangelicals and to oppose the reactionary theologians of the Sorbonne. Georges d'Armagnac's preferment as bishop of Rhodez in 1529 owed much to Margaret, as everyone knew.

Of course Rabelais was socially far below Georges d'Armagnac, but the allusion to such a nobleman in the letter to Erasmus suggests that he was already under the protection of members of the entourage of Margaret of Navarre and that he had contacts with the very highest society. He repaid his debt to Margaret by dedicating the *Tiers Livre de Pantagruel* to her in 1546.

Soon – we do not know when, but certainly before January 1534 and perhaps long before – Rabelais came under the direct and powerful protection of the du Bellay family. Jean du Bellay, both as Bishop of Paris and later as cardinal, took him on visits to Rome as his personal physician. (To visit Italy for a Frenchman was to be exposed to the full enthusiasm of the Renaissance. Rabelais was never quite the same again.) The bishop's brother, Guillaume du Bellay, the *Seigneur de Langey*, was one of the most influential statesmen of his day: Rabelais developed a profound veneration for him, working for him when he was French viceroy in the Piedmont. Another brother, René du Bellay, though less colourful a figure, was a major force in Paris, directly concerned with protecting the du Bellay interests, advancing their causes and enforcing a major review of the ancient University's statutes and curricula.

Within the households of Jean and Guillaume du Bellay Rabelais, as a scholarly physician, probably had confidential duties to perform quite outside the bounds of medicine. Doctors frequently acted as confidental secretaries or special advisers.

[4] Text and facsimile of letter in P. S. Allen, *Erasmi Epistolae* x, p.129f. Translation in various *Oeuvres de Rabelais*.

Rabelais, during the whole of his literary life, was either on the fringe of the households of great men such as Georges d'Armagnac, the du Bellays or, later, of the Cardinal de Châtillon, or else indeed even more firmly attached to their interests. He was a man who normally worked for patrons. And these patrons included some of the greatest, most powerful and most learned men of the time. His connexions with Margaret of Navarre show him aspiring to the highest patronage of all, as do his in-jokes and special pleadings addressed to the French Court, and probably to the monarch in person, in several parts of *Gargantua* as well as in the *Quart Livre*.

Since his patrons were, in the main, royalist Gallicans, it is the Church in France which most concerns him when laughing at religious error. The purer Church which Rabelais envisaged for France was not one dominated by the theologians of the Sorbonne, whose concerns for a particular conception of Gallican rights and privileges, which enhanced their independence of both pope and monarch, he never shared. It was one in which the King of France had the last word. Royalist Gallicans were no 'papists' – a term which then was not simply a rude protestant word for Roman Catholics but a hostile term used also among Catholics for those who attached more importance to papal powers and pretensions than Gallicans thought to be right. I use it with that sense in this study.

Pantagruel is a comparatively slight book. But it is already the work of an erudite humanist, seeking to provoke rich and varied laughter. Some of its jests seek their matter in rare concerns of scholarly knowledge. The laughter it so delightfully aroused is much less committed, as a rule, than what we find in the later Chronicles. But when it was reprinted with additions in 1533 and again in 1534, it became much more *engagé*. Its open 'engagement' shows its author to be a humanist strongly enough supported by the du Bellays to make common cause with them against the Sorbonne.

In the early 1530s Rabelais was poised on the brink of a new career. Life, for Rabelais, was about to begin again at fifty. The main fruits which this new life bore, as far as we are concerned today, were the four Chronicles of Gargantua and his son Pantagruel.

3

Pantagruel

1. *A humanist book*

Most of Rabelais's readers today know more or less what to expect when they open *Pantagruel*. In this we have a considerable advantage over those who first bought the book in Claude Nourry's shop in Lyons. The book that the first readers bought, the first edition of *Pantagruel*, aroused different expectations. It was in French and evoked the name of a popular dwarf, Penthagruel. If Renaissance habits allowed prospective purchasers to flip through the pages, they would have seen enough allusions to traditional French books in the Prologue to convince themselves that they were buying another comic transposition of the old chivalrous tales. On the other hand they would have had their comic appetite aroused by a feature unique to *Pantagruel* as it first appeared. The original *Pantagruel* did not *look* like a parody of the chivalrous tales: it looked like a learned Latin law book! An elegant classical framework, composed of two columns with pediment and tympanum, had long been used by Jean David *dict la Mouche* on the title-pages of Latin law books which he printed for two Lyonese legal booksellers, Vincent de Portonariis and J. and F. Giuncta. When David went bankrupt in autumn 1531, he sold his printing material. From January 1532 it was in the hands of another Lyonese printer Benoît Bonnyn, specialising in Latin law books for the same publishers. It was this David-Bonnyn frame which appears on the title-page of *Pantagruel*. Did Claude Nourry own it for a brief period – in which case *Pantagruel* would seem to date from the winter of 1531? Or did Bonnyn lend Claude Nourry his recently acquired material? Did he even print *Pantagruel* for Claude Nourry, who died before the second edition and might have been already ailing? Whatever the reason, *Pantagruel* looked like a hybrid, a funny cross between a popular comic tale of chivalry grossly parodied and dense heavy works of Latin jurisprudence. There is so much legal humour in *Pantagruel* that we can assume it was part of the original comic design to give this little book both the outward format of technical law books and a French title promising all sorts of comic high-jinks.

It is normally believed that *Pantagruel* appeared in autumn 1532; but we are not sure of this.

The few fugitive allusions to real events seem to make autumn 1532 a reasonable guess; bibliographical considerations might suggest a date somewhat earlier.

About the composition of the book we know even less. We do not know whether it arose out of a single flurry of creative zeal or whether it was written and conceived over many years. On the whole I incline towards the belief that it was written over a fairly long period; but I may be quite wrong.

Pantagruel is a short book, originally divided into twenty-four chapters numbered I to XXIII, with *two* chapters numbered IX. These were later broken down into thirty-four. It tells the tale of the birth of the little giant Pantagruel to Gargantua and to Badebec his wife. This took place during a period of prolonged drought. The giant soon grows up and travels through French university towns. On his journeys he meets many people, including a silly scholar from Limoges, who attempts to hide his provincial speech behind pretentiously Latinised French: he is trapped by fear into revealing his ignorance, messes his trousers and dies of thirst (as is appropriate to an enemy of both Pantagruel and 'Penthagruel'). This death from 'the death of Roland' – acute thirst – is jocularly presented as an act of divine vengeance; it confirms what both 'the Philosopher' (Aristotle) and Aulus Gellius said: that we ought to confine ourselves to customary linguistic usage. This is the first hint of several themes which are destined to be considerably developed in these Chronicles.

The visit to Paris is the most important of all. It is made the occasion for a good satirical laugh against old-fashioned scholarship, by listing the alleged holdings of the library of St Victor's monastery; a letter from Gargantua introduces a new moral and theological dimension, praising the fertile marriage and a humanist conception of education. In Paris, too, Pantagruel meets Panurge 'whom he loved all his life'. He too becomes a major source of laughter – the comedy is based upon theories of language which were both ancient and current.

A legal debate between Baisecul (Kiss-my-arse) and Humevesne (Suck-fart) is resolved by Pantagruel, occasioning more linguistic and legal laughter. Panurge gives an uproariously amusing account of his escape from the wine-hating, Moslem Turks; we are told how befouled female pudenda would make good walls for Paris; and then, in a major episode, Thaumaste comes from England to debate with Pantagruel. The debate is to take place by means of physical signs not with words. The innocent Englishman debates with Panurge instead. This comic episode can be shown to be extraordinarily complex in its meanings and terms of reference; once more it has important connexions with linguistic theories which are to be fully developed only in later works, especially the *Quart Livre*.

Panurge falls in lust – love is the wrong word – with a pretty, married

Parisian social climber, who knows how to use her beads in Church while giving men the glad eye. She resists, 'crying out, but not too loud'. Panurge gets his revenge by making the stray dogs piss all over the bitch. This acts as a foil to Pantagruel's brief affection for a noble lady, an *affaire* which, once again, leads to reflexions on language, hermetic writing and symbolism.

The book ends with Pantagruel and his disciples fighting the Dipsodes (the Thirsty Ones). Readers in the nineteenth and early twentieth centuries were struck by the occasional coarseness of the language, but it did not put them off. Today's readers, inundated with 'obscene' linguistic usages, may fail to be artistically arrested by the outspoken comedy; they also sometimes fail to notice that the 'obscenity' is not erotic in form or in its effects. (*Pantagruel* did seem foul-mouthed to a few contemporaries.) The contrast between the occasional coarseness of the comedy and the elevation of its theology and morality is of the essence of the book. As well as being an amiable parody of the Arthurian stories, there are episodes with wider-reaching intellectual aims, including a visit by Epistemon to a Lucianesque underworld whilst he is half-dead, with his neck partly severed, and an important prayer to God by Pantagruel, which raises fundamental questions of Christian faith and practice.

This little comic book proves to be unexpectedly profound in its implications. It is occasionally satirical and sometimes overtly serious. It is the first-born Chronicle of an ex-Franciscan, ex-Benedictine religious turned secular priest, who had recently graduated as a doctor and was enjoying an honoured status as physician to a major hospital. Yet it contains next to no laughter at the expense of the religious orders and betrays little interest in medicine, except towards the end, when Pantagruel is prescribed pills 'by the counsel of the doctors'; (these pills contain men who dig out his excrement with shovels). One might suspect that its main preoccupations are that of an earlier period: Rabelais was a student of the law before becoming a student of medicine. If any professional interest may be said to dominate in *Pantagruel* it is the law. This holds true of Rabelais's acute awareness of the comic potentialities of human speech and argumentativeness: in all the four books we are about to study, concern for language (in this sense) is presented in a legal context. Rabelais was sharply aware of the gulf which may separate sound from sense, flighty words from concrete deeds, actions, symbols, gestures, signs.

He shared with many of the best minds of his day an interest in alternative means to words for signifying or conveying truths. Language, precisely because it is a God-given faculty, is open to rhetorical and argumentative abuse; the corruption of the best is, we know, the worst. Moreover, since Babel and its famous Tower, sounds which mean much to some are downright gibberish to others.

The first edition of *Pantagruel* exploits such matters for comic ends. It gives sure indications of being a work written by a humanist who did not take himself too seriously. Most of the concerns of contemporary humanists find some echoes in these pages, including an interest in abstruse Judaeo-Christian scholarship, in education, in Evangelical theology. Yet *Pantagruel* is not a humanist book, typographically speaking. Its print is gothic not roman; it has none of the visual charm of books of far less importance. It is well printed though, carefully composed and comparatively free from errors. The print sits densely on the page, relieved only by ornamental capitals at the beginning of the chapters. The printed word here is not intended to be particularly exciting visually, as it had been in so many mediaeval manuscripts and still was in so many printed books. The printed page is above all the vehicle for conveying to us an account of the spoken word. Many forces were at work on Rabelais and some of his contemporaries encouraging them to look upon writing and printing as primarily the recording of speech. And Rabelais's Chronicles are works which derive their greatest comic effects from the spoken tongue.

A great deal of education was aural and *viva voce*, a tendency encouraged by the new pedagogy of the humanists which Rabelais himself championed. Classical theory emphasised the rhetorical nature of literary writing. Legal scholarship and jurisprudence as the humanists conceived them led to an interest in actual pleading in court, however un-aural their own technical writings were.

Rabelais's Chronicles are influenced by the traditional genres of *conte* and farce, both of which were widely enjoyed right into the sixteenth century. It would be wrong to class such interests as 'mediaeval'. The genres flourished during the French Renaissance, not least because of the spread of printing. By convention the *contes* may be presented as stories told by a teller. As for farces, they are by definition 'spoken' and regarded as being so, even when read in print or manuscript. This concern with the spoken word as reported in farce and story leads Rabelais to relate his first Chronicle through a fictitious storyteller called Alcofrybas Nasier, an anagram of his own name, and to present many episodes as dramatic monologues, debates or plays. We need constantly to remember that Rabelais is never speaking directly in his own name before 1546 (the date of the *Tiers Livre*) and hardly even then. *Pantagruel* and the other novels do not have Prefaces but Prologues, a word with possible connexions with play-acting among other things.

The prologues, presented in every case as humorous monologues, are certainly 'Prologues de l'auteur', but the author in this sense is not the Reverend Dr Franciscus Rabelaesus; he is the serio-comic Alcofrybas Nasier who is built up in the course of the books as a kindly, slightly doddering figure, capable of outbursts of passion but essentially amiable and harmless. The first two Chronicles are related by him. This pleasant fiction is partly maintained even in the *Tiers* and *Quart Livres*, where the author is no longer Alcofrybas but Maistre François Rabelais from the title page onwards. But in the prologues to the *Tiers Livre* and the *Quart Livre* Rabelais the storyteller shows many of Alcofrybas's characteristics, and is clearly differentiated from the Rabelais of real life. Only once in the novels does Rabelais entirely drop this pleasant pretence in order to speak directly in his own name: that is in the dedicatory letter to Cardinal Odet de Châtillon, prefixed to the completed *Quart Livre* of 1552. Even in that book, the 'author' has, in the prologue, those characteristics we have learned to associate with Maistre Alcofrybas, not with Rabelais himself.

Within the tales, monologues, dialogues, debates and discussions which make up a large part of these comic Chronicles, the spoken effect often intended is emphasised by the constant use of the verb *dire*, frequently without any attempt at variety, apart from an occasional *répondre* when the context calls it forth. The grotesque and comic nature of so many of the interlocutors serves to make the fundamentally farcical quality of much of the dialogue in *Pantagruel* stand out in strong relief.

For contemporaries there was the additional salt of archaism: there is at times an element of 'gadzooks' and 'ye olde worlde' in the speech of Rabelais's characters. Inevitably, this is less striking for us today, when even the modern French of the 1530s has become irremediably archaic. We also probably fail to savour as fully as his first readers did his numerous neologisms, provincialisms, comico-pedantic usages and other linguistic *tours de force*. This is a pity, for the charm of Rabelais's writing is sometimes to be found in the judicious mixture of these various elements. Plays on words are a sustained feature of the Chronicles, in the serious parts as well as in the more obviously funny parts.

Why Rabelais chose to place a certain distance between himself and his comic creation can be inferred but not definitely known. I suspect that, precisely because he conceived his *Pantagruel* as a series of essentially narrated episodes, he preferred to think of his novel as being read ideally by an actor or a skilled professional reader, just as Terence's plays (for example) were then thought not to have been acted by players but recited by an *histrio* called Calliopus. The *histrio* does not show his real self; he hides behind his comic mask. This wearing of a 'mask' has the unexpected result of allowing Rabelais the man to appear in his own novels: under his real name in a most seriously moving part of the *Quart Livre*; again under his own name in the *Tiers Livre* when he appears in a list of medical actors in Montpellier; and anagrammatically, as Seraphin Calobarsy, in a serious part of *Gargantua*. It may be important that in these cases Rabelais should appear as a doctor: an honoured fictional one in *Gargantua*, a very real one in very real historical contexts in the *Tiers Livre* and the *Quart Livre*.

Whether Rabelais actually intended *Pantagruel* to be listened to rather than read as we read today is a disputed point. Reading out loud seems to have been a common practice in the sixteenth century. Insofar as he was hoping to attract an aristocratic audience, Rabelais would have known that the great often preferred listening to reading. Not all French noblemen in the 1530s read even French fluently; anyway, getting someone else to read for you conserved the precious gift of sight: Renaissance *besycles* (spectacles) were not a patch on modern glasses. When Calvin read *Pantagruel*, we can be reasonably sure that he read it as we do today; but, when Francis I wanted to find out for himself whether Rabelais's Chronicles were dangerously heretical or not, he had them read out to him by the best *anagnostes* (reader) of the kingdom, that is by Pierre du Chastel, bishop of Mâcon. Writing to the Cardinal de Châtillon in 1552 Rabelais alludes to this event, boasting that Francis found none of his passages in any way suspect. It is a nice conceit to imagine Rabelais's Chronicles read aloud to his king by a bishop. If the bishop of Mâcon was as good a reader as Rabelais says he was, then he probably aroused great laughter from one of the parts of *Pantagruel* that many find dull to read: I mean the passages in strange tongues, real and invented, which Panurge pours forth when he first meets Pantagruel. A clever comic may get a great deal of laughter out of this cascade of strange sounds: reading the words silently over, as we sit in armchairs or in libraries, hardly gives them a chance to make us laugh.

Worse: when we read them silently we are tempted to understand them, to squeeze a meaning out of the old German, Scottish, English or Danish, as well as out of the Greek, Latin and Hebrew. Yet whoever in sixteenth-century France knew German *and* Scottish? On the other hand, the general sound of these languages would have been known to many who lived in university towns or who came into contact with foreign mercenaries.

Imitative skill is required to make the noises of these foreign languages sound ridiculous to French ears. Later in the century, Etienne Pasquier, a good and sensitive admirer of Rabelais, believed Panurge's comic use of foreign tongues to be an imitation of a scene in the farce of *Maistre Pathelin*. Rabelais gives a broad hint that this is so.

The meaninglessness of foreign tongues when spoken outside the areas in which their conventions apply is presented comically and dramatically; hence the value of a good *anagnostes*. But that is not the whole story. The reader or listener who laughed at the strange sounds of English or German also no doubt laughed even more at the strange sounds of the languages Rabelais invented (Antipodaean and Lanternish) or re-invented (Utopian). But as Emile Pons has shown, these invented languages can be deciphered ('Les langues imaginaires dans le voyage utopique', *RHLF*, 1931, pp.185–217). To those in the know, they are not mere strings of nonsensical sounds, any more than Scottish or Hebrew are. Rabelais, by inventing these tongues, has imposed his meanings on the verbal signs of which they are composed. This way of looking at his languages is confirmed by what he writes about language and meaning in later works. While awaiting his explanations, nothing stops the reader or listener from simply laughing.

Many Renaissance scholars were preoccupied by secret ways of writing, by ciphers and cryptograms. Thomas More gave a fillip to imaginary tongues when he invented Utopian. By giving his invented languages real decipherable sense, Rabelais may have been partly indulging in a private joke; but it can hardly be that and no more. Even those who have not deciphered the tongues can recognise the proper-names transferred into them out of the French. Duly deciphered, the passage in Lanternish starts as follows:

I first of all have the most pressing need for you to listen to the request of my distress, O noble possessor of the lands of Gravot-Chavigny-Pomardière as well as the lordly domain of La Devinière near Naÿs (*Pant., TLF* IX, 61 *var.*; *EC* 74).

These words associate Pantagruel with lands owned by the Rabelais family; nothing else in the first Chronicle does this so closely – hence the feeling that a private joke may be involved. Certainly nobody simply hearing the book read aloud would have had time to decipher the language itself. It must have been a rare bird who made anything out of these invented tongues. And yet the place-names *would* have been recognised. If Rabelais's links with Gravot, Chavigny, Pomardière or La Devinière were known at all, allusions to these possessions could be recognised from the unknown and undeciphered Lanternish as readily as from the French. The allusions to real but tiny hamlets in both *Pantagruel* and *Gargantua* were lost on all but a handful of people who knew Rabelais's home and its immediate surroundings. Perhaps Rabelais was showing us how vital it is to know the conventional meanings attached to sound and symbol before we can hope to understand. Unless we do know them, human language, meaningful to some speakers, is laughable gibberish. Some of the du Bellays' correspondence is in cipher. If Rabelais was acting at times as a confidential secretary to them, that would help to explain his interests in secret writing.

In *Pantagruel*, concern with the comic potential of language is sometimes paramount. This becomes explicit later; in *Pantagruel* it is implicit in the comedy. It leads Rabelais to create a vehicle of astonishing richness. Over and over again the effect that Rabelais evokes in his audience is one that can only be obtained by using a rare word, a direct borrowing from classical tongues, a lightly gallicised version of a word current in school Latin, an Italianism, a Germanicism, an Anglicism even. Other effects can only be produced by foreign tongues the reader does *not* understand.

Where French is concerned, words are constantly being associated together in *Pantagruel*, independently of their meaning, by pure qualities of sound. This playing with words may also take the form of associating words by etymology, not seriously in this first Chronicle but by etymologies known to be far-fetched, by punning, by deformation. Series of expressions follow upon each other in which sense can only be made out of parts of a sentence, not out of the whole. The more one knows the idioms of Renaissance French, the more amusing (say) does Baisecul's hovering round about a meaning become: the more not less meaningless his utterances appear to be.

Rabelais reserved until later his exposition of the linguistic theories he worked by. But at least something must be said about them now, if the reader is not to be all at sea.

The theories of language he worked within were the dominant ones in Western Europe since the thirteenth century, being widely accepted in theological and philosophical circles as well as in the law. Dante applied them to the vulgar tongues with conspicuous success. The theories are Aristotelian, as harmonised with Platonism by Alexandrine Greeks in late classical times.

Put simply, this theory maintained that words have no natural connexions with the things they signify. Speaking *is* a natural human activity, but the languages which men speak are not natural creations: they all result from the arbitrary imposition of meaning on aural symbols, these 'arbitrary impositions' subsequently being accepted by informed convention. Rabelais does *not* mean that each and every speaker can make up his own language as he goes along, imposing any old meaning on any old sound. On the contrary: to do that is to make yourself both comic and incomprehensible. The words of French, Latin or any other tongue derive their senses from the mysterious word-makers who founded the various languages and imposed meanings found acceptable by general convention. Only neologisms had, as it were, private founders: for this very reason they were often suspect. It is precisely because authoritatively imposed meanings, accepted by convention, are normative that departures from the norm are laughably comic. Anyone who divorces established sense from verbal signs in this way is mad, diabolically wicked or just comic. A great deal of Rabelais's comedy of language depends on this concept. To misuse a word through malapropism is funny: to link it unexpectedly with others by a certain kind of punning is comic, whereas to show its origins by serious etymology is mysteriously informative. Since convention is what consolidates language-groups, it is always potentially comic to employ the sounds of one language in contexts where the conventions are unknown – by talking in Scottish and Danish to monoglot Frenchmen. More refined comedy can be made by detaching the words of a particular language – in

Rabelais's case, French and occasionally Latin – from the things and concepts on which they had been imposed.

The theory of language adopted by Rabelais often made an exception for Hebrew: some believed it was the original natural language of man, exempted from the confusio of Babel. Other exceptions concerned proper-names. It was widely believed that proper-names could sometimes have real, not arbitrarily imposed, links with the person, place or thing signified. The main authority of this was usually derived eventually from Plato but, again, through the intermediary of the Alexandrine Greeks. This belief explains the underlying assumptions of Rabelais's jesting explanation of the name which Gargantua 'imposed' on Pantagruel. He uses the technical term *imposer*; with his tongue in his cheek the narrator tells us that the name 'imposed' has real and appropriate links with the character of the young giant: 'for *panta* in Greek means *all* and *gruel* in Hagarene means *thirsty*'. This joke would best be appreciated by those who knew how the admired Erasmus was protesting against the misuse of Plato to try to justify fanciful explanations of Biblical and other names, in terms of etymologies drawing on languages different from the one in which the name appears. (*Pant., TLF* II; *Garg., TLF* VI; cf. *Erasmi Epistolae* IX, 289).

Rabelais's theories of language move into prominence in the *Tiers Livre*; in the *Quart Livre* they occupy the centre of the stage. Until we reach those books in this study it is enough for the reader simply to keep his eyes and ears open when reading Rabelais; quite a lot of humour is aroused by stupid etymologies; some significant and deeper meanings are suggested by serious ones.

Except when thinking linguistically, we tend to make a fairly sharp distinction between spoken symbols (words) and all others. It is a distinction of doubtful validity and certainly not one which a Renaissance humanist who was legally trained would easily make, since important legal glosses dealt with the question.

The ability to speak has a place of honour in the affairs of man: it is a gift recalling the Word of God himself. But it is not alone, totally isolated from other means of communicating meaning or enshrining concepts. There are many other 'signs' besides verbal ones: ecstasies, miracles, precious stones, paintings, hieroglyphics, emblems, devices, armorial badges and colours. . . . Such things will frequently concern us. But, thank goodness, Rabelais did not stop there. One of the ways in which he enlarged his field of comedy was to link sign and symbol to gesture. Once more this step was encouraged by his legal studies. It was also encouraged by Quintilian, the first-century writer on rhetoric, who, as Erasmus pointed out, gave a large place to gesture in his *Institutio Oratoria*. Yet another way in which Rabelais enriched his comedy was to stress the real significance of actions compared with the often slender evidence of speech. By making actions significant in this way Rabelais saved his comedy from a dangerous over-concern with matters so temporally circumscribed and, to later minds, so trifling that without this ethical enlargement his works might have sunk into oblivion. An evangelical humanist who sees the comic potential of men who say one thing and do another is assured of making men laugh for centuries, not for a few decades.[1]

The readers of the 1530s had no prior warning of the philosophical and linguistic bases of Rabelais's concern with the comedy of language, symbol and gesture. When, in *Gargantua*, this comic concern was enlarged to embrace ethical activity, it was still presented with the barest minimum of supporting theory.

2. The anonymity of Pantagruel

Pantagruel appeared without clear indication of its paternity. It did not have a famous name on its cover but the self-evidently false name of Alcofrybas Nasier. Some no doubt knew whose name hid anagrammatically behind this vaguely Arabic pseudonym. Others, noting the clear allusion in the text to specific people and places – to du Douhet, Tiraqueau, La Devinière – could have found out who the author was if occasion arose. *Pantagruel* is not a book whose author seriously tried to hide his identity: the Sorbonne could soon have made the necessary inquiries if they wanted to identify the author. It is a book promising laughter. Just as a famous comic actor like Jean du Pont-allais abandoned his own name for the pseudonym *Songecreux* when acting or writing professionally, so too Rabelais adopts a pseudonym when he takes time off to make us laugh.

Most of the first hesitant purchasers of *Pantagruel* doubtless asumed that it was a Chronicle of comic giants in the mock-heroic prose tradition. The legal title-page would have seemed a mere spoof. Nothing would have reminded them of Lucian, until they read the book. Everything would apparently be linking *Pantagruel* with unpretentious French works, especially with the recent and quite unliterary *Grandes et inestimables Cronicques: du grant et enorme geant Gargantua*. The earliest dated copy of this little book to come down to us is '1532'. It may have been written by an otherwise unknown François Girault, whose name appears in an acrostic poem at the end of at least two later versions. It was printed in Lyons by François Juste, but bears no name or address. It has been argued that these *Grandes Cronicques* incorporate elements of folklore and popular legend; it would be unwise to date the original stories, as distinct from the book of François Juste, from 1532; but if there were earlier dated editions then they

[1] In *Pant*. II, *TLF* 76f.; *EC* 65f., the 'sign' is a comic miracle. In the Latin New Testament, *signum* is the normal word for miracle. Erasmus, *Adagia* I, 3.21: *Manum non verterim. Digitum non porrexerim*; Quintilian XI. iii. 64f.: gestures are almost another language, replacing words.

were read to pieces, for they have left no trace. There were certainly other editions later – perhaps very many editions, for some have come to light only very recently. These *Grandes Cronicques* were a great success. It is not easy to see why. They are poor stuff aesthetically, slackly written, restricted in vocabulary and sometimes syntactically weak. Yet they appealed not only to a popular audience but also to a highly literate one. The Renaissance reader in general loved the chivalrous romances; he was all the more readily able to appreciate their being grossly parodied. The Arthurian romances especially enjoyed great favour in the sixteenth century, both in modernised French prose versions and in the new Italian poetic versions of Ariosto and Boïardo. Noël Béda, the syndic of the Sorbonne, fulminated against them: that would make them all the more attractive to a man such as Rabelais, for Béda also fulminated against Plautus and Terence. Again, it would be wrong to think of an interest in those romances as a case of pure mediaevalism: the romances had a secure place in the Renaissance bookshop – not only as escapist reading but in hard politics. The Field of the Cloth of Gold (1519) was a triumph of knightly splendour; much later, in England, the 'King of Great Britain' drew heavily on Arthurian legend to sustain the mystique of the newly united Kingdom. It is during a time when such legends are appreciated at many levels of human life, including the highest, that parody of them (not necessarily destructive) is most appreciated too. Mock-heroic epics such as the *Opus macaronicorum* of 'Merlinus Cocaius' (Folengo) flourished when real knightly epics flourished as well: many humanist readers no doubt loved them as a relaxation or just as a change.

Rabelais, while making his main comic appeal in the prologue of *Pantagruel* to the new and popular *Grandes Cronicques*, alludes to many other romances – to the *Orlando Furioso* (which had appeared in 1516) to *Robert le Diable*, *Fierabras*, *Guillaume sans Paour*, *Huon de Bourdeaulx*, all figures of chivalrous romances, intermingled with less noble figures such as *Fessepinthe* ('Pint-guzzler', with an inevitable echo of the word for the behind, *fesses*) or to *Monteville*, an allusion to the tall stories of Mandeville which had been published by Claude Nourry.

This simultaneous appeal to serious and far-from-serious figures in chivalrous romance, apart from being delightfully funny in itself from the very fact that romantic and grotesque are jumbled together, leads the reader to expect to find in *Pantagruel* a light-hearted tale similar to the simple comedy of the *Grandes Cronicques*. Even the more literate contemporary might still not even have thought of Lucian. There is little or no hint in the prologue of a desire to emulate him.

Presenting *Pantagruel* as a successor to the enormously successful *Grandes Cronicques* doubtless boosted sales. But the reader whose intellectual horizons were really limited to the *Grandes Cronicques* must have been puzzled and resentful when he came to *Pantagruel* itself after struggling through the prologue. He had expected to find an amiable, gross, coarse and undemanding parody of the chivalrous stories he enjoyed: he got this certainly, but so much more, including much which he could not understand. Leaving aside more complex episodes, the quite straight-forward mockery showing up the hollowness of the pretentiously Latinate French of the *Ecolier limousin* means little to a reader who has no Latin. Even gross parody in *Pantagruel* draws upon linguistic and cultural resources which are undreamed of by the author of the *Grandes Cronicques*; and Rabelais knew his chivalrous romances well, later including listening to them at mealtimes as an enriching relaxation in his ideal system of education in *Gargantua*. This basic chivalrous matter he embroiders with borrowings from widely assorted sources, classical, Jewish and tradition-ally French. The popular element in *Pantagruel* is but one among many, and not always the most important, though hardly ever entirely lost from view.

3. *Pantagruel: a dwarf turned giant*

The comic promise of the book does draw upon traditional and popular matter in at least one way now lost to the casual reader, for whom the name 'Pantagruel' evokes inevitably and exclusively thoughts of Rabelais's giant. For the men and women of the time Penthagruel was no giant; he was a very small devil whose job it was to go round throwing salt into the mouths of sleeping drunkards, giving them hangovers and drying out their throats as a prologue to further drinking. By naming his giant 'Pantagruel' Rabelais was inviting his reader to enjoy the same sort of simple joke which leads schoolboys to call the biggest boy in the class Titch or Tiny Tim. The change of spelling from Penthagruel to Pantagruel could well have been unintentional (there was no orthographic norm for such names, or indeed for spelling in general). But we may suppose that Rabelais preferred the form Pantagruel in order to facilitate a comic etymology, *Panta* and *gruel*, where the first element looks Greek.

The thirst-raising power which Rabelais's Pantagruel owes to the little legendary devil is a major source of comic unity in the novel. It recurs as a *leitmotiv*. When one is least expecting it Pantagruel will be catching someone by the throat (literally and figuratively), pouring salt into mouths or otherwise causing heroic thirsts. This contributes to the unity of the book by drawing episodes only loosely connected with the giant hero back into the context of the Chronicles of Pantagruel; as a comic device it has much in common with the delight we find in the unexpectedly repeated catchphrase, whether in Molière or in many comedians in modern times.

The association of Pantagruel with Penthagruel also leads to the concern with merry drinking in this thirsty novel. Devotees of this new Pantagruel, the thirst-raising giant, are naturally great drinkers of wine; his enemies, equally naturally, acquire epic and unquenchable thirsts – not least the Greek-named *Dipsodes*, the Thirsty Ones. There is no sign here of the great importance Rabelais is later to attach to the liberating powers of wine. Merry drinking lends the same sort of laughter to *Pantagruel* that Shakespeare provides in the drinking scenes with Sir Toby Belch in *Twelfth Night*. There is indeed in *Pantagruel* a great deal to remind us of Twelfth-night revels, of that world of fantasy and comedy where normal standards of right and wrong, good and evil, the done and the not done, simply do not apply, being put away for a season of indulgence and relaxation. To this world of Twelfth-night revel is added the topsy-turvy world of Shrove-tide, an aspect of the novels clearer at some times than at others. Another world of fantasy and indulgence, linked in *Pantagruel* with Twelfth Night and Shrovetide, is the world of the student – not the sad reality of student life as lived in the Collège de Montaigu, not the rather scruffy and tawdry image of student life fairly current today, but of a young, entirely male, irresponsible, international, poorer but happier world, in which sprees and tricks and pranks of the type associated with the Villon of fact and legend formed the norm (whatever the reality was really like); in which the town serjeants were the natural butt of comedy; in which conventions can be flouted and authority deflated; in which women (when not being worshipped as mistresses) are coarse objects of lustful but uncomplicated amusement; a world of licence, laughter and *gaudeamus igitur*.

When Rabelais was studying medicine in Montpellier, he and several other medical students (some destined to become quite famous) put on a play, *The Farce of the Man who Married a Dumb Wife*, in which the medical profession was guyed and treated with scant respect (*TL* XXXIV). *Pantagruel* as a whole has analogies with that farce, though here it is the legal world which gives rise to much of the humour. Both the farce in which Rabelais once acted and *Pantagruel* itself share the quality of in-joking: of professional men taking time off to laugh, not too seriously, at the profession whose dignity they maintain most of the year. In this mood one can laugh, therapeutically, at one's profession and even at one's ideals.

This probably explains the importance for both *Pantagruel* and *Gargantua* of the *Farce de Maistre Pathelin*. Just as the *Farce of the Man who Married a Dumb Wife* was a comic comment on the medical profession enjoyed by doctors, so *Maistre Pathelin* was a farce deriving from a comic view of the legal profession and enjoyed by lawyers. The dominance of legal jesting in *Pantagruel* – in several episodes it is paramount – has much in common with *Pathelin*, being just the kind of mockery of the law, which one would have expected Rabelais, du Douhet, Tiraqueau, Bouchard and other students of jurisprudence to enjoy during periods of permitted licence. Over and over again Rabelais's serious interests in real life find a comic counterpart in his Chronicles. When archaeology and epigraphy become a passion for him, they duly appear as comedy in *Gargantua*; his serious Almanacs are paralleled in comedy by the *Pantagrueline Prognostication*. The Jewish jokes in *Pantagruel* are best seen as a reflexion of this tendency, arising out of some real concern for Hebrew, some real (if partly second-hand) knowledge of the Talmud, the kabbala and rabbinical writings.

Several of the strands which go to make the woof of *Pantagruel* would have been effective at almost any time: tales of giants, echoes of gaily romanticised student life, are not confined to the 1530s. But there is one aspect of *Pantagruel* which was strikingly apposite to the time in which it appeared: the extraordinarily dry weather which greeted the birth and childhood of the giant. It was Abel Lefranc who, in his introduction to the *EC Pantagruel* (1922), first pointed out that 1532 was a year of scorching drought – a thirsty year, in fact. One can go further: the drought was not limited to 1532; it lasted from late 1528 until early 1534. Mézerai's testimony about this is clear: he tells us that from the end of 1528 until the beginning of 1534 the heavens were so angry against France that there was a perpetual disordering of the seasons: you could say that summer took the place of all the others; over a period of five years there were not two days of frost in a row. This tiresome heat enervated Nature, making her powerless. She allowed nothing to come to maturity; trees brought forth their blossom immediately after the fruit; corn did not multiply in the ground: as there was no winter, vermin ate the seed as it germinated, so that at harvest-time there was nothing even to sow for the following year; this dearth caused widespread famine, followed by an outbreak of an unknown illness called 'stoop-gallant'; then came the plague. These three scourges (Mézerai says) carried off a third of the population.[2]

We tend to think of a series of mild winters and hot summers as good weather. A peasant agricultural society does not. In the late 1520s and early 1530s this prolonged heatwave was a national disaster – one of the factors forcing Francis I to sign the harsh Treaty of Madrid with Charles V. Rabelais, writing a comic book, uses it as a source of humour, not as an excuse for breast-beating: 'Mieulx est de ris que de larmes escripvre', the true comic tradition by which we are often made to laugh, not weep, at

---

[2] Paraphrased translation of Mézerai, *Histoire de France depuis Pharamond jusqu'à Louis le Juste*, 1685 II, p.447f. Cf. *Police Subsidiaire à celle quasi infinie multitude de pouvres survenus à Lyon Lan Mil cinq cens trente ung*, Claude Nourry, Lyons (Baudrier, *Bibliographie Lyonnaise*, s.v. Claude Nourry p.94f.) 1531 or 1532 (?). Many of the starving people could not swallow anything: 'Many running hither and thither through the churches and cross-roads made such lamentations day and night that you heard nothing but "I'm dying of hunger, dying of hunger".' The town of Lyons was like an *un famélicque hospital* – an hospice for the starving. Rabelais, a doctor working in the aftermath of this and distinguishing himself by his devotions to his patients, prepared *Pantagruel* for the press at this very time.

what we are really afraid of. A good comic writer can find his comic matter in the stuff of high tragedy. Such a prolonged dry and thirsty period, stretching over years, suggested to Rabelais's comic imagination that the dwarfish Penthagruel had been superseded by a giant of heroic proportions, whose birth evoked epic legends of biblical and ancient days.

This dwarf-turned-giant, Pantagruel, must not be judged (by anticipating what he is to become in the later books) by the standards of the inerrant Stoico-Platonic Christian sage. For the reader who comes back to *Pantagruel* from the *Tiers Livre* or the *Quart Livre* this can be refreshingly disconcerting. Yet most giants that I know are not very bright. An intelligent giant is the exception. The giant in Rabelais's first book can be even a bit of a booby; he is the reverse of the stoically unmoved dispenser of profound truths, being at one moment 'so sad that he wanted to kill himself'; he is an amoral, gigantically indulgent looker-on at pranks and practical jokes; for most of this first book he is anything but a philosopher. His keywords are words of uncritical amusement, stressing how he 'laughed at everything' and 'took pleasure in everything': 'Et le bon Pantagruel ryoit à tout'; 'Et Pantagruel prenoit à tout plaisir.' He is so far removed from the later idealised princely Pantagruel, the wise man dominating not by rank but by wisdom and moral authority, that in *Pantagruel* he can cry out for help – to Panurge; he can, for page after page, act almost as the comic stooge of Panurge rather than as his Master.

This conception of Pantagruel as a great uncomplicated guffawing giant is much truer to tradition than the highly original developments of the later books. Behind the latter-day Pantagruel, from 1546 onward, we can catch glimpses of those heroic qualities which Rabelais admired in Guillaume du Bellay: it would be a bold man who saw in Pantagruel, as he first appeared in Rabelais's novel, an idealised portrait of such a powerful, wise and admired contemporary, or indeed of anybody else who had qualities demanding our respect.

This comparative closeness of *Pantagruel* to the tradition represented in part by the *Grandes Cronicques* is not a weakness. This rollicking giant of farce and parody already opens horizons on to other possibilities: he is sporadically learned, even though the learning is itself, in this first book, more a source of laughter than of true admiration; yet episodically, both Pantagruel and Gargantua take on a completely different rôle as propagators of the New Learning. But little or no attempt is made to integrate these characteristics into one complex whole. This apparent hesitation about the rôle of Pantagruel is essentially an extension into the moral and intellectual spheres of a wider ambiguity current throughout mediaeval and Renaissance writing about giants. This ambiguity is most obvious when we try to imagine how big these giants are meant to be. Rabelais shares with numerous other writers a complete inconsequentialness about their size. At one moment Pantagruel can lift an otherwise immovable bell with his little finger, or cover an entire army with his tongue. At other times he can walk about quite normally and converse easily with his peers. This convention, which Rabelais and his contemporaries inherited from the past, is a liberating one, well adapted to the constantly shifting preoccupations of his first two books. He exploits it to the full. We are, happily, far removed from the cold and meticulous concern with relative size which marks out *Gulliver* as so new and (for me at any rate) so chilly a conception of gianthood.[3]

4. *A comic Utopia*

A radically new departure, rich in consequence, was to make the giants royal. Although Gargantua is 'le roy Gargantua' in some versions of the *Grandes Cronicques*, the gigantic Gargantua of French tradition was not a king: it was Rabelais who invented the dynasty of kings – Grandgousier, Gargantua, Pantagruel – with roots going back to the giants and heroes of antiquity. This kingship was to become an important device for Rabelais, opening up his novels to the possibility of political comment. Already in the *Pantagrueline Prognostication* for 1533 (the next book he wrote) these possibilities were being exploited. From *Gargantua* onwards they are an essential part of the intellectual content of his books.

It is also noteworthy that the kingdom of Pantagruel's royal father – definitely in *Pantagruel*, less clearly so in the later books – is Utopia. At a single bound Rabelais places his heroes in a new perspective, one which could be appreciated (and only be appreciated) by the literate. More's book had appeared in Paris in 1517, having first been published in Louvain in 1516. In 1518 it again appeared in print, this time at the scholarly press of Froben in Basle, prefaced by Latin epigrams contributed by More himself and by Erasmus. Rabelais could not have failed to be familiar with the writings of More. But outside learned circles *Utopia* remained nothing but a name, if that. More's book was not done into French before 1550, when Jean le Blond published *La Description de l'isle d'Utopie*. The mention of Utopia in *Pantagruel* – and of such names as the *ville des Amaurotes* also borrowed from More – could have meant nothing to the Latinless reader, let alone the Greekless.

Such allusions serve to remind us, as they reminded literate contemporaries, that *Pantagruel* has pretensions far beyond the limits of the *Grandes Cronicques* and of popular literature generally. Thomas More was (as all the learned would know) the intimate friend of Erasmus. At the very time that Rabelais draughted his beautifully orthographed letter to Erasmus, many

---

[3] Cf. C. S. Lewis, *The Discarded Image*, Cambridge (1964) 1970, p.127. An excellent introduction to some of the problems discussed here.

reactionary theologians of Europe (and not least of Paris) were continuing their vicious attacks on him and his writings. As for More, the Chancellor of England was still a human figure, controversial, bold and sharing some of the suspicion that the hyper-orthodox felt for Erasmus, and some of the hatred that schismatic extremists felt for Erasmus's respect for Catholic unity. The heavy hand of martyrdom and the deader hand of sainthood had not yet been laid upon him and his memory. What Rabelais thought of More's execution we do not know. His royalist Gallicanism would not have encouraged him to admire the policy of a man who set himself and his Church against his King – especially over the matter of the Henrican divorce, where all the du Bellays supported Henry's case through thick and thin. But Rabelais never struck out the allusions to *Utopia* and so remained publicly loyal to the work of the stubborn ex-Chancellor of England when it was not always fashionable to be so in France, where More eventually became the cynosure of some of the theologians most opposed to his 'darling', Erasmus. More himself probably never read *Pantagruel*. He would doubtless have enjoyed it if he did. He would certainly have understood it.

5. *Comic chivalry*

Stories of heroes in chivalrous romances had long since followed a general pattern: the birth of the hero is related, sometimes with accounts of early events which foreshadowed his heroic greatness or knightly valour. The childhood is quickly skipped over – no writer seems to have been much concerned with childhood between Augustine, the first author to write about his own childhood, and Jean-Jacques Rousseau – and then we are plunged into colourful accounts of battles and knightly prowesses. *Pantagruel*, as a good parody, follows in outline this general convention, the *Enfances Gargantua* leading fairly quickly to the *Prouesses Gargantua* (all of which are marked by the cankered muse of satire – more laughing, though, than hating – the gaiety of farce, the sustained mockery of Lucianesque laughter). The sheer joy and playful amusement of the gigantic episodes in *Pantagruel* would be hard to equal. Later additions and expurgations made *Pantagruel* into a different book: the 1532 *Pantagruel* surprises by joy; the 1534 edition is already the work of a man under attack, occasionally taking refuge in bitterness. In the original version the satirical is always subordinated to the funny; there is no suggestion of bitterness from one end of the book to the other. This playfulness is enriched by the ease with which Rabelais moves in and out of the framework of chivalrous parody, making prolonged forays into serious or comic matters, of no concern whatsoever to the romances but of great concern to legal humanists and evangelical Christians.

In practice the gigantic chivalry of *Pantagruel* occupies mainly the beginning and the end of the book. It is a sort of sandwich, the filling of which has little or nothing to do with comic knightly tales, being made up of a variety of succulent episodes less concerned with funny Utopian giants than with mockery of what a humanist scholar found laughable in some of the intellectual movements of the France of his day. In this respect *Pantagruel* is like both *Gargantua* and the *Tiers Livre*, in having beginnings and ends which have much in common with each other, less in common with many of the chapters which separate them.

6. Scriptural laughter

What strikes the modern reader of the earlier chapters of *Pantagruel* most forcibly is not so much the parody of the Arthurian romances – he may not know them all that well anyway – but the parody of the Bible. The giants of the Old Testament are to the forefront of Rabelais's mind when the genealogy of Pantagruel is established. The genealogical list which Maistre Alcofrybas draws up, stretching from Chalbroth, Sarabroth, Faribroth and Hurtaly ('who was a good eater of sops, and lived at the time of the Flood') right up to Grantgousier, Gargantua and 'le noble Pantagruel mon maistre', is the work of a humanist scholar who, for the comic purposes of his book, recalled the genealogies of the Book of Chronicles and Deuteronomy through the distorting glasses of Lucian. In few parts of his writings is the Shrovetide revelling more evident than here: it is no accident that one branch of the monstrous creatures brought forth by the Great Drought produced that barrel-bellied race of whom it was written *Ventrem omnipotentem* – a laughing echo of the *Patrem omnipotentem* of the Creed; from this stock came 'Saint Guts' (the jocular *saint Pansart* duly venerated in fun at Shrovetide) and Mardy Gras himself (*Pant.* 1).

This traditional familiarity with religion lingered on longer in England than in France. The combined forces of Calvinism and of the equally sober Counter-Reformation effectively drove good-hearted jesting on religious subjects right out of French literature for at least two centuries. For Rabelais this jesting is in part a left-over from his years as a Franciscan (and doubtless as a Benedictine too). The very awe felt for liturgy and Holy Writ encouraged those who lived with them in daily intimacy to turn to them also for comedy or light relief. The Franciscans ('God's Gleemen') were famous for the vigour, joy and humorous coarseness of their sermons. Men who knew their breviaries off by heart – and often, if we can believe Rabelais, knew nothing else – acquired an easy intimacy with them which made it natural to allude jestingly to them during convivial wine-bibbing, or even when making a sexually risky joke. Rabelais's drinker in *Gargantua* was certainly not the first to have 'Christ's words in his mouth: "I thirst"' when wine is called for. Frère Jean was certainly not the first to call on the incipit of the Psalm *Ad te levavi* ('I lifted up unto thee') to refer, in priapic vein, to the privy member (*Garg.*, *TLF* IV, 84 *var.*; XXXVIII, 95; *EC* V, 106; XL, 76).

There is nothing necessarily destructive in this parody and jesting, which scholarly convention calls 'monastic humour'. As the years went by it did seem so in French-speaking countries. In France, especially perhaps during the nineteenth century, this humour was so little understood that it gave rise to the legend of an atheistic Rabelais, destructively mocking the religion of which he was a priest. At the same time, in England, the Anglican clergy delighted so much in Rabelais that Trollope noticed it – does Archdeacon Grantly ever read anything else but *The Thunderer* and *Pantagruel*? The Reverend Charles Kingsley loved Rabelais too: a simple reading of the *Water-Babies* leaves no room for doubt about that. Yet the belief that Rabelais was parodying Christianity in an atheistical spirit is not merely a nineteenth-century aberration, however difficult it is to sustain in the light of his later books. The Sorbonne (wrongly) suspected that *Pantagruel* was destructively parodying scripture in the genealogy of Christ; the new puritans of Geneva were even more opposed to Rabelais and his group – Rabelais had to run the gauntlet all his mature literary life between Geneva and the Sorbonne. He was to have the distinction of being execrated in Geneva, put on the Index in Rome, yet loved and appreciated in Amsterdam and London. Writing from Geneva, Andre Zébédée in a letter to Charles de Candeley, dated 31 July 1538, says darkly: 'I well remember *Dolet*, *Rabelez*, and *Marot*; and I am astonished when I recall what they said of them in Lyons.'[4] But Rabelais more than once got his own back on Calvin and his like. As for the Sorbonne, from 1533 onwards, Rabelais made them a principal butt of his laughter, and they answered him with hatred and attempts at suppression.

The fact that some of the Scriptural parodies are maintained even in the 1542 edition of *Pantagruel*, when Rabelais carefully expunged matter judged too controversial, confirms that the jests were not considered dangerous or destructive by those who mattered. In a nonsense passage, even the Sermon on the Mount can give rise to good jokes: as when Baisecul cites the burlesque lawyer Maistre Antitus and then makes an alleged quotation from the specialists in canon law which reads, 'Blessed are the heavy, for they have stumbled' (*Beati lourdes, quoniam trebuchaverunt*). Not only does this remain in the prudent text of 1542, but the word *ipsi* is inserted before *trebuchaverunt*, an addition which makes the joking parody of the Beatitudes quite transparent: compare *Beati lourdes, quoniam ipsi trebuchaverunt* with

---

[4] Texts in Mlle Gabrielle Berthoud, 'Lettres des Réformés saisies à Lyon en août 1538', in *Etudes et Documents inédits sur la Réformation en Suisse Romande*, Lausanne 1936. This study has often been overlooked by students of Rabelais, Dolet and the *Cymbalum Mundi*.

'Blessed are the meek, for they shall inherit the earth' (*Beati mites, quoniam ipsi possidebunt terram*). Other Scriptural jests did have to go, less out of respect for the Gospel (that was never in question) than because of the theological issues raised by the use of the texts: Alcofrybas's claim to be telling the truth in his Chronicle was, in the first editions of *Pantagruel*, supported by a light-hearted citing of St John ('J'en parle comme Sainct Jehan de l'Apocalypse, *Quod vidimus testamur*' – 'We testify to what we have seen'). That brings to the fore the whole question of when, where and in what the Christian has faith. Already in 1534 that was too dangerous; it had to go, to be replaced by a much more technically precise theological joke in *Gargantua* on just this question of the nature of true faith (*Pant.*, *TLF* IX *bis*, 184; prol., 77; *Garg.* V, end; *EC* XI, 32; prol., 64; *Garg.* VI, end).

Parodies of Scripture and jokes, sometimes quite obscene, based upon allusions to Scripture had long been a common type of humour. In an age when few would have possessed a Bible or have read one, they tend to exploit those parts of the Bible known through popular devotion or through the liturgy: the Psalms, the main outlines of the Old Testament (the Creation, the Fall, the Flood, Solomon and Sheba), the Nativity and so on, which were a frequent subject of artistic illustration in stone and on wood or canvas, or else the pericopes of the mass, which correspond in the main to the passages still appointed to be read in the Book of Common Prayer. Refined jests based on misapplications of Scripture were quite pleasing even to the fastidious Erasmus – witness the *Praise of Folly* – though he disliked Franciscan *scurrilitas* such as Rabelais delights in. Rabelais's profound respect for Erasmus was quite unfeigned. But there were parts of his mind not satisfied by an exclusive devotion to the New Learning. Perhaps that is why, unlike Erasmus, he wrote with originality only in the vulgar tongue. Rabelais the humanist and Alcofrybas the chronicler coexisted in an easy and quite stable relationship. But although Erasmus would not have liked the coarser parts of Rabelais's parodic jesting, the two men were not really far apart in their attitudes towards large sections of the Old Testament. Erasmus thought that, taken literally without the enrichment of spiritual and prophetic exegesis, the Old Testament was often no more convincing than tall stories out of Homer. The deep feelings of respect and awe that men like Erasmus experienced for the inner, moral and spiritual senses of the Old Testament did not necessarily lead them to respect the literal meanings of many of the episodes. Rabelais is not all that different: he cites the Old Testament seriously – either purely historically or else assuming our acceptance of a moral or spiritual inner sense. But he is prepared to get plenty of fun from some of the literary conventions of Biblical writers, as well as from the literal sense of Old Testament writ.

3. Pantagruel

7. Hebrew laughter

An interest in rabbinical and other Jewish writings was an important aspect of the Renaissance, as it had been of mediaeval Biblical scholarship from the thirteenth century onwards. The attempt in Germany to suppress all Jewish writings except the Old Testament – an attempt associated with the converted Jew Pfefferkorn – had rallied most humanists to the cause of Jewish studies, giving rise to one of the funniest books of the sixteenth century, the *Letters of Obscure Men*. This anonymous collection of silly letters in bad Latin is presented satirically as an answer to an authentic collection of *Letters of Famous Men* written to support Reuchlin against the anti-humanist, anti-Hebraic obscurantism of ignorant theologians. (It was translated into English, with a good commentary, by F. G. Stokes – London 1925.) Rabelais borrows several jokes from these *Letters of Obscure Men*. His support for Reuchlin does not have to be guessed at or inferred: in the joyfully satirical catalogue of the Library of Saint-Victor his sympathy for Reuchlin and his school is quite open. Already in the first edition the library list includes an *Art of Politely Farting in Society, by Magister Ortuinus*, an allusion to a theologian of Cologne widely mocked for his hostility to Reuchlin and Jewish studies generally. In 1534 the list of books is extended to include (among other things) clear allusions to notorious anti-Reuchlinists: Magister Jacob Hocstraten, 'measurer of heretics' (*hereticometra*) contributes a book on the *Hypocrisies of Genitals*; Magister Lupoldus, *Moralisations on the Hoods of Sorbonne Gowns*; the doctors of theology of Cologne, collectively, contribute *Fuss and Bother against Reuchlin* (*Tarraballationes adversus Reuchlin*). The author of *Pantagruel* wanted his support for Reuchlin and the studies of Hebrew texts (including rabbinical glossists and the kabbala) to be clear beyond doubt (*Pant.*, *TLF* VII, 57, etc.; *EC* 135, 166, 169, etc.). If we were to wonder why Rabelais increased his open support for Jewish studies in 1534, we might note that in the January of that year the Sorbonne had unwisely allowed Béda (its syndic who had been temporarily recalled from exile for quite other reasons) to attempt to stop the Royal Professors of Francis I's Trilingual Academy from lecturing on the Hebrew Old Testament. Royal authority put Béda and his fellow theologians firmly in their places. It was a good moment to declare one's support for the school of Reuchlin and for Hebrew studies generally.[5]

In his ideal educational system, Rabelais allows an important place to the study of Hebrew and cognate semitic tongues, including Arabic. These languages are studied primarily to open up the real meanings of the Old Testament. Exactly how much Hebrew Rabelais knew is not clear. He can make mistakes – confounding for example such rabbinical scholars as Aben

---

[5] Texts in Bulaeus, *Historia Universitatis Parisiensis* VI, 239–45, etc.

Ezra with the massoretes, more modest students of the Hebrew texts. That he was favourably disposed towards Jewish contributions to medical studies he shows by including them in his scheme of humanist education. But more important perhaps than guesses about how sound his Hebrew learning was, is the fact that *Pantagruel*, in more than one episode, is clearly concerned with Hebrew studies, including midrashic and kabbalistic traditions. This reminds us that some serious knowledge of both ancient and more recent Jewish commentaries and legends had filtered through to Christian scholars, thanks in part to mediaeval theologians such as Andrew of Saint-Victor, commentators such as Nicholas of Lyra, converted Jews such as Gironimo of Santa Fè. The school of Reuchlin carried this mediaeval interest in Hebrew right into the heart of the Renaissance. Precisely because some knowledge of these writings was widely available, at least at second-hand, Rabelais can make jokes which presuppose a fair acquaintance with Hebrew tradition and exegesis.

For example Pantagruel's genealogy goes back to beyond the Flood, as so many great princes' did. Yet how, asks Alcofrybas, did such a gigantic race survive, since no giant is known to have been saved within Noah's ark? Rabelais gives the answer in terms which strike some modern readers as anti-Christian: the ancestor of Pantagruel was a giant called Hurtaly, who rode astride the ark. Alcofrybas cannot give the answer on his own authority – he does not date from the Flood – so he relies on Jewish sources:

I will cite you the authority of the Massoretes, interpreters of the Hebrew scriptures, who say that, without error, the aforesaid Hurtaly was not *inside* Noah's ark – he could not have got in anyway, being too big – but was on top of the ark, with one leg one side, one the other, like little children on hobbyhorses. In this fashion he saved the ark from foundering: for he made it move with his legs, and turned it about with his foot as one does with a ship's rudder. And those who were inside sent him up ample food through a chimney, as people who recognised the good he was doing them. And sometimes they exchanged conversation, as Icaromenippus did with Jupiter, according to the report of Lucian (*Pant.* I, end).

There is plenty of irreverence here. But not anti-Christian irreverence. Rabelais is not comparing the Old Testament account of Noah's ark with the tall stories of Lucian: he is enjoying playing with Jewish lore, just as elsewhere he plays with other branches of learning which, in other moods, seriously concerned him. Rabelais's Hurtaly is based on Og, King of Bashan, the giant who was overthrown by the children of Israel and whose name appears in several books of the Bible. Og was the subject of many legends and rabbinical myths. The story of Hurtaly in *Pantagruel* is a paraphrase of the tale of Og in the *Pirkei of Rabbi Eliezar ben Hyrcanus*. These *Sayings of Rabbi Eliezar* were not printed until later – an edition appeared in Venice in 1544 – but parts were fairly well known from references made to them in Christian theological writings several generations before Rabelais. In Gerald Friedlander's translation Rabbi Eliezar's tale is given thus:

And all living things which were upon the face of the earth decayed, as it is said, 'And every living thing was destroyed which was on the face of the ground' except Noah and those who were with him in the ark, as it is said, 'And Noah only was left, and they that were with him in the ark', except Og, King of Bashan, who sat down on a piece of wood under the gutter of the Ark [*variant versions say, closer to Rabelais*, 'on a rung of one of the ladders']. He swore to Noah and to his sons that he would be their servant for ever. What did Noah do? He bored an aperture in the ark, and he put through it his food daily for him, and he also was left, as it is said, 'for only Og, King of Bashan, remained of the remnant of the giants' [Deuteronomy] 3:11.[6]

That rabbinical legends about Og were 'foolish' was a commonplace of Christian scholarship. J.-J. Lenfant in his *Histoire du Concile de Pise* ends his account of the writings of the converted Jew Gironimo of Santa Fè with a sharp condemnation of Jewish superstition. Apart from the 'extravagancies' of the Talmud, he condemns 'gross stupidities' which go against the reliability of Holy Scriptures, 'as when they say, for example, that Og, King of Bashan, was pulled out of the waters of the Flood by Noah. There are other fables about this Og, more worthy of fairy tales or the Arabian Nights than of a Law attributed to God himself.'[7]

Sebastian Muenster, a good Hebrew and Biblical scholar, also found Jewish legends about Og to be amusing. Commenting on Deuteronomy 3:10 in his *Hebraica Biblia* of 1534, he says: 'The Jews write marvellous things about the stature of this giant, but you cannot read them without laughing.' That was Rabelais's opinion too.

It is just possible that Rabelais calls *his* Og *Hurtaly* from an unexplained corruption of the Hebrew *Ha-palit* ('he who survived'), a scriptural phrase vital to the legends about Og; it was interpreted as meaning he had indeed survived the Flood.[8] Or perhaps he changed the name of Og precisely in order to avoid any confusion with the authentic Biblical accounts, though I doubt this explanation. That he had the Biblical Og in mind as well is clear from his Hebrew sources: and he later cites Nicolas of Lyra's gloss on Og and his famous 'bedstead of iron' (*Pant.*, TLF IV, 62; EC IV, 51).

Unless Rabelais had access to Hebrew sources, it is not known how he

---

[6] *The Pirkê de-Rabbi Eliezar*, trans. G. Friedlander, London 1916. Consult Louis Ginzberg, *Legends of the Jews*, Philadelphia 1913, I, p.160; IV, p.181.

[7] J.-J. L'Enfant, *Histoire du Concile de Pise*, Paris 1724, II, p.167. For the *Contra Judaeos* of *Hieronymus a Sancta Fide, ex Judaeo Christianus*, see *Bibliotheca Veterum Patrum*, ed. M. de la Bigne; 3rd edition, Paris 1610, IV.

[8] L. Sainéan, *La Langue de Rabelais*, Paris 1923, II, p.33; *Pant.*, EC I, 6, note; *Pant.* IV, TLF 63; EC 50.

could have alluded in detail to Rabbi Eliezar's tale of Og riding on the ark since, almost alone among the tall stories about Og, this one seems to have been fully available only in Hebrew. I doubt if Rabelais had enough Hebrew to read it unaided. Perhaps the acquaintance who wrote Panurge's Hebrew speech for him supplied him with details. Or perhaps he heard the story from Amaury Bouchard.[9] Another tempting hypothesis proves to be an impossibility – namely that Rabelais had access to the earliest known Latin translation of the *Pirkei*. This was made by Conrad Pellican (1478–1556), himself a Franciscan who became a follower of the Zurich reformer Zwingli. But the original manuscript of his version is still in the library of Zurich (at Ms. Car. C.60; fol. 201–250). Pellican adds at the end that he finished it on 24 September 1554, and that it was 'the work of 15 days'. So it is far too late for *Pantagruel*.

Christian accounts of Jewish lore may have inspired more than just the tale of Hurtaly riding astride the ark: they may also have inspired the whole beginning of *Pantagruel*, with its comic *Old Testament* genealogies and its series of comic gigantic growths of various parts of the body. Chapter four of the second book of Gironimo of Santa Fè's treatise *Against the Jews* is entitled *Of the Vanities, Inaccuracies and Errors contained in the Talmud*. His list includes the story of how God made Nebuchadnezzar's penis grow three hundred cubits long in order to put a stop to his urge for sodomy with Zedekiah; we are also told how Rabbi Eliezar and Rabbi Ismael had bellies so enormous that when they stood facing each other two oxen could pass between them. Being told that their sons could not really be theirs, since men so fat could never lie with their wives, they replied that their wives' bellies were even fatter still. This did not matter, as they had penises proportionately enormous and so could manage quite well.[10]

This is the world in which Rabelais, in search of laughter, places his giant hero. It is neither destructive of Jewish legend – there is no trace of the intolerant impatience of Gironimo of Santa Fè – nor destructive of the Canonical Old Testament. It is an excellent example of the way in which Rabelais's erudition and that of his readers opened up new fields of comic reference in the widely curious Renaissance.

In this Jewish dimension, as in so many others, Rabelais was very up-to-date. In 1530 Francis I established in Paris his *lecteurs royaux*, professing Hebrew, Greek and Latin. Despite the hostility of many traditional

[9] In *Tēs gunaikeias phutlēs*, 1522, p.23rº, Bouchard calls Rabbi Eliezar 'the most fruitful fountain of all the Talmudists'.

[10] Gironimo of Santa Fè: *Contra Judaeos*, lib. II, chap. IV, *De vanitatibus, decisionibus et vitiis contentis in Talmut* (cf. note 7 above). Rabelais marries Jewish jokes to similar Christian ones. The giants with long noses, added in 1534, derive from the *Dicté joyeux de tous les nez*, in which Vulgate phrases containing the word *ne* (not: lest) are treated as though it meant *nez* (nose). *Pant., EC* I, 60, note.

theologians, these *lecteurs*, seen rightly as first steps towards the founding of a royally-favoured Trilingual Academy, made the Greek of the Septuagint and the Hebrew of the Old Testament a study approved by the High and Mighty. Tools for learning Hebrew were becoming increasingly available. For example, just before Rabelais published *Pantagruel*, a knowledge of Hebrew grammar had been made more accessible. Elias Levita, who had taught Hebrew to Sebastian Muenster and many others in Germany, had written several works on Hebrew grammar, vulgarised by his famous pupil. In 1531 Cratander published in Basle Muenster's Latin translation of Moses Kimhi's *Grammatica* together with a commentary by Elias Levita. This explains the topicality of Panurge's lame excuses for robbing the pardoners' boxes, by playing on an elementary point of Hebrew grammar, by which the future tense sometimes serves as the imperative:

So when the pardoner said to me *Centum accipies* ('Thou shalt receive a hundred'), he meant *Centum accipe* ('Take a hundred.'). And thus it is expounded by Rabi Kimy and Rabi Aben Ezra and all the Massoretes; and there we find old Bartolo (*et ibi Bartholus*).[11]

    This is comic at a fairly self-evident level. Is there a more learned joke as well, reserved for those who really did know Hebrew grammar? Panurge asserts that the future is used as an imperative in Hebrew, but he omits to state that this only applies to negative commands! The example he quotes is a positive command. By no stretch of linguistic ingenuity can *Thou shalt receive a hundredfold* be made to mean, 'Help yourself to a hundred pounds'. And what are these 'rabbis' doing commenting on a text of Christ in the Gospels! If we do not recognise that Panurge is twisting words from Matthew 19, 29, and if we think of *Rabi Kimy* merely as a mediaeval rabbi with no contact with the interests of Rabelais's humanist contemporaries, we miss the point. *Rabi Kimy* is very up to date: he had just been published in an important Latin version whose very existence reminded humanists of the victory of Reuchlin and his allies against the obscurantist theologians of Cologne and against those in the Sorbonne who were still only too keen to emulate them by opposing the teaching of the regius professors in Paris. The allusion to Rabbi Kimhi is one of those glancing references in *Pantagruel* which show us that it was aimed at a public who knew what was in the bookshops. It was not of course necessary to have read Rabbi Kimhi to get the point of the fairly straightforward joke; but it was necessary to know

[11] *Pant.*, *TLF* XII, 227; *EC* XVII, 44. Up to 1537, Rabelais cited at this point Christ's summary of the law (Luke 4, 8). The text was not omitted as too hot to joke with – several similar jests remain. Panurge's phrase *Centuplum accipies* remains scriptural, echoing Matthew 19, 29: *Omnis . . . centuplum accipiet* (Everyone . . . shall receive an hundredfold). By changing the verb from the third person to the second, he gives it a jesting imperative meaning: hence the joke.

who, or rather what *Rabi Kimy* was: a recent humanist Hebrew grammar rather than just some old rabbi.

Rabelais had a deep respect for Hebrew as a language; he saw it as a vital, indeed indispensible, tool for the study of the Old Testament. Towards Hebrew-based mysticism, the kabbala and rabbinical studies generally, his attitude was more ambivalent but certainly not just mockingly and ignorantly hostile.

8. *Comic ecstasy*

Artistically, the relaxed sporting with Jewish legend which is so marked a feature of the beginning of *Pantagruel* is in easy harness with an intimate knowledge of scripture. Throughout *Pantagruel* the meanings of entire episodes are pointed by scriptural allusions: the very person of Pantagruel, who has wisdom greater than Solomon's and who receives answering voices from heaven, inevitably evokes associations with Christ. This odd juxtaposition of the central person of the Gospels and the humorous and grotesque hero of *Pantagruel* is not the least of the obstacles that some readers find in the way of their enjoying and understanding *Pantagruel*. But there is really no problem. In *Pantagruel*, Rabelais takes to its logically comic limits that jesting with scripture which monks had made their own. In the amoral comic climate of this first book – so conspicuously different from the later ones – the contrasts and comparisons between the fictional giant and Christ form part – often a vital part – of the comic tension. That these tensions are resolved in later books is intellectually satisfying, but Rabelais had to pay a price: in the first novel and in parts of the second the giants are genuinely and profoundly comic: in the *Tiers Livre* and the *Quart Livre* the comedy is drained out of them and poured into other characters. The comic tension will no longer be within Pantagruel but between him and the error round about him.

One of the ways in which Pantagruel (and to a lesser extent Gargantua) appear in this first Chronicle as what may seem to be a parody of Christ or of patriarchs and apostles is easy to overlook. It is the way they cause ecstatic reactions. It happens too frequently to be a mere accident.

At Pantagruel's birth, Gargantua is moved to foretell 'en esperit de prophetie' that he will be the dominator of the Thirsty Ones; a few lines further down, one of the midwives is similarly moved 'en esperit propheticque'; in the next chapter, when Gargantua sees his wife's funeral cortège, he is 'tout soubdain ravy ailleurs' – a clear allusion to ecstatic transports. When Pantagruel pronounced judgment in the case of Baisecul *versus* Humevesne, the counsellors and doctors of law 'remained swooning in ecstasy for a good three hours'; and 'All were ravished in admiration at the more than human prudence of Pantagruel'.

The kind of ecstasy that Pantagruel provokes is specifically that caused by *admiratio*, astonishment.[12] It is the specific kind of ecstasy produced by Solomon in the Queen of Sheba when she came to try him with hard questions. It is also the ecstasy which seized the three astonished Apostles at the Transfiguration. Yet here it is a comic ecstasy, parallel to that awesome true ecstasy of the Old and New Testaments but transmuted by comedy into a source of amusement which has nothing to do with destructive parody. One could believe (in the generally Talmudic Old Testament setting of much of *Pantagruel*) that the hero was being presented as a sort of funny Solomon; and indeed he might be just that part of the time. But this cannot be the whole answer. In the episode of Thaumaste scriptural texts are applied to Pantagruel which originally applied to Christ, precisely to show that a *greater* than Solomon was present among men. Rabelais does not even parody ecstatic pretensions in the later ravishments of Thaumaste. The ecstasy induced by the sight of Pantagruel or by his achievements is not a parody of ecstasy at all: it is the removal of true ecstasy from a real context of awe into a world of laughter and comic intimacy.[13]

9. Scatological laughter

Another aspect of *Pantagruel* and *Gargantua* which strikes us forcibly is the frequent reference to the grosser bodily functions. We notice especially the defecation and the urination, but it is right to insist that these obviously grosser functions are frequently intertwined by Rabelais with others which we find less startling: with sweating, dribbling and so on. From *Gargantua* onwards all grosser functions, including sometimes urination, are used as a means of comic condemnation. In *Pantagruel* this is not so, although at least one of the changes Rabelais introduced in 1542 suggested that he wanted to divorce the fun of oceans of urine from the comic condemnation he increasingly associated with faeces. In general *Pantagruel* offers us oceans of urine not so much to condemn as to provide

[12] *Pant.*, TLF II, 80; III, 40; IX *bis*, 486 (*EC* II, 69; III, 36; XIII, 61). Cf. *Garg.*, TLF VI, 45; *EC* VII, 40: at the sounds of the glasses clinking, the young giant 'entroyt en extase', as though tasting the joys of paradise. In *Garg.*, TLF XIII, 4; *EC* XIV, 4, Grandgousier is specifically 'ravy en admiration'. Ecstasy caused by *admiratio*, astonishment, is lower in the scale than the ecstasy which raises the soul up to heaven. The two sorts of *ecstasy* figure in Rabelais, in contexts both serious and comic.

[13] *Pant.* IX *bis* title (omitted later, *EC* X). Pantagruel judges the case so equitably that his sentence was considered 'more admirable than Salomon's'. In *Pantagruel* (TLF XIII, 290; *EC* XX, 7) Thaumaste applies to Pantagruel words which Christ applied to himself: 'le mot evangelicque. *Et ecce plus quam Solomon hic.*' Cf. Matthew 12, 42.

opportunities for uncomplicated laughter and for deflating pomposity.[14]

Faeces are another matter altogether. This particular grossness is virtually absent from *Pantagruel* but may be conveniently treated here in a digression. In *Gargantua* scatology appears when Rabelais is bending his comedy away from pure amusement into the direction of carefully pointed comic satire. In this he is making masterly use of a human tendency. To refer to the arse *is* a means of deflation; to mess your trousers (whether from fear, anguish, complacency or self-indulgent guffawing) is laughable and seen to be so, even when decorum temporarily bans the words to describe such a plight from drawing-room and printed page. Fecal references belong at times to the category of 'signs'. Rabelais needs words to describe the fecal situation, but the situations as such have natural rather than imposed meanings.

The ease with which Rabelais uses such words should not really surprise us. Any reader of Rabelais who is puzzled by his easy references to faeces and similar bodily unpleasantness might ponder on the gulf separating our own domestic offices (bare and hygienic, synthetically redolent of pine-forests) and the foul jakes which even noble ladies had to put up with in Renaissance palaces. It sometimes seems as if an intolerance of bad smells and of the body as it really is is a feature of our deodorant age, going hand in hand with an unwillingness to face other aspects of the human condition, such as death and decay. A Renaissance author lived among fetid odours and ghastly stenches. He was at home with pain, deformity, illness, starvation and death. He did not like them, but he was not averse to referring to them. The body was a constant reminder of the corruption and humanity of such creatures as we, crawling betwixt heaven and earth. Incidentally, medical and other serious writing makes it plain that one did not have to be a Renaissance D. H. Lawrence to call bodily things by their proper names.

Laughter on lavatorial subjects was not confined to literature in French. One famous contemporary example of it in Latin was the so-called Sainte-Barbe War, the *Barbaromachia*, which set the Parisian Colleges of Montaigu and Saint-Barbe at each other's throats over the open sewer which ran down hill from Montaigu to the very doorstep of Sainte-Barbe, where it formed a large stinking mire.

Rabelais's deluges of urine are in the same spirit of good simple amusement. His giants are giants, and so piss copiously. By a sort of comic

---

[14] Cf. *QL* LIII, 96: 'At this Homenaz began to fizzle, fart, laugh, slaver and perspire.' All these physical excretions are signs of his fatuous joy at his weak joke designed to support a ridiculous theological assertion. *Pant.*, *TLF* XIV, 212f.; *EC* XXII, 48f. The dogs befouled Panurge's social climber with both urine and faeces until 1542, when Rabelais struck out the fecal reference (in italics): 'Ces villains chiens *la conchioient et* compissoient tous ses habillemens.'

contamination, so do the dogs and Gargantua's mule. Since Pantagruel
(when Rabelais wants him to be so) is immensely big, his urine is
immensely copious.[15]

Giants and stories about giants are intimately connected with childhood.
This is I suppose because we all as children live a significant part of our
lives as pygmies among giants who are erratic and incomprehensible. The
gigantic element in Rabelais is clearly associated with childhood memories
in *Gargantua*, and probably already so in *Pantagruel*. This seems to encourage
Rabelais to dwell on urine as little boys do, pissing against the sun. The
micturating dog, which canine anthropomorphism has encouraged adult
society to ignore while it looks the other way, is a good traditional means
of comic debunking. The 'refeeed' Lady of Paris in *Pantagruel* is getting her
deserts with a copiousness appropriate to a comic book about giants when
the dogs piddle all over her; even the fastidious age of Racine can get a
laugh out of the dog in *Les Plaideurs* which cocks its leg at the wrong
moment. In Rabelais we are far from the perverse sexual snigger of Pope,
very much nearer to the 'schoolboy malice' of Platonic views of laughter.[16]

Rabelais was a doctor, however much law dominates *Pantagruel*. A
Renaissance doctor lived with urine and faeces. In comedy his symbol of
office was not the stethoscope but the enema. Part of his duty might consist
in tasting his patients' urine. When Molière makes a character condemn an
uncouth doctor for not being used to looking people in the face, the
audience got the point: doctors (in comedies anyway) were more used to
looking at their patients' behinds.

The omnipresence of the signs and symptoms of human corporeality and
corruption could have led men and women to bury such unpleasant things
beneath polite periphrases and euphemisms. There certainly was such a
tendency in a Renaissance during which Christian realism about the body
was being overlaid with Platonic spirituality. But Rabelais is an author
who knew his Greek and Latin comedy and his Latin satirists. Such
literature is not given to taking refuge in the evasions of our polite
drawing-rooms or of the salons of Renaissance ladies.

10. Anti-feminist laughter

More difficult for a modern reader to appreciate with unbuttoned guffaws
is the comic antifeminism of parts of *Pantagruel* which is closely associated

[15] *Pant.*, TLF XIV, 249 *var.*; EC XXII, 83. In 1534, Rabelais makes the dogs' urine pass by the
abbey of St Victor (where it becomes the river Bièvre). Gobelin's scarlet cloth was believed
to owe the secret of its colour to the waters of this stream and to urine, supplied, it was said,
by students who were given free drinks beforehand.

[16] Cf. Pope's, *On a Lady who P-st at a Tragedy of Cato. Occasion'd by an Epigram on a Lady who
wept at it* (*Poems*, ed. L. Bult, London 1963, p.283). For Plato's 'schoolboy malice', see
below, p.231.

with gross 'body' humour. In each age, man in this mood seems to laugh at women within the idiom of his own time. Ever since St Jerome in the fourth and fifth centuries gave antifeminism a place in the sun in his writings against Jovinian, antifeminism occupied a large place in Christian writing. There was plenty of classical material to call on as well. Inevitably perhaps, this writing, while never ceasing to be potentially moral in intent, became allied to laughter. Jankin, the clerkly fourth husband of the Wife of Bath, laughed when he read his antifeminist tracts (until the Wife of Bath put an end to all that nonsense, incidentally proving the truth of much that her wretched husband was reading):

> He hadde a book that gladly, night and day,
> For his desport he wolde rede alway:
> He cleped it Valerie and Theophraste,
> At whiche book he lough alwey ful faste.
> And eek there was som-tyme a clerk at Rome,
> A cardinal, that highte seint Jerome,
> That made a book agayn Jovinian. . . .

Long and apparently ramshackle poetic compositions such as Gratien Dupont de Drusac's *Controverses des sexes masculin et femenin* and the much lighter pseudo-Rabelaisian work jocularly entitled the *Louenge des Femmes*, had an appeal corresponding in part to the appeal of James Thurber in antifeminist mood. It was agreed on all sides that antifeminism could be funny; we often laugh at what we are expecting to laugh at, and among the oldest of conventions was the one which made antifeminism comic, antifeminist attitudes a source of amusement. This is an area of laughter we may even now be losing.[17]

11. Taboo laughter

Anti-feminist humour of the kind we find in *Pantagruel* seems to have been particularly appreciated precisely because in other moods men were placing women on pedestals, killing dragons for them or, in the Renaissance, abusing Platonism by turning them into goddesses.

There is in all this bawdy or coarse antifeminism an element of happy taboo-breaking, though what exactly Renaissance taboos were is not all that easy to determine at any level of society. That a taboo was being mildly broken by even mentioning the female pudenda by their proper name is suggested by the long currency of such genteel paraphrases as *belle*

---

[17] Cf. the pseudonymous and ironical *Louenge des Femmes. Invention extraicte du Commentaire de Pantagruel sus l'Androgyne de Platon* (1551): reprint, 1967 by Ruth Calder, S.R. Publishers, Wakefield.

chose and *comment-a-nom*, the latter all the more amusingly effective from its first syllable then being fully nasalised and so corresponding in fact to *con*, the *syllable sale*.

Minor authors find a manifest delight in using the word *con*. A generation later Montaigne informs us of a genteel female taboo over the word *foutre*. These are just the taboo-breaking words which we find making us laugh in the French-speaking scene of *Henry V*.

The refinements of 'platonic' love encouraged refinements of language. Renaissance *Précieuses* were beginning to prefer to allude to sexual climaxes under the platonic term of 'dying'. In such a climate, comedy and satire react by increasing the grossness and directness of their terms of reference.

How far polite language avoided direct allusions to defecating and similar matters is not easy to discover. Certainly the actual facts of the body's functions were not hidden as they often are now. In the *Heptameron*, Margaret of Navarre has to explain why one of her ladies visited the jakes alone.

In serious vein, Gargantua's tutor goes to the privy with him, purging his mind of error with the Greek New Testament while the young man purges his body of its natural impurities.

That noticeably breaking wind was frowned upon by polite usage and so was potentially funny is shown by the title of one of the books in Rabelais's Library of Saint Victor. Schoolboys were warned against breaking wind in public by a schoolbook such as Johannes Sulpicius's *De moribus in mensa servandis*. As far as urinating was concerned, there seems to be little evidence to suggest that there was much of a taboo on words alluding to it. In this respect polite modern English, which seems weak in words derived from *to piss* used literally or figuratively, is significantly different from French and from popular and older English usage. I have no explanation of why this is so: but the fact itself might explain why deluges of comic urine strike us in English-speaking countries as more outlandish than Rabelais could have expected.

Rabelais's laughing allusions to the body in its sexual or its more grossly functioning rôle are comic at several levels. Some can be explained as taboos being broken, but not all that many. Other allusions remind us that 'what is Natural is not obscene'. This is no tolerant modern cant: *naturalia non sunt turpia* was an honoured adage. If pretentious convention denies this, then comedy will have its revenge through laughter. The words that Rabelais wrote are all ones which a Renaissance bishop could read out in court for the delight of his king.

Faeces are a sign of our humanity; copious faeces and urine may be signs of gluttony and excessive wine-bibbing; jesting allusions to the nates conjoined at all our conceptions may serve as a brake on the excessive spiritualisation of conjugal love; such things are, or may be, moral indicators, whether or not they are allied with laughter.

Like other platonising Christians, Rabelais held a high view of man. In Christian thought living man is a body plus a soul, neither of which makes full human sense without the other. The swing from body-humour to spiritual seriousness is an example of a Renaissance harmonising of extremes in a golden mean.

For Rabelais God was in the very mind of man; human sexuality was, in marriage, the most precious of the gifts of God. The apparent corollary of this higher view of man was that his grossly bodily nature seemed odder and odder. Montaigne, reacting against an excessive platonising of Christianity, was moved to wonder: 'nous sommes merveilleusement corporels.' Predisposed as his age was to seek the essential man in his soul, he was amazed to find how corporeal we all are. Montaigne, a humorous not a comic thinker, uses smiles and wit to bring this home. A comic writer prefers to work through the sudden glory of laughter awakened by thoughts of the bodily dross of humankind so oddly allied to an immortal soul.

The body and its grosser functions are above all potentially comic when men and women regret the existence of their corporeal reality. In a society such as the Renaissance, with its tolerance of the extremes of Lent and Carnival, the tolerance of interludes of bodily humour within the longer periods of soul-and-mind-centred seriousness seems natural enough. It was also one of the ways in which the corporeal religion of Christianity brought Platonism back to earth.

Rabelais calls on Greek and Latin to tell his readers that the most god-like aspect of man's person is his mind, 'his *nous* or *mens*' – and this mind is set in a body which is lower in the scale of excellence (*TL* XIII, 73). It is because the most divine part of man is his mind, that the body and its works can be made funny. A pornographic view of mankind sees the essential man or woman not in the mind, not in the soul, not, as Christians do, in the body and soul conjoined, but in the genitals or the backsides. It is serious to the point of boredom about such things, finding its laughter in the spiritual and mental aspirations of man, his religion, his ideals. That is almost the antithesis of Rabelais's position. Almost, but not quite. As a Christian he finds a concentration on either the body or the mind potentially comic. Man is both at once.

The association of certain verbal taboos with middle-class attitudes may lead to the assumption that bodily comedy is popular. If this is coupled with a political assumption that the people are the repository of goodness, vigour and virtue, it leads to a false interpretation of Rabelais as a popular and praiseworthy naturalist. In the comic Chronicles there is little reason to believe that Rabelais saw naturalism or the common people this way. As the Chronicles progress it becomes more evident that it was not as a champion of the people but as a platonising Christian that Rabelais found the body's functions, when overstressed or exaggerated, potentially laughable. Normally the common people are dismissed *en masse* as silly boobies, as the people of Paris are in *Gargantua*, or seen as amusing and odd, as they are most of the time in Brueghel or in Shakespeare, for whom an appropriate name for an artisan is Bottom. In the case of any one author or artist, I would not be inclined to read deep sociological meanings into this: it was too widespread a convention for that. *Pantagruel* fits snugly into a Renaissance dominated by erudite humanist Christians, often moving at least on the fringes of noble society and writing for almost anybody but 'the people'.

Rabelais tells us that he wrote his Chronicles during his spare time; that his main aim was to encourage the therapeutic joy of laughter; that indeed it was a highly important aspect of the doctor's calling to do so. I find no reason to disbelieve him (*Garg.*, prol.; QL, *Epistre Liminaire* – important for being in his own name). As his art matured, laughter did become more problematic to him; in the *Quart Livre* he betrays a sharper awareness of what it implies: then, the specially human property of laughter is no longer seen as always simply good and desirable. But that is some fifteen or sixteen years after *Pantagruel* was published.

12. Pantagruel: *an episodic chronicle*

Pantagruel is a novel of episodes sandwiched between the fantastic chronicles of giants. Such a book could simply have been a *roman à tiroirs*, of infinitely varying length and of no essential unity. The ease with which Rabelais later expanded some of his episodes suggests that the notion of *Pantagruel* as such a *roman* was not entirely absent from his mind. But this aspect of *Pantagruel* should not be exaggerated. Individual episodes are later expanded, but no new ones are slipped in or old ones slipped out. The advantage of the episodic structure is not, for Rabelais, that it meant he could put anything in anywhere, but that he could switch suddenly and effectively from subject to subject, style to style, laughter to sober reflexion. By the simple device of quoting a letter, pedagogical propaganda and glorying in the joys of wedlock can be introduced at will into the Chronicle without lengthy preparation. A comic battle can rapidly move from the mock-heroic into the densely religious and back again, by the simple and effective device of having the hero say his prayers. This movement from one set of emotional and intellectual concerns to another, or even their coexistence at one and the same time, need not be particularly challenging or confusing. Rabelais can be in deadly earnest when jests are coarser and thickest on the page.

Unity would not be a quality that one would spontaneously look for in a work constructed as *Pantagruel* is. Yet it is there. Partly this unity derives from the self-contained and entirely personal world that these Chronicles represent. The world of Rabelais's books, and the language he uses to build it up for us, are *sui generis*: they belong together; they belong nowhere else. There is also in each of the books a bundle of themes which tighten the structure at least as successfully as an imposed structure would do. In *Pantagruel* there is for example the thin red line of a comic concern with the failure of men to communicate their thoughts; a comic concern with language in general, a concern which overspills into other traditionally associated means of communication.

This concern with the comedy of language and gesture sometimes dominates over the other satirical concerns with which it is associated in the Chronicle. In later books it becomes even more dominant and more explicit. That such things intrigued Rabelais doubtless partly explains why there is often a gulf between the satirical points made explicitly in *Pantagruel* and the episodes which develop these points comically. The explicit concerns may be less comic than the language used to communicate them.

An attack on a legal abuse may be made quite unambiguously: yet ensuing pages which apparently develop this satirical attack may abandon satire in favour of pure comedy. A chapter devoted to educational propaganda, such as chapter VIII (Gargantua's letter), does not lead to a series of episodes in which Pantagruel's humanist learning is used to show up satirically the ignorance of the Old School. Such a technique is a later development, soon to be successfully employed in *Gargantua*, but finding no place in this first book.

A great deal of *Pantagruel* can be enjoyed with no more help than that of the footnotes in good editions, especially by readers sensitive to plays on words and forewarned of Rabelais's ideas about meaning and language. But there are some episodes particularly difficult for us to understand and enjoy: others which need special consideration because of their interest for the understanding and enjoyment of the book as a whole. They can conveniently be looked at now.

13. *Gargantua's perplexity*

The first of these episodes concerns Gargantua's inability to decide whether to rejoice over the birth of his son or lament over the death of Badebec his wife (*Pant.* III). Traditional educational methods encouraged two-sided debate, giving scholars the ability to develop 'both sides' of any argument, *pro et contra*. In this way it encouraged the belief that there were two sides to any question; that arguments of force could be mustered to defend even a case clearly opposed to the the true and the good. Traditional methods did not provide the means of resolving the problems posed by the existence of two weighty sets of mutually exclusive arguments towering up on either side of a decision. They encouraged forensic skill and scepticism rather than a quiet seeking after truth. This *pro et contra* method is especially associated by Rabelais with scholastic dialectic and the Sorbonne, the faculty of theology of the University of Paris, the *bête noire* of European humanist scholars in general and increasingly of Rabelais personally, as it had long been of Erasmus and of the entire du Bellay family. The hopeless inadequacy of *pro et contra* debating as a means of reaching truth often moved Rabelais to laughter not entirely devoid of bitterness. The bitterness can partly be explained by the secure hold that such sterile dialectic had on school and university syllabuses. A full generation later, Montaigne (in *De l'incertitude de nostre jugement*) humorously showed that anyone can use such a method to be wise – after the event. Arguments can be found in plenty, and with ease, to support the *pro* as well as the *contra*. What have such superficial skills which delight the pedagogical talking-shops – the *écoles de la parlerie* – to do with wisdom?

Gargantua, until he cuts the Gordian knot, is a good example of the man who can spin out arguments on both sides of a question, but not resolve his problems by their help. We are treated to a comic deformation of a standard lament for a dead wife – the comic writer can make anything laughable. Rabelais succeeds delightfully: Badebec is so depersonalised, so absurdly gigantic, that any feeling of pity for her which might have spontaneously arisen in real life, or have been artistically aroused in tragedy, is effectively eliminated. The yokelish delight of the giant over the birth of his son, coupled with his easy resolution of his sadness over Badebec's death, after duly marshalling simplified or grossly exaggerated versions of the stock-in-trade of consolatory commonplaces, effectively communicates the laughing tone. It also communicates to us, in the lightest of ways, a moral concern with the acceptance of the divine will which will be enriched and deepened in the following books.

One point is worth stressing: *Pantagruel*, for all its excellences, is Rabelais's first chronicle. His comedy will later blossom into the profound philosophical laughter of the *Tiers Livre*. In *Pantagruel* the giants are ambiguously comic, sharing qualities which will, in the later books, be those of Panurge or of some other butt of satirical laughter. That is because the very notion of the giants as 'exemplars of perfection' has not yet developed beyond a very sketchy possibility. In *Pantagruel*, Gargantua, dangling between the opposing extremes of suasive rhetoric, is close both to the mockingly treated *magistri nostri* of the Sorbonne in the next chronicle and – even more – to the risible Panurge of the *Tiers Livre*. He was caught like a mouse in pitch: 'et par ce moyen demouroit comme la souriz empeigée. . . .' This last phrase was added in 1542. Such a position is a comic one, meriting, and getting, our laughter. When Rabelais deepens and widens his comedy in the *Tiers Livre*, it is unthinkable that his new-model giants should remain in such a predicament. Then it will be Panurge who marshalls the arguments *pro et contra*; Panurge who cannot resolve his dilemma; Panurge who (in a telling return of the same proverbial phrase) evokes the thought of a mouse ensnared, 'une souriz empegée'. And unlike Gargantua, he will stay like one (*Pant.*, *EC* III, 11; *TL* XXXVII, beginning).

In his subsequent works, Rabelais so successfully adapted his comic techniques to the satirical ends, so successfully made laughter a vehicle for theological and philosophical comment, that one might be tempted to think of his art in *Pantagruel* as being in some ways incomplete without these characteristics. This is an anachronistic judgment, as coarse as to regret that (say) the *Fourberies de Scapin* is amoral in a way that the *Misanthrope* or *Le Tartuffe* are not. *Pantagruel* (until the 1534 edition made it partly so) is hardly ever satirical in the way that *Gargantua* often is. The first sustained application of comedy to satire that Rabelais made seems to have been his *Pantagrueline Prognostication* of 1533, which was followed closely by the additions to *Pantagruel* for the edition of 1534, unless *Gargantua*, as some think, was published in between. The first version of *Pantagruel* is a book of pure laughter, in which there is little or no fundamental moral comment implied in the act of laughing.

Laughter is, in itself, morally neutral at most. A good comedian can make us laugh at virtue as easily as he can make us laugh at vice – more easily perhaps, since virtue is often rigid and singleminded where vice may be pliant, multiform and diffuse. A comic writer who wishes to make us laugh satirically at vice, while keeping our respect for virtue intact, has got to guide our laughter along the paths of righteousness. This Rabelais increasingly does in later books by placing a quite unfunny norm of excellence side by side with a butt for our amusement, a butt whose every action, thought or hesitation may be exposed to the full gusts of our laughter. How he does this is best left until we look at the *Tiers Livre*: here it is enough to notice that one could draw up quite a list of laughable devices which are spread apparently at random through *Pantagruel* but will be strictly reserved for the comic butts in the later books. To give but a few examples: in the prologue of *Pantagruel* Alcofrybas briefly defends the value of the *Grandes Cronicques* with just such terms as Homenaz uses to defend the hated papal decretals in the *Quart Livre*.[18] Similarly Panurge who, in *Pantagruel*, is not at all the comic butt he will become in the *Tiers*

---

[18] Compare *Pant.*, prol., *TLF* 52f., (*EC* 43) with *QL*, *TLF* LIII, 8f.: *Pant.*: 'Est-ce rien cela? Trouvez moy livre, en quelque langue, en quelque faculté et science que ce soit, qui ayt telles vertus, proprietés et prerogatives, et je poieroy chopine de trippes. Non, Messieurs, non!' – this is pleasant banter. But cf. Homenaz in the *Quart Livre*: 'Est-ce rien

Livre, amuses Pantagruel with his *patelinage* and then is snugly packed off to bed heavy with food, where he remains 'jusques au lendemain l'heure du disner': in *Gargantua* Rabelais uses such terms to make us laugh at the ignorance of the young giant, before humanist education reformed him, or to round off the satire of Janotus de Bragmardo. In *Pantagruel* the good giant is allowed to make just those diabolical accusations of heresy for which Panurge will be noted and condemned in the philosophical laughter of the *Tiers Livre* . . .[19]

The hesitations of Gargantua in this part of *Pantagruel* are more comic than satirical. They do contain the seeds of the moral laughter of later books, but are not consistently moral here at all, except in the lightest of ways.

14. *The Library of Saint-Victor*

One episode which will repay patient study is the list of titles of comic books in the Library of Saint-Victor. The presence of this episode in a humanist book is at first sight puzzling. The library of Saint-Victor's Abbey was probably the most important in the whole of France. It was a storehouse of valuable manuscripts and early printed books; its catalogue (drawn up by Claude de Grandrue in 1513) has come down to us, and is positively mouthwatering in its richness. Why should Rabelais have mocked this Library, when he might have been expected to venerate it?

The first reason is, I suspect, connected with the tendency of most ages to be most critical of their immediate predecessors. The late mediaeval manuscripts of the Abbey Library, like many early printed books also, represented just that old-fashioned learning which the New Learning rashly dismissed *in toto*. A second and perhaps more cogent reason is purely hypothetical: it is not connected with any of the books the library possessed but with the fact that the Abbey to which this Library belonged was

---

cela? [. . .] Mais trouvez moy livres on monde, soit de philosophie, de medicine, des Loigs, des Mathematicques, des letres humaines, voyre (par le mien Dieu) de la saincte Escripture, qui en puissent autant tirer. Poinct. Nargues, nargues!' The techniques are closely parallel: the moral imports very different.

[19] *Pant*. ix, *TLF* 144; *EC* 161. Compare with *Garg*., *TLF* xx, 267; *EC* xxii, 249. In both cases the characters go tipsy to bed and sleep 'jusques au lendemain, heure de disner' or, 'jusques au lendemain, huict heures'. – *Pant*. vi, *TLF* 30; *EC* 30: Pantagruel uses the words *dieu* and *diable* as Panurge does in the later books. Faced with the Latinate jargon of the 'Ecolier Limousin' he exclaims, 'Tu es quelque heretique'. Again this is typical of the later Panurge: cf. his reactions to the good dying poet Raminagrobis (*TL* xxii). Similarly, in *Pantagruel* (*TLF* xiii, 103f.; *EC* xviii, 91f.) both the naïf Thaumaste and the gigantic hero are equally 'elevated and transported in thought' the night before the debate. Again, the phrase with which the author comically defends the 'truth' of his tall stories in the prologue to *Pantagruel* (*TLF* 84f.; *EC* 68f.) is a variant of the same phrase used to end the history of the death of Pan (*QL* xxviii, 66).

associated with open hostility towards Erasmus and humanism in general. The anti-Erasmianism of the monks of Saint-Victor in 1532 is known from a letter of John Spyractes to Boniface Amerbach dated 21 April. 'There are here,' he writes, 'the very worst kind of monks in the monastery of Saint-Victor near the walls of Paris. They have compiled and stuck together the most stupid and criminal of volumes against Erasmus; they brought it to Badius begging him to print and publish it, but he flatly refused. This I learned from an honest and learned German in charge of booksales for Badius.'[20] In wishing, unsuccessfully, to join in the printed attacks on Erasmus, the monks of Saint-Victor were allying themselves with the supporters of the recently dead, princely cardinal Albert Pio da Carpi and, especially in 1532, with John Genesius Sepulveda, whose *Antapologia pro Alberto Pio* had just appeared in both Rome and Paris, being published by Antoine Augerau on 22 March 1532. In the light of this, it is understandable that Rabelais should make fun of the Abbey Library for its old-fashioned theology. It *is* odd, though, that an enthusiastic Erasmian such as he was should make no direct allusion to their still-born book if he knew about it. Perhaps this is because he had set the episode in a vaguely distant past. There are few direct allusions in the first version of the comic catalogue to books written or published in or about 1532. Insofar as the satire of the Abbey Library has a period flavour, it seems to recall the time from the end of the fifteenth century up to the early years of the 1520s. It could be that Rabelais wanted to leave his readers with the feeling that the monks of Saint-Victor had been obscurantist from time immemorial.

Some of the jests in the catalogue simply parody good-naturedly old-fashioned works of moral theology, still read in the 1520s and 1530s, such as a poem by the late fifteenth-century poet Olivier de la Marche entitled the *Parement & triumphe des Dames*. The first chapter of this poem is headed, the 'Slipper of Humility': Rabelais invents several other titles by comic analogy. They all deserve a laugh. Other parodies take us on to more controversial ground. Among the imaginary figures cited as authors of silly books in the first version of the library catalogue are five very real theologians: Tartaretus, Bricot, Major, Béda and Sutor. Peter Tartaretus, a pillar of the Sorbonne and an authority on Aristotle and on the dethroned, old-fashioned, scholastic philosopher Peter of Spain, probably figures in this list less as a representative of an out-dated theological approach (there were many such) than because his name led to an easy pun on *tarter*, a current slang word meaning – inevitably – to defecate: hence the title of his book: *De modo cacandi*. Bricot may well be Thomas Bricot, another Aristotelian, whose *Tractatus insolubilium* appeared in Paris in 1511. (A better candidate would be Guillaume Bricot, the *pénitencier* of Notre-Dame

[20] *Die Amerbachkorrespondenz*, ed. Hartmann, IV, pp.127f.

de Paris, an enemy of Reuchlin and hence of all good humanists concerned to defend Hebrew learning.) The 'Beda', whose book on the *Excellence of Tripe* suggests the gross feasting attributed to the Sorbonagres as well as the quality of his thought, is Noël Béda, the syndic of the Sorbonne, not the Venerable Bede who had, in general, a good press among humanists. Jests against Béda were welcome at any time among supporters of Erasmus or of the du Bellays; and Rabelais was both. Already in the early 1520s Noël Béda was publishing books which Rabelais would have considered worthless and stupid. In 1532, under Béda's leadership, the Sorbonne sought to place an interdict on Erasmus's 'most Christian and most elegant' defence against the recent condemnations of his writings by the theological faculty; that gave added zest to any mockery directed against him. As befits someone of his power and authority, Béda appears in the title of another comic book, given additional importance by being cited outside of the Abbey booklist: *Concerning Hunchbacks and the Deformed: In Defence of Our Masters of the Sorbonne*. Béda was a cripple and a hunchback, defects which contemporary satirists exploited without mercy (*Pant.*, TLF x, 102; *EC* xiv, 96).

The most clearly pro-Erasmian of the satirical gibes in the first version of the Library is the seventh from the end – the last entry to laugh at a Sorbonne theologian by name: 'Sutor: *Against Someone who called him a Wretch, and, That Wretches are not Condemned by the Church.*' For a humanist such as Rabelais, Sutor was almost the archetypal figure of monastic reaction. As a Carthusian he represented monasticism at its most severe; his book against translating the Bible (1525) is obscurantist to a degree surprising even when we read it today, with all passion spent; his taste for controversy seemed endless – witness his *Counter-defence against the defence of Erasmus entitled, Against the Ravings of Peter Sutor* (1525).

The kind of satire we have here – a large part of the laughter is provoked by the poor quality of the very doggy Latin – owes much to the *Letters of Obscure Men*. The debt is not hidden. The famous letters were supposed to be addressed to Magister Noster Ortuinus Gratius. The same 'Maistre Ortuinus' is credited with a fecal book in the Saint-Victor catalogue.

The success of this list of comic books was clearly great. Rabelais added and added to it until the definitive text of 1542. But despite the great increase from some forty-two titles in 1532 to nearly a hundred more in 1542, the spirit of the list remains the same: satirical certainly, but with the accent on laughter. The theological satire is one element only, and by no means always the dominant element, in an ever-changing comic concern. The law is well represented: the second title *Braguetta Juris* ('The Codpiece of the Law'), is a deformation of the *Brocardica Juris*, an elementary law book which figures again in a major episode of the *Tiers Livre*. Other titles aim to raise a laugh and little more: laughter for its own sake needs no excuse in

Pantagruel, though it does later. Such titles as the *Decree of the University of Paris concerning the Gorgeousness of Filles de Joie* still get their well-deserved smile; to appreciate a later title such as *Franctopinus, De re militari*, one above all needs to recall that *Franc taupin* was the familiar name given to a militia-man of the part-time citizens' 'train-bands' of the period: it would be equivalent to making a clownish inexperienced militiaman write a treatise on military strategy. The joke is better still if one knows that a real book entitled *De re militari*, by Robertus Valturius, appeared in Paris in 1532.

Time spent with the footnotes of the *Edition Critique* (still, with all its faults, the best guide to this chapter) can bring a great deal of the laughter back to life, at least for the reader who has retained a modicum of Latin. The reader of the period would not have needed the footnotes, but he would have needed both to be able to read Latin and to have some acquaintance with humanist movements in Germany and France.

15. Gargantua's letter to his son

The laughter of chapter VII ends with a rather confusing allusion to 'ceste noble ville de Tubinge'; a formula recalling the great printing centre Rabelais seems to have associated with superstition and ignorance. But Pantagruel was in fact in Paris. With the laughter still ringing in our ears we suddenly come across the sustained and stately earnestness of chapter VIII: the letter of Gargantua to his son, written 'from Utopia, on the seventeenth of May' . . . and we supply such year date as we wish.

Attempts have been made to make even this chapter 'funny' too, to see in it mockery and laughter, where most see the Renaissance at its gentle best.

The art of letter-writing was highly developed in the Renaissance. This letter follows all the rules of composition. It is a clear, balanced, earnest statement of a recognisably liberal, humanist theology, honouring learn-ing, honouring matrimony, and above all honouring the liberal Catholic view of man's moral and religious place in the divine scheme, all of course in the context of divine grace.

For us who know that Rabelais, a friar turned monk, a priest vowed to celibacy, was the author of this book, the opening words are particularly challenging: 'the greatest of God's gifts' is man's ability to find, through his children, a species of immortality and so, 'even in the course of this transitory life,' perpetuating his name and his seed. This is God's way of partially restoring to man what he had lost when the sin of disobedience brought death into this world.

God, the sovereign *Plasmateur*, decreed that the glorious *Plasmature* he had made man out of should return to nothingness: that is, that man should die and his body rot, returning to the dust from whence it came. The terms *Plasmateur* and *plasmature* sound Greek, but are not so really, being modelled on early Latin Christian usage: since the time of Tertullian God was *deus hominis plasmator* – the Moulder of man's body – a term sometimes paralleled to God's other rôle in the creation of man, the *Afflator animarum*, the Inspirer of souls.

For man, death is the separation of body and soul. At the Fall the soul, created immortal, saw its body, the 'magnificque plasmature, en laquelle avoiṭ esté l'homme créé', reduced to dust. Only through legitimate marriage can this personal loss be made up from parent to child, through the divinely ordained channels of 'seminal propagation' within 'lawful wedlock'. It was opinions such as these which underpinned the determination of many Renaissance Christians to abolish compulsory celibacy. Yet such ideas should not be seen as 'protestant' – not simply because 'protestant' as an adjective has no sense at all when applied to the 1530s in France, but because many Catholics held them strongly as well. These are traditional ideas which critics of the Church's comparatively newfangled compulsory celibacy could press into the service of their cause, whether they were 'Protestants', 'Catholics' or any other variety of Christian.

This letter is often rightly cited as further proof of contemporary enthusiasm for the Renaissance. It reminds us that people at the time were aware that they were living in an age of intellectual and spiritual renewal. The notion of there being a Renaissance in France in the sixteenth century is not merely one foisted on to the period by a later taste for historical compartmentalisation: Frenchmen of the time gloried in the restoration of learning, as did more international figures such as Erasmus. Yet this letter also reminds us that some aspects of the Renaissance in France were almost as much evolution as revolution.

Gargantua's categories of thought are essentially those of traditional philosophy, going back directly to Aristotle and Plato and enriched by Judaeo-Christian glosses and interpretations. Gargantua is singing the praises of 'generation'. Since Aristotle, the notion of 'generation' almost inevitably calls forth the twin notion of 'corruption'. For centuries the best scholars were making such an association and were still doing so. *Generatio* and *corruptio* are aspects of one and the same process in the physics which Christians took over from Aristotle. If there were no 'corruption', then there would be no need for 'generation'. This process of generation-and-corruption will last until the end of this world, when in the words of Rabelais and St Paul, Jesus Christ 'shall have handed his peaceful kingdom back to God the Father'. In this way, Aristotle and St Paul are in easy harness. Rabelais's allusions to scripture need to be carefully noted. Both some of his best jokes and some of his profoundest assertions depend upon our recognising the Biblical authority behind the words. A precise knowledge of the fullest senses of scripture was the major aim of most of the humanists in their educational policies.

Here the allusion is to both I Corinthians 15 in general and to verse 24 in particular: 'Then cometh the end, when he [Christ] shall have delivered up the Kingdom to God, even the Father.' Thereafter there will be no more sin; no more death; no more corruption – so no more generation. All will be at rest in perfect and consummate peace. This chapter 15 of I Corinthians – still read at the service for the burial of the dead – is the great resurrection chapter, refuting (with II Timothy) any notion that the succession of one generation to another is really what resurrectional immortality means. It is therefore a useful corrective to any misunderstanding of Rabelais's enthusiasm for the 'species of immortality' that God has granted to man through his children born in lawful wedlock. Immortality through one's legitimate children is not a substitute for that fullest immortality that man will find at the end of the world; it is a compensation which will last until Christ's final victory and the Resurrection of the dead (*Pant.* VIII, *TLF* 21f.; *EC* 19f).

In Aristotelian thought, *generatio* is twinned not only with *corruptio* but also with *educatio*. The man and woman who together exercise their God-given privilege of sexuality and 'generate' a child, have an inescapable moral obligation, which in that man-centred age was especially incumbent on the father: the duty to 'educate' their progeny. This duty Gargantua joyfully assumes. The twin concepts of generation-and-corruption and generation-and-education form the intellectual structure of the letter.

At death, Gargantua's soul will, at the bidding of God, leave 'ceste habitation humaine'. It is wryly amusing that a theologically illiterate school of criticism used to see proof of Rabelais's atheism in this passage, for it continues to be anchored in the language of scripture. In this case we are referred to II Corinthians 5, 1–2. There the body is seen as the *oikétèrion*, the *habitatio*, the 'temporary dwelling place' of the soul, until it is called heavenward (*Pant.* VIII, *TLF* 35; *EC* 30).

Gargantua when he is dead (that is, with his body returned to the dust, while his soul is in the Divine Presence) would see his son on earth; he would feel that he had not 'totally died' (that is, that his body and soul had not been totally severed in and from this transitory world); it would be as though he had transmigrated from one place to another, living on as body-and-soul in this world also, through his son.

But his son, inevitably the image of his father's body, can only be made, under grace, into an image of his father's blameless life, if properly educated. It is through the educated soul especially that the immortality of the family name is safeguarded; through the soul (not the lower part, the body) that 'our name remains blessed amongst men'. Rabelais, with Melanchthon and many others, apparently thinks that 'seminal propagation' not only gave a child his body but his soul as well. This doctrine, known as traducianism, is quite an orthodox assumption, though one not universally held. The thorough education of the soul as well as the body will make Pantagruel a worthy image of his father: 'ung mirouer representant la *personne* de moy ton pere.' *Personne* (*'persona'*) is a technical theological word meaning that unity of one body and one soul which makes the full individual man so much more than a mere 'thing' (*Pant.* VIII, *TLF* 64; *EC* 63).

All this is placed in the context of lawful wedlock, 'mariage légitime'. We can glimpse why Rabelais's first-born son was no casually spawned bastard but Théodule ('Slave-of-God') Rabelais. His later children, François and Marie, were destined to be fully legitimated, 'as though born in lawful wedlock', and to bear the surname of their father. How an ex-monk and a celibate priest could perhaps have considered his own children legitimate, his marriage legitimate, will be clearer when we come to the *Tiers Livre*. The 1530s were, after all, a time when criticism of traditional western Catholicism was growing in momentum; reformed Christianity, in all its principal manifestations, introduced the optional marriage of priests and ministers. Celibacy is not a doctrinal matter but a disciplinary one, one the Church can change at her corporate will. Many loyal Catholic Christians hoped with Erasmus that the Church would relax its discipline, the proven cause of concubinage, whore-mongering and vice. Erasmus's only hope was that monks, if they did leave their cloisters to marry, should do so officially with Papal blessing – and if possible leave their wickedness behind them.

The influence of Roman law is also important. Roman law had no time for love-matches. The central question was one of authority where marriage was concerned: had the *paterfamilias* given his consent? This letter of Gargantua's is entirely patriarchal. In the *Tiers Livre* we shall see why.

The parallel paean in praise of education was part of the spirit of the times too. In the 1520s and 1530s educational treatises were in the air, being written and published by a great many writers, known and unknown, including Budé, Erasmus, and Vivès.

Educational ideas in *Pantagruel* are not fully worked out as they are some two years later in *Gargantua*. There is in Gargantua's letter a committed, occasionally aggressive, note which reminds us that, however much the humanists might be in general agreement among themselves, the battle was far from won, especially the battle for Greek and for the Bible made accessible.

That Rabelais's giant should see the restoration of learning as an act of God's goodness ('la bonté divine') or that printing should be seen as an invention directly attributable to divine inspiration – as indeed a divine counterblast to the devilish promptings which led to the invention of gunpowder – is at one with his age: they are humanist commonplaces. The notion once current that the Renaissance was a pagan affair was based on a series of misunderstandings. In France as elsewhere the Renaissance was shot through and through with the divine, especially in the earlier years, when all the main exponents of the New Learning were religious men. But commonplace or not, it took a committed humanist to propagate these ideas in 1532, at the very moment that the Sorbonne was censoring books, condemning Erasmus, marshalling its still formidable powers against the New Learning and, specifically, trying to persuade Francis I to forbid printing altogether throughout his domains. (In February 1535 they were temporarily successful: Francis did forbid printing; and the New Learning was – temporarily but for a while successfully – equated with heresy and error.) For Rabelais's giant, on the contrary, sound learning is as 'manna from heaven', something which even women and girls have learned to aspire to. The placing of women and girls after male criminals in the list of seekers after the New Learning is not simply humorous: everything in due order! But to approve of the educating of women at all was by no means a routine commonplace, as Erasmus's delightful colloquy *The Abbot and the Learned Woman* shows.

The standard scholastic notion that man has the duty to educate his child becomes suddenly revolutionary when we look at the educational content.

The details of the syllabus are clearly set out: Greek, Latin and Hebrew are to be learned, together with 'Chaldaïcque et Arabicque', the last three languages in order to understand the scriptures better. The full Renaissance encyclopaedia of learning is presented, including geometry, arithmetic, music, botany, geography, medicine, law. Astronomy is honoured; divinatory astrology and the Art of Ramón Lull are unique in being condemned, together with corrupt writings from the time of the *infelicité des Gothz* – the learning of the later Middle Ages. (The 'Art of Lullius' condemned here is a kind of derivative kabbalistic magic, using a lettered wheel.)[21]

The quiet enthusiasm comes to a first climax in medicine – including frequent dissections by which the microcosm which is man can be known, and Arabic medicine which was causing a flurry in the Lyonese bookshops at this time. There are a 'few hours a day' spent on a study of the New Testament and the Old in the original tongues. In this way the young giant – now the full image of his father – is enriched with the New Learning, and so becomes (in an ancient and honoured Latinate phrase) an *abysme de science*, an *abyssus sapientiae*.

Yet this is not all. The fuller climax comes, as is right, at the end. *Scientia sine conscientia: ruina animae* was a scholastic axiom honoured by the New School also: without a trained moral sense, mere learning leads to the

[21] *Pant.* VIII, *TLF* 132; *EC* 103. The 'art of Lullius' condemned is the magic art of combinatory divination based upon his *Liber de articulis fidei*. It had been attacked in the fifteenth century by Gerson (*Contra Raymundum Lulli*), but remained in favour among many Renaissance magicians.

downfall of the soul. Gargantua cites it as a reminder of man's duty to serve, fear and love God, to place all his hope in him, so to join himself to him that sin for all its reality can never separate man from his Saviour. This, in a phrase redolent of Catholic orthodoxy and consciously anti-Lutheran, is achieved by 'foy formée de charité', by *fides charitate formata*, that is, by a faith which is incomplete until it finds its solid 'form' in Christian Love.

This religious ending to the letter evokes Christ's summary of the Law and the Prophets, that kernel of Renaissance evangelical Christianity frequently present in Rabelais's novels. Gargantua then recalls the words of II Corinthians 3, 1, in order to remind his son that reliance on grace does not mean standing idle while God does all the work: 'Et les graces que Dieu te a données, icelles ne reçoipz point en vain.' In other words, God's gifts will be received 'in vain' if the Christian does not put them to effective use. In this letter each and every good thing is presented as a gift of grace: marriage, seminal generation, the blessing of children, moral integrity, sound learning, printing – even of course the writings of pagan or pre-Christian writers such as Plutarch. But these gifts have to be used; and used aright. Used wrongly they lead to the downful (*ruina*) of the soul.

This is the earliest example in Rabelais of what is to become a major aspect of his thought: all that is good and true comes from God, the Giver of all good gifts; but man is not a passive vessel for this grace abounding; he is a responsible *persona* who must 'work together' with grace if it is not, to his greater peril, to be received in vain.

This letter, carefully and cogently written, stands out from its context, without being detached from it. It is not Rabelais's last word on many of the questions raised; it is, on the contrary, lopsided and incomplete when set against some of his subsequent writings. The education is mainly book-ish; so bookish that a boy or man who followed it through would be better equipped for a life of scholarship than for kingship. The closest of parallels may be established between Rabelais's pedagogy in *Pantagruel* and the new educational ideas championed by lawyers. It is probable that the ideal education outlined in the first Chronicle arose fairly directly out of legal treatises and was more appropriate for a budding legal expert than a prince.[22] The education of the body and the preparation of the giant for his future rôle as Christian Knight are passed over in a very few lines:

[22] Cf. the legal education outlined by Jean de Coras in *De Jure Civili in Artem Redigendo*: chap. 5: *Quibus artibus literisque tinctus esse debeat Juris studiosus*, in *Tractatus Universi Juris*, Venice 1583. Nowhere does Rabelais include specific training in traditional rhetoric, dialectic or logic; he does not see them as appropriate to gentlemen or humanist scholars, who base their style on sound classical models and treatises. He himself had certainly studied both.

For since you are becoming a man and growing up, you must emerge from the tranquillity and leisure of study, learning chivalry and arms so as to defend my household and to succour our friends, in all their affairs, against the assaults of evil-doers (*Pant.*, *TLF* VIII, 154f.; *EC* VIII, 121f.).

This is not entirely an afterthought, crammed in at the last minute, but the ideal is less satisfying than the fully developed education of the Christian prince in *Gargantua*. Here study is conceived, as many of the late Romans thought of it, as an 'honourable leisure', an *otium honestum*, to be followed later by a separate training in chivalrous virtues and duties. In *Gargantua*, book-learning and princely chivalry are acquired together, interpenetrating the whole system of education to their mutual enrichment.

The next sentence, which again bears richer fruit in *Gargantua*, is not really an integral part of the education system of *Pantagruel* at all, but a glide enabling the letter to fit more snugly into the context of the following chapters:

And I want you briefly to try out how you have profited: something you cannot do better than by publicly defending theses for debate, on all matters, against all comers, and by haunting the educated men to be found in Paris and elsewhere.

But however much we criticise the detail of the pedagogy, this delightful letter is the first indication that Rabelais saw his novel not simply and totally as a comic relaxation from more exacting matters, nor merely as a Lucianic romp through contemporary foibles, but as a richer work in which laughter and mockery could be allied to positive and instructive propaganda.

16. Panurge and Pantagruel

The contrast between the Gargantua and Pantagruel of this letter, and the wordy arrival of Panurge in the following chapter (IX) is striking; apart from its own intrinsic delight, Panurge's arrival forms a buffer between the serious giants of the letter and the first public encounter of Pantagruel with the 'gens lettrez' of Paris: which (as is normal in this book, where the prosaically expected never happens) is not a serious demonstration of the superiority of the education he has received, but a good piece of legal laughter, with a pinch of something more. The case of Baisecul versus Humevesne is legal and linguistic comedy. But first we meet the equally unexpected Panurge, where the linguistic humour dominates.

Whether Rabelais had in mind a permanent rôle for Panurge in later books is anybody's guess. He may not even have had further French books in mind at all. Nevertheless, Pantagruel finds Panurge 'lequel il ayma toute sa vie', though we should not expect those words to have a meaning extending into books yet unwritten. There is little sign that the subsequent developments of Panurge in the *Tiers Livre* and the *Quart Livre* are present even in germ in Rabelais's artistic consciousness. Panurge in this first Chronicle is the crafty one, as befits a man whose name is a light gallicising of *panourgos* – a Greek term applied, rarely in a good sense, to a man ready to do anything. The word is fully classical, but New Testament Greek knows both *panourgos* and the general term *panourgia* ('craftiness, cunning'). The terms appear also in the Greek Septuagint, which in practice was at least as influential in humanist circles as the Hebrew original. Anybody who knew Greek in any of its forms would have 'placed' Panurge at once: a trickster ready for anything. Not perhaps *a* trickster, but *the* Trickster: craftiness personified.

His name, though Greek in meaning, was known to the Latin-educated from its appearing in Cicero's *Pro Roscio Comoedo*, where *Panurgus* is the surname of the actor or pantomime (*histrio*) that Cicero's lawsuit was about. From the outset, Panurge's use of many languages is part of his 'trickery', based upon his mastery of word and persuasion. A *légiste* such as Rabelais probably connected the trickster with the late classical *impostores* ('deceivers') to whom Budé devoted an interesting note in his *Annotations on the Pandects*: such *impostores* were the delight of kings; the prototypes for Frenchmen were not so much the classical figures of Ciphissodorus, Pantaleon or Matreas, as François Villon – not the real Villon only, but the Villon about whom had coalesced a whole series of merry pranks and practical jokes. 'Our own fathers' time', Budé writes, 'saw an outstanding *impostor* in François Villon: his name alone is as good as a definition' (*Opera* III, 255AB).

It is appropriate that Panurge should be no Baisecul trapped in his own fluent incoherence, but a clever impostor who can impose upon others. In *Pantagruel* he is amoral; all is forgiven so long as he makes us laugh. This is as it should be: moral considerations do not normally apply to the farcical world of the impostor. Whether we are dealing with the mediaeval or the Renaissance farce, Rabelais's Chronicles or Molière's comic delights, morality is introduced skilfully into the comedy by a conscious artistic decision, if it is there at all. On the trestles we expect the servants to cheat their masters; the sons to cheat their parents; the Sganarelles to cheat the lot of them, outrageously. The more such characters break the conventions the more we laugh. Their very presence is enough to banish tragedy and seriousness: even imprisonment under the Turks – a real hazard at the time – becomes amusing when Panurge is the prisoner and Panurge the storyteller.

Modern reactions to Panurge are mixed. Many quite sensitive readers find him unappealing, even unfunny; this is a pity since it suggests that irrelevant, moral or even humanitarian concerns are slipping in between the laughter Rabelais sought to evoke and our own reactions. It is true that there are signs that Rabelais himself soon felt he had exhausted the potentials of his first conception of Panurge as the embodiment of *panourgia*. His absence from the next novel, *Gargantua*, can be explained on chronological grounds – though Rabelais would have ignored such matters if he had wanted to do so. In the *Tiers Livre* and the *Quart Livre* there is a character called Panurge of course, but he is not simply the natural extension or development of the character we meet in *Pantagruel*, any more than the new, wise Pantagruel is the logical or aesthetically natural development of the original jolly giant. The comedy later acquires intrinsic moral implications which remove Panurge far from the Panta-leons and the Villons. Yet there are probably few better ways open to the reader who wishes to study Rabelais's art as a storyteller who enjoys telling a story for its own sake, with no other apparent motive than to provide amusement and provoke laughter, than to concentrate on those parts of *Pantagruel* where Panurge dominates, especially in the absence of the hero.

His escape from the Turks is an almost perfect example of its *genre*, a world where nothing at all has the same resonances as in real life; where fire does not burn, death does not matter, prisoners escape against impossible odds, the clever weak outwit the stupid strong.

This totally unreal world in which Panurge moves is in striking contrast with the episodes in which Pantagruel dominates: these often have undertones of serious concern which occasionally come to the surface in explicit statement. The tour of the universities which Pantagruel makes in search of legal learning is light-hearted enough and a delight to read. Yet for all its exaggerations it deals with the real world of the wandering scholar and with the symbols of student life (such as the *Pierre levée* at Poitiers, a large menhir which played a part in student rags and initiation ceremonies). When Pantagruel is about, reality may break through at any time – real people may make their appearance in the book: 'le noble Ardillon', Rabelais's Benedictine abbot at Fontenay-le-Comte, to whom his friend Bouchet, the poet and chronicler, dedicated his *Annales d'Acquitaine*; or 'le docte Tiraqueau', a man whose name will be linked with Rabelais's as long as he is read. Places that Rabelais is known to have been connected with – Maillezais for example – crop up in some profusion. This has not unnaturally led readers to wonder whether there is some sort of autobiographical basis for the university tour in search of law, or even for Pantagruel himself. It would be unwise to press the point so far as to use these episodes as material to fill in the many gaps in our knowledge of Rabelais's real life: there is much to place against so easy an assumption. One of the few allusions we *are* able to check to some extent concerns Pantagruel's visit to Montpellier. There – unlike Rabelais – he decides not to stay, rejecting the law school because of the inferiority of the professors

– but also rejecting medicine as an alternative because the professors stink of enemas.[23]

It is jokes such as these which make one wonder whether part at least of *Pantagruel* does not go back to student farces and play-acting: such a jest would have gone down well in the world of a medical students' farce. This farcical quality may explain what may otherwise seem the casual heart-lessness of one of the few possibly dateable allusions in *Pantagruel*: the reference to Toulouse as a university where Pantagruel refused to linger, 'because they burn their regents like red herrings'. Depending on dates, Rabelais is presumably alluding to the burning at the stake of Jean de Caturce, a graduate in law, in June 1532, or to the events leading up to it. It was a truly awesome outburst of persecution involving many others, including a close friend of Rabelais's, Jean de Boysonné, whose Latin poems are our only source of knowledge about the life and death of Rabelais's little son Théodule. Yet Pantagruel's reaction to the burning of regents is that of an enlarged Penthagruel: 'God forbid that I should die that way, for I am naturally thirsty enough, without warming myself up any further.' If Panurge had made such a remark one could have shrugged it off as part of his amoral *panourgia*; but Rabelais has so interwoven reality and fantasy in the episodes where Pantagruel is to the fore, that such a solution is not possible. Perhaps what we have here is an example of comic understatement such as Swift used in his *Modest Proposal*, where it is suggested that the English solve the Irish problem by eating Irish babies. One way of protesting against huge abominations is to understate their seriousness with a laugh.

Renaissance Christians were, on the whole, highly selective with their pity. But the repression of heresy in Toulouse in 1531–2 was particularly harsh; simply to be a supporter of Erasmus was sufficient presumption of heretical leanings. Jean de Boysonné, despite his legal dignity as professor-regent in law, was obliged to make a solemn and humiliating abjuration; his house was confiscated and he was fined the then enormous sum of one thousand pounds. Perhaps that is why he is not mentioned in *Pantagruel*. We are told nothing of Toulouse fining her regents, but of her custom of burning them.

Boysonné's fate may have defied even Rabelais's comic genius. But if he is alluding definitely and unequivocally to Jean de Caturce – and he may not be – then we might remember that Jean de Caturce was not simply a

[23] *Pant*. v, *TLF* 59f.; *EC* 52f. At Montpellier, the medical professors stank of enemas: the *légistes* were a shovelful of nonentities. Since Pantagruel is presented as the 'possessor of the lands of Gravot, Chavigny and Pomardière' – and since he becomes a lawyer – it is at least arguable that he is partly a comic transposition of Rabelais's father rather than of Rabelais himself, who never apparently possessed these lands and who, unlike his father, was not a practising lawyer, despite his legal erudition.

liberal Catholic. He stood for much that Rabelais abhorred, especially when in a Twelfth-night farcical mood. For Caturce was a declared enemy of Twelfth Night. Instead of announcing the ritual Twelfth-night toast, *Le Roy boit*, he had called out, 'Christ regne en nos cœurs'; the 'accustomed dances and dissoluteness' of Twelfth Night he wanted to replace by Gospel readings. This religious zeal, with its gloomy puritanical flavour, did not then simply appear as the excesses of a glum sectarian with a bad sense of timing; it seemed like heresy and, at least in Toulouse, was readily punished as such. Jean de Caturce was a sectarian extremist whose death would not call forth Rabelais's pity as a matter of course.[24] All the great figures of the time seem impervious to the sufferings of those they fundamentally disagreed with. The kindly More was not opposed to burning heretics; even Montaigne, who was no trimmer, and who protested against cruelty used against American Indians and between French opponents during the Wars of Religion, makes no reference at all to the massacre of St Bartholomew; the gentle bishop Amyot, translator of Plutarch, was not worried by the harsh and zealous persecution of error in his diocese; Rabelais, in *Gargantua*, positively incites Francis I to send the Principal of the Collège de Montaigu to the stake, together with his cronies. The burning of the zealous and sectarian Jean de Caturce in a wave of inquisitorial bigotry would not have recommended Toulouse to Rabelais: but the death of Caturce himself may have left his pity quite untouched: an enemy of Twelfth Night finds no allies in *Pantagruel*. And once pity is absent, laughter is possible.

17. *Legal laughter: the glossators*

This allusion to the burning of doctors-regent at Toulouse serves to emphasise that the whole of Pantagruel's tour was dominated by a quest for legal learning in a spirit of comedy. Toulouse was above all famous for its faculty of law. Jean de Caturce, Boysonné and other sufferers at the University of Toulouse were *légistes*, a point made by the historian of the city. Pantagruel's tour of the universities takes him to Bourges, also famous for its faculty of law; but it is at Orleans that he finally graduates: it would be nice to know why. Anyway, Pantagruel, now a *légiste*, is given the title *Maistre* (*TLF* IX *bis*, 105; *EC* X, 53). In the *Tiers Livre* this title will be dropped; then it is Panurge who is the *légiste* – one more example of how Rabelais later redistributes his rôles. In *Pantagruel*, however, the legal dimension must be borne in mind all the time, at least until we are brought back into the mock-chivalry of the final chapters.

[24] Cf. J. Crespin, *Histoire des Martyrs*, Geneva 1619, p.106r.; Baum and Cunitz, *Histoire ecclésiastique* (dite, de Bèze), 1883, p.20; E. V. Telle, *L'Erasmianus sive Ciceronianus d'Estienne Dolet*, Geneva 1974, p.25; *Pant.*, *TLF* V, 54f.; *EC* V, 47f.

Major explicit propaganda passages in *Pantagruel* are concerned with law. The new and unaccustomed dominance of humanist French juris-prudence, the *mos Gallicus* of which Budé and Alciati were exponents, was a source of pride for the French. It freed the French from their former heavy dependence on the tradition of Italian legal scholarship. This pride was not limited merely to legal circles. The law was not simply a professional mystery, restricted to those who earned money by it. It was an integral part of the educated man's intellectual accomplishments. Rabelais's legal jests are not just jokes meant for legal professionals to enjoy. The Roman *Pandects* as annotated by Budé formed the basis of that great scholar's national and international fame as a humanist and were widely read. Roman law plays a definite and recognisably humanist part in the educational ideas expounded in Gargantua's letter. Pantagruel is to study Roman law, learning its 'beautiful texts' off by heart. Their justice he will appreciate by combining the study of law with the study of philosophy (*Pant.* VIII, *TLF* 134; *EC* 105). This is both a little – it is after all only one part of the circle of learning to be mastered by Pantagruel – and also a lot. It shows Rabelais championing in a wide-ranging educational scheme, made easily accessible by being written in the vulgar tongue, Budé's contention that sound jurisprudence required not only a firm grasp of the law in its original tongues but a knowledge of philosophy. The adjective *beaulx* applied to the legal *textes* is by no means only a piece of padding; it recalls Budé's insistence on the beauty and elegance of the language of Roman law which form both its charm and its challenge. This stylistic beauty made the copious glosses of the lawyers of the *mos Italicus* seem all the more grossly ugly and irrelevant to legal partisans such as Rabelais and many of his friends. The objections of men like Rabelais to the Italian school of Accursius and Bartolo were not simply aesthetic. They accused the partisans of the Italian school of a fundamental misunderstanding of the basic texts of the law and, because of their ignorance of philosophy, of the very nature of justice.

The people Rabelais moved among, the people he was in correspondence with, his friends, included a fair sprinkling of *légistes*. The names of Budé and Tiraqueau remain well known; in their day others, such as Briend Vallée, Seigneur du Douhet and Amaury Bouchard, were men of prestige, power, importance and wide erudition. All seem to have been in varying degrees committed supporters of the *mos Gallicus*, the 'French method' of legal scholarship, though Tiraqueau was too good a scholar to be confined to it alone. This method sought to explain the basic texts of Roman law with the aid of the widest possible, the deepest possible, philological philosophical, scientific, literary and historical knowledge. Scholars working in this tradition were not all French, but the French were proud that, at last, they were not simply pupils of the dominant Italian school.

The new 'French method' sought to establish in the fullest possible detail what the ancient texts really meant when they were promulgated; exact historical knowledge, exact philological knowledge, were the foundation-stones of their studies (Budé, *Opera* III, p. 12f.).

The *mos Italicus* on the other hand was more exclusively 'professional', above all seeking to understand legal texts with the help of successive generations of legal glossists and the opinion of practising lawyers and judges. To the humanists this seems like relying on the weakest of reeds. However conversant they were with the law, men like Accursius were quite ignorant of Greek; ignorant too of the finer shades of meaning of classical Latin. When writing about them Budé and Rabelais do not act as historians of legal scholarship, duly and unavoidably impressed by Accursius's achievements; they are committed men, lambasting the gods of a rival school. These scholars by no means always deserved Budé's and Rabelais's contempt, as a fairer French methodologist, Tiraqueau, is prepared to admit in later life. But fair or not, the contempt of the new school was totally understandable in an age which was rightly proud of its restoration of classical philology, proud also of its growing sense of history – often an achievement of legal scholars striving to arrive at the real meaning of their legal authorities. The greatest of the glossists of the *mos Italicus* school clearly had little or no sense of history, as Budé delights to show. How else could he have applied to the dignitaries of the Christian Church enactments which, historically, were clearly pre-Christian, applying to the pagan priests of the Roman State? (Budé, *Opera* III, 12f., 14, 15, etc. His index draws attention to *Accursiana ignorantia*, to *Accursiana errata* and *nugae*.)

Although Budé had been fighting his legal battles for well nigh two decades before *Pantagruel* appeared, Rabelais's legal satire was no stale exercise in fighting battles definitively won. It was no mean achievement to take legal propaganda out of Latin into French. The partisans of the new school continued their propaganda, while the despised texts of the *mos Italicus* continued to be edited. In 1533, the year that *Pantagruel* was first officially reprinted, Rabelais's own learned printer Sebastian Gryphius published an oration by Nicolaus Beraldus *On the Old and New Jurisprudence*; the following year Charles Girardus's treatise *On Purging the Legal Tomes* was ready for Gryphius to print (it appeared in 1535). These books are fighting the same battle for the new law as *Pantagruel* is. Meanwhile, what should be published in Lyons in 1533, with title-pages exactly like *Pantagruel*'s, but two of Bertachino's old *Tractates*! That no doubt explains why Bertachino, who was already classed among the ignorant glossists in 1532, comes in for additional mocking in 1533.[25]

[25] J. Bertachinus: *Tractatus de Episcopo* and *Tractatus de Gabellis*; both printed by Benoit Bonnyn of Lyons. Cf. *Pant.*, *TLF* IX *bis*, 89; *EC* X, 76, where 'Bertachin' is included among *Accursius's* old 'mastiffs' (a pun on Accursius's name and *chiens coursiers*). In 1533, Rabelais

The quarrel between the two schools of legal scholarship was virtually the twin of the bloodier quarrels between the two main schools of theological thought. A theologian such as Erasmus who wished to rediscover the real sense of the Gospel texts in their historical setting would pour scorn on Peter of Spain or Thomas Aquinas in exactly the same way in which Budé belittles Accursius or Bartolo. Humanist lawyers and humanist theologians were natural allies. There are, for example, fundamental criticisms of the Vulgate in Budé's *Annotations on the Pandects*. His scathing condemnation of old-fashioned theologians for their ignorance of Greek, and hence their total ignorance of the real meaning of the texts of the Gospel, are sometimes overlooked by historians of religion. These criticisms of scriptural scholarship were all the more influential for their being made outside the main stream of professional theological controversy. The converse applies when humanist evangelicals concern themselves with the law: Erasmus for example shows how necessary it is to know what texts really mean by reminding his readers of the injustice done by lawyers ignorantly applying to *larrons* (thieves) the harsher penalties that Roman law reserved for *latrones* (highwaymen). In other words a French evangelical humanist was almost certainly at this time a committed partisan favouring the new humanist approach to legal studies. Rabelais is no exception.

18. Legal laughter: Baisecul v. Humevesne

Mockery of a list of legal glossists of the *mos Italicus* was a standard method of satire for partisans of the *mos Gallicus*. There is nothing odd about Rabelais's satirical broadsides – except that they were made so much more widely understandable by being in French. But however clear the overt satire is, the actual case of Baisecul *versus* Humevesne is more complex, and goes beyond the apparent objectives suggested by this overt satire.

Before we even start to hear the case of Baisecul *versus* Humevesne the piles of legal documents are swept aside – what need is there of depositions when the parties can appear in person? We then are treated to a highly partisan attack on a string of glossists (all Italian) including of course Accursius, Baldus and Bartolo. These glossists are condemned for their ignorance 'of everything that is necessary for the understanding of laws'; why, the simplest law of the *Pandects* was beyond their ken (*TLF* IX *bis*, 78; *EC* X, 66). The *Pandects* (the sixth-century abbreviated collection of Roman laws made by order of the emperor Justinian) was both the delight and the

---

brings 'Bartachin' into Pantagruel's genealogy: *EC* I, 99. For views on law similar to Rabelais's in *Pantagruel*, cf. N. Beraldus, *De Vetere ac Novitia Jurisprudentia Oratio*, Paris 1533; and C. Girardus. *De Juris Voluminibus Repurgandis*, Lyons 1535.

despair of humanist jurisconsults: the delight, because it brought them close to the original fount of Roman law in its most reliable form; the despair, because Tribonian the 'architect of the *Pandects*' was believed to have made a deliberately bad job of cutting up the laws into snippets in order to weaken their force. Tribonian will come in for attack in due course in the *Tiers Livre*. Here in *Pantagruel* the emphasis is on the delight.

To be understood, Roman law needs classical knowledge. How then can these glossists, who lack such knowledge, dare to claim authority? The cry rings out again and again in the Renaissance:

For (as is quite certain) they had no knowledge of language, neither Greek nor Latin, but only Gothic and barbarous. And yet the laws were first taken from the Greeks, as Ulpian testifies, *l. posteriori, de orig. juris.* (*Pant.*, *TLF* IX *bis*, 94; *EC* X, 80.)

Greek is liberally cited in the text of these laws; the Latin in which they are written is elegant in the highest degree, and hence not understood by these glossists with their chimney-sweep's Latin; the full understanding of these basic texts requires, moreover, a knowledge of both natural and moral philosophy, since good law itself has its roots in these disciplines.

The disputes encouraged by such legal ignoramuses are seen as just another case of specious *pro-et-contra* debating. At another level they open the way to the diabolical influences of smart immoral lawyers such as the Italian Cepola, whose *Cautelae* ('Precautions') included advice on how to avoid justified suspicions of heresy. They had a very cool reception among humanists, who saw the law as a moral force not to be twisted for private convenience or for the securing of unmerited acquittals. (The large collection of such *Precautions* published in Lyons in 1572 admits in its first sentence that the very word *cautelae* has become almost proverbial as a term of abuse.) The adjective *diabolicques* which Rabelais applied to the *Cautelles de Cepola* is not just comic exaggeration. Twisting the law was, for Rabelais, one of the ways in which the Devil works in this world: the point will be made specifically in a later book; in *Pantagruel* the bare adjective suffices (*Pant.*, *TLF* IX *bis*; *EC* X).

Few parts of *Pantagruel* more clearly remind us of the educated readers that Rabelais must have had in mind than his legal propaganda. He proudly and publicly makes common cause with Budé, Tiraqueau and others. And not in vain. A generation later Jean de Coras, a legal force to be reckoned with, still adopts essentially the same attitudes as Rabelais. His book *On the Art of the Law* contains attacks similar to his; while his educational requirements for the formation of a lawyer are almost identical to those set out by Gargantua in the letter to his son. When writing about the law Rabelais shows himself abreast of the major movements of his time.

The contemporary reader of this part of *Pantagruel* would have thought above all of Budé. Any mention of the word *Pandects* inevitably evoked his *Annotations*. From the earliest version published in 1508, Budé attacked Accursius in the very first words of the very first sentence for his simple-minded interpretation of the axiom, *Law is the art of the good and the equitable*. Throughout the *Annotations* Budé ridicules Accursius and others like him for their ignorance of the basic tools required to do their job: Greek, Latin, at least an elementary knowledge of all the major fields of human inquiry and endeavour. Above all he emphasised the need for legal studies to go hand in hand with philosophy: a point clearly taken by Rabelais.

The only legal authority favourably cited by Rabelais at this juncture is *Ulpian., l. posteriori, de orig. juris*. This was the standard way of referring to legal texts, though it can disconcert Rabelais's readers now. Rabelais is alluding to the widely admired classical Roman jurisconsult Ulpian and to the second title of the first part of the *Pandects*, *On the Origin of Law*. This is itself divided into two parts, *lex prior and lex posterior*. The abbreviation of *lex* as *l.* was normal; the titles themselves were so well-known that they are invariably shortened as here. Ulpian is highly praised by Budé in his *Annotations* as the greatest of the ancient commentators. It is normally said that Rabelais slipped up in his haste to attack the bad glossists, citing Ulpian when he should have cited Pomponius. Pomponius, certainly, was the author of explanations of the *lex posterior* of *On the Origin of Law* in which the Greek origins of law are stated. But it was Ulpian who was the strongest ancient defender of the need for profound philosophical learning in the jurisconsult; Ulpian who, from the very outset of Budé's *Annotations on the Pandects*, is contrasted with Accursius. If Rabelais is wrong, he is wrong because he had not checked an enthusiastic recollection of Budé's opening pages and had conflated the ideas of Pomponius and Ulpian.

It is one of the delights of *Pantagruel* that nothing seems to follow an expected course. After a diatribe such as the one which opens this episode, the reader expects to find a comic expansion of the same ideas – a scene showing up the stupidity of Accursius and his followers, or else scenes contrasting the confusion of lawyers who work from paper depositions with the clarity of French Renaissance *légistes* calmly confronting the parties in a spirit of legal philosophy. It may be that Rabelais, in this earliest of his books, had yet to learn how to make his explicit satire and his comic pages coincide. But I doubt it.

What we meet in this reported farce of Baisecul *versus* Humevesne – for such it is – is not a parody of the burrowing away of old-fashioned, French Italian-style lawyers into the *faeces litterarum*, the literary dung, dropped by Accursius and his pack of mastiffs, but something quite different. Baisecul (with not one single allusion to one single glossist) bumbles fluently and confusedly on; Humevesne gives him an even more confused reply; and Pantagruel out-Greeks them both in his summing up and final judgment. The general framework of the comedy (a variant of the theme of the 'deceiver deceived') is an adaptation to the exigencies of 'Pathelinage' of the legal adage: 'Two deaf men went to law; the judge was deafer than both of them' (*Surdaster cum surdastro litigabat: judex autem erat utroque surdior*). Erasmus, who comments on the axiom in his *Adages*, makes it apply to matters where both sides are 'ridiculous and stupid' (*Adagia* III, 4, 83).

Within this episode we are treated to three speeches in which language is thrice used in such a way as to mean nothing – or more correctly, where three speakers in a row claim to be speaking coherent sense but where in fact there is only a jumble of nonsense and 'near-sense'. Neither Baisecul nor Humevesne 'make sense'; they 'mean not, but hover round about a meaning'. They concatenate ready-made phrases used just incorrectly enough for us to feel that at any moment sense may break through; but it never does.

Baisecul and Humevesne speak languages appropriate to their names. We might apply to them the suggestion put into our heads by a 1542 addition to the text of *Pantagruel*, where to the languages spoken by Panurge is added Danish. Eusthène comments: 'I believe that the Goths spoke thus: and thus too, if God so wished, would we speak with our arse'. The grossly named Lords are (as it were) speaking 'Danish' or 'gothic' in French (*Pant.*, *TLF* IX, 80 *var.*; *EC* IX, 106).

The climactic surprise comes when Pantagruel plays them at their own game, and sends them both home happy. (Happy endings dominate when Pantagruel is about.)

How amusing we find the detail of the three speeches will depend on how well we know the idiom which is being misused. The speeches undoubtedly become funnier as one's knowledge of Renaissance French and its commonplaces is increased. I must confess to finding parts of them rather heavy going.

From the point of view of legal satire, in the speeches of the parties to this law-suit Rabelais seems to be showing, in comic action, that contempt for meaning which Budé and others attributed to Accursius and his pack. According to Budé they claim to get at the 'blood' of the law and not to remain on the surface 'skin'; they claim to have the right to ignore the meaning of the words in detail, as long as they follow the general sense. They are mere despisers of words – *verborum contemptores* – who apparently do not know that words (*verba*) are images of things (*res*); that complex ideas require most precise use of language. These followers of Accursius worship their illiterate authorities as oracles – they do indeed use that very word; Budé was too fastidious in his elegant *Annotations* to use the fecal language of Rabelais's condemnation, but he says much the same thing.

Why, he asks, when they could model themselves on Ulpian and others, do they prefer to use such sordid language, Gothic and barbarous?[26]

These ideas of Budé were not reserved only for those who could get access to his copious *Annotations on the Pandects*. Other authors took them up. To give only one example: 26 March 1533 Benoît Bonnyn finished printing an edition of a fairly elementary *Vocabulary of Both the Laws*, meaning of both civil and canon law. The prefatory letter is closely based upon Budé; it is entitled *Adversus infantes Jurisperitos: verborum cultum non esse aspernandum*: 'Against inarticulate legal experts: the cult of words is not to be despised.' So in 1533, the Lyonese public could read the same legal propaganda in Rabelais's French or in several Latin treatises. Anyone who owned both the 1532 *Pantagruel* and the 1533 *Vocabulary* would have noticed that the frames on the title-pages are identical.

But this farcical concern with words emptied of content, of *verba* divorced from *res*, certainly does not exhaust the comic possibilities of this lawsuit. The setting is a semi-realistic one. There are enough clues for the contemporaries to get the point: we are still partly fumbling in the dark, but can at least see the general context of Rabelais's comic comments.

This lawsuit is not the first encounter of Pantagruel with the Parisian pundits. In one of those little phrases which often serve in Rabelais to tie one episode in with another, Pantagruel 'bien records des lettres et admonition de son pere' challenged the faculty of arts to debate on any of 9,764 theses. Having shown up the *Artiens*, he then shows up the Sorbonne, keeping these theologians busy for seven weeks, from four in the morning till six at night – though even he could not stop them from breaking off for drinks, a reflexion which prudence obliged Rabelais to drop in 1542. The Sorbonagres were soon shown up as be-robed idiots, and then we quickly move on to the legal wrangle.

The speed with which Rabelais dismisses the arts men and the theologians is interesting: the *Artiens* never concern him much; in 1532 even the Sorbonne theologians are only one butt among many: the law is his prime concern, and so we move quickly and irrevocably out of the university into the High Court of Parlement in Paris. There assemble the luminaries not only of the Parlement de Paris but of the provincial parlements of France. Invited as well were members of the Grand Conseil (the high, royally sponsored legal body with vague but ever-growing authority even over the parlements). Present also were the principal regents of the universities of France and – surprisingly – of England and Italy (*Pant.*, *TLF* IX *bis*, 38f.; *EC* X, 34f.).

[26] Budé, *Annotationes in Pandectas*; *Opera* III, p.14. He mocks Accursian lawyers who do not make their words (*verba*) correspond to the things (*res*) meant by them. Valla made the theme current among both philologists and lawyers in his *Dialecticae Disputationes* (*Opera*, Basle 1540, I, cap. 2, p.648; cf. ibid., I, cap. 14, p.676).

Attempts to identify today what is being held up to our amusement are not helped by the deliberate confusion about the time in which the events portrayed took place. In a less whimsical Chronicle we could assume that the events satirised occurred before 1519 (when one of the real people mentioned in the episode as being present, the celebrated Italian glossist Jason de Maino, died). But we are also told that Briend Vallée, the Seigneur du Douhet, was present as a provincial 'Parlementarian': 'le plus sçavent, le plus expert et prudent de tous les aultres.' He is not known to have been a counsellor of the Parlement of Bordeaux before 1527 (though he already held high legal office in Sainctes). Rabelais's close friendship with du Douhet goes back to the early days of his association with Amaury Bouchard. The chronology of the real world would lead us to expect the case of Baisecul *versus* Humevesne to be both before 1519, because of Jason de Maino, and yet perhaps later than 1527, because of Briend Vallée. I would opt for the earlier date, not arbitrarily, but because of the appearance of yet another real-life figure in the episode: 'Philipe Dece.'

Decius (as he is normally called) died in 1538. He was best known in France and his native Italy for the advice he gave to Louis XII of France in a famous *Consilium* requested by the king and published in Pavia and Paris in 1511. An allusion to 'Philipe Dece' in a French book in the vulgar tongue is almost certainly an allusion to the very important events attendant on that *Consilium*.

Louis XII, exasperated by the tergiversations of pope Julius II, asked Decius for legal advice on whether or not a Council of the Church could be called without papal support. Decius, in a long and complex judgment, said, Yes. Louis XII took the advice and called the Second Council of Pisa (normally known to Roman Catholic historians as the *Conciliabulum* of Pisa, since its catholicity was denied by Julius II and, much later, by the Church in general). For his part in encouraging the calling of this Council, Decius was banished by Julius II, but recalled by his successor, a former pupil, Leo X.

Decius's 1511 *Consilium* is known by the title *Pro Ecclesiae auctoritate*. It is a triumph of conciliarism against papism, placing the ultimate authority of the Church in ecumenical councils not in unsupported papal decisions. This anti-papist Catholicism found many eager supporters in France. Rabelais's Cardinal, Jean du Bellay, was (in his own words) 'not much of a papist';[27] satire of excessive papalism plays a great rôle in Rabelais, not least in the *Quart Livre*. It is worthy of mention that Decius's 1511 *Consilium* was republished in Paris in 1612, in an anti-papist volume entitled, *The Acts of the first Council of Pisa held to end the schism of 1409, and, of the Council of Sienna,*

---

[27] *Correspondance de Jean du Bellay*, ed. R. Scheurer, Paris, I (1969), no. 173. Seeing the Pope in such a state of perplexity over the Henrican divorce, Bishop Jean du Bellay comments, 'Je ne suis pas trop papiste' – but even he could not help feeling a bit sorry for the pope in his frightened indecision.

1423, from a manuscript Codex. Also, Constitutions enacted in various sessions of the Second Holy General Council of Pisa, 1511. From the Royal Library. The volume ends with the full text of the satire against Julius II attributed to Erasmus: *Julius exclusus e coelis*, in which Pope Julius II is shut out from Paradise. Whenever one comes across Decius's name in France one comes across anti-papist conciliarism.[28]

The debate of Baisecul *versus* Humevesne raises problems of university autonomy and ecclesiastical authority. Rabelais emphasises that his sympathies lie with the Church and University policies of the French monarchy. If one looks at Rabelais's text with these facts in mind, certain things jump to our notice. First Baisecul, among all his *galimatias*, alludes to the Pragmatic Sanction of Bourges.[29] This was King Charles VII's royal decision, promulgated on 7 July, 1438, subordinating papal authority, as far as the French were concerned, to that of the Councils. Humevesne, among all the confusion of *his* reply, refers to 'l'an trente et six', which can hardly be other than an allusion to 1436, that is to the date of the stormy sessions of the Council of Basle which sought to restrain papal authority and, again, to subordinate it to that of Catholic Councils. Another date in Humevesne's plea is given as 'l'an dix et sept'; that must mean 1517, a date Humevesne asks his judge to keep in mind. The date 1517 completes the circle. The movement to control Papal power was started in the Council of Basle in 1436; papal authority was subject to arbitrary French royal decree in the Pragmatic Sanction of Bourges in 1438; the matter was raised again, in an acute form, in the allegedly heretical Second Council of Pisa (1511), which was called by the French on the advice of Decius. The whole matter of the relative powers of king and pope was decided 'once and for all' by the Concordat of 1517 (Old Style) and submitted to the fifth Lateran Council (1512–17), itself called partly as a rival to the Conciliabulum of Pisa. In 1519 the Concordat was submitted to the Parlement of Paris, but not without riots and dissension. The Concordat essentially shared out power between pope and king, abolishing in France the rights and privileges of Church and University established by law in the pragmatic sanctions. It was hated by many French churchmen and university men. Only after bitter wrangles, including a battle of propaganda posters and noisy and sometimes violent opposition from the Sorbonne and the clergy, was peace restored in Paris by royal might and the Concordat registered by Parlement, thus becoming

[28] *Acta Primi Concilii Pisani celebrati ad tollendum Schisma Anno M. cccc. ix etc.*, Paris 1612 (Bodley, F. 2.31, Linc., and 4° C. 37 Th. Seld.). Note the title given to the Second Council of Pisa – *Sacer* (Holy) and *Generalis*. In spite of papal condemnations, it is presented in France in 1611 as orthodox.

[29] *Pant.*, TLF ix *bis*, 226f.; EC xi, 67: 'Seeing then, said Baisecul, that the Pragmatic Sanction made no mention of this, and that the pope gave everyone freedom to fart as he wished. . . .'

law in France. This ought to have put a stop to protests, but it did not. The theologians of Paris were Gallicans almost to a man, but, in this respect, by no means patriotic royalists. They still clung desperately to the pragmatic sanctions as the ghost of a defence of their important university privileges. In this they were supported by most of the clergy, including influential clerics of Notre Dame de Paris, and, for some time, by a majority of members of the Paris Parlement.

The forcible registration of the Concordat undoubtedly made it the law of the land, though the Parlement continued to express its reservations. And so did the Sorbonne, whose liberties were very much put at risk, reduced or even abolished. To make this aspect of his satire clearer, Rabelais in 1534 inserted an allusion to them in Baisecul's pleading: 'par la vertuz' guoy' (an amusing attenuated oath, 'By Golly's virtue') followed immediately by 'des privileges de L'université'.

The du Bellays were monarchists: firm supporters of the Concordat. They were determined also that the University of Paris, for all its privileges, should obey the law and, more than that, do what the king of France ordered. The details of the sometimes gallant but essentially pathetic attempts of the University to resist bullying make interesting reading. Since the du Bellays cut such dashing and such noble figures; since the opposition to the royally backed *ukases* was led by the despised Béda; little modern sympathy is normally given to them. In this we find ourselves at one with Rabelais.

In the 1530s, René du Bellay was compelling the university to reform its statutes and its teaching. Francis I was deploying his increasingly almost limitless authority. Somewhere behind the satire of Baisecul and Humevesne making their pleas before the Parlement of Paris, reinforced for the occasion by delegates from other Parlements, from the universities of France and from Italian and English universities, we almost certainly have echoes of real legal battles over the jurisdictional privileges of the university.[30]

It should be possible to identify more certainly such an important

---

[30] *Pant*. ɪx *bis*, 36; *EC* x. 33f.: 'The controversy was so high and difficult, that the court of Parlement understood it no more than high German. Whereupon, by the command of the king, were assembled four of the most learned and fat men of all the Parlements of France, together with the Grand Conseil, and all the principal regents of the universities, not only of France but of England and Italy such as Jason [Mainus], Philip Dece [Decius], Petrus de Petronibus [an imaginary name] and a lot of other old rabbinists.' They were joined by Du Douhet – a friend of Rabelais's – 'the most learned, the most expert and prudent' of the lot. One thinks either of the Second Council of Pisa itself, or of such a gathering as the Council of Tours, called by Louis XII in 1510. It brought together 'all the bishops and prelates of the kingdom and the greatest doctors of all universities, not only of the faculties of theology but also of civil and canon law'. Its aim was to oppose Pope Julius II (Bouchet, *Annales d'Acquitaine*, 1545, p.cxlvi).

international jamboree of parlementarians and university men. But so far I
cannot. We can be sure that the contemporaries of *Pantagruel* saw in the
case of Baisecul against Humevesne not only a delightful mockery of
opaque legal language; not only an overt championing of the new method
of French legal exegesis; but also an allusion to wranglings in the Paris
Parlement arising out of their enforced acceptance of the Concordat. At
the centre of the controversy lay the ancient privileges of the University of
Paris, weakened by papal and royal collusion. In the *Tiers Livre* glancing
allusions to 'le grand bon homme Concile de Latran' and to the 'bonne
Dame Pragmaticque Sanction' show that these questions still remained live
issues in 1546. Some of the allusions in *Pantagruel* were themselves added in
1542; this was Rabelais's way of updating his satire. But what was relevant
in 1542 was even more relevant in the 1530s. Rabelais's comic lawsuit
becomes clearer when one looks at the history of the publication of the
Concordat, and of the pragmatic sanction. The Latin text of the
Concordat did not appear in print until 1 June 1518. The French
translation, restricted by a royal *privilège* to the printer Durand Gerlier,
appeared on 13 July 1521. On the expiry of his monopoly, editions appeared
in Toulouse, 1523; Paris, 1532; Lyons, 1535. The texts of both the
Concordat and the pragmatic sanctions were printed, with copious
commentaries, by Benoît Bonnyn of Lyons on 15 June 1532: *The Pragmatic
Sanction with concordant texts. A Commentary by Côme Guymier of the famous
Parlement of Paris.* [. . .] *Together with* [. . .] *the Concordat between the most holy
Pope Leo X and Francis the First, the Most Christian King of France.* . . . Such a
book, coming in 1532 from a printer closely associated with *Pantagruel*, is
indicative of intellectual currents in Rabelais's circle.

As for Philip Decius, he remained a luminary for Gallican lawyers of
royalist convictions: his *Writings on the Rules of Law* were republished in
Paris in 1532 or 1533. It is doubtless also relevant that Rabelais's publisher
Claude Nourry brought out in 1531 a little book entitled, *Extraict de toutes les
Ordonnances Royaulx de France depuis le regne de Philipe le bel jusques au regne de
Françoys premier de ce nom.* In it, with a separate title-page, is an edition of *Les
Ordonnances Royaulx sur l'abbreviation des procés et aultres matieres. Publiées en le
court de parlement de Paris le penultime jour de Novembre l'an Mil cinq cens dixneuf.*
Where Baisecul and Humevesne were concerned, these royal *ordonnances*
were dead letters!

The printing of these works shows that Rabelais's funny lawsuit dealing
with interminable legal wrangling in the context of the pragmatic
sanctions and the Concordat corresponded to the preoccupations of the
reading public at the time that *Pantagruel* appeared. Historical fact
reinforces this impression of contemporary relevance. The rearguard
action against the Concordat by the 'privileged churches' – those
traditionally exempt from royal nomination to benefices – did not end

until the early 1530s. Francis at first transferred their right of appeal to the royally-dominated Grand Conseil and away from an often too independent Parlement: this right and the other privileges were finally denied altogether. Francis obtained a Bull from Pope Clement VII on 9 June 1531. It was 'lue, publiée et enregistrée' by the Grand Conseil, the forum of the Baisecul lawsuit, on 12 May 1533. This Bull of Clement VII's joined the Concordat agreed in 1517 with Leo X, Decius's pupil, as part of the law of France when, after sustained Royal bullying, it was finally registered by Parlement. In this way the Gallican Church and the University of Paris were brought under royal authority. But the memories of powerful corporations are long and bitter. Hope of reversing the balance in their favour was maintained for decades. Where the university was concerned, the royal control was being effectively exercised by René du Bellay, brother of the bishop of Paris, who knew when to bully, threaten and use troops. This triumph of the Concordat over the Pragmatic Sanctions was a bitter pill for many within both University and Parlement. While Francis I was imprisoned in the Spain of the Emperor Charles V after his defeat in Pavia (1525), his mother, Louisa of Savoy, when acting as Regent, was expressly noted in the registers of the Paris Parlement as agreeing that the 'abolition of the Pragmatic Sanctions was the principal cause of the downfall of the Church and of the reverses which the King her son had suffered'. She went on to give an assurance that, once released from captivity, 'this prince would so act as to revoke the Concordat and to restore her ancient dignity to the Church'. But the hopes of Church and university, naturally raised to great heights by so authoritative a public promise, were dashed to the ground by Francis I at his *lit de justice* of 24 July 1527. He absolutely refused to honour his mother's promises. Tension between the king and the town and university of Paris ran high for many years. The town was believed to have been unwilling to help pay the king's ransom; the church and university were believed to have used the king's enforced absence as an opportunity for regaining their lost privileges. On his return, Francis used tough means to show who was master.

The imprisonment of Francis by Charles V, his release and all that these traumatic events brought in their train, were still searing memories for the French of the 1530s. There are several references to them in *Gargantua* to remind us of this. Rabelais's writings show that he was consistently and consciously a defender of royalist interests. Baisecul *versus* Humevesne is an episode of happy satire at the expense of opponents of royal policies, making us feel that these opponents were obscure and obscurantist pettifogging lawyers, crawling out of self-interested universities.

The entire episode has a legal flavour: the *pro et contra* methods of legal dialectic are held up to ridicule; laws renowned for their difficulty – fourteen of them – are listed; and Pantagruel ends his judgement with an

allusion to 'legal spikes' – an expression borrowed from Roman law, taken
up again in the *Tiers Livre*.[31]

19. The visit of Thaumaste: kabbalistic laughter

The judgment of Maistre Pantagruel is so heavenly that the hearers swoon,
rapt in ecstasy – specifically in that form of ecstasy caused by wonder and
astonishment. For Pantagruel is a new Solomon. Chapter IX (*bis*) of
Pantagruel was later broken up into no less than four chapters, numbered X
to XIII. The original title made the comparison of Pantagruel with Solomon
quite specific: *Comment Pantagruel equitablement jugea d'une controverse merveilleusement obscure et difficile, si justement que son jugement fut dict plus admirable que
celluy de Salomon.* The point is made again at the end. The case is described as
a 'most perplexing one'. This term becomes of central importance in the
Tiers Livre but is lightly passed over here. (A 'perplexing case' involved the
maximum of obscurity.) So when Pantagruel did make his startling
judgment everybody went about saying that 'Salomon' was not so wise as
Pantagruel. Pantagruel is therefore even greater than the wisest king of
Israel. Only one person is called to mind when a 'greater than Solomon' is
mentioned: Jesus of Nazareth. Rabelais can be seen lifting the most
awesome of scriptural sayings out of their contexts, as he places them in
unexpected settings dominated by comedy and laughter.

The lawsuit between Baisecul and Humevesne is eventually followed by
another debate, this time in sign language between Panurge and the
Englishman Thaumaste. The two debates are separated by three chapters
devoted to Panurge. We are told of his Villonesque tricks against the
university and church dignitaries; of his escape from the Turks; his
ingenuity about the walls of Paris. These pages form a sort of interlude, of
most delightful uncomplicated comedy: they do not seem to need the long
commentaries required today if we are to recapture the meanings of the
two debates. When they are over and Thaumaste comes across from
England, Pantagruel is even more closely tied, by specific Biblical texts, to
the Man who was greater than Solomon himself.

Here again we are invited to join in a complex romp where amusement is
evoked at several levels; where superposed layers of meaning have to be
recognised and appreciated, before the comedy can be seen for what it
is.

The most obvious comedy concerns the signs used in the debate. The

---

[31] *Pant.*, *TLF* IX *bis*, 84: ten mediaeval jurists mocked; 430f.: fourteen obscure Roman laws
cited; (*EC*, X, 70; XIII, 13f. Useful notes). The allusion to *chausses trapes gutturales* (*TLF*, IX *bis*,
481: *EC* XIII, 53) is to the term *murices* (iron spikes set in the ground), a word used by lawyers
to represent metaphorically the snares of the law. Budé also translates *murices* as
chaussestrappes.

very idea of debating esoteric unutterable truths by an exchange of mystical signs is certainly funnier to us than it was then. Rabelais makes it funny: it was not comic in itself. The signs used divide into two groups: those used by Panurge and those used by Thaumaste: Thaumaste's are meant to reveal profound and arcane truths, which either surpass the powers of human speech or at least by-pass them. The meanings of Thaumaste's signs are esoteric, only known to the initiate. Panurge's are obscene, clearly and evidently so except to the mind of Thaumaste, who seeks to interpret them too according to esoteric principles. They make us laugh at the English Thaumaturge's gullibility and naivety, as he confounds signs having natural meanings with signs having secret, imposed, conventional ones.

'Words are the signs of things' – a commonplace of classical, mediaeval and Renaissance linguistics. This notion encouraged theorists, including lawyers, to pay attention to the non-verbal signs through which men may communicate with each other. There are times in law where the meaning of a gesture may be the point on which an entire case revolves. It was quite natural for a legal mind, when treating of the nature of speech, to turn its attention to the nature and meaning of gesture. Text and gloss encouraged it. Most considerations of these problems in Rabelais's life-time are locked away in technical hermeneutical treatises or hidden in the denser glosses of legal books; but an idea of the way in which words, signs, symbols and gestures went together can be readily seen from Francis Bacon's *Advancement of Learning* (1605), which has the advantage of being written in English and of being in the same intellectual current as Rabelais several decades nearer to us. It is worth quoting at some length for the light that Bacon can throw on the signs in the episode of Thaumaste and, when we come to them, on important sections of *Gargantua* and the *Quart Livre*.

De notis rerum. These notes of cogitations are of two sorts; the one when the note hath some similitude or congruity with the notion: the other *ad placitum*, having force only by contract or acceptation. Of the former sort are hieroglyphics and gestures. For as to hieroglyphics (things of ancient use, and embraced chiefly by the Egyptians, one of the most ancient nations), they are but as continued impreses and emblems. And as for gestures, they are as transitory hieroglyphics, and are to hieroglyphics as words spoken are to words written, in that they abide not; but they have evermore, as well as the other, an affinity with the things signified. As Periander, being consulted with how to preserve a tyranny newly usurped, bid the messenger attend and report what he saw him do; and went into his garden and topped all the highest flowers: signifying, that it consisted in the cutting off and keeping low of the nobility and grandees. *Ad placitum*, are the characters real before mentioned, and words: although some have been willing by curious inquiry, or rather by apt feigning, to have derived imposition of names from reason and intendment; a speculation elegant, and, by reason it searcheth into antiquity, reverent; but sparingly mixed with truth, and of small fruit. This portion of knowledge, touching the notes of things, and cogitations in general, I find not inquired, but deficient. And although it may seem of no great use, considering that words and writings by letters do far excel all the other ways; yet because this part concerneth as it were the mint of knowledge (for words are the tokens current and accepted for conceits, as moneys are for values, and that it is fit men be not ignorant that moneys may be of another kind than gold and silver), I thought good to propound it to better inquiry. (*Advancement of Learning and New Atlantis*, Oxford 1974, ii, 16:1, p.131.)

Like Bacon later (and like the majority of his own contemporaries, probably) Rabelais sees words as signifying *ad placitum* ('by contract and acceptation'); but gesture he sees as having at times 'some similitude or congruity with the notion': but not always.

Rabelais's ideas are not identical with Bacon's – in the *Quart Livre* he has more faith in etymology as a source of truth than Bacon has – but they are very close. However, Rabelais, while fully acknowledging that many gestures do have natural or congruous meanings, bases his comedy on the fact that there are other esoteric signs, the meanings of which are as arbitrary as the meanings imposed upon words. Such were the kabbalistic signs used between Solomon and the Queen of Sheba, a major biblical episode which Rabelais has in mind in these chapters. So Thaumaste comes to Paris as an erudite but gullible kabbalist; his head is so chock full of high, esoteric, conventional signs that he is quite unable to recognise the natural or congruous meanings of the coarse gestures made by Panurge in reply to his own kabbalistic ones. He is so determined to find veiled kabbalistic truths behind Panurge's signs, that the crudest of gestures sets him sweating after secret wisdom.

The example which Bacon gives of Periander's gesture of chopping off of the heads of the highest flowers, as a clear sign that the nobility and grandees should be cut down, is the very one used by Rabelais in the *Quart Livre*. It was apparently a standard *exemplum* showing that gestures may have a real affinity with the things signified and so were not, as words are, simply examples of arbitrary and conventional impositions of meaning on to indifferent aural signs. Rabelais probably got it from Erasmus.

But not all gestures are clear, natural and congruous. There are signs and gestures which have to be interpreted, like the symbolic gifts sent to Darius from the Scythians in the *Quart Livre*, which only Captain Gobryes could make sense of. Others can be purely and simply misunderstood. The classical example among lawyers of such misunderstanding of signs and gestures is one which also enabled them to laugh at Accursius. It was therefore very popular among humanists. It underlies the comedy of these pages, concerning as it does a widely known example of legal gullibility revealed in Accursius's commentaries on the part of the *Pandects* known as *On the Origin of Law*. This was precisely the section cited earlier in *Pantagruel* when Accursius was mocked together with other 'ignorant mastiffs'. It is a pity that Accursius's silly bit of fake history is now all but forgotten; but as it is, it must be briefly resumed here.

Accursius relates after earlier sources how the idea of law was brought from Greece to Rome. The Greeks, he tells us, sent a wise man to find out whether the Romans were worthy of learning law. Not knowing how to communicate with the Greek emissary, the Romans sent forth a fool (*stultus*) to dispute with him by signs and gestures; if the Greek were defeated in argument it would be all the funnier: if the Romans were defeated, they could say it was only a fool who acted for them. The wise Greek began with a nod, and then raised one finger, to signify One God. The fool, thinking the Greek was trying to poke one of his eyes out, defended himself by sticking forth two fingers with the thumb 'naturally' raised as well, as though he were going to poke out both the Greek's eyes. The Greek sage interpreted the fool's gesture as having a deeper theological significance: the Trinity. So he opened the palm of his hand, to show that all was naked and open to God; the fool, thinking the Greek was going to clout him one, raised a clenched fist as though to strike him back. The wise Greek took this to mean that God held all things in his hand. He went back to Athens convinced that the Latins were worthy of learning law. 'And so law had its origin with the Greeks, as all learning did.'[32]

Sophisticated humanists not unnaturally found such daft nonsense laughable. It became a commonplace among them to show up the total nullity and the immeasurable ignorance that they attributed to the legal glossists of the old Italian school. This story and Accursius's gullibility about the 'fortuitous gesticulations' taken to mean the Trinity are used by Budé in his commentary on *De Origine Juris* as crushing proof of Accursius's total ignorance of even the elements of history, an ignorance passed on by him to the host of his followers (*Opera* III, 31B).

This well-known episode forms a backcloth to the Thaumaste chapters. Thaumaste comes to debate with Pantagruel, who is replaced by a 'fool' (Panurge). Panurge's gross gestures Thaumaste interprets, without exception, as profound religious truths. But Rabelais has taken the scene out of its ancient legal setting, in order to place it within a context which opened the way for wider and more up-to-date amusement.

Thaumaste is an Englishman. His name is, at one and the same time, a gallicising of the Greek word for a magician or wonder-worker, *thaumastos*; an allusion to the last letter of the Hebrew alphabet, *Thau*, from

---

[32] Resumed from Accursius's gloss on *De Origine Juris*, s.v. *Constitui*, Digest, I, tit. II; in *Pandectae*, Lyons 1569, I, col. 64.

time immemorial the sign of signs; and finally a play on the name Thomas, at this time as standard a nickname for an Englishman as Taffy is now for a Welshman or Jock for a Scot. It was Henry VIII's determination to devalue the memory of that troublesome priest Thomas Becket which led to the apparently permanent decline of the name Thomas among Englishmen.

Behind Thaumaste have been seen allusions to specific Englishmen, especially to Thomas More, though why Rabelais should want to mock More is not explained. A tempting interpretation which does not seem, alas, to fit, would see him as a parody of Thomas, duke of Norfolk, who was indeed in and out of Paris at this time, well received in court and constantly putting pressure on the Sorbonne to vote, as it eventually did, in favour of the Henrican divorce. But more likely in a context steeped in kabbalistic magic and secret lore is Thomas Anglicus – a Franciscan like Rabelais, and the author of a mediaeval book on natural magic, whose influence was great, not least from its being sometimes attributed to Thomas Aquinas, probably from a confusion of *Anglicus* and *Angelicus*, the doctoral surname of Aquinas.[33]

But whether Thaumaste should remind us or not of this mediaeval Franciscan Thomas Anglicus is less important than our recognising the intellectual context of the comedy: that of legal laughter at the expense of erroneous approaches to kabbalistic magic and the *prisca theologia*.

That there was an 'Ancient Theology', a secret and hidden revelation of God's truth available to initiates, parallel to the scriptural revelation, complementary to it but not identical to it – and certainly not to be confused with Catholic *traditio* – was a major belief of many Renaissance platonists. It was sympathetically expounded by many writers, including Budé in his *Annotations on the Pandects*. Through a series of misdatings of late pagan and early Christian writings, adherents traced this 'Ancient Theology' back to Moses and his 'contemporary' Hermes (or Mercury) Trismegistus. This theology gave pride of place both to arcane pre-figurations of Christian truth and also to additional magic lore, all of which was attributed to revelations made to Hermes (who may even have taught Moses), as well as to Egyptian priestly sages and Indian gymnosophists. This was syncretised with Jewish and Christian doctrine, making a heady perennial philosophy, which did not necessarily offend orthodoxy but which was not pleasing to everybody.

Two of the most influential of the adherents of the Ancient Theology were Ficino – who liked to think of himself as a Christian *Magus* – a good 'magician' – and the Elder Pico, the earl of Mirandola, though Pico's

---

[33] Cf. G. Naudé, *Apologie pour les grands hommes soupçonnez de Magie*, Amsterdam 1712, p.349. Naudé also advances the claims of the Franciscan Thomas Bungay.

nephew Gianfrancesco insists that his uncle later abandoned this path to God as false. The influence of the thought of such men was immense, embracing not only scholars such as Budé and princely cardinals such as Pio da Carpi but a host of writers, major and minor, throughout Europe. Thomas More himself made the elder Pico his life's exemplar, but he does not seem to have had much time for the Ancient Theology; nor indeed did Erasmus. Rabelais had not a little sympathy for the arcane movements of his day. His mockery of Thaumaste's gullible search for hidden knowledge in the fields of 'magic, alchemy, kabbala, geomancy, astrology and philosophy' does not mean that he rejected such studies as purely nonsensical.

But, despite this sympathy for arcane symbolic wisdom, he saw its weaknesses and the openings it gave for the gullible to be deceived by the charlatan.

Rabelais's partial sympathy for this magical philosophy was, to some extent, attributable to its avoidance of the tedious pyrotechnics of Sorbonne debating. His reading both of Plutarch and of the New Testament led him to reject alleged quests for truth which merely sought the plaudits of men.[34] But how is one to tell the wheat from the chaff, the truth from the error, in all this magical and secret learning? His friend Marot, whose kabbalistic interests were revealed not by his poems, but only after his books were seized when his rooms were searched, answered his accusers by saying that one could tell truth from falsehood in such matters by using the touchstone of scripture. But what then was the value of this complementary revelation, which could only be judged from the touchstone of Holy Writ? For a platonising Christian such as Margaret of Navarre the answer was not in doubt: Hermes Trismegistus was the best of authors for producing quiet Christian certainty – better by far than the floods of theological controversy.[35] But many authors saw its dangers. Not

[34] *Pant.*, TLF XIII, 58f.; *EC* XVIII, 535. Thaumaste declines to debate *pro et contra* 'like the sophists of this town' of Paris and elsewhere, or by declamations, as the Academic Platonists do. Nor does he wish to debate 'by numbers, as Pico della Mirandola wanted to do in Rome'. He wished to debate 'by signs alone': the matter was too hard for words to express. Pantagruel approves of this: 'I greatly praise the manner of argument that you have proposed, by signs, without speaking. For by so doing, you and I will understand, and we shall be quit of the applause which the sophists make' just when the crux is reached. The dismissal of the methods of the Sorbonne derives partly from evangelical interpretations of St Paul (II Timothy 2, 14), 'Strive not with words' – *Noli contendere verbis* – cf. the terms *contention* and *contentieusement* in *Pantagruel* (*TLF* XIII, 189, 172 and *EC* XVIII, 154, 146). Plutarch also specifically condemns the applause of the sophists (cf. *Œuvres de Plutarque*, trans. Amyot (1572), reprint, S.R. Publishers, Wakefield 1972, I, 142E). Plutarch's condemnation of sophistical disputations is to be found in the treatise cited by Gargantua in his letter to his son: *How to Praise Oneself without Envy*. For a satirical account of Sorbonne debates cf. Glareanus's letter to Erasmus, 5 August 1517 (*Erasmi Epistolae* III, pp.35f.).

[35] Clément Marot, *Au Roy Du temps de son exil à Ferrare*, lines 143f.; Marguerite de Navarre, *Dernières Poésies*, ed. A. Lefranc, Paris 1898, p.208.

least Erasmus, who rejected the *prisca theologia* outright; he had no time at all for Ficino and his magic rings or for Pico and his number mysticism; number mysticism he saw as just as bad as scholastic theology! 'Those sin no less who set before us *fumos cabbalisticos et talmudicos*.' As for Hermes, he was probably an impostor.[36]

Rabelais, seeing both the attractions of the kabbalistic *prisca theologica* and its dangers, poses the problem comically. Thaumaste arrives to debate, 'crossing the seas', as so many classical exemplars of seekers after hidden wisdom had done in ancient days. Like the Greek sage, he debates with a 'fool' (Panurge). The Pantagruel he wanted to meet – still the raiser of extraordinary thirst, still a comic giant, still far from even a hint of the sage of the *Tiers Livre* – swots up books, real and imaginary, on arcane means of communication. The Hebrew *Thau* ('sign') is represented in Greek by *sēmeion* and in Latin by *signum*. So the books which Pantagruel consults before meeting Thaumaste have such titles as *De numeris et signis* and *Peri semion* (for *Peri sēmeion*). When Thaumaste uses special conventional signs, whose sense is known only to the initiate – including signs which the venerable Bede wrote about and which Erasmus was excited to rediscover just about this time[37] – Panurge wags his codpiece about, pokes out his tongue, turns up his eyes. The difference between the two sets of gestures is underlined by Rabelais with jokes and by false comic *naïveté*. Panurge blows in his palm, makes a ring with his left hand and pushes his index finger in and out of it – an evidently sexual gesture, here indicative of lack of respect; he then cocks up his chin. The narrator innocently adds:

Whereupon, the audience who understood nothing of such signs, understood that, by this means, without saying a word, he was asking Thaumaste: 'What do you mean by that?'

Thaumaste, as befits a seeker after hidden truth, is rapt in ecstasy ('ravy en haulte contemplation') and eventually breaks the agreed rule of silence, shouting out – significantly – 'Ha, Messieurs, le grant secret' (*Pant.*, TLF XIII, 220, 224–5, 267; *EC* XIX, 74, 77–8, 114).

Subsequent additions to the episode increase the mockery of the Sorbonne, but also make the 'Ancient Theological' setting of the satire much more clear. In the final version of *Pantagruel* (1542) this aspect of the satire is made more obvious still, by a comic dotting of the i's. With amusing elaboration we are told how Panurge cocked a snook at

---

[36] For the magic rings and incantations, cf. Erasmus's *Paraphrase* on James 5, 13–14. For his judgment on Hermes Trismegistus, see D. P. Walker, *The Ancient Theology*, London 1972, p.125. For the 'kabbalistic and Talmudistic smoke' see *Annotationes in Novum Testamentum*, 1535 edition, p.166.

[37] See *Opera* of Jerome, ed. Erasmus, Paris 1533, I, p.25v and 20v,f.

Thaumaste as we still do it today, by extending both hands in line from the nose and waggling the fingers. At this Thaumaste bursts out into speech, referring to the authority he has so much in mind: Hermes (or Mercury) Trismegistus: *'Et si Mercure.'* Whereupon, after other gestures, Panurge waggles about his 'trismegistical codpiece'. The subject could hardly be indicated with greater precision: we are being made to laugh at the way in which those who seek the hidden revelation of 'Mercury' – Hermes Trismegistus – may take the false for the true; the silly for the serious. They are laughed at for this, but preferred to the Sorbonne with its noisy, empty debates, the quest for plaudits and a quite unevangelical contentiousness. Already, at this level of meaning, the episode of Thaumaste is a storehouse of laughter. But this still does not exhaust the comic potential of these densely comic pages (*Pant.*, TLF XIII, 193 *var.*; EC XIX, 24, 34). There are other layers of meaning, even less clear today.

The scriptural quotations in these pages are vital clues to what Rabelais is getting at. Thaumaste's travelling in search of knowledge is justified with the standard *exempla* taken from Aelian and St Jerome. The first *exemplum*, however, and by far the most important, comes from the Old Testament: from the Queen of Sheba's visit to Solomon, narrated twice in scripture, in II Chronicles 9, 1–12, and in I (IV) Kings 10, 1–13. As Rabelais resumes the story: 'The queen of Saba [Sheba] came from the limits of the East and the Persian sea, to see the order of the house of the wise Solomon and to hear his wisdom.'

The visit of the Queen of Sheba to Solomon acquired special importance for Christians from its being alluded to by Christ. This fact is emphasised by Rabelais in the words cited above. There he quotes directly from Christ's words in the New Testament to explain the sense of the Old. In Matthew 12, 42, Christ alludes to the Queen of Sheba's visit to Solomon when he says: 'The Queen of the South shall rise up in the judgment with this generation, and shall condemn it: for she came from the uttermost parts of the earth to hear the wisdom of Solomon: and behold a greater than Solomon is here.'

That this awesome condemnation by Christ is important to the sense of Thaumaste's visit is further indicated by the Englishman's exclaiming at the end of the debate, the last words of this text of Matthew: *'Et ecce plus quam Solomon hic'*; 'And behold; a greater than Solomon is here.'

We could simply stop there: Maître Pantagruel, the new Bachelor of Laws, had already given a judgment 'plus admirable que celui de Salomon'. This episode could be simply an extension of that reputation, made by applying to him words which Christ actually applied to himself. But when in Chapter 12 of his Gospel Matthew alludes to the Queen of the South – the Queen of Sheba – it is to report the words with which Christ makes a strong condemnation of those who seek after *signs*. Jesus was surrounded by men who sought to trap him, asking him for a *sign*. Jesus 'answered and said unto them, An evil and adulterous generation seeketh after a *sign*; and there shall no *sign* be given unto it, but the *sign* of the prophet Jonas. The Queen of the South shall rise up in the judgment with this generation and shall condemn it: for she came from the ends of the earth to hear the wisdom of Solomon; and behold, a greater than Solomon is here.' Commentators of this passage draw attention to the emphatic repetition of the word *sēmeion*, *signum*, 'sign'. In other words, the gospel passage alluded to more than once in this episode refers to the Queen of Sheba in a way which punningly recalls the *signs* sought by Thaumaste on his visit to Pantagruel. Both Matthew and Rabelais condemn the official repositories of religious truth, the Jews and the Sorbonne respectively. They both, on the other hand, warn against the seeking of *signs*, other than the sign of Jonas – doubtless the Resurrection – and recall the visit of the Queen of the South to Solomon as an example of a modest seeker after truth. Of course the senses covered by the word *sign* are very wide: in the Gospel a *sign* is a principally miraculous event confirming a religious truth: for Thaumaste as for lawyers, signs are mainly gestures. The comedy of these chapters lies partly in the ambiguity of the word *sign*. So, too, does the more serious impact: for there are good signs and bad signs: signs with real meanings and signs with conventional ones: signs condemned outright by Christ and other signs – kabbalistic ones – which, whilst not to be condemned absolutely, are possible sources of error, precisely because their senses are not natural but conventional ones, restricted to the initiate.

It is this aspect of the episode which is hardest for us to see. The Gospel condemns the seeking after signs; yet the sign-language of Thaumaste is laughed at sympathetically: for he too will rise up in the judgment against the Sorbonagres. He is comically and ludicrously wrong, since he is still acting as though Solomon and his signs had not been superseded by Christ and his Gospel. One might wonder what this has to do with the Queen of Sheba. And why is the purpose of Thaumaste's visit twice stated to be a search not for 'signs' but for hidden knowledge? – to 'conferer . . . d'aulcuns passaiges de philosophie, de magie, de alkymie et de caballe'; later, 'pour conferer . . . tant de magie, alkymie, de caballe, de geomantie, de astrologie, que de philosophie' (*Pant.*, TLF XIII, 48f., 249f.; *EC* XVIII, 45f.; XX, 10f.).

The answer lies in the traditional rôle of the Queen of Sheba. Her visit to Solomon was no idle one. She went to 'prove him with *hard questions*' (I Kings 10, 1). The Vulgate rendering is more suggestive: 'venit temptare eum *in enigmatibus*.' In this it echoes the Greek Septuagint, which also uses a word meaning enigmas. Both the Latin and the Greek give to the words we render as 'hard questions' a sense closer to 'riddle' or 'dark saying'. She came in other words to treat of arcane matters. In the Renaissance it was sometimes taken for granted that her visit led to an exchange of secret lore with Solomon and that they communicated with each other through esoteric gesture, not words. Several paintings of the Queen of Sheba 'trying Solomon with hard questions' were made in the Renaissance. In most of them that I have seen, including copies, Solomon and the Queen are making signs to each other with their hands: just such signs in fact as Thaumaste had hoped to exchange with Pantagruel.[38] If we were to wonder why Rabelais and other Christians linked her with the kabbala and with magic, the short answer is that the Queen of Sheba's visit to Solomon was seen as a mystical prefiguration of the visit of the Magi to the infant Christ – and the study of the *Magi* was *magic*. Like them, she was concerned with magic which then (in its good Christian form) included a great deal of kabbala, a great deal of Ancient Theology. The episode of Thaumaste is one which, sympathetically but trenchantly, mocks Thaumaste the seeker after magic; he should have gone forward to the fuller truth – and he should not have had such purblind confidence in even good and permitted esoteric signs. He himself sees – and yet does not see – this, when he exclaims, using Christ's words to praise Pantagruel above his servant Panurge: 'The Servant is not above his Master.'

It is probable that somewhere behind the moral import of this comic debate lies the example of the elder Pico. When Pantagruel first meets Thaumaste, Rabelais alludes to a most famous episode of his early days – his desire to debate on all areas of knowledge (*de omni re scibile*) through numbers. Since the elder Pico later renounced his interest in arcane revelation, he may have contributed not a little to Rabelais's conception of this complex episode (*Pant.*, TLF XIII; EC XVIII).

It is possible to see Rabelais playing in *Pantagruel* with ideas which were both excitingly up to date and, as far as we can judge, of real interest to him in his scholarly life. The kabbalistic knowledge which Thaumaste sought was connected with Jewish studies, and so with the name of Reuchlin. Reuchlin's mystical treatise *De verbo mirifico* was reprinted in 1532 in Cologne, just as his *De arte cabbalistica* had been reprinted in Haguenau in 1530. His books were still very much in Rabelais's mind after *Pantagruel* first appeared.

To sum up: Rabelais takes a matter of concern to thinkers of his time and treats it comically. Sign language interested him as a means of communication and as a means of getting at arcane truth. He shows how gullibility in such matters can, when tricksters are about, be a source of comic delight for those who are not taken in by trickery. In this he is recalling the stories which humanist lawyers told against Accursius. But Thaumaste shows that

---

[38] Cf. iconological collection in Warburg Institute, University of London. Relevant pictures include works by Lucas de Heere, Tintoretto, Raphael's studio, etc.

even a gullible man, who honestly and modestly seeks the truths hidden in the Hermetic symbolism of the kabbala and similar fields of inquiry, is much to be preferred to the noisy and arrogant Sorbonagres, who in their wordy debates seek the truth less than they seek the plaudits of men. Thaumaste is at least like the Queen of Sheba, travelling far to learn secret truths from Solomon. As such, he will rise up in the judgment against the despised theologians of the Sorbonne. Yet what was good for the Queen of the South may no longer be good for Christians, who follow not the veiled wisdom of Solomon but the fuller revelation of Christ. The kabbalists and the magicians are potentially on the wrong track: their studies, insofar as they are a seeking after signs, may come within Christ's condemnation of a generation of vipers for whom 'signs' were everything. In the Gospel, *sēmeion*, sign, includes miraculous confirmation of doctrine or authority through special revelation. To seek or demand such a sign is to go flat against the express commands of Christ: it is purely and simply forbidden to Christians from the earliest times. Rabelais seems to suggest that kabbalist signs, once honourably sought by the Queen of Sheba, may be included among the forbidden signs. They must certainly be sought with prudence. And they are certainly comic when used or abused by the ignorant. In this way, Rabelais defends Hebrew studies, as well as good magic and the Ancient Theology, from the hostility of the Sorbonne, while at the same time leaving us with the feeling that they merit the words Erasmus applied to them: 'kabbalistic and talmudistic smoke.' Smoke (*fumus*) in Latin, implies not only obscurity but empty promises. One is reminded of an adage Erasmus used towards the end of the *Praise of Folly*: *magus cum mago*: 'magician meets magician' – Greek, as we say, meets Greek.

Once more Pantagruel, without being a destructive parody of Jesus, is placed in a context where what he stands for draws on the Bible, in order to establish its fuller meaning by allusion to the Christ of the Gospels. The grotesque giant's full and rounded force lies partly in his being able to break unexpectedly into a world where the Queen of Sheba and Jesus of Nazareth were at home and where, thanks to Rabelais's genius, his interloping creates laughter, not hatred, indignation, scorn or shocked piety. At any point in *Pantagruel* informed scriptural reference may whisk us away to theological heights and provide laughter of a quite unexpected kind.

20. *A visit to the underworld*

Not all the chapters present us with this kind of jig-saw puzzle of meaning to put together. Time has left many as clear now as they were then, though changes of taste have led some to see blasphemy in such an episode as the

ring with its false diamond (*diamant faux*) and its inscription LAMAH
HAZABTHANI. The ring was sent to Pantagruel and taken to mean, 'Tell
me false-lover (*dis, amant faux*) why has thou forsaken me?' Rabelais would
doubtless have been surprised that men of goodwill, not mere Sorbonagres
could have seen in this good tale, retold from the Italian of Masaccio, proof
of hidden atheism! He would doubtless have been more than surprised –
shocked and indignant – that others should have seen in the resuscitating of
Epistemon a secretly destructive parody of Christ's resurrection of
Lazarus. Such a scene may certainly remind us of popular books claiming
to be by Lazarus, but that is another matter. In fact the account of
Epistemon's recalling to life from the underworld contains no echoes of the
scriptural account of the death and resurrection of Lazarus. Epistemon's
account of what has happened to the great in the topsy-turvey state of
Underworld owes little if anything to the New Testament, something to
Lucian's *Menippus seu Necyomantia*, something to mediaeval popular song
and story, and something to Erasmus. It could certainly be an amused
comment on such unevangelical writings as *Les peines & horribles tourmens
d'enfer comme racompta le Lazare*. But an age which appreciated the little
masterpiece *Julius excluded from Paradise* would not have found much to
trouble it in Rabelais's underworld, a world turned upside down. The
changes that Rabelais subsequently made to his text show that in one way
only had he overstepped the mark: in referring too light-heartedly to the
douzepers of French national epic and to the legendary founder of the
French monarchy, Pharamond. These he soon replaced by less patriotic
names. Either Rabelais was a bad judge of jokes on national and royal
subjects, or else Francis I became touchier about them as time went by.
The persons selected for praise in *Pantagruel*'s underworld include
Diogenes. The chosen few whom Epistemon saw enjoying the underworld
are all characters who remain important in the later Chronicles.[39]

21. Pantagruel's prayer

An episode of *Pantagruel* which needs some detailed explanation for the
import to become clearer is the giant's prayer before the battle with
Loupgarou. It is so densely theological, so charged with meaning, that
readers who have not already noticed the dense scriptural references in the
episode of Thaumaste are surprised, finding it hard to explain why such a
compact sermon should find its way into so comic a book. A Franciscan was
seldom averse to giving his sermons in jocular form. Perhaps Rabelais
remained in this respect a Franciscan unto the end. The sermons which

[39] *Pant.* xx; *EC* xxx. Names which disappear in 1534 include Pharamond, Fierabras,
Charlemaigne and 'les douze paires de France', who did nothing in Hades but get their noses
tweaked. The good characters are Diogenes, Pathelin, Jehan Lemaire de Belges and Villon.

Rabelais attached to the serious interludes of the funny war against the Dipsodes concern the theology of man's relationship to God. He rejects totally the pagan cynicism of 'God helps those who help themselves', a cynicism he attributes to the *'caphards'*.[40] *Caphard* (black-beetle) was a term regularly applied to hypocrites. There is a delightful picture of Brueghel's in which the hypocritical devotees of Lent are humanised black-beetles. In Rabelais the term normally means either monkish hypocrites or hypo-critical doctors of theology– or of course both. Here he is condemning those who refuse to place all of man's life within the hands of God, especially those hyperorthodox Catholics who were so terrified by the implications of Lutheran theology that they were prepared to condemn as Lutheran the very theology of St Paul. The Christian, as Rabelais insists, trusts in God; he does not trust in his own might. But – and the but is vital – he does not leave God to do for him the work that he should do for himself. This sermon is 'preached' by Pantagruel in his prayer: the matter made subject to theological clarification is the relation of man to God in the context of war:

Therefore as Loupgarou was approaching in great fierceness, Pantagruel, casting his eyes up to heaven, commended himself to God with a right good heart, making a vow as follows: 'O Lord God, who hast always been my protector and my saviour, thou seest the distress in which I now am. Nothing brings me here except that natural zeal which thou hast allowed to men for the guarding and defending of themselves, their wives, children, country and family, in cases which do not concern thine own affair, which is faith; for in such a matter thou wantest no fellow helper [*nul coadjuteur*], except the confessing of the catholic religion and the ministry of thy word; for thou art the Almighty, who, in thine own proper affair, and where thine own proper cause is drawn into action, canst defend thyself very much more than one can estimate – thou who hast a thousand thousands of hundreds of millions of legions of angels, the least of which can kill all mankind, and turn the heaven and earth at his pleasure, as well appeared in the army of Sennacherib. Wherefore, if it pleaseth thee to come to my aid at this time, since in thee alone is my total trust and hope, I vow to thee that, throughout all the lands where I have power and authority (both in this country of Utopia and elsewhere), I will have thy holy Gospel preached purely, simply and entirely, so that the abuses of a mob of hypocrites and false prophets, who have poisoned the world with the constitutions of men and depraved innovations, shall be banished from around me.'

And there was heard a voice from heaven, saying: '*Hoc fac, et vinces*', that is, 'Do this, and thou shalt have victory.'[41]

[40] *Pant.*, *TLF* XVIII, 26; *EC* XXVIII, 25: 'I do not say like the hypocrites, *Ayde toy, Dieu te aydera*: for it is quite the reverse: Help yourself, and the Devil will break your neck. What I say is, put all your hope in God, and he will not leave you.' (You need a good army – the giant has – but you trust in God, not in your own might.)

[41] *Pant.*, *TLF* XIX, 62ff.; *EC* XXIX, 54ff.; cf. Erasmus, *Opera Omnia*, 1703–6, V, 1127; Ch. de Bouelles, *De Prophetica Visione*, 1531, ch. XXI; Lefèvre d'Etaples, *Commentarii Initiatorii in Quatuor Evangelia*, 1522, on Matthew 14, [53] ff.

Pantagruel makes the only bargain with God, the only vow, which Erasmus believed that scripture allowed: if God will spare him, he will preach the Gospel, whole, in all its purity and simplicity, uncorrupted by merely human notions. War is seen as a natural right of man to self-defence; but it is totally forbidden to man as a means of spreading the Christian faith. There is no playing about with concepts here: Pantagruel will preach the faith if he is spared; but the war is emphatically not a religious war; it is not undertaken in order to force the Christian religion (or any particular conception of it) on to others.

If force is required in religious matters, then God himself will provide it. From man God wants no 'help' at all in matters such as these, except that he should confess Catholic truth and minister to his word. This theological conclusion, while quite orthodox, did not seem so to the Sorbonne. It is nearer to Lutheran doctrine than to Erasmus's, for Erasmus hated all wars, not simply, as Luther did, religious ones. Rabelais draws his theology once more from definite scriptural sources: Christ's refusal to avoid arrest in the garden of Gethsemane, and the example of the single angel who alone overthrew the vast army of Sennacherib. In placing these texts together in this way he was acting as a very competent theologian.

When Christ rebuked Peter for drawing his sword to defend him, he said to him: 'Thinkest thou that I cannot now pray to my Father, and he shall presently give me more than twelve legions of Angels?' The twelve legions of Angels, one per apostle, are glossed by the theologians in such a way as to insist that Christ could have called on *more* than twelve legions, a finite number: God is served by an infinite number of Angels represented by multiplying together the largest numbers known to the Jews or the Greeks: hence the numbering of the elect as

> Ten thousand times ten thousand,
> In sparkling raiment bright,

in Alford's famous hymn. The scriptural commentators, after opening to our religious awe the infinite power of a God whose heavenly messengers are infinite in number, proceed to try to give us some slight notion of this might, by alluding to the one, single, unaided angel of the Lord who (in II Kings 19, 35) 'went forth, and smote in the camp of the Assyrians a hundred and fourscore and five thousand: and when they arose early in the morning, behold they were all dead corpses.' These are the authoritative commonplaces around which Rabelais constructs Pantagruel's sermon-prayer.

The word *coadjuteur*, which Rabelais derives from I Corinthians 3, 9, he later finds inadequate, preferring with many other Renaissance theologians a translation which avoids any suggestion that man is *helping* God, as though God could not do everything, always, by himself. But in 1532 such precision was not required of him; it was not required in fact until 1552. At one and the same time he rejects any such notion as the pagan cynicism of *Ayde-toy, dieu t'aydera* and yet holds man capable of working to further the purposes of God. Rabelais's hero does not find, like La Fontaine's carter, that the help he gets from God is really what he does for himself. We are shown that it pleases God when human effort is made, but not when it is relied on. Human effort is always a vital yet a modest collaboration with the almighty power of God. Only one exception is made by God: he wants nobody to fight to spread the faith. The faith is spread by precept and example. This is a very important exception. In most cases where Rabelais juxtaposes words and actions, words come off second best. In *Gargantua* Rabelais makes his thought on this subject more precise and more complex.

Theological points such as these could have been read by Rabelais's contemporaries in Lefèvre d'Etaples' *Commentaries on Saint Paul* and in his *Initiatory Commentaries on the Four Gospels*. Others could have read them in Charles de Bouelle's treatise *On Prophetic Vision* which was published in 1531, probably just before *Pantagruel*. It is not unlikely that a far larger number of Christians in need of such moral theology were reached by this sermon in *Pantagruel* than by Lefèvre, Bouelles and a whole regiment of scriptural exegetes. Perhaps that is why Franciscans, for all Rabelais's irregularities, listed him among the 'writers of this Order'. They would certainly have liked his *synergism*, that is his theological insistence that God normally requires man to 'work with him' – war being a partial exception in that the faith is spread by precept and example and not by force of arms in wars wilfully started for this purpose.

A Sorbonne in which Rabelais's *caphards* dominated would probably have seen Lutheranism in all this. The same Sorbonne had already included among Luther's damnable errors his rejection of the use of force in spreading the Gospel. But they would have been wrong. For all the importance Rabelais gives to grace, he calls upon men to be coadjutors of God in ways displeasing to stricter Lutheran orthodoxy, though not to Melanchthon in one camp or to Erasmus in another.

When Pantagruel finishes his prayer, the heavens open and a voice declares *Hoc fac, et vinces*. Rabelais may be alluding to an epoch-making event in the life of the fourth-century emperor Constantine, who was said to have been converted to Christianity by the appearance in the sky one evening of a radiant cross, bearing a Greek inscription regularly rendered in Latin as *Hoc signo vinces*, 'By this sign thou shalt conquer'. The cross and inscription were adopted as the imperial *labarum* – the official standard of the empire. The allusion to the labarum is probable but conjectural; more certain is an allusion to a key text of the gospel, widely used at the time by Catholics, since it was known to worry Luther, being held to defend the rôle of free will in the divine plan for man and his moral activity. Rabelais may, of course, have conflated St Luke and the inscription on the labarum.

Anyway, the echo of Luke, 10, 28 could hardly be closer. There we find not *Hoc fac, et vinces* but *Hoc fac, et vives*: 'Do this, and thou shalt live.' It was Christ's answer to the crafty lawyer who asked: 'What shall I do to inherit eternal life?' He was told to recall the Ten Commandments and then to obey them. It is a good text to quote here, defending man's duty to serve both God and his neighbour, while warning against over-clever legalistic quibbles.

Rabelais, it should be noted, does not think that wars can be avoided: his hero fights because he was attacked. And although Rabelais does not believe that religious wars should be started by Christians, he insists that, once a victory has been vouchsafed, the victor can and must grasp such a heaven-sent opportunity to preach the Gospel, in all its purity, within those territories which he rightly governs. By doing so he will banish (*exterminer*) those 'doctrines of men' with which the 'false prophets' have poisoned the world. The language is, once more, biblical.

Rabelais's comedy, an increasingly Christian comedy, depends heavily on this limited and unequal co-operation of God and man. The man who leaves it all to God is as comic as the man who thinks he can do it all himself, without the aid of God and his grace.

22. *The end of the first chronicle*

The serious core of moral theology in Pantagruel's prayer surprises the reader, just as the letter of Gargantua surprised him: the surprise is of course a highly pleasurable one, not least because it introduces yet another *nuance* into the series of scriptural parallels between Pantagruel and Christ or Old Testament heroes. The urgency of the prayer, and the clarity of the theological distinctions made in it, suggest that there was some genuine need at this time to make a wider public aware of the difference between political and religious wars, and to discourage any traditional assumption that the rôle of France was to fight 'crusades' for orthodoxy, however right it was to preach the Gospel freely and purely within one's rightful domains. The theological and political quality of this prayer is undoubtedly enhanced by the new dignity given to the Pantagruel-Christ parallelism; by and large, until these pages the parallels have been a source of humour and laughter: here they add an epic flavour quite beyond anything we had been led to expect. But once the point is made, we are whisked away again into a world of laughter – Epistemon's account of the underworld and Maistre Alcofrybas's trip down Pantagruel's throat (which has been hailed by one scholar as a model of the Aristotelian ideal of art as *mimesis*, creative imitation). Here, again, we find a mixture of traditional themes and Lucianesque 'True History', gently taking off the 'je qui vous fais ces tant véritables contes' of traditional pseudo-history and story-telling. A by-product of some of the laughter is to make the Turks less formidable; this period saw an increasingly close French *rapprochement* with the Sublime Porte, as French self-interest and fear drove them to find allies outside the boundaries of Christendom.

The end of the book comes quickly upon us. In the language of a fair-ground huckster, Alcofrybas gives us detailed promises of how the story will be continued in a next horrific Chronicle. These promises remain in later editions, but are neither kept nor meant to be kept. The arbitrariness of Rabelais's endings are of the essence of comedy; they are as arbitrary as Molière's. Once the comic world has unveiled its actors and made them strut and dance before us, there remains nothing to do but to call down the curtain. Pierre Jouvet strongly defended the 'arbitrary' ending of Molière. Rabelais's endings, too, are entirely satisfying, belonging to comedy in its purest form. We have been taken through a world of many-sided laughter. And then *Pantagruel* finishes as it began: with funny tales about giants and promises of more to come.

The debt to Lucian, to Aristophanes, to comic story-tellers both French and Italian, to the *Letters of Obscure Men,* to the traditional farce, to lawyers' books and lawyers' jokes is there for all to see. But Rabelais's art absorbs these borrowings, transmuting them into laughter new and unforeseen. Not for centuries, if ever, had anyone in Rabelais's class as a scholar and thinker devoted his comic talents to making learned laughter so open and so vastly enjoyable.

23. The success of Pantagruel

Pantagruel was probably the most successful of all the books which Rabelais published (learned works apart). It was quickly pirated, appearing in Paris as well as Lyons. Yet this wide appreciation of its comic worth seemed to go hand in hand with a failure to recognise its uniqueness. It was so little recognised as the glorious reflexion of one man's comic vision, that lesser men sometimes felt free to add to it and change the text at will. In this respect it was treated almost like the *Grandes et inestimables Cronicques.* Throughout his lifetime, and even more so afterwards, Rabelais's writings were freely altered or added to by some publishers and often appeared in collected editions interlarded with supposititious works of obvious mediocrity. Only since the nineteenth century has the Rabelaisian *corpus* appeared pruned of most, though not of all, of its adventitious accretions.

Habent sua fata libelli. No sooner had *Pantagruel* appeared than two groups of people showed an interest in it, an interest that was to dog Rabelais's footsteps: Sorbonne theologians at one extreme and French schismatic reformers at the other. In the spring of 1533 at the latest, the Sorbonne impotently set its censors on to *Pantagruel*; in the same year, the printer

Pierre de Wingle, the extreme evangelical son-in-law of the late Claude Nourry (the bookseller who first sold *Pantagruel*), brought out in Neuchâtel a provocative work of theological propaganda, which he hoped to sell better by associating it with the name of Alcofrybas's giant: *Le Livre des marchands fort utile à toutes gens, nouvellement composé par le sire Pantapole bien expert en tel affaire, prochain voysin du seigneur Pantagruel.* All later editions drop the allusion to *Pantagruel*, as it became increasingly clear that Rabelais was no friend of the schismatic reformation which later became associated with the name of Calvin. However much he might laugh in later books at the superstitious errors of the Sorbonne or papist extremists, he remained quite divorced from the *Eglise réformée* and its French-speaking antecedents. Only by tampering with his text could Rabelais be made into safe anti-papist reading for puritans.

4
L'Almanach pour l'an 1533, *the* Pantagrueline Prognostication pour l'an 1533 *and early* modifications *to* Pantagruel

1. Rabelais: a learned and a comic astrologer

After what may have been a few months' delay, *Pantagruel* was followed by the *Prognostication*, which bears the new giant's name. The use of the adjective *Pantagrueline* reminds us that the success of *Pantagruel* was immediate and real enough to encourage a different publisher and printer, François Juste, to take it over from the dead Claude Nourry, and for Rabelais to conceive his comico-satirical prognostication in a way which permanently tied it to his first Chronicle, not to the second, which he was presumably gestating at the same period.[1]

Rabelais seems always to have had a firmer regard for *Pantagruel* than for *Gargantua*: the *Tiers Livre* hops over *Gargantua* to become the *Tiers Livre de Pantagruel*; so too the fourth book is the *Quart Livre de Pantagruel*. His comic philosophy he called 'pantagruélisme', not 'gargantuisme'. Perhaps this is because he actually created Pantagruel as a giant out of the legendary imp, whereas Gargantua was already existing as such in popular legend. The close links of the *Pantagrueline Prognostication* with *Pantagruel* are emphasised by the nature of some of the stylistic devices which the two works share. Additions made to both the works in 1534 emphasise the links further still. These books go together and need to be read together in appropriate editions.

The first known edition of the *Pantagrueline Prognostication certaine, veritable et infalible* is for the year 1533, and so was almost certainly written in 1532. It was a work of immediate relevance: in this it is very different from the form in which it is most widely printed nowadays. After the first edition, specific references to the state of the heavens in 1532–3 are all expunged. In later editions, the satire becomes essentially timeless, and the comedy weaker in the process.

The new work remains pseudonymous, the work of 'Maistre Alcofrybas, architriclin dudict Pantagruel'. *Alcofrybas* has already lost his *Nasier*,

[1] For text and study, see the *Pantagrueline Prognostication pour l'an 1533*; TLF, Droz, Geneva 1974; also gives the text of Rabelais's *Almanachs*. Specific references are not given here to documents cited there.

and so is no longer an anagram of Françoys Rabelais. The word *architriclin* is exclusively associated with the 'ruler of the feast' in charge of the wine for the wedding at Cana of Galilee, the occasion of Christ's first miracle. With this word the curiously complex comic associations of Pantagruel with the Gospel are suggested from the title-page, but not specifically developed in the pages which follow, which are, however, openly, evangelical. The association of ideas meant something profound for Rabelais; the prologue to the *Tiers Livre*, after a deepening of the philosophy of *pantagruélisme*, returns to the same rare word for the 'ruler of the feast' and to the miracle associated with it. Rabelais seems to consider his comedy as in some way a contribution of wine to an evangelical feast.

The *Pantagrueline Prognostication* differs most from *Pantagruel* in having some clear, over-riding satirico-comic end in view: the debunking through laughter of the widely consulted almanacs and prognostications which come within the category of judicial astrology. Particular reference is made to contemporary prognostications containing gloomy forecasts for the year 1533.

Judicial astrology – *astrologie judiciaire* or *divinatrice* – claims to foretell the future by a study of the heavens; great importance was attributed to eclipses, both lunar and solar, and to comets; ever since Arabic astrology became acclimatised in Europe in the thirteenth century, considerable attention was focused on planetary conjunctions.

Throughout the later Middle Ages and the Renaissance an air of exoticism and mystery hung over astrology. All the planets bear the names of pagan deities; men still felt, after one and a half millennia, that their lives might be influenced by Jupiter, Saturn, Venus, Mars or Mercury. Astrology also brought to ordinary people's attention mathematical calculations of extraordinary complexity, whose bases were hardly understood – the very word *mathematicus* regularly meant astrologer. The constant allusions to such Arabic authorities as Albumasar, Abenragel, Avenzoar, Averroës and Avicenna, gave to astrology an air of the potentially dangerous; some felt that Christian authorities were being devalued to the advantage of 'Punic' Moslem ones.

The influences of the heavenly bodies were believed, when orthodoxy was maintained, to incline the human will to courses of action, not to be inevitably causatory. The distinction was not always actually maintained in practice. Judicial astrology claimed that its forecasts covered not only human decisions and the weather, but major changes in politics, war and religion.

The concern with sustained propaganda in the *Pantagrueline Prognostication* suggests that Rabelais was already working in the interests of the du Bellays. They certainly did not like the enervating effects of astrological fatalism on political decision, especially as the judicial astrologers were often making forecasts increasingly favourable to Charles V.

In the 1530s Rabelais attacked trust in judicial astrology on two fronts: with informed laughter in the *Pantagrueline Prognostication*; seriously and specifically in Gargantua's letter (*Pant.* VIII) and in his own scientific almanacs, two of which have come down to us, incomplete, in a late manuscript transcription.

At the time, the serious scientific almanacs would not have been associated with *Pantagruel* or with the *Pantagrueline Prognostication*, except by those who knew who Maistre Alcofrybas really was. About the almanacs, there was no doubt. Scientific almanacs were required by law to bear their author's name and signature: Rabelais's are attributed on their title pages to 'Moy, François Rabelais, Docteur en medecine, et Professeur en Astrologie' (1533), and to 'Maistre François Rabelais, Docteur en Medecine et Medecin du grand Hospital dudict Lyon' (1535). Rabelais's claim to be a professor of astrology is almost certainly not a jest; the writing of almanacs was, in France and some other parts of Europe, the legal monopoly of doctors; the earliest reference we have in literature to Rabelais's skill as a physician is a Latin ode of Salmon Macrin published in 1537 and addressed to *The Most Learned Doctor François Rabelais of Chinon*. It praises his astrological learning in the highest terms. Later Rabelais will be mentioned with modern astrologers worthy to be classified with the great ancients: Pythagoras, Joseph the Patriarch, Daniel the Prophet, and Ptolemy; praise indeed. Salmon Macrin makes his medical skill and astrological knowledge equally profound and equally honourable. And indeed he composed genuine almanacs.[2]

We inevitably place the *Almanach pour l'an 1533* and the *Pantagrueline Prognostication pour l'an 1533* side by side. They are certainly complementary. In an idiom appropriate to their *genres*, both undermine trust in judicial astrology; both deal with real astrological data; both seek to detach their readers from astrological forecasts and fears based upon them.[3]

Opponents of judicial astrology were of many kinds: those who were shocked by the impiety of trying to foretell what God had in store for man or for his world; those who were shocked by the Arabic sources of modern astrology; those who felt that the unique power of God as Lord and First Cause was being eroded; those who were sceptical about all types of

[2] Salmon Macrin *Odae*, Sebastian Gryphius, Lyons 1537, *Ad Franciscum Rabelaesum, medicum peritissimum*: 'I pass over your art of healing and the astrology, which you have acquired by the sweat of your brow.' Rabelais is praised 'above Galen' for his saving so many from the jaws of death – an allusion, no doubt, to his work as a doctor in Lyons during the recent plague. For the placing of Rabelais with Daniel, Ptolemy and so on, see Prof. V. L. Saulnier, *BHR* XVI (1974) pp.142f.: 'François Rabelais, patron des pronostiqueurs', and *Pant. Prog.* (*TLF*), *ad loc.*

[3] Nothing in the 1533 almanac is a retraction of what we find in the *Pantagrueline Prognostication*. The almanac is not *parodied* in the *Prognostication*. Both books take the same line, in styles appropriate to Rabelais's professionally medical and private worlds.

astrology because of proven errors in the past; those who were groping their way out of astrology into astronomy.

Scientific astrologers like Rabelais were also sound astronomers: to be able to chart the phases of the moon, eclipses, the situation of wandering planets, all one needed was enough mathematical knowledge to interpret the tables of Johannes Stoeffler, the great *mathematicus* of Tubingen. Even the most astringent moralists conceded to scientific astrologers the right to forecast the weather and to note the days particularly propitious for the taking of medicines, for bleeding and so on. Rabelais's *Almanach* for 1541 (parts of which have survived in bookbindings) does just that. We can be certain that both the 1533 and the 1535 *Almanachs* did the same, though all we have of them is a copy of their prefaces, not the astrological tables themselves.

It is possible that the 1533 *Almanach* was more immediately successful than the *Pantagrueline Prognostication* in allaying the fears of Frenchmen who were aware of the bleak predictions for that year. But it was the *Pantagrueline Prognostication* which went triumphantly forward to form an often neglected part of the Rabelaisian corpus.

These astrological works of Rabelais, both comic and serious, both with their evangelical earnestness, are best explained by looking at the time in which they appeared.

Comic almanacs were quite an established *genre*, being written by anti-astrological moralists and by practising astrologers. Rabelais borrows extensively from a comic almanac by Johannes Fortius Ringelbergius, entitled *Some Ridiculous but Amusing Prophecies*, appended to a serious *haute vulgarisation* of the main outlines of astrology published in his *Opera* by Gryphius in 1531. Rabelais draws as well on the Latin versions of comic German prognostications by Starrenwadel and Henrichmann, especially known from their being included in Bebel's well-thumbed Latin book of *Jokes* (*Facetiae*).

French comic prognostications were mainly in verse. Most which survive are without any striking merit, either artistic or intellectual; but it is certain that Rabelais knew some of them and even took some of his jokes from them. Alongside these modest comic almanacs were the serious, evangelical, anti-astrological ones, best studied in the German *Christian Almanach* of Otto Brunfells. This kind of almanac is a stranger to fun and laughter; it reflects the horror of a certain kind of Christian of the Renaissance – a minority, probably – when faced with the terminology of judicial astrology, which selected a particular planet as the *Dominus Anni*, the Lord of the Year. They feared, with some reason one would suppose, the harmful effects of such superstition. Wherever astrology of this kind flourished, fatalism was encouraged too; the ultimate fear of the anti-astrological party was that God's unique power as Ruler of the World, as

Lord of Life, as the First Cause to whom all other causes are subjected, was being undermined not merely by superstition but by the Powers of Darkness. Mézerai, in his *Histoire de France depuis Pharamond jusqu'à Louis le Juste* duly notes, when dealing with the death of Louisa of Savoy, the baleful comet of 1531: 'The death of this Princess was preceded by a comet, which appeared during the previous month of June, presaging or engendering a furious plague.' Powers which could foretell or lead to the death of princesses and to the unleashing of an historically well-attested plague were not to be trifled with.

Things had come to a head when Stoeffler's calculations had shown that there were to be no less than twenty planetary conjunctions in February 1524, sixteen of which had aqueous associations. Men – reasonable men – feared the worst: floods, of course, but also great religious and political upheavals. When the danger was over men still argued, for it had been a dreadful year. On top of the usual run of calamities there had been the Peasants' Revolt in Germany; as for France, in 1524 (o.s.) the Most Christian King had been taken prisoner by Imperial troops at the battle of Pavia. Whether these events had been caused or foretold by the planets was an open question, hotly debated. That is why Rabelais makes an amused allusion to 1524 in the *Pantagrueline Prognostication*.

Astrologers normally strove to remain within orthodox limits; they denied that they were dealing with rigid causality; they placed all, in the last resort, in the hands of God. But that did not stop very many men, from the highest to the lowest, from believing, or half-believing, in the causatory power of the heavenly bodies. It was worrying enough for those who believed that the power of the heavenly bodies was merely one which 'influenced' us – the very word 'influence' was once exclusively astrological, a fact which testifies to the widespread nature of the belief. The battle between, say, the plans and projects of the king of France on the one hand and the influences of comets or of the conjunction of Saturn and Mars on the other, might well seem an unequal one to the king himself, let alone to his subjects.

1524 had been a frightful year – that is why Rabelais mentions it satirically in passing, reducing fear by the comic effects of sane laughter. But predictions saw 1533 as a frightening year too. There had been comets in 1531; from September 1532, there were still more troublesome comets in the heavens. According to astrological forecasts, the effects of the great comet of 1532 were to be felt into 1533, betokening 'generally many evil influences, as well in the ayre, water, persones, sexes, trees, frutes and religions.' This evil was to be reinforced by the lunar eclipse due on 4 August 1533, and the generally malign influences of Saturn and Mars. The awesome planet Saturn was to be retrograde (and hence more malign) in 1533; there were to be no less than twenty-six conjunctions between the moon and either Saturn or Mars. Saturn, named by astrologers *infortuna major*, and Mars, *infortuna minor*, exerted fearsome influences. Some of the leading astrologers of the time foresaw disaster: earthquakes, storms, wars, religious disturbances.

It is to quash such fears that Rabelais twice put pen to paper. In both cases, the 'sermon' he gives is basically the same: do not trust in the stars; trust in God.

The *Almanach pour l'an 1533* is striking for the first appearance in Rabelais's writings of the theme of the *Conseil Privé*, the 'Privy Counsel', of God. This phrase successfully likens God in his majesty to a great monarch. But whereas kings have their privy counsellors, God keeps his own counsel: for man to wish to trespass into such divine secrets is stupid and blasphemous. God's wisdom and his plans for men are hidden: it is sacrilegious to presume God's ways to scan. It is a major aspect of Rabelais's theology (quite orthodox, though primarily associated now by scholars with Augustine, Luther and Pascal) that God is a Hidden God, a *Deus absconditus*, who can only be known insofar as he reveals himself. Few sermons make the case for this more cogently, or on more telling evangelical authority, than Rabelais does. He gathers together texts which had become authoritative commonplaces, taken from the Book of Tobith, from the Psalms, from Proverbs and from the Acts of the Apostles. The climax of his case is built upon the Prayer of prayers:

Wherefore, in every case, it behoves us to humble ourselves and to pray (as Christ our Lord has taught us) that there may be done not what *we* wish and ask for, but what pleases *him* and what he has established before the creation of the heavens; so only that his glorious name be hallowed (*1533 Almanach; Pant. Prog.,* TLF p.41).

The tone and savour of this almanac recall those of Pantagruel's prayer before the battle with Loupgarou. We may also note Rabelais's skilful use of a semitic variant of Psalm 64(65). Astrologers were currently called Chaldaeans. To condemn their officious and wicked pryings into the counsel of God, Rabelais cites against them 'the Chaldaean reading' of the first verse of this psalm. The Greek and the Latin versions claim that it is *praise* which 'belongs to God in Zion'; the 'lettre chaldaique' asserts that what belongs to God in Zion is not praise, but *silence*: 'Silence t'appartient en Sion.' In the face of God's 'privy counsel', men – especially Chaldaeans – should hold their peace (*1533 Almanach; Pant. Prog.,* TLF p.41).

There is a certain tension between Rabelais's alleged targets (the *Prognostications de Louvain*) and his own comic *Prognostication*. The dire forecasts for the year 1533 were not in fact primarily those of Louvain, to judge from those which have chanced to survive. The *Grande et Vraye Prenostication de Louvain* for 1533 produced by the famous mathematician

Henry de Fine is not particularly worrying: nor is the French *Grande pronostication* for that year by Jehan Laet (son of the more famous Gaspar Laet), 'docteur en medecine et Astrologue en l'université de Louvain'. On the other hand, an English translation of *The Pronostication calculed by Maister Jaspar Laet* – not his son Jehan – is very disturbing: so, too, no doubt, was the original. It foretold 'strife amongst people . . . intendying secret sedicyon', international and national 'discensions'; the 'estate of relygion' was threatened; war was likely in countries East of Antwerp – that would include France; and there would be 'conspiracy or distaunce amonge princes'.

Prognostications by Italian astrologers such as Ludovico Vitalis expected an increase in devil-worship and harm to religion generally.

There was plenty of justification for Rabelais's desire to play down the dire forecasts for 1533. But, curiously enough, the formal parody which gives its shape to the *Pantagrueline Prognostication* is not modelled on the Italian almanacs, on Jehan Laet's nor on Henry de Fine's Louvain *Prognostications* for 1533; where formal considerations are concerned, Rabelais based the *Pantagrueline Prognostication* on earlier *Prognostications de Louvain*. All ephemerides tend to be discarded when the year to which they apply has passed. Of the flood of prognostications and almanacs from this period, only a handful have survived. Of those that I have read, none combined the form which Rabelais is satirising with the dire previsions he is mocking. Rabelais seems to be drawing on his memory of older Louvain prognostications for the shape of his *Pantagrueline Prognostication*, while reserving his debunking of actual astrological previsions on ones made in prognostications of a rather more modern format.

At all events, the astronomical information on which the 1533 *Almanach* and the 1533 *Pantagrueline Prognostication* are based, as well as the astrological forecasts that they are attacking, are as accurately outlined in the satirical *Prognostication* as in the evangelical almanac. But in the satirical work, laughter is to the forefront, with an effective but sparing use of scriptural authority to dot the i's and make clear to the reader that God has no rivals in the heavens or on earth.

The comic techniques of the *Pantagrueline Prognostication*, indebted to several sources – French, Latin, and, perhaps through intermediaries, German – are all delightfully marshalled to the single end of demolishing respect for judicial astrology through laughter. This very singleness of purpose makes the book seem light-hearted, even naïf, after some of the complexities of *Pantagruel*. A knowledge of the type of *Prognostications de Louvain* that he is laughing at is a great help in appreciating his humour.

But those who are unacquainted with the prognostications being parodied can still enjoy the solemn statements of the obvious and the Shrovetide revelling of the jesting: 1533 will be a year in which (as usual)

Quaresmeprenant (Lent) 'will win his lawsuit' against Carnival; masked figures will be out in Carnival dress, as one part of the population comes out in disguise to deceive the other ('l'une partie du monde se desguisera pour tromper l'autre'). Never did nature see such disorder ('L'on ne veit oncques tel desordre en nature').

But the evangelical and political implications deserve our serious attention too. St Paul is cited as proof of the unique governance of God; we are also reminded that he, who had been privileged to visit in ecstasy the third heaven, gave the clearest of messages: 'If God is with us, who can be against us?' Behind all the laughter we can also see a political concern as well, with Rabelais suggesting that France would gain a great deal if news were censored at the frontiers of the kingdom (was he thinking of troublesome prognostications flooding into France?) Pantagruel had done just this in his kingdoms of Utopia and Dipsodia, we are told. Increasingly in Rabelais what was done in the kingdoms of the giants has relevance to what ought to be done in France.

2. *Gaiety compromised*

The *Pantagrueline Prognostication* is not weighed down by its propaganda. It is a happy work. All this gaiety was soon to be compromised, however. By the spring of 1533 the theological censors of the Sorbonne were already turning their attentions towards *Pantagruel* and finding it worthy of condemnation. Their attempts were frustrated, but notice of what they were up to certainly reached Rabelais in Lyons.

We first learn definitely of the Sorbonne's interest in *Pantagruel* in a letter which young Calvin wrote in October 1533. Rabelais is only of interest to him incidentally. The main concern of Calvin in this part of his letter is to tell his correspondent, Lambert Daniel, how the king of France, learning that the theologians had dared to censor *Le miroir de l'ame pecheresse*, the pious poem of his sister, Queen Margaret of Navarre, had come down on the university like a ton of bricks. The attempts to censor the *Miroir* occurred in 1533, but we do not know exactly when – in May no doubt. On being challenged in October 1533, one after another the faculties denied ever authorising the censoring of Margaret's poem; the wretched Nicole le Clerc, a Sorbonne doctor, curate of the Parish of Saint-Martin-des-Arcs in Paris, was left alone to explain how Margaret's *Miroir* had been allegedly placed to one side; as a work of theology published without the authorisation of the theological faculty, it had 'accidentally' become mixed up with certain obscene books – *obscoenos illos Pantagruelem, Sylva cunnorum* – and other such stuff.

This account, as it stands, is not convincing. The wretched Le Clerc is attempting to deny that there had been any attempt to censor the writings of the king's own sister. This no doubt leads him to belittle the books the *Miroir* allegedly got mixed up with; it is presumably Le Clerc (though it could be Calvin) who supplied the adjective *obscoenos*. Even though the exact nuance of the adjective is difficult to determine, it would clearly apply to a book with some such title as *La Forest des cons*; but did the faculty of theology really only wish to censor *Pantagruel* because it was *obscoenus*, whatever sense one actually attaches to the word? Calvin is often treated as our only direct source of what went on. A clearer idea of what happened in Rabelais's case can be inferred from his own writings.

The first clear inference is that the Sorbonne's attempt to censor *Pantagruel* was quite abortive. *Pantagruel* not only reappeared in 1533 and 1534 in Lyons (where their writ did not run directly), but in Paris where it did. This does not mean that the Sorbonne had never made the attempt. In *Gargantua* there are definite indications that the criticisms which the Sorbonne made of *Pantagruel* went beyond 'obscenity', which might not indeed even have been mentioned at all in his case. On at least one matter, they made a specifically theological condemnation.

'I refer you' (says Rabelais in chapter II of *Gargantua*) 'to the *grande chronicque Pantagrueline* to learn the genealogy and antiquity from which Gargantua had come to us.' After pleasant banter he adds:

By a sovereign grace of God, the antiquity and genealogy of Gargantua have been kept safe for us, more completely than any others – I do not speak of God, for such does not belong to me, and the devils (namely the *caffards*) are against it.

This implies that the calumniating, devilish hypocrites of the Sorbonne had accused him of parodying the genealogy of Christ in *Pantagruel*. This is an amusing coincidence, since he was also thought to have done so by critics in much more recent times. Rabelais denies that he had any such intention: his genealogy has nothing to do with Christ's. And he is right. The genealogy in *Pantagruel* is not even remotely like either of the genealogies of Christ in the New Testament. In 1532, and much more in 1533, Gargantua's genealogy is an Old Testament joke, deriving amusement from Old Testament family lists, with one eye, as we saw, on Midrashic glosses. But it seems likely that the Sorbonne had actually tried to condemn *Pantagruel* on the grounds that it parodied the 'genealogies of God'. Rabelais was sufficiently well protected not to have to worry, and sufficiently sure of his innocence to be righteously indignant.

To make this point clear, he introduced a few – a very few – changes in the edition of *Pantagruel* published in 1533 (the second version of the text authorised by himself). Claude Nourry now being dead, he turned to François Juste, the printer and publisher of the *Pantagrueline Prognostication*, to print and publish his revised work. In a very special sense Juste now became Rabelais's French-language printer, while Sebastian Gryphius remained his Graeco-Latin one.[4] Clearly François Juste did not put pressure on Rabelais to tone down *Pantagruel*. The 1533 *Pantagruel* is more aggressive than the first edition, though less so than the one Juste will offer the public in 1534. Changes of some importance are introduced. In the comic genealogy of the giants, all these changes emphasise still further the Old Testament savour of the jesting. After the name Eryx, Rabelais adds, 'qui feut inventeur du jeu des gobeletz'; after the name Etion, 'lequel premier eut la verolle pour n'avoir beu frays en esté, comme tesnfoigne Bartachim'. These clauses recall descriptive asides in the Old Testament, not the New. The last shot is aimed at the Accursian legal glossist Bertachino.

There are several other of these descriptive asides, amiably parodying similar ones in Deuteronomy and other Old Testament books. Apart from being amusing in themselves, these numerous additional phrases make it quite impossible for anyone who knows his Bible to think that the parody refers to the family-tree of Christ.[5]

Here, it seems, is practical proof that the Sorbonne made a theological objection, not merely a vague accusation of obscenity, and that Rabelais heard of it in time to leave no doubt at all in the mind of a reader of the 1533 text of his first Chronicle. Other 1533 additions – the speech of Panurge in very mangled English for example – had no ulterior motive other than to amuse. But that Rabelais was in no mood to tone his book down is shown by his expanding of the list of books in the Abbey of Saint-Victor's Library. Not all these new books are theologically aggressive, but many are: *La profiterolle des indulgences*, with its easy play on *profiterolle* (the cake) and the *profit* which certain churchmen seek to make out of Indulgences, does not suggest a desire to compromise. One Sorbonne luminary is mentioned by name, in a book laughing at the Sorbonne's taste for eating and drinking: *De brodiorum usu et honestate chopinandi* – *Concerning the Use of Gravy and the Honourableness of Tippling*. This gem is attributed to a former Sorbonne fellow who died in 1523, Sylvester de Priero. He was a famous opponent of Luther and a defender of Indulgences. A work of his, *Silvestrina*, was republished in Lyons in 1533; hence his resurrection in this mocking catalogue.

One of the books added to the library was perhaps too bold to last. It appears in 1533, to be dropped in 1534: *Nine Books of Aristotle on How to Say the Canonical Hours* (*Pant.*, *EC* VII, 87–98 *var.*). It was a commonplace sneer among evangelicals that the Sorbonne attached more importance to Aristotle than to St Paul. The fact that this accusation was made in a

[4] Claude Nourry's successor at bed, board and press, Pierre de Sainte-Lucie – also called the *Prince* after he had married Nourry's widow – published an edition of *Pantagruel* in 1535: it does not seem to have been authorised.

[5] The descriptive asides increase the parallel between *Pantagruel's* genealogy and those of the Old Testament, where they figure frequently.

contemporary evangelical forgery, daringly attributed to the disgraced syndic of the Sorbonne Noël Béda and presented as his reformed Confession of Faith, probably explains why it was dropped. The *Confession de Foy de Maistre Noël Béda* was printed and published in Neuchâtel by the brother-in-law of Claude Nourry, Pierre de Vingle, on 20 December 1533. Guilt by association is not a new thing. Francis I had been deeply angered by the book, not even knowing for certain whether it was actually a forgery or, in very deed, a true *Confession et raison de la foy de maistre Noël Béda*, as its title proclaimed. He took energetic action to find out.

Another author and book added to *Pantagruel* in 1533 (*Jabolenus: Concerning the Cosmography of Purgatory*), lasted until 1537, but was then quietly dropped too. Open disbelief in Purgatory was becoming increasingly Lutheran in the eyes of the Sorbonne, despite widespread doubts about the traditional theology amongst many orthodox humanists (*Pant., EC* VII, 87–98 *var.*).

The clearest indication that neither Rabelais nor his printer was in a mood to compromise, once it had been made obvious that there was no question of confounding Pantagruel's comic genealogy with Christ's, is the title-page which Juste gave to this volume. Juste's new motto was JESUS MARIA, which was printed in capitals within the tympanum of the ornamental columns which decorate his title pages. He keeps them there for the 1533 *Pantagruel*, and prints his full name and address. He also cheekily claims that this new edition of *Pantagruel* is 'Augmenté & Corrigé fraichement, par Maistre Jean Lunel docteur en theologie'. The exact meaning of the phrase is not clear. One's first reaction is to take it all as a joke. This is probably the right one. But there *was* a French theologian named Jehan Lunel living in Rome. Was Rabelais alluding to him? Or was he laughing at the Sorbonne by inventing a name suggestive of lunacy which turned out to be a real one? The sentence came out in 1534, never to be restored; but in 1533, when the Sorbonne would have dearly loved to have *Pantagruel* banned, Rabelais claims that a specific theologian had 'corrected' his newly augmented text. Whatever else the phrase means, it certainly means no kowtowing to Our Masters of Paris.

The 1533 *Pantagruel*, published despite the known disfavour of the Sorbonne, proves that Rabelais and his printer were strongly supported. Without such support it would have been idiotic rashness to expose oneself to their powerful enmity, which could in unfavourable circumstances lead by quite rapid steps to prison or the stake. Sure of this support, from Jean du Bellay certainly and doubtless from the entire du Bellay faction, Rabelais prepared yet another edition of *Pantagruel*, the richly interesting text of 1534, refurbished the *Pantagrueline Prognostication*, and put the finishing touches to at least some episodes of *Gargantua*.

The *Pantagrueline Prognostication* was modified just as *Pantagruel* was. The original *Prognostication* was 'for 1533'. A major revision and expansion was 'for 1535': this text was presumably printed in 1534, and if this was '1534, old style' it could have been printed as late as Easter 1535, though it probably was not. In between these two versions there was a third, now lost, dating no doubt from late 1533. The traces of this lost *Prognostication* which have come down to us show that Rabelais was already making detailed stylistic changes to his texts.

The same concern for style is clear in all his French works from now on. The text of *Pantagruel* published by François Juste in 1534 is in some ways the most rewarding text of that Chronicle. A comparison between it and the earlier versions shows that Rabelais desired to make his text both more archaic and syntactically tighter. There is also a marked tendency to gallicise some ancient names which appear in more classical guise in both the earliest *Pantagruel* and in some chapters of *Gargantua*. An analogous concern with detail also leads him to strike out some traditional French forms and to replace them by more humanist ones. Changes such as these, occurring in more than one text at approximately the same period, can perhaps serve as pointers to the periods in which Rabelais wrote or revised his texts. Some of the changes suggest a wish to eliminate ambiguities: thus, after Panurge's allusion to the 'jardin de France' as the place where he was born, Rabelais adds 'c'est Touraine' (*Pant.* IX, *TLF* 122 *var.*; *EC* 141).

These detailed revisions suggest a work of loving care, undertaken at leisure. One addition here and there, even a major addition here and there, would be compatible with haste: detailed stylistic revision required time. This fact is suggestive; for *Gargantua*, when published, shows, on the contrary, every sign of haste – of lack of detailed supervision or revision.

As well as the detailed revisions, the 1534 *Pantagruel* contains important interpolations, which can be loosely classified into two groups: those which increase the laughter without adding significantly to the satire; those whose intention is manifestly satirical.

The 'fun' additions include the race of giants who grew large noses – with two personal allusions to people Rabelais knew – and some of the many additions to the Library of Saint-Victor, not all of which by any means are satirical in any committed sense.

The lack of bitter satire in the original *Pantagruel* makes the satirical additions of 1534 stand out in sharp contrast. Not that all the additions are bitter. They include further amused glances at legal glossists – Accursius himself appears in one of the longer titles. Some of the titles show that Rabelais had recently been to Rome.[6] But there is an underlying seriousness in the continuing intention to mock scholastic enemies of Luther (Johannes

[6] *Pant.*, *EC* VII, 88–90: *Praeclarissimi juris utriusque Pilloti Racquedenari de bobelidandis glosse Accursiane baguenaudis repetio enucidiluculidissima.* For 'Roman' titles, cf. in chapter VII: *Poiltronismus rerum Italicarum, Auctore magistro Bruslefer; Les pettarades des bullistes, copistes, scripteurs, referendaires et dataires, compillées par Regis*; a work *'cum privilegio papali'* etc.

Eck, for example, who would also figure as an enemy of Erasmus) or to keep alive the satirical objectives of the *Letters of Obscure Men* by mocking the anti-Hebraicist enemies of Reuchlin.[7] Interspersed among 'merely funny' new books in 1534 are silly books attributed to Sorbonne scholastic theologians: in the climate of 1534 such jests could never be just amusing: the laughter, even when open and free from underlying hatred, can hardly fail to imply commitment.[8] And some bitterness there now is, transpiring through the apparently jocular word play. When Thaumaste agrees that he wants to avoid contentious debates, leaving that to the 'maraulx de sophistes', his meaning was clear from the start: evangelicals to a man, as well as Lutherans, regularly used the term *sophistae* for reactionary scholastic theologians. But in 1534 there is no doubt who these *sophistes* are, for they are called *Sorbillans, Sorbonagres, Sorbonigenes, Sorbonicoles, Sorboniformes, Sorbonisecques, Niborcisans, Borsonisans, Saniborsans* (*EC* XVIII, 155 *var.*). One would dearly love to know the full mocking force of the *contrepèteries* (*Spoonerisms* sounds too English); *Niborcisans* and *Borsonisans* are anagrams of *Sorbonisans*; so too is *Saniborsans* (almost), with the first *a* replacing an *o*. The comic disintegrating of such words for 'worshippers of the Sorbonne' is enjoyable and effective; but without the final grasp of what lies behind the last three comic deformations the comic effect is partly muted. There may be a play on the dog-Latin *borsa* (*bourse*: scholarship award, 'exhibition'), accusing the Sorbonne of being 'Sansbourses', pilferers of scholarship-money. If so it would fit into René du Bellay's pressure on the Sorbonne to put its house in order.

The most effective of these satirical *contrepèteries* are reserved for the last paragraph added to the very end of the book, where they are maintained through thick and thin; no pressure or prudence brought him to remove them even in 1542. This last paragraph, from its very position as the last words to be read before the book is closed, greatly alters the feel of *Pantagruel*, which ceases to be a book ending gaily with hucksterish promises. It now ends with bitter indignation, even with venom. We are now, in the last words of a book so given over to joy and laughter, finally invited to hate: 'Fly from such men, abhor them and hate them as much as I do.' And we are told to distrust those men 'qui regardent par un pertuys', who spy through holes. The accusations pile up. These hated people are the monkish censors of the Sorbonne, readers of 'Pantagrueline' books in

---

[7] Ibid.: *Manieres ramonandi fournellos, per M. Eccium; Taraballationes doctorum Colonensium adversus Reuchlin,* etc.

[8] Ibid.: cf. *De usu et utilitate escorchandi equos et equas, auctore m. nostro de Quebecu; Magistri n. Fripesaulcetis de grabellationibus horarum canonicorum lib. quadraginta; Chault couillonis de magistronostrandorum magistronostratorumque beuvitis, lib. octo gualantissimi; Badinatorium Sorboniformium,* and so on. These jests allude to Marot's character *Fripesaulce* and to the *Epistolae Obscurorum Virorum*.

secret; persecutors of them in public. They are hypocrites; not only disorderly monks, the technical word for whom was *Sarabaites*, but bovine examples of such; *Sarrabovittes* in fact. They are disguised; they are servants of the devil, the Father of Lies, seeking to harm the innocent, 'sçavoir est articulant, monorticulant, torticulant, culletant, couilletant et diabliculant, c'est a dire calumniant'. Amongst all the hatred, it is a relief to find even bitter laughter.

With this play on words we start with the real threat of the Sorbonne, summed up in the word *articulant*: their right to draw up 'articles' of accusations for heresy; within this word, Rabelais isolates the syllable *cul*; in this way we see a usual adjective for hypocrite, *torticol* ('twisted-necked'), became laughably *torticul* ('twisted-arsed'); the *cul* remains when we are told that they act as little devils, *diabliculant*. The quick transposition from devilishness to *calumniant* (where the *c*, the *u* and the *l* of *cul* are suddenly and meaningfully rearranged) brings us to a learned comic climax. The wider realisation that the word 'devil', *diabolus*, had a sense; that it was, in Greek, the word for calumniator, slanderer, false accuser, was an important rediscovery of the Renaissance. Even the greatest authors such as Erasmus and Rabelais felt they were unveiling a deep truth about Satan and his ways when they brought this etymology out into the light. For example, in a letter to Willibald Pirckheimer, Erasmus asked rhetorically: 'Where does the Greek word for Devil come from? Not from usury, adultery, theft, or any other vice, but from calumny.' And he applies this lesson to the Devil's agents in this life (*Erasmi Epistolae* III, p. 118).

With this final paragraph, for all its linguistic delights, there is an inevitable feeling of happiness deceived; of confident joy turning sour; of a romp becoming a rough-house.

In some ways the change is a permanent one. There are many parts of subsequent books in which Rabelais shows greater comic mastery than in *Pantagruel*. But his comedy is rarely if ever so innocently and uncomplicatedly joyful as it was in the *editio princeps* of *Pantagruel*. Yet it is precisely in that version that *Pantagruel* has been least read. It was an important event when V. L. Saulnier established the text of his edition of *Pantagruel* for the *Textes Littéraires Français* on the first version, even though the variants are incomplete. To acquire the full authentic savour of Rabelais's works it is necessary to read each of them in their first versions; to follow them through all their changes to their final versions; to look at the backcloth of the history of his time to find clues to what he meant by what he first published, as well as what was implied by subsequent additions to or subtractions from his texts.

5

Gargantua *and* L'Almanach pour l'an 1535

1. Gargantua: a courtly book rushed into print

At first glance *Gargantua* is very like *Pantagruel*: a tale of giants, giving us once again a mock-heroic account of the birth of the eponymous hero, of his childhood and of his knightly deeds. Certain subjects which played an important part in the first book, education for example, reappear in the second. We find the same genius for creating a rich, flexible and learnedly playful language – creating it as only those authors can whose genius flowers when the literary language is not fixed and settled. In outline *Gargantua* seems almost to be cast in the same mould as *Pantagruel*. These similarities are emphasised by the names of the family of giants, Grandgousier, Gargamelle and Gargantua all having associations, real or imaginary, with eating and drinking, with the *gosier* (throat) of French or the equivalent words in Provençal and Languedocien (*gargamallo* and *gargamela*).

   Yet these similarities are, on the whole, fairly superficial. The differences are even more striking. The erudite comic obscurity of parts of *Pantagruel* – the Baisecul *versus* Humevesne lawsuit or the foreign languages of Panurge – has little or no counterpart in *Gargantua*. When Rabelais feels the urge to do that sort of thing again he usually expands *Pantagruel* or refers back to it. Chapter II, the enigmatic poem entitled *Les Fanfreluches antidotées* is a partial exception. It is quite incomprehensible today. Was it so when it appeared? The gross rustic eating and drinking of *Pantagruel* and in the various versions of the *Grandes Cronicques* are conceived quite differently in *Gargantua*. In *Pantagruel* the massive eating and the horrific thirsts are intimately bound up with the basic conception of the characters. In the first book the giant Pantagruel cannot be totally detached from the thirst-raising imp from which he derives, as Rabelais's repeated reminders serve to show. In the *Grandes Cronicques* the eating and drinking merely emphasise the huge size of the giants. In *Gargantua* the enormous eating and drinking are comic in a new and deeper sense: they are things which are at first related with joyful indulgence but on which eventually the heroes turn their backs, as resolutely and as totally as Henry V turns his back on the companions of his riotous youth. Eating and drinking to excess become activities we are finally brought to laugh at. They are typical of the giants in the earlier chapters only, those chapters which find a warm place for rustic indulgence before the new humanist education changes Gargantua from a lazy, ignorant, stupid lout into something approaching the sage of the *Tiers Livre*. This semi-miraculous metamorphosis – only made possible by the intervention of a 'learned doctor of the time called Seraphin Calobarsy' (Phrançoys Rabelais in person) – works like a charm on other characters too (*Garg.* XXI). Grandgousier is at first as boobishly indulgent of Gargantua's laughable coarseness as Pantagruel ever was of Panurge's in the first book; before *Gargantua* is over he is a worthy exemplar of Plato's ideal of the Philosopher-King. The novel, which finds a place in its earlier pages for the bucolic tripe-feast of rustic giants, finishes with the refinements of the Abbey of Thelema and a moving call to resist religious persecution 'unto the end'.

Interwoven into the fabric of the tales are comic, Lucianesque and satirical delights of great artistry. The abundant comedy is shot through with other, equally deep, non-comic insights into the human condition. Classical and evangelical studies now bear fruit in new and exciting applications of humanist learning to situations comic and serious. The world of *Pantagruel* is static, as pure comedy's world often is; *Gargantua's* world is one of transition. The transition is fundamental: we pass once and for all out of the world of *Pantagruel* with its largely a-moral revels into a world of increasingly moral laughter, into which we are led by a Christian humanist bent on meriting Horace's description of the greatest authors, according to the meaning which Renaissance thinkers read into their *Ars poetica*: *Omne tulit punctum qui miscuit utile dulci*, He wins the highest approval, who mingles the morally useful with the aesthetically pleasing.

The differences between *Gargantua* and *Pantagruel* are quite remarkable when one remembers how hard upon the publication of *Pantagruel* the writing of at least part of *Gargantua* must have followed. Some scholars would make the first edition of *Gargantua* appear less than a year and a half after the first edition of *Pantagruel*; others would go up to about three years. Even the longer period is strikingly short. Rabelais was not a full-time author or pampered recluse; he was a busy man, busy as doctor, scholar, botanist, diplomatist; travelling to and from Rome; editing scholarly books; writing the *Pantagrueline Prognostication*; revising *Pantagruel*. He was a man deeply involved in the active life of his time. He tells us – or more correctly 'the author' tells us in *Gargantua's* prologue – that these Chronicles were dictated during the time set aside for rest, while eating and drinking. This may well be the strict truth, though probably it needs a little modification.

Pantagruel is a polished work; *Gargantua* in its first version is not. Rabelais did not see it through the press; the kind of errors it contains show that neither compositor nor publisher had access to him to clear up difficulties in reading his manuscript. The manuscript itself must have contained inconsistencies attributable to speed of composition, lack of revision and changes of intention. It retains stylistic and grammatical forms or constructions that Rabelais was progressively eliminating in revisions of *Pantagruel*, from 1534 onwards. Many chapters and the prologue are already in the 'new style'; others retain his older practices. Some references are made to Touraine, when the logic of the story required them to be placed in Paris. Rabelais put much of this right in the second edition, which bears the year-date 1535. The shift of scene to Paris seems to have been a late decision, made so as to include a full-scale mockery of the Sorbonne in a Chronicle where it previously had little place; the subsequent need to change the odd phrase here and there elsewhere in the story escaped Rabelais when he hurriedly handed his manuscript to François Juste, his new printer-publisher.[1]

It is tantalisingly difficult to know why he was so careless, so rushed. Did he leave the manuscript with François Juste in January 1534, when he set off for Rome with Jean du Bellay? Or did he publish his work much later, either during a temporary absence from Lyons, or during his precipitate departure from the Hôtel-Dieu in February 1535? The question of dating is not an idle one. The new horizons of *Gargantua* are such that we cannot always know for certain what national and international events are being exposed to the laughter of this Christian Lucian unless we can date more accurately the publication of his second Chronicle. If *Gargantua* appeared in January 1534, then it seems in many ways to be actually prophetic; if it appeared late in 1534 or early in 1535, that upsets a lot of preconceptions. I prefer a later date, though not without misgivings. If a later dating proves unacceptable, then January 1534 has its attractions.

Pantagruel belonged to a static world and also to a closed one; a world of books (real and imaginary): a world many of whose landmarks were only recognisable to men of some professional learning. Later revisions of the book emphasise these qualities. *Gargantua* on the other hand makes fewer calls on the technical and professional knowledge of its readers; its legal jesting moves on to broader and more spacious grounds; its medical jesting and its theological comedy leave the scholar's workroom for the world of the informed noble layman. *Gargantua* is a courtly book, treating of matters

[1] Changes include a preference for a French form of many (but not all) classical names – already visible in the prologue to *Gargantua A* – the frequent omissions of *pas, poinct*. Substantive alterations include the change of *la riviere de Loyre à Montsoreau* to *la riviere de Seine*, and *la porte de Besse jusques à la fontaine de Narsy* to *la porte Sainct-Victor jusques à Montmartre* (*TLF* XXI, 172, 210; *EC* XXIII, 141, 175). The compositors of *Gargantua A* were often foxed by Rabelais's handwriting, reading for example *histes* for *gestes* and *Endemon* (frequently) for *Eudemon*.

of interest to a mighty evangelical nobleman such as Philippe Chabot and
appealing (perhaps quite directly and personally) to the relaxed delight of
men like Guillaume du Bellay, the great diplomatist, and Jean his prelate
brother. This helps to explain why major episodes of this apparently joyful
book are placed against a sombre political background, reminding the
reader of that worried preoccupation with divisive tendencies threatening
the unity of church and state, which is so marked a feature of the
correspondence of the du Bellays and the declarations of Francis I in the
first five years of the 1530s.

At the theatre we are sometimes agreeably surprised when the flats fall
back to reveal a wider deeper stage. *Gargantua* several times gives us similar
surprises: first when we come to the prologue from the last pages of
Pantagruel and pass from the huckster's language of the 1532 version, or the
bitter mockery of the 1534 one, into the spacious humanism of the new
book; again, for example, when the mockery of the education Gargantua
received from his two old coughers suddenly opens up into the satire of the
Sorbonne; yet again, when we suddenly leave the *Enfances Gargantua* and
enter the field of battle with the Picrocholine War.

Changes so fundamental doubtless had many causes. One of these causes
seems to be Rabelais's more intimate connexions with the du Bellay clan,
which enabled him to seek his public among the highest in the land. Not
that the Rabelais of *Pantagruel* was a mere grub-street scribbler of no social
standing. He was a man of real but limited reputation: a provincial scholar
and doctor who, without his masterpieces, would have earned footnotes in
the history of scholarship. *Pantagruel* remains in many ways a provincial
book almost in a pejorative sense; the real people mentioned in it are local
men like Ardillon, the abbot of Rabelais's Benedictine monastery at Ligugé,
or André Tiraqueau, still a relatively minor jurisconsult at Fontenay-le-
Comte, though destined to higher things. The learned books that Rabelais
published in 1532 show the same local loyalties and limitations in their
dedications to Tiraqueau, to Bishop d'Estissac of Maillezais and to Amaury
Bouchard, who, as King's Counsel and *Maître des Requêtes* was perhaps the
most exalted of his friends of earlier days. But the edition of Marliani's
Typography of Ancient Rome that Rabelais procured in 1534 was dedicated to
the very great: to Jean du Bellay, bishop of Paris. So too, in *Gargantua*, we
move on to a level where Rabelais can know of the interests of the Admiral
of France and allude to them. Allusions can even be made to the Most
Christian King's imprisonment by Charles V after the disastrous defeat at
Pavia in 1525; to the burden of his ransom, and (most telling of all) to the
actual defeat, in such a way as to make it clear that Rabelais justifiably
hoped not only to win the ear of great courtiers and diplomatists but also to
have the awesome duty of amusing and influencing his monarch. Even the
allusions to some lesser mortals are governed by this new ambition. When

Rabelais mentions the actor 'Songecreux' (Jean du Pont-allais), we can be sure that he was fully aware that Songecreux, from 1532 to at least 1534, was following the court with his players, delighting Francis I with his farces. Songecreux's joyous farces may indeed have had a direct and enriching effect on Rabelais's conception of his art.

This is the audience, as well as a wider one, before whom Rabelais could make Charles V strut about the stage with schemes of world conquest, or show the professors of theology at Paris to be stupid, vicious, bumbling fools.

2. L'Almanach pour l'an 1535

The deepening and widening of Rabelais's interests in Gargantua mirror a deepening and widening of his cultural and spiritual awareness. This fact can be most easily seen from a comparison of specific parts of *Pantagruel* and *Gargantua*: of the two prologues (say), or the issues raised by the two wars. Even more clearly, since we are then dealing with very short, self-contained works, we can grasp the new dimensions of Rabelais's interests by comparing the *Almanach pour l'an 1533*, closely contemporary with *Pantagruel*, with the *Almanach pour l'an 1535*, whose intellectual links with *Gargantua* are striking, a fact which probably suggests that it was written about the same time.

The 1533 almanac seems primarily designed to strengthen French resolve in the face of quite worrying astrological predictions for the year 1533. It works within a traditional astrological framework, that of Ptolemy and Arabic science.

The *Almanach pour l'an 1535* on the other hand starts off with a bang. We are reminded from the outset of what was traditionally thought to be the strongest rational proof of the immortality of the soul. This argument has the same starting-point as several Latin philosophical treatises, as well as Dante's *Convito*; later it became the starting-point of *De l'experience*, that most probing chapter which brings Montaigne's *Essais* to a close. It is borrowed from the opening words of Aristotle's *Metaphysics*, as read and interpreted over the centuries by some of the best Christian minds: 'All men naturally desire knowledge.' We are brought by quick authoritative steps to the conclusion that the afterlife simply must exist: man's natural desire for knowledge is manifestly not slaked in this world; yet Nature gives us no appetite which cannot be satisfied, if not in this world, then perforce in the next. We are confronted with scriptural texts used cogently, skilfully and emotively; they lead by rapid stages towards an allusion to the first of Hippocrates's *Aphorisms*, which Rabelais had edited in Greek and Latin in 1532: 'Life is short, art is long'; and then on to Socrates's gnomic saying (cited in Latin not Greek, as it had become an authoritative Latin adage, not least thanks to Erasmus): 'What is above us, does not concern us.' Next, at the climax, we are presented with Plato as a worthy complement to the teachings of Christ (*Pant. Prog.*, etc., *TLF* 45–7).

This is one of the clearest of the earlier examples of Rabelais welding together into a single Christian system elements taken over from non-Christian cultures, especially Graeco-Latin ones. Some such syncretism was a marked feature of the religion of Renaissance humanists. In the sixteenth century this syncretism was often platonising, just as it was Aristotelian for many the mediaeval scholastics and for those Renaissance philosophers who were unsympathetic towards Platonism, neo-Platonism, or their modern descendants. In the hands of Rabelais platonising Christianity does not lead to any weakening of the essential tenets of the faith, nor to a rejection of Aristotelianism; what it does do is to reconcile much of the thought of the ancients with Christian revelation, seeing the light of Christian truth shining, albeit fitfully, on other places than in the Old and New Testaments or in the Church. The ultimate authority for such a theology, so strongly attractive to minds which were rediscovering most of what remains of what the ancients wrote and thought, was the practice of early Christian thinkers. Important in this group were Greek fathers such as Origen and, for those who knew it directly or indirectly, the wide tolerance encouraged by Justin Martyr in his *Apology for the Christians* (about A.D. 150). There Socrates is shown as a man touched by the divine Logos, the Reason who was incarnate in the Word of God; 'Whatever has been uttered aright by any men in any place,' he wrote, 'belongs to us Christians; for next to God we worship and love the reason which is from the unbegotten and ineffable God.' The ordinary Renaissance Christian could not read such words in print until just after Rabelais's death. But scholars knew their manuscripts, while the works of Greek theologians who had been exposed to such ideas were flooding into the west, not only ancients but relative moderns like Theophylact.[2] Such notions accord with attitudes in Erasmus, whose *Antibarbari* was influencing liberal humanists from 1520 onwards. He was so deeply moved by Socrates, his moral purity and his piety, that he felt he could make one of his characters *almost* exclaim: 'Pray for us, Saint Socrates.' When Rabelais held that all sound learning and wisdom was a manna from heaven, vouchsafed to many through grace, he included the ancients in this benediction.[3] Rabelais's

---

[2] Justin Martyr is the earliest Christian theologian whose works survive. He was first published in the 1550s. Cf. *Apology for the Christians* II, xiii; I, xlvi, etc. (Theophylact, the mediaeval archbishop of Bulgaria (*Ochrida*) was a major influence on Erasmus and, partly through him, on the sixteenth century generally.)

[3] Cf., in context, such phrases as *Manne celeste de bonne doctrine* and *celeste manne de honeste sçavoir* (*Pant.*, *TLF* VIII, 106; XIII, 78; *EC* VIII, 83; XVIII, 67).

world was no absurd universe of modern fashioning; his thought presupposes a divinely ordered universe, against which mankind's folly may be judged with tears, if need be, but often with laughter. God was at work in Egypt, Greece and Rome as well as in Israel and the Christian lands.

When Rabelais counsels his readers to be suspicious of astrology and to refrain from inquisitiveness about God's unchanging providence, his authorities are both Platonic and biblical. After citing the Socratic saying, 'What is above us does not concern us,' he goes straight on to defend his case:

It remains therefore that, following the advice of Plato in the *Gorgias* or, better, the teaching of the Gospel (Matthew 6) we should refrain from curious inquiry into the government and changeless decree of Almighty God, who has made and disposed all things according to his holy pleasure (*arbitre*); supplicating and beseeching his holy will to be done in earth, as it is in heaven (*TLF* 47f.).

At this point, Rabelais's syncretism reveals a real debt to Erasmus. What Rabelais wrote can be directly compared with the philosophy of Christ to be found in his annotation on Luke 12, 29 which is probably the direct source. This text (which in English reads differently) in the original reads, *kai mē meteōrizesthe*. The sense is obscure – perhaps, 'Do not exalt yourselves'. The Greek verb is cognate with the adjective *meteōros* (lofty, sublime), from which we derive *meteor*. Because of this astrological sense, this was an important verse of scripture for a Greek-reading humanist to turn to when seeking advice on astrology. The Latin Vulgate translates these words as *Nolite in sublime tolli*, possibly with the sense of, 'Be not borne aloft', or, 'Do not exalt yourselves'. Erasmus, following the Greek, sees in this text a warning against astrological predictions; like Rabelais after him, he cites Socrates's adage, states that it 'agrees with teaching of Christ', and then refers the reader to Matthew 6.[4]

3. Gargantua: *the prologue*

Analogous concern with an Erasmian syncretism dominates important parts of *Gargantua* too. This is especially striking in the prologue. Prologues

[4] Luke 12, 29: (AV) 'Neither be ye doubtful in mind.' Erasmus accepts the astrological suggestions of the Greek original, *Mē meteōrizesthe*: 'This applies not so much to that 'pompous commotion', *tumor*, which the Greeks call *megala phronein*; it means, rather, that we should take no care for that which is above us.' [The words he uses here, *ne curemus ea quae supra nos sunt*, prepare the way for the Socratic adage.] 'For *meteōra* is the word for those things which are in the clouds and in the upper region of the air, about which Aristotle wrote his *Meteorologica*. The saying of Socrates, *Quae supra nos, nihil ad nos* agrees with Christ's teaching.' Erasmus cites also Theophylact's interpretation of *meteōrizesthai*, making it refer to those 'who are not content with the present but always gape after greater things'. He wonders whether the phrase has not been displaced, suggesting that the reader complete what is lacking in Luke with Matthew 6.

and prefaces tend to get written last; in the prologue of *Gargantua* we probably have the last part of the new Chronicle to be written, just before publication. It is certainly in Rabelais's newer style, and hence has much in common grammatically with the revised *Pantagruel* of 1534. But *Pantagruel* in all its versions starts off with a reference to the *Grandes et inestimables Cronicques* and succeeds in getting right to the end of its prologue without a single erudite classical allusion. *Gargantua* on the other hand plunges the reader straight into Alcibiades's praise of Socrates in the *Symposium*; as befits the master of Plato, whose doctrines are consonant with Christ's, Socrates dominates the prologue to *Gargantua*. He is treated as a man inspired: his learning was 'divine'; his wisdom was 'more than human', fit to be compared with a 'heavenly medicine'. This prepares the reader to find in parts of *Gargantua* something not seen in *Pantagruel* : precisely that platonising Graeco-Christian syncretism which may, at this time, have been Rabelais's chief debt to Erasmus and which was widespread among Christian humanists. From now on Rabelais will make comments in his comic writings which are committedly syncretistic and profoundly evangelical, being marked by an informed evangelism, in which a knowledge of the Bible is enriched with borrowings from those authorities the Christian humanists tended most to revere, Socrates, Plato, Plutarch, Cicero, Seneca among them. (Neo-Platonism, as well as the magic-centred Platonism associated with Ficino's name in late fifteenth- and sixteenth-century Italy, appealed to him less, but leaves its mark upon his writings too. His suspicions may owe something to Erasmus.)

The reader who does not expect to find this marriage of classical and Christian in a comic Gothic book written in the vulgar tongue might well be disconcerted or put off. He might not be able to find his way through the banter and the jesting to the ever-deepening philosophy of Pantagruelism.

The tone adopted by 'the author' in this new prologue, and in the book which follows it, is no longer the one of pure relaxed laughter which characterised *Pantagruel*. The old Shrovetide revelling breaks through very effectively and very often, but *Gargantua* is openly satirical in ways that *Pantagruel* never was in its original form. It is more clearly the work of a humanist with lessons to convey; *Gargantua* is much more obviously the work of a doctor and of an ex-monk, in that medicine and monastic satire, for the first time, occupy prominent places in the new book. It seems as if *Gargantua* represents a completely new state of mind: the mind of a newly liberated man, free to champion his new profession of medicine; free to rejoice publicly in that new-found freedom with which evangelical learning had set him free; free to revel in his knowledge of Greek; free to make fun of the very Benedictine Order in which he had once sought refuge from local Franciscan anti-intellectualism. It may even be said that *Pantagruel*, as published in 1532, represented the pre-medical, pre-

Benedictine, legal Rabelais of earlier days, whereas *Gargantua* represents a man who had come to terms with his past and with his present. *Pantagruel* contains just enough allusions to near-contemporary events for it to be highly improbable that it was written in its entirety long before it was published. But much of it could have been written, or at least conceived, fairly early. *Gargantua* on the other hand has episodes closely related in time to the period in which it was published. It is the work of a man who lives in the world and who has learned how to judge it with laughter.

Perhaps because of this, the story-teller's mask of Rabelais is now more than a little awry. The 'author' is no longer *Alcofrybas Nasier* on the title-page, if we can judge from that of 1535, the earliest to come down to us. Already on the title-page of the *Pantagrueline Prognostication* (1532) the *Nasier* was dropped in favour of 'Maistre Alcofrybas, architriclin dudict Pantagruel'. From the 1534 edition onwards, *Pantagruel* is the work of 'Maistre Alcofrybas, abstracteur de quinte essence', a jocular title alluding to alchemical attempts to extract a 'fifth essence'. *Gargantua* is simply attributed to 'L'abstracteur de quinte essence', with no proper name; and when 'Alcofribas' does appear – once – in the story he is referred to in the third person.[5] In other words, Rabelais's authorship of *Gargantua* could only be reached at two removes; by knowing that 'l'Abstracteur' was *Alcofrybas*'s new title; and by knowing that *Alcofrybas* plus a no longer mentioned *Nasier* was an anagram of Françoys Rabelais. This casual dropping of a pseudonym so successfully used earlier is a little puzzling. It cannot be that Rabelais seriously wanted to hide his authorship: if he had wanted to do that he would have avoided alluding in the text to a good doctor Seraphin Calobarsy (which is another anagram of his name) and would not have sited the battlefield for the Picrocholine war in his own back-garden at La Devinière. It seems as though he wanted to set a certain distance between the world of *Pantagruel* and that of his new book. The new book is at times more closely associated with Rabelais's life in a more real world, so his 'author' wears his comic mask at a jauntier and more ambitious angle. A comic Utopia is progressively abandoned for France, or for the serious utopism of the Abbey of Thelema; the very giants become, in the course of the story, less like figures of legend and more like ideally noble Frenchmen.

The success of *Pantagruel* doubtless made Rabelais surer of his talents. His highly-placed patron Jean du Bellay gave him scope for his new ambitions, both as a doctor, by taking him to Rome, and as an author, by affording him much needed protection. Few patrons in the whole of France were better placed to appeal to a humanist evangelical of Gallican and royalist loyalties than were the du Bellays. For Rabelais they had the enormous advantage of

---

[5] *Garg.*, TLF VII, 124; *EC* VIII, 105: 'All was done by the good captain Chappuys [Michel Chappuy, a sailor in the royal service] and by Alcofribas, his good agent.'

being great families from his part of France, as well as international figures. France in the sixteenth century remained a country of deep provincial loyalties. The du Bellays were Touraine magnates and it was natural that they should have accorded Rabelais their protection, not least after he had given proof of his skill as a doctor and of his potential use as a comic propagandist. His connexions with the du Bellays probably go back to his earlier days as a Franciscan friar; after January 1534 at the latest, the du Bellays become a major factor in his life. His life was touched at many points by these astute and wise diplomatic servants of the king's interests at home and abroad, men for ever concerned to advance the cause of humanism in France, men constantly preoccupied with politics, with church affairs, with university reform. For these men, reactionary theologians such as Béda and their Sorbonne were troublesome pests; Erasmus and Melanchthon, whom Béda hated, were scholars to be courted and admired.

Working for the du Bellays was in itself a liberating experience for Rabelais. The local links they shared created confidence and a certain intimacy. Perhaps this helps explain why a book like *Gargantua*, which takes most of the European world as its stage, contains several jests which could best be understood by a man such as Guillaume du Bellay, Seigneur de Langey, who knew the hamlets, villages and the local monuments which Rabelais scatters through the pages of this Chronicle.

The prologue to *Gargantua* betrays none of the signs of strain between the the old Rabelais and the new which are still visible in some of the earlier chapters of the book itself. It has a striking unity of tone and style. The bantering, shifting arguments, the air of quiet amusement, make it immediately arresting and profoundly satisfying. The argument is based on a saying of Alcibiades in Plato's *Symposium*. Erasmus includes it, with an important essay attached, in his *Adages*. By alluding to Alcibiades's saying about Socrates, Rabelais was following the acknowledged interpreter of a well-known classical commonplace. Even an ambitiously erudite comic author cannot make his jests too learned, if he wants to be understood. He must take account of the common stock of culture of the audience he seeks to amuse. Rabelais's medical jokes, for example, show him to be what we know him most certainly to have been: a good humanist doctor; but the matter of these jokes had already entered into the awareness of all reasonably educated men. Similarly, Erasmus's *Adages* were a common fund of classical lore available to these readers he had most in mind.

Both the adage and the mainly classical apophthegm enjoyed an immense prestige in the Renaissance. They were not simply seen as wise old saws. Whether attributed to the great sages of the past or simply found imbedded in lesser classical writings, they took on the nature of gnomic utterances, darkly and deeply meaningful, often having inner senses far more moral than it would ever occur to a modern reader to give to them. Whether known from their original contexts or gathered together in compendious 'gnomologies', they formed a set of independent moral and philosophical 'commonplaces': that is, they were far more important than the private opinions of even great men; they were part of a common store of wisdom, open to all who were duly initiated into their deeper meanings.

The adage and apophthegm played next to no part in *Pantagruel*: in the prologue to *Gargantua* they are central to the structure of the ever-shifting argument. Later, in the *Tiers Livre*, Rabelais's most complex chronicle, they at last come fully into their own. The path from the prologue of *Gargantua* to the philosophical comedy of the *Tiers Livre* is a long one, but a direct one.

The two Erasmian adages to figure prominently in the prologue to *Gargantua* are *Sileni Alcibiadis* (the Sileni of Alcibiades) and *Pythagorae symbolae* (the Symbols of Pythagoras). There are several other adages, including two listed by Charles de Bouelles in a contemporary collection of proverbs: *ossa infringere* (to break the bones) and *eruere medullam* (to extract the marrow). The 'Sileni of Alcibiades' go back as an adage to Plato's *Symposium*, which begins with Alcibiades comparing Socrates to little images (*Sileni*) which have ridiculous and ugly carvings on the outside, but which can be opened up to reveal within the figure of a god. The name of these *sileni* derives from Silenus, the fat, old, ugly, wine-bibbing follower of Bacchus. There is an element of wilful, playful paradox on Plato's part, when he applies the term *silenus* to Socrates, his teacher, the wisest and the best of men. But then, Socrates was himself a paradox within platonic philosophy: his inspired soul was clad in a startlingly ugly body. Outwardly he was gauche, ridiculous and ugly; inwardly, he possessed a divinely philosophical soul, 'despising all those things for which other men run, sail the seas, sweat, go to law and fight'. Rabelais borrows from Erasmus the main points of his explanation of how Socrates was a Silenus, numinous in his wisdom, full of an unbelievable contempt for the things for which men 'veiglent, courent, travaillent, navigent, bataillent'. With artistic originality, he equates the *Sileni* themselves not with ancient statuettes, which only a few of his readers could have known, but with those ugly-ornate boxes containing precious drugs which were to be seen everywhere on the shelves of Renaissance apothecaries. The contrast between the ugly outside and the inner beauty was held to show off the art of the carver. *Gargantua* resembles Socrates in also being like one of those: a book ugly outside, profoundly and divinely wise below the surface.

What struck many Renaissance scholars so favourably when they contemplated Socrates was not simply his goodness but his humanity. 'Divine' he was in his learning and moral integrity; but he remained human and approachable. This aspect of Socrates is touched upon in a way which makes a lasting contribution to the charm of Pantagruelism. Socrates was human enough to like his glass of wine; he delighted in feasting moderately with his friends. The French name of Plato's *Symposium, Le Banquet,* helps Rabelais to establish his Socrates as a 'divine' philosopher with a human face. Rabelais works in many allusions to the gentle joys of drinking wine, exploiting the fact that Socrates's goodness as a man was perfectly compatible with the elevating pleasure of good wine drunk among friends.

From the opening words of the prologue we realise that *Gargantua* is to be a very different kettle of fish from *Pantagruel,* much more classical in its terms of reference, potentially deeper in its meanings. The language is playful and happy, but Rabelais betrays a manifest pride of authorship. He had pretended that *Pantagruel* was just another book like the *Grandes Cronicques*; now he is afraid that his readers really might believe that his comic Chronicles are no deeper than *Fessepinthe* or imaginary works such as *On Peas and Bacon; with a commentary.* If readers will only open the Silenus which is *Gargantua* they will find the matters treated are not so trivial or ugly as the title might suggest. This puts Rabelais's new book in good company: when More's *Utopia* appeared in English it too was compared by its translator to the *Sileni* of Alcibiades. Rabelais's defensiveness about the profundity of his new Chronicle is quite understandable; it is not at odds with the assured humour of the book. He knew that his aims were high; that at his best he could rival Lucian in his comic vision and handle his own language with a comic richness analogous to Aristophanes's pliant use of Greek. But he was writing in French, a language despised, for literary works, by the first generation of humanists in France. And his Chronicles when they appeared were not set up, as his learned works were, in Gryphius's humanist type but in that very Gothic type that humanists abhorred.

With comic profundity the 'author' of the prologue goes on to play with several other adages: the reader should look for the inner sense of his 'Pythagorean symbols' (which were enigmatic indeed), seeking in his book for that 'deeper sense' which wise men find below the surface triviality of Pythagoras's gnomic utterances. They will find in his new book 'most high sacraments', 'most horrific mysteries', treating matters of concern to 'our religion' as well as politics and 'economics', that is, 'private life at home'. Of course, the over-ingenious will find in his works senses he never dreamed of – just as they do in Homer or in Ovid. But the wise reader will be like Plato's dog, that most philosophical of animals, who gnaws the bone in order to get through to what really matters: the essential 'substance-making' marrow, the *substantificque mouëlle* – 'c'est à dire, ce que j'entends par ces symboles Pythagoricques'. The adages which he exploits ('To break the bones' and 'To extract the marrow') are explained by Charles de Bouelles with just such a sense.

In the prologue Rabelais shifts his argument with delightful comic illogicality, with deliberate humorous ambiguity. He wants the reader to see in his book the inner seriousness that the gothic format and the legendary gigantic setting might lead him to ignore; but he does not want to encourage anything like the perverse ingenuity which led ancient and more recent critics to find cryptic meanings in Homer and which encouraged recent theologians like Pierre Lavin to find the whole Christian religion latent in Ovid's *Metamorphoses*.

The book lives up to its promise: it does look on the surface like the unpretentious books it was partly inspired by; it does contain much comment on matters of religious, political and domestic concern; and it has been interpreted over and over again in ways which are no less arbitrary than those in which the over-ingenious have interpreted the *Iliad* or the *Metamorphoses*. Books do indeed have their own fates.

4. Gargantua: *another episodic chronicle*

Gargantua, even more than *Pantagruel*, is a book of episodes, dividing sharply into major sections, themselves subdivided. As often as not Rabelais makes little or no attempt to lessen the aesthetic shock when we pass from one major section to another. When we come to the quiet almost timeless end of the ideal educational programme (chapter XXII), we are suddenly plunged into the laughably petty beginnings of the Picrocholine War with the words: 'At this time, which was the season of the grape harvest. . . .' There is of course no 'time' to which these words can actually refer; Rabelais the artist either did not care to make a gliding passage from one section to another (simply using a formula perhaps intentionally analogous to the words *In illo tempore* – 'At that time' – with which it was customary to introduce the Gospel-reading at Mass), or else he deliberately sought to amuse the reader by jumping about in this way. This frequent arbitrariness of his passage from section to section is never more clear than at the end of the Abbey of Thelema, which nearly ends on a fairy-tale note ('And they loved each other to the end of their days, as much as on the first day of their marriage'), only to be followed by two sentences making the most arbitrary of transitions: 'I don't want to forget to describe you an enigma, which was discovered in the foundations of the abbey, on a great bronze tomb. It was as follows.'

The impression I have from these sudden changes of direction is that Rabelais has juxtaposed in *Gargantua* episodes written at different times and with different purposes. That does not mean that the arbitrariness of the passage from section to section is necessarily only the effect of hasty composition: the aesthetic shock that these changes cause could well have been quite deliberate. But deliberate or not the divisions of *Gargantua* are evident enough for us to be sure that we are not ourselves acting arbitrarily if the book is studied natural section by natural section.

5. Gargantua: *the earlier chapters*

It is the earlier section of *Gargantua* which, on the whole, is closest in technique to *Pantagruel*.

Chapter I succeeds in both taking a swipe at the hypocritical devils of the Sorbonne for misinterpreting the genealogy of the giants – so linking the book with the confidently aggressive end of the 1534 *Pantagruel* – and, at the same time, making patriotic claims for the French right-of-succession to empire on the collapse of Byzantium, so introducing the theme of rivalry between Francis I and Charles V, which is to dominate parts of *Gargantua*. Renaissance·political theory accepted the notion of a rightful 'transfer of empire'. That Charles V, as Holy Roman Emperor, should claim even shadowy suzerainty over France was intolerable to French nationalism: the imperial prerogatives ought to have been French anyway. Rabelais's jests would have gone down well at court. The enigma which follows (the *Fanfreluches antidotées*, 'Sweet nothings, with an antidote',) has not been adequately deciphered for modern readers; it is probably a continuation of this theme of empire. It is written in the style of poetic enigmas composed by the court poet Mellin de Saint-Gelays. There are textual similarities between the *Fanfreluches antidotées* and a particular poem of Mellin's, but we cannot tell who copied whom. As befits a poem 'found' in the course of a humanist's comic book at a time when archaeology was a growing passion, it was discovered, we are told, during ditching at Chinon, Rabelais's own town. We can be reasonably certain that the *Fanfreluches antidotées* were not all that obscure for the readers of the time: the poem comes close to the start of the book, where any author normally seeks to win and retain his public's attention. Whatever we may find it to mean one day, we may note that it is balanced by the other enigma at the end of the book. That too has connexions with Mellin de Saint-Gelays, being written in the style of 'Merlin le Prophete', as Rabelais pointed out in an addition of 1542. These two enigmas give to *Gargantua* an aesthetic balance like that of *Pantagruel* and the *Tiers Livre*, where the beginning and the ends have artistic similarities with each other.

Today the incomprehensibility of the *Fanfreluches antidotées* undoubtedly puts many readers off, not least those undergraduates who may be reading *Gargantua* as their first French Renaissance book. They may not even know that the pundits get no more sense out of it than they do. Some syllabuses simply strike out the first chapters entirely from their prescribed reading. This is understandable but regrettable, since the earlier chapters take us to the heart of some aspects of the Renaissance, as well as containing quite a lot of very accessible amusement. Even an opaque chapter like the *Propos des bien yvres* (which consists of a series of clerkly jokes) can be found amusing with the aid of a few footnotes.

6. The birth of the hero: eleven-month pregnancies

As an example of the unexpected richness of Rabelais's comic concerns in the earlier chapters of *Gargantua* we could take the birth of the hero. The basic story is told in a vein which, for all its literary and linguistic art, is in keeping with the spirit of *Pantagruel* and the *Grandes Cronicques* – Gargamelle, like Badebec before her, is polished off, though long after giving birth to the young giant. The comic ruthlessness of Gargamelle's death may be connected with Rabelais's lack of interest in female characters – there is only one noble and gracious lady in the four books, outside the Abbey of Thelema, and she has a Priapic name in Hebrew. I suspect also that Rabelais was impatient with both the newfangled Italianate lady-centred courtliness and the continuing mediaeval cult of the lady in the still popular courtly romances. To adopt *en passant* an anti-feminism of the kind that his friend Tiraqueau had been accused of was good for a laugh – and could be more than atoned for later in the Abbey of Thelema.[6]

Gargantua is born after an eleven-month pregnancy as the result of his mother's eating a surfeit of tripe. The gigantic comedy of the birth, which is set not in Utopia but in Touraine, is in no ways diminished by its being used as an excuse for Rabelais to have his say on the clash between lawyers and doctors on the centuries-old problem of the maximum duration of a pregnancy. This is a lawyers' joke, but a problem of real concern to real men and women as well. Legal opinion on the maximum possible duration of pregnancies had been divided for nearly a thousand years, ever since the emperor Justinian in the sixth century had overthrown the judgment of the emperor Hadrian and somewhat arbitrarily rejected, with the whole force of law, the possibility of a pregnancy lasting more than ten months. Ten months – probably lunar months – were for a variety of reasons the normal classical equivalent of our nine. But judges have their ways of dealing with bad laws. In the course of the centuries, understanding judges and glossists, faced with apparently chaste and loyal wives whose children were born ten months or more after their husbands' deaths or prolonged absence, gradually extended the ten classical months to mean at least eleven!

---

[6] After giving birth to Gargantua, Gargamelle is not mentioned again – except to approve of Grandgousier's choice of name for her son (*Garg.*, TLF vi, 13; *EC* viii, 11) – until she probably dies of joy at the news of the successful outcome of the fighting against Picrochole (*TLF* xxxv; *EC* xxxvii): 'For the *supplement* to the *Supplementum Chronicorum* says that Gargamelle died there of joy. For my part I know nothing about it, and care very little about her or any other woman there is.' All the upbringing and education of Gargantua is dependent on his father alone, who enjoys the prestige of the Roman *paterfamilias*.

Doctors in general and traditionalist lawyers agreed with this, defending pregnancies lasting eleven, twelve or even thirteen months. Many humanist lawyers opposed this; some defended it. Much later, in the *Apologie de Raymond Sebond*, Montaigne uses this clash of expert opinion as a central example of how little agreement he finds in professionally-based knowledge.

The problem was made newly topical at the highest level in a study which Andrea Alciati included in his *Paradoxes* of 1531. Rabelais's friend Tiraqueau also treats the subject at length in his best-selling *Commentary on the Law, 'Si unquam'*; it was not published until 1535 but was already completed at Fontenay-le-Comte on 1 August, 1534. Rabelais's erudition seems to have been entirely borrowed from his friend's book, which, if *Gargantua* was published first, he must have read in manuscript. These works are only the tip of an iceberg. A flood of books treat the subject in the sixteenth and seventeenth centuries, frequently continuing to defend the legitimacy of children born after pregnancies of up to thirteen months.

The central argument of the 'tolerant' traditionalist school was based on the law known as the *Lex Gallus*, a law called by Rabelais *robidilardicque*, partly because it enabled the merry widow, in a jocular idiom, to rub her bacon (*lard*) in secret (*en robbe*) for two whole months after her husband's death, and then to palm off her bastard on her husband's estate. There may also be an allusion to a certain Robillard who held the traditional 'tolerant' view. That Rabelais is in favour of the restriction of 'legal' pregnancies to nine months is not made the subject of moral thundering but of learned humour, much of which still comes straight across to us. It is striking that the humour apparently commits Rabelais to a total acceptance of a limit of nine months; humanist lawyers were themselves divided on this matter, some siding with what, for Rabelais, were old-fashioned traditionalists. On the whole, medical opinion favoured the longer period. But the laughter does not deform the ideas he is mocking. In 1529 Marius Salomonius Albertiscus published in Lyons *Paradoxes on the Lex Gallus*, in which, as a compromise, he limited legitimacy to children born ten months after the day of the putative father's death. Everybody knew then, of course, that a normal pregnancy lasted nine months. The legal and medical quarrel concerned what was the maximum possible duration of a pregnancy which could lead to the birth of a legitimate child. The legality of children born after pregnancies lasting eleven months was strenuously defended right through the Renaissance, not only by doctors but by such a sceptical man as Montaigne. Others rejected them with no less vigour. Rabelais's book-learning is sound, but he chose a subject for his humour which was of such concern that it was known far outside the chambers of the legal experts or the surgeries of the doctors. (For Robillard, see E. V. Telle, *ER* XII.)

The gross amusement that he gets out of the permissive ambiguities of the law may be related to his placing the birth of Gargantua on 4 February, that is eighteen days before Lent in 1534 and a mere ten days before Lent in 1535. At such a period, jesting is more appropriate than moral exhortation. Both the wily wife and sexual relationships generally had long been themes of comic writing, giving rise to good uncomplicated laughter; the wife who cuckolds her husband is a regular figure of comedy in *conte* and farce; to cuckold a husband after his death is simply an extension of the theme. But this is an example of how Rabelais jests at matters which, in other moods, are topics of earnest moral concern for him. In serious vein no writer has written more enthusiastically about the gift of procreating legitimate children within lawful wedlock: in the *Tiers Livre* the finding of a wife who fears and loves God, and so refuses to commit adultery, is a wise and honourable quest in itself.

7. *The birth of the hero: a lesson in faith*

Another unexpectedly deep example of humanist laughter occurs when Gargantua is actually born; Grandgousier and Gargamelle prefer the solid comfort of the Gospel to the legends of St Margaret associated with childbirth: that is in keeping with evangelical ideas and so with the whole spirit of *Gargantua*. But the episode suddenly becomes an exercise in laughing propaganda, as Gargantua is born in a most extraordinary fashion, finally popping out of his mother's ear and crying out for a drink. Rabelais challenges us to say why we believe the tall story of the nativity of Christ, yet do not believe his equally tall story of the nativity of Gargantua. This challenge leads directly to evangelical propaganda at its best. It raises problems which were already latent in *Pantagruel* and which become of central importance in the *Tiers Livre* and in the closing chapters of the *Quart Livre*. Rabelais is a full Christian sceptic much earlier than scholarship normally allows such a philosophy to flourish. He believes that there is *no* argument based on natural reason which enables the Christian to pick and choose between the miraculous birth of Gargantua, the monstrous births related by Pliny and the tall story of Christ's nativity. What enables the Christian to find his way through such errors mimicking the truth is divine revelation. Hence the importance of the scriptures with their uniquely revealed doctrine. Hence also the importance of fully understanding what Christians mean, or should mean, by faith.

Traditional theologians tended to think of faith as a kind of gullibility: humanists of all persuasions followed the New Testament in seeing it as trust: trust in the promises of God. Rabelais is contrasting the teaching of Sorbonagres, misled by the Vulgate and by their ignorance of Greek, with what he, Erasmus and many others believed to be the true meaning of faith to be found in scripture. The theologians of the Sorbonne based their contention that faith is good credulity on a misunderstanding of the Epistle to the Hebrews 11, 1. This reads, 'Now faith is [. . .] the evidence of things unseen'. They wrongly take this to be a *definition* of faith. Erasmus made short shrift of that error: the Epistle to the Hebrews does not give a definition of faith at all; it is a eulogy of it. The Sorbonagres are accused of totally misunderstanding the meaning of this important scriptural text by relying on the Latin Vulgate and then having inadequate Latin or Greek to extract the right meaning from it. The Greek of Hebrews 11, 1 is opaque. The Authorised Version says that faith, the substance of things hoped for, is the 'evidence of things unseen'. The Vulgate attempts to render the Greek by saying that faith is the *argumentum non apparentium*. Anyone whose French is better than his classical Latin could wrongly take this to mean that faith is an *argument des choses de nulle apparence*, thereby making faith into something believed because it is *'not very likely'*. With such a so-called definition how could one possibly defend believing in Christ's birth without being obliged to believe in Gargantua's too? Both are quite unlikely events, events *de nulle apparence!*

Rabelais mockingly answers these confused errors with the verse of scripture which was indeed held to show what true faith is, namely trust in the power of God to carry out his promises. He quotes the reply which the Angel Gabriel made to the Blessed Virgin when she at first, quite rightly, refused to believe his extraordinary annunciation. Gabriel confirmed his divine authority by alluding to the specially-favoured, unlikely pregnancy of Elisabeth who was called barren: 'For with God nothing shall be impossible' (Luke 1, 37). Gabriel's assertion of confidence in God's promises is strengthened by its being an echo of the words to be found in the Greek Septuagint version of Genesis 8, 14, confirming the unlikely pregnancy of the ageing Sarah, who in this matter was a prototype of Mary. Abraham trusted that his seed would be as numberless as the sand of the sea-shore, even when his wife remained barren into extreme old age. Faith believes that God *will* fulfil his promises, come what may, even if the son eventually born to the barren old wife has apparently to be sacrificed as Isaac was.

Rabelais's final quip, 'For with God, nothing is ever impossible, and, if he so willed, women from now on would have children through their ears', reminds us that not only was Gargantua born through his mother's ear but so too was Christ – in popular legend. That the Word of God was conceived through the ear was a commonplace of popular theology; to make him be born through the ear was a natural extension of this, condemned by the Church of course but well-enough known to be worth a laugh, precisely because it was not Catholic.

The propaganda here would inevitably have struck the Sorbonne as Lutheran. Almost as inevitably they would have been wrong. Luther certainly held the same opinions as Rabelais on the nature of faith; but so too did the Catholic Erasmus (an author whom diehards of the Sorbonne considered just as bad as Luther himself). And the very orthodox Jean Bouchet, an early friend of Rabelais's, was equally convinced that in matters of birth, like everything else, God can do what he wills.[7] Actually Rabelais was probably in his own mind being as much a lawyer as a theologian. Erasmus pointed out in his sharp reply to criticisms of the *Praise of Folly* by Edward Lee, where he too had mocked those who misunderstood Hebrews, 11, 1, that it was the experts in canon law who spread misunderstandings of this text in their stormy glosses on the first title of the first book of the papal decretals, *De Summa trinitate et fide catholica*, claiming it to be a definition and then criticising it for not being a good one. As recently as 1532 Andrea Alciati (in his legal commentary on the words *De summa trinitate* which figure also in the title of the standard editions of the emperor Justinian's legal *Codex*) had translated the Greek much as Erasmus and Rabelais did, condemning the Vulgate rendering and 'those recent theologians who do not understand St Paul'.[8]

It is a persistent error of some literary and historical methodologies to tend to isolate theology in the Renaissance, making it only a concern of exceptionally dedicated Christians. Theology penetrated deeply into all areas of scholarship; conversely, scholars in all disciplines had their say in theological matters. Some of the most fundamental criticisms of the Vulgate Latin text of the New Testament appear in Budé's *Annotations on*

[7] Cf. Jean Bouchet, *Epistres Morales et Familieres du Traverseur* (1545), reprint, ed. J. Beard, Wakefield 1969; second part, 36v.; Bouchet stresses that, *Si dieu vouloit*, children would be born without sexual intercourse; men would all live without food or drink; the earth would produce its fruits without husbandry, for God can do what he will. A useful *résumé* of contemporary legal opinion on eleven-month pregnancies in Marius Salomonius Albertiscus: *In L. Gallus, et in Responsa prudentum Paradoxa*, Lyons, July 1529; see especially p.6, paragraph 51 r. Cf. also Cardano, *Contradicentium medicorum lib. I; Contradictio VIII*, in *Opera*, 1663, x, pp.344f.; also *Opera* ix, pp.9f. – The *Lex Gallus* was cited in *Pantagruel* ix *bis* (*EC* xiii) as one of the laws difficult to interpret.

[8] Erasmus, *Responsio ad Annotationes Edvardi Lei*, Basle 1520, ad. *CCXX*: He condemns the legal experts who, in their glosses on the title *De Sancta Trinitate et fide catholica* make a storm about the so-called definition in Hebrews 11, condemning it, by dialectical and scholastic standards, as insufficiently 'magisterial'. Lee thinks it is a 'definition' by the standards of his 'topics' [dialectical commonplaces]. He is wrong. It is an encomium of faith. If opponents object that Jerome and Augustine called it a definition, Erasmus has nothing against such men, only against those who treat the matter in a sophistical fashion (*tam sophisticè*). Cf. A. Alciati, *Codicis Justiniani Imp. Aug., Liber Primus* (published by Rabelais's learned printer, Sebastian Gryphius in Lyons, 1532) *Rubrica: De Summa Trinitate*, gloss: 'Faith is the foundation of those who hope and the proof (*indicium*) of things not seen. This conforms better to the meaning of St Paul in Hebrews [11, 1] than the Vulgate rendering. It is not surprising that more recent theologians, failing to understand Paul, offer a different definition' (cf. Aquinas, *Summa Theologica* iiia, xxxvi). For Budé's strong criticism of the Vulgate, cf. *De asse* (*Opera* ii, p.284).

the Pandects. One of the features of the Renaissance which most offended and disturbed the old-fashioned theologians of Paris, Louvain and elsewhere, was that their theological certainties were being overthrown not by other theologians (that would have been bad enough) but by mere philologists, who knew Greek and Hebrew as well as the classical Christian Latin of St Jerome, say, or St Augustine, and so could prove them and their scholastic authors wrong.

By the time we have reached chapter v, *Gargantua* can be seen to be living up to its promise: treating deeper matters than its gothic title would suggest.

8. Gargantua's attire

Other examples of Rabelais's combining lawyers' jokes with the less technical interests of his public may be found in the chapters dealing with Gargantua's attire. The growing giant has yet to be reformed; he is still nearer in conception to the hero of *Pantagruel* than he is to his own self later in the Chronicle. This explains why some of the precious stones he wears may have comic rather than moral qualities. Renaissance men and women knew the hidden qualities of precious stones either from such popular books as Mandeville's *Lapidaire en françoys* or else, directly or indirectly, from classical and post-classical authorities, especially the mediaeval bishop Marbod of Rennes or modern scholars such as Cardano. Precious stones are yet another example of things having real meanings and real properties, not meanings or properties arbitrarily imposed. The things they signify and the powers they possess were discovered, it was thought, by the specialist scholars, not simply attributed to them by authority or convention (*Garg.*, *TLF* VII, 37; *EC* VIII, 31; cf. Cardano, *Opera*, 1663, X, pp.520f.).

But the humour soon becomes more serio-comically up-to-date. Renaissance nobility were interested in the meanings of colours, especially in heraldry. It was widely believed that colours (unlike words) also had real, not imposed, meanings. There were sharp differences over what these real meanings were, coupled with a sharp reaction to anyone who sought to impose upon colours arbitrary meanings of his own.

Very many treatises, printed and in manuscript, poems, popular works and scholarly works, deal with the meaning of colours at every level of human inquiry. A popular supplement to the mediaeval herald Sicile's *Blason des couleurs*, which was printed several times in 1530s, is used by Rabelais as a peg on which to hang a disquisition which combines the bantering art of the declamation with sound legal scholarship.

This supplement to the *Blason des couleurs* was the work of a certain Carroset, but Rabelais did not know that. For him the treatise was (understandably, given its tyrannous ignorance) anonymous. This treatise, he says, sought to impose its own meanings on to colours, arbitrarily making Blue signify faith; White, firmness. This is inexcusable, since, we are told, the real meaning of White is happiness and delight, while the real meaning of Blue is heavenly things. The subject could seem barren enough to those who do not share the passionate concern of Renaissance men with symbolic meaning. Rabelais brings it alive in several ways: by linking it with the Renaissance cult of emblems; by linking it with humanist legal and scriptural concerns; and by treating the topic with humour. The question of the meaning of colours is directly connected with the preoccupation with natural and imposed symbolic meaning. Colours are *not* like words, kabbalistic signs or emblems, in having imposed meanings accepted by convention; they have real natural meanings, indications of which are given in the Bible and elsewhere, or else attainable through reason. That this chapter is to be read as an extension of Rabelais's sustained concern with natural and imposed meaning is emphasised by the terms used. In *Gargantua* VI, we are told how a name was *imposed* (*imposé*) on the baby giant; in *Pantagruel* II a name was similarly 'imposed' on the baby hero. That is the right way to give a name to one's son. But where colours are concerned there is no room at all for such private 'impositions' of meaning, for *impositions badaudes*. Colours have real meanings, which may be discovered. Such meanings have *not* been decided on by human beings: *Et n'est poinct ceste signifiance par imposition humaine institué.*

The chapters which deal with colours and emblems enable Rabelais to show his virtuosity as a writer of a *declamatio* in favour of the real meanings of colours and of the dignity of authentic symbolic heraldry. That he has chosen the form of a declamation rather than a sustainedly serious *exposé* sometimes puzzles modern readers, although this is just what one would expect in a humorous book. The basic seriousness of the subject he is treating seems clear in the first edition; it is made still clearer in 1542, when Rabelais links it with the 'restitution des bonnes lettres', that battle-cry of the humanist;[9] but the declamation was precisely a literary form enabling authors to treat serious topics in a mixed, partly bantering manner.[10] Two

[9] *Garg.* VIII, 54–5 variant; *EC* IX, 100. Mocking rebuses based on such puns as a broken bench (*bancq rompu*) to mean bankrupt, he declares that those who tolerate such inept and tasteless homonymies deserve to have a cow's turd plonked on their faces for holding to such nonsense 'after the restoration of good literature'. Of course jokes based on such homonymies – ingenious not inept ones! – abound in the Chronicles; but they must never be confounded with humanist emblems or with the cap-badges (*images*) with which they were so often connected.

[10] Cf. Henry Cornelius Agrippa: *Apologia adversus calumnias propter Declamationem de Vanitate Scientiarum et Excellentia Verbi Dei, sibi per aliquos Lovanienses Theologistas intentatas,* 1533, ch. XLII: 'Moreover a *declamatio* does not judge, does not dogmatise'; it remains within its conventions: 'it says some things in jest, some seriously, some aggressively; sometimes the

of the most popular books of the Renaissance were declamations: Henry Cornelius Agrippa's *On the Vanity of all Learning and on the Excellence of the Word of God* and Erasmus's *Praise of Folly*. This literary form, exemplifying Horace's question, 'What forbids you from speaking the truth while you smile?', intermingles the serious and the trivial; the true and the false; the weak argument and the strong; the deep personal conviction and the odd idea borrowed light-heartedly from others. A reader not used to this convention notices the weakness or the jocular detachment of some of the arguments and wrongly dismisses the whole treatise as simply a joke. Rabelais does not merely jest when the *restitution des bonnes lettres* is at stake. . . . He takes his argument moreover into legal territory, linking it with the fifteenth-century humanist Lorenzo Valla and his scathing *Book against Bartolo* (published for the first time posthumously, in 1517), which was dedicated to the learned Candido ('White') Decembrio. This enables him to mock yet again those who think that a knowledge of the Latin Vulgate suffices when one seeks truth in scripture. Bartolo of Sassoferrato was a legal scholar, as uncritically ridiculed by humanist lawyers like Budé and Rabelais as Accursius was. He had written a book on the meaning of colours whose very title was in non-classical Latin (that was enough to damn him). Like a donkey who would not raise his head to look at the sun, he had thought that light was of the colour of gold, so wrongly attributing to Gold the meaning which rightly belonged to White. This he tried to support with a quotation from St Matthew's account of the Trans-figuration. But unfortunately for him, the Vulgate contains a definite error, saying that Christ's vestments became 'as white as snow', whereas in the Greek original they became as 'white as light'. The fact that other Gospels use the phrase 'as white as snow' is irrelevant: nobody denies that snow is white; the point is that Saint Matthew makes light to be white as well.[11]

In all this Rabelais was probably rejoicing the heart of his friend Tiraqueau and mocking one of his enemies, Barthélemy de Chasseneux, who, in his legal study on heraldry, pompously called *The Catalogue of*

---

author expounds his own opinions; sometimes other peoples; sometimes he proclaims the truth; sometimes falsehoods; sometimes things which are doubtful.' Agrippa stresses these points: 'A *declamatio* does not always give my opinions; . . . it often adduces many weak arguments.' He adds that anyone who ignored these conventions could not possibly understand a *declamatio* – a salutary warning against superficial readings of such texts.

[11] By classical standards Bartolo's treatise *De Insigniis et Armis* misuses the word *insignis* 'emblem', which in the ablative plural, should be *de insignibus* not *de insigniis*. Valla's treatise forms part of his concern with words as 'signs'; in his *Opera Omnia*, Basle 1540, it is placed immediately before his *Dialecticae Disputationes*. In the Greek original, Matthew 17, 2 tells how Christ's raiment was *leuka hōs to phōs*, 'as white as *light*'. The Vulgate reads *alba sicut nix*, 'as white as *snow*'; at some early stage *lux*, light, was misread as *nix*, snow, and became established as the standard reading among the Latins. It is one of the cases where the Vulgate is demonstrably and incontrovertibly wrong.

Worldly Glory, ignorantly fell into the same error as Bartolo, whom he quotes on this point. Much later, Tiraqueau was prepared to make allowances for Bartolo's bad Latin and absence of Greek; but that was in the days when his international professional reputation made him more circumspect. Towards the end of the episode, Rabelais claims to want to write a whole book on the subject of colours, treating blue as he had treated white. He makes only one proviso: *Le Prince* must command him to. The treatise will be written, 'si le Prince le veult et commende, cil qui en commendant, ensemble donne et povoir et sçavoir'. That he was in fact sufficiently interested in symbolism of all kinds to write such a treatise, his works clearly show. But he struck these words out in 1535. By *Le Prince* did he mean his king as I once thought? Probably not, despite the fact that *prince* was a current latinism applied to Renaissance monarchs. The phrase *Le Prince le veult* is based on the standard formula for giving regal authority to a law, *Le Roy le veult*, but is probably used in jest. For Rabelais's first publisher was nick-named *Le Prince*. So too was his first publisher's successor at bed and board, Pierre de Sainte-Lucie. It would be nice to know whom he meant and why he crossed the sentences out. For Claude Nourry, the first to be surnamed *Le Prince*, died in 1533; Sainte-Lucie was using the name early in 1534. Such clues could help to date *Gargantua*.[12]

Renaissance scholars know of the importance attached to colour symbolism, but on the whole find the subject fairly arid. Emblems, on the other hand, have a passionate following today as in the past. Luckily for us Rabelais is at his comic best when dealing with the gross ignorance of those who confound Renaissance emblems with fustian riddles.

It was Alciati who made emblems widely appreciated, reinforcing a tendency already encouraged by such works as Colonna's *Dream of Poliphile* and by Erasmus's *Adages*. His book of *Emblemata* was first published by him in Lyons in 1534, though it was inefficiently pirated in 1531. Rabelais does not use the term *emblème*, preferring *ymage* when the emblem is worn in the cap, or *devise* and *divise* in a more general sense. Both these terms had wide currency. Claude Paradin, in an influential treatise (1551), specifically calls Francis I's emblem a *devise*.[13] But the term emblem is now consecrated by usage and it would be absurd to try to change it. Emblems frequently consist of a picture with a moral saying or poem attached. They can also be pictures without words, or even the words without the pictures, though this latter meaning is both early and rare.

Alciati's *Emblemata* consist of a series of woodcuts symbolically

---

[12] The question of the interpretation of *Le Prince* (*Garg.*, *TLF* viii, 80; *EC* ix, 66 *var.*) as Rabelais's printer was first raised by G. Defaux. See bibliographical notes to this chapter.

[13] Claude Paradin, *Devises heroïques*; first edition 1551, Cf., for Francis I's *devise*, 1557 edition, a 8v°, reproduced in *Harvard Library Catalogue*, Ruth Mortimer, 1964, ii, p.511, entry no. 410.

representing a moral or philosophical truth; they are accompanied by verses explaining the symbolism which the pictures enshrine. He himself thought of the enigmatic moral picture, not the verse or the motto, as the essence of the emblem. This fact is proved by what he writes about his little book of *Emblemata* in his weighty legal study *On the Meaning of Words*: his *Emblems* constitute a book where *things* have direct meanings. Normally it is words (*verba*) which signify: things (*res*) which are signified. But exceptionally things can signify directly, as his book shows. His emblems prove that pictures, although classifiable as *res*, can have meanings in themselves, without calling upon words to express them. His basic theme is a commonplace, spread, for example, by St Augustine in his treatise *On Christian Doctrine* and touched upon by many Renaissance authors.

Emblematic pictures, with or without accompanying words, were worked in precious metals as badges to be worn in caps; they were used to decorate palaces and castles; they were woven into tapestries, used as printers' devices. Some of the greatest poets of the Renaissance used the concept of the emblem in their poems, conjuring up emblematic pictures to convey their concepts, though in this case they had to call upon the magic of words to describe them.

For the Renaissance Humanist the emblematic picture was akin to the 'sacred writings' (hieroglyphs) of ancient Egypt. They could therefore elaborate them with the help of the fourth-century treatise *On Hieroglyphics* by Horapollo, who claimed to explain the sacred writings of a civilisation even older and more mysterious than that of Greece, and whose sages (as many Renaissance thinkers believed) had been taught their secret lore by Moses.

Horapollo's treatise was frequently printed in several languages; it was known to the circles which Rabelais now frequented. As early as 1521 it was edited by Johannes Angelus in Greek and Latin and dedicated to Jean de Mauléon, bishop of Comminges. Angelus, an admirer of Margaret of Angoulême's protégés Briçonnet, Lefèvre d'Etaples and Girard Roussel, was a member of the group of Meaux, who, protected by the king's sister, hoped to establish an evangelical, Catholic reformation throughout the diocese of Meaux. With the learned support of such a venerable treatise and the work of Alciati, the emblem becomes no mere fad or fashion. Emblems were a means of 'sacred writing' able to convey a moral idea otherwise only knowable through discursive reasoning. The fact that these portrayals of moral ideas were neither arbitrarily personal nor yet knowable to anyone but the initiate was one of their charms. On Plutarch's authority emblems (once they had been identified with Egyptian hieroglyphs) could be seen as close to Pythagorean symbols, whose meaning could not be known except to a privileged few.[14]

[14] Cf. *Garg.*, TLF VIII, 62; *EC* IX, 52: 'Very differently [from the inventors of the silly rebuses] did the sages of Egypt behave in days of yore, when they wrote by letters which

A major courtly use of the emblem was as an *ymage* to be worn in the beret, proclaiming to the initiate one's philosophy of life. In giving Gargantua an *ymage* to wear in his cap, Rabelais was following the practice of the great. Guillaume du Bellay certainly wore one, as is shown in his portrait in Versailles.[15] Bartolomeo Veneto's *Portrait of a Courtier* in the National Gallery in Rome is reproduced by Mario Praz precisely to show a typical emblem as worn in court.[16] Rabelais ends his account of the dignity of emblems with a reference 'to the device of my Lord the Admiral, which was first worn by Octavian Augustus'. This flattering reference to Philippe Chabot, Admiral of France, Britanny and Guyenne, a power indeed at court, is no chance allusion. He was known to be interested in emblems; the one he wore as Admiral of France was of ancient dignity, consisting of an anchor with a dolphin entwined about it. It signified *Festina lente*, Hasten slowly. When Jean le Fèvre published his French translation of the *Emblems* of Alciati in 1536 its title was: *Le Livret des Emblemes de Maistre Alciat, mis en rime françoyse et presenté à Monseigneur l'Admiral de France*. Not only is its dedication appropriately fulsome, but like Rabelais it sees emblems as a source of *images* for courtiers.[17]

Rabelais found it intolerably stupid and worthy of hearty mockery that some of his contemporaries should confound these hieroglyphic emblematic *ymages* and devices with punning fustian rebuses. That was to rob them of their splendour and to trivialise a mystic form of pictorial symbolism, reserved for informed initiates. The scholar-printer Geoffroy Tory was one who made the silly confusion Rabelais laughs at. He confounded with hieroglyphic emblems such nonsense as an *S* written large, signifying *largesse*, or a broken bench signifying *bankrupt*. Such puns are a fair source of laughter and Rabelais widely uses them as such in his writings. But to confound such laughable nonsense with true devices is to misunderstand a

---

they called hieroglyphical; such letters no one understood who did not understand – and everyone understood who *did* understand – the virtues, property and nature of the things which were figuratively represented by them.' Such a concept is basic to the Renaissance emblem. (For Plutarch, cf. *On Isis and Osiris*, 354, 10: Pythagoras admired the Egyptian priests, copying their symbolism, incorporating their teachings in his enigmas. Plutarch adds that Pythagoras's precepts are indeed like Egyptian hieroglyphs – in other words, the good, humanist emblems which Rabelais links also with the hieroglyphs are of the same nature as the *symboles Pythagoricques* of the prologue to *Gargantua* and of the gnomic sayings interpreted in the *Tiers Livre*.)

[15] Reproduced in Plattard, *Vie de François Rabelais*, 1928, plate facing p.168.

[16] Mario Praz, *Studies in Seventeenth-Century Imagery: Second Edition considerably increased*, Rome 1964, p.9.

[17] *Garg.*, TLF VIII, 68; *EC* IX, 56. Of emblem-hieroglyphs Rabelais writes: 'Horapollo composed two books in Greek about them, and Poliphilo in his *Dream* [*Hypnerotomachia*] expounded more about them. In France you have a fragment of them in the shape of the *devise* of Monsieur l'Admiral [Chabot], which was first worn by Octavian Augustus.' Such associations are found in the scholarly interpretations of Renaissance emblems.

vital aspect of the Renaissance, confounding the serious and the risible. The confusion could easily arise out of a confusion of terminology. Emblems are *res*: things which signify without words. The *rebus* calls upon the same word *res* in an oblique case. But for those who take emblems seriously rebuses are stupid parodies of something good, venerable, mysterious and ancient.

The emblematic *ymage* that Rabelais gives Gargantua to wear in his cap was of enamel set in gold. As befits the newly syncretistic Rabelais who cites *The Symposium* in his opening words, the *ymage* consists of the androgyne also borrowed from Plato's *Symposium*; it is held to symbolise the mystical sense of Greek words forming a quotation from St Paul: 'Charity seeketh not her own.' Appropriately for Gargantua in this stage of the book the androgyne is described quite comically, as having 'two heads, one turned towards the other, four arms, four feet and two arses, such as Plato says in the *Symposium*' (*Garg.*, TLF VII, 95f.; *EC* VIII, 80f.). Plato is a little less explicit. But the humour is not destructive and leads us on to the solid defence of the new humanist cult a few pages later. I think it likely that Rabelais, in comically emphasising the posteriors of the androgyne, was showing how the emblem was appropriate to the bottom-centred young giant, while the inner religious profundity of the emblem is the potential later realised through the new humanist education. Erasmus certainly saw the androgyne as both 'indecent' and yet a possible symbol of true Christian love in marriage, making two persons into one; this can be seen from his annotation on Matthew 19, 6: 'Wherefore they are no more twain, but one flesh.' Like Rabelais he refuses to be overawed by his Platonic source: 'Aristophanes's fable in Plato's *Symposium* does not entirely disagree with this statement. But it is rather indecent (*obscoenior*).' Gargantua's emblem is in the fashion represented by the highest in the court, but marked by the comic grossness appropriate to this stage of the second Chronicle. Margaret of Navarre's own emblem consisted of Cupid with the legend 'By him all things were made', bringing together Christ as Love and the well-known phrase from the Creed.[18]

These chapters devoted to the real meanings of colours, and the true nature of emblems for those duly initiated into their mysteries, show Rabelais in a new mood: still interested as ever he was in symbolic representation of meaning, but extending his interests away from the by-roads of legal controversy into the main avenues of Renaissance culture.

9. The adolescence of Gargantua

With chapter x, at least for modern tastes, Rabelais's art takes a great leap

[18] See *Marguerites de la Marguerite des Princesses*, Lyons 1548 (reprint, ed. Ruth Thomas, Wakefield 1970), the emblem of Margaret is on the title-page of each volume as printed by Jean de Tournes.

forward. From now on, through several chapters, the footnotes can become less insistent while Rabelais's incomparable language can speak to us more directly over the centuries. Some of his most enduring comedy and some of his most attractively humanist thinking lies just ahead. In more than one sense these chapters make the final break with the concept of comedy dominant in his writing until now. The grossness and the coarseness still raise their belly-laughs, but as a prologue to our condemning them against higher and purer ideals.

The young giant does everything absurdly wrong, going against proverbial wisdom in all its forms: yawning at the flies, pissing in his shoes, not looking (as it were) before he leaps. The list of proverbs that he turns inside out – greatly expanded in the second edition – is a *tour de force*. These proverbs, as well as laughingly condemning Gargantua (for proverbs, even popular ones, may partake of the dignity of the classical adage so treasured in the Renaissance) also introduce movement into Rabelais's novel.

The earlier chapters are, like much of *Pantagruel*, essentially static; now all is movement. The young rustic clown of a giant is never still for a minute. His language is of the earth, earthy; his main concern is with excrement. In this he joins many a real child, puzzled by adult convention which makes breaking wind or going to the lavatory subjects not to be laughed at but discreetly ignored. In *Gargantua* the comic exaggeration of it all is designed to make us laugh; but the laughter is by no means gratuitous.

Gargantua is negligently allowed to read scatological poems in delicate Marotic rime-schemes scribbled on the walls of his jakes; he spends his ingenuity in inventing caressingly gentle substitutes for lavatory-paper; he is brought to think of himself in terms of his anus and of women in terms of excreta. Grandgousier, in his indulgent ignorance, is as tolerant a looker-on at all this as Pantagruel was tolerant of Panurge; and like many a character in *Pantagruel* he becomes ecstatic, 'ravy en admiration', as he considers the high understanding and marvellous intelligence of his son (*TLF* XIII, 1; *EC* XIV, 1). This recurrence of the theme of comic ecstasy is one of the many features linking these earlier chapters of *Gargantua* with *Pantagruel*.

Appropriately, Gargantua is put to study under dirty, doddering old tutors who were Parisian theologians; the first, Thubal ('Worldly') Holofernes died of the pox 'in 1420', having wasted his pupil's time reading the silly boring books in bad Latin traditionally mocked by humanists throughout Western Europe for over half a century. Rabelais's innovation was to do the same comically; and in French. Thubal Holofernes was a stupid man as befits a theologian who was placed first in his finals by Our Masters of the Sorbonne. Jobelin Bridé, his successor, was another 'old cougher' out of the same stable. He continues the bad work, so that Gargantua becomes more and more ill-educated. A boy, already besotted with faeces, is forced to acquire such learning as he has among books which humanists condemned as so much literary dung (*faeces litterarum*). This can lead to no moral or spiritual improvement, not even to progress in the natural sciences or in social graces. All the boy learns – as Ponocrates discovers when he watches Gargantua live as his Sorbonne mentors had taught him to – is how to be lazy, how to be dirty, how to take a delight in food which raises an excessive thirst for wine, while giving canting 'moral' reasons for all this slackness. Gargantua woke up at the then very late hour of 8 or 9 o'clock, 'whether it was light or not'; for so his theological teachers had ordered, citing as their authority the words of David in Psalm 126 (127): 'It is vain for you to rise up early.' He got dressed with the absolute minimum of toiletry, simply running his fingers through his hair as old Professor Almanus used to do in Paris: 'for otherwise to comb, wash or clean himself was to waste time on the things of this world. . . .'

What made Grandgousier see the error of his ways in bringing up his princely son so negligently was the arrival on the scene of Eudemon, the Fortunate One. This handsome young page, educated according to humanist principles, is presented as a living condemnation of the ideas of old-fashioned, idle pseudo-theologians of the universities. Clean, healthy, modest, eloquent, his formal address to Gargantua was made with gestures so appropriate, with so clear an enunciation, with so elegant a voice and in Latin so correct and properly ornate, that he was more like a Gracchus, a Cicero or an Aemilius than a young man of this century!

All Gargantua can do in reply is to bellow like a cow and hide his face in his hat. It was no more possible to get a word out of him than to get 'a fart from a dead donkey' (*Garg.*, TLF xiv, 33f.; *EC* 27f.).

The arrival of Eudemon is an excellent example of the way in which Rabelais gets the maximum of comedy out of unlikely circumstances. Eudemon is certainly an ideal. His arrival is a pivotal point in Gargantua's life. Yet we are struck by the inappropriateness of his praise of Gargantua, stressing as it does his virtue, his good manners and his physical beauty! The comic tension created makes us smile, without however rejecting Eudemon as a mere Rosencrantz or Guildenstern adept at flattery.

It is possible that this comic tension partly arises out of a sudden change of direction on Rabelais's part, whilst writing this episode. Eudemon was praised, as we saw, for being unlike 'a young man of this century'. Yet a mere page before, the products of the Sorbonne education were contrasted unfavourably with this paragon, precisely in order to show up their ignorance against 'the young people of today'.

Grandgousier would willingly have killed Jobelin Bridé when he saw what a mess he made of his son's education. But, with that mixture of kindliness and negligence which Rabelais delights us with in one of his comic veins, he is paid his wages, allowed to tipple away 'theologically' and then sent to the devil.

The new humanist education makes a total break with dirt, squalor and slackness. Never again will the giants be the gross boobies they have been up till now. But the change has to be a semi-miraculous one, operated by Rabelais's appearing in the novel as 'a learned doctor of that time called Seraphin Calobarsy'. In this way Rabelais intervenes in his own creation, purging Gargantua with hellebore from the island of Anticyra, making him forget all the nonsense he had learned (*Garg.*, *TLF* XXI, 12; *EC* XXIII, 9 *var.*).

Rabelais's legal and rhetorical training would probably have led him to follow this comic mockery of pre-humanist education by a direct statement of the ideal which had already, in humanist eyes, superseded it. In fact several chapters are intercalated into this episode, all given over to mocking the Sorbonne. It is reasonably probable that the story as first conceived did not contain these chapters: that the good and bad education were placed side by side, both taking place in Touraine. That would explain why Rabelais inadvertently first left in Touraine references – to the Loyre, to the *porte de Bessé* and to Narsay – which he changed into Parisian allusions (to the Seine, to the *porte Saint-Victor* and Montmartre) in time for the second edition.

The new education answers the defects of the old, point by point for the most part. The new young man will be given a full day, marked by cleanliness, godliness and hard work – his new preceptor's name, Ponocrates, being derived from *ponos*, toil, intense desire and *kratos*, force, power, dominion.

Whereas the old Gargantua started his day late, in physical and spiritual squalor, half-hearing twenty-six or thirty masses while mumbling his beads with his dirty tipsy chaplain, the new Gargantua gets up at 4 a.m. (which *was* early); he is rubbed down while he listens to the scriptures read aloud with full regard to their meaning; then he purges his body of its superfluities while his tutor purges his soul with recapitulations of the harder scriptural texts he had just heard.

This is, as far as the heroes are concerned, a definitive farewell to faecal grossness. From this point onwards, whenever that kind of physical grossness appears in the Chronicles, the character involved is held up for comic condemnation. Two more floods of urine are allowed to enliven the tale of the giants, but before the book is over even they cease to be compatible with the wise heroes they have become. The change is marked by the striking change in language: deliberately and comically specific for the old Gargantua, medically and chastely generalised for the new. The old Gargantua, before tackling breakfasts of fried tripe, goat-steaks, ham and monastical bread-and-dripping, 'Shat, pissed, coughed up phlegm, farted and let snot drip from his nose like an archdeacon'. The new Gargantua does not eat anything at all for hours after getting up; and his bodily purgations are not only discreet in language but plainly subordinated to his spiritual welfare: 'Then he went off to the privy in order to excrete his natural digestions. There his preceptor went over again what he had read' – that is, the passages of scripture. The comic grossness of the heroes is about to pass into other characters – in *Gargantua* it becomes a dominant trait of Frère Jean, while Grandgousier and his son soar upwards to increasingly moral heights (*Garg.*, TLF xx, 30; xxi, 38f.; *EC* xxi, 24; xxiii, 30f.).

The detail of the new learning is clearly spelled out: a thorough knowledge of Greek and Latin is simply taken for granted (and there is no more talk of Syriac and Arabic). The young man will learn all that a gentleman should: all *honneste sçavoir*, including music, mathematics, astronomy, botany. He will, as befits a young gentleman rather than a young giant, play courtly games like tennis; he will prepare himself to be the Christian knight that befits his rank by constantly having God's goodness before his mind while he follows a kind of army assault-course. This training is meant to be a serious preparation for knightly duty. In *Pantagruel* the education was more appropriate to the formation of a professional lawyer than of a gentleman. Once acquired it was swallowed up in the mainly comic encounters with characters such as Thaumaste. But in *Gargantua* the hero ends as a wise commander in charge of his father's armies, in a war in which by no means all the tale consists in fun and games. There are no time-wasting joustings: 'Then,' we are told, 'Gargantua broke no lances; for it is the greatest nonsense in the world to say, "I have broken ten lances in tournament or in battle" – a carpenter could do just that – but praiseworthy glory there is in breaking with one lance ten of your enemies' (*Garg.*, TLF xx, 133f.; *EC* xxiii, 107f.).

In poor weather various trades and professions are visited and studied, public lectures are listened to; so too are the pleas of 'noble barristers', and the sermons of 'evangelical preachers'.[19]

In propagating this humanist educational system Rabelais is both copying and rivalling the new pedagogical theories which many of the great and not-so-great humanists of his day had formulated; some were being published at this very time. Budé's treatise was published in 1532; Erasmus's in 1531; Vivès's broad and attractively humanist ideas were widely available; so too were Melanchthon's and many others. These humanist systems (often indebted to ancient platonic educational theories) all had in common the determination to bring a young nobleman into an appropriately virtuous Christian manhood. While all partly sharing the platonic assumption that sin and moral error are more akin to ignorance

[19] *Garg.*, TLF xxii, 23f.; *EC* xxiv, 24f.: 'They went to hear public lectures, formal learned discussions [*actes solennels*], speeches [*répétitions*], declamations, the pleas of noble barristers and the addresses of evangelical preachers.'

than to deliberate wickedness, they in practice remain firmly Christian, both overtly and in their clear intention not only to expose the child to the morally good but to shield him from the morally evil.

As befits the liberal education of a free-born gentleman, there is an insistence on the joy of learning; on sport; on practical lessons. There is a distrust of passive reading: all that can be done *viva voce* is done that way. As so often in the Renaissance, when the art of memory was highly cultivated, great importance is attached to knowing things off by heart. Writing is in fact only mentioned in order to insist that it was in the humanist hand, not old-fashioned gothic. The writing of one's own manuscripts is replaced by the printed book.[20] There is also a sustained intention to defend elegance and culture from accusations of worldliness. It was not only the diehards of the Sorbonne who murmured about worldly vanities when young men were taught to be clean, sweet-smelling and gorgeously attired. Rabelais answers this kind of criticism in many ways: by openly suggesting that they were based upon lazy ignorant cant, not upon true religion, or by having the young pupil do two things at once – being dressed by his servants while yesterday's lessons are gone over. A good example of how the new system answers the old concerns the long list of games in chapter xx. These games – and the hundred-odd of the first edition are expanded considerably in the next – are a copious example of lawyers' jesting at legal methodology. Tiraqueau made several such lists in his legal studies (once, for example, drawing up as complete a list as possible of all feminine jewellery and knick-knacks mentioned in ancient literature; this was to show that women are naturally spendthrift). This list of games, which is funnier when listened to than when read coldly from the page, shows the hundred-and-one ways in which the young can waste their time. It is answered in the new and ideal system in two ways: cards are brought out in the new system too – but not to be played with: – 'non pour jouer, mais pour apprendre . . . Arithmeticque'; only when thanks have been given to God after a cultured dinner is there any question of 'pastimes', such as playing musical instruments or else indulging (before a final look at the sky, a final recapitulation of the day's events and fervent prayers before bed) in 'ces petitz passetemps qu'on faict ès chartes, ès dez et guobeletz'.[21]

The evangelical fervour of the new system is perhaps best represented

---

[20] *Garg.*, *TLF* xxi, 123f., *EC* xxiii, 97f. Contrast *Garg.* xiii, 39f.; *EC* xiv, 31f.: In the old educational system Thubal Holoferne taught Gargantua 'to write gothically'; the young giant 'wrote out all his books. For the art of printing was not yet current.'

[21] It is important that Rabelais cites Leonicus Thomaeus's book on the ancient game of *Tali* (a form of dice) and the practice of 'our good friend Lascaris' who enjoyed playing it. (*Garg.* xxii, 11f., *EC* xxiv, 10f.) This gave humanist dignity to such relaxations. Lascaris, a Greek who taught both Erasmus and Budé, might have been met by Rabelais in Rome; or he may have known him in France.

by the contrast between the old Gargantua, mumbling through his graces while he drinks and picks his teeth with a pig's trotter, and the new Gargantua, whose graces at dinner consist of several beautiful canticles praising the munificence and kindness of God. Now, cleanliness is literally next to godliness; these 'beautiful canticles' are preceded by a careful washing of the face and eyes 'in beautiful fresh water' (*Garg.*, TLF XX, 87; EC XXII, 1; cf. TLF XXI, 91; EC XXIII, 72).

The censors of the Sorbonne may well also have noted that Gargantua's thirty-odd masses are not counter-balanced in the new ideal by a single mass, attended with devotion, but by Scriptural readings, evangelical prayers and evangelical sermons. Rabelais as a priest duly said his daily mass: so at least he claims in his *Supplication for his apostasy* and I am inclined to believe him. But in his Chronicles the mass is evidently played down, while evangelical prayer and preaching are advocated with energy and fervour. He was treading on dangerous ground if he really held the doctrine, duly and in this case not surprisingly condemned by the Sorbonne, that 'it is better to hear one good sermon than to hear a hundred masses' (*Garg.*, TLF XXII, 25, note).

Laughter had pushed the old system of education so successfully off the stage that the new system sweeps triumphantly in to replace it, without a word of discussion. As a means of propaganda Rabelais had found a powerful artistic vehicle. To answer him effectively it would not be enough to counter his arguments: an opponent would have to make his system as laughable as he made theirs. And only an equivalent comic genius could do that. In some ways the seriousness of these chapters is surprising. Not that a humanist would take education other than seriously, but the explanation of the ideal system was occasioned by a comparison between the tongue-tied boorish young Gargantua and the fluent latinate Eudemon. His set-piece of polite flattery has defects of its own, defects not untypical of some humanist trends: it is more ornate, elegant and courteous than truthful. Rabelais's ideal system of education ought to produce a much less shallow, much less facile, character than this healthy young flatterer.[22] It does. And with Jobelin Bridé's death we are made to feel that the bad education is a thing of the past, dating from the fourteenth and fifteenth centuries, when Gargantua was born and bred in gothic darkness. The only date mentioned is 1420. It cannot be taken literally as it is part of a jingle.[23] Then, unexpectedly, Rabelais lifts us out of the early fifteenth century

[22] *Garg.*, TLF XIV, 33; EC XV, 27. (Rabelais may have got the idea of his name from Plutarch; *On the Virtues of Woman*, 260D: 'Battus, who was surnamed *eudaimōn*.' The term is current in Greek with the sense of happy, blessed, fortunate.)

[23] *Garg.*, TLF XIII, 57; EC XIV, 45; Jobelin Bridé died of the pox, 'Et fut l'an mil quatre cens et vingt – de la verolle que luy vint'. Rabelais is citing two verses of Marot, from a comic epitaph on the Franciscan brother Jean Levesque.

right into the time when he was writing. The main enemy soon ceases to be the laughably inadequate old-fashioned pedagogy of former days that was largely discredited already in weighty and authoritative Latin treatises; it is now that of the Sorbonne, the conservative theologians of Paris. Contempt for the Sorbonne, far from dominant in the first version of *Pantagruel* (1532), just more perceptible in the second (1533) and so triumphantly scathing in the third (1534), becomes the main preoccupation of chapters XV to XIX of *Gargantua*. Their being embedded in the section devoted to education suggests most successfully that the evil effects of the tutors Thubal Holofernes and Jobelin Bridé are to be laid at the door of the faculty of theology of the University of Paris which taught them. For humanists who respected Erasmus, the Sorbonne was the centre of all that was bad, ignorant, incoherent and old-fashioned in theology. For many humanists of the time, its ignorance and aggressive intolerance were summed up in the personality of its syndic Noël Béda, though he was far from being alone in his views.[24]

These chapters, which events could easily have made bitter in the extreme, are the clearest examples of Twelfth-night or Shrovetide humour in the whole of *Gargantua*. Rabelais apparently wrote them when the party of the Sorbonne was, at least temporarily, in decline and that of the du Bellays in the ascendancy.

10. *The borrowing of the bells of Notre-Dame*

The tale of how Gargantua took the great bells from Notre-Dame and hung them about the neck of his mule belongs to the Gargantua legends related in the *Grandes et inestimables Cronicques*. Rabelais briefly alluded to it in *Pantagruel*, just before amusing us at the expense of the Library of Saint-Victor:

Having done this, Gargantua came to Paris with his men. Upon his entry, everybody came out to see him – for, as you well know, the people of Paris are daft by nature: and they looked at him with great amazement, and not without great fear lest he should carry the Palais somewhere else, to some country *a remotis*, just as his father had carried off the bells [*campanes*] of Notre-Dame to attach them to the neck of his mule.

The story was all the more amusing because the bells of Notre-Dame were proverbially large: Loupgarou's club had thirteen diamond points, the least of which was 'grosse comme la plus grande cloche de Nostre-Dame de Paris'.[25]

---

[24] Erasmus, in his *Responsio ad Notulas Beddae* (*Opera Omnia* IX, 706D) wrote: 'If the Most Christian King were to need a fool, who could do this better than Beda, so seriously ridiculous?'

[25] *Pant.* VII; *TLF*, 28f.; *EC*, 25f. For Loupgarou's club, 'aussi grosse comme la plus grande cloche de Nostre-Dame de Paris', see *Pant.*, *TLF* XIX, 51; *EC* XXIX, 45.

The tale in *Gargantua* takes up this theme, also commenting on the remarkable daftness of the people of Paris. But the scope of the story is now much wider. When and why Rabelais decided to retell this story of the bells in a major episode of *Gargantua* is impossible to know for sure. Since Gargantua seems to be given a mule rather as an afterthought, it is at least possible that the tale was not part of the original conception of his new Chronicle. Anyway, a mule is quickly acquired for the young giant – out of Africa, whence something new always comes. She is described in ways which increase the local flavour of Rabelais's yarn: her tail was twice as large as a monument in Rabelais's part of the world, *la pile Sainct Mars auprès de Langest* (*TLF* XV, 1; *EC* XVI, 1). Rabelais delights in situating his giants' prowesses and the great war against Picrochole in the lands of his childhood. There is also an artistic complicity between Rabelais and his patrons, sharing as they all did a local knowledge of the same part of Touraine. The pillar of Saint-Mars was near the village we now spell as Langeais. Jean du Bellay's brother Guillaume du Bellay was always known to his contemporaries as the 'Seigneur de Langey'.

The swishing tail of the mule which knocks down the proverbially lacking forests of Beauce provides good simple laughter in the tradition of the *Grandes Cronicques* on which it is based; so too does Gargantua's sitting on the towers of Notre-Dame and drowning polyglot crowds of silly Parisian students in a flood of comic piddle. The account of the great drowning is told in mock-heroic Biblical style, a point emphasised by the vast number of the slain being given 'not counting the women and children'.

The excitement that this tale of Gargantua's visit to Paris probably aroused in contemporaries lies no doubt in the skilful blending of a delightful variant of a well-known story with shrewd and direct political comment.

To deal with the story first.

In the *Grandes et inestimables Cronicques* the tale of the borrowed bells is told in the usual unrealistic timeless fashion. No mention at all is made of the University of Paris in general let alone of its faculty of theology, the famous and infamous Sorbonne. Rabelais on the contrary made the Sorbonne central to the whole story. This enabled him to link his earlier chapters, consecrated to educational matters, with this major episode of comic satire. Gargantua's private tutors were both products of the Sorbonne, both old coughers. Janotus de Bragmardo, the University's public orator, is a Sorbonagre too, the very archetype of the doddering old phlegmy, catarrhal professor. Naturally he begins his confused harangue *en toussant*. We are treated at the end to a fine piece of slapstick in which Janotus bullies a wretched minor dominie for his ignorance of the *Parva Logicalia*, that scholastic 'labyrinth of useless difficulties' to which Vivès attempted to give the *coup-de-grâce* in 1531 in his treatise on education, *De tradendis disciplinis.* The *Parva Logicalia* and its author, Peter of Spain (Pope John XXI) had dominated mediaeval dialectic since the thirteenth century: both became symbols of old-fashioned scholastic ignorance. The effects of such studies on scholars devoted to them is a sustained element of the humour of the harangue of poor old Janotus. The mediaeval manuals of dialectic claimed to teach men to argue logically. This Janotus attempts to do. Even logic at its best often gets short shrift in Rabelais. His wise giants, when expounding their moral, religious or philosophical certainties, never have resort to dialectical syllogisms or rhetorical enthymemes. It is left chiefly to his windy fools to do that! When Maistre Alcofrybas is logical, he is light and to the point. As for Janotus, he has completely forgotten what little useless logic he did know. After a cascade of words meaninglessly ringing the changes on the low-Latin word *clocha* (bell), he complacently adds:

Ha! ha! ha! That's speaking, that is! The argument is in *tertio prime*, in *Darii*, or somewhere (*Garg.*, *TLF* XVIII, 48; *EC* XIX, 39).

A Sorbonne professor devoted to the *Parva Logicalia* who does not know whether or not his argument was to be placed in *tertio prime* – in the third mood of the first figure of syllogisms – was ignorant indeed. As for *Darii*, it is a mnemonic vocable used in an otherwise meaningless jingle invented by mediaeval scholastic philosophers to help students of logic to remember the different forms of syllogisms: *Barbara celarent Darii ferio baralipton.* The Sorbonne theologians who chose Janotus as their orator did so after having 'said their *ergos* both *pro* and *contra*', after which they 'concluded in *baralipton*'. At least they did know that they had based their argument on the form of syllogism represented by the first three vowels of the made-up word *baralipton*: that is, on the first indirect mood of the first figure of syllogisms, in which the two premisses are universal affirmations and the conclusion a particular affirmative. Janotus, who outshines them in ignorance and disarray, cannot remember whether or not his argument was in *Darii*, that is, in the first mood of the first figure of syllogisms, in which the major premiss is a universal affirmative and the minor premiss and the conclusion particular affirmatives.

If we find such terms confusing and jargon-ridden, that is precisely the effect that Janotus and his cronies are there to produce.

This mockery of the *Parva Logicalia* and of the whole system of dialectic which mediaeval scholastics had painstakingly built up on the basis of Aristotle, is one of the most successful episodes in Rabelais – so successful that he never felt called upon to do it again. Mediaeval dialectic is laughed out of court, its basic text-book lumped together with the silly, turgid, stultifying books which had made young Gargantua into an ignorant lout, just as they had made Janotus into a vicious, bumbling fool, tying himself up in knots as he impotently sets about sniffing out heresy. The mockery of the scholastic taste for chop-logic – for conclusions reached in *modo et figura* – was gentle and indulgent in *Pantagruel* III. Now the laughter is a full-blooded guffaw – and much more dismissive (*Garg.*, TLF XVIII; XIX, 40f.; EC XIX; XX 36f.).

The chapters devoted to the borrowing of the bells for Gargantua's mule develop into an uproarious farce, complete with comic movement, comic monologue, slapstick and unexpected laughter. The glorious muddle of Janotus's speech contains some of the best comic writing Rabelais was ever to produce.

This farcical element is doubtless connected with the enthusiasm which Rabelais already showed for this traditional French *genre* in his days as a mature undergraduate at Montpellier. It is also connected with his sustained admiration for the *Farce de Maistre Pathelin*, that mediaeval masterpiece which was enjoying a new lease of life in the 1530s, among other things being made widely available by being translated into Latin. Rabelais, whose eyes were now raised high above a public who bought their books and lived out their lives in Lyons or Touraine, also took care to connect his farcical story with Songecreux, that is with the great actor-manager Jean du Pont-allais whose talents had delighted Francis I in the years 1532–4 as he and his troupe followed the court from place to place, honoured by the patronage and privy-purse of his king. Rabelais is inviting the court to compare his own story with farces as acted by the most acclaimed actor of the day before the most exalted company, when he declares that Janotus had provided better pastimes and more laughter than Songecreux himself (*Garg.*, TLF XIX, 22; EC XX, 18).

To this striking claim for his creation, Rabelais adds yet another element: an element of carnival. It contributes a great deal to the savour of our laughter.

Rabelais's tale is set in carnival. That is shown in several ways. When for example Janotus de Bragmardo weaves his slightly tipsy way in due academic procession towards Notre-Dame, our reactions are ones of amusement as he drives before him his silly *vedeaulx* who are half beadles (*bedeaulx*), half stupid heifers (*veaulx*). His M.A.s, his *maistres inertes*, are slovenly, dirty and ignorant – just as Tubal Holofernes was. The reactions of Ponocrates to this farcical procession would be hard to understand if we did not appreciate the carnival allusion:

At their entrance, Ponocrates met them and was frightened within himself, seeing them thus disguised, and thinking them to be madcap masked revellers [*masques hors du sens*]. Then he asked one of the *maistres inertes* of the band, what this mummery was trying to do (*Garg.*, TLF XVII, 12; XVIII, 9).

The word *mommerie* reminds us of the trestles. That is timeless enough, though often connected with periods of feasting, such as Twelfth-night.

But one period of the year only was connected with *masques hors du sens*: carnival.

The carnival flavour is maintained until the end. Janotus had bet on the success of his joyous harangue. He stood to win a length of cloth and a string of sausages if successful. The length of cloth refers to an episode in *Maistre Pathelin*; but the string of sausages is a well-known symbol of Carnival in his battles with Lent. Meaty sausages are as unmistakably a symbol of Shrovetide laughter as sad fish are of Lenten gloom. Again we find the language of the trestles in alliance with the language of carnival (*Garg.*, *TLF* XVIII, 18; *EC* XIX, 14).

Janotus's actual address continues to emphasise the farcical flavour of these chapters: it is a monologue conceived dramatically and presented as such: it ends, as is both funny and right, with a double parody of formulas used to mark the end of a barrister's speech in the lawcourts and of the phrases used to mark the end of the classical Latin comedies of Terence.

To enjoy the episode of Janotus at this level is in itself very rewarding. There are no excessively erudite obstacles to understanding; only the completely Latin-less can fail to enjoy the pompous ignorance and confusion of this silly old professor, who can unwittingly compare his faculty to the ignorant mules of the psalm or fall into heresy out of sheer grammatical confusion. He is rambling, incoherent, impotently vicious and surprisingly pathetic. His attempts to blind his hearers with science merely reveal the language of scholastic philosophy to be, as humanists to a man proclaimed it to be: ugly, silly and barbarous; his attempts to bribe them with money pinched from the poor-box or with absolutely free Indulgences are closer to the bone, more open to accusations of Lutheranism from the people he is laughing at, but funny and innocent enough; such jokes do not attack the Catholic religion itself: nobody believes that dons should rob the poor-box or dish out pardons for nothing! Even the heresy which Janotus falls into is comic heresy, arising out of his mechanical use of pious formulas or from confused and bumbling syntax. It would have been easy, and indeed almost normal, to twist these accusations into something more serious. Rabelais is satisfied with a happy laugh.

But readers who knew their satirical literature would have been alerted to a potentially more ambitious aim in this laughable portrait of a Sorbonne diehard. Several of Rabelais's jokes show that he was modelling himself partly on the side-splitting *Letters of Obscure Men*. These letters were natural reading for Rabelais in 1534, when Hebrew was again under attack and when he felt obliged to redouble his mockery of anti-Jewish obscurantism by expanding the 'Library of Saint-Victor'. The links between the Library, the Bells of Notre-Dame and the otherwise irrelevant Sorbonne may well have arisen in Rabelais's mind from his expansion of the Saint-Victor catalogue, following hard, as it does, upon the original allusion to Gargantua's mule and its borrowed bells.

11. *The bells of Notre-Dame: contemporary satire*

Amusing and effective as Rabelais's tale of the *cloches de Nostre-Dame* is when read in this way, we cannot simply stop there. The text invites us to place the episode against a definite background. Without ceasing to be an almost timeless piece of amusement at the expense of academic rambling and incoherence, set in a vaguely mediaeval past, these chapters also evoke memories of ,real and recent events which mattered to Rabelais and his patrons and affected them closely.

We are first alerted to this contemporary relevance by the words with which Rabelais introduced Gargantua's visit to the great city:

. . . the people of Paris are so daft, so doltish, so naturally inept, that a juggler, a pardoner, a mule with her bells [*cymbales*] or a fiddler at the crossroads will draw more people together than a preacher of the Gospel [*un prescheur evangelicque*] (*Garg.*, TLF xvi, 1f.; *EC* xvii, 1f.).

The sting lies in the tail, in the allusion to evangelical preaching. Such preaching caused riots or disturbances in Paris in both 1533 and 1534 – especially in 1533. This is doubtless why Rabelais stresses that upon the bells being stolen, 'toute la ville feut esmeue en sédition. . . .'

An historical excursus is necessary to make this background clearer. It underlines what may be called the '1533 flavour' of parts of *Gargantua*.

Paris was out of favour with the court. Francis believed his capital city had been disloyal during his captivity in Spain. He further believed the city to be less than enthusiastic in paying the huge ransom which released his children held hostage by Charles V. This royal distrust spread to both university and church. The immediate predecessor of Jean du Bellay as bishop of Paris, Etienne Poncher, died in prison, where he had languished at his king's command. Jean du Bellay's loyalty was clearly a factor in his preferment to the see of Paris and he consistently showed his devotion to his monarch.

All the du Bellays identified themselves with the royal interests, though their quarrels seem to have been more with the university than with the Town. In these quarrels they were supported both by the king of France and by Margaret his sister, the Queen of Navarre, whose interest in the day-to-day skirmishes was direct and real. Part of the quarrel lay in the unwise attempts of Béda and his cronies to censor even Margaret's works; part of it arose out of royal attempts to enforce a reform of the university curriculum and statutes; part of it came out of the royal determination to overcome the University's delaying tactics and its scruples so as to compel it to vote (as it eventually did) in favour of the legality and morality of Henry VIII's divorce. The du Bellays were exasperated by the constant plottings (*menées*) and the successful party manoeuvring. The university quarter was almost a law unto itself. Royal authority had often to be asserted there with royal might.

In 1533 the situation took a turn for the worse. Riots, mobs, propaganda and counter-propaganda boiled over into apparent *sédition* ('divisive disorder'). The years 1532–5 aroused memories of 1516–18, when posters and disturbances in the Latin quarter challenged royal policy over the Concordat and again gave rise to accusations of *sédition*. In 1533 these disturbances were connected with the evangelical preaching of Girard Roussel, chaplain to Margaret of Navarre. What made these circumstances so dangerous for the Sorbonne was an unexpected grouping together of their enemies. The Sorbonne had earned the lasting hostility of the du Bellays, the enmity of Queen Margaret and the unremitting mockery of Rabelais. What the Sorbonne could not have foreseen is that these opponents, so widely separated in status, rank and wealth, were to make common cause against them, bringing attacks upon them right into satirical literature, before a wide public, including the highest in the land.

Evangelical preaching was a recent feature of Lent in Paris. From at least Easter 1532, royally protected, evangelical sermons formed a public aspect of court devotion. The faction of the University led by Béda stepped up their protests. In the Lent of 1533, when Girard Roussel was preaching, they were moved to read violent sermons against the new evangelical trends, for Girard Roussel was an old enemy of theirs.

The sermons against Girard Roussel and other preachers provoked riots against the evangelical party. Francis intervened. There had already been disturbing reports of students overstepping the mark in their traditional Twelfth-night revels: an undergraduate play had mocked Margaret and Girard Roussel; another had jeered at Béda, laughing heartlessly at his physical deformities. In December 1532 Francis had forbidden unauthorised assemblies in Paris *pour quelque cause que ce soit*; and here, in Lent 1533, were riots and disturbances caused by university preachers rousing the rabble against sermons listened to by King Henry of Navarre and Margaret his consort, as well as by many members of the royal court of France.

The king was absent from Paris. But encouraged by Margaret, the du Bellays and others, he reacted sharply to the disturbances, not least because they were the work of the hated faction (*monopole*) of Béda and his supporters. The king's partiality was clear: Girard Roussel was placed under house arrest in the care of his patroness Margaret; Béda and two fellow theologians were cited before the Parlement and banished from Paris on 26 May 1533. Girard's case was duly examined: he was exonerated and cleared of all charges, resuming preaching in Paris by Easter 1534, among new but lesser outbreaks of violence.

It is against this backcloth that Rabelais has Janotus and his cronies process, debate and make their protests. It is this fact that gives added force to such words as *schismes*, *monopoles* and *menées* found in the story. They repeat accusations actually made against the Sorbonne by king, bishop and royal agents. Even when Rabelais makes the faculties debate *pro et contra* over who should have the troublesome privilege of acting as official orator, he is alluding to actual recent quarrels between the *Artiens* and the *Théologiens*. But when the aged Janotus totters home to college in apparent and pathetic triumph, Rabelais unveils the full force of his satire of the Sorbonne as a hot-bed of *sédition* and anti-royalist wickedness. The theologians of the Sorbonne try to cheat Janotus out of part of his bet, wanting a share in his broadcloth and some of his sausages. Like a nasty overgrown schoolboy, he threatens to split on them.

Wretched traitors, you are worth nothing; the earth bears no people more wicked than you are – I know it well. Stop limping before the lame! [*Ne clochez pas davant les boiteux*]. I have done wickedness with you. By God's spleen, I will warn the king of the enormous abuses which are fabricated here by your hands and plottings [*par voz mains et menéez*]; and may I be a leper if he does not have you burnt alive as buggers, traitors, heretics and seducers, enemies of God and of virtue.

Four hundred years later the pyres sound metaphorical. They did not do so then (*Garg.*, *TLF* xix, 60f.; xxv, 25f.; *EC* xx, 52; xxxvii, 19f.).

Recently a new and attractive suggestion has been made: could not these *grosses cloches de Nostre-Dame* of Rabelais's farcical story be more than mere bells? Could they not allude to the three theologians whom Francis exiled from Paris in May 1533, because of the preaching against Girard Roussel? Béda was lame: *il clochoit*; he was therefore in older usage *un cloche*. In other words can this whole episode have a double meaning, punningly adapting the story of *les grosses cloches de Nostre-Dame* to the (masculine) *cloches* of the Sorbonne: theological exiles who were literally *lame*?[26] If two or more of the theologians in exile can be shown to be lame, the cap would fit. But so far only one, Béda, is known to have been crippled this way.

The accusation that the Sorbonne was associated with *beaulx placards de merde* (that is, with posters pejoratively described) can be reconciled with this new interpretation. When the reactionary theologians were arrested and exiled in the early summer of 1533, posters were stuck up in the Latin Quarter protesting against this royal action. Clément Marot, the elegant and evangelical court poet, seized upon the event to write a parody of one of them (*Oeuvres Poétiques*, ed. Guiffrey, 1911, i, pp.186f.). Could it be these

---

[26] This attractive suggestion is that of G. Defaux.

particular *placards* that Rabelais is alluding to, only dropping the reference in the second edition of *Gargantua* when the more famous *placards* of 1534 and 1535 made even the word *placard* something to avoid at all costs? It seems very likely. Yet many of the details do not fit. In the case of the sermons against Girard Roussel, Francis I acted with vigour, both against disturbers of the peace and against the Sorbonne theologians; but in *Gargantua* the king of France is accused of tolerating sedition, going beyond the virtue of patience into its excess (*'stupidity'*).[27]

The attractiveness of this hypothesis obliges one to tread with care. In favour of this interpretation is the appearance of the Sorbonne in an episode where it does not traditionally belong. There are also the double meanings that can be read into the latinate language of the theologians: *La . . . feut remonstre l'inconvenient des cloches transportées*, which could refer to 'bells' not 'carried away' but 'transported' into exile. Similarly too with the phrase, *ilz demandoient les cloches leurs estre rendues*; that could mean 'bells' returnable to the faculty not to Notre-Dame. *Delivrer les cloches*, also, could mean to set them free, to liberate them, not simply to hand them over. And so on.

The main objections to this hypothesis (apart from those connected with the lack of proof that other theologians beside Béda were lame) are ones of detail. Above all there is the Shrovetide setting of the story in Rabelais, whereas the sermons which caused the uproar in 1533 were apparently all preached during Lent (that is, after the second of March). As for the posters and other protests over the exile of Béda and his fellows, they were later still, towards the end of May.

Nevertheless Rabelais may obviously have so arranged his story that, despite differences of chronology, it was designed to arouse memories of recent events involving the Sorbonne. I think he did just that.

---

[27] *Garg.*, TLF xvi, 72; *EC* xvii, 46: 'All the town was in seditious disorder (*esmeue en sédition*) – as you know they are so prone to this that foreign nations are amazed by the patience (or to put it better, the stupidity) of the kings of France, who do not otherwise curb them by good justice.' The contrast between *patience* and *stupidité* is between good and bad forms of the same quality. It is wrong to read modern meanings into the word; Calvin, as cited by Littré, throws light on Rabelais's usage: 'Those who turn *patience* into *stupidité* must lose heart and fall into despair, when they wish to devote themselves to patience.' (Patience itself is a minor virtue, subordinate to all the theological and cardinal virtues; cf. Aquinas, *S.T.*, 2a 2ae, cxxxvi, art. 2.) (Later, the good orator Gallet asks Picrochole whether he found his royal master *si ignave et stupide* as to put up with unprovoked attacks.) Having stressed the troubles which arise from excessive royal patience – *stupidité* that is – the narrator adds: 'Would to God I knew the workshop where these schisms [divisive tendencies] and *monopoles* [party factions] are forged, to see whether I could not make some beautiful *placards* of shit there.' These accusations echo actual condemnations of Béda and his cronies by the du Bellays and Francis I in person. But the whole sentence was struck out in *Gargantua B*; either it was too bold, or else circumstances had changed enough to make it no longer applicable.

There were many occasions when the University sent delegations to Notre-Dame or to the dignitaries of the town of which the Provost was the exalted head. The University also sent delegations to Francis to beg the return of the exiles. In 1534 they again sent a delegation begging Béda's release from prison. Echoes of some or all of these may doubtless be heard in Janotus's troubled and muddled oration. But the text of Rabelais obliges us to forget about delegations sent to the king in person. This delegation appears not before the king but before real people, people identified by their office. These officers are apparently accomplices of Gargantua and his companions: wittingly or unwittingly, they allow Janotus to make his speech after events had already made it superfluous, since the bells had been quietly returned to their keeping:

. . . so that the cougher should not enter into vainglory from the bells [*cloches*] having been returned at his request, they sent off, while he was having a tipple, to seek the provost of the town, the rector of the faculty and the vicar of the church . . .

To these dignitaries, before the speech was made, the bells were delivered (*Garg.*, *TLF* xii, 26f.; *EC* xviii, 20f.).

There is an earlier reference to what also appears to be a real person, a Commander of the Order of St Anthony who wanted to take the borrowed bells away from Gargantua, giving up the idea 'not because they were too hot but because they were too heavy'. Part of the joke is obvious enough: there is laughter arising from an idiom taken literally; moreover St Anthony's order was particularly concerned with swine, taking pigs and swineherds under their protection and receiving gifts of pigs in return; the symbol of the religious order was a lanyard with staff and *bell* attached. But was the Order of St Anthony in some way involved in the real events which lie behind the tale of the bells? If so, it has still be to identified. The other persons mentioned by these officers pose fewer problems (*TLF* xvi, 69; *EC* xvii, 40f.).

The Provost of Paris (*le Prévost de la ville*) was a man of importance. As bailiff of the university, he had great disciplinary powers that had been contested for centuries. Throughout the period that doubtless concerns us here, the Provost of Paris was Jean de la Barre; during Béda's exile he had searched his lodgings at Queen Margaret's request, looking for evidence that the rash syndic had alleged that Henry VIII and Francis I 'did not live like Christian kings'. He died in the spring of 1534. The *recteur de la faculté* gives some trouble, since Rabelais seems to have confounded *Dean* of the Faculty and *Rector* of the University. The error seems elementary. If error it be, he nevertheless did not correct it in later editions. But the *Vicaire de l'eglise* raises an exciting possibility. Did Rabelais mean René du Bellay, vicar-general of the bishop of Paris? Or was the post of *Vicaire* a separate one in Notre-Dame cathedral itself?

The bells are handed over to those real men. If the *cloches* were limping theologians as well as bells, this could only allude to the recall of the three theologians in the very last days of 1533. Béda was recalled because it was strangely thought he might have written a schismatic evangelical book entitled *La Confession de foy de maistre Noël Béda*. The intention was to punish him further if he had written it: to make him preach against it if he had not. It may seem odd that Béda should have been exiled as an arch-Sorbonagre and yet later have been suspected of being a recent convert to a schismatic Reformation. But nothing seemed unlikely in late 1533 after Nicolas Kopp, the Rector of the University no less, had fled to Geneva and abandoned the old religion in favour of what was later to be known as Calvinism. Picart, another exile, was summoned back to Paris at the same time.

At this point we must recall two historical events: the Parisian *masques* of 1533; the evangelical preaching of 1534.

Carnival *masques* were not allowed to roam the streets of Paris at the whim of individual revellers. The town officials had to give their consent. This applied even to the magnificent and quite exceptional Shrovetide banquets of 1533, organised in Paris by the King and Queen of Navarre as well as by the dauphin. Full accounts of these splendid entertainments have survived.[28] So too has the explicit permission given by the *Prévôté de Paris* on 6 February 1533 to *porter masques par la ville de Paris*. It is this that lends importance to Janotus and his procession's being mistaken, in these streets of Paris, for men disguised as *masques*, *hors du sens*, as madcap carnival revellers.

The implication may be that Rabelais wished his story of the bells to allude to events associated especially with Shrovetide 1533. If so, he intended to keep the memory green in other works too: in 1534 he added to *Pantagruel* a mocking attack on *Sarrabovittes*, *Hypocrites*, *Caffards* and other censoring monastic hypocrites, *qui se sont desguizez comme masques pour tromper le monde*. The same evil beings appear again in late 1534 or early 1535, in the freshly adapted *Pantagrueline Prognostication* for 1535, which reminds us that Quaresmeprenant will win his lawsuit, with one half of the world disguised, dashing through the streets like *folz et hors du sens. . . .*[29]

---

[25] For the festivities, see the *Diarii di Marino Sanuto*, vol. 57, Venice 1902, col. 596f.; P. Jourda, *Marguerite d'Angoulême, duchesse d'Alençon, reine de Navarre*, Paris 1930, I, 173.

[29] *Garg.*, TLF xvii, 12f.; *EC* xviii, 9: When Janotus and his procession entered, Ponocrates was frightened, 'seeing them so disguised, and thought that they were *masques hors du sens*'. Cf. *Pant. Prog.*, TLF ii, 15, variant (1535 onwards): 'One part of the world will disguise itself to trick the other, running through the streets like fools and people who are *hors du sens*.' In additions made to the 1534 text of *Pantagruel* (*EC* xxxiv, 30f.) there is reference to

Was the Sorbonne believed to have done something underhand – putting up controversial posters during the weeks before the Lent of 1533 perhaps, using agents disguised as Shrovetide *masques*? It seems possible though we may never know for certain. But we *do* know that in the later and graver *affaire des placards* of October 1534 and the even graver ones of January 1535 Margaret of Navarre was convinced that the Sorbonne had acted as *agents provocateurs*, themselves provoking the dreadful events which they then egged on both king and Parlement to punish with the utmost rigour. . . .[30]

If Rabelais was recalling in *Gargantua* events which happened in the days preceding Lent in 1533, that ought to rule out the *cloches* being taken as lame theologians sent into exile; but Rabelais is quite cavalier with time when he wants to be. He certainly had good cause for keeping the memory of these events alive in 1534 and even later, for Easter 1534 was curiously parallel to Eastertide 1533. During Lent 1534 particular note was taken of the evangelical fervour of the sermons of a bearded religious sent to the French court by Pope Clement VII. He was seconded by Girard Roussel, newly vindicated and released. A letter dated simply 'January' and apparently written in 1535 to the Earl of Wiltshire, a keen observer of the Paris scene, tells of Girard Roussel preaching not only at Easter but throughout the summer, although 'bothe the doctors of ye universite of parres and the comman peple also did greatly resist'. If this were written in January 1535, the Easter and summer alluded to must be those of 1534. It is known that, when Maistre Girard attempted to mount the pulpit of Notre-Dame to preach on 1 April 1534, chaplain of Queen Margaret though he was, he was jostled by the crowd and prevented from doing so, 'comme estimé suyvant la doctrine du Lhuter'.

This, or something like this, is the context in which Rabelais set the simple story of *Gargantua* and the bells of Notre-Dame, which he found in the *Grandes et inestimables Cronicques*. By introducing the Sorbonne, its *monopoles* and the riots caused by evangelical preaching, he makes the joyous harangue of Magister Noster Janotus de Bragmardo into more than a simply happy farce.

'Sarrabovittes' and other hypocrites 'who have disguised themselves like *masques* to deceive the world'. It seems that the 1534 *Pantagruel*, *Gargantua A* and the *Pantagrueline Prognostication pour l'an M. D. xxxv* are all alluding to the same events and reveal the same sense of outrage, partly transmuted into comedy within a context of masked revels.

[30] Cf. Margaret's letter to her brother Francis I, written in late 1541: 'Thank God, my Lord, none of our people were found to be sacramentarians, even though they have borne hardly less punishments; and I cannot refrain from saying that you should recall the opinion I had, that the wretched *placards* were the work of those who want to visit them upon others [estoient faits par ceuls qui les cherchent aux aultres]. F. Génin, *Nouvelles Lettres de la Reine de Navarre* . . . , Paris 1842, p.196f.

There are so many things we do not know about these years. But we do know that the chapter of Notre-Dame was in conflict with Béda's Collège de Montaigu and had summoned him to appear before them where he was publicly humiliated. There is nothing unreal in Rabelais making a delegation of university theologians plead on the parvis of Notre-Dame before an audience which included the Provost of Paris and the Vicar of the cathedral. But there is an unmistakable feeling of strife being o'er, of battles won. Janotus is allowed to win his sausages and, by allusion to an old proverb, allowed wine, a soft bed and a deep dish to comfort his old age. The episode in general is marked by a remarkable degree of indulgence. A Sorbonne professor worrying about sausages is a carnival figure of fun rather than a figure of hatred.

Laughter in Rabelais can sometimes win forgiveness even for a Sorbonagre! Janotus had made his audience laugh 'as much as Songecreux'. The great actor was a hunchback; on account of this he had been compared with Béda – both being like a crooked letter *S*. Could it be that Janotus in his pathetic comic rôle is a distillation of characteristics of Béda (who hated Terence and Plautus) and of other old Sorbonne coughers, who earn in Rabelais's pages an amused compassion they never earn in real life? Perhaps he even owes something to the doddering principal of Montaigu, whom Béda admitted to be too gaga to do his job. In carnival mood the Sorbonagre Janotus may be indulgently treated in *Gargantua*. In real life such men were not so treated by their enemies – not even by Rabelais. Later in *Gargantua*, in a more realistic but still carnivalesque context, Ponocrates evokes the scandalous ill-treatment of students in Béda's own Collège de Montaigu. He wishes he were 'king of Paris' so that he could burn the principal and the regents who tolerate such scandalous conditions (*Garg.*, *TLF* XXXV, 22; *EC* XXXVII, 25f.). The expression *roy de Paris* adds an element of humour; Ponocrates wishes to be not king of France but 'king of Paris', a title which evokes comparisons with such festival kings as the *Roy de la Basoche*. But in the circumstances of the years 1533–5 (when Béda, a regent of the Collège de Montaigu, illegally claiming precedence even over the principal, was for most of the time in disgrace, either in exile or else dragging out his life in prison), the invitation to royal repression is not a pretty one. But that comes later in *Gargantua*; such violence is foreign to the spirit of the episode of Janotus and the bells. It seems that Rabelais wrote these pages when he and his patrons could be generous even to their bitterest opponents.

Our enemies' impotent wrath can be generously treated as both humorous and pathetic when we are victorious and conscious of having disarmed them. Before *Gargantua* is finished a new and more tragic note will be sounded.

12. *The Picrocholine War*

The chapters devoted to mocking mediaeval education and its antiquated champions in the Sorbonne end positively but statically: the last chapter gives a timeless account of how Gargantua spent rainy days and how, once a month, he picnicked in the country, enjoying a day off books and lectures. On those fine days his intellectual powers were given a rest: he simply confirmed some ancient experiment, recalled to mind passages from the rustic parts of Hesiod, Virgil and Politian, or else composed a few Latin epigrams, turning them and the rustic verses into traditional French poetic forms. . . .

The quarrel between the flat-bun makers of Lerné and Gargantua's men, which eventually leads to the Picrocholine war, starts abruptly by telling us that 'at that time' it was the season of the grape harvest in early autumn. Gargantua (if we were silly enough to take Rabelais's chronology literally) was born in 1380, since, when his first tutor died in 1420, he was a big bouncing schoolboy of forty. The chapters devoted to the Sorbonagres take us out of the mediaeval past into Rabelais's own time, but do not actually give us a year-date. At what season of the year Janotus made his speech can safely be inferred by the Shrovetide references perceivable behind his comic masquerade. There are analogous suggestions of date in the account of the war as well. Grandgousier's letter to Gargantua, recalling his son to fight in the war, is dated '20 September', with no year given. But during the war, a laughing allusion is made to the holy sindon at Chambéry which was 'burned three months later' than the attack on Seuillé by Picrochole's men. This suggests that the Picrocholine War was first set in autumn 1532, that is, soon after the probable publication of *Pantagruel* (*Garg.*, TLF XXVII; XXV, 133; *EC* XXIX; XXVII, 109).

It would be unwise to press such points too far. Rabelais delights in playing with time, making it behave according to the laws of an *Alice Through the Looking-glass* world rather than to the spirit of pedantry. The whole of the events narrated in *Gargantua* 'ought' to precede those in *Pantagruel*, since Pantagruel is Gargantua's son. Yet *Gargantua* is clearly, in all respects, a later book than *Pantagruel*. That Rabelais intended his sporting with time to be a definite feature of his writings is shown by his subsequent publication of the two books in a reverse order to their original publication, so making the learned *Tiers Livre* pick up the threads from the end of *Pantagruel*. It is only an hypothesis – stylistic factors may confirm it – but what seems to have happened is that the first outline of the Picrocholine War was written in an 'autumn 1532' setting; that, just as what may be 1533 or 1534 events concerning the Sorbonne and Janotus were interpolated into the education section, so too Rabelais, seeing wider potentialities in the character of Picrochole and his war, brought that nearer in time to the date of publication of *Gargantua* by expanding it and adapting it, making it refer as well to events later than autumn 1532, events which took place on a wider world stage.

The Picrocholine War is fought around the area of the Rabelais family's farm of La Devinière. When one sees how tiny the real ford is at the Gué de Vède (which Picrochole's marauding soldiers have to cross); when one realises how much of the comic battlefield can be seen from Rabelais's own kitchen door; it brings home forcibly the very personal humour of Rabelais in this war, a battle of mighty armies, of a giant and his acolytes, all fought out in the miniature world of his childhood. There is here, far more clearly than in *Pantagruel*, a vital element of private humour, shared with a few friends, the family, and powerful patrons whose roots were in the local soil.

Some of the corrections Rabelais made to the text of the second edition of *Gargantua* indicate, as we saw, that the education chapters had first been given a local Touraine setting, which had only been incompletely adapted to a Parisian one in time for the first edition. Analogous changes, even more striking, seem to have been made to the account of the Picrocholine War. A local war, apparently taking place in Rabelais's backgarden in autumn 1532, explodes into something much greater, embracing satire of Charles V, the Holy Roman Emperor, and alluding to later events of European concern. There is a truly comic and aesthetically satisfying quality in Rabelais using his private little local world to serve as a battlefield for the armies of a parodied Charles V, the fearsome enemy of the French, the most powerful and successful of European monarchs, who seemed fated to triumph in all his enterprises. I wonder if this is symbolised by the name of Gargantua's ambassador Ulrich Gallet. He has a local Touraine surname (local names abound in the story), but a Christian name recalling that of Ulrich of Württenberg, who was restored to power by Philip of Hesse, with French support, in June 1534.

Picrochole is a bitter man of choleric nature: that is what his name means. We should think of him in terms of the typical choleric as the medical theories of dominant humours would describe him: tall, lean, easily moved to anger. Early local tradition insists that the person originally mocked is Gaucher de Sainte-Marthe, Rabelais's contemporary as Seigneur de Lerné. Since Lerné is a real place with its own lord of the manor, the tradition seems a likely one. Abel Lefranc discovered a real quarrel hiding behind the comic war, a legal battle concerned with rights of navigation on the Loire, imperilled by Gaucher de Sainte-Marthe's high-handed protection of his alleged fishing-rights. The quarrel, of wide and passionate concern in the valley of the Loire, involved Antoine Rabelais, the father of the author and a very important legal and political figure in Touraine (*Garg.*, EC *Préface*, liv f., lxii f.).

But if Gaucher de Sainte-Marthe is laughed at, he is in most illustrious company; for Picrochole is most certainly also a joke at the expense of Charles V; it is this aspect of the satire that most Frenchmen at the time must have seen more clearly. The reasons which lie behind Rabelais's widening the scope of his satire so that Picrochole can be a ludicrous choleric, a laughable local lord and, at the same time, a parody of the emperor Charles and of his plans for world conquest, can be partly inferred. The same shift of emphasis towards the interest of a courtly audience which we saw in the education chapters seems to have been at work here.

Ever since his release from captivity after the defeat at Pavia, Francis I's rivalry with Charles V took on a new dimension: Charles was convinced of French treachery; Francis was embittered by the crippling ransom imposed upon the kingdom and the obligation to send his two eldest children as hostages to the imperial court. The royal children were not released until 1530. The war in *Gargantua* contains overt allusions to these events and is partly conceived as propaganda. The conduct of the giants contains lessons for French statesmen. Their wise combination of prudent appeasement and a religiously responsible use of armed might, followed by a balanced fusion of justice and mercy when war is thrust upon them, serves as a condemnation of the policies and person of Charles and an example to Francis. The general influence of Erasmus's balanced pacifism, and also probably of More's, is there to be seen; so too is the condemnation of the imperial design. Charles liked to be thought of as a new Alexander the Great; Picrochole does too: the laughter at his expense is increased, to make this clear, in the second edition. Similarly Grandgousier condemns modern imitations of Hercules, Alexander, Hannibal, Scipio or Caesar as contrary to the profession of the Gospel; it is simply wicked brigandage, a term (*latrocinium*) which St Augustine applied to the conquests of the Roman empire which he saw collapsing.

In *Gargantua*, rivalling the Scipios and the Pompeys is acceptable only in terms of parody and comedy: Charles V in real life must not and should not have such aims. Frère Jean is the battling monk of chivalrous tale who can get caught up in a tree by his ears as surely as Absalom was caught up by his hair; so his prowesses *can* be compared to those of Camillus, Scipio, Pompey, Caesar and Themistocles. The responsible giants know better and would never make the claims that Picrochole and Charles V make.[31]

The mockery of Charles V, the *Rex catholicus*, does not have to be dug out

---

[31] Cf. *Garg.*, TLF xxi, 8 (text of 'B' – 1535); *EC* xxviii, 6: '*Cyre*, today we will make you the happiest, the most chivalrous prince there has ever been since the death of Alexander Macedo. – Put your hat on, put your hat on, said Picrochole. – Many thanks *Cyre*, we are at your service.' This fatuous scene equates Picrochole-Charles V with Baisecul: cf. the similar jest in *Pant.*, TLF ix *bis*, 154; *EC* xi, 6. (The spelling *Cyre* (for *Sire*) increases the comedy, suggesting that Picrochole is a new Cyrus the Great, as well as indicating the

of cryptic hidden allusions in the tale of the Picrocholine War. As Gargantua told both victors and vanquished, his father always behaved with the noble generosity he had shown towards a former enemy, Alpharbal: 'In cases where other kings and emperors – who indeed call themselves Catholic – would have treated him wretchedly, imprisoned him harshly and ransomed him excessively, he treated him with courtesy.' Grandgousier could have demanded, *tyrannicquement*, two million sovereigns in ransom – the actual sum extorted by Charles V; he could have taken his enemy's eldest children hostage; but he did not. With such words the conduct of Charles V is condemned as tyrannical. Mediaeval and Renaissance politics made the greatest of distinctions between the rightful king and the lawless tyrant. The blow against the Catholic king is meant to be a grievous one (*Garg.*, *TLF* XLVIII, 28f., 69f.; *EC* L, 21f., 50f.).

Rabelais develops his mockery of Charles's imperial design with the aid of Lucian. Picrochole, in the headlong self-deception encouraged by his flatterers, passes from future to present and then to past tenses, as though his conquests had already been made. But the core of his satire does not go beyond the sober reality of Charles's chivalrous dreams. That is what makes the setting of the war – a parody of mediaeval chivalrous romances – so comically appropriate (*Garg.*, *TLF* XXXI; *EC* XXXIII). Charles saw himself in chivalrous terms; he wanted to establish the Christian empire championed by Dante in *De monarchia* and kept alive in a host of literary works, not least in Italy. His imperial emblem – two pillars with the 'wider, yet, and wider' device of *Plus oultre* – symbolised an empire beyond the conception of the ancients, stretching beyond the pillars of Hercules (the straits of Gibraltar) into the new world. France was newly allied with the Turkish piratical captain Barbarossa in her desperate desire for help against the imperial menace. That is why Picrochole's captains egg him on against the Turks: he will have the straits of Gibraltar named after him: 'and there you will erect two columns, more magnificent than those of Hercules.' Having crossed this newly renamed 'Picrocholine Sea', behold, Barbarossa becomes his slave:

– I (said Picrochole) will have mercy upon him.
– Yes (they said) provided he has himself baptised. And you will attack the kingdom of Tunis and Hippo [*de Tunic, de Hippes*,] indeed of all Barbary. Then proceeding further – *passant oultre* . . . (*Garg.*, *TLF* XXXI, 28f.; *EC* XXXIII, 26f.).

The laughter at Charles's expense could not be less inhibited, going down well in the French court, we can be sure. One of the most politically

current (false) Greek etymology of *Sire* from *Kurios*, 'lord'.) For serious and comic allusions to the ancient heroes, cf. *Garg.*, *TLF* XLIV, 10f.; XXXVII, 1f. (*EC* XLVI, 9f.; XXXIX, 1f.). Rabelais is close to Erasmus's influential essay in the *Adagia* (III, 7, 1) on *Scarabeus aquilam quaerit*. (Picrochole's command, '*Qui m'ayme, si me suyve*', is a parody of Cyrus's; cf. Montaigne, III, 5: '. . . ou à la guise de Cyrus, *Qui s'aymera, si me suyve*.')

endearing, though theologically shaky, assertions of Frère Jean will be his condemnation of *Messieurs les Apostres* for letting their Master down – especially inexcusable since they had just had a good Supper! If only he could be king of France for eighty years or so! He would whip those curs who fled the battlefield at Pavia, when Francis was captured by imperial troops, and left 'their good prince in such straits. Is it not better and more honourable to die fighting manfully than to live fleeing ignobly?'[32] Rabelais shows through laughter that even the defeat at Pavia was not proof of Charles's military genius: it was all the fault of a few cowardly scapegoats on the French side. This was a standard royalist assertion.

The Holy Roman Emperor did not plan to convert Barbarossa by force. But it was good propaganda to pretend, with a laugh, that he did! The parody of Charles's alleged policy of forcibly converting the Moslems – Barbarossa will only be pardoned by Picrochole if he gets baptized – might have seemed semi-Lutheran to some, since Luther was known to be strongly opposed to converting anyone at all by force. But French policy at this time relied increasingly on an alliance with the Sublime Porte, and in particular with Barbarossa. The French could not allow themselves the luxury of only having Christian allies against the Holy Roman Emperor; when Khair ed Din (the real Barbarossa) seemed to get the better of the Emperor in 1534 and 1535 there were cynical rejoicings in the entourages of the Most Christian King and the Defender of the Faith. Among the strong supporters of the French alliance with the Turks were Guillaume du Bellay and Jean, bishop of Paris. The sincerity of the Christian convictions of Rabelais's patrons cannot be impugned; for many centuries – not least since the establishment of French-speaking states in *Outremer* during the Crusades – alliances of Christians with Moslems against other Christians and Moslems were a fact of diplomatic and military life. With the fall of Byzantium to the Turks, such alliances became both more urgent and more attractive.

Francis I's policies at home and abroad entailed reconciling several different trends and managing several difficult allies. He supported Henry VIII's divorce and, to some extent, his schism; at home, he occasionally yielded to the pressures of illiberal and repressive conservative theologians or of the Cardinal de Tournon, while supporting evangelical tendencies under the influence of Margaret of Navarre. At the interview of Marseilles, where he was the host to pope Clement VII in October and November 1533, he undertook to put down heresy in France; in general the persecution was largely directed against sacramentarians – those more extreme reformers for whom the sacraments of the church were signs or memorials, not efficacious liturgical means of grace. This did not

[32] *Garg.*, *TLF* xxxvii, 66f.; *EC* xxxix, 66f. His heart is in the right place. But, as he asserts later in the chapter, 'the biggest clerks aren't the wisest' (*Magis magnos clericos non sunt magis magnos sapientes*).

necessarily worry the German Lutherans whom he sought as allies against the Emperor, since Luther himself had sharply condemned them too; but many of the theologians of Paris tended to lump all heretics together, calling Lutherans sacramentarians and vice-versa, and yearning to suppress them both. They had to be watched. And above all was the fear of Charles V's encircling might, against which the Turk was an ally to be courted and won over.

These policies were well understood in the chancelleries of Europe. The du Bellays were active supporters of them all, with a devotion which earned for the bishop of Paris a reputation for being soft on heretics and even of Lutheranism.[33] Jean du Bellay was not a Lutheran, but both he and his brother saw much that was good and true in Lutheran theology, a fact which underpins the entire pro-Melanchthonian policy of the French king. But the common people of France and of Germany were disturbed by repression of Christian sects in France, just when, in late 1534, Barbarossa's envoys were flitting exotically about. In February 1535 Guillaume du Bellay wrote an elegant Latin letter under the king's name to the German states and municipalities, defending and explaining his policies. *Gargantua* seems to be preoccupied with the same questions.[34]

There may be a specific allusion to the most resounding events of 1534 or even 1535 in this satire of Imperial schemes concerning Barbarossa and Tunis. On 22 August 1534 Barbarossa captured Tunis; its ruler Mulley Hassan fled, called on Charles for help and got it. Charles, over many months, assembled the greatest fleet Europe had ever seen and recaptured Tunis in person in July 1535, reinstating Mulley Hassan, who did him homage. Charles stood poised, at least in the opinion of the French and English monarchs, to press on to capture Constantinople. Sustained attempts to belittle Charles's achievements were made in France as in England.

Is Picrochole's Lucianesque scheme designed to mock Charles's preparations for this war against Barbarossa and Tunis – or indeed the war itself? Or did Rabelais strike lucky – mocking, early in 1534, imperial schemes which turned out to be prophetically true in 1535? The answer depends on the date when *Gargantua* first appeared. When this problem is resolved – probably on the basis of material bibliography – *Gargantua* will be easier to interpret with greater certainty.

---

[33] Cf. a letter of Cifuentes to Charles V, opposing Jean du Bellay's elevation to the cardinalate on the grounds that he had 'tocato en las cosas de Lutero'. In December 1534, there was a rumour – false of course – that 'a brother of my lord of Paris' – Langey no doubt – 'had been imprisoned as a Lutheran'. It is specifically stated by Ferrufini, who reports the rumour, that it was spread by the Paris Parlement. (See R. Scheurer, *Correspondance du Cardinal Jean du Bellay*, ı (1529–35), Paris 1969, p.491, note; p.451, note.)

[34] *Christianissimi Galliarum Regis . . . Epistola qua confutantur calumniae a malevolis in eum per totam Germaniam disseminatae*, dated 1 February 1534 (old style, = 1535). Copy in B.L. at 1193, h. 47.

The second known edition of *Gargantua* is dated 1535, with no day or month. The readers of that edition must have inevitably made the connexion between Charles's capture of Tunis – and his rout of Barbarossa – and Picrochole's scheme to capture the same town, only being prepared to show mercy on the same famous piratical ally of the French 'provided that he gets baptized'. In 1535 Europe was flooded with news-sheets bringing news of Charles's projects and exploits against both Barbarossa and Tunis. Some bear his device – so like Picrochole's 'two columns, more magnificent than those of Hercules'. In 1542 Rabelais emphasised further the satirical laughter at the expense of the Holy Roman Emperor. He finally revised this chapter, inserting allusions to Algiers and Bona (Bizerta); this brings the mockery of Charles's African aspirations up to date by alluding laughingly to the Emperor's abortive African campaign of autumn 1541, which, to the delight of his enemies, ended in disaster before the walls of Algiers.[35]

Many parts of the Picrocholine War show how the Holy Roman Emperor appeared to loyal monarchist Frenchmen in the 1530s, still smarting under the defeat of their king at Pavia, still resenting the loss of Milan, while they helplessly watched Charles's apparently unstoppable triumphs. Ulrich Gallet, the giants' ambassador, in a cogent Latinate speech, expounds a profoundly religious and moral view of kingship such as appealed to many Christian thinkers of the Renaissance – not all were to become Machiavellians. The artistry of his oratory is emphasised by its being called an *harangue*, just as Janotus's feeble effort had been, a fact which contrasts true humanist rhetoric and dialectic with the coughing inadequacies of those whose powers of reasoning were based on the sorry techniques of a despised, and recent mediaeval past. Ulrich Gallet sees Picrochole – and hence Charles – as a man 'emancipated from God and reason', perhaps even being deceived by diabolical illusions.[36] Similarly Grandgousier saw him as a man whom God had 'abandoned to his own free will' which, as a sound evangelical Catholic, the good giant knew to be irremediably evil unless guided by grace.[37] These sentiments appear to echo standard French reactions to the Emperor. When Charles later

---

[35] *Garg.*, TLF XXXI, 36 *var.*; EC XXXIII 33. Already in a letter from Rome [28 January 1536] Rabelais noted that Barbarossa had fortified 'Bona and Algiery' against the Emperor. Text in P. Jourda, *Œuvres de Rabelais*, Garnier, II, p.547.

[36] *Garg.*, TLF XXIX, 69f.; EC XXXI, 55f. There is no excuse to be found in blaming it all on fate. God will judge. If l'*esprit calumniateur*, trying to lead Picrochole astray, had deceived him by *phantasmes ludificatoyres*, then he should first have inquired into the matter and found out the truth.

[37] Garg., TLF XXVII, 30f.; EC XXIX, 22: Grandgousier realised that God has abandoned Picrochole to 'his free will and his own sense' (*son franc arbitre et propre sens*) 'which cannot be other than evil, if it be not continually guided by divine grace'. The theology is Augustinian: the will is free, but so vitiated by sin that it must be *guided* by grace.

challenged Francis to single combat – another example of his choleric romanticism – Nicolas Raince wrote to Jean du Bellay (24 April 1536) saying: 'It is probable that he is out of his mind [*alliéné*] and entirely without a good will' (*Correspondance*, ed. Scheurer, II, 1973, p.322).

Perhaps the deepest condemnation of Picrochole is one which antici- pates Rabelais's philosophico-comic techniques in the *Tiers Livre*. Picro- chole's courtiers encourage his dreams of wider yet and wider conquests. They are all blinded by self-love, though that is not yet spelled out. The moral blindness self-love proverbially causes leads them to defend their madcap schemes by perverting that very wisdom of antiquity which served to warn prudent kings against such folly! Picrochole's enthusiastic reactions to his advisers' projects leads even them to act flittingly with a parody of prudence:

Not (they said) yet: wait a little. Do not be too sudden in your undertakings. Do you know what Octavian Augustus said? *Festina lente*: Hasten slowly.

The very courtiers who proffer this sound advice go flat against it, feeding the follies of their imprudent monarch with their flattering nonsense. That is part of the comedy of the episode. Rabelais prepared his readers to see this, by earlier picking out for praise the emblem of the anchor and the dolphin. Admirals of France had taken it over, duly aware that it had been the device of Octavian Augustus himself. *Hasten slowly* was the 'significance' of this uniquely illustrious emblem. Philippe Chabot, the current admiral of France, whom Rabelais names in this connexion, took his device seriously. Such a man will make short shrift of Picrochole – and Charles V. Or so we are made to feel.[38]

13. Frère Jean, the battling Benedictine

Political satire is only one element in this richly embroidered parody of the romances which Rabelais and his age enjoyed. For many readers today the lasting value of these chapters lies above all in the amused parody, especially as embodied in Frère Jean, a battling monk who carries on in comic vein a theme reaching back beyond Archbishop Turpin in the *Song of Roland*. This aspect of the episode is indeed a constant delight. Frère Jean is a

[38] *Garg.*, TLF VIII, 71; *EC* IX, 58. See Erasmus *Adagia* II, 1, 1, *Festina lente*. Renaissance scholars regularly associate the anchor-and-dolphin emblem with both Augustus Caesar and Admiral Chabot. Cf. B. Aneau's French edition of *Les Emblèmes* of Alciati, Lyons 1549; note to this emblem. Rabelais had already underlined Picrochole's military imprudence: his flattering courtiers advise him to 'divide his army in two as you know so well how to do' (*TLF* XXXI, 15; *EC*, 14). In a letter written from Rome [30 December 1535] Rabelais condemns the Sophy for doing just that: 'Voyla qui fait mauvais advis partir son ost devant la victoire.' Text in P. Jourda, *Œuvres de Rabelais*, Garnier, II, p.538.

cloistered monk, fully worth thirty eggs now he has left his monastery – he and other cloistered monks were scarcely worth two eggs before. This monastic status of Frère Jean we are never allowed to forget: as often as not he is simply called *le Moyne*.[39]

Frère Jean is a Benedictine, the Order to which Rabelais, for all his irregularities, still canonically belonged. His monastery is at Seuillé (Seuilly, a stone's throw from La Devinière). These facts may explain the loving detail with which he is portrayed as a lean, amorous, flighty monk having all the faults traditionally laid against bad monks by satirists – he is gluttonous, ignorant, lecherous, uncouth – but also having virtues which redeem these faults. He knows how to amuse his friends; when the right time comes, he knows how to stand up and fight when under unprovoked attack. It is part of the meaning of this chapter that he should bring the reader to accept that the traditional criticisms of the monks are justified but theologically trivial. Monks do indeed have these faults, as Frère Jean is the first to show: but such shortcomings pale into insignificance beside the lazy uselessness of superficially better monks, who pointlessly stick to the verbal ritual of their calling and claim to intercede for men, while the men themselves know how to act.

Frère Jean is a great and attractive creation, a character who can be placed against Pantagruel, Gargantua and Panurge, losing nothing in the comparison. He is endowed with virtues and vices writ so large that he himself is larger than life, an appropriate companion to giants in process of being humanised and leaving their old ways. As Gargantua detaches himself from the vices of his first education, becoming less comic and more exemplary, Frère Jean jumps in to provide comedy, having precisely those qualities of coarseness, gluttony and so on that Gargantua was purged of.

Within the novel he plays several rôles: he gives rise to some of the best laughs in the book; he is an informed but often naïf condemnation of both 'bad' monks and 'good' ones, enthusiastically agreeing with the heroes' condemnation of monkish idleness, triviality and venality, while himself acting as an example of action not words. More surprisingly to modern minds, he is an actor in a moral parable.

The chapter in which he first appears starts off seriously. Rabelais invites us to wonder why it is the good priests and the good doctors who die of the plague (which was then endemic in France, raging particularly in 1531 and 1533), whereas the *diables pilleurs*, the devilish pillaging soldiers of Picrochole, get off scot-free. The answer is given by implication: the plague is not the work of God and his saints; it is the work of the Devil who knows how to look after his own in this world, of which he is the Prince. Of

---

[39] No less than five chapters in the original text of *Gargantua* start with the words, *Comment le Moyne . . .* And Frère Jean is introduced in chapter xx under the title *Comment un Moyne de Seuillé. . . .*

course, all events in this world, even apparently evil ones, form part of the divine Providence. But many hoped to take the moral responsibility away from God by making the Devil the agent of evil, leaving God to turn this apparent evil into actual good. How satisfactory this is theologically may be debated, but Rabelais apparently adopts this view. The word *diable* in Rabelais often has a deeper sense than that of a mere expletive, even when it is apparently used in a traditionally expletive way. Phrases like *ces diables pilleurs*, here soon to be followed by *les paouvres diables de moynes*, are often more meaningful than the mindless usage of colourful speech might lead us to think.[40] Rabelais uses allusions to both God and the Devil in unexpected ways. Simple expletives such as *diable* may point to real devilishness. That is the case here: both the pillagers and the monks are devilish people. But there are other times when Rabelais uses pious or blasphemous language to different ends. His Chronicles suggest that there is no merit at all in simply verbal piety without moral activity. Similarly, when active virtue is displayed, there is little demerit in purely verbal cursing and swearing. The contrast established in this episode between the fearful empty prayers of the passive 'good' monks and the foul-mouthed active virtue of the 'bad' one is fundamental, destined later to be the subject of much comic elaboration.

We probably do not notice much of this at first, being more immediately delighted by the contrast between Frère Jean's religious profession and the ornate variety of his very ripe language. But he stands for something more than just another ignorant randy monk in the tradition of mediaeval satire best known to Englishmen through Chaucer. That is hinted at when he throws off his habit and attacks the enemy with the butt-end of a venerable cross – a weapon which surprises us, and is meant to surprise us. We are carefully reminded of this weapon later on, when the monk, after disarming enemy troops and shutting them up in churches, seized *tous les bastons des croix* (*Garg.*, TLF XXV, 80; *EC* XXVII, 67; cf. TLF XLVI, 79; *EC* XLVIII, 61).

The butt-end of Frère Jean's cross is covered with faded *fleurs-de-lys* and made out of wood of the service-tree (*cormier*: the Latin *cornus*). This is one of those learned jokes which Rabelais delights in when we least expect it. *Cornus*, as readers of Virgil know, is no ordinary wood: it is the *bona bello cornus*, 'a wood good for war' (*Georgics* II, 448). The *fleurs-de-lys* suggest that Frère Jean is acting in the royal interest. That the cross is old and the *fleurs-de-lys* faded probably suggests that he is going back to good old patriotic ways, long fallen into disuse among the monastic brethren.

That his weapon is a cross may be seen to be significant in another sense:

---

[40] *Garg.*, TLF XXV; *EC* XXVII. Later (*TLF* XLIII, 53f.; XLV, 43f.) Grandgousier condemns the superstitions which make 'the just and saints of God like devils', by attributing to them powers over pestilences.

it drives home a lesson dear to evangelicals, and not to reformers only: that no *object* is sacred in itself. Everybody knows that both Catholic evangelicals and schismatic reformers were sceptically hostile to relics and the popular superstitions associated with them. It is less widely known that the same distrust was felt for crucifixes and crosses generally: they could all too easily be thought of as sacred, when, at best, they merely symbolise a sacred truth of which they form no part. For many such Christians crosses, and not merely crucifixes, were especially blasphemous objects.

The headlong valour of Frère Jean reminds the reader of the tough fighting monks of traditional epics. It lends to the Picrocholine War that indulgent laughter we reserve for parodies of *genres* that we like. Phrase after phrase, formula after formula, serve to remind us of the old stories and chronicles as surely as the *Morte d'Arthur* does with its refrain, 'As the Frenche book says'. Frère Jean's war is as full of incident as any *chanson de geste*. But it is a war which is only serious when he is not there, all of whose incidents raise a laugh when he is present. The Picrocholine War is like a rope, made up of many strands, which form a single whole but never merge completely. Frère Jean's strand is one of parody and laughter; he wounds without pain; kills without our feeling the presence of death; fights a war against an enemy who is fitfully a local squire and Charles V as though it were a war of grotesque puppets, with himself partly the puppet-master, partly a bigger and more successful puppet-warrior. With him the war becomes the setting for more than one example of comic cruelty. This is a feature which Rabelais develops more fully in the *Quart Livre*. Rabelais's particular brand of comic cruelty seems to be a literary variation on the cruelty of the traditional farce – still successfully employed by Molière in plays like *Sganarelle* – enriched by laughably inappropriate medical precision. Frère Jean's *ad hoc* club does not simply smash his opponents' heads in; it makes them split apart at the lambdoïdal suture; his mighty sword does not simply slice an archer dead; his blow 'entirely severed the jugular veins and the sphagitid arteries of the neck' – the same blood vessels by two different names; then it opened up the spinal marrow between the second and the third vertebrae . . . (*Garg.*, *TLF* XLII, 44, 18; *EC* XLIV, 37, 14).

Cruelty is probably inseparable from all comedy, ranging from the comedian who knocks his head against a shelf, through custard-pies in the face to the merciless unmasking of a Tartuffe or the heartless mockery of a Malvolio. The comic writer who takes sustainedly cruel situations as his subject is not being cruel – and certainly not encouraging cruelty by example, unless he deliberately moves his comedy into areas where pity and the higher emotions rightly dominate over our sense of the ludicrous. The cruelty of comedy acts in a world dehumanised, where sympathy would be as ludicrously out of place as it would be if we were to weep when Punch is knocked about the head by a puppet policeman.

This attitude is not a modern one, based on a reading back into the past of our own predilections, prejudices or insights. It is that of a medical theorist of the generation after Rabelais, Laurent Joubert, a professor at Montpellier and author of an impressive French *Treatise on Laughter*. He himself was deeply indebted to numerous thinkers writing over the centuries before him. Joubert believes, with the ancients, that we laugh when we perceive something to be indecent, ugly or out-of-keeping – but only when it is unworthy of pity or compassion. He insists that pity and compassion are quite foreign to laughter, an idea which reappears in Bergson's *Le Rire*. An example he gives is particularly useful for the understanding of Rabelais's art; it is, he writes, indecent to bare the behind; so, if there is no factor which compels our pity, we cannot help laughing if somebody does so unnecessarily. But if someone were to come and realistically stick a hot iron on that naked backside our laughter would give way to compassion – unless, that is, the act were made to seem small and trivial, for that would reinforce the laughter (L. Joubert, *Traité du Ris*, Paris 1579, p.18f.).

Rabelais dehumanises the characters of Picrochole's soldiers, just as he had done for Gargantua's tutors. They act as puppets or clowns, not as real men. Their wounds are made, in Joubert's terms, to be trivial; and their deaths similarly do not and cannot compel our pity. *Tripet* is the name of a captain destined to be *de-triped*! (*TLF* XLI, 2; *EC* XLIII, 2). A cowardly guard who flatters Frère Jean, a mere monk, by calling him *Prior* is rewarded with talk of *Posteriors*; when he persists, calling the monk 'Cardinal', he becomes a medically precise comic example of what *faire cardinal* meant in idiomatic speech: to give someone a bloody cock's-comb, red like a cardinal's hat (*TLF* XL; *EC* XLIV). This aspect of the comedy is reinforced with all the verbal art at Rabelais's command. The bare statement of the first editions, *Les uns mouroient sans parler*, becomes much more amusingly dehumanised in 1542: *Les uns mouroient sans parler, les aultres parloient sans mourir. Les ungs mouroient en parlant, les aultres parlant en mourant* (*TLF* XXV, 142; *EC* XXVII, 116). Such figures of fun do not really suffer and die. They are knocked about like marionnettes and are finally put back in their boxes or strewn about like broken toys that a child has tired of. Only when an element of humanity is included in their make-up (as was the case with Janotus de Bragmardo) are the butts of our humour eventually worthy of compassion and, as a reward for making us laugh, safely tucked up in bed at the end.

Other insights can also help us to understand better what Rabelais was at. Laughter can be a means of avoiding fear, bringing the awful and the frightening not merely down to our level but firmly below us. Charles V was as disturbing to the French in his day as Hitler was to us in ours. Rabelais, like a Charlie Chaplin, brings the terrible enemy low by making us laugh at Picrochole. Renaissance war was a beastly, painful business, with wounds which doctors hardly began to know how to treat, so in *Gargantua*, written when war seemed unavoidable, death and wounds in war are made to seem comic. The laughter is not that of a heartless man; it is that of a doctor who has learned how to live with life and death as they are, comforted by the profound strength that humour and laughter can supply, especially to a Christian man. Laughter is the distinguishing property of man: so it is better to write of laughter than of tears: *Mieulx est de ris que de larmes escrire*. One can either laugh or weep at human folly. In Rabelais's Chronicles when the laughter ceases, death and woundings cease to be comic too. At the end of the Picrocholine War, when the grotesque gives way to reality, the dead are honourably buried and the wounded are treated in a classically named *nosocomium* (hospital). Similarly, at the beginning of the story, the good doctors and preachers who tend the dying, themselves die of the plague – to some purpose in a divinely ordered world. The frequent changes of tone from laughter to seriousness in these chapters stop the war from being merely trivial or merely frightening. And over all there is the injection of a religious dimension, unexpected as so much else in this surprising Chronicle.

Some of the religious propaganda needs little comment: the mockery of the cult of relics for example – readers of Erasmus realise that there is nothing necessarily 'protestant' about it. Other aspects of the satire do need a word of explanation. When the war against Picrochole is treated earnestly in the closing stages, Rabelais quotes Plato *via* Erasmus in order to condemn war between Christian states as *sédition*. The vanquished troublemakers of Picrochole's army are similarly called *séditieux*. In fact much of *Gargantua* may be said to be concerned with *sédition*. There was *sédition* in Paris when Gargantua arrived there; among the enemies excluded from Rabelais's ideal abbey are *séditieux mutins*. Rabelais has much in common with those humanists who insisted upon seeing all war and strife between Christians in essentially moral terms. Three major episodes of *Gargantua* – the *cloches de Nostre-Dame*, the Picrocholine War and the final Enigma – are concerned with *sédition*, with party-strife troubling the peace of the Christian common weal. This concern with *sédition* is echoed in the letters of Francis I and of the du Bellay brothers. Sedition was not then simply a political crime: it was a vice, acknowledged as such by theologians and duly classified in Christian manuals, often with reference to the 'tumults' (*seditiones*) condemned by St Paul in II Corinthians 12, 20. Perhaps it was from an association of ideas that Rabelais, knowing that the Sorbonne professors were accused of being seditious by his king and his patrons, made it an appropriate punishment for Picrochole's vanquished *sédicieux* to work the printing-presses newly established in Grandgousier's realm.[41]

[41] *Garg.*, *TLF* XLIV, 32f.; XLX, 1; LII, 48; *EC* XLVI, 26f., LI, 1; LIV, 47. Cf. Erasmus, *Institutio Militis Christiani* in *Opera Omnia* IV, 608D: 'Plato calls it *sedition*, not war, whenever Greeks

But the religious issue most obviously prominent in these chapters concerns the irrelevance of monasticism. Rabelais is at pains not to allow the ignoble cowardice of these monks to be confounded with the armed evangelical appeasement he had expounded in Pantagruel's prayer in his first book. In *Gargantua* it is the nobly appeasing Grandgousier who exemplifies this doctrine, not these cowardly shavelings. The monks of Seuillé do nothing to help repel the invaders, though the novices are prepared safely to slit the throats of the helpless wounded; they meet in their chapel, decide to take out processions and to sing responsories for peace, as though they had all the time in the world, yet the enemy is at the gates. When they timorously chant an October responsory from their breviary, *Impetum inimicorum ne timueritis*, they are wrong at all levels. They chant 'Fear ye not the onslaught of your enemies', yet are very afraid; they passively sing when they should be doing; they are so concerned with the musical settings of their antiphon that they repeat syllables with total disregard for sense. These accusations are all taken up later. Frère Jean and his doings, for all their comic delights, are not set before us gratuitously.

It is in the *Quart Livre* of 1548 that Frère Jean, referring back to his battles in Seuillé, reminds us that he has always stood for the need of men to work together with God, not simply to badger him with passive prayers. This is one of the *plus hauts sens* of his story. There are others (*QL*, *TLF* XXI, 54 *var.*; cf. XXIII, 48).

The most detailed condemnation of monks is delayed to chapter XXXVIII, where, in a masterfully written episode, the theological basis of contemplative monasticism is overthrown. Monks are simply drones, an accusation which may owe something to Plutarch's platonic condemnation of idlers. They are rightly rejected by ordinary people just as worker-bees (in Virgil's phrase) drive the lazy herd from their abodes; they attract evils (as the Latin adage says) like the wind called Caecias attracts the clouds; their monasteries are isolated from contact with polite society, just as lavatories are in our houses: rightly, since monks eat the faecal droppings of the world – a scathing allusion to auricular confession. Then, with a sustained application to monks of Plutarch's condemnation of flatterers, we are told that monks – the lazy ones anyway – 'do not plough like the peasant, do not guard the land like the soldier, do not cure the sick like the doctor, do not preach or teach sound doctrine to the world like the good evangelical

---

fight against Greeks.' It is even worse when Christians fight Christians; Cf. II Corinthians 12, 30: 'Lest there be debates, envying, wraths, strifes, backbitings, whisperings, swellings, tumults [*seditiones*].' In the *glossa ordinaria*, these '*seditiones*' are explained as *tumultus ad pugnam* – disorders leading to fighting (*Patrologia Latina* CXCII, 89); cited by Aquinas, *Summa Theologica*, 2a 2ae, 42, *De Seditione*: sedition (except against a tyrant) is a mortal sin, opposed to the unity of a people, state or kingdom.

doctor or schoolmaster, do not transport goods and things needed by the state like the merchant' (*TLF* XXXVIII, 1f; *EC* XL, 1f.).

These phrases are restricted to lazy monks alone, whereas schismatic reformers applied some of them to all the Roman clergy, secular and religious. They link this chapter with the good Christian men who died of the plague while tending the sick; they also, with the allusion to the *bons prescheurs evangelicques*, bring back to mind the earlier pages devoted to mocking the Sorbonne, and the gawky seditious citizens of Paris who preferred jugglers to sound evangelical preachers.

This important adaption of Plutarch is introduced with words which raise a smile today:

But if you understand why a monkey is always mocked and teased in a family, you will understand why monks are avoided by everybody, both young and old.

The idea of referring to a pet monkey, as though it was the most natural thing in the world, just because Plutarch had done so might seem unintentionally laughable. But we would be wrong. Pet monkeys were a feature of the sixteenth century. An elegant engraving in Macault's French translation of Diodorus Siculus, dedicated to Francis I in 1535 and based on a manuscript presented to the king in 1534, shows Francis with his three sons, surrounded by his nobles, listening to Macault reading his work; a pet monkey sits on the table. If the monkey was there when the bishop of Mâcon read *Gargantua* to the king, the points made here would have been particularly apposite. It probably was. (A pet monkey also figures in Holbein's portrait of the family of Thomas More.)

The monasticism which is rejected is the kind of monkery affected by the lazy (*ocyeux*) monks. In its turn, this important limitation is swept aside. The notion that any monk may redeem inactivity by 'praying for us' as Grandgousier suggests is roundly dismissed by Gargantua, with the comically innocent support of Frère Jean. All monastic orisons are said to be ignorant, full of superstitions, undertaken for the sake of the rewards: fine loaves and bread-and-dripping (a simple enough luxury one would have thought, but not treated as such).

The word applied to their kind of ignorant routine prayers is *mocquedieu*. It emphasises, after the laughter, the seriousness of the charge: for 'God is not mocked'. The monks sang their responsory with vain repetitions. *Im, im, im, pe, e, e, e, e, e, tum, um, in, i, ni, mi, co, o, o, o, o, o, rum, um.* Laughable; yes. But also precisely that *battologia* ('vain repetition') which Christ condemned as pagan when he taught his disciples how to pray. Then, with a bold and theologically much oversimplified use of Romans 8, 26 and 34, Gargantua declares monastic intercession to be impertinent: 'All true Christians, of all estates, in all places, in all times, pray to God, and the

Spirit prays and makes intercession for them, and God takes them into his grace' (*TLF* XXXVIII, 41f.; *EC* XL, 33f.).

The thought that monks, though otherwise idle, might be worthily praying for the sinners of the world is not dismissed with sneers about ignorant routine and bread-and-dripping. In order to make his point with the greatest emphasis, Rabelais gives the suggestion that monks 'pray for us' not to some sleazy, comic, religious layabout but to the increasingly esteemed Grandgousier. This is a way of showing that the idea was one influentially held. It needed first to be advanced by a respected character and then to be refuted seriously and evangelically.

A long-term aim of the diplomacy of the du Bellays was to heal the major schism of their time by bringing together moderate French Catholics and moderate Lutherans in a spirit of loving Christian understanding. (The Anglican schism seemed nothing like so serious.) To do this they had to clip the wings of traditionalist, authoritarian extremists such as Béda and the conservative Sorbonne generally, while encouraging in the French church those evangelical tendencies which were reconcilable with true Catholicism and absolutely indispensable in the eyes of moderate Lutherans. Their policy was to be triumphant in 1535 when Melanchthon was invited to Paris.

Such policies do not mature overnight. It is unthinkable that the du Bellays in 1534 – or in 1533 for that matter – would have allowed an author whom they patronised to stand in the way of so vital an achievement. On the contrary, one would expect such an author to advance their policies. That is what Rabelais does in parts of *Gargantua*. We do not know for certain at what stage of the negotiations *Gargantua* was written, but Rabelais is mocking and challenging just those aspects of popular Catholic devotion, and of the far more respectable traditional piety, which had to be devalued and overthrown if the du Bellays' hopes for an ecumenical understanding with Melanchthon were to bear fruit. On the whole, humanist Evangelicals heartily disliked these practices anyway, considering them as mere 'traditions of men' passing themselves off as true religion. From the point of view of the bishop of Paris the obstacles to an understanding with the theology of the great preceptor of Germany were not negligible – they were formidably entrenched – but intellectually and theologically trivial. These obstacles included the stubborn anti-humanist conservatism of professors of theology in Paris; pilgrimages to saints venerated superstitiously or wickedly; monastic pretensions to prayerful intercession on behalf of mankind; the numerous masses of the slack old devotion. Surprisingly, papal authority was not a central matter of dispute or disagreement. On the other hand, Catholic evangelicals would need to be reassured that Catholic synergism would not be replaced by the enslaved will of Luther and more extreme schismatics.

Francis I approved Melanchthon's confession of the faith with only minor reservations. Rabelais must have recommended himself greatly to his patrons, with his strong, joyful propaganda in favour of just that synergism which Catholic humanists could heartily share with Melanchthon. Philippists (followers of Philip Melanchthon) were known to be synergists and often so called. Melanchthon was a loyal friend of Luther, but on issue after issue he was not content simply to echo his master's voice. Almost unbelievably he succeeded, without breaking with Luther, in reconciling a clearly and openly synergistic theology of salvation with broad Wittenberg doctrine. In this he is at one with Rabelais, whose religious beliefs, to judge from his writings in the 1530s, were royalist-Gallican, truly Catholic within the wider tolerance of pre-Tridentine theology, yet close indeed, on major issues, to the Philippists on whom the du Bellays pinned their hopes. Rabelais's Chronicles, in the most unmistakable of terms, both through laughter and sometimes through less joyful propaganda, continue to defend the doctrine that man can and must 'work together' with the grace of God.

An official royal approach to Melanchthon did not come until 1535, in a letter from the king in person dated 23 June. After a few days' discreet delay, letters followed from both Jean du Bellay and Guillaume du Bellay, Seigneur de Langey. These overtures to Melanchthon were the crowning achievement of the policy of the du Bellays. It was hoped that, with the worst of the Sorbonne theologians in prison, Melanchthon would be able to hammer out an agreed theology with the Sorbonne, so ending the Lutheran schism and, at the same time, reforming the church in France. The du Bellays had earned public respect for both their international policies and their effective restraining of religious persecution in France. As the German scholar Johannes Sturm wrote to Melanchthon from Paris, after the dreadful persecutions of winter 1534–5 which followed upon the *affaire des placards*, were it not for the influence of Barnabé de Voré, Seigneur de la Fosse, a frequent ambassador to German lands in 1535, for the bishop of Paris (Jean du Bellay) and his brother Langey, 'a most prudent and good man', Germany would have been full of exiles from France. It was the patient work of the du Bellays, and especially perhaps of the Seigneur de Langey, which made approach to Melanchthon possible.

Rabelais was advancing causes of which they approved. His own life suggests that the religious views advanced in *Gargantua* were very much his own as well. We can see why Rabelais, holding ideas such as those we find in *Gargantua*, left his cloister and became a doctor. Doubtless it was his Franciscan training, reinforcing a fundamentally evangelical drive to spread the Good News in an uncorrupted form, which led him to conceive his Chronicle as a means of joyfully propagating specific evangelical beliefs.

The du Bellays's main ecumenical hope was to reconcile liberal Lutheranism and liberal Catholicism into a renewed and reunited, truly Catholic Church. It was their influence, their diplomacy, which, after a period of harsh repression, brought Francis I to approve (with only a few reservations) the confession of faith of Melanchthon. Guillaume du Bellay made the most of this in a speech at Smalkalden in December 1535. The king of France, he insisted, was in many places close to Melanchthon in his *Theological Commonplaces*. Despite minor and sometimes major setbacks, the influence of the du Bellays, supported as it was in various degrees by Margaret of Navarre, Budé, Dolet, was dominant whenever liberal views prevailed in France. We can barely believe today the extraordinary veerings and tackings of the king's religious policies. At the time they must have made humanist evangelicals soar with hope, plunge into despair and soar with hope again. In 1535, after a frightening outburst of persecution and intolerance for which observers thought the king had no true zeal, with what surprise men learned that Melanchthon had actually been invited to come to Paris and debate with 'selected theologians' from the University. Selected was a euphemism: Béda was in permanent disgrace (destined to die imprisoned in the dungeons of Mont Saint-Michel); his party was in disarray, though by no means powerless. In the end conservative forces in both Germany and France brought the overtures of Francis and his liberal counsellors to naught. But that is to look into the future.

Rabelais's ideas sometimes seem Lutheran: so did those of Jean du Bellay. It is as gross an oversimplification to call Rabelais a Lutheran in *Gargantua* as it is to call the bishop of Paris one. Both he and his patrons were Catholics who had much in common with the tolerant theology of Melanchthon. None of them was ever a 'papist', as far as we know. All were loyal Frenchmen; their first and last religious loyalty was probably to the Church in France, but they hoped, for both ecumenical and for political reasons, to heal the schism that divided France from her natural allies within Charles's German empire. It was natural that evangelicals, even Erasmians, should feel some sympathy for Luther and a *fortiori* for Melanchthon, as they saw the Sorbonne lumping Luther, Erasmus and Lefèvre d'Etaples together, and even condemning the very ideas of St Paul as heretical.

Chapter xxxviii makes some of these theological points more clearly. The prologue to *Gargantua* invited us to look below the surface, not to stay content with the literal meaning. Nowhere is it more necessary to do this than when we try to interpret Frère Jean's rôle in the Picrocholine War. It has so many levels of meaning. Immediately after quoting St Paul on the subject of that intercession of the Holy Ghost which makes monastic prayers utterly superfluous, Gargantua turns his attention to Frère Jean, contrasting him with those lazy monks which St Paul's statement was held to condemn.

Now such is our good Frère Jean. Wherefore everyone hopes to have him in their company. He is by no means a bigot; he is not shabby; he is honourable, joyful, determined and a good fellow. He toils; he labours; he defends the oppressed; he comforts the afflicted; he succours the needy: he protects the abbey's close.

This eulogy ends like a military citation: 'il garde le clos de l'abbaye.' It is steeped in the language of Christian virtue. Frère Jean, we are told, 'defend les opprimez; il conforte les affligez; il souvient [*succours*] es souffreteux.' (*Garg.*, TLF xxxviii, 57f.; *EC* xl, 45f.).

Few, if any, of us would have drawn such a lesson from the conduct of this foul-mouthed soldier monk. But that does not mean that we have to assume that Gargantua has gone out of his mind. Rabelais has not given him words to say that are merely obscurely funny. Frère Jean is acting out a parable. The time has come for Rabelais to reveal its meaning. Today we may misunderstand what parables are: a more theological age did not. The model of all parables are those of Christ in the New Testament. These parables are *not* self-evident, though after two millennia they might seem so: Christ had to explain them to his uncomprehending disciples; others heard them but did not understand them either; and to them the meaning was *not* revealed, so that seeing they might not see and hearing they might not understand. Parables are not a means of explaining a religious belief: they are a means of veiling it, until it is revealed. This is true of all parables. All parables moreover contain many details which do not apply to the doctrine they are veiling in deliberate obscurity: the kingdom of heaven is likened in a parable to the actions of an *unjust* judge; Erasmus reminds us that Christ in his Second Coming will be as a thief *sneaking* into a house at night. It is a commonplace of exegesis that the detail of a parable is not to be closely pressed; judgment is to be applied and the meaning to be found not in the detail but only from the end. This is even more true of a parable in a comic book.[42]

Just as it would be a serious error, trivialising the nature of *Gargantua*, to ignore or play down this parabolic rôle assigned to Frère Jean, so it would be equally gross error to limit him to it. He plays not only the part of condemner of monks by his active defence of the oppressed and the succouring of the needy; he is himself an unwitting witness to the truth of much of the other criticism levelled at the religious orders. When Gargantua praises him for his activity, he amusingly agrees with naïf enthusiasm, stressing that indeed he is never idle:

[42] Matthew 13, 10f. Maldonatus points out, in his commentary on Mark 4, that parables are a form of *enigma*. (On the need not to press the details, cf. Erasmus, *Annotationes*, on John 7, 1.)

For in hurrying through our mattins and anniversaries in the quire, I make cords for crossbows at the same time, I polish arrows for crossbows; I make nets and snares for capturing rabbits. I'm never idle! (*Garg.*, TLF XXXVIII, 64f.; *EC* XL, 51f.).

Can it be a coincidence that the gossipy old Brantôme should attribute such a criticism of monks to King Francis himself, who based, it was said, his moral right to the monastic patronage he acquired through the Concordat with Pope Leo X in 1516 on precisely such a judgment of what monks were really like?

Cloistered monks are useless people (he would say), who were good for nothing except eating and drinking, visiting taverns, gambling, making cords for cross-bows and ferret nets, catching rabbits and whistling down linnets – those are their excercises, as well as the debauchery their idleness brings in its train (Brantôme, *Mémoires*, 1665–6, I, p.251f.).

Through the comedy of Frère Jean, Rabelais amusingly shows that these accusations are true; but they pale into insignificance beside the impertinent uselessness of the intercessory prayers that cloistered monks claim to offer on behalf of Christian men.

This emphasis on active virtue in *Gargantua* helps to explain the theological comedy of the end of this significant chapter XXXVIII. Rabelais's theology gives a vital place to divine grace, but insists that man must 'work together' with God, except when God forbids it. This theology of synergism has no necessary connexions with opposition to classical determinism; what it is opposing are certain concepts of predestination to salvation which make man a passive recipient of saving grace. Forerunners of Calvin's *Eglise réformée* were moving towards this doctrine. They are more thorough-goingly consistent than even Luther with his 'enslaved will'. For them there could be absolutely no working together with God where salvation was concerned. God's predestination of the elect is absolute, unfettered and quite unmerited by the elect themselves. Catholics of all kinds, and even Lutherans such as Melanchthon, denied this, leaving some small rôle for the individual Christian to play in the scheme of divine predestination.

The key Pauline proof-text which was held to justify the theology of absolute predestination which formed the corner-stone of the theology of stricter Lutherans and later of Calvin and the *Eglise réformée*, was Romans 9, 21: 'Hath not the potter power over the clay, of the same lump to make one vessel into honour, and another unto dishonour?' It is by no means an easy text to explain away; yet those who wanted to defend a synergistic theology had to do so. It was a basic rule of exegesis shared by Christians of all persuasions that no part of scripture, properly understood, could contradict another. Erasmus found a means of interpreting this fearsome text in such a way as to save free will by glossing Romans 9, 21 with II Timothy 2, 20–1. This text of Timothy reads: 'But in a great house there are not only vessels of gold and silver, but also of wood and of earth: and some to honour, and some to dishonour. If a man therefore purge himself from these [errors], he shall be a vessel unto honour'; and so on. In this way the vessels made by the Potter, God, are shown as able to 'purge themselves'; they are not passive objects, but can make themselves 'meet for the Master's use, prepared for every good work'. About the time that *Gargantua* appeared, Guillaume Budé admits that, before he was told by an unnamed man how to interpret Romans 9, 21 in such a way as to safeguard free will, the authority of the text had seemed to lead inescapably to the enslaved will he dreaded (Budé, *De Transitu Hellenismi ad Christianismum*, in *Opera* I, 168D).

Rabelais, writing a comic book with more than one eye on Lucian, succeeds in countering the great text of Romans 9, 21, not by argument but by comic means. He makes no allusion to Erasmus's exegesis; he simply takes the dread text as the basis for laughter.

Grandgousier is at times a model of evangelical wisdom, but not always. He is shown in this chapter to be dignifiedly wrong in his theology. He was wrong, totally wrong, about monastic prayers, and accepted correction; now he is wrong about Romans 9, 21, a fact which once again suggests that we are dealing with an error not self-evidently stupid but one which even a Grandgousier can hold, until he is further enlightened. Gargantua asks a comic question, 'Why has Frère Jean got such a fine nose?' The question is a laughable one, because of a by no means only popular belief that the size of a man's nose was in proportion to the size of his penis, being an indication of the degree of his lustfulness. A nose like Frère Jean's was a sure sign of exceptional lechery. But Grandgousier replies to Gargantua's question with complete innocence:

Because God wished it so, he who has made us in such a form and to such an end as a potter makes his vessels.

Frère Jean strips this text of its aweful isolated power by giving a rival, light-hearted explanation of his nose's ample size, an explanation more in keeping with the current belief: his wet-nurse had soft breasts, so his nose was able to grow while he was suckled; snub-nosed babies are caused by hard bosoms.

With a jest based on the incipit of the 123rd Psalm (*Unto thee I lift up*) he informs his hearers that it is the size of the nose by which we judge the size of old *Ad te levavi*.[43]

---

[43] *Garg.*, TLF XXXVII; EC XXXIX: end. Cf. Erasmus, *Responsio ad Albertum Pium* (*Opera Omnia* X, col. 1111D). Defending his scriptural jests in the *Praise of Folly* he comments: 'But Folly misuses texts of Holy Scripture – as though certain priests and monks do not take

This light-hearted coarseness on Frère Jean's part successfully takes away from Romans 9, 21 that frightful and austere authority which made synergistic Christians approach it with worried awe; men knew that, on this text above all, was based that totally passive theology of pre-destination to eternal salvation and eternal reprobation which was becoming the corner-stone of an increasingly schismatic reformation. Without in fact being irreconcilable with some traditionally Catholic theologies, it was destined to become one of the hallmarks of the major forms of Protestantism.

14. The pilgrims in the salad

The return to mockery of more obviously popular deformations of evangelical purity as Rabelais saw them comes with Lasdaller and his fellow pilgrims. We at first have a marked revival of an earlier style, reminiscent of Alcofrybas's journey into Pantagruel's mouth. The pilgrims are eaten in a salad by Gargantua, now fully a giant again. Washed about between his teeth with water and with wine, they escape, only to be cut off by one final deluge of urine – the last one in all the Chronicles. Simple-mindedly applying scriptural texts to their own situation, the pilgrims believe these events to have been prophesied in the 124th Psalm – the psalm following *Ad te levavi*: 'Then the waters had overwhelmed us, the stream had gone over our soul. . . . Blessed be the Lord, who hath not given us as a prey to their teeth . . . ' (*Garg.*, TLF XXXVI; *EC* XXXVIII).

The pilgrims are then forgotten for six chapters which are largely devoted to the amusing chatter and bold adventures of Frère Jean, until, in fullness of time, they are brought before Grandgousier. Frère Jean still supplies plenty of good comedy, but with Grandgousier the tone rises once again to that of evangelical homily. The old king, with sounder theology than he showed over monastic intercession and Frère Jean's nose, condemns those who blasphemously preach that 'the just and saints of God' cause plagues: to believe that is to turn them into devils. Such preaching is the work of 'false prophets'; their teaching is akin to that of the pagans who invented a host of evil deities. Grandgousier, taking matters into his own royal hands, had stopped the mouth of a hypocrite who had dared to preach such a doctrine in his lands. He did this despite the *caphard*'s calling him a heretic. We are once again made aware that Rabelais is daring to attempt to influence royal policy in France:

---

almost all their jests from scripture. As when they say, 'What is Charity? A monk's cloak. Why? Because it covers a multitude of sins' [based on James 5,20]. Similarly, the man who was asked whether he liked wine said 'Go up higher', and got the reply 'Go up higher. Then shalt thou have glory' [play on Luke 14,10]. Erasmus's examples are chaste enough, but they give an idea of the use of Scriptural commonplaces in jokes.

I am astonished, if your king [the King of France, that is] allows them to preach such offensive doctrines [*scandalles*] throughout his kingdom, for they are more to be punished than those who should spread the plague throughout the land by magic or other craftiness. The plague only kills the body: but these devilish preachings poison the souls of poor simple people (*TLF* XLIII, 52f.; *EC* XLV, 42f.).

This can be placed against other outspoken parts of *Gargantua*, where the comedy gives way to unveiled counsel to the Most Christian King. These words were written by a man who had, in Lyons, witnessed the plague. They were addressed to a public still mourning the countless deaths caused by two recent outbreaks of this dreadful scourge, by a doctor soon to be praised by Salmon Macrin for the lives he had striven to save. They give some indication of his evangelical commitment. So too does his aim of winning over his king to the cause of evangelism.

Grandgousier's advice to the pilgrims is theologically interesting: the king himself judged the theology of the false prophet, found it unevangelical and punished him, despite cries of 'Heretic!' All over northern Europe there were moves towards royal or state authority in religious matters. Henry VIII, without over-worrying the du Bellays, had declared the royal supremacy in England in February 1531; Lutheran and, later, Calvinist doctrine gave wide powers to the state for the repression of blasphemy; the Concordat of 1516 had resulted in a sharp increase in the royal prerogatives over the church in France; royalist theologians who strove to extend these prerogatives into the field of theological decision recalled how it was no bishop or pope but a monarch, the emperor Constantine, who summoned the great Catholic council of Nicaea in 325 and presided over it. What is revealing, since it gives us more than a hint of Rabelais's theological loyalties at this time, is the scriptural basis for Grandgousier's contention that pilgrimages are otiose and useless, St Paul having told us to stay at home to work and bring up our children. That is a doctrine which can only be extracted from St Paul's letters by means of a Lutheran or quasi-Lutheran interpretation of verses of I Timothy and Galatians.[44] Erasmus was prepared to mock the cult of relics and the practice of pilgrimages on

---

[44] *Garg.*, *TLF* XLIII, 94f; *EC* XLV, 58f.: 'Go, wretched people, in the name of God the Creator; may he be for you a perpetual guide. And from henceforth be not so ready for these idle [*otieux*] and useless journeys. Look after your families; toil, each one in his calling, and live as the good Apostle St Paul teaches you to do. Doing this, you will have with you the protection of God, the angels and the saints, and there will be no plague nor evil which can harm you.' Cf. I Timothy 5,8: 'But if any provide not for his own and especially for those of his own house, he hath denied the faith and is worse than an infidel'; Galatians 6,10: 'Let us do good to all men, especially unto them who are of the household of faith.' The original Greek does not lend itself to propaganda against pilgrimages or the need to stay at home to look after one's family. Reformers and evangelicals were prepared to ignore this fact when it suited them.

Platonico-Christian grounds: such perversions concentrate on bodily shadows not on the invisible spiritual reality. Rabelais too holds this opinion; but he goes beyond it, making Grandgousier claim the explicit authority of St Paul for his pious interventions. Evangelicals tending towards the Reformation were all convinced that relics and pilgrimages were sub-Christian; they were equally convinced, for the most part, that they must somewhere have been condemned in Scripture. But where? Not with ease, but only with more than a little shuffling, could two passages of St Paul be twisted into the meaning that Rabelais – with Lutherans generally – read into them. No part of *Gargantua* so clearly advocates a theology pleasing to Melanchthon, or to the du Bellays who placed their ecumenical hopes in him. To the Sorbonne, on the other hand, it would have seemed flat heresy; what Rabelais writes about pilgrimages is indeed close in theology, and in the actual detail of his expression, not only to Luther but to what could be read in the bitterly satirical *Livre des Marchands*, which attacked the Church of Rome as a group of merchants putting Christ and his religion up for sale.

The two giants, whose theology of monasticism was not at first identical, are at one over pilgrimages. Grandgousier's address to the pilgrims leads Gargantua to compare him to the ideal philosopher-king of Plato's *Republic*. The comparison was by no means a hackneyed one; nor is it out of place in an evangelical context: Erasmus cites it several times, once in his commentary on the 2nd Psalm, *Quare fremuerunt*. After condemning a king whose qualities are strikingly like Picrochole's, Erasmus alludes to republics happily governed by philosopher-kings who know how to rule others because they have learned to control their emotions.[45]

From this point forward, Grandgousier does indeed give proof of his kingly wisdom: he treats the prisoner Toucquedillon with generous humanity, condemns imitations of the ancient conquerors as un-Christian and constantly has the name of God on his lips. The war ends with an address to the vanquished, in which veiled allusions are cast aside. Gargantua makes a sharp contrast between his noble, generous, kingly and clement father and – not Picrochole, but now, specifically, the emperor Charles V. This forms the climax to the royalist propaganda of the book, a climax in which the Most Christian King of France is exhorted to merit the title of philosopher-king by pursuing evangelical policies, tempering justice with mercy, and, in all things, acting contrary to the Holy Roman Emperor.

[45] Erasmus, *Opera Omnia* v, col. 228 E. The bad king is 'a fool, lacking judgment, taking the worst for the best', dominated by anger, hate, pride and stormy passions. 'But to be a philosopher is to lack these *perturbationes*.' Hence Plato's judgment on philosopher-kings. Later Amyot (dedication of Plutarch's *Œuvres morales* to Charles IX) links Solomon and Plato in this context.

Rabelais succeeded in giving to a wide public, including the French court, through amusement and laughter, the Christian message which Erasmus gave in an elegant letter to Sigismund, king of Poland, dated 28 August 1528. The letter was widely read, being published in an edition of Erasmus's letters by Froben of Basle in 1529. Erasmus is sometimes regarded as an absolute pacificist, never countenancing war in any circumstances. He hated war, of course, but he was not so impractical as to pretend that it was always avoidable. In his letter he reminds Sigismund that kings are in the hands of God; that (in the words of Proverbs 20, 28), 'Mercy and truth preserve the King: and his throne is upholden by clemency'. Clemency, says Erasmus, consists in not going to war as soon as there is a *casùs belli*; in leaving no method untried which might avoid war: it is often wiser to dissimulate an injury than to follow it up with arms. It is clement, if war can in no wise be avoided, to wage it so as to shed the minimum of human blood and to finish it as soon as possible. These words of Erasmus could serve as a partial summary of the politico-moral meaning of the Picrocholine War. Erasmus goes on to remind Sigismund how wisdom fit for kings had been expressed by the ancient Egyptians in their hieroglyphs. No wonder that Rabelais considered the restoration of true emblematic hieroglyphic devices to be part of the 'restitution des bonnes lettres' (*Erasmi Epistolae* v, p.457).

Only when Rabelais had in this way exhorted Francis I to emulate the philosopher-king does *Gargantua* take us back to the miniature world round about La Devinière; we find ourselves once more with giants amongst pygmies. It is a most successful and pleasing technique, bringing us lightly out of realist propaganda back to the world of fantasy and of humour. And it prepares us for the monk's reward: the Abbey of Thelema, to be built on the banks of the Loire, two leagues from the Forest of Port-Huault, between (we may note) the farmstead of La Devinière and the manor of Langeais.

15. The Abbey of Thelema

Gargantua draws to an end with the famous chapters devoted to the Abbey of Thelema and the prophetic Enigma discovered in its foundations.

Thelema is a complex episode, having several levels of meaning. It is also a well-written one – one which Rabelais was clearly proud of – despite the fact that its parts are juxtaposed rather than interlocked. In form it consists of six chapters, five in prose, one entirely in old-fashioned complicated verse, noted for the ingenuity of its rimes. This kind of verse, known today as 'grand rhétoriqueur' poetry, was already giving way to Marot's courtly, fluent verses. These 'rhétoriqueur' verses form an inscription set above the doorway to the abbey. The poetry of the Enigma is far less complicated.

The general flavour of the abbey is that of platonising Christianity –

with the Christianity less immediately noticeable in the prose chapters but dominant in parts of the verse inscription, as well as in the ensuing Enigma. The platonism is marked by what Frère Jean says before the abbey is described as well as by the main episode, with its optimistic association of goodness and truth with beauty. Both the Christian assumptions of the abbey and its concern with the will of man are emphasised by its name, *Thélème. Thelēma* means 'will'. It does not bear this sense in classical Greek; it is essentially a New Testament word. One of its many uses is well-known through the Lord's prayer: 'Thy will (*thelēma*) be done.'

The abbey is an abbey of the 'will'; it is also a monastery turned on its head, devoted to a proper use of freedom. In Thelema, the individual wills of men and women are freely used, with paradoxical results. This freedom of the will is a matter of daily, hourly, decisions made by noble men and their ladies. In the chapters devoted to the abbey proper, there is no question of 'free will' in that technical theological sense which the term has in controversies about the predestination of the elect to salvation and of the reprobate to damnation. Those theologians who defended man's free will, under grace, in that sense, maintained that Christians can contribute something of their own to the redemption operated by Christ. Rabelais does not even mention predestination until the very end of the book – in the closing verses of the Enigma and subsequent comments of Gargantua; there the context is different and the theological matter has a different urgency and intensity. In the abbey proper we are concerned with the liberty of the Christian man who has been set free from the bondage of the law of Moses and of all those crippling ecclesiastical duties which evangelicals claimed to be usurping their God-given privilege to be free. Evangelicals such as Erasmus joined with more extreme schismatic reformers in claiming that the corrupt church of late mediaeval times had become a 'judaïcising' church, seeking to bind Christians with a mass of regulations and obligations analogous to the precepts of Mosaic law. They were determined to free themselves from these bonds, reasserting their Christian liberty to live in accordance with their own will, 'abounding', as St Paul puts it, 'in their own sense'.

The Abbey of Thelema shows us men and women freely using their will and rejoicing in their *libertas Christiana*.

Rabelais became openly concerned with freedom, in this sense, after the first version of *Pantagruel* had been published. An addition to his first Chronicle in 1533 makes this clear. In *Pantagruel* the good giant, in evangelical mood, roundly condemns those hypocritical *caphards* who dare to assert that man can be independent of God by cynically declaring that God helps those who help themselves. 'On the contrary,' says Pantagruel, 'help yourself, and the Devil will break your neck.' It is at this point that his prisoner begs to be ransomed. Pantagruel refuses to ransom him:

His end was not at all to pillage and ransom human beings but to enrich them, restoring them to complete freedom [*les. enrichir et remettre en liberté totalle*].

The religious overtones of this 'total freedom' are emphasised by the context and by the words which follow – added also to the 1533 *Pantagruel*:

Go (he said) in the peace of the living God, and never follow bad company, so that evil may not befall you (*Pant.*, *TLF* XVIII *var.*; *EC* XXVIII, 37f.).

Christian freedom was a battle-cry of all who believed with St Paul that Christ had set man free from subjection to the law. In the Renaissance the rediscovery of Christian liberty was a revolutionary idea: so many of the traditional practices of the Church – and of monasticism in particular – were widely held to be neo-judaïcising snares, trapping men into losing that freedom with which Christ had set men free. Naturally, the extreme reformers took up extreme positions. Rabelais may not go beyond Erasmus, but the presentation of his case in Thelema is not unlike that of Luther himself. There is, indeed, much in common between Erasmus, Luther and Rabelais in their devotion to the liberty of the Christian man.

The surface meaning of the Abbey is obvious enough: the three monastic virtues are stood more or less on their heads. Poverty is replaced by riches: this enables Rabelais to develop in loving detail the splendour of the abbey, with its fountains, baths, libraries, sculptured graces, ornate carvings and all the beauty sought by a French Renaissance prepared to go to school in Italy. The description of the physical beauty of the abbey, including the gloriously ornate clothing, conveys both courtly splendour – the Thelemites are young ladies and gentlemen – and that aesthetic appetite which is one of the most striking characteristics of the Renaissance. This beauty also has inner symbolic force. For example the abbey is hexagonal, dominated by the mystical powers that ancient and modern mathematics attributed to the perfect earthly number six. The kitchens of Rabelais's Benedictine monastery at Maillezais were hexagonal. It would be pleasant to think that this was also in his mind. But the mystical powers of six dominate.

After poverty, chastity is overthrown – not true chastity, a state perfectly reconcilable with wedlock, but that monastic perversion of it which identifies chastity with compulsory celibacy. The ladies and the gentlemen of Thelema live together in harmony, equal in numbers; if they leave they marry and live happily ever after. Snide remarks about monks who wash the floors down when decent women walk over them are placed side by side with contemptuous allusions to real monasteries as places fit only for the bungled and the botched. Once more a platonising concern with beauty leads Rabelais to emphasise that the Thelemites are all handsome and beautiful. Beauty and goodness go hand in hand in Platonic philosophy; the contrast between the beauty of the good and the ghastly ugliness of the evil is a central one.

Rabelais is so determined to make Thelema contrary to established monastic practice that women are given a rôle in the abbey greater than what is suggested by any other parts of his very masculine books. Rabelais was not (I think) the violent anti-feminist that some made him out to be, but he was closer, most of the time no doubt, to the distrustful attitude of Tiraqueau than to the enthusiastic feminism of Amaury Bouchard. Not however in the Abbey of Thelema. The harmony of the ladies and gentle-men of Thelema, shown in their balanced, united, gracious lives and leading to their happy marriages, makes a strong contrast with Rabelais's tendency to kill off his female giants when they have served their purpose. Antifeminist quips are foreign to the spirit of the Abbey of Thelema, though even there, in one of the many smiles to be found below the surface, the women are described as the 'least boring of ladies', as *dames moins fascheuses*. There are elements of amused sexual punning even in apparently straightforward praise of these young gentlemen and their ladies: no young gentlemen were ever *plus vers* ('more full of sap'), *mieux remuans* ('more full of movement') or 'better able to handle their weapons'. And the ladies are very good at 'the needle' (*Garg.*, TLF LV, 38f.).

The crucial point of the philosophy of Thelema is expounded when obedience is overthrown; for this is the abbey of total freedom. Monks are governed by laws, statutes, rules, bells; so in Thelema the rule will have only one clause: *Faictz ce que vouldras*, 'Do what you will.' Rabelais is following Cicero's celebrated definition of freedom (*Paradoxa*, 5, 1, 34): *Quid enim est libertas? potestas vivendi ut velis*; 'What is freedom? The power to live as you will.' '*Fay ce que vouldras, Il sera tard quand tu mourras* was a moral jingle of the time – not encouraging men to eat drink and be merry for tomorrow they die, but thought fit to be placed on the title-page of books of hours.'[46]

This one clause, *Faictz ce que vouldras*, does not lead to anarchy; it leads to a noble desire on the part of all the Thelemites freely to conform to the general will. After a while they all dress the same, of their own free will replacing personal arbitrariness by accepted conformity, under the direction of the ladies. All enjoy the same sports; at the same time, all agree to ride or to eat. This somewhat chilling concept of freedom is not a stranger to other utopic ideals. The freedom offered us by Utopists hardly ever ends up by meaning what ordinary people think freedom to be. In Thelema this unforced, accepted, unifying conformity in all things is a

---

[46] *Garg.*, TLF LV, 10; *EC* LVII, 9. Cf. *Heures a lusaige de romme tout au long sans riens requerir* [1522?]. *BL*, C, 41, e. 6. This was brought to my attention, independently, by John Jolliffe, Jenny Beard (Mrs Britnell) and Sally North.

positive good, a fact perhaps not unconnected with the 'seditious' party spirit of the Gospel's enemies. It is worth following how Rabelais reaches this egalitarian conclusion for the Thelemite élite.

Faictz ce que vouldras is not a clause which could apply to all men and women. It applies to carefully selected inmates. These young Thelemites are *gens libères*, people born to freedom; they are *bien nez*, 'well-born', probably with the double sense of nobly born and well-endowed intellectually (Amyot in his translation of Plutarch's *How to bring up children* uses the phrase in the second sense). On top of this they are *bien instruictz*, having received therefore something like the education reserved for young Gargantua under Ponocrates. They are shielded from bad influences, being *conversans en compaignies honestes*, a phrase which recalls to mind both the moral assumptions of the educational practice outlined in Gargantua's letter in *Pantagruel* and the 'total freedom' addition to the 1533 *Pantagruel*.

The young gentlemen in Thelema are *beaulx, bien formez et bien naturez;* the young ladies are *belles, bien formées et bien naturées.* It is because the Thelemites are all handsome, lacking in deformities and 'good natured', that they can be given a rule with only one permissive clause. For 'good natured' does not have its easy-going modern sense; it refers to natural goodness of character, to natural virtue. It is the Platonic term *euēthēs* that Rabelais seems to be rendering by *bien naturé*. Plato uses it to contrast the 'well born' honourable man with the rascally *panourgos*.[47] In Thelema, such good people, educated and shielded from bad company, are motivated by a sense of honour. It is here that Rabelais is perhaps most difficult to follow; behind the word *honneur* – an appropriate one for ladies and gentlemen to be guided by – hides the more complex theological concept of 'synderesis'. Synderesis is that aspect of moral judgment and persuasion in the soul of man which, although weakened at the Fall, was not obliterated. The traditional description of its function was to *murmurare contra malum et stimulare ad bonum*: 'to protest against evil and urge towards the good.' So, too, Rabelais's Thelemites 'ont par nature un instinct et aguillon qui tousjours les pousse à faictz vertueux et retire de vice': Honour. This force in man is both an *instinctus bonus* and an *instinctus naturae*. To make the then semi-technical word *instinct* clear, Rabelais uses it with its French doublet, *aguillon* (goad). It is amusing to think that some have seen in this part of Thelema a denial of original sin! The interpretation of synderesis as a good natural instinct, encouraging good conduct and discouraging evil, is totally at home in Christian philosophy; it was almost certainly when he studied St Bonaventura in his Franciscan days that Rabelais learned to respect this preserving moral force in man. In Aquinas synderesis is largely a habit of

---

[47] *Euēthēs* means good hearted, open-minded, guileless, *honnête*. Plato contrasts the man who is *euēthēs* with the *panourgos* in *Lysias* 100, 17. (I suspect also a general influence in this chapter of Plutarch's treatise, *How to Bring up Children*.)

moral judgment; in St Bonaventura it is more than that: as for Rabelais too, it is a basic orientation of the will towards the good.

It is of course never suggested that Rabelais's 'good-natured' Thelemites are free from sin! They exemplify what Gargantua could rightly say of himself in his letter to his son: that he had so lived among 'men of honour' that his way of life had been, with the help of God's grace, 'not without sin' as he must confess, 'for we all sin and constantly beseech God to wipe out our sins; but without reproach.' In Thelema young *Chevaliers sans reproche* and their ladies are examples of just such a way of life among *gens d'honneur* (*Pant.* VIII, *TLF*, 39f.; *EC* 33f.).

Repressive, so-called educational restraints, and a plethora of rules forced upon people like the Thelemites, merely encourage the very things they are supposed to discourage or suppress. The words Rabelais used, *vile subjection* and *asserviz*, show that he is contrasting the slavery of rules with the noble freedom appropriate to the inhabitants of Thelema; repressive rules 'divert the noble desire by which they freely [*franchement*] tend towards virtue', leading them to 'put off the yoke of slavery', *à deposer ce joug de servitude*. With the phrase *joug de servitude*, the freedom of the Thelemites specifically becomes the freedom of the Christian Man: one of the most explosive of evangelical doctrines.

It is only when the noble characters have put off the 'yoke of slavery' that freedom can lead to praise-worthy harmony and unifying (not divisive) emulation. The term *joug de servitude* is not a classical common-place: it is a direct allusion to St Paul's defence of Christian freedom, and his warning not to slip back again into the slavery of the law, given in Galatians 5, 1: 'Stand therefore, and *be not entangled again in the yoke of bondage*'; in the words of the Vulgate which Rabelais echoes directly: *Nolite jugo servitutis contineri.*[48]

We can be sure that Rabelais was aware that Erasmus had made this call to Christian Freedom even more urgent, by interpolating at this point, after *therefore*, the words we read translated in the Authorised Version: 'Stand therefore *in the liberty wherewith Christ hath made us free.*'[49]

Such Christians, standing in their freedom, avoiding the yoke of bondage, are freely able *servire invicem*: 'to serve one another' (Galatians 5, 13). The concept of freedom that we are dealing with in Thelema is this New Testament *eleutheria*: the *liberty* to do or not to do things having no relation to salvation; the *freedom* from the tyranny of the Mosaic law; the

---

[48] *Garg.*, *TLF* LV, 16f.; *EC* LVII, 13f. Cf. *Garg.*, *TLF* XXVI, 56; *EC* XXVIII, 43: Grandgousier prays for help in restoring Picrochole to the *joug*, 'yoke', of God's 'holy will' by teaching him a sharp lesson (*par bonne discipline*). There the language is generally pious rather than specifically scriptural.

[49] In the Vulgate, *qua libertate Christus nos liberavit* is attached to the end of the previous chapter. It is missing from some Greek mss.

freedom which, by liberating man from corrupt desires, enables him to do, by the free impulse of the soul, what the will of God requires. It is *ho nomos tēs eleutherias*, the perfect 'law of liberty' (James 1, 25). Some Renaissance scholars perceived a mystical relationship between freedom (*eleutheria*) and the name of Luther. But the German reformers had no monopoly over Christian freedom.

That Rabelais is evoking the great defence of Christian freedom in Galatians 5, 1 is certain. It is tempting to think that he went on to develop the Abbey of Thelema in the light of the whole of this chapter; but that is less certain. The battle between flesh and spirit impedes *eleutheria* (says St Paul), 'so that ye cannot do the things that ye would'. The highly Platonic Christianity of Thelema would provide an environment in which fleshly desires did *not* war against the spirit in disharmony; and the words used by St Paul ('so that ye cannot do the things that ye would') include the verb *thelō*, cognate with *thelēma*.

The rightly refractory nature of free-born men and women in face of slavish repression is expressed by Rabelais not only in terms of the Gospel but also in the words of Ovid: *Nitimur in vetitum, semper cupimusque negata* ('We strive towards what is forbidden and always desire things that are denied us'). These words appear, directly translated, at a crucial point in the exposition of the philosophy of the abbey: *Car nous entreprenons tousjours choses defendues et couvoytons ce que nous est denié.*

It is not odd that a line of Ovid should be quoted in defence of a Christian's moral freedom. Both in patristic times and in the Renaissance it was a commonplace to use this text this way. Luther quotes with approval the use that St Augustine made of it in his treatise *On the Spirit and the Letter*. Like Rabelais he does so in defence of Christian freedom, commenting on Romans 2, 2: the Mosaic law with its Thou-shalt-not actually entices men to sin, whereas the Christian in his freedom is freely led to goodness. In his commentary Luther quotes 'Blessed Augustine's' remark: 'I do not know how it happens that the things we desire become more seductive when they are forbidden. The Poet says: "We strive towards what is forbidden and always desire things that are denied us." '[50]

Rabelais was no Lutheran, in the sense that there are doctrines in Luther he never accepted; but, when developing this paradoxical freedom which leads to each subjecting himself to all, could he have been unaware how close he was to the great paradox which Luther wrote in large letters at the beginning of his treatise *On the Freedom of the Christian Man*: 'The Christian man is most free, lord of all, subject to none: The Christian man is most unfree, a servant of all, subject to all'? For Rabelais to base his Thelemite

---

[50] *D. Martin Luthers Werke*, Weimar 1883 (in progress), LVI, 200f. Cf. Augustine, *Patrologia Latina* XLIV, 204; Thomas More, *English Works*, London 1931, II, p.301.

freedom on the overthrowing of the *jugum servitutis* was to go back to the same Pauline texts as Luther did, clearly and unmistakably.

'And this (wrote Thomas More, attacking the Lutherans) they call the liberty of the Gospel: to be discharged of all order and all laws, and to do what they list.' Not an unfair summary of the philosophy of the Abbey, as long as one adds to it a platonic alliance of beauty and goodness; a delight in beauty as a morally enhancing environment; a perhaps stoic belief that good men subordinate their private will, in all things great and small, to the general will; and a Bonaventurian synderesis.

In Thelema noble youth lives free from *vile subjection*; Francis I wanted his sons brought up in *liberté* to free them from the fear of *subjection* acquired as hostages. Is this a coincidence? (*Soc. hist. France: Notes et Documents*, 1884, p.329).

16. The persecution of the elect

There is a sharp contrast between the optimism of the five prose chapters devoted to the abbey and the grim inscription written over its portal. There are no walls in Thelema – why should there be? There is no intention to keep anybody in against his will. Yet, with the verse inscription, things abruptly and suddenly change. This abbey of beautiful people is threatened from without. The verse still stresses that Thelema is a timocracy, a *séjour d'honneur*; it welcomes *nobles chevaliers* and *dames de hault paraige . . . fleurs de beaulté . . . à maintien preude et saige.* But the ugly and the deformed beset it round. It may have no walls to keep people in, but it needs them to keep a frightening crowd of uglies out – *caffards* and the progeny which in the *Quart Livre* is attributed to Anti-Nature: *cagotz, matagotz* and so on. The complex rime-scheme of Rabelais's poem emphasises the horror of the serried ranks of enemies waiting outside. The abbey is intended for those who are 'All sound of body'; it is, in a repeated refrain, the home of 'honour, praise and delight', of *honneur, los, deduict.* The forces hostile to it are ugly and dishonourable – hypocrites, crooked lawyers, old-fashioned judges who send good parishioners to die a dog's death, monastic tramps with abuses to sell, scribes and Pharisees. As befits enemies of the good and the beautiful, they are not only evil; they are deformed as well: *Tordscoulx, courbez, camars* (men with their noses smashed in), people with a *face non humaine* (*Garg., TLF* LII; *EC* LIV).

Merely to read this dreadful list suggests that Rabelais's enemies are no longer simply comic Sorbonagres and Sorbonicoles, hideously deformed as wretched Béda was; people like that could once be laughed out of court or dismissed with bitterly contemptuous plays on their name. The field is wider now; the Gospel really is now under serious attack.

With the verse inscription above the portal the rôle of the abbey as a church sheltering from persecution is brought to the fore. The inmates who are welcomed are addressed as 'you who actively preach the Gospel, however much people may scold' ('qui le sainct evangile, en sens agile anoncez, quoy qu'on gronde'); Thelema is a *réfuge* and a *bastille*, not only against error, but against the *hostile erreur* which is poisoning the world. Within the abbey, the foundations of deep faith will be laid. It will then be ready to counter attack: 'then one may confound, by speech and by writ, the enemies of the holy word':

> *Puis, qu'on confonde, et par voix et par rolle,*
> *Les ennemys de la saincte parolle.*

Nothing, literally nothing, in the optimistic prose chapters of Thelema gives even a hint of all this. Even when we notice that their freedom is a Christian one, the notion of persecution for the sake of the Gospel is elicited from the verse alone: 'May the holy Gospel never be extinguished in this most holy place: may every man be girt around with the holy word, and every woman be pregnant with it.'[51]

Is it fanciful to imagine Thelema suddenly being metamorphosed into the courtly evangelical entourage of Margaret of Navarre? There, too, men like Marot, devoted to the Gospel, suddenly found themselves under attack from powerful enemies in university and Parlement. The happy, stable protection they once found there proved a weakish reed. By 1535, Marot and many others had fled, seeking protection in foreign lands.

17. The Enigma

The grim message of the *Inscription* is continued in the *Enigme*, abruptly presented at the end of the episode.

This Enigma, which, apart from its first two lines and its last ten, may or may not be by Mellin de Saint-Gelais, is a double-bluff.[52] Its language is apocalyptic; yet it is about a tennis-match, the royal game. Amusing enigmas, which seem to be dealing with great matters but which turn out to be merely hidden ways of alluding to trivial, ordinary or obscene things, were widely appreciated. Without its first two lines, its last ten, and its context, the Enigma can be safely taken to be one of that type. But Rabelais

[51] The line *Chascun en soit ceint* (*Garg.*, *TLF* LI, 85; *EC* LIV, 84) echoes Ephesians 6,14: 'Having one's loins girt about (*succinti*) with truth.'

[52] Nicolas Bourbon (*Paidagogein*, 1536, p.36, *Ad Rabelaesum*), asks Rabelais to greet several friends, including *Sangelasius*. The enigma of *Gargantua* LVI (*EC* LVIII) appears in a posthumous edition of the works of Saint-Gelais, but without the first two lines and the last ten. These are by Rabelais. The others may or may not be.

gives a double-twist to the Enigma: it *is* a veiled description of a tennis-match – for Frère Jean; but for Gargantua it is something far more tragic: an authoritative scriptural call to resist persecution unto the end. This gives an additional value to the apocalyptic element in the Enigma itself: now it not only amusingly veils the actions of a mere game of royal tennis; it serves as a reminder that persecution of the faithful elect will precede the end of the world.

The last ten lines of the Enigma, together with Gargantua's interpretation, spell out this meaning: not the least of the surprises of this complex book is that its gaiety, its optimism, its laughter, bring us in the last chapter face to face with Christians suffering unto death for the sake of the Gospel. In this it is not unlike the later *Pantagruel*, which was a book of joy ending, in 1534 but not before, with a call to hate. In *Gargantua* the hate implied in the inscription is transmuted into the gold of Christian suffering.[53]

In Rabelais's day, as in our own, the sense of the end of the Enigma and of Gargantua's comments on it is only 'revealed' to those who have a knowledge of the Gospel; it is expressed through a series of interlocking scriptural proof-texts, all encouraging and strengthening the persecuted elect of God.

In these last pages of *Gargantua*, we are told that God's will (his *thelēma*) is that those who 'toil, travail and bear afflictions' shall be 'refreshed' – (*refaictz*), an echo of Matthew 11, 28, 'Come unto me all ye that travail and are heavy laden, and I will refresh you'. We then move on to the parable of the sower: the seed that falls on good ground 'brings forth fruit with patience' (suffering); it is by the suffering of the elect, in Rabelais's verse, that 'one shall see, with certain knowledge, the good and the fruit which comes from patience': *Le bien et fruict qui sort de patience*. Those who have suffered will then find their reward: 'Oh, how much to be revered is the man who shall be able to persevere unto the end!':

> O qu'est à reverer
> Cil qui pourra en fin perseverer!

This resumes the most important of all the proof-texts comforting the persecuted Christian (Matthew 24, 13):

But he that shall persevere unto the end, the same shall be saved.

---

[53] The lines under discussion (*Garg.*, TLF LVI, 102f.; EC LVIII, 102f.) may be literally and prosaically rendered thus: 'It remains afterwards that these folk, exceedingly burdened, suffering, weary, travailed, afflicted, should – by the holy will of the Eternal Saviour – be given rest from such labours in due time. Then will we see, by certain knowledge, the good and fruit which come forth from suffering. For he who shall have suffered most toil

Gargantua, deeply moved, comments that it is not only in recent times that people are persecuted when they are 'led back to Gospel truth'; and he adds, 'Bien heureux est celluy qui ne sera scandalizé'. Rabelais is quoting Matthew 11, 6 and Luke 7, 23: 'Blessed is he who shall not be offended in me.'[54] *Offended* in English and *scandalizer* in Rabelais's French are renderings of the Greek verb *skandalizein* (in Vulgate Latin, *scandalizare*). In evangelical exegesis, this great text was intimately bound up with the words from St Matthew that appeared in the last lines of the Enigma. Its full force lies in the sense of the verb. *Scandalizer* means to make someone lose his faith through fear of persecution. It was in this sense that Peter was 'offended' or 'scandalised' by Christ's arrest.[55] Gargantua sees the Enigma as signifying the way the Gospel must be upheld, the 'decours et maintien de verité divine'. He remarks that the Christian must not be 'scandalised', always striving towards the target (*au but, au blanc*) that God has set up before us through his 'dear Child'. That powerful image of the true Christian's striving to 'hit the target' through an imitation of Christ is an example of Rabelais's sense of nuance: the word for 'to sin' in Greek, *hamartanein*, literally means 'to miss the target'.

Gargantua interprets the Enigma as a call to resist persecution for the Gospel 'unto the end' – to be prepared to suffer for it and, if needs be, to die for it. Frère Jean does not accept all this; with two clipped sentences he interprets the Enigma as a game of royal tennis. The book ends with his briefest of brief explanations of the Enigma in a sporting sense and the call for 'good cheer'.

Frère Jean's 'harmless' interpretation provides a good escape hole; if hostile forces, who are not meant to understand the evangelical call, do break its code and recognise it as a comforting of the persecuted elect, then Frère Jean's innocent interpretation can be blandly put forward as the real one.

In 1542, when persecutions were not so much in the air, Rabelais rewrote the ten last lines of the poem – one of the few parts of any of his books destined to be fundamentally rewritten, as distinct from having some words cut out or many others put in. In these new lines the principal persecution proof-texts are still retained, but a new emphasis stresses that true Christians are indeed an elect, each of whom will have his predestined

---

beforehand, will receive more of the share then offered. O, how to be revered is he who can persevere unto the end!'

[54] *Garg., TLF* LVI, 112; *EC* LVIII, 112. The scriptural commonplaces in the last lines of the Enigma and in Gargantua's exegesis are all interlocking ones, often found glossing each other.

[55] Matthew 26, 33. Peter, before the Crucifixion, said: 'Though men should be offended (*skandalisthēsontai: scandalizati*), yet will I never be offended.' Christ retorted that he would be; and he was.

lot (*son sort predestiné*). These, too, are significant scriptural commonplaces, as is the 'heavenly manna' promised to the faithful.

This new version is sometimes misunderstood. Because the theology of both Luther and Calvin gave pride of place to the absolute predestination of the elect, it is at times assumed that any use of such terms suggests reformist tendencies. But both the word *elect* and the word *predestination* are fully scriptural. No evangelical can avoid them. The schismatic Reformation had no monopoly of such concepts. Indeed, St Augustine made the predestination of the saintly elect to consist in their receiving from God the gift of persevering unto the end (*Garg.*, TLF LVI, 102–11 *variants* and notes).

Frère Jean's exposition is expanded too in 1542. He notes that the Enigma is in the style of 'Merlin le Prophete', an allusion to the court poet Mellin de Saint-Gelais, (often called Merlin by reference to the prophet of Arthurian legend). In keeping with the monk's amiable theological crassness throughout the book, he adds: 'Give it any grave allegories and meanings that you will, and dream away – you and everybody else – as much as you like.' For him, with greater detail than in the original version, the Enigma still is a royal tennis match.

The comedy here is very refined. One needs a theological mind not to get tied up in knots. The last ten lines of the poem, in both its versions, make a very different use of Scripture from that of the body of the Enigma. The body of the Enigma *is* an allegory; it is an account of a tennis match veiled in the terms which the Bible applied to the end of the world. But in the last ten lines and in Gargantua's comments there is no need of *allégories* to extract from them obscure *intelligences tant graves*. The grave tragic meanings of the texts quoted *is* their undoubted and undeniable literal scriptural sense. As for the Enigma proper it is, without peradventure, an account of the end of the world in apocalyptic terms – its scriptural sources are clear, though less cogent than those of the last ten lines. So it is Frère Jean who reads allegories into the text, not Gargantua. Only through the allegorisation that Frère Jean condemns can the poetic Enigma be made to refer to the royal game! Without the allegory, it is purely and simply apocalyptic.

The refinement of Rabelais's humour at this point is lost on those who do not know their rules of scriptural exegesis, especially as conceived in the circle of Jacques Lefèvre d'Etaples, the French Aristotelian scholar turned Biblical translator and scriptural exegete, whose reputation in France often surpassed even Erasmus's. His influence on Queen Margaret of Navarre and on Guillaume Briçonnet, Bishop of Meaux, her spiritual counsellor, was profound and lasting. Naturally he was dubbed a heretic by Béda and his cronies. Lefèvre and others held complex views about the literal meaning of scripture. And indeed, the expression 'literal meaning' is not as clear as it might sound. The literal meaning of an episode intended to be allegorical – there are many such in the Bible – is the allegorical one. All the allegorical texts quoted in the last ten lines of Rabelais's Enigma and in Gargantua's comments are scriptural allegories, explained as such in the Gospels. Their allegorical meaning is therefore, in theological terms, their literal one: the parable of the sower, for example, is not a lesson in horticulture, but a lesson about faith and persecution. Christ tells us so.

Similarly the literal sense of the Enigma as such is, paradoxically, allegorical: the Enigma, as Frère Jean says, is a description of a game of royal tennis veiled under apocalyptic allegories. Its inner sense, its *plus haut sens*, consists, as Gargantua shows, in bringing it back to the true literal meaning of the scriptural sources which the Enigma amusingly exploits allegorically. The road for this is prepared by the last ten lines added to the Enigma – lines tellingly absent from the version attributed to Mellin de Saint-Gelais.

The reader comes to the Enigma after having already read the complex verse of the inscription above the abbey portal. He cannot fail to see that both the inscription and the Enigma are preoccupied with the persecution of good Christians by ugly, hostile, powerful forces.

After reading the inscription, the *altior sensus* of the Enigma becomes tragic indeed, without, at another level, losing the pleasure that Renaissance readers found in breaking enigmatic codes. Indeed, they had two codes to break.

Why does the abbey, joyfully, peacefully, utopianly untroubled, without a hint of toil, travail or persecution within its dominant prose-chapters, lead to a conclusion which opens up a window on to the appalling sufferings of the elect? Only the inscription in verse paved the way for such an ending.

There are hints to be gleaned from a study of the text. History provides further clues.

The prose chapters are carefully written, though not without minor blemishes, nor without the odd construction suggestive of an early date of composition. The original conception of the abbey may date from the period of the 1533 *Pantagruel*, where Rabelais first revealed his concern with *liberté totalle*. There certainly are aesthetic tensions which give rise to the hypothesis (which may seem cogent) that the prose chapters of Thelema were first written without any idea of persecutions being in Rabelais's mind – but only an optimistic, untroubled joy in that Christian freedom which, in art and in real life, had released him from the *jugum servitutis*.

The finished abbey is more problematical. Not the least of the paradoxes of Thelema is that we must accept that the noble, beautiful, well-born, virtuous, honourable Thelemites, free with St Paul from the *jugum servitutis*, should apparently have the uncouthly lecherous monk as their abbot, however much his vices are redeemed by action and laughter. Yet the abbey is created to provide a reward for the monk who had battled so bravely. *Restoit seulement le Moyne à pourvoir* (*Garg.*, *TLF* L, 1f.; *EC* LII, 1f.).

There are moments when a text needs to be pressed close. The boon that Frère Jean requests is *not* that he should become abbot – he made a clear reply, denying any wish to have charge or governance of monks: *le Moyne fist response peremptoyre que de moynes il ne vouloit charge ne gouvernement*; he asks to be allowed to found an abbey to his own liking. The new religious order is in fact Gargantua's: Frère Jean simply requests, 'that Gargantua should institute his religious order on contrary principles to those which usually applied: *au contraire de toutes aultres*'. From then on Gargantua makes all the decisions; the monk, after cracking jokes in the first prose chapter – one of them interpolated into the middle of a long periodic sentence of Gargantua's – disappears completely from view for the rest of the book, not being even alluded to for six whole chapters – for seventeen pages in the original edition – until he appears in order to give his interpretation of the Enigma in the last thirteen lines. It is Gargantua alone to whom is attributed the vital decision to make the abbey's ladies and gentlemen pass their lives, not under laws, statutes or rules, but in accordance with both their will (*vouloir*) and their free will (*franc arbitre*). It is Gargantua alone who, with the single clause of their rule, freed them from the yoke of slavery: *ainsi l'avoit estably Gargantua.*

In fact, we do not actually know for sure that Frère Jean is Abbé de Thelème until 1546 (in chapter XLIX of the *Tiers Livre*.) This could be an example of yet another switching of rôles.

The Enigma is introduced, not by Gargantua or Frère Jean, but by a narrator (*Je*), with a laconic phrase bearing all the signs of an afterthought which Rabelais – with his tongue in his cheek – did not bother to hide (*TLF* LV; *EC* LVII – end). There is not a single suggestion after the monk's second joke to remind us of his presence.

So, in the abbey, Frère Jean is totally eclipsed. The abbey is indeed appropriate to a Gargantua purged by Seraphin Calobarsy and taught by Ponocrates; to place Frère Jean over it would make him as conspicuous as Hurtaly riding on Noah's Ark. As we read the episode we forget him. He is not only inconspicuous; he is not even there.

And yet he is, especially at the beginning. No modifications to the later editions of *Gargantua* change his rôle; on the contrary, later books recall it to us. There is a challenge here. This snotty-nosed, amusing good-fellow, *vray moyne si oncques en feut depuys que le monde moyna*, knows nothing except his service books; he is 'a clerk up to his teeth in breviary stuff'. He shows no sign of being fundamentally changed as Gargantua was, either in this book or the following ones. Yet, at the outset of this episode, for the first and last time, Frère Jean bases himself on wisdom attributed to Socrates: 'How can I govern others when I do not know how to govern myself?' These words are more at home in the mouth of a philosopher-king; and indeed Erasmus alludes to them in just such a context: '. . . this is what Plato meant, when he said the happiness of states lay in their having kings who were philosophers. For who can rightly rule over others, who is himself a slave to blind emotions?'[56]

At no time in the Renaissance can a Socratic parallel like this one be ignored, least of all in a book which starts off, as *Gargantua* does, with Socrates as an inspired exemplar.

Nothing that Frère Jean ever says or does has prepared us to expect him to appear even fleetingly in Socrates's garments. Yet there he is, inspiring Gargantua's foundation of Thelema.

One explanation is that Rabelais is the master of surprises, spinning off the stage on his toe when we think we have pinned him down. Like Shakespeare, he can so intermingle laughter and tears that the art is immeasurably impoverished if one is seen without the other. Thelema is quite obviously an ideal to which Rabelais attached great importance: it is one of the few episodes in the earlier books kept alive by references in the later ones. The presence of Frère Jean becomes understandable when we pass through his literal rôle to his parabolic one. The abbey is, unexpectedly, an evangelical group of the elect, beset by ugly, vicious, hostile forces in a world where Christians are tormented and oppressed. These Christians are sorely tried. They are *lassez, travaillez, affligez*; but they persevere. The terms used at the end of the Enigma recall in detail the same words used when Gargantua ascribed a parabolic meaning to Frère Jean. Such words bear repeating:

. . . *Il travaille, il labeure; il defend les opprimez; il conforte les affligez; il souvient es souffreteux; il garde le clous de l'abbaye* (*Garg.*, TLF XXXVIII, 57f. Cited above in translation, p.181).

In both cases we find words recalling the toil and travail of the afflicted. Insofar as he has a *plus-haut sens* in such matters, Frère Jean defends those who travail and are heavy laden; he comforts the afflicted and succours the needy. And he also 'guards the abbey's close'. Does this parabolic interpretation of Frère Jean's prowess in defence of the abbey of Seuillé also quietly look forward to his rôle in the Abbey of Thelema? There too will he protect the abbey's close? If so, we may recall that, however gross he is in literal fact, Gargantua called him both joyful and *honeste*.

18. Sedition, persecution and the 'affaire des placards'

That Rabelais should have turned his art from the gay confident laughter

[56] *Garg.*, TLF L, 9f.; *EC* LII, 6f. Erasmus, *Opera Omnia* v, col. 228 E.

of most of *Gargantua* into the deep channels of the toil, travail, and hostility towards the faith revealed in the Inscription and the Enigma can be partly explained by the events of his time.

If *Gargantua* appeared early in 1534, there were fears that Francis I's meeting with the pope at Marseilles in autumn 1533 could lead to the suppression of liberal theology in France, if humanist, evangelical, Catholic religion became effectively smeared with the taint of heresy. As far as the pope was concerned there was no real need for these fears, despite the agreement to repress heresy in France: many noticed the evangelical nature of the Lenten sermons preached in 1534 by the monk he sent to the French court. But there were sticky moments, not least because of royal waverings. In the winter of 1533–4, even Jean du Bellay found his rights and duties as bishop of Paris publicly questioned by those who wanted heretics to be more vigorously oppressed and who had gained the ear of the king. Jean's brother, René du Bellay, was for a while justifiably disquieted, as was the bishop himself.[57] If *Gargantua* appeared early in 1534, thoughts of persecution could have been aroused in his mind, as he saw his admired patron attacked, wondered why Béda had been recalled and saw the Sorbonne adopting a censuring posture. But if *Gargantua* was first published late in 1534 or even in 1535, then the persecutions alluded to could be the dreadful ones known to us as the 'affaire des placards'.

The 'affaire des placards' is, a little too easily, treated a watershed for French evangelism. On the night of 17 October 1534, Zwinglian posters against the 'idolatry of the Mass' (a new kind of poster with books attached) were strewn about the streets and crossroads of Paris. The shock was profound. The repression that was started by this imprudent and aggressively stupid action was great – hundreds were said to be arrested, houses were searched; we know of sixteen heretics burnt in Paris between 10 November and 24 December. But dreadful as this repression was, it was not indiscriminate and is sometimes exaggerated. This results from the conflation of two different, but related, outbursts of religious intolerance.

The posters of October 1534 were sacramentarian, the work as we now know of Marcourt of Neuchâtel. Provided the Paris Parlement and the Sorbonne did not succeed in smearing Catholic evangelicals or Lutherans

---

[57] On this important matter, see the letters in R. Scheurer, *Correspondence du Cardinal Jean du Bellay* I, pp.332f., starting with the letter of Jacques Groslot to the bishop, 25 November 1533. In another letter, dated 11 December 1533, Groslet writes in a state of fear. To reinforce the suppression of heresy, which the king believed to be 'pululating in Paris', the bishop's jurisdiction was compromised by the appointment of two commissioners from the Paris Parlement. The matter blew over. Jean du Bellay was in favour throughout the disturbed events of winter 1534–5. Cf. Scheurer, I, p.451, note. Throughout these difficulties the king's support of the Trilingual Academy did not waver: Rabelais's satire of the anti-hebraic attitudes of the Sorbonne in the 1534 *Pantagruel* would have pleased the court and was not over bold.

with the guilt of the sacramentarians there was no reason yet for men such as Marot, Rabelais, or Catholics generally to feel immediate danger. While the du Bellays were influential in court there was no fear of such a confusion being easily made. Throughout the period in question all the du Bellays were back in royal favour. But evangelical Catholics knew their enemies only too well. Deep anxiety they could not, and justifiably could not, avoid. The Sorbonne, smarting from being laughed at and devalued, smelt blood and power.

For some reason, scholars have attached the term 'affaire des placards' so closely to the events of 17–18 October 1534 that the far worse events of January 1535 have been frequently ignored, played down or even passed over in silence or in a footnote. The real climax of the 'affaire des placards', the one which made persecution and repression cruelly relevant to men such as Marot and Rabelais, occurred on the night of 13–14 January 1535. Posters, again with little booklets attached to them, both attacking the Mass in sacramentarian terms, were again strewn through Paris. This time the royal reactions stunned the kingdom. Francis ordered all printing to cease – though it was soon permitted again owing to the influential intercessions of Budé and the du Bellays. An imposing act of national expiation was led by the monarch through the streets of Paris to Notre-Dame on 21 January 1535. Six heretics were publicly burned on that day alone. The repression did not slacken off until May; it was said – though on what authority is not clear – that the pope had intervened to stop the killings. The moderate influence of the du Bellays certainly played a decisive rôle, persuading the king to reverse his policies abruptly. The Edict of Coucy, promulgated on 16 July 1535, freed prisoners and allowed exiles to return – provided that they abjured heresy; property formerly confiscated was restored. From February 1535 these influences were already at work.

The events of October 1534 should not be conflated with the graver repressions of January 1535. The January *affaire* was on another scale altogether. Even highly protected evangelicals had to flee or disappear. But events moved with bewildering quickness, taking extraordinary directions. A fortnight after 13 January Langey wrote, and printed under the name and authority of the king of France, the famous letter of 1 February 1535, aimed at reassuring the German states of the Holy Roman Empire; there was, he said, nothing sinister in French relationships with the Grand Turk; no Germans were being troubled in France for their religion; the only French people being punished were madmen (*furiosi*), lunatics (*amentes*). (Marot – one of the men who had to flee in 1535 – also attributed the *placards* to idle fools – *Au Roy. Du temps de son exil à Ferrare,* line 160f.) The king's actions were aimed only at putting a stop to 'horrible sedition' – (*teterrima seditio*). Johannes Sturm, who strongly supported the initiative of the du Bellays, mentions this fear of sedition in two letters to Melanchthon written in March 1535. In the first he stresses the seditious aspect of the events of October 1534. In the second, after emphasising how, in 1535, the evil minded were lumping together Anabaptists, Erasmians and Lutherans, he ventures the opinion that the king made a real distinction between the *seditiosi* and those who merely held untraditional opinions about the Mass. Bartholomew Latomus, writing to Erasmus on 29 June 1535 says that 'last winter' – not 'last autumn' – Germans as such had been in some danger from the indiscriminate repression.[58] This explains the urgency of the king's (or rather Langey's) circular letter. Preoccupied as it is with Barbarossa, with persecution, 'sedition' and Christian diplomacy, it has close connexions with the concerns of Rabelais in *Gargantua*. It acknowledged the stresses and the strains, but still held out hope of peace and concord.

The height of the influence of the du Bellays was their persuading Francis I to write to Melanchthon on 23 June 1535. The king went out of his way to praise Guillaume du Bellay, expressed delight that Melanchthon should agree to come to France to discuss a 'union of doctrine' with French theologians, and looked forward to the re-establishment of religious harmony. In Jean du Bellay's own letter, sent four days later, he urged Melanchthon to come to France, fully associating himself as bishop of Paris, recently made a Cardinal, with these ecumenical overtures.

Whenever *Gargantua* first appeared, the second edition can only have come out after the du Bellays regained the initiative in February or March 1535. In the light of these events, the propaganda in the last chapters of *Gargantua* can be seen to be consonant with the du Bellay interests in both 1534 *and* 1535.

It is a book which would be pleasing to evangelicals who were not schismatic, but nevertheless sympathetic to the du Bellays' confidence in Melanchthonian synergism. Duly shorn of such indiscreet words as *stupidité* applied to the tolerance of French Kings for Parisian unrests and, above all, of the very word *placard*, it continued to advance the cause of evangelism through amusement and laughter, interrupted with moments of deep seriousness.

That a book by Rabelais so openly hostile to the Sorbonne, a book so evangelical, so openly defending the oppressed and the persecuted, could appear, or appear again, after the dreadful explosion of intolerance

[58] All letters in Herminjard: *Correspondance des Réformateurs* (1870), reprint, Nieuwkoop 1965, III, p.249f.: Letter of Langey (abbreviated): p.252: ' . . . contagious pestilence and *teterriman seditionem*.' First letter of J. Sturm, p.267: the state and people were disturbed by *stultissimis et seditiosissimis rationibus* in October 1534; p.273: the king is principally acting against the *seditiosos*. Sturm is concerned to put the best face on things; for his close relationshp with the du Bellays and Melanchthon, see letter no. 515; see also no. 531.

following the January *placards*, can only be understood in terms of the effective protection afforded by the du Bellays and of the policies they stood for. The 1535 *Gargantua* is no fly-by-night publication: it bears François Juste's name and address, as though it were the most innocuous of books imaginable. So too, probably, did the first edition, but the only known copy lacks the title-page. (I wonder whether it is significant that this *unicum* came to light in Italy, in the nineteenth century. Rabelais and Jean du Bellay were there in 1534 and 1535.)

Rabelais published the second edition of *Gargantua* in the course of a year which had seen the ugly enemies of the Gospel on the rampage, sedition openly at work and, eventually, the appeasing policies of the du Bellays newly strengthened. This second edition has nothing on the title-page or elsewhere which 'places' the book in 1533 or 1534. A purchaser had to know he was reading the second edition of a 1534 book, if such were indeed the case. From one point of view the defence of Christian freedom is a timeless thing; Christian freedom is always under attack. Comforting those who suffer persecution for the Gospel's sake is also not linked to the odd month here or there. But the terms in which Thelema's verse inscription and the Enigma describe the persecution unleashed by the unlovely enemies of the Gospel would certainly fit the most violent outbursts of persecution imaginable. And such persecution the purchasers of 1535 had recently witnessed with their own eyes. If watershed we must have, then 13 January 1535 has a much greater claim to that description than 17 October 1534.

Rabelais did not intend to remain silent when Gospel truth was at stake. The October 1534 persecutions drew open condemnations from his pen. His *Almanach pour l'an 1535* is a work which one would expect to be published late in 1534 at the earliest. It bears his name and titles; in it Rabelais shows himself a fully committed man. We do not find him cowering in silence.[59] Similarly, the *Pantagrueline Prognostication* was brought up to date *pour l'an M.M. xxxv*. Among his additional material is an attack on persecution (*TLF* VII, 1f.);

During the whole of this year there will only be one moon; and she will not be 'new' either. That makes you very upset, you who do not believe in God and who persecute his holy and divine word, together with those who uphold it. But go and be hanged!

This is the very language of the end of *Gargantua*.

Gargantua is a complex book: it attractively and clearly syncretises Platonism and evangelism in a way unknown to *Pantagruel* in any of its

---

[59] *Almanach pour l'an 1535*, *TLF*, p.47, line 77: 'I say, on my part, that if kings, princes and Christian communities hold in reverence the holy word of God and govern themselves and their subjects according to it, then . . . ' 1535 will be a good year for body and soul.

versions, but very much like that of the *Almanach pour l'an 1535*; its gay laughter and early optimism lead to emotive reflexions on the tragedy of those who suffer for the Gospel. Its happy mockery of the divisive activators of religious and political 'sedition' leads, in the end, to an identification of sedition with the dreadful powers of darkness.

6

The Tiers Livre

1. *Rabelais between* Gargantua *and the* Tiers Livre

Between the second edition of *Gargantua* and the first edition of *Le Tiers Livre de Pantagruel* (1546), Rabelais published little that was new. Editions of *Pantagruel*, *Gargantua* and the *Pantagrueline Prognostication* were printed and sold by François Juste in 1537 and also, the same year, by a Parisian printer (almost certainly Denis Janot). François Juste's *Pantagrueline Prognostication* was now said to be 'for 1537'; Janot's 'for 1538'. Juste's edition shows no clear signs that Rabelais had revised it or otherwise worked on it; he may not even have authorised its publication. Chapter XIII (the bottom-wiping chapter) disappears altogether from *Gargantua*, leaving a gap in the chapter-numbering. It is hard to believe that Rabelais authorised such an omission, occurring as it does in this edition only. The Janot edition, which is much more elegant than the new Juste one, gives essentially the same texts as those which last appeared – that of the 1534 *Pantagruel*, the '1535' *Gargantua* and the *Pantagrueline Prognostication* 'for 1535'. But a change or an addition here and there do allow us to believe that Rabelais had personally revised his texts. Some comic book-titles were added to the catalogue of the Library of Saint-Victor, for example; these titles (which are retained in subsequent editions) include what appear to be memories of Rabelais's stay in Rome – an allusion, say, to the statue of Pasquillo where satirical pamphlets and poems were traditionally displayed (the famous *pasquinades*). Other titles take up and develop jokes made earlier, including an allusion to Jean du Pont-allais, Songecreux, under the comic professorial title of 'Magister Noster Songe Crusyon', a satirical quip which would keep alive this actor's resemblance to the once powerful theological syndic, Magister Noster Noël Béda and his hunchback.[1]

Rabelais's comparative neglect of his works, his failure fundamentally to revise them or to write a continuation, can be partly explained by the life he was leading as an influential doctor actively working in the du

---

[3] *Pant.*, *EC* VII, 76; also 112: '*Prognostication que incipit "Silvi Triquebille", balata per M. n. Songecrusyon.*'

Bellay interest and concerned as well with the great responsibility of looking after his patrons' health. His first visit to Rome (January to May 1534) perhaps preceded the first publication of *Gargantua*, though it may not have done so. His second visit to Italy kept him out of France from at least July 1535 to the summer of 1536. He visited Ferrara; worked in the household of cardinal Jean du Bellay in Rome, arranged (with the connivance of his patrons) to be relieved of the canonical penalties he had incurred by his apostasy in abandoning his monastic profession. This was all part of a complicated manoeuvre; Rabelais was received back into the Benedictine order by François Bribart, in Jean du Bellay's monastery at Saint-Maur-les Fossés; within months, the monastery was duly secularised, turning Rabelais once and for all into a secular priest, free forever from monastic obedience. He was now authorised to practise medicine, provided that, as a priest, he did not shed blood; if benefices eventually came his way he could, as a priest, draw upon their income; protected as he was by so influential a cardinal, his surviving children François and Junie were eventually fully legitimated (in 1540). His medical career advanced – from bachelor of medicine he became doctor of medicine at Montpellier in May 1537. He moved among the great – a life not always without its difficulties, as is shown by the danger he ran when a letter of his, indiscreetly written to a turncoat friend in Italy, fell into the hands of the Cardinal de Tournon, an opponent, an enemy even, of the du Bellays. The affair is obscure, but Rabelais was, for a while, in serious trouble.

The greatest influence on his life at this time seems to have been his period in Turin, stretching from at least the summer of 1540 until December 1542. Here he developed his profound admiration for his hero, Guillaume du Bellay, the pacifier of the Piedmont, the French viceroy in Cisalpine Gaul. When Guillaume du Bellay died on the way back to Paris (on 9 January 1543, near Roanne) Rabelais was with him and doubtless witnessed the plundering of his baggage-train and the tragedy of the destruction of his diplomatic and private papers.

During this period in Italy with Guillaume du Bellay, Rabelais finally recast his two Chronicles. *Gargantua* and *Pantagruel* were shorn here and there of satirical shafts considered too indiscreet. His real concessions to Sorbonne were few, however. That he changed (several times) the word *theologien* into *sophiste* showed that he was in no mood for fundamental compromise, despite what is often said; such changes merely emphasise that he was no enemy of true theology, but only of that kind of theology represented by Our Masters of the Sorbonne. Both Catholic humanists and schismatic reformers regularly condemned the Sorbonagres as *sophistes*, men not really interested in truth but paid theological hacks, as far removed from true theology as the Greek sophists had been from true disinterested philosophy. Nevertheless all the explicitly anti-Sorbonne jokes disappear, in the sense that every single allusion to the Sorbonne by name is stricken out. Artistically we can deplore all the changes, the most regrettable being no doubt the loss of the belittling word-play on *Sorboniste* in the Thaumaste episode of *Pantagruel*.

As well as apparently wishing to avoid any head-on collision with the Sorbonne, Rabelais took care – almost excessive care, one might think today – to avoid any possible offence to regal dignity. As early as 1534 he had cut out of *Pantagruel* jesting allusions to characters who formed part of the legend and mystery of the French monarchy and so were not to be treated lightly by an author with courtly ambitions. In 1542 Rabelais even found it prudent to drop any suggestion that a king had a bottom that needed wiping: Gargantua's new means of wiping his tail remains *le plus seigneurial, le plus excellent, le plus expedient*, but it ceases to be *le plus royal*.

The *Pantagrueline Prognostication* is now finally removed from any particular year-date: from now on it is *pour l'an perpetuel*.

So, in 1542, the French public found itself able to read Rabelais again in a new, less openly aggressive, revision.

But it could also read the old, less prudent text, since Etienne Dolet, totally without authorisation, produced his own edition of Rabelais, following the earlier unexpurgated texts of 1537 and throwing in a pseudo-Rabelaisian *Voyage et navigation que fist Panurge, disciple de Pantagruel* into the bargain, fathering it off on Rabelais. A few pages entitled *L'imprimeur au lecteur* were added to the stocks of Juste's edition, scathingly attacking Dolet and his sharp practices. This attack was reproduced in a further reprinting, also in 1542, probably by François Juste's successor, Pierre de Tours.

This stormy rebirth of *Gargantua* and *Pantagruel* in 1542 was only a prelude to more serious trouble. The Sorbonne, invited by the Paris Parlement, took official notice of *Gargantua* and *Pantagruel*, proceeding to condemn them. The title given in their censure makes it plain that it was Rabelais's less aggressive revised text that they were condemning, not simply the injudicious pirated reprint of Etienne Dolet. Corporations like the Sorbonne have long memories and do not forgive easily. Some of the men Rabelais had mocked in his Chronicles in the 1530s were still very much alive, only too keen to pay off old scores. Picart, one of the theologians exiled in 1533 with Béda, was now an influential fellow of the Collège de Navarre, a close friend and admirer of Gabriel Dupuyherbault, an unshakable enemy of Rabelais and all that he stood for.

As though it were not enough to have the Paris Parlement and the Sorbonne taking up a censuring stance which could have had serious consequences, Rabelais found himself violently attacked in 1543 by Guillaume Postel, a distinguished but erratic orientalist who was himself only saved from the stake later on by being declared insane, but who throughout his life retained considerable influence in high places. Postel, in a book declaring that the so-called evangelicals were in fact thinly disguised Moslems, attacked Rabelais as an enemy of Christ, an 'atheist' like the authors of the *Cymbalum mundi en françoys* and of the *Novae Insulae*. There indeed Rabelais perhaps finds himself in good company, since the *New Islands* may refer to More's *Utopia* (*De nova insula Utopia libellus*), though I doubt it. One of the crimes Postel lays at Rabelais's door is that in the episode of the 'Abbey of Thelema and the Tennis Match' he declared that true Christians must suffer persecution – sure proof that he was no better than a disguised follower of Mahomet. Another proof that the evangelicals were Moslem infidels he saw in their assertion that Christian doctrine must be based on the gospel, since there is nothing in the Gospels which says any such thing. In the *Quart Livre*, Rabelais dismisses him as an 'anti-natural' maniac.[2]

We might be tempted to do just the same. In modern terms it does seem the act of a maniac to call another man both a Moslem infidel and an atheist, because you do not approve of his basing his Christianity on the authority of an infallible book, the Bible, and especially on the New Testament. But Postel's virulent attack on Rabelais makes better sense when read in the light of contemporary religious controversy. Postel is feeling his way towards an argument which was soon to become a major one among those Catholics who based their religious assurance entirely on the authority of an infallible Church. Rabelais is a sceptical Christian, a generation before such attitudes are said to be current. As we saw, he wove his way through the complexities of faith in relation to Christ's and Gargantua's nativities not under the guidance of reason but of a Christian assurance based on the Bible. This infallible book enabled him to reach firm conclusions in matters where reason was impotent; it also enabled him to criticise adversely the abuses rampant in the Catholic Church, against an authority higher than herself.

[2] *QL, TLF* XXXII, 119: '*Les Maniacles Pistoletz*' refers to *Postel*. Cf. G. Postel, *Alcorani et Evangelistarum Concordiae Lib*, Paris 1543; p.14: the 'false evangelicals' are accused of Manichaean tendencies as condemned by Augustine, wickedly maintaining that 'when some of them are burnt for the public peace' this is a sign that they are in fact the persecuted elect of God; these false evangelicals, 'as though they were, by the consensus of everyone, most holy people, call princes tyrants and bishops pharisees when they suppress their lusts: Mahomet said the same', Ibid., p.72: the false evangelicals work craftily. They first insist that nothing must be believed except what is in Scripture: they then undermine Scripture. Only the Church gives authority to many of the principal dogmas, and to Scripture itself. Without the *prior* authority of the Church, there is no way of knowing the Gospel to be the Gospel, nor God to be God. The books attacked are '*Villanovani de tribus prophetis, Cymbalum Mundi, Pantagruellus et novae insulae*', whose authors had once been leaders of the 'false evangelicals'. Ibid, p.74: the 'false evangelicals' frequently profess the Gospel, 'but so that they can live (as that Scourge of Christ expressed it in the abbey of the Thelemites and the tennis-match), "as they will"'.

Postel is a forerunner of those many Catholic apologists who attempt to demolish the simple authority of the Bible, seen as a rival to the authority of the Church when privately interpreted.

The attacks on Rabelais do not seem to have exposed him to any immediate danger, despite the fact that he had lost not only his great patron Guillaume du Bellay, but, in the same year, another patron, Geoffroy d'Estissac, who died in May 1542. Rabelais still enjoyed the support of Cardinal Jean du Bellay; but was this support always effective? Cardinal Jean's influence was now sometimes less than that of his rival, the Cardinal de Tournon. Rabelais's continued loyalty to the du Bellay family is underlined by two major allusions to Guillaume du Bellay in the *Tiers Livre* and the *Quart Livre*, as well as by a work which he wrote in Latin but which appeared in a French translation in 1542, published by Sebastian Gryphius at Lyons: *Stratagemes, c'est à dire prouesses et ruses de guerre du preux et tres celebre chevalier de Langey, on commencement de la tierce guerre Cesarienne.* (This work is lost, though it was seen in modern times by a scholarly bibliographer of impeccable reliability – M. Charles Perrat, on a bookstall, when a young man.)

2. *The Royal Privilege for the* Tiers Livre

Rabelais was discouraged by these attacks on his works; that is natural enough. But he was not now a man who could simply be silenced by a committee of professors or even by the influential Paris Parlement; he was a man with strong backing from the king and his sister. When the *Tiers Livre de Pantagruel* appeared in 1546, it bore a fulsome *Privilege* signed by Delaunay in the name of Francis I, dated 19 September 1545. Whoever wrote the privilege on behalf of the king, it shows us a Rabelais triumphant and at the height of his literary reputation. His two previous 'volumes of the heroic deeds and sayings of Pantagruel' are described, in an adaptation of Horace's words, as being *non moins utiles que delectables* – as works which blend the morally useful with the aesthetically delightful. Such terms place the *Tiers Livre* in the highest literary category of all (*TL*, *TLF Privilege*; and notes).

The phrasing of the *Privilege* suggests that Rabelais had already written the sequel to the first two volumes, but was put off from publishing it, despite the daily badgering of the 'learned and studious people of our kingdom', by the irresponsible conduct of printers who had corrupted and perverted his texts. It was on these grounds that Rabelais was given a monopoly of his works for six years, Francis 'desiring that good literature should be encouraged throughout our kingdom, for the use and erudition of our subjects'.

When the *Tiers Livre* finally appeared, printed by Chrestien Wechel of

Paris *A l'escu de Basle*, it was no hole-in-the-corner affair. Unlike the earlier
works which more or less hid behind pseudonyms, the title-page of the
Tiers Livre proudly bears the name of its author: *M. Franç. Rabelais docteur en
Medicine*; the colophon tells us it was printed 'For, and in the name of M.
Franç. Rabelais, doctor of Medicine'. And – final accolade – the *Privilege*
was preceded by a *dixain* from Rabelais's pen, addressed to the ecstatic
spirit of the king's sister, Queen Margaret of Navarre. And this time the
ecstasy is not merely comic; it is a foretaste of things to come.[3]

There are clear signs of a battle of interest between court and the Paris
Parlement where Rabelais was concerned. The catalogue of proscribed
works drawn up by Sorbonne and Parlement was published by the town
criers on 28 June 1545, after nearly two years of delay. In it *Gargantua* and
Pantagruel are condemned. Yet Rabelais's *Privilege* for the *Tiers Livre* was
signed less than three months later; it specifically gave him authority not
only to publish the *Tiers Livre* but to 'correct and revise' the first two books.
It is even an open-ended *Privilege*, in that it gives Rabelais the right to
publish not simply the *Tiers Livre* but *ses dictz livres et œuvres consequens des
faictz heroicques de Pantagruel, commençans au troisieme volume*. In other words,
Rabelais had the king's permission to republish *Gargantua* and *Pantagruel*, to
publish the *Tiers Livre* for the first time – *and* to publish a continuation of the
Tiers Livre itself. (Can this mean that the first version of the *Quart Livre* was
already partly written in 1546?) Despite the royal Privilege the censors
refused to be intimidated: the *Tiers Livre [de] Pantagruel fait par Rabelés
MDXLVI* was included (oddly under the heading of works by unknown
authors) in the supplement to the *Catalogue of Books Censored*, printed by the
faculty of theology of Paris on 31 December 1546. Rabelais was already
safely in Metz, then outside France; safely, but in much reduced
circumstances. Whether he actually fled or found it wise to disappear is not
known.

It was increasingly the practice for books published in Paris to be given a
visa by the censors. At least in theory, even to possess a copy of a book
which had no *visa* was an offence. The *Tiers Livre* first appeared – with its
royal *Privilege* – before Easter 1546, apparently without a *visa*.[4] At least two
other editions appeared during the same year – both without the *visa*. It is
not clear what personal risks Rabelais was running, supported as he was by
Francis I and Margaret of Navarre; but the Sorbonne was certainly going
through a period of aggressive hyperorthodoxy. The writ of the Paris
Parlement did not run directly in Lyons, which remained a safe town for

---

[3] The opening line *A l'Esprit de la royne de Navarre* stresses ecstasy three times: her spirit is
abstraict (*abstractus*: taken outside of her body in ecstasy); *ravy* (ravished in ecstasy) and,
finally, *ecstatic*. The *Tiers Livre* treats such themes sympathetically as well as humorously.
[4] On these and allied subjects mentioned here, consult the study of Robert Marichal,
prefixed to his fascimile of the 1548 *Quart Livre* (*Etudes Rabelaisiennes* IX, 1971, p.135f.).

Rabelais to publish in. Yet it was in Paris, not Lyons, that he chose to publish his new book. Anyway royal policy was fairly consistently to clip the wings of the Parlement by setting against it the growing authority of the more amenable Grand Conseil. Nevertheless, although the *Tiers Livre* duly appeared in Paris, as well as Lyons, in 1546, 1547 and 1552, no Parisian printer seems to have cared to publish *Gargantua* and *Pantagruel* again after the revised editions of 1542.

If Rabelais were cautious that is only too explicable. The secretary of Jean du Bellay, François Bribart – who had played a part in Rabelais's metamorphosis into a secular priest – was burned at the Place Maubert on 8 January 1545, a mere year before the *Tiers Livre* first appeared in print. Tiraqueau, for all his friendship for Rabelais, dropped his flattering allusion to him and omitted his Greek epigram from the revised and expanded edition of *The Laws of Marriage*, the *Privilege* of which is dated 6 January 1546. No wonder that, by March, Rabelais had discreetly left France for Metz. Johannes Sturm, in a letter to Cardinal Jean du Bellay dated 28 March [1546?] lamented that 'we are but men, even when we want to be wiser than others and more experienced. The times have driven Rabelais out of France; fie on such times'. Rabelais went to Metz, an Imperial free city in which Jean du Bellay's agents, Saint-Ayl and Sturm himself, were men of importance (Heulhard, *Rabelais*, 1891, p.224; Rabelais, *Oeuvres*, ed. Marty-Laveaux, III, p.390).

If the Sorbonne had succeeded in suppressing the *Tiers Livre de Pantagruel* they would have deprived the world of what is arguably its most profound comic book. Yet it would be unwise to exaggerate their effective powers. Rabelais might be safely in Metz, but the printers who set up his books in type and then sold them remained in Paris, apparently unharmed and untroubled. Attempts to link the 'state of the times' which had ' driven Rabelais from France' directly with the renewed alliance of Francis I and Charles V against the Lutheran heresy should not be pressed too far. The Treaty of Crépy between the French king and the Holy Roman Emperor was signed a year and a day before Rabelais obtained his royal *Privilege* for the *Tiers Livre*. Insofar as the anti-Lutheran intention of the treaty affected him, it represented no sudden change of government policy in 1546. Nor had Jean du Bellay and his agents given up their aim of detaching the German Lutheran states from the policies of the Holy Roman Emperor and aligning them with the interests of France and with the liberal wing of the Roman Church. But, for whatever cause, Rabelais was in genuine difficulties. He wrote to Cardinal Jean du Bellay from Metz on 6 February [1547?]; the letter was conveyed by Saint-Ayl, one of du Bellay's energetic agents, who had assured Rabelais of the Cardinal's desire to grant him 'some alms':

Certainly, my lord, if you do not have pity on me, I know not what I may do, other than put myself into service of someone over here, with harm and evident loss to my studies. It is not possible to live more frugally than I do. You could not give me too little of the goods which God has put into your hands; that little would help me to get by, barely living and maintaining myself honourably, as I have done up to the present, for the honour of the household from whence I came on leaving France. . .

Such a request for financial help is not without its dignity.

Knowing as we do, if those letters are correctly dated, how Rabelais's life altered sharply for the worse in 1546 after the publication of the *Tiers Livre*, is a matter of hindsight. The *Tiers Livre* itself shows none of these strains. Indeed, if the documents which treat of Rabelais's exile in Metz were not so cogently relevant to this period – despite their absence of year-dates – one would even be tempted to discount them, making them refer to another period of his life. For the *Tiers Livre* is a confident book, a book showing signs of mature reflexion, of leisurely study, of loving care in composition. And however much Rabelais himself may have been at risk, his new book circulated freely, protected as it was by royal authority.

3. *The* Tiers Livre: *a learnedly constructed book*

The *Tiers Livre* divides naturally into several sections. First there is the prologue, much longer than the previous ones, more ambitious and more overtly humanist. Then follows chapter I, which loosely links the new book to *Pantagruel* by referring back to the conquest of Dipsodie; it also makes comments on kingship and colonisation which have relevance to contemporary statecraft. The third section is dominated by Panurge. It consists of a long mock eulogy or encomium, in which Panurge attempts to defend the indefensible by praising debts and debtors. Pantagruel alone supplies his audience and his interlocutor; he expounds a fuller and rounder version of Pantagruelism. The fourth section is an extension of the third; in it Panurge is encouraged to seek a resolution of his hesitations over whether or not to marry – he fears he will be cuckolded, beaten and robbed by his wife if he does. He consults many of the methods of divination respected or feared in Renaissance times. This section stretches from chapter VI to chapter XXV, with an extension into chapters XXVI–XXVIII, during which Frère Jean makes his monkish contribution to Panurge's dilemma. In the course of this section, the book suddenly ceases to be a dialogue between Panurge and Pantagruel. The fifth section abruptly changes the subject, being less concerned with whether Panurge should marry than whether any man should – and with what are the risks of cuckoldry and so on awaiting any married man. It stretches from chapter XXIX-XXXVI. We are treated to a series of consultations with wise scholars: a theologian, a doctor and a philosopher. There are indications that Rabelais conceived these consultations as a transposition, in comic terms, of a Platonic 'banquet' – a *symposium*. Panurge still remains undecided. Worse. He becomes entangled and perplexed. The sixth section moves into the curious territory of Christian folly, a form of enlightened 'madness' which fascinated Renaissance Christians. Two Christian 'madmen' act the wise fool before us: the lawyer Bridoye, who has nothing to do directly with Panurge's worries but who moves the whole question of decision on to a higher plane; then we meet the court fool Triboullet, who, at this late stage, rounds off the fourth section by giving the fullest and best advice to Panurge directly. The seventh section occupies one chapter – XLVII; in it the decision is taken to visit the oracle of the Bottle (an oracle which subsequently becomes not simply La Bouteille but La Dive Bouteille and La Dive Bacbuc). In the eighth section Gargantua brings us back to reality and the direct religio-political propaganda, by making an onslaught against clandestine marriages; again it occupies one chapter only: XLVIII. The ninth and final section is entirely devoted to an enigmatic praise of a mysterious herb, *pantagruelion*, which turns out to be hemp. This curious and arresting comic eulogy stretches from chapter XLIX to the end of the book; it artistically balances Panurge's praise of debts with which the *Tiers Livre* begins after the important introductory matter of chapter I.

It will become clearer that these structural divisions of the *Tiers Livre* are not arbitrary ones. They correspond to several of Rabelais's preoccupations, arising out of his rhetorical, legal and religious studies.

Valid as this outline of the structure of the *Tiers Livre* may be, it gives no idea whatsoever of the variety of the new book, with its surprising paradoxes, its ever-shifting emphases, its astonishing range of comic devices. The book makes great demands upon the reader – greater now, of course, than when it first appeared. Even at the time many found it too hard to manage. But if ever a book was worth the effort required to read it, that book is the *Tiers Livre de Pantagruel*.

4. *The prologue of the* Tiers Livre

The *Tiers Livre*, after making its poetic bow to the emphatically ecstatic spirit of the Queen of Navarre and flourishing its fulsome Royal *Privilege*, starts off with a *Prologue de l'auteur*; the author now is Maistre François Rabelais, with no pseudonym. But Rabelais still does not stand back from his fictional creation in order to tell us soberly in a preface what his aims are. The comic monologue which again forms the totality of the prologue does tell us much about the book, much about Rabelais's hopes and fears in placing his new work before the public, much about the dominant philosophy of the *Tiers Livre*. Yet the real scholarly Dr Rabelais still does not talk to the reader directly; he continues to wear a mask as certainly in the prologue to his third Chronicle as he did in the two earlier ones. This time, the mask he adopts is that of a modern Diogenes, energetically rolling his barrel while others defend the kingdom.

This choice of Diogenes is interesting for several reasons.

First of all, it links the *Tiers Livre* to both *Pantagruel* and to *Gargantua*: when Epistemon visited the underworld in *Pantagruel* he found there a world turned upside down: those who had once been great lords on earth were eking a subterranean living in a multitude of lowly comic jobs, while an élite of philosophers and good men who had been poor in this world had become great lords. The chosen few form an attractive group: Diogenes, Pathelin, the Gallican theorist Jean Lemaire de Belges and François Villon. In 1534 they were joined by Epictetus the Stoic. In this underworld, Diogenes enjoys lording it over Alexander the Great, the man of power he had once snubbed so famously. This is the character, as seen through the eyes of Lucian and Budé, who dominates the new prologue.

The episode of Epistemon's visit to the underworld is in keeping with the spirit of *Pantagruel*. But Diogenes, even when seen from accounts in Lucian's *True History*, was a complex character for any Renaissance humanist who was on the lookout for deeper meanings. In the commentary on the adage 'The Sileni of Alcibiades', Erasmus (just after the passage which also inspired the prologue to *Gargantua* with its praise of the divine wisdom of Socrates) picked out two characters for special praise: Diogenes, a *Silenus* purer in soul than Alexander the Great, and Epictetus, dear to the gods for the purity of his life and the wisdom of his philosophy. Diogenes and Epictetus were almost certainly interpolated into the 1534 *Pantagruel* at the same time as Rabelais was working on the prologue to *Gargantua*. His source was doubtless, in both cases, the same text of Erasmus. Here is a strong hint that even in *Pantagruel* (not least in 1534) Rabelais had taken the Cynic Diogenes to be more than a 'dog'; with Erasmus he saw him as a philosopher worthy to be placed beside Epictetus, the first-century Stoic sage whom Christians honoured for his resistance to Nero. Both Diogenes the Cynic and Epictetus the Stoic are *Sileni* worthy to be cited by Erasmus in the same breath as Christ, the most wonderful (*mirificus*) *Silenus* of them all. The *Tiers Livre* is marked by a Christian version of both Stoicism and Cynicism, taking these ideas one stage further than *Pantagruel* and *Gargantua*. It is also, even more so, a work of Christian scepticism.

The *Tiers Livre* is more marked by Christian Stoicism, perhaps, than by Christian Cynicism, though both find their place in this eclectic work. Diogenes is not out of place in such a book; long since he had become almost as much a hero for the Stoics as for the Cynics; he can rightly head a book whose hero marries together the philosophy of Christ and markedly Stoic-flavoured wisdom inspired by the ancient world. An eclectic respect for the ancients led Erasmus to see Socrates, Diogenes and Epictetus not as professors of rival philosophical schools but collectively as *Sileni* in some way prefiguring the hidden wisdom of Christ, the Man who had no beauty that we should desire him. Rabelais, deeply influenced by Erasmus in general and by the 'Sileni of Alcibiades' in particular, does the same (Erasmus: *Adagia* III, 3, 1; especially *Opera Omnia*, 1703–6, II, col. 771).

Immediately after citing the example of Diogenes in the first sentence of the prologue to the *Tiers Livre*, Rabelais passes on to a smiling allusion to Ecclesiastes – which is by far the most sceptical book of the whole Bible – and then on to the blind man of the Synoptic Gospels whose sight was given him by Christ – by 'him who is Almighty, and whose word is in a moment made apparent'. It is hard to find an expression which more fully and gratuitously emphasises the godhead of Christ than this paraphrase, which expands the simple name of *Jesus* in St Mark whose Gospel is Rabelais's direct source. The link between Diogenes and the blind man of the Gospels seems to lie in their common acceptance of basic priorities. Diogenes showed how few are the things that man needs to live fully and well; the blind man, by asking Christ not for riches or power but for the natural gift of sight, shows the same thing more authoritatively.

The readers for whom the *Tiers Livre* was written would have seen more in this allusion to Diogenes placed at the very beginning of the prologue. First of all they may be supposed to have recognised Rabelais's source of the comparison in Lucian's *True History* and to have wondered whether Rabelais were inviting comparison between his works and Lucian's. The many readers who had studied law would have seen a parallel in the use made of Lucian's Diogenes by Budé, in the preface to the *Annotations on the Pandects*. The *Tiers Livre* is a book which presupposes a genuine knowledge of Renaissance law; both many of its jests and much of its erudition and Christian wisdom draw heavily on legal knowledge and arise out of reflexion on legal texts. A place of honour is reserved for a philosophy of religious madness which owes a great deal to Guillaume Budé; Rabelais's philosophy of language has legal terms of reference; and so on. Budé, precisely in the Preface to the *Annotations on the Pandects* which Rabelais and his learned readers had in mind in more than one passage of the *Tiers Livre*, exploits the theme of Diogenes and his barrel in a way closely analogous to that of Rabelais, whose choice of words proves that he was following him directly.[5] Was Rabelais suggesting that his new book was, in some ways, just as important as Budé's? If so, later judgements would support his contention. With both Lucian and Budé open before him, he uses the example of Diogenes rolling his barrel up and down the Cranian Hill outside Corinth as justification for writing his book, while great political and military matters were being energetically pursued all round him.

Budé of course writes with the restraint due to the Latin language and a legal preface. Rabelais uses Budé's Lucianic text as a peg on which to hang an example of comic copiousness, partly designed to make us laugh at language itself when detached from conventional meaning. Noticing the military activity of all about him, as France set about mending her frontiers and establishing a chain of fortresses well able to defend the kingdom and render France *superbement bournée*, Rabelais, with all the resources of his art, makes his excuses for doing nothing but write a masterpiece. The laughter is erudite, playing on such classical commonplaces as the lecherousness of Corinthian women given over to the worship of Venus. A series of puns raise much innocent laughter from sexually ambiguous military expressions. But most striking of all, a cascade of words succeeds in giving us an impression of purposeful activity on the part of the military Corinthians, while another cascade of words – used for their sound not their sense – leads us both to see and to hear Diogenes trundling his barrel up hill and down dale in a flurry of apparently purposeless activity. But the activity is not purposeless. Rabelais (all of whose novels contain some statement about war relevant to the time in which they were published) takes care to dissociate himself from those 'pickers-over of old Latin scrap-iron' who assert that war was called 'bellum' by antiphrasis (since it was anything but beautiful, *bellum*). War can be the means of showing, in a Platonic alliance of words, the 'good and the beautiful' for what they are; for showing up, too, the bad and the ugly. Not that Rabelais has become a warmonger: France's military activity on both sides of the Alps he saw as a means of bringing peace and security to the kingdom, an aim in keeping with the wisdom of the peaceful Solomon, who, in the *Song of Songs*, anagogically compared the unutterable perfection of the divine wisdom to 'an army with banners'. The starting-point of this important praise of the good and the beauty which can come out of war is yet another classical adage, *War is the Father of all things*. Duly catalogued by Erasmus, it is mainly associated with Lucian's *True History*; Erasmus (no lover of war) believes it to mean that war encourages the renewal of all things (*TL, TLF*, prol., 133f.; *EC* 118f.; Erasmus, *Adagia* III, 5, 36).

[5] *TL* prol., *TLF* 100, *EC* 84; Rabelais's Diogenes *roula son tonneau fictil* (rolled his 'fictile', that is, his *earthenware*, barrel). Cf. Budé, basing himself on the same text of Lucian: *dolium illud suum fictile* (*Opera* III, sig. alpha 3).

Fate has left Rabelais, he tells us, with no resources apart from his art. His only source of inspiration (*Enthusiasme*) lies in his draughts of wine. In this he bears out the truth of the saying, *He is no dithyrambist who drinks water.* This adage (the explanation of which by Erasmus Rabelais takes over in his prologue) appears just before *To act like a Corinthian.* There is in this prologue a mildly Bacchic quality; Rabelais may indeed compare himself to Diogenes and invite us to use the adjectives *Pantagruelicque* and *Diogenicque* as though they were interchangeable; but *his* barrel contains wine, not the water which sufficed for Diogenes. As we saw, Alcofrybas Nasier was formerly described as Pantagruel's *Architriclinus.* Now Rabelais is, in his own name, the *Architriclinus* of the gallant French warriors, alluding once more to Christ's first miracle, changing water into wine. That is partly why, a few sentences later, he invites his readers not to fear that *his* wine will run out as did the wine at the marriage of Cana in Galilee. That Rabelais liked his glass of wine seems certain enough; his frequent references to wine are not always metaphorical; but, here at least, the word is used metaphorically for 'un vray Cornucopie de joyeuseté et raillerie'. And since, in the *Tiers Livre,* Rabelais does change some of the more brackish waters of Renaissance pedantry and scholarship into the wine of intellectual comedy, the *plus hault sens* of the allusion seems very appropriate.

In general the prologue appears assured, gay and poised. But there is another side to it. Rabelais expresses fears that his new book may be too 'monstrous' to be understood and fully appreciated. He retells after Lucian the tale of Ptolemy, son of Lagus, who had hoped to win the love of the Egyptians by showing them a rare, black, Bactrian camel and a curiously bi-coloured slave. The Egyptians reacted with mockery, hostility and contempt. This example made Rabelais vary between hope and fear: his book is of a new kind, with no model against which it could be judged; it is a new and monstrous mixture of laughter and seriousness. With a hostility which is only partly comic, he allowed himself to select the readers he wants. As a new Diogenes he takes up his stick to drive off venal judges, ignorant lawyers and pox-ridden, tippling, gluttonous hypocrites – the *caphards* of his previous books. They are not only evil, but diabolical, being servants of that Evil One from whom we beg to be delivered in our daily prayers. This evocation of the last clause of the Lord's Prayer is quite powerful. So too is the passing from the comic *Goutteux* ('Poxy Blades') of Rabelaisian jest to truly syphilitic hypocrites; from the gentle civilised wine of Rabelaisian delight and metaphor to the *altération inextinguible* of his ugly enemies; from the simple comic feastings and bucolic gorgings which Rabelais had made a feature of his earlier comedy, to the *manducation insatiable* of his diabolical foes. We are told that the chief enemies are *caphards*; the fact that they 'sometimes counterfeit tramps' suggests that these hypocrites were professed religious, especially those of the mendicant orders.

Ptolemy, son of Lagus, and his ill-fated attempts to amuse, worried Rabelais as they worried Lucian before him. But it would be an inadequate reading of the new prologue to see in the example of Ptolemy no more than anxieties about the reception of a book which combined philosophy and laughter in a 'monstrous' genre new to the Renaissance public. It has a more precise import.

The prologue to the *Tiers Livre* opens with allusions to Lucian's Diogenes, closes with an allusion to Lucian's Ptolemy. Lucian is being paraded as source and model. Alerted by this we may be inclined to look more closely at Lucian's works.

The story of Ptolemy, son of Lagus, dominates Lucian's short dialogue entitled, *To one who said to him, 'You are a Prometheus in words'*. This little work expounds his worries about the reception awaiting the new genre he formed out of the marriage of comedy and dialogue. Before Lucian, dialogue was the preserve of philosophy and therefore poles apart from comedy.

Any reader of the *Tiers Livre* who knows *You are a Prometheus in words* must be struck by the appropriateness of Rabelais's allusion.[6] The *Tiers Livre* is quite unlike *Gargantua* and *Pantagruel* in that its first thirteen chapters are *entirely* given over to a sustained comic dialogue. There are only two interlocutors: Panurge and Pantagruel. Nobody else is present. Nobody is even lurking in the wings. Not until the last sentence of chapter XIII is Frère Jean brought in to say a few unimportant things. We are given not one word of explanation for his sudden appearance. Then, in haste, and again without a word of explanation, the companions are mentioned one after another: Epistemon, Frère Jean, Ponocrates, Eudemon, Carpalim 'and others'.

From then on the *Tiers Livre* ceases to be a comic dialogue between two characters only. But for its first quarter it was nothing else; and the following three-quarters are largely given over to monologue, dialogue and conversation generally. The author of the *Tiers Livre* felt the urge to recreate Lucian's art of philosophico-comic satirical dialogue in French. Like Lucian he felt anxieties about the reception of such a new *genre*, so he turned to Lucian for means of showing this too.

[6] Lucian, *Works*, Loeb ed. (1959) 1968, VI, p.424: 'I am afraid that my work too is a camel in Egypt [. . .] since even the combination of two very fine creations, dialogue and comedy, is not enough for the beauty of form if the blending lacks harmony and symmetry. The synthesis of two fine things can be a freak. . . .' Dialogue and comedy do not naturally go together: Dialogue 'used to sit at home', while 'comedy gave himself to Dionysus and joined him in the theatre, had fun with him' and so on. Readers might like to study the whole of this short work of Lucian's with the *Tiers Livre* in mind.

Pantagruelism is defined in the prologue (*TLF* 255; *EC* 204) as a 'specific and individual quality' known to our ancestors; as, that is, a natural disposition belonging to mankind as a species and to each man as an individual person. This quality, akin it seems both to laughter as a property of man and to Christian charity, leads us never to take exception to anything whatsoever which has its origin in a 'good, frank and loyal heart'. This charity does not pretend that evil is good, or that good and evil do not matter. Rabelais, for all his Pantagruelism, never confounds the boundaries of good and evil. But Pantagruelism does take note of intentions and of goodness of heart. The fuller force of this is not realised until later, when Pantagruel explains how the mind of man is a battleground for good and evil spirits, a notion particularly at home in the platonising Christianity which, from sub-Apostolic times, endowed each man with two personal angels: a good one prompting him towards the good and the beautiful; an evil one, seeking to lead him, *via* evil and ugliness, to eternal damnation. Such notions appealed to tough-minded humanist lawyers as much as to theologians and moral philosophers. The *Tiers Livre* opposes, with sustained art and unswerving clarity, the good and the beautiful on one side; the bad and the ugly on the other. In this sense it takes over where *Gargantua* left off.[7] The harshest condemnation of all is reserved for those who 'turn the white into black'. Such immoral and skilful spinners of words mislead the good, the faithful, the unwary and can even tie the wiser men in knots. They are a real butt of the philosophical laughter of the *Tiers Livre*. The chief of these is Panurge. Many accepted Cicero's definition of dialectic (*De Oratore* II, 157) as the art of discussion, the end of which was to distinguish between the true and the false (*ars disserendi . . . cujus finis est verum a falso discernere*). Panurge, by using his rhetorical gifts not to arrive at truth but to cloud the issues, is serving devilish ends. But Rabelais succeeds in making us laugh at him; we are not led by his diabolical skill into the lesser ways of fear and trembling.

[7] For the good and bad angels, see *Regula S. P. Benedicti, cum commentariis* by Martène: *Patrologia Latina* LXVI, col. 272 BC. The belief that men have two angels 'of which one is a good one, given as a guardian, the other a bad one, given as a trial' is expounded with reference to the Book of Hermas, Origen, Bede, etc. Catholics are certain of the good angel; the bad is more controversial. Maldonatus discusses this (*Commentaria in Quatuor Evangelistas*, Venice 1597, col. 413). The source of the doctrine is Matthew 18,10: 'Take heed that ye despise not these little ones; for I say unto you, That in heaven their angels (*angeli eorum*) do always behold the face of my Father which is in heaven.' The good angel, he notes, is certain, although the Calvinists deny it, saying that all angels are concerned with all men, not being allocated one for one. The bad angel is supported by Hebrew tradition (Rabbi Moses) as well as the Shepherd of Hermas and the apocryphal Epistle of Barnabas. 'And it is credible that the Devil, the prince of the demons, should, in the administering of his kingdom [the world] imitate God; and just as God sets individual angels above individual men, so Satan should oppose them by individual demons.'

The terms which Pantagruel uses to condemn Panurge are helpful here.
They suggest – as indeed does so much else in Panurge's rôle in this book –
that Panurge is above all conceived, so far as his talk is concerned, as a bad
rhetorician within the definitions of Quintilian. He is a fluent speaker,
more given to monologue than to the cut and thrust of good classical
dialectic. When Panurge has talked non-stop for two whole chapters (III
and IV), Pantagruel finally makes his comment on all this verbiage at the
outset of chapter V:

'I understand (replied Pantagruel); you seem to me to be a good topicker, devoted
to your cause. But preach and plead from now to Pentecost, yet in the end you will
be astonished to find you have persuaded me not at all; by your fair speech you will
never get me to run into debt . . . You use me here fair *graphides* and *diatyposes*, and
they please me well enough . . .'

But persuade him to borrow money, except in cases of unforeseen
disaster? Never.

The word *topiqueur* might imply that Rabelais was holding Panurge up to
ridicule primarily as a bad dialectician, since a 'topicker' – a student of the
Topics – was a student of dialectic. In my edition of the *Tiers Livre* (1964) I
woefully underplayed dialectic at the expense of rhetoric, having only just
seen the relevance to Rabelais of Aristotle's *Peri Hermeneias* and its exegetes.
Nevertheless Panurge is presented in his praise of debts and debtors mainly
as a rhetorician. What he seeks to do is to 'persuade' (*persuader*) by his 'fair
speech' (*beau parler*). His declamation is an example of suasive rhetoric. The
figures of speech which Pantagruel notices – his *graphides* and *diatyposes* – are
rhetorical ones, aimed at decorating an oration. His monologue is a *cause* –
a *causa* – a term of rhetoric as well as a term of law. (In Quintilian it is used as
the Latin equivalent to the Greek *hypothesis*, in the sense of a definite
question.) Similarly, the problem which besets Panurge, *Should he marry?*, is
one which Quintilian, amongst others, cites as a standard rhetorical theme
(III, 5, 16). On the other hand Pantagruel does call his wordy and argumentative follower a *topiqueur* – and a knowledge of the *Topics* is one of his
boasts (*TL* V, 5; XXVIII, 20f.).

Perhaps it is best, in a book when law is so dominant, to accept as a guide
the divisions we find in such treatises as Hegendorphinus's *Dialectica Legalis*
(Paris 1547 edition), in which quite a deal of space is devoted to
distinguishing between dialectic and rhetoric. In most cases Panurge comes
closer to the conception of the rhetorician. It is not simply that he has
nothing of the Janotus de Bragmardo in him – at his worst he is no chopper
of logic in the wake of the *Parva Logicalia* – for there is a classical dialectic
in Cicero and Aristotle for him to abuse, purer and more attractive than
that of the mediaeval scholastics. But Hegendorphinus and others follow

Cicero in seeing dialectic as a condensed form of eloquence (*contracta et quasi adstricta eloquentia*). He adds that 'rhetoric is truly a kind of dialectic', but it 'disputes on a matter with many words, varying the bare face, as it were, of dialectical subjects with rhetorical figures (*schemata*)'. The standard contrast was between dialectic as a concise form of speech, whose image was the closed fist; rhetoric, an ample flood of elegant words, its image an open palm. In Quintilian's terms (II, 20, 7) Panurge is more adept at the *oratio perpetua* (continuous speech) of the rhetoricians than at the *oratio concisa* (broken up, short, concise speech) of the adepts of dialectic.[8]

All Panurge's verbiage is swept aside by Pantagruel with the revealed wisdom of Scripture, elaborated by inspired philosophy.

5. *The themes of the* Tiers Livre

The original public, in 1546, read the book in isolation: it was a sequel to the two previous Chronicles but not published with them. In 1547 it found its place as the third book in a collected edition, beginning with *Gargantua*. Ever since, the *Tiers Livre* has normally been read after *Pantagruel* not *Gargantua*.

The pleasurable aesthetic shock we feel in passing from *Pantagruel* to *Gargantua* is nothing compared with what we feel when passing from *Pantagruel* to the *Tiers Livre*. This shock was clearly intended. Despite its humanist typography, despite its elegance and its philosophical ambitions, the *Tiers Livre* lightly and paradoxically picks up the threads of *Pantagruel* and twists them unexpectedly into the stuff of a very different book. Why Rabelais wanted to do this can only be inferred. He could so easily have managed without both Panurge and Pantagruel, as he did in *Gargantua*, inventing new characters for his new book. Until Frère Jean makes his first fleeting and comparatively trivial appearance, the *Tiers Livre* is essentially a comic and dramatic debate between two characters who are indeed called Panurge and Pantagruel; but this new Pantagruel and this new Panurge have hardly anything in common with their original namesakes. It was Maistre Alcofrybas who was rewarded with the Manor of Salmigondin in *Pantagruel*, a rôle now assumed (without a word of explanation) by Panurge. Alcofrybas Nasier does not appear in the *Tiers Livre*, though he will surface in the *Quart Livre*. Gargantua, who in *Pantagruel* had been

---

[8] Consult (apart, of course, from Quintilian and Cicero) Valla, *Dialecticae Disputationes* (in *Opera*, Basle 1540); Christopher Hegendorphinus, *Dialectica legalis, Francisci Jametii diligentia repurgata* (together with Calcagnini's *commentarii*), Paris 1547. A work I have found particularly useful is Mario Nizolio's *De veris principiis et vera ratione philosophandi contra pseudophilosophos*, edited by Quirinus Breen (*Edizione Nazionale dei Classici del Pensiero Italiano*, Rome 1956.)

whisked out of this world like Enoch and Elijah and borne away to the Land of the Faeries, unexpectedly walks on to the stage halfway through the book completely changed into that philosopher-king we could expect him to become from the rôle he played at the end of *Gargantua*. We can further note that while the first chapter of the *Tiers Livre* ostensibly deals with the wise measures taken by the victorious Pantagruel and his Utopians at the end of the conquest of Dipsodie, the political tone of the chapter has far more in common both with the serious reflexions on king-ship, and politics generally, which brought the episode of the war against Picrochole to a close in *Gargantua*, and with the realities of Guillaume de Bellay's royally supported military aims of a France happily secure within its powerfully defended natural boundaries.

Rabelais seems to want us to see that the comic mould of *Pantagruel*, with its gay and largely amoral laughter, has been finally broken; that the pieces are now rearranged and the rôles re-distributed; that the passage we saw in *Gargantua* from a world of burlesque giants to a world more akin to real life has now been completed. This change is emphasised by the conscious humanism of the first chapter of the *Tiers Livre*, with its sustained indebtedness to Plutarch – from now on a major influence on Rabelais's art and thought – with its citing of Hesiod, Homer, Virgil and a string of classical names – Jupiter, Pamyla, Alexander of Macedonia, Thrasybulus and so on; with its classical gods interpreted euhemeristically as great men of old. There is an easy use of Greek terms *Demovore* (Dēmoboros), 'Devourer of the People'; *Evergetes* (Euergetes), 'Benefactor'; *kosmētor laōn*, which Rabelais renders 'Ornament of the Peoples'.

Rabelais's concept of the ideal general or the ideal monarch is close to Erasmus's thought in such an important adage as *The Beetle Searches for the Eagle*, a fact which forges another link with the end of the Picrocholine War in *Gargantua* rather than with the war against the Dipsodes in *Pantagruel*. The giant's newly enhanced moral and philosophical stature takes over and develops further characteristics increasingly attributed to his father in *Gargantua*. In the case of Panurge the change amounts to a positive transfiguration. From being the accomplice of Pantagruel, a man able to eclipse his master, a man on whom his master can call for aid in a decisive moment in battle, he becomes the antithesis of all that Pantagruel stands for. It is no doubt partly to emphasise this fundamental change in the concept of a character who is to dominate two thirds of the book, that chapters II to XII are given over to a confrontation between Panurge and Pantagruel, which guides our laughter authoritatively into desired philosophical channels by telling us a great deal about the new Panurge, his speech and his ways.

The *Tiers Livre* is a book about decision and indecision; it centres round the problem of how men can, or cannot, reach right decisions in a divinely

ordained universe in which God reigns supreme but the Devil remains
prince of this world. Within this framework we are treated to a complex
series of kaleidoscopic episodes, artistically interconnected in the most
skilful of fashions, episodes which start as often as not from dry-as-dust
controversies or obscurities in Renaissance law, medicine, theology or
philosophy, all of which are almost miraculously changed by the genius of
laughter into a source of comic insight into problems human and divine.

Panurge is presented as a man defeated by his problems; his argumentative skill, his unwise erudition, serve only to obscure issues not to resolve
them. But his character – one of the main comic vehicles of the book – is
not suddenly revealed all at one go; it is unrolled for us as the book
progresses and as Panurge's indecision leads him deeper and deeper into
those darker, madder areas of the mind where the Devil has his sway. The
man whose hollow confidence in his verbose parody of wisdom leads him
at the outset of his quest for certainty to proclaim 'It is from me that
counsel must be sought' (*TL*, *TLF* II, 55), is soon shown begging advice
which he can never bring himself to accept or profit by, spiritually blinded
as he is by qualities and forces recognised as evil by the inspired philosophy
of Greece and the revealed wisdom of Christianity.

In many ways the *Tiers Livre* is Panurge's book; he and his dilemma
dominate the stage from chapter II to chapter XXXVIII. But from then on
he is virtually eclipsed, except for his climactic consultation with the court
fool Triboullet in chapter XLV. This is a reminder of a vital fact: although
the *Tiers Livre* can indeed loosely be called Panurge's book, the book itself is
greater and profounder than any problem which Panurge alone could
conceivably represent.

Panurge is no Rabelaisian Hamlet, a good man driven distracted by
hesitation, unable to distinguish for certain between a spirit of health or
goblin damned. He is a fool from start to finish, a darker and more
disturbing fool as diabolical madness takes over his mind. His folly is
always laughable, but, progressively, far from merely laughable.

6. The praise of debts and debtors

Panurge appears as essentially a new character from chapter II, where he
embarks upon his praise of debts and debtors. This carefully structured
eulogy is not so much a satirical one as a comic one, akin to some of the
classical models which inspired Erasmus to write his *Praise of Folly*. It is a
lusus, a 'game', a mock encomium, a comic declamation. Comic encomiums were much appreciated by Renaissance admirers of Lucian and
Erasmus. They are written with great art, despite the convention which
encouraged authors to present them as little trifles thrown off in a moment
of idleness or whilst on a journey separated from one's books. As often as

not the literary framework of a comic encomium conforms to the artistic
ideal represented by Lucian, as well as to the advice which Aphthonius or
Quintilian gave for the proper ordering of a serious eulogy. Not least in the
Renaissance, the audience for which a comic encomium was written was a
knowledgeable one, appreciative of the niceties of rhetorical elaboration.
Panurge's *Praise of Debts* is no exception. Rabelais shows himself to be
at home with both the *Progymnasmata* of Aphthonius and the *Rhetoric* of
Quintilian, works which freed humanists from scholastic stylistics.

Panurge (whom we last met in *Pantagruel*, some fourteen years earlier,
mocking the defeated King Anarche of Dipsodia) has now become an
object of intellectual laughter. He ostensibly sets out to prove that it is
mutual indebtedness which makes the world go round; that the 'little
world', the microcosm, of man, like the 'great world', the macrocosm, of
the Universe, is maintained in harmony by mutual indebtedness, without
which man's body, his *persona*, the entire human race, the vast sublunary
world, the whole fabric of the Universe, would collapse and their
harmony clash into discord.

Whether Rabelais himself took these ideas seriously cannot be told from
Panurge's praise of debts alone. A mock eulogy intermingles arguments of
all sorts, ranging from self-evident error to wilful misapplications of
arguments which, when properly used, are worthy of profound respect.
The general context of the ideas which Panurge outrageously misapplies is
a Platonic one, with more than a nod towards Ficino's *Commentary on Plato's
Symposium*, in which love is said to bind the world together. I doubt
whether Rabelais took Ficino's Commentary without a large pinch of salt –
it muddles together so many types of love. The Platonic system, in a purer,
less Ficinian form, he seems to have held in the great veneration we would
expect from a platonising Christian. But the whole point of large tracts of
Panurge's praise of debts is that he misapplies arguments which, when
properly applied, would condemn him out of hand. The peculiar intellectual mixture which Panurge misapplies in his eulogy – to his readers'
great delight – is strongly reminiscent of parts of Pomponazzi's treatise *On
the Immortality of the Soul*, which intertwines arguments and themes
borrowed from Platonic sources and from Galen's medical writings.
Pomponazzi may have been one of the sources which Rabelais drew upon
when seeking material for Panurge to misuse in his outrageous eulogy. On
the other hand, the ideas are too much a part of Renaissance philosophical
commonplaces for them to be easily traceable to one single source. It is the
very fact that they are venerated commonplaces which makes the reader
able to smile as he sees through the deceptions and self-deceptions of
Panurge's suasive rhetoric.[9]

[9] In *Pant.* (*TLF* XIII, 62; *EC* XVIII, 55), Pantagruel declined to 'dispute by declamations as

A comic eulogy is successful in so far as we realise that it is comic. It would be aesthetically and even morally disastrous if Lucian's encomiums of the parasite or of the cruel tyrant Phalaridis were taken straight! Rabelais is concerned to imprint upon the reader's mind the new rôle he has given to Panurge – that of the foolishly erudite spinner of words who can turn black into white by crafty argument. He carefully stacks the cards against him. That the praise of debts is a mock eulogy is clear from the outset: it follows hard upon the presentation of Pantagruel in his new rôle as the Stoico-Christian sage, calmly secure within his God-given reason and totally unmoved by all that the world contains. Panurge is soon defending his case by reference to the University of Paris of all places! For him Rabelais's *bête noire* is the fountain-head of 'all theology', of *panthéologie*. (The word recalls the title of an old-fashioned treatise of *Pantheologia*, which enjoyed some success in the 1470s.) Panurge, an admirer of old error and of the Sorbonne, has learned his lessons well, crying 'Heretic!' against those who will not believe him. As the chapters succeed each other we see that he is acting against the most authoritative doctrines of ancient and Christian wisdom, wisdom polished and refined in apophthegm and adage. Against all this Panurge marshals arguments which show his case to be so much laughable nonsense. But the laughter he arouses is not the safe, clear, cut-and-dried laughter provoked by Janotus de Bragmardo and his exploded scholastic chop-logic. Panurge is not a scholastic fool: he is an erudite one as humanists were erudite. His errors are altogether more serious because of this.

On the portals of the oracle of Delphi which declared Socrates to be the wisest of mortals were inscribed three commandments as influential as the ten given to the Jews on Mount Horeb. They were:

> Know thyself;
> Nothing to excess;
> The companion of borrowing and litigation is wretchedness.

Throughout the *Tiers Livre* Panurge will be shown as acting against these divinely revealed maxims. Naturally, in the eulogy of debts and debtors it is the third of these injunctions which is being most openly broken; but in fact they all are. For while Panurge is ostensibly defending a Ficinian conception of a universe based on mutual love and harmony in delicate balance, he is using these fashionable and attractive ideas as a smoke-

---

the Academics did'. That is just what Panurge is doing here, but no early humanist dismisses the *declamatio* in its entirety; there are good and bad ones in Rabelais's Chronicles. (The treatise of Pomponazzi has been translated into English: E. Cassirer, *The Renaissance Philosophy of Man*, Chicago 1948; J. Randall: *Pomponazzi on Immortality* XIV, pp.350f.)

screen: the debts that he is really defending are common-or-garden money ones; and they are all one-way debts: money he has borrowed and never intends to repay. In other words, an improvident pleasure-loving Panurge, with his tongue in his cheek, is striving to make out a case for borrowing money which his creditors will never see again. A culture which gave pride of place to the Greek adage *Blessed is he who owes nothing* could be in no doubt about the criminal folly of what he is doing (Erasmus, *Adagia* II, 7, 98: *Felix qui nihil debet*).

That he is wilfully on the wrong tack is emphasised by the heading of the chapter in which his eulogy abruptly begins: *Comment Panurge . . . mangeoit son bled en herbe*, which tells us how Panurge squandered his resources by selling off his corn when it was merely green sprouting shoots. The expression *manger son blé en herbe* is a proverbial one: Panurge was (as we would say) eating the very seed-corn. Such conduct, amusingly and of course unconvincingly defended by Panurge, goes right against Persius's adage, *Messe tenus propria vive* – 'Live within your own harvest' (Erasmus, *Adagia* I, 7, 88). Panurge is improvident, running up debts which he can never repay in order to finance his immediate, sensual pleasures based on extremes of self-loving indulgence. We are delighted by his impudence when he proclaims that his rash and improvident conduct conforms to the four cardinal virtues of prudence, justice, fortitude and temperance, as well as to the three theological virtues of faith, hope and charity. We are morally satisfied when Pantagruel condemns such profligacy by calling upon the adage *Proterviam fecit* as Erasmus explains it. Protervia is shameless imprudence and wantonness. Rabelais reminds readers that the Protervian Feast was in some ways like the Passover, in that all food that cannot be eaten must be destroyed, leaving nothing for the morrow. Panurge is wantonly squandering his resources like some foolish Roman at such an imprudent feast. Rabelais follows Erasmus in contrasting such shameless extravagance with the wise provisions of Roman sumptuary laws which regulated expenditure and moderated luxury (Erasmus, *Adagia* I, 9, 44).

Panurge sees himself as a little tin god, creating debts *ex nihilo*, where nothing was before. Humanist readers would have known where he found this particular gem of wisdom! It is taken straight out of Plutarch's treatise entitled *Do not Borrow*, which dominates Erasmus's explanation of the adage *Blessed is he who owes nothing*. (Plutarch's treatise is a great help to our understanding of Rabelais's wise commonplaces).

Panurge shares with other characters in Rabelais who admire the Sorbonne a taste for cant and a positive genius for twisting moral maxims. When he cuts down his timber – until very recent times *the* visible sign of the improvident squire – it is in order to turn his land into fair barren moorland, incapable of hiding outlaws known to lurk in shady forests;

when he defends, in the name of distributive justice, his late-night banquets with the local girlies, he outrageously claims that his girl-friends were following the moral dictates of one of the greatest of the Romans and one of the greatest of the Greeks: had not Cicero quoted with approval Plato's saying *Nemo sibi nascitur*, according to which 'No one is born for himself alone', since part of our birth is legally claimed by our country, part by our friends: *partem vendicat patria, partem amici?* Similarly Panurge's girl-friends 'do not believe that they were born into this world for themselves alone, but keep a part of themselves for their country . . . and a part for their friends'. We can guess which part (*TL* II; *TLF* 88f; *EC* 68f.; Erasmus, *Adagia* IV, 6, 81).

This comic misapplication of *Nemo sibi nascitur*, one of the most authoritative of ancient maxims, is a good example of a technique which Rabelais probably learned from Erasmus's *Praise of Folly*, where Folly (when actually speaking foolishly) misuses Plato's myth about the cave in which men dwell in ignorance, only to use it properly and tellingly later on, in the moral climax to the eulogy where mere folly is replaced by the heights of Christian folly. So too, in a moral climax to the *Tiers Livre*, Pantagruel will show what the maxim *Nemo sibi nascitur* really means, syncretising it with evangelical doctrine in the true Christian humanist tradition. (See below, p.256.)

That Rabelais should have chosen to reveal the new Panurge to us through his long monologue in praise of the indefensible is in keeping with an important Renaissance belief that speech is a mirror of character. The platonising smoke-screen eventually parts to reveal a Panurge as comically coarse as young Gargantua once was, before he was taken in hand and purged of his error. Just at the point where Panurge is about to be reduced to joking about anuses, wind breaking and other tokens of the viler aspects of our humanity, Pantagruel reminds us of our higher aspirations, finally squashing Panurge with St Paul's command to 'Owe no man anything but mutual *agapē*' (Christian love), bringing to bear infallible scripture on to a problem already largely resolved by appeal to the authority of Plato as developed by Plutarch. Plutarch was an authority whom Bishop Amyot also thought fit to place beside scripture (as indeed did Erasmus who, like Rabelais, often expands a peremptory Evangelical precept with the elegant help of the *Moralia*). The delicate ears of princes (Amyot tells us) are sometimes offended by the imperious commands of scripture. Plutarch and other ancient moralists, who sought – like Rabelais we might add – *à plaire ensemble et à profiter*, enter more easily into royal ears because of the beauty of their language and their numerous *exempla*.[10]

[10] *TL* V (*TLF* 9; *EC* 7). Cf. Plutarch as translated by Amyot (*Oeuvres Morales et Meslées*, 1572, reprint Wakefield, 1971; especially, I, pp.130 and 131 – a major source of Rabelais's condemnation of Panurge's borrowing proclivities.

Panurge's reaction to Pantagruel's syncretic truth and beauty is to break wind, it being vulgarly current then to say *Voy là pour les quittes* ('That's for those who are out of debt') when loudly doing so. This descent to bodily grossness is in keeping with a standard comic device which Cicero noted and which underlies all of Panurge's eulogy: taking higher or metaphorical ideas in a literal or physical sense. Not that there was ever a higher sense to the coarse jesting of *Voy là pour les quittes*; but the praise of debts, which Panurge affected to conceive of in Platonic terms and to develop with high-flown rhetorical elaboration, ends up with the language of the jakes (*TL* v). There is indeed much of the Old Adam, of the original coarse Gargantua, in the freshly redrawn Panurge.

After reading a few chapters of the *Tiers Livre* the perceptive reader is made quite aware that Panurge is a fool by what he actually says. As early as chapter II readers are alerted to Panurge's wrong-headedness by his praise of the Sorbonne! And he dares cheekily to misuse one of the most venerable arguments of Cato in favour of prudent and frugal economy.[11]

Pantagruel's reaction to Panurge's grossness is to order him, for the second time, to shut up. The taciturnity of Pantagruel in the presence of Panurge, his repeated silences, are proof of his wisdom; as Plutarch noted, quoting Euripides: 'Silence is the answer wise men make.' The wise man has arguments and *exempla* ready, but he does not waste them on irrational men (*Oeuvres morales*, trans. Amyot, I, 179 BC).

Stultus stulta loquitur (*Adagia* I, 1, 98): 'A fool speaks foolish things.' What Panurge says is the express image of his character. Erasmus in his comment on this adage also quotes Euripides: 'The speech of the fool is foolish.' He goes on to note that 'Our own prophet Isaiah says the same thing in so many words. Seneca wrote to Lucilius that the way a man talks is like the way he lives. [. . .] Democritus the philosopher called speech "the mirror-image of a man's life". Nothing is truer than this. No looking-glass reflects the shape of a man's body more truly and more clearly than his speech reflects his disposition. A man can be judged by his speech as surely as a bronze vessel by its ring.' It is in the context of a culture for which such ideas were high moral commonplaces that Rabelais makes the

[11] *TL* II (*TLF* 77; *EC* 60). Pantagruel reproaches Panurge for his lack of *Mesnaigerie* (wise home economics). Panurge's reply is to misuse a famous saying of Cato the Censor in his *Mesnagerie* (*De re rustica*): 'The paterfamilias must be a perpetual seller' – which in context means he must be frugal, putting aside produce for the market. Erasmus (on *Adagia* IV, 4, 99, *Quod non opus est, asse carum est*, 'What you do not need is dear') ranks the sentence misused by Panurge with *Nosce teipsum* – no less. Panurge's declamation only seems ambiguous to those who do not know their commonplaces and the immense authority of the texts misused by him.

opening third of this philosophically ambitious book into an exchange of speech between two men, interlarded with the pregnant silences of the Sage.

The constant opposition of Panurge and Pantagruel gives to the first half of the *Tiers Livre* both its structural solidity and its sustained comic profundity. When Panurge is about, Pantagruel now plays a rôle rather like those of the *raisonneurs* in Molière, though he is more successfully and vitally integrated into the *Tiers Livre* than the *raisonneurs* are in all but Molière's greatest comedies. By adapting the two companions of his earliest Chronicle into the protagonists of the first part of the *Tiers Livre*, Rabelais subtly brings his readers to accept without question the curious relationship which exists between these two unlikely companions. In the course of the *Tiers Livre* Panurge is condemned as totally as it is possible to condemn a man by the standards of Renaissance philosophy. Yet he is not hated. He retains something at least of the sheer comic impudence of the *panourgos* he was when Pantagruel first met him. In *Pantagruel* the young giant 'found Panurge, whom he loved all his life'. He was Pantagruel's friend. And despite the metamorphoses of both characters, he still remains somewhat of a friend in the *Tiers Livre*. This is important, since Rabelais's conception of comedy deepened in the years that separated the first versions of *Pantagruel* and *Gargantua* from the *Tiers Livre*. In his reading of Plato he had come across the *Philebus* in time to insert an allusion to that dialogue in the second edition of *Gargantua* (*TLF* I, 13). By making Panurge – a friend not an enemy – into the butt of the mockery of Pantagruel and his companions in the *Tiers Livre*, Rabelais is putting into practice that concept of comedy outlined by Socrates, for whom intellectual laughter was a special kind of 'boyish jesting malice' which essentially consists in recognising a man's false conceit of his wisdom. Since laughing is usually regarded as a somewhat dubious activity, we cannot be laughing at an enemy: if we were, there would be nothing to be dubious about! Laughing at a friend provides just that element of dubiousness which Socratic laughter requires and which the *Tiers Livre* supplies in measured quantities.[12] As a reader of Plutarch, Rabelais also knew that the wise man's reply to a foolish friend is either silence . . . or a rebuke. Friendship and flattery will not mix.

7. *Panurge's dilemma*

The praise of debts gives no hint of what is to be Panurge's dominant quality in the *Tiers Livre*: his inability to make up his mind. On the contrary

[12] See H. Hackford: *Plato's Examination of Pleasure. A Translation of the Philebus, with Introduction and Commentary*, 1945, p.92. Cf. Plutarch, *Oeuvres Morales* I, 79c.

he at first appears deceptively settled in his views. But, in keeping with the paradoxical nature of the *Tiers Livre*, Panurge's granite turns out to be clay; we see him, throughout the book, rushing from extreme to extreme quite unable to decide, once and for all, whether he should marry or not. These hesitations, which in one way or another occupy most of the book until the episode of Bridoye begins in chapter XXXIX, are treated in the two standard ways: first as an 'hypothesis', 'Should Panurge rightly take a wife?'; then as a 'thesis', 'Should any man take a wife?' These divisions into *hypothesis* and *thesis* are rhetorical ones, taken straight from Aphthonius. Panurge rushes from yes to no and back again, blown about with every wind of doctrine.

Like so many other Renaissance writers, consciously rejecting the misogyny of a mediaeval Church dominated by celibate priests and monks, Rabelais is philogamic, though not stupidly so. In the *Tiers Livre* at this point Rabelais's technique is to establish a climate favourable to marriage by quoting and expounding Old Testament authority to show wedlock in so good a light that even marriage to a barren woman, even re-marriage, are treated sympathetically. Many traditionally-minded theologians would not have liked that at all.

Matrimony and paternity were so highly valued by the Jews that even in time of war the newly-wedded husband was exempted from military duty for a full year. Rabelais seizes on this (*TL* VI; the Scriptural sources are *Deuteronomy* 20, 5–7 and 24, 5). But marriage can either be a foretaste of heaven or else quite hellish. Such a theme links the *Tiers Livre* with the centuries-old *Querelle des Femmes*, a quarrel by no means exhausted in the Renaissance, but renewed, rather, by the greater accessibility of ancient texts, including Jerome's diatribe *Against Jovinian*; by the facultative marriage of most reformed priests and ministers; by such studies as Tiraqueau's work *On the Laws of Marriage* and the reply to it by Amaury Bouchard.

There was a flood of books and pamphlets giving the *pro* and *contra* of the married state; the whole question of women and their rôle in life, in marriage and about the Court, was delightfully and lightly renewed by the elegant poems of the *Querelle des Amyes*, an exchange of verse in which one of the poets claimed to be a follower of Rabelais.

It would be quite wrong however to limit the import of Panurge's dilemma to the scope of the *Querelle des Femmes*. The marriage question was one of the standard examples of a dilemma listed by the rhetoricians since classical times. Rabelais's interest in the marriage question is real and sustained; but more real still, and more fully sustained, is his interest in the problem of the man who cannot finally and irrevocably make up his mind, so allowing the Devil to profit from his hesitations.

The comedy of Panurge's dilemma does not lie in his initial hesitation –

anyone who has read a number of the copious treatises stating the *pro* and the *contra* of wedlock, yet unacquainted with the Renaissance man's genius for 'harmonising' extremes, must wonder how anybody who took them seriously ever made up his mind at all. The comedy and the theological error lie in Panurge's sustained hesitation, in his rash swings from one extreme to the other, in his repeated ifs and buts. There is also the deliberately farcical context in which Panurge is placed. He is an old man in love – a traditional butt of the farce and of theological disapproval; he is not even lusting after a particular woman; any woman who legitimises his orgies will do. Yet he is afraid of being beaten, robbed and cuckolded: farcical worries, not heroically borne philosophical ones.

There is, I suspect, an echo here of the dilemma stated by St Jerome in *Against Jovinian*: it is displeasing to have a wife nobody else deigns to look at; it is as bad to have a wife other men find attractive. In the face of such arguments you simply cannot win! Panurge, until he finds his match, intends to give up wearing breeches and codpieces; appearing in a comic toga, with 'a flea in his pierced ear' (a suggestion of his being enslaved to lust). He intends to look after his genitals, though, defending his contention that the codpiece is the main armour of the soldier with arguments taken from Galen (which followers of Hippocrates found laughable), according to whom the testicles are a 'principal member' more vital to man than even his head. All this word spinning, with its subordination of the individual man to the blind good of the species, is a comically damning presentation of Galenic doctrine on human sexuality; it will be taken up later and answered platonically: at this stage we simply laugh such ideas out of court, as another example of Panurge making black seem white (*TL* VIII).

The farcical flavour of Panurge's dilemma is enhanced by Pantagruel's wisdom and also by his playfulness. He repeatedly throws Panurge back on to his own duty to decide, amusingly echoing the end of all his sentences throughout one whole chapter (*TL*, IX).

Pantagruel bases his philosophy of decision on firm evangelical doctrine, with Stoic and Platonic overtones. His pronouncements are occasioned by the strange garb of Panurge, who dons a rough brown toga. Pantagruel does not condemn him too severely, despite his distaste for giddy novelty.

The starting-point of the giant's homily is St Paul's Epistle to the Romans 14, 5: 'Let every man be fully persuaded in his own mind.' In the Vulgate this injunction reads, *Unusquisque in suo sensu abundet*. Pantagruel echoes these words directly: *Chascun abonde en son sens*, using an idiom which can mislead modern readers, as it now means something different (*TL*, *TLF* VII, 44f.).

To appreciate the force of his argument, it is necessary to know that Romans 14, 5 was a proof-text, lending authority to a particular concept of Christian freedom. On the basis of this text many evangelicals believed that man is morally free to make his own decisions in any matter whatsoever which is neither good nor bad in itself. Such matters, in Stoic terms, are classed as 'external' and 'indifferent'. They can be good, if man's attitude towards them is good; bad, if his attitude is bad.

This is the theology which Pantagruel expounds:

Let every man be fully persuaded in his own mind, especially in matters which are extraneous, external and indifferent; which things are neither good nor bad in themselves, since they do not come from our hearts and thoughts, which are the 'manufactory' of all good and all evil: good, if the 'manufactory' be good and our emotions governed by the clean spirit (*l'esprit munde*); evil, if the emotion be depraved from equity by the devil (*l'esprit maling*). But novelty and contempt for common usage do displease me (*TLF* VII, 44–52).

Evangelical humanists included almost every human activity within the category of 'external things'. What matters is not the thing in itself but one's attitude towards it. Amongst such externals were classed dress . . . and matrimony. This idea is an important one in the *Tiers Livre*. Panurge is obsessed by marriage and the fear of cuckoldry. Yet marriage is an external thing, *une chose foraine, externe et indifferente*; what matters is one's emotional attitude towards it. Depending on one's attitude, it can be either (in theological terms) a part of God's kingdom or of Satan's. It is again left to Pantagruel to make this point. 'A good many people' are so happily wed that in their marriage 'there seems to shine some idea or representation of the joys of paradise'. But others are so wretched, that 'the devils who tempt the hermits in the deserts of the Thebaid or Montserrat are not more so' (*TL, TLF* X, 19f.).

Such terms are Christian and Platonic – both *idée* and *repræsentation* being terms used to render the Platonic theory of *ideas*, according to which an object on earth is a reflexion of a true prototype in heaven. The good and bad spirits – the clean spirit and the evil one – are at home both in Christian and Platonic psychology. As for the *equity* out of which man's mind may be diabolically depraved, this too is a classical notion. *Aequitas* means that which is *aequus*: level, plain. Its legal sense is accompanied by others: by the notion of what is just, humane, balanced in attitudes towards others. A man like Panurge who has been devilishly 'depraved out of equity' will be selfish, inhumane, unfair and 'unbalanced'.

The refusal of Pantagruel to become annoyed at Panurge is part of his Christian Stoicism. The conservatism of the last phrase, by which Pantagruel disapproves of innovation and contempt for common usage, shows that his 'apathy' (*apatheia*, freedom from emotion) is a Stoic one. A pure Cynic flouts convention on principle.

Since a man's decision is vital in moral terms – on it depends whether indifferent things become either good or bad in his case – it is essential that he should be aware of the limits imposed upon human beings, making a firm decision in the light of this fact. Pantagruel stresses this. 'Are you not confident in your will? The principal point lies therein. All the rest is fortuitous, depending on the fatal dispositions of the heavens.' Precisely because marriage can be heaven or hell, man must leap into the unknown, undertaking it *à l'adventure* – accepting the hazards, 'with your eyes bandaged, bowing the head, kissing the ground and commending yourself meanwhile to God – once you have decided to enter upon it'. The language is military in its metaphors. The wise man acts as a Christian soldier, battling onward, accepting the inevitable for whatever it proves to be. There is no other assurance possible (*TL* x).

8. Self-love

It becomes progressively clear that Panurge is dominated by the *Esprit maling* (the same diabolical spirit who had set Picrochole on the rampage). Fairly early on in Panurge's quest, Pantagruel remained silent for some little time and seemed deep in thought. Then he said to Panurge, 'You are seduced by the devil'; '*L'Esprit maling vous seduyt.*' (*TL* xix, 1f.). The way that this evil spirit misleads Panurge is to inflate his self-love, which then, as always, proceeds to blind him to the light of truth and to a just assessment of his own real interests.

That Panurge is deceived by self-love is brought to our attention in many ways. We are shown its deluding powers at work in all the consultations, both in the hypothesis and in the thesis. Even the plainest of statements that he will be beaten, robbed and cuckolded is twisted by him into favourable prognostics of wedded bliss. Epistemon (the mouthpiece of classical wisdom) spells it all out in terms of the fable of Aesop most authoritatively held to condemn self-love and proverbially summed up in Catullus's words, used as an adage, *We do not see the wallet on our back*. In the fable men have a double wallet slung over their shoulders; the pocket in front is kept for the faults of others; the one on our backs, for our own faults. Aesop, now often banished to the children's bookshelves, was the only one of the 'eight moral authors' of mediaeval teaching to retain his prestige during the Renaissance and actually to enhance it. He was admired as representing the cream of ancient thought by authors as diverse as Luther, Erasmus and Montaigne. His weight alone would have served to lend virtually unshakeable authority to the basically evil nature of self-love.

When Epistemon cites Aesop in the middle of the series of Panurge's consultations he is peremptory and condemnatory. His style is appropriately Latinate:

A thing very common and popular it is amongst mankind the misfortunes of others to hear, foresee, recognise and predict. But oh, how rare a thing it is one's own misfortunes to predict, recognise, foresee and to hear. And how wisely Aesop said in his fables . . . [and so on] (*TL, TLF* xv, 97f.).

His conclusion is, that it is only those who see their own faults who enjoy 'the benevolent aspect of the heavens.'

When Rabelais consulted the *Adages* to see what his admired 'father and mother' had to say about Aesop's fable of the beggar's wallet, he found open before him, on the very same pages, a mass of interconnected adages condemning self-love. He seized upon them with both hands, exploiting both adage and commentary to develop the shrewdest philosophical comedy in the book. To see it at work we need to jump ahead to the meeting with Her Trippa, the monomaniacal comic magus.

It is worth reading chapter XXV closely; it is a masterpiece of intellectual farce. At first Her Trippa seems to be the butt of the comedy, and indeed he is laughable right to the end. But Panurge outshines even him in his folly. 'Her Trippa' is a play on the name of the German magus Henry Cornelius Agrippa, the author of a standard book *On Occult Philosophy* (1533) as well as of commentaries on the Art of Ramon Lull – that *art de Lullius* that Gargantua condemned in *Pantagruel*. Rabelais was well-informed about magic, however much he distrusted it.

We laugh at Her Trippa, but it is never suggested that his dubious magical methods are all inefficacious. They confirm the answers given by nobler, more legitimate, safer methods: Panurge will be cuckolded, robbed and beaten. Driven to rage and despair, Panurge takes the ultimate step of the man blinded by *philautia*: he accuses Her Trippa of his own blinding vice! This he does by launching against the silly magus the whole group of Erasmian adages which he ought to have applied to himself.

Socrates said: 'Things are done rightly or wrongly *at home*.' This was taken to mean that a man should put his own affairs in order, not meddle with other people's. Instead of taking it to heart, Panurge applies it – in the spirit of Aesop's beggar's wallet – to Her Trippa! Socrates's saying is paralleled by one of Christ's. Erasmus lists that too: 'To cast the mote out of a neighbour's eye.' Panurge is more concerned with Her Trippa's mote than with his own beam. Indeed, he makes Her Trippa's mote into the beam! Socrates and Christ lead on to *Know thyself*, also explained by Erasmus on this page of the *Adagia* as a clarion call to avoid *philautia*. Panurge, again, uses this against Her Trippa, instead of himself acting on its advice. A busybody such as Panurge was called by Plutarch a *polypragmōn*, a meddlesome man 'busy over many things'. This too figures on the same page of Erasmus and is gleefully used by Rabelais: Panurge the *polypragmōn* calls Her Trippa just that.

Panurge is a learned fool: he knows the adages off by heart: what he cannot do is to learn wisdom from them. Instead, he exemplifies the self-loving man with his own faults kept behind his back, lovingly gloating over those of others. He shouts out against Her Trippa:

He doesn't know the first point of philosophy, which is 'know thyself'. And boasting of seeing a splinter in someone else's eye, he fails to see a great tree-trunk poking both his eyes out. He's just the sort of *polypragmōn* Plutarch wrote about . . .

Erasmus – still in the same page – said that Diogenes the Cynic (the dominant character of the prologue to the *Tiers Livre*) used to compare self-loving men to a certain Lamia. Lamia could take her eyes out. She did – at home. When she went out she put them in again, the better to see the faults of others. And since she was wilfully blind to her own faults, Rabelais remembered that Erasmus also explained the adage 'Blinder than a mole' in a moral sense. These adages supply Panurge with his next set of attacks on Her Trippa:

He is another Lamia, who, in other people's houses, in public, among the common people, was able to see more clearly than a lynx [another adage!], but who, in her own house, was as blind as a mole – at home seeing nothing, for, returning to her own dwelling she took her eyes out of her head – they were exemptile like glasses – and hid them away in a clog hung behind her door.

This wily, rustic Lamia should have taught Panurge a lesson on the dangers of *philautia*. Instead, he is the very pinnacle of self-loving blindness. A better example of the 'beggar's wallet' in action would be hard to find. Panurge is the antithesis of the combined wisdom of the ancient world and of Christendom. Since the adages he misapplies are associated with Socrates and Christ, the condemnation is severe. The comedy, without ceasing to be extremely laughable, carries with it a condemnation so basic that only a fundamental cultural shift could make it seem in any way obscure today. It remains for Pantagruel to make a serious etymological pun in true Renaissance taste: *'philautie ou amour de soy vous deçoit'* – *amour de soy* (self-love) is a love that 'deceives' (*deçoit*). (*TL* XXIX; *TLF* 15; *EC* 13).

Philautia seems so classical a concept that we might overlook its total acceptance as a root of all evil by Renaissance Christians of all persuasions. Whatever separated the theologians of the various confessions into which mediaeval western Catholicism split up, from papism at one extreme to Calvinism and Zwinglianism at the other, an acceptance of the evil of *philautia* within the framework of Christian doctrine united them. Erasmus, in his *Sermon on the Child Jesus*, written for St Paul's School in London, compares the Christian's progress in Christ with Socrates striving after knowledge even in old age: 'And so too with us, the more we are in Christ, the less we shall be pleasing to ourselves if we have really made progress in him. So *philautia* is a plague for both studies and piety. . . .' Bullinger uses the notion that self-love is a 'fountain of all evil in the world' in his commentary on St Luke 18; Zwingli, in his treatise *On True and False Religion*, opposes *philautia* to the love by which we love our neighbours as ourselves: against our truly loving our neighbour there cries out our 'old man, our infirmity, our flesh, our Adam; for it is by these names that the teachings of the Apostles call the vice of *philautia*'. So too Calvin, in his commentary on the second great commandment, Thou shalt love thy neighbour as thyself: even God can only help us by tearing *philautia* from our hearts – an idea repeated in his commentary on Isaiah. And there are innumerable commentaries linking condemnations of *philautia* with I Timothy 3, 2, where the first of the signs of the perilous Last Days to come is that men shall be 'lovers of their own selves'.[13]

The inevitable product of self-love is moral, philosophical and spiritual blindness. A man who loves himself can get nothing straight; he certainly cannot both love himself with *philautia* and know himself. Since the height of wisdom is to *Know thyself*, this great Delphic commandment is used to condemn Panurge; that Panurge is a man who does not 'know himself' is the thread running through the book. Once again Rabelais is basing his intellectual comedy on Socrates's description of philosophical laughter in the *Philebus*. There Socrates explains to Protarchus the nature of the ridiculous: it is a certain kind of 'badness', in fact, 'that species of the genus *badness* which is differentiated by the opposite of the inscription at Delphi'. Protarchus asks, 'Do you mean KNOW THYSELF, Socrates?' and gets the reply, 'I do. Plainly the opposite of that would be for the inscription to read, BY NO MEANS KNOW THYSELF'. It is this antithesis of Delphic wisdom that Panurge exemplifies.

9. *The advice of divination*

Panurge is 'ridiculous' by the most Socratic of definitions. It follows for an Erasmian Evangelical (and for many other varieties of Renaissance Christians) that he is also and more deeply wrong in the light of

[13] Erasmus: *Opera Omnia* v, col. 603; Zwingli, *De vera et falsa religione* (1530?), p.117v°; Bullinger, *Commentaria in Lucam*, Zurich 1548, on Luke 18; Calvin, *Corpus Reformatorum*, XXIV, col. 724; XXVI, col. 243. Cf. Lefèvre d'Etaples, *Commentaria initiatorii*, on Romans 15, (*homines seipsos amantes*). The list is potentially inexhaustible. G. Estius (*Commentarii*, 1679, p.822) stresses that the Greek original of St Paul's 'lovers of self' is *philautoi*. The apostle places this vice first, 'since it is the *fons et origo* of all the others. This is weightily supported by St Augustine near the beginning of the *City of God*; the philosopher Plato held the same doctrine.'

Christianity. He consults the various means of divination open to Renaissance scholars; before us pass a series of authorities, wise and less wise, which together form the greater part of Renaissance lore concerning prophetic or mystical means of reaching decisions, all of which ways had their powerful and influential partisans: neither Virgilian and Homeric lots, nor dreams interpreted neo-platonically, can satisfy him, yet these are ways highly honoured in the Renaissance, discussed at length by Tiraqueau in a weighty legal study. Less honoured ways – but ways which, for all his light-hearted treatment, Rabelais is careful not to condemn outright – do not satisfy Panurge either: a comic (but by no means uninstructive) Sibyll, a deaf-mute and the uproariously funny (but again instructive) Her Trippa leave Panurge self-wilfully unenlightened. Epistemon cannot help him in this field: Christ put an end to the ancient Oracles which in former times he might – or might not – have advised Panurge to visit.

All the methods of divination which Panurge consults mean to everybody but himself that he will be cuckolded, beaten and robbed. To the explanations of Pantagruel and his wise companions Panurge opposes explanations of his own, weaving a web of self-deluding nonsense. *Au rebours* becomes his comic refrain. A great deal of the amusement and laughter in this part of the *Tiers Livre* arises out of our recognition of his wordy and ingenious powers of self-deception. We see through his arguments: we are not taken in by his twists and turns. In other words, we recognise his self-loving 'blindness' for what it is.

Renaissance authorities agree that divinations can only work for people who consult their advice in a calm, dispassionate and 'indifferent' state of mind. That Panurge approaches the consultations with his heart in his mouth simply serves to emphasise that he is riddled with *philautia*, incapable of acquiring that indifference which alone might enable a man to learn anything from the enigmatic counsel that divination affords.

That Panurge consults any of these means of divination merits our attention; he himself would have rushed in and thrown a set of three dice as a means of consulting the appropriate sections of Lorenzo Spirito's *Livre de la Fortune des dez*. This disturbing book is condemned by Pantagruel with a vigour which carries conviction: it is truly diabolical, worthy to be totally and inexorably suppressed and the woodblocks from which it is printed smashed to pieces (*TL* XI).

This condemnation of Lorenzo Spirito's book is in keeping with Rabelais's awareness of the ingenious ways in which the Devil may lead poor souls to perdition. But not all means of divination are diabolical. It is Pantagruel who counsels that the future should be reconnoitred by approaching other means of divination. The term reconnoitre (*explorer*) is a technical one: it is as though one were sending forth scouts into the territory of the future: they can give counsel, but are not infallible or fully informed. In fact, highly persuasive and probably correct as some of the means of divination are, none of them is presented as infallible; collectively they give results whose truth can be gauged from the fact that they all agree: *All truth is consonant with all other truth* is cited to make the point (*TL* xx, end).

Renaissance attitudes to the use of lots to reach decisions were largely favourable, though there were many provisos and *distinguos*. Rabelais turns our attention to these divinatory aids in order to make several aspects of Panurge's dilemma stand out in relief. His real, indisputably real dilemma, one which is only dishonourable and comic because of his prolonged hesitation, is that he cannot decide whether to marry or not. To consult oracles to help one make up one's mind on such a question is quite respectable; the subject was amply treated in numerous legal treatises and glosses. But, as Pantagruel insisted, all but the decision is outside man's control: the rest is 'fortuitous' – dependent on fate. Pantagruelism requires men to despise such things. As Pantagruel knows, this concept of the *casus fortuitus* was at home in Roman law since Ulpian.[14] Such fortuitous matters are to be treated as *adiaphora*, as indifferent in a philosophical sense: neither good nor bad in themselves. Cardano (*Opera*, 1663, II, p.301) insists that wisdom, friendship and so on are real goods which no wise man would renounce; but so-called goods which depend upon chance or fortune are not true goods at all. Yet it is these *adiaphora* – whether once married he will be beaten, robbed and cuckolded – which preoccupy Panurge so much that the final decision to marry or not to marry eludes his grasp. To consult oracles to help one reach a decision was theologically and legally unexceptionable; to use them to foretell such things as trouble Panurge was almost universally condemned, except when it could be shown that knowledge of such future contingencies was rightly and directly relevant to the decision itself.

Lawyers and theologians placed lots into three main categories. First came *sortes divisoriae*, distributive lots, by which property might be divided, rights of succession decided, selections made for office by a controlled use of approved lots; under stringent safeguards that method was legal and orthodox. The second category (*sortes consultatoriae*) applied 'when one inquires what should be done or avoided as good, safe, useful or the reverse'; these too were quite acceptable under due safeguards, provided that they were undertaken *sub ratione consilii*, that is, when considered as advisory only, as a means of making up one's mind. The third çategory, *sortes divinatoriae*, was far more dubious, theoretically meriting severe condemnation, whether one was divining by means of the heavens, fortune or spirits. But – and the *distinguo* is important – *sortes divinatoriae* can often be

[14] Cf. Oldendorpius, *Opera*, 1559, p.173; Spiegel (*Lexicon Juris Civilis*, 1541, s.v. *Fortuitus casus*) cites the standard authorities since Ulpian. Rabelais is working within the legal definition.

reclassified to make them orthodox; this is done by consulting them *sub ratione consilii*, as a means of seeking advice in reaching a decision. They are not then regarded as infallible prognostics but as means of establishing probabilities.[15]

Panurge could rightly seek help in making up his mind by turning for advice to *sortes consultatoriae*; such lots should be able to help him decide whether to marry or not. With greater prudence he may also consult *sortes divinatoriae* about the probable behaviour of his wife. But – and Pantagruel is careful to underline the distinction when counselling Panurge to try the most respected of all methods, Homeric and Virgilian lots: they are not infallible; to think they are is to let oneself be 'abused' and opens the way to diabolical error.

Divination by *games* – whether games of dice or games of *tali* (a form of knucklebones) – is sharply condemned in the legal treatises as well as in the *Tiers Livre*. *Tali*, honoured and innocent in themselves, cease to be innocent when used for divination.

The view of the universe on which respect for such methods of decision and divination depended is a Platonic and neo-Platonic one, widely held by Renaissance humanists. It was no mere 'mediaeval left-over'. The universe of many humanists was full of spirits, daemons and intelligences as well as dominions and powers. The main source of Christian doctrine about the angels was still Dionysius the Areopagite, who brought neo-Platonic doctrines right into the centre of Christianity. Luther and Erasmus doubted his authenticity, but they were in a tiny minority. So when a man turned to lots for advice, counsel or fore-knowledge, angelic powers might answer him. But so too might diabolical powers, for the Christian can never forget that his wrestling is not merely against flesh and blood but against spiritual wickedness in high places – evil spirits in the heavenly regions (Ephesians 6, 12). Scholars sympathetic to spiritual magic such as Pico della Mirandola and Henry Cornelius Agrippa were careful also to write against such sympathies.

Sortes consultatoriae and *sortes divinatoriae*, had to be treated as uncertain if they were to remain within the bounds of orthodoxy. *Sortes divisoriae* on the other hand were treated in law as final in the sense that, once an appeal had been made to them, once a decision had been made with their aid, no appeal against them was legally or theologically admissible. These legal

---

[15] Consult (since it concerns the customary law of Paris) Charles Molendineus: *Commentarii in consuetudines Parisienses*, Paris 1542, ɪ, p.100v°f; see also Troilus Maluetius, *Tractatus de Sortibus* (in *Tractatus illustrium Jurisconsultorum de Judiciis criminalibus*, Venice 1584, xɪ para. 2, p.400f. For a theological view, consult Luke Lossius, *In Novum Testamentum Commentarii*, ɪɪɪ, p.58, *De sortitione*. This is the tip of an iceberg: there is a vast literature on the subject during the Renaissance, as well as myriad legal glosses. For a good study of the rôle of the devil in such matters, see Paulus Grillandus, *Tractatus de Heretics et Sortilegiis*, Lyons 1536, pp.xiiii–xvii.

attitudes correspond exactly to those found in the *Tiers Livre* and are emphasised by Pantagruel.

It is important for our understanding and appreciation of the *Tiers Livre* that Panurge always fails to make the right distinctions. Where his 'little worry' about the future conduct of his putative future wife is concerned, he consults lots for their divinatory revelations, striving to twist them into a favourable prognostication of certain bliss. When he consults lots about whether or not he should marry, he seeks to twist them into *sortes divisoriae*, as a means of putting his decisions into the hands of Fortune – provided of course that Fortune will promise him what he wants! He is wilfully and petulantly ignorant of the stern limitations of such lots. He will consult them and accept their advice – but only provided that the decisions go in his favour. And since he is inclined to treat both *sortes consultatoriae* and *sortes divinatoriae* as though they were capable of giving the clear-cut decisions reserved for *sortes divisoriae* alone, the whole of his consulting of the powers lying behind the various lots is potentially impious and certainly foolish. Using the language of the law, Panurge insists that he *will* interpret the lots according to his own self-interest. If they go against his wishes, he intends to lodge an appeal: *Autrement j'en appelle.*

Pantagruel's rejoinder is a crushing one, backed up by the full force of humanist jurisprudence.

To appeal against judgments made by lots and Fortune is never possible, as our ancient jurisconsults attest and as Baldus says, *L.ult. C. de leg.* The reason is because Fortune does not recognise any superior to whom an appeal can be made against her or her lots. And so, in such a case, the inferior cannot be restored to its former state, as Baldus clearly says on the *L. Ait Praetor, § ult. ff. de minoribus* (*TL* XII, end).

Exactly such an argument, based as the same authorities, may be found in Tiraqueau and other legal experts. The authority lies in the 'ancient jurisconsults', not in the unsupported testimony of Baldus, one of the glossators laughed at in *Pantagruel.* They may be found quoted in Baldus's gloss on the *L. ult. C. de leg.* (that is, on the last law of that section of the Roman *Codex* entitled *Concerning legates*) and in his gloss on the *L. Ait Praetor, § ult. de minoribus* (that is, on the last section of the Roman *Pandects* entitled *Concerning minors*, in the paragraph beginning, the *Praetor said*). The abbreviations are troublesome, but were absolutely routine, used by lawyers and non-lawyers alike.

This must not be dismissed as legal pedantry of marginal interest only. The *Tiers Livre*, in addition to showing up Panurge against the great moral commonplaces of ancient and Christian morals as syncretised by Christian humanists, also shows him up against the relevant commonplaces of Roman law, one of the most treasured of the riches which the Renaissance inherited from the ancient, and early Christian, world. A knowledge of the commonplaces of the law was an important and integral part of the culture of the *gens sçavans et studieux* for whom the *Tiers Livre* was written. When Tiraqueau came to publish his great commentary *On the Law of Primogeniture* he uses words so close to Pantagruel's that it seems likely that Rabelais read his treatise long before it was published. But they were commonplaces. He could have read them elsewhere.

Later, the section of the *Tiers Livre* dominated by Bridoye will return to these questions with a new profundity, but on the basis of the same legal texts and others traditionally associated with them.

10. The rôle of the Devil

Renaissance Christians took *philautia* one vital stage further than the ancient Greeks. For them it was not enough that *philautia* should be the fountain of evil and error, the great obstacle to self-knowledge. It was seen to be the way the Devil worked in man, cutting him off from God himself. Luther is clear on such points. Others agreed with him.

Luther (in terms which Rabelais would have approved of) rejects Duns Scotus's contention that *philautia*, love of self, is a step towards the love of God, since it is at least love of a lesser good: 'If arguments are based on human feelings which are depraved, they are evil. Such is the argument of Scotus: "I love a lesser good [myself]: therefore I love a greater good [God] even more." Here I deny the conclusion, because my loving is not a divine ordinance but a demonic depravity. It should indeed be that, when I love myself or some other creature, I love God the creator more; but it does not happen that way, because self-love is something wicked, by which I love myself in opposition to God' (*Luthers Werke*, Weimar, XL, p.461; English translation: Concordia edition, XXVI, p.297).

Panurge is dominated by the *Esprit maling*, as Pantagruel expressly tells us. This diabolical deception of Panurge by his self-love is never clearer than when he meets the good dying poet Raminagrobis. Great and good men might be endowed on their deathbed with prophetic powers: Rabelais knew that from personal experience. Not only did such a belief have great authority behind it including Plutarch's; it had recently been vouchsafed to Rabelais to hear the dying utterances of the Seigneur de Langey. His deathbed prophecies had already partly been proved true; Rabelais confidently waited for the rest to be vindicated by events (*TL* XXI).

The consultation with the dying poet Raminagrobis is the most holy one of all: his reply is the best one of all. Panurge's reactions to this consultation are among the most searching ones in the whole book. Just before he meets this holy man, he shows himself up in his silliest, and in religious terms his most erroneous state, claiming to be preordained to happiness in dealings with 'women and horses'! As Cardano points out in his work *On taking a wife* (*Opera* II, p.238), it was proverbial that a man was at greatest risk when choosing either of these creatures! That is why, when buying a horse or choosing a wife, he should 'close his eyes and recommend himself to God'. Those words are Cardano's, but that is just what Pantagruel told Panurge at the outset of his quest. The silly erudite fool still has not learned this basic lesson (*TL* XXIX, beginning; XX, end).

The good dying poet is called Raminagrobis, a name appropriate to a hypocrital fat-cat. That is in keeping with the paradoxical nature of the *Tiers Livre*, where the unexpected often happens. It is also a linguistic joke, the import of which may be left aside for a while. This saintly poet, dying like an Erasmian evangelical, gives Panurge good advice: *Prenez-la; ne . . .* ; *Take her; don't. . . .* All about him is redolent of the peace, trust and tranquillity of a man already tasting the joys of heaven, now that he has finally chased away hordes of monkish beetles trying to get him to make a will in favour of their Orders. Panurge's reaction to him is both comic and linguistic proof of diabolical possession. The Devil in him is deeply troubled by the holiness of Raminagrobis, whose soul (in Plutarch's Platonic metaphor) is already entering its home port, descrying its friends waiting to welcome it on the quayside. In chapter XXIII, where Panurge reaches a paroxysm of laughable indignation over Raminagrobis and his holy way of dying, he makes a defence of traditional scholastic doctrines of contrition and repentance. That Rabelais is mocking this view and laughing at Panurge's devilish error is shown by Panurge's language. He employs the word *diable* twenty-seven times, to which may be added *diabolologie* (twice) and *diabolologicque* (once). We also learn, for the first time, that Panurge had studied *diabolology* at Toledo, under his Reverend Father in the Devil Picatrix (who takes his name from a famous mediaeval book of magic which influenced H. C. Agrippa). Panurge's theology and his language become that of the hated and despised Sorbonne; he several times shouts *Houstez vous de là*, a magic spell designed to drive away devils, but used by Panurge not against the devils who possess him but against the good influences emanating from Raminagrobis. After this climax of 'talking of the Devil' (marked, though less strongly so, in chapters XXII and XXV), he slips back to his average of one devilish allusion per chapter, whenever he appears throughout the book.

Pantagruel, by contrast, only uses the word *diables* once in the entire book, and then seriously. His other allusions (five in all) are made in great earnest to *l'esprit maling* (twice), to *le Calumniateur ennemy*, to *l'Ange de Sathan* and to *l'esprit maling et seducteur*. Speech is indeed the mirror of character in the *Tiers Livre*, for these terms are scriptural.[16]

---

[16] *TL* VII (*l'esprit maling*); X (*diables qui tentent les hermites*); XI (*le calumniateur ennemy*); XIV (*l'ange de Sathan; l'ange maling et seducteur*); XIX (*l'esprit maling*). All these uses are serious, condemnatory and free from any element of swearing. (There are learned jokes as well. Cf. *TL*, XXII, 9; Panurge's praise of the *circumbilivagination* (*circum* + *umbilicus* + *vagina*, with pun

The diabolical *philautia* of Panurge makes his hypothetical inquiries delightfully and disquietingly comic. We can count on his being on the wrong side, championing all the errors which Rabelais found hateful or merely stupid – throwing out accusations of heresy, falling into the obscure pretentiousness of scholastic philosophy; placing Maître Ortuinus of the *Letters of Obscure Men* in the same category as Socrates; inclined to believe that there is a natural language whereas words signify by arbitrary convention; delighting in the counsel of silly women; seizing upon a wide range of superstitious beliefs, while at the same time disbelieving in good sound Platonic Christianity (*TL* XVI; *TLF* 84f.; *EC* 69f.; XLIX, 5f.; etc.).

It is only after this series of consultations is over, when we have laughed our fill at Panurge's misplaced ingeniousness, that we are told why Pantagruel had sent him off on this wild-goose chase: it was to show up his self-love for what it is. Never is this done more clearly than when Panurge rejects the counsel of Raminagrobis, for this dying sage gives the best reply of all whom he has consulted so far. When Pantagruel studied the prophetic poem of Raminagrobis, he declared that none of the advice given to Panurge pleased him more: 'He means, in short, that when undertaking matrimony every man should be arbiter of his own thought and take his own advice.' That, we are told, was always Pantagruel's opinion, conforming to the advice he gave 'the first time you talked to me about it'. But (he adds) 'you quietly mocked it I remember'. That was how he realised that '*philautia* and self-love' – one complex idea – was leading Panurge into error (*TL* XXIX, beginning).

11. The rhetorical thesis: Hippothadée's advice

After the hypothesis comes the thesis: should any man marry? must all men risk being cuckolded? Panurge still asks questions in terms of himself, but the replies he gets are all in the general terms appropriate to a thesis.

Traditionally man's interests were divided into three categories, with three professions established to look after them: the soul (the concern of theologians); the body (the concern of the doctors); his property (the concern of legal experts). Panurge's borrowed sarcasms against the three professions are rejected by Pantagruel: we are to get the advice of a truly Christian theologian, a good prophylactic doctor and a selfless lawyer. A philosopher is thrown in for good measure. These men are all scholars whom Renaissance lawyers classed as *periti*, 'experts' in their disciplines.

---

on *vagare*, to wander) of the scholastic monks; he uses the adjective *gyrognomonicque*. This is perhaps a deformation of *ouranognomenos*, a coinage of Lucian (*Menippus*, 5) meaning 'skilled in the heavens'. Erasmus uses it (*Commentary on Psalm 38* in *Opera Omnia* V, 438F) to condemn ignorant censors who cry scandal and heresy. Rabelais makes the first element *gyro* because of the 'gyrations' (gaddings about) of the mendicant orders.

Epistemon confirms that, in all the country, you could not have chosen better men (*TL* XXIX). With some awe we realise how wide-reaching Rabelais's aims are in this book. He has just made the whole procession of the means of divination and of lots which humanists had cogently classified out of the legacy of the ancient world pass before our eyes, in an everchanging pattern of subtly differing emphases, from serious exposition to farcical laughter. Now comes the turn of the rest of the Renaissance encyclopaedia of metaphysical and physical knowledge. We expect, and get, a kind of Platonic *symposium*, with learned men quietly and interestingly discussing problems during or after a banquet. Rabelais makes the parallel himself: in Plato's *Timaeus* the guests are counted at the beginning; in his symposium they are counted at the end (*TL* XXXVI; *TLF* 148; *EC* 125). Rabelais is aided in his artistic and philosophical aims both by his comic insight, which can find subjects for laughter in the most arid of Renaissance treatises, and by his gift for condensing complex ideas into a few meaningful words. All Rabelais's readers are aware of his verbal copiousness: perhaps only those who have read their Renaissance treatises at their most technical can fully appreciate his equally important gift for concentrating on essentials.

One of the main ways in which Rabelais achieves such condensation of complex issues in this part of the *Tiers Livre* is, yet again, to base his comedy on theological and medical commonplaces which had left the verbose technical works of professional scholars and entered into the public domain of condensed general knowledge. Through such works the expertise was appreciated by a wider readership, without undermining its authority. It is a technique closely analogous to his preference for the adage, the apophthegm, the exemplum, the fable: condensed forms in which ancient wisdom can be found quintessentially distilled.

Hippothadée speaks first. When Panurge asks for advice on whether he should marry, the good theologian, like Pantagruel, throws him back on to his own duty of deciding for himself, of finding out for himself what he really wants. He must be his own counsellor: *mais premier fault que vous mesmes vous conseillez*. The advice he gives is based on evangelical doctrine, according to which celibate chastity is an exceptional gift, vouchsafed to very few men. It is each man's duty to judge for himself whether he has this 'special gift of continence'. Those who do not have it must marry: it is very much better to wed than to burn with lust. This favourable and markedly liberal paraphrase of standard scriptural texts by-passes both traditional monastic misogamy and any notion that a man without the gift of celibacy should pray to be given it, rather than seek the remedy of wedlock.

Panurge is momentarily happy. Here is a clear reply! But he has a little unimportant scruple: will he be cuckolded, *Seray je poinct coqu?* Hippothadée's reply is a general one, based on the Lord's Prayer. Panurge should pray that God's will be done in earth, as it is in heaven, for that is how we hallow his blessed name. There are times when that would be the end of the matter, as in the *Almanac for 1535*, where curious astrological inquiries into God's 'privy counsel' had been condemned with just such texts. But marriage is one of those matters which God has *not* reserved for his own 'privy counsel': it has been vouchsafed to man to enjoy a general revelation from God where marriage is concerned. Panurge, if he were wise, could know God's will.

God has revealed man's lot in marriage in the scriptures: take a wife who fears and loves the Lord and then you will not be cuckolded. Such a wife would never commit adultery. But the wife must be helped by the example of her husband. Hippothadée adds exacting moral counsel adapted from Plutarch: a wife is a looking-glass reflecting the moral comportment of her husband. A man who wants his wife to be faithful to him had better be faithful to her first (*TL* xxx).

12. Dr Rondibilis

Such advice is quite unwelcome to Panurge, who dismisses both it and the good theologian with a few superficial quips. He now turns to Dr Rondibilis, the expert in natural knowledge as Hippothadée had been in supernaturally revealed knowledge. Rondibilis's answer to the question whether a man should marry leads to a summary of Platonico-Hippocratic teachings on the nature of semen. From a doctor's 'natural' point of view, marriage is the God-given, morally acceptable way of emitting semen. There are also various means open to a man to impede the production of semen in his body.

Rabelais bases his comedy on the clash between two rival schools of spermatology. It dated from classical times. Mediaeval European and Arabic medicine had somewhat complicated the views, but the two schools of thought still remained sharply divided.

The followers of Hippocrates believed that semen was a product of the brain. It descended the spinal column, reaching the testicles in which it was stored. The experiments with which Hippocrates had confirmed this doctrine were well-known; Dr Rondibilis cites them.

Galen, already in antiquity, had scornfully rejected this teaching. For him, semen is a product of the testicles themselves. In essentials, Renaissance doctors had to choose between one or other of these schools. The disciples of Hippocrates sometimes strengthened their case by insisting that Hippocrates had received special revelation.

Two opposing moral consequences follow from these rival doctrines. The platonising doctors, who followed Hippocrates, believed that Nature was more concerned with the perfection of man as an individual person than with the perpetuation of the species. The followers of Galen denied this: for them, Nature was not concerned with the individual man at all; she was concerned to perpetuate the species. (This was often supported by the authority of Aristotle, in *Oeconomica* III. 4.) Galen was led to marvel at the ingenuity of Nature, who had made this vital matter so easy, that even idiots knew how to lie together.

For the disciples of Galen, the production of semen in the testicles was outside the moral control of man. For platonising doctors, on the contrary, the production of semen was not totally independent of the will. A man, by taking certain drugs, say, by doing hard physical work or by giving himself over to deep thought, could prevent the formation of semen in the brain or its descent to the organs of generation through the spinal column.

Rabelais takes these two directly opposing views and builds his moral comedy round them. Both were readily available in compendia, often conveniently set out with the main arguments in their defence. These are the arguments Rabelais uses.[17]

In a matter as morally important as this, Rabelais prepared the way carefully. In the light of what the good Dr Rondibilis stands for, we can now see why Rabelais made Panurge undertake so wrong-headed a defence of the codpiece, for that enabled him to laugh Galen out of court, long before he expounded the morally acceptable doctrine of the rival school through the mouth of Rondibilis:

Consider (said Panurge) how Nature inspired man to arm himself, and what part of the body he first began to arm. It was, by God's virtue, the balls [. . .]. This is testified to by Moses, the Hebrew captain and philosopher, affirming that he armed himself with a brave and gallant codpiece ingeniously made out of figleaves, which are naturally appropriate, and entirely apt – by their hardness, cut, curl, polish, size, colour, smell, virtue and properties – for the covering and the arming of balls (*TL*, *TLF* VIII, 51f. and notes).

Having thus misused the account in 'the first book of Moses, called Genesis', of how Adam and Eve, realising they were naked, 'sewed figleaves together, and made themselves aprons,' Panurge proceeds to cite his Galen.

That is what moved the gallant Claudius Galen, in his first book *On Semen*, bravely to conclude that it would be better – that is to say less bad – to have no heart rather than to have no genitals.

Rabelais did not make that up; Galen said just that. He believed the testicles to be a primary organ more important than the head, and had

---

[17] E.g. in Peter of Abano's *Conciliator*, Differentia 34, 'Whether or not semen is abstracted from all the body or from all members'; plus other relevant *differentiae*. The subject is discussed in a host of medical and legal treatises.

trapped himself into irritably declaring that it was better to have no head than to have no testicles (*De Spermate* I, 15). The Platonic doctrine, on the contrary, as sympathetically and energetically expounded by Dr Rondibilis, leads to the morally attractive conclusion that Nature is primarily concerned with the individual man, and only secondarily with the perpetuation of the species. As medicine in the person of Dr Rondibilis is given the responsibility of expounding natural wisdom in the symposium of the specialists, we are bound to take particular note of what he says at this point, before the episode merges delightfully into farce (cf. *TL, TLF* VIII, 78–88; contrast XXXI, 52–70).

But even sound Platonic medicine has no comfort to give to Panurge over his 'little problem' of cuckoldry and marital bullying. According to Dr Rondibilis's unexceptionable natural reasoning, the only way for any man on earth to be certain of avoiding being cuckolded is to remain unmarried. Any married man is, was, will be, or may be cuckolded.

The advice that Rondibilis gives is partly borrowed from Plutarch, partly from Plato and Hippocratic medicine: a man who wants his wife to be faithful must make her desire to be so; he must not provoke her, hold her on too tight a rein, spy on her, impinge upon her freedom, make her desire forbidden fruit. The basis of Rondibilis's sound moral (as distinct from medical) advice is a fable of Aesop's, twice found in Plutarch (*Opera* I, 122Af.; 609Ef.). In the fable, it is Grief whom Jupiter made into a god who visited only those who set about worshipping him. Rabelais changes Grief into a god called Cuckoldom, who deigns to visit only those men who distrust their wives and spy upon them. The man who would avoid being cuckolded must learn to trust his wife – learn also to make her *want* to be loyal to him. This advice is not based upon romantic idealisations of women: for Rondibilis woman is a '*sexe tant fragil, tant variable, tant muable*' (*TL, TLF* XXXII, 47). She is, in other words, the ever-fickle woman of Virgil (*Aeneid* IV, 569 – *varium et mutabile semper foemina*). Rabelais's doctor draws the logical conclusion from sound medical beliefs. Women may well contribute a weakish semen to supplement the male's – so Galen and Panurge believed (*TL* IV, end) – but the production of semen is not of the essence of her sexual desires. She is largely at the mercy of her womb. The woman, however moral she may be, is swayed by her womb, an awful force dwelling within her body but not obedient to her mind. Woman, unlike man, cannot really control her sexual drive without risking that dreadful form of hysteria ('womb disease') which mimics death. Woman's physical sexual yearnings arise out of the nature of the womb, which was widely held by both Galenic and platonising doctors to be capable of self-movement and to be able to distinguish between smells. On account of these properties platonising doctors classified the womb as an independent *animal* yearning for the act of generation; Galenic doctors accepted the mobility of the womb but denied its independent animality. The distinction is entirely verbal. Both schools of medicine based their views about woman's sexuality – and their cures of hysteria – on these properties of the womb. An unsatisfied womb might rise up in a chaste woman's body, producing a state mimicking death.

Dr Rondibilis expounds the doctrines of platonising medicine: Nature was certainly concerned with man as an individual person but seems not to have been so concerned with the perfection of individual womanhood. In the case of womankind Nature *was* chiefly concerned with the propagation of the species; that is why sexual morality comes so much harder to a woman than to a man; why a wife so signally needs the understanding and support of her husband; why she needs to be sexually satisfied. For the ageing Panurge none of this is good news; sexual inadequacy is one of his fears. We may note that what Rondibilis is insisting upon in medical terms is the due fulfilment by the husband of the 'marriage duty' – that Pauline concept which Panurge used for merely joking ends at the close of his praise of debts and debtors (*TL, TLF* XXXII, 76f.; IX, 89f.; IV, end).

The opposition between man's sexual organs, which by a control of the semen-producing processes were held to be amenable to rational restraint, and woman's which were not so amenable, was universally thought to go straight back to Plato. Curiously enough Plato makes no such distinction. For him both male and female sexual organs were deaf to reason (*Timaeus* 91A-D). But over many centuries medical treatises had wrenched Plato's judgment on male and female sexuality right out of context. I know of no author before Montaigne – let alone one writing in French – who spotted the error and put the passage from Plato back where it belonged. As soon as this was done, Plato ceased to be an authority decreeing that woman was more dominated by irrational sexual urges than was man; male and female sexuality ceased to be seen on his authority as totally different things. Montaigne ends his chapter *Sur des vers de Virgile*, in which he discusses these matters at length, by saying that 'males and females are cast in the same mould; upbringing and custom apart, there is not much difference between them'. But for Rabelais, still basing himself on hallowed medical intermediaries, no such conclusion was possible.

13. *The techniques of the farce*

So far the *Tiers Livre* has been essentially dramatic in that characters come and go before us, make their speeches and get answered by others. The basic technique had been one of dialogue or monologue. Drama in a more stagey sense only occasionally broke through, notably in Panurge's encounter with Her Trippa, all of which reads like the book of a company about to act out a moral comedy on the trestles (*TL* XXV). The comic devices in the Her

Trippa episode are very successful. One example will suffice to show this: the monomaniac magus, running headlong through all his methods of divination, offers to use lecanomantia. This method – successfully tried, we are later told by the much admired fifteenth-century Italian humanist Ermolao Barbaro – shows the future through shadows in water held in a basin. Panurge is promised a vision of his future wife carrying on with a couple of peasants. He explodes into gross, meaningless, petulant abuse:

When you put your nose up my arse (says Panurge) remember to take off your glasses.

A moment or two is needed for these words – quite misunderstood – to penetrate through to Her Trippa's self-inebriated consciousness:

By catoptromantia (said Her Trippa, continuing). – You won't need any glasses (*TL* xxv; *TLF* 94f.; *EC* 74f.).

With Rondibilis the farcical flavour at last becomes dominant, to the great enhancement of our pleasure. Before the episode is over, Ponocrates and Eudemon remind Dr Rondibilis how, during their student days in Montpellier, they had acted together in 'the moral comedy of *The Man who Married a Dumb Wife*. Their fellow actors were students, several destined to become famous doctors, including, by name, François Rabelais. An echo of *Pathelin* (*Retournons à nos moutons*) leads to a farcical confrontation between Rondibilis, the representative of medicine, and Panurge now, somewhat unexpectedly but so very appositely, the comic representative of the legal profession. The quarrel concerns which of them has the professional right to examine the future Mrs Panurge's urine. In the end, when Panurge pays the doctor for his consultation, slipping four rose-nobles into his hand, we find ourselves a very long way from the cogently Platonic doctor with which the episode began; we are joyfully back in the happy atmosphere of medical undergraduates having a good laugh at the expense of their own profession:

Rondibilis took them well enough, then said in amazement, as though indignant: 'Hé, hé, hé, monsieur, I didn't want anything. Many thanks all the same. From bad people I never take anything: from good people there is nothing that I refuse. I am always yours to command.'
– So long as I pay (said Panurge).
– That's understood (replied Rondibilis) (*TL* xxxiv, end).

14. Christian scepticism and legal harmony

From now on, through many chapters, we shall never be far from the savour of the farce. This fact by no means implies that the comic philosophy of the *Tiers Livre* becomes less profound. On the contrary, the *Tiers Livre* is approaching its first climax, which takes the form of a dramatic conversation between the wise heroes, Gargantua and Pantagruel, and the professional experts, the *periti*, we have just heard expounding their views.

This conversation is not only sandwiched between scenes of pure farce, dominated by the sceptical Regius Professor of Philosophy, Trouillogan: it derives from Panurge's refusal to take the professor's advice seriously. Once again Rabelais traps his readers into laughing at a character who is then shown to be, paradoxically, the height of wisdom. This section is marked by an assumption shared by many of the best thinkers of the Renaissance: that unsuspected depths of wisdom may lie beneath apparently silly or trivial gnomic utterances. In this way one gets the best of both worlds; we may laugh at the surface silliness of the utterance and then be soberly impressed by the depth of the meaning hiding within (*TL* xxxv).

Panurge asks Trouillogan whether he should marry or not; he is told, *both* and *neither*: *Tous les deux*, then, *Ne l'un ne l'autre*. Not unreasonably Panurge is put off by Trouillogan's clipped replies. Since the farcical nature of the dialogue is clear beyond question, we as readers are at first no more inclined to take the sceptical Trouillogan's *both* and *neither* any more seriously than Panurge does. This *both* and this *neither* are soon glossed in philosophical ways quite foreign to our habits of thought, but very much at home in Renaissance ways of thinking. In the Renaissance a philosopher or a jurisconsult, faced with mutually exclusive authorities or opinions, as often as not sets about 'harmonising' them. A convenient way for a reader of the *Tiers Livre* to appreciate this habit of mind would be to read some of the numerous sixteenth-century treatises dealing with the *pro et contra* of marriage or of the goodness or badness of women. As often as not the *pro* and the *contra* are followed by a third section, seeking to reconcile the two extremes in a harmonic concord.

That a climax is at hand we suddenly realise when Gargantua – of all people – appears, preceded like the scriptural Toby by his little dog called *Dog*. Pantagruel, rising to his feet with his companions, is invited to sit down again; he expounds to his courteous royal father the point they have reached in Panurge's quest. (Nobody ever explains how *Gargantua* has got back from the Land of the Faeries.)

Pantagruel's *résumé* of Trouillogan's reply is a model of fairness; all that he leaves out is the farcical dialogue:

When Panurge asked him, 'Must I get married or no?' Trouillogan replied, 'Both at once,'; the second time he said, 'Neither one nor the other' (*TL*, *TLF* xxxv, 37f.).

The key phrases are 'both' (*tous les deux ensemblement*) and 'neither' (*ne l'un ne l'aultre*). In words the full significance of which will appear a page or so later, he adds that Panurge finds these replies unsatisfactory:

Panurge complains of such incompatible and contradictory replies, protesting that he can understand nothing.

The language at this point is technically precise; it needs to be borne in mind:

Panurge se complainct de telles repugnantes et contradictoires responses, et proteste n'y entendre rien.

None of the other characters are in Panurge's position. They do understand; they do not find mere opposition and contradiction in Trouillogan's apparently silly and mutually inconsistent answers to straight questions.

Panurge 'protested that he could understand nothing'. Gargantua counters this, with kingly courtesy but quite firmly; he does understand: *je l'entends en mon advis*. For his interpretation, he draws on the *altior sensus* of a classical apophthegm as duly explained by Erasmus: to a man who objected that Aristippus, a philosopher, should have been sexually possessed by the courtesan Laïs, Aristippus retorted, 'Not at all: *I* possessed *her*'. The deeper meaning of this reply, which in no wise detracted from its epigrammatic surface humour, was thought to be a lesson in philosophical and moral moderation, with a tinge of *apatheia*: there is nothing reprehensible in enjoying such pleasures as are rightly allowed; what is disgraceful is to be enslaved by them (*TL, TLF* xxxv, 50–4, and notes).

Pantagruel agrees, citing another ancient apophthegm from Erasmus's collections: a Spartan serving-girl was asked whether she had anything to do with men. She replied, 'No. But men occasionally had something to do with her'. This Erasmus took to mean, in its *altior sensus*, that she did not have sexual relationships with men out of lust but out of obedience to the law and to her parents: another lesson in indifference and moderation. Behind the smiles of the literal and surface meaning can be seen the foundations of something spiritually and morally important (*TL, TLF* xxxv, 55–9).

Rondibilis, with a certain amount of wordy obfuscation, reveals the meaning in medical and philosophical terms. Trouillogan's *both* and *neither*, like the gnomic apophthegms just cited, signify that man should remain within the golden mean.

In the same way (said Rondibilis) we establish the *neuter* in medicine and the *mean* in philosophy, by participation of one or other extreme, by rejection of one or other extreme, or by division of time, being now in one extreme, now in the other (*TL*, *TLF* xxxv, 60).

The technical phrases which Rondibilis uses are: *par participation de l'une et l'aultre extrêmité* and, *par abnégation de l'une et l'aultre extrêmité*.

The ideal of the golden mean was not then applied to some inexacting middle course. That is not how mediaeval and Renaissance philosophers ever saw it. Following their classical models they conceived of the mean, not as a static middle way, not as some grubby highest common factor, but as an elastic position, consisting of an everchanging balance. The mean could be reached *per participationem*: in that case both extremes are, in various ways or at various times, dominant, as the follower of the golden mean *participates* in one extreme or the other depending upon circumstances. The golden mean could also be reached *per abnegationem*: in which case both extremes are *rejected* in a similar manner. And the two ways can be combined. In other words, the golden mean between being married and not being married does indeed consist in Trouillogan's *both* and *neither*: by being *both* married *and* unmarried *per participationem*, yet being also *neither* married *nor* unmarried *per abnegationem*.

Aurea mediocritas, the golden mean, had long since found its honoured place in Christian wisdom. It was normally recognised as a classical ideal, applicable to the moral life of mankind, capable of governing the cardinal virtues recognised by all men of good will. At times it is even at home amongst the revealed theological virtues of faith, hope and charity. Rabelais's works show here, and even more clearly later, that there need be no tension between this ancient Greek ideal and the demands of the Christian faith.

Rondibilis's reply is by no means a model of clarity. His terms are latinate and technical. Dr Rondibilis, while being a good and wise physician, is not averse to a little flattery in the bedside manner; nor, as here, is he above a tendency to blind his hearers with science. That is why the modest and courteous Hippothadée gently rebukes him: 'The Holy Apostle seems to have put it more clearly when he said, "Let those who are married be as though they were not married; they that have wives be as though they had them not".'

In other words, the good theologian explains Trouillogan's apparently silly replies in terms of the actual words of St Paul in I Corinthians 7 (in some ways the most important part of the New Testament dealing with marriage):

It remaineth that both they that have wives be as though they had none; and they that weep, as though they wept not; and they that rejoice, as though they rejoiced not; and they that buy, as though they possessed not.

Hippothadée's concept of celibacy or chaste matrimony as a gift of grace is also partly to be found in this chapter. It is peculiarly right that this *locus classicus* should supply the solution to Trouillogan's paradoxical advice: that is where any evangelical would expect to find authoritative help towards a resolution of a Christian's hesitations over matrimony – advice which, in context, applies to the whole of human life. In Rabelais's hands, St Paul himself becomes a champion of scepticism.

Trouillogan proves to be the perfect sceptic in the ephectic tradition. As a Pyrrhonian, he corresponds exactly to Montaigne's conception of this ancient school: say that snow is white, they will say it is black;

If you say it is neither – *ny l'un ny l'autre* – they maintain it is both – *tous les deux*.

Tell them that honey is sweet:

The Pyrrhonists would say that they do not know whether it is bitter or sweet, whether it is neither – *ny l'un ny l'autre* – or both – *tous les deux* – for they always reach the highest point of doubt (*Essais* II, 12; ed. Plattard, II, 2, pp.250, 378).

The Christian scepticism of Rabelais is in the direct tradition of Gianfrancesco Pico della Mirandola's *Examination of the Vanity of Pagan Teaching*. Soon Trouillogan refuses to be pinned down by Panurge – to Gargantua's great amusement. Scepticism on the ancient Greek model is sometimes wrongly said not to have been widely known or developed in France until later. Gargantua positively declares that sceptics abounded among the leading philosophers of the day. And he is not at all worried by it (*TL* XXXVI; *TLF* 133f.; *EC* 114f.). Why should he be? In the Renaissance classical scepticism was an ally of Catholic Christianity.

Two partial translations of Sextus Empiricus, the fountain-head of scepticism, were made in fifteenth-century Italy. About the same time, Savonarola advocated his being translated, a fact which gave Greek scepticism advanced Christian credentials. In France, as early as 1514, Guillaume Budé had written that we should follow the *ephectici* more, so restraining the arrogance of our judgments (*Opera* II, 12v°). Like Pico before him, Rabelais used Pyrrhonism as a tool for defending revealed knowledge, especially knowledge as revealed in scripture. The success of Rabelais's methods as early as *Gargantua* is shown by the virulence with which Guillaume Postel attacked him. Rabelais sees the Christian revelation as percolating even wider than the pages of the Gospel, which has primacy without being totally unique. Whether it is a question of strange nativities, marriage, or what you will, only the Gospel, or other revealed wisdom and knowledge, can enable man to pick his way between truth and multiform error. Both truth and error alike will seem to be mere opinion to the wise man's unguided reason.

Since the resolution of Trouillogan's sceptical impasse is to be sought in revelation, one might have expected the central role to be alloted to Hippothadée, the professional exponent of scriptural learning. By giving this rôle of final arbiter to Pantagruel, Rabelais enhances his giant's authority. He also creates a situation in which revealed knowledge triumphs, without being restricted to the biblical revelation, which nevertheless remains normative.

The sceptical bases of Rabelais's philosophy are remarkably like the foundations of Montaigne's more easily recognised sceptically based Catholicism: but whereas Montaigne's post-Tridentine scepticism leads him to place ultimate authority in an infallible Church, sole custodian of authentic revelation, Rabelais's scepticism leads him to see the manna of revealed knowledge and wisdom more widely sprinkled over enlightened humankind.

It is artistically appropriate that the full and complete explanation of what Trouillogan meant should be made not by any of the episodic characters but by Pantagruel in a masterful summing-up. No other character in the book, not even Gargantua, has the requisite moral and philosophical stature. Pantagruel draws on the advice of the other speakers in the symposium to expound with exact humanist learning what St Paul means when he was inspired to tell Christians to have a wife as though they had her not. He does so in a dense statement, interweaving together the advice of the Old Testament, the New Testament and the Classical world. In his reply Genesis and the New Testament find themselves in easy harmony with the *aurea mediocritas* of classical Greece and Rome.

To have a wife means to have her as Nature intended: as a source of joy, recreation and companionship. *Not to have a wife* means not to be always dancing attendance on her, nor for ever trying to please her at the expense of other duties; it means not to allow one's love for her to corrupt that unique and highest love that man owes to God alone; not to neglect the duties one naturally owes to country, state and friends, to one's studies and avocations. At the climax of this classical-Christian synthesis, Pantagruel's wisdom is, as usual, totally opposed to Panurge's mere opinions. The last words of Pantagruel's speech – the last words of the chapter – show how the advice of the wise, when properly understood and harmonised, deny all force to Panurge's complaint that Trouillogan's replies were mutually exclusive: *repugnantes et contradictoires:*

Taking in this way *to have*, and *not to have, a wife*, I can see no contradiction in the terms – (*je ne voids repugnance ne contradiction es termes*) (*TL* xxxv, end).

15. Perplexity and its legal remedy

It is now possible to sum up this part of the *Tiers Livre*, to recognise how it is constructed and to understand it more fully. In these important chapters, Panurge is wrapped fast in the bonds of 'perplexity'. In order to help him escape from so anxious and inhibiting a state, Pantagruel arranged for him to consult the leading *periti*, the acknowledged experts in the relevant fields of knowledge. Panurge, having heard their advice through the cloud of his distorting self-love, declares the replies of the best sceptic philosopher to be *repugnantes et contradictoires*. Pantagruel on the contrary, after the replies of the *periti* and the wise glosses that all the speakers make to resolve the extreme Pyrrhonist doubt of Trouillogan, then *harmonises* all the replies in the light of revealed wisdom.

Rabelais is using technical terms and presenting a technical remedy. He has constructed his solution in accordance with standard legal methodology.

Perplexitas is a legal term, subject to much commentary. In law, this kind of perplexity exists when the problem a man has to solve is surrounded by diverse and mutually contradictory authorities – *diversi authores sibi invicem repugnantes*. There we have Panurge's actual terms. And at the outset of his quest he was not wrong: standard authorities were contradictory in their advice about marriage. But the wise man knows how to find his way out of this maze. The recommended legal way to escape from the bonds of perplexity was, precisely, first to take the advice of the appropriate experts (*per consilium peritorum*) and then to harmonise the contraries (*per contrariorum concordantiam*).[18]

Rabelais has conformed to this jurisprudential wisdom in every detail. Panurge's perplexity has been resolved in accordance with the best advice the law has to give. The *periti* are consulted; the contrary extremes of *both* and *neither* are brought into harmony by the wisdom of Gargantua and all the other interlocutors, as a prologue to the masterly and climactic

---

[18] Consult Albericus de Rosate, *Lexicon Juris*, s.v. *perplexitas*. He bases himself primarily on the standard authority, Raymundus de Peñaforte, *Summa*, titulus xxx, §2, *De Perplexitate*. Panurge's perplexity is a copy-book example of *perplexitas juris* according to Albericus's normative definition: '*Perplexitas juris* is when one finds, in relation to what has to be done, divers authorities which contradict each other (*sibi invicem repugnantes*). This *perplexitas* is to be resolved by the counsels of the experts (*consilium peritorum*) and the harmonising of contraries (*contrariorum concordantia*).' Panurge is faced with contradictory views about marriage – he himself exposes them especially in ch. ix (the echo chapter). The various '*periti*' do *not* of course expound contradictory advice; their advice is sound, needing only to be beaten out into one complex judgment by Pantagruel.

harmonising of Pantagruel. The two great allies of Pantagruel in his quest for truth within his legal framework are scepticism and revelation.

This full reply of Pantagruel's, drawing as it does on such sound authority, makes the wife into a wise man's helpmeet, a fit companion for a good and wise man. It shows how shallow the view is that would make the *Tiers Livre* into the tract of an antifeminist extremist. Rabelais's attitude to women and to the wife is more akin to that of the liberal spirit of the Renaissance, an age when, for the first time for over a millennium, the great, the good, the saintly and the learned included many married men and women, such as Guillaume Budé, Thomas More and Margaret of Navarre: an age when some of the most profoundly committed priests and monks hoped to bring back the marriage of the clergy, so rashly forbidden (in their opinion) a few centuries earlier.

Throughout the *Tiers Livre* the wise characters show considerable respect for marriage as an honourable estate and for the moral wife. This respect for the wife and for matrimony reminds us that the philosophical and religious heroes of Rabelais's time were as often as not married men who showed by their good and scholarly lives that marriage was no impediment to moral and intellectual greatness. Many reformers either married, as Luther did, or else held their fellows' marriages in honour, as did Melanchthon. The firmly non-schismatic Catholic theologian whom Rabelais most venerated, Erasmus, was by almost any standards a feminist, a man intuitively sensitive to female aspirations and openly respectful of the marriage state, infinitely preferring chaste wedlock to unchaste celibacy.

The rôle given to the husband by such men and by Pantagruel is an exacting one, quite distinct from the double standard traditionally applied to the sexual lives of men and women. In Pantagruel's explanation there is no hint of the misogynist 'monastic' contention that to have a wife as though one had her not implied the desirability of abstaining from coïtus. There is no hint either of the Augustinian notion, widely held, which would restrict the help a woman can give her husband to the begetting of children. Nothing in Pantagruel's speech ties the wife down to being no more than a mother to his children. Barren or fertile, she is a potential source of joy, happiness and companionship. Throughout the *Tiers Livre* theological commonplaces are consistently interpreted in ways favourable to the married state. The authority of the husband over the wife is interpreted in terms of example, understanding and freedom. It is, however, never questioned in itself. Only the rejection of New Testament authority can enable Christians to do that.

Rabelais brought the golden mean of classical wisdom into the very text of the apostle whom he most admired. His explanation is redolent of Stoico-Christian apathy; it shows what is really meant in a Christian context by that great Platonic and Ciceronian adage *Nemo sibi nascitur*: the Christian is indeed not 'born for himself alone', fulfilling his duties to his country and his friends within a hierarchy of duties where love for his wife finds an honoured place. But even more highly is placed the love he owes to God (*TL* XXXV, end).

16. *Panurge's madness and Christian prophecy*

That is the full reply to Panurge's perplexity in terms of the thesis. He has his answer. But the man who had earlier abused St Paul's marriage chapter and had twisted the wisdom of Plato and Cicero into material for sophistical jesting is not likely to profit by Pantagruel's syncretistic wisdom. On the contrary, it sends him mad.

Yet even now Panurge is not abandoned to his own devices. Among the major sources of revelation is prophecy, which is, traditionally, a spiritual gift sometimes vouchsafed to the pure and simple-minded. We are now to be taken into new territory: that of Christian prophecy and Christian folly.

The *Tiers Livre* is a book concerned with prophecy in many of its senses. Pantagruel is prophetic within a definition, very much at home in Erasmian Biblical exegesis, according to which the true sense of prophet, in Holy Writ as in Holy Church, does not consist in a mere foretelling of the future; the prophet is the man who is inspired to reveal the true inner sense of scripture. Pantagruel is a prophet in this sense; his ability to prophesy is a function of the gift of wisdom with which God has endowed him. The highest sense of the word *prophētēs* in Biblical Greek is one who speaks out for God and interprets his will. Pantagruel does that here.

Panurge, confronted with Pantagruel's prophetic exegesis, is on the point of being driven insane by Trouillogan. His reaction to Pantagruel and to Trouillogan is, as usual, to spin words. While Panurge waffles, Trouillogan answers him with comic literalness. When Panurge begs for advice, he is thrown back on the counsel most pleasing to Pantagruel and which had been confirmed, amongst the others, by Hippothadée.

> – But counsel me, by grace – What must I do?
> – What you will (*Ce que voulez*).

Trouillogan's attitude to his own marriage is a comic model of indifference. Was he ever cuckolded? Was he happy? His reply is, that his marriage accorded to his fate: *Comme porte mon sort fatal* (*TL* XXXVI). These words all take us back to Pantagruel's original contention, when Panurge first hesitantly begged him for advice about his marriage:

Are you not certain about your will (*votre vouloir*)? The principal point lies there: all
the rest is fortuitous and dependent on the fatal dispositions of heaven (*TL, TLF*
x, 10f.).

Trouillogan is particularly sceptical about the faithfulness of Panurge's
future wife: an amusing example of sceptical doubt if ever there was one!
Panurge, meanwhile, returns to his diabolical concerns.

17. *Panurge's melancholy madness*

Throughout his encounter with Trouillogan, Panurge is worsted at all
levels. On the surface he remains cockily amusing, and so in comic terms
he is not totally squashed. He pops up for more, but differently each time.
His situation is now a dire one. At a deeper level Rabelais is moving him
into yet another and profounder level of error. Through his own mouth
Panurge is shown to have been driven genuinely and disturbingly mad.
When Trouillogan refused to be definite and committed in his replies,
Panurge burst out into self-revealing agitation, as different as possible
from Stoico-Christian tranquillity of mind, from that freedom from
emotional concern and turmoil which characterises the Pantagrueline
ideal. Panurge is supremely agitated and distressed. His *phrenes*, *metaphrenes* and *diaphragmes* are in a state of acute turmoil. In medical
terminology, both *diaphragme* and *phrenes* are connected with the mind (the
mens). Rabelais uses these words both for comic effect and to prepare the
way for the recognition of Panurge's madness. To translate the outburst of
Panurge would be misleading. It would suggest his words have a meaning.
They do not: they reveal his agitation and the madness which caused it:

*Toutes mes phrenes, metaphrenes et diaphragmes sont suspenduz et tenduz pour incorni-
fistibuler en la gibbessiere de mon entendement ce que dictez et repondez* (TL, TLF xxxvi,
101f.).

We laugh at him – made-up words such as *incornifistibuler* are used by
Rabelais to good effect; but we should be aware that we are now laughing
at incipient madness. Panurge has become an alienated melancholic. He is a
particular kind of fool, a *phreneticus*: a man about to slip down the slope into
continuous and sustained insanity. Budé, every bit as sharply as Rabelais
does, makes the contrast between the calm sort of wisdom, which typifies
Pantagruel, and Panurge's *phrensy*. He bases himself on Cicero and the
ancient medical writer Celsus:

According to Cicero madness (*insania*) is what the Greeks call *mania*; raging (*furor*)
is what the Greeks call *melancholia*. Elsewhere, interpreting madness philosophically, he asserts that the soul's health is said to be found in tranquillity and

constancy. A mind empty of those qualities is called mad, because there can be no health in a disturbed soul or body. Celsus, in his third book, says that the Latins call *insania* what the Greeks call *phrenesis*. For *phrenesis* (frenzy) or as the Greeks say, *phrenitis*, is an acute illness accompanying fever, by which the sick become silly and say strange things (*aliena*). (Budé, *Opera* III, 254D-55A)

The tense state of Panurge's *phrenes, metaphrenes* and *diaphragmes* amusingly reveals, with medical precision, the state of his *nous* or *mens*, that divinest part of man. We now realise that he is not only self-lovingly blind and diabolically misled; he is no longer rational.

Through many chapters, Rabelais is now concerned with madness of all sorts. The number of fools, we are told, is infinite. With great art and much laughter, Rabelais disentangles the main categories: mere insanity, diabolical possession, the self-loving errors with which a learned fool can deceive himself, that irreligious foolishness that counts for wisdom in this world. Panurge is touched by them all and so is placed at the opposite pole from the philosophical apathy of the Christian sage, whose mind is bathed in the light of pure angelic powers, and also from that wisdom which is madness only in the eyes of the worldly. One of the firmest of convictions of Christians who knew the scriptural exegesis of Erasmus was that there exists a good Christian form of madness, a good divinely ordered Christian folly, which is one of the great charismata of a loving God who moves in a way mysterious indeed to those whose wisdom is simply the wisdom of this world. Such Christian folly is not incompatible with true wisdom, which is also a gift of the Spirit: on the contrary, as befits gifts freely given by the same Spirit, diversity does not mean incompatibility. Divinely given wisdom and divinely given folly reach the same goal by different routes.

Christian folly, that neglect of this world which enables Christians so to pass through things temporal that they finally lose not the things eternal, is associated nowadays above all with Erasmus's *Praise of Folly* but is far more authoritatively supported. That the Christians' way of life should appear mere folly in the eyes of the worldly is scriptural; the great exemplar of Christian folly was St Paul; Christ's own behaviour made his very family think he was a madman. To be a 'fool for the sake of Christ' is an ideal associated more with the eastern than the western Church: but precisely in the Renaissance the richness of eastern theology, and not only ancient patristic theology, was being avidly discovered or rediscovered in the west. Men of unimpeachable orthodoxy such as Thomas More held Greek theology to be far richer than that of the Roman west; Erasmus discovered in the platonising Christianity of the east justification for a concept of Christian folly which permeates much of his work. It was in no wise restricted to the *Praise of Folly* but informs some of his best theological writings. This good folly not only leads a man to overcome his *philautia*, to neglect his self-interest in this world; to suffer, if necessary, as St Paul suffered; it may ravish him in ecstacy, bringing him to a prophetic knowledge of the truth; it may enable him to tap sources of divine wisdom from which the worldly are totally excluded, but which may be revealed to particular types of 'fools'; its truth and its import are not at variance with the learning of the truly wise, but it will seem sheer lunacy to those whose master is the Devil, or whose values are those of this world, not the next.

18. Good and bad madness

The *Tiers Livre* now embarks upon a sustained examination of folly, an examination again marked throughout by Rabelais's marriage of evangelical learning and legal erudition with pure comedy.

The first of the two inspired fools we meet in Triboullet.

In a linguistic game Pantagruel and Panurge cap each other's epithets for the word *fool* in one of those long litanies which gave so little joy to most readers today but which can still provide a store of quiet amusement, as well as being pointers to deeper meanings within the books. Artistically they are a form of prose *blason* and *contreblason*, of sustained praise and dispraise. All the adjectives which Pantagruel uses to describe the court fool Triboullet – a real person as well as a character in the *Tiers Livre* – are highly favourable and positive ones: for Pantagruel, Triboullet is a fool worthy of such favourable epithets as *fatal*, *celeste*, *eleu*, *ecstaticque*, *autenticque*. He is – and the word is worth noting from its being a technical one in Roman jurisprudence – a *fanaticque*, a word deriving from *fanaticus*, a god-inspired fool dwelling in temples. In other words Pantagruel praises Triboullet's madness as a god-sent religious folly, marked by that form of ecstatic revelation reserved for the elect. Panurge, on the other hand, is no Renaissance follower of the old prophetic Faunus and Fatua of ancient mystery. He would have no place in the paradoxical wisdom of the Feast of Fools for he is a fool of another kind.[19]

Panurge's *contreblason* shows that his view of Triboullet's folly is quite wrong. For him Triboullet merits such dispraising adjectives as *terrien* (earthy), *papal, à simple tonsure*; he is a *sommiste*, a scholastic expert in Thomas Aquinas's *Summas*; he is like Tubal Holofernes, *premier de sa licence*; with a pun laughing at papal law consolidated in both authentic and forged

---

[19] Rabelais borrows some rare erudition about the prophetic Faunus, and Fatua his wife or sister, from the commentary on Ovid of Fanensius and Marsi (15th century). For the importance of such notions in a legal context, see B. Brisson, *De Verborum quae ad Jus pertinent Significatione libri XIX*, Francfort, 1683, s.v. *Fatuus vel morio*; cf. *TL*, *TLF* xxxvii, 37f. and xxxviii, 125f. Rabelais links together the prophetic Fatuus, Fatua, the Roman Quirinalia and the Feast of Fools. (See below, p.299.) The Feast of Fools fell during the twelve days of Christmas, often on 1 January.

decretals, including the collection entitled *Extravagantes*, he is *extravaguant*. In other words he is the mere jester, a fool *à sonnettes*, complete with his bauble (*marotte*). That is Panurge's wrong-headed opinion about Triboullet; his own diabolical folly blinds him to the divine nature of Triboullet's folly, leading him to apply to the good court fool terms which really apply to himself.

This verbal play is not gratuitous. Panurge and Pantagruel are to be just as opposed in the realm of folly as they were in the realms of prognostication and of wisdom. We expect to return to his catch-phrase *Au rebours*, and are not disappointed. Pantagruel eventually accepts Triboullet's prognostication as the fullest of all: Panurge refuses to believe it and blames Pantagruel for wasting his precious time! (*TL* XLVI).

This blasoning of Triboullet is an artistic device which confirms the reader in his knowledge that the *Tiers Livre* is now to be dominated by many forms of folly. Earlier, when the *Tiers Livre* was preoccupied with human sexuality, another *blason* and *contreblason* were devoted to praise and dispraise of the testicles, a punning device based on the fact that *couillon* can mean either *balls* or *old chap* (*TL* XXVI and XXVIII). Panurge applied to the randy Frère Jean – surprisingly present and surprisingly episodic in the *Tiers Livre* – epithets suggesting testicular confidence, health, vigour and copiousness; Frère Jean answered with adjectives applied to Panurge, all suggestive of slackness, sickness, wretchedness and inadequacy. On this occasion both Panurge and Frère Jean were right. But in the blasoning of Triboullet, Pantagruel is right, Panurge wrong.

19. *Panurge ensnared 'like a mouse in pitch'*

Once Panurge has been shown to be mad, his perplexity ceases to dominate the *Tiers Livre* for a good many chapters. After his *contreblason* of Triboullet, he disappears from view, only surfacing occasionally until he eventually consults Triboullet in person. There are reasons, legal, philosophical and artistic, which go far to explain Panurge's apparent eclipse.

The great contrast now is not between Pantagruel's gift of wisdom and Panurge's self-loving, diabolical silliness; it is between various kinds of madness including at least two forms of good, divine madness. Rabelais is leading his readers by rapid stages into the deep waters of Christian folly. It is vital that Panurge's diabolical folly should not for a moment be confused with the variations of Christian folly represented paradoxically by Bridoye and Triboullet.

Before he is condemned to pages of silence we find him in a truly sorry state: the once-confident spinner of words, who thought he could turn black into white, is now reduced to impotence and idiocy, by an invincible ignorance which his rhetorical fluency and wide erudition can no longer hide. Even Pantagruel can see no other way for him to escape from his perplexity than by seeking the advice of an inspired fool (*TL* XXXVII). We know of course with an unshakeable certainty that Panurge will twist this good inspired fool's advice and then reject it, just as he has twisted and rejected everything else: comic characters such as Panurge are leopards which never really change their spots.

In order to show us how serious Panurge's position is behind its surface comedy, Rabelais, with lightness of touch, links him with notable errors associated with characters in the two earlier Chronicles. We already know that he is dominated by the *Esprit maling*; we now see him in terms of the stupid and laughable young Gargantua of the bad old days. Pantagruel, disturbed to hear the news that Bridoye, the good old judge, has been summoned before the court of appeal to explain a clearly erroneous sentence, comes across the melancholy Panurge, acting like a dreamer (*en maintient de resveur*), with his head wagging up and down (*dodelinant de la teste*). He compares him to 'a mouse caught in pitch'. By such means Rabelais shows that Panurge has been rendered as stupid as young Gargantua once was by his Sorbonne teachers, in those far-off days when he used to amble off on an old mule looking for rabbits caught in a snare, while *dodelinant de la teste*. Only the purgative properties of Dr Rabelais's hellebore had saved Gargantua from otherwise incurable stupidity. Panurge is afforded no such way of escape. He is now in the position of agitated indecision which characterised Gargantua when he could not decide whether to laugh over the birth of his son or weep over the death of his wife. Gargantua – in the 1542 *Pantagruel* – was stuck 'like a mouse in pitch'. Now it is Panurge who is in precisely that state of inextricable hopelessness (*TL* XXXVII). (Cf. above, Chapter Three, section thirteen, pp:57ff., *Gargantua's perplexity*.)

20. *Panurge still more deeply perplexed*

Panurge is *perplexe*. His dilemma is *une perplexité*. This is his state throughout the *Tiers Livre*, not only in the chapters studied so far. These words, pregnant with legal meaning, are now used to form a bridge which takes us into the territory of Judge Bridoye. The term *perplexe* and its cognates have technical legal meanings which are about to be further developed, but they also retain the full sense of the Latin *perplexus*: 'thoroughly entangled.' In law and in moral philosophy, *'perplexity'* means a state of complete bewilderment, leading to a total inability to think correctly, to anxiety, to mental perturbation and eventually to madness. His perplexity is a snare (*lacs*), the strings of which are drawn ever more tightly around him by his own silliness (*TL*, *TLF* XXXVII, 10).

The legal precepts followed by Pantagruel, when he sought to free

Panurge from his perplexity by consulting the experts (*periti*) and harmonising contraries, do not exhaust the resources of legal wisdom on this matter. So far Rabelais has been concerned with simple perplexity, a state of acute confusion and bewilderment for which the law prescribed a remedy. Pantagruel followed this legal remedy; that it did not work was attributed to Panurge's deep-rooted, self-loving folly. But now Rabelais is about to take his readers into the more technical field of what mediaeval and Renaissance jurisconsults termed a 'perplexed case'. In law a *casus perplexus* is not just a case difficult to resolve but one marked by the 'maximum possible uncertainty'. In such perplexed cases, when all other ways had been tried, but not before, legal authority admitted that the solution lay beyond purely human means. It was acknowledged that there was literally 'no way out' of the snare, except by having recourse to the divine.[20] When this stage was reached it was right to lay aside all human knowledge – including knowledge generally but not specifically revealed – and to have direct recourse to God as represented by Fortune in her legal guise.[21] One does not have the right to do this in the face of each and every difficult problem. (Whether a man should marry or not is a dilemma which should *not* lead a wise man into a *casus perplexus* – though it could well perplex a fool, especially the kind of fool whose silliness is magnified by his unwise erudition.) Such a method – it is worth repeating – was reserved for perplexed cases when there was 'no other way' open to man.

21. Judge Bridoye: a Christian fool at work

Panurge is abandoned at this stage of the *Tiers Livre* because the book is about to play with profounder notions than any suggested by his dilemma. We are to be treated to comedy arising out of the madness revealed by his last kind of perplexity; the Christian folly we are to be shown behind a screen of laughter is much more positive than anything immediately and directly suggested by Panurge's matrimonial hesitations. Panurge is persistently and wilfully ignorant about the marriage state and its corollaries. He refuses to accept the natural limits placed on human certainties. He has refused the ways out of perplexities such as his which were hallowed by jurisprudential wisdom. He is the very embodiment of insane, diabolical

[20] *Institutiones Juris Civilis* with annotations of Silvester Aldobrandinus and others, Venice 1568, p.192v°: 'In addition, in law it is wrong to admit lots, *unless* the matter is so perplexed and uncertain that there is no other way out.' This is given on the authority of the same law of the Codex of Justinian cited by Pantagruel at the end of chapter xii of the *Tiers Livre*. Cf. also Albericus, *Lexicon*, with additions by J. F. Decianus, Venice 1601, s.v. *Sors* (additions).

[21] Cf. J. Viguerius, *Institutiones ad Christianam Theologiam* . . . , Antwerp 1565, ch. 5, §4 (*De Speciebus Divinationis*) p.71. Viguerius is even more favourably disposed to lots than Rabelais.

philautia. The ground has been prepared for us to move on away from Panurge and his self-love into the comic, selfless world of the foolish judge Bridoye. Panurge's perplexity will not be mentioned again, until Christian folly emerges triumphant in his absence.

Nothing in all Rabelais's writing is more paradoxical than the episode of Bridoye. We are told at the outset what qualities are required of a man who makes himself 'apt to receive the gift of divination': they are unmistakably those of Christian folly. Of all the gifts of the Holy Ghost the gift of prophetic utterance is most clearly charismatic. On this gift was based a theology of impressive intellectual and moral integrity, far from the anti-intellectual self-indulgence characteristic of later 'charismatic movements'. Platonising Christians, especially, believed that this charisma was mediated to an elect amongst Christians through angelic powers – through good *daemons* and those heavenly 'intelligences' who govern the stars in their courses. A man does not passively wait for such a hallowed gift of the Spirit; he can and must make himself 'apt to receive it'. This he does by so living that his character is pleasing to the angelic 'intelligences', who are the highest of all the spirits in the angelic hierarchy to deign to concern themselves with the affairs of men. Such a man rejects the standards of this world and refuses to accept the self-centred, self-advancing suppositions of the worldly-wise. The wisdom of this world is recognised by the heavenly intelligences for what it really is: sheer stupidity in the sight of God. A man who wishes to appear wise in the estimation of the angels must be selfless and foolish after the manner of Christians. To vulgar men he will appear a fool in the usual pejorative sense. But a man, in Pantagruel's belief, lives his life in the sight of these *Intelligences coelestes.* Rabelais makes his point with the help of serious word-play, linking together *sage* (wise) and *praesage* (endowed with prophetic wisdom through foreknowledge):

And so, to appear wise before the intelligences – I mean *sage* and *praesage* by divine inspiration, and apt to receive the gift of prophecy – a man must forget himself, be beside himself, empty his senses of all earthly passions, purge his spirit of all human solicitude, and take no heed of anything – such conduct is vulgarly imputed to folly (*TL, TLF* XXXVII, 30).

After such words we expect, if we do not know our Rabelais, to be brought face to face with a transparently saintly man to set directly against Panurge; a man who not only totally forgets himself and neglects his own interests but who may be 'beside himself' – ravished in prophetic ecstasy. What we get is Bridoye, apparently no more than a silly old judge who has decided all his lawsuits for forty years by casting dice – and who sees nothing odd in what he has done. We are given a broad hint. We are warned how often 'the counsel and prediction of fools' have saved princes and stages from destruction, as well as helping to 'resolve perplexities' (*TL*, *TLF* XXXVII, 17).

As we laugh at Bridoye we notice that the laughter he arouses has a very different savour from that which we associate with Panurge. Simplicity and single-minded certainty can arouse laughter as surely as duplicity and hesitation. Rabelais is, once more, so ordering his novel that we laugh at a character who is later shown to be worthy of our awe or our respect. It would be totally inadequate to laugh at Bridoye's single-minded simplicity without recognising, with the heroes' help, its links with Christian folly.

When Bridoye appears before the centumviral court at Myrelingues, he does not deny the charge: he simply excuses his error on the grounds that his eyes have grown dim in old age, making him misread the spots on the dice. With touching innocence he assumes that all his fellow judges have always done as he has done, deciding their cases by casting dice. His catch-phrase, *Comme vous aultres, Messieurs*, is one of the comic delights of his defence, recurring over and over again as he explains to the astonished court how he had decided his cases and pronounced his sentences. Yet not one of his crazily-reached judgments had been reversed on appeal for over forty years (*TL* XXXIX).

It is satisfying that Rabelais should be at his most profound when he is being so wilfully paradoxical and so learnedly comic. Legal knowledge now dominates the *Tiers Livre* again for several chapters: it supplies the jokes; equally important, it builds up the case for Christian folly with the help of authoritative and fundamental legal texts.

The legal jokes are largely lost on modern readers; they can be recovered, though not without much effort. Bridoye's defence consists of a string of legal commonplaces – used *more* sparingly, by the way, than is normal in the contemporary legal treatises, however densely strewn they may seem to us. Most of the actual legal allusions are taken from a little Latin memory-book variously known as *Flowers of the Laws* or *Brocards of the Law*. We are meant to know this: it is the point of Bridoye's statement that he had studied law in Poitiers under 'Professor Brocardicum Juris'! (Rabelais had long since had his comic eye on the *Brocardica Juris*: as we saw, a book-title of the Library of Saint-Victor, *Braguetta Juris*, the 'Codpiece of the Law', is a jest at the expense of this widely read little legal crib.) Bridoye strews his legal brocards throughout his plea with simple-minded literalness. The legal injunction, 'In matters obscure we follow what is least', he takes to mean that a judge uses his smallest dice when the case is a particularly difficult one; the metaphorical expression the 'dice of judgments' he believes to refer to real dice, not to the chanciness of going to law.

A few of the legal jokes do still come across fairly easily, provided we

retain a modicum of Latin and are not put off any attempt to enjoy them by
the cryptic abbreviations traditionally used when citing legal sources. For
example Bridoye introduces one of his most longwinded developments
with the brocard which had for centuries reminded learned counsel that
'modern men delight in brevity'. Rabelais's contemporaries laughed more
knowledgeably, since they knew of works which really did, in all
seriousness, cite this brocard in passages of almost unbelievable long-
windedness.[22] Other jokes were chestnuts, having the delight of an old,
well-tried jest, re-used in an unexpectedly new way. We may not
experience this particular enrichment of the humour, since not one single
standard joke of Renaissance legal laughter seems to have entered into the
common domain of modern comedy. But we can certainly laugh at
Bridoye's confused use of an authentic but silly gloss on the legal phrase,
'The horse flaired the mule'. It appears in the law known as the Lex Agaso,
which determined the responsibility of owners for the amorous propensi-
ties of their horses on public thoroughfares. Bridoye cites the then well-
known gloss on this phrase – quite dottily, since he is reminded of the Lex
Agaso and its infamous gloss by a French verb he uses, sentir (TL, TLF XLI,
50f.). In the context of his own speech, sentir means 'to be sensible of', 'to
feel'. But sentir can also mean, 'to smell', and it was the classical Latin verb
for 'to smell', olfacere, which the mediaeval glossator felt called upon to
explain. Olfecit equus mulam means, 'the horse flaired the mule' whilst in rut.
The glossator, distrustful of the latinity of mediaeval lawyers, explained
that the horse approached the female mule and nasum ad culum posuit, 'put his
nose to her arse'. The five-letter basic words still remain comic and
laughable; but there are some fifty-odd legal commonplaces amusingly
misapplied by Bridoye! An age like our own, in which even a cultured man
who is not an expert knows little or no Roman law, finds the humour heavy
and excessive.

22. The defence of Bridoye's Christian folly

The legal jokes, numerous as they are, are only half the story. Rabelais's
readers are brought to laugh at Bridoye as a prologue to his being
paradoxically defended by both Pantagruel and by Epistemon. Their
explanations of Bridoye's long string of successful verdicts reached by
means of his 'dice of judgment' are based mainly on Roman law interpreted
in the context of Christian folly.

[22] TL xxxix, 49f.: 'I (said Bridoye) will reply briefly, in accordance with the teaching of
C. Ampliorem, § in refutatoriis, C. de appella, and what is said in the gloss on C.1, ff., quod met.
cau., namely: Gaudent brevitate moderni ("Modern men delight in brevity").' For a serious,
long-winded defence of brevity based on the same locus classicus, cf. Johannes de Deo,
Cavillationes, ch. 1 (in Juris Tractatus Cautelarum, Lyons 1577, p.279).

Renaissance jurisconsults writing on the matter made the sharpest of distinctions between irresponsible attempts to appeal to Fortune through gaming-dice – they are rigorously condemned – and the correct legal use of *sortes* (lots) in deciding perplexed cases. Panurge, gaily wanting to use *trois beaulx dez* in conjunction with Lorenzo Spirito's diabolical *Livre du passetemps de la Fortune des dez*, falls squarely within the category of the legally and theologically unacceptable. Bridoye on the other hand, once comic exaggeration has reaped its harvest of laughter, is seen to be using, with startling success, a perfectly legal and quite acceptable method of deciding cases of genuine perplexity. Bridoye is at one and the same time an object of our laughter and an object of our awe. None of the heroes doubts for a minute (though Panurge does) that legal perplexities may sometimes be resolved by appeals to Fortune through lots (*TL*, *TLF* XLIII, 77f.).

In practice, appeals to Fortune were restricted by the legal scholars. As Renaissance law books point out, lots should only be used when the facts of the case were clear, but the application of the law to those facts was not at all clear. Rabelais knew this perfectly well, and later cites a standard example of a *casus perplexus* of this kind in a context of sustained seriousness: an Athenian woman discovered that her second husband had murdered the son she had had by her first husband; overwrought, she understandably but illegally took the law into her own hands, killing the murderer, her new husband. Should she be punished? The highest court of Athens, the Areopagus, was baffled, effectively adjourning the case *sine die* by ordering the parties to appear before it, in person, a hundred years later. Such a case, according to Rabelais, could rightly have been decided by lots (*TL* XLIV).

Rabelais simplifies the issues where Bridoye is concerned; but he does so with what were established legal terms, permitting a pious recourse to dice when there was 'no other way' open for reaching a decision.

Years earlier, Thomas More, a very competent lawyer, made the distinction Rabelais is making, in a book written in English, which Rabelais could not have read. More knew the limits to be placed on appeals to Fortune. He naturally accepts that such appeals can be made, but laughingly rejects the idea that any sensible person would take a wife on the advice of lots. Lots may only be used, he held, 'to avoid the perplexity . . . if there were none other way' (*TL*, *TLF* XLIV, 85 and notes).

In Panurge's case the use of lots would not be appropriate: his anguish does not arise out of that kind of legal perplexity in which the facts are clear and the application of the law is unclear. Nor is he left with 'none other way' out of his dilemma. It is meet and right that he should consult a Christian fool, Triboullet, as his last resort. Pantagruel simply takes it for granted in this knowledgeably legal book that a straight use of *sortes divisoriae* is not the ultimate appeal open to Panurge. In his case both right and wrong uses of dice prove irrelevant. But not for all men at all times.

Bridoye is too silly and laughable a man to be limited by legal erudition. He decides *all* his lawsuits by casting dice. For him, all cases are *casus perplexi*! He always has done this and thinks nothing of it. The element of exaggeration is part of the comedy. But it is also an essential part of the paradox we are confronted with. It leads to a serious puzzlement on the part of the heroes, who come to hear him summoned before his legal superiors to explain a manifestly erroneous verdict. The problem he poses is not that of one or two judgments successfully made by lots. In rare cases of genuine legal perplexity the idea of having recourse to lots, which include a reverent use of dice, would have occurred to anyone experienced in the ways of Roman law. The problem lies in his forty-year-long run of uninterrupted successes. In a divinely ordered world such a long run cannot be attributed to mere chance, not least when it is recalled that Bridoye's one wrong judgment did not mean that the dice had let him down at last. Because of his failing eyesight, he had merely misread the small dice he had felt constrained to use. There is no suggestion that the dice were no longer guiding him to a correct verdict.

For legal scholars, Fortune was the ultimate court. Against her judgment no further appeal could be entertained. This classical notion of a deciding Fortune had been christianised along with the rest of Roman law, as it was adapted to the needs of Christendom in Rome and the New Rome of Byzantium. The standard text authorising the use of *sortes* to obtain the judgment of Fortune in matters perplex was the law of the Codex of the emperor Justinian known by the title of *Communia de legatis*. We met this text at the outset of Panurge's quest. This is the legal authority with which Pantagruel had squashed his hesitant follower, when Panurge had declared his intention of appealing against the Homeric lots if the judgment went against him (*TL* XII, end). In other words the paradox of Bridoye had been prepared very early on in the *Tiers Livre*. Panurge's rash desire to reach his decision with three sporting dice and Lorenzo Spirito's book was sharply condemned as opening the way for the Devil. This makes any comparison between Bridoye's 'dice of justice' and Panurge's three dice quite impossible for anyone who knows his law. Similarly the evocation of the law *Communia de legatis* placed the whole of Panurge's quest within a wide-embracing legal context in which lots found an important place.

Another way in which Rabelais amusingly and lightly prepared his readers for the paradoxical defence of Bridoye's method of judgment is revealed in the first legal source cited by Bridoye in explanation of his 'dice of judgment'.

– What dice (asked Trinquamelle, the grand president of the aforesaid court) do you mean, my friend?
– The dice (replied Bridoye) of judgments, *alea judiciorum*, of which it is written by *doct.26.ii.c.sors* (*TL*, *TLF* XXXIX, 34f.).

The comedy aroused by Bridoye's literal interpretation of the 'dice of judgment' is straight-forward enough. But most readers today are likely to be foxed by the last words just quoted. They allude to a famous commonplace of canon law, to be found in Gratian's *Decretum*. This compilation, made by an Italian monk at Bologna in the twelfth century, was the foundation of a great deal of Church law. It was the basis of a system of ecclesiastical jurisprudence, claiming precedence over all civil law, both written and customary. The work was so authoritative, so frequently cited by scholars in so many disciplines, that it was absolutely normal to allude to it as Rabelais does here, mentioning neither Gratian by name nor the title of his book.

The sections into which the *Decretum* is divided are often cited with the minimum of explanation. *26.ii.c.sors* sounds cryptic to us; but we should not think that Rabelais – or Bridoye – is being unnecessarily technical. All he is doing is alluding, in a standard way, to a key text of the *Decretum*. The part of this work which concerns him is divided into *Causae*. These *Causae* are subdivided into *quaestiones*. These *quaestiones* are further subdivided into *canons*, known either by their number or by their first words (or, of course, by both). Bridoye seeks his authority not in the text itself but *per doct.*, that is, in the glosses of the *doctors* of canon law on that section of the second *quaestio* of the 26th *Causa* which begins with the word 'lots' (*sors*).

In parts of the *Tiers Livre* Rabelais may seem opposed to canon law as such – but that is an ill-informed judgment, based upon ignorance of the quarrels of his day (see below pp.281f.). The text which Bridoye cites was held to be authoritative by civil lawyers as well as the canonists. *Causa 26, quaestio 2, canon 2, Sors*, lightly touched on by Bridoye in his rambling speech, does not justify his particular dotty use of dice, but it does deal with appeals to Fortune; it becomes important later, when the serious defence of Bridoye's conduct is undertaken by Pantagruel and Epistemon.

Causa 26, quaestio 2, canon 2, Sors, when read in isolation does not strike one as particularly favourably disposed towards the use of lots. Nevertheless it did provide ammunition for scholars seeking support for deciding matters by lots, since it did allow the use of this method in certain circumstances. Moreover, Bridoye's case is not based on *Causa 26* itself, but on the interpretations placed upon it by the doctors of canon law in their glosses. Some glossators interpreted *Causa 26, quaestio 2* in ways much more favourable to the consultation of lots than the text itself seems to allow. One of the doctors of law worth reading on this point is Sebastian Brant, the humanist author of the *Ship of Fools*. His gloss on the relevant text would make a good commentary on the *Tiers Livre* itself (*Decretum Gratiani*, Basle 1500). His additional glosses bring *26 qu. 2, Sors* and the existing glosses much closer to Rabelais, making them very favourable to the use of lots. Having cited the classic scriptural case of the casting of dice to select Matthias as the apostle to succeed the traitor Judas, Sebastian Brant adds: 'So when no human help is left, we can then have recourse to divine help, as in [another *Causa*] *22 qu. 2, quaeritur*; and, according to the laws, in cases of doubt, recourse may be had to lots, as in *ff. de judi, Sed cum ambo* and *C. Communia de legatis, lege, Si duobus.*' These last two authorities from Roman law – from the Pandects (*ff*) and the Codex (*C*) – are cited by Bridoye from the outset (*TL*, *TLF* XXXIX, 42–6). The second also echoes the authoritative statement of the law by Pantagruel earlier in the *Tiers Livre* (*TLF* XII, 143) to condemn Panurge's claim to a right to appeal against Fortune. Inevitably, in an age when many scholars had studied 'both the laws' (civil and canon), *26 qu. 2, Sors* was often glossed by reference to such civil texts as Brant and Bridoye cite. Brant is quoted here as a guide, not necessarily as a source. But as he was one of the first to come to the support of Erasmus and his *Praise of Folly*, it is by no means unlikely that Rabelais knew his work, respected it and, possibly, drew some of his inspiration from it when treating of Christian folly in a legal context.

23. Bridoye and the gift of prophecy.

Roman law (honoured, but not above criticism) and canon law (the glossators of which are not always honoured, but known to Rabelais and sometimes pressed into service) form the learned framework of the sections of the *Tiers Livre* which develop the theme of Christian folly. Appealing to a christianised Fortune is, of course, a religious act to be undertaken with humility. Bridoye's use of dice to decide all his cases is an example of humility, but not of even ordinary human responsibility. That is where the comedy lies. So we laugh at his simple-minded and quite irresponsible appeals to Fortune, until we are suddenly made to see that his power of resolving perplexities is one special form of Christian prophecy. This fool is no ordinary fool. Bridoye is an humble man specially favoured by the celestial intelligences. His ability to decide his cases aright by the use of dice can only be explained tentatively in terms of gifts of the Holy Ghost. Prophecy in all its forms is charismatic. So too is the Christian folly which often accompanies such spiritual gifts. This explains why Pantagruel's wisdom, which is also a gift of the Spirit, is not hostile to Bridoye's curious powers, nor *a fortiori* opposed to Triboullet's prophetic madness: for though there is a diversity of gifts there is in each case the same Spirit. True God-given wisdom and Christian folly are allies not opponents. Bridoye's Christian folly is probable and conjectural, not certain (*TL*, *TLF* XLIV, 47f.). But we are left in no doubt whatsoever that Pantagruel's wisdom is charismatic, and he inclines to accept that Bridoye is an inspired fool. Trinquamelle specifically alludes to Pantagruel's 'bon sens, discret jugement et admirable doctrine que le grand Dieu, dateur de tous biens, a en vous posé'. Pantagruel finishes the speech which follows hard upon this solemn invitation to adjudicate, with yet another reference to God as the giver of all good gifts (*TL*, *TLF* XLIII, 10f., 60f.).

The tension between the scriptural seriousness of the language and the actual name of Trinquamelle is in keeping with the paradoxical nature of so much of this part of the *Tiers Livre*. *Trinquamelle* barely hides the venerable name of the great and erudite *Tiraquellus* (Tiraqueau), now a power in the land as a member of the Paris Parlement as well as a scholarly jurisconsult of great reputation. Calling Tiraqueau by the funny anagram *Trinquamelle* ('Bagatelle') is analogous to the paradoxical name given to the dying poet *Raminagrobis*, who was clearly not a hypocrite. All Rabelais's Chronicles supply examples of arbitrary imposition of names. There is method in his paradox, but this is not the moment to discuss it. We may simply note *en passant* that we no more think that Trinquamelle is a mere bauble, because he is called after one, than we thought Raminagrobis was a hypocrite.

Pantagruel's defence of Bridoye is embued with charity and compassion (*TL* XLIII). But there is no question of totally condemning Bridoye, and then merely asking for a light sentence. His numberless correct decisions had all been upheld by the higher court, despite his then unsuspected use of dice; this suggests divine guidance on the part of a God whose ways are mysterious and who works his miracles as and when he wishes. The Christian God, as the liturgy of evensong daily reminds the faithful, puts down the mighty from their seats, exalting the humble – not the 'humble and meek' of English worship but *les simples et humbles*, an alliance of words peculiarly appropriate to the simple and selfless Bridoye. Such terms open the doors to Christian folly. The divine blessing given to those who in English are called 'the poor in spirit', in both French and Latin more clearly applies to people who are 'simple' in the sense of intellectually wanting: *les pauvres d'esprit*, the *pauperes spiritu*.

Bridoye is modest; his character is a pure one. Rabelais uses to describe it the term *sincerité*, a word which retains the sense of the Latin *sinceritas*: cleanness, purity, soundness, wholesomeness. He has been found worthy of the guidance of the intelligences because of his purity, his simplicity and his conspicuous lack of self-love.

These august spirits, agents of God, make Bridoye into a man set apart, a man chosen to receive a variant of the gift of prophecy and so to be, in his Christian folly, wise above the wisdom of this world. He is 'beside himself', mad, that is, with that divine madness which Erasmus eulogised through Stulticia in *The Praise of Folly*.

The gift of prophecy that he has received is not the major prophetic gift, so valued by Erasmus; it is not, that is, the gift of 'speaking out' in such a way that the fuller sense of Scripture is authoritatively revealed. Rabelais reserves that kind of prophecy for Pantagruel. Bridoye is not prophetic in the sense that Pantagruel is; neither is he endowed with knowledge of the future. His form of spiritual gift is one which enables him to act as a vehicle for God's judgment. Elsewhere, Rabelais also interprets the gift of prophecy in a more traditional, less technically correct way, as a gift of divination. Such a prophet does have specially bestowed powers of foretelling the future. That is the sense in which Triboullet the fool is shown to be prophetic at the end of Panurge's search for counsel. But Bridoye is not *praesage*; he is, paradoxically, *sage* – wise as a Christian fool may be, *par aspiration divine*. To him is given the power of miraculously judging aright by the aid of lots. Faced over the years with cases which were all, for him, *casus perplexi*, Bridoye finds a way out of his perplexity through the special revelations of the angels of God.

What Panurge could have learned from Bridoye, if he were not so dominated by the Devil and self-love, would not be anything about his future wife, but how to put oneself and one's future in the hands of God, by accepting the rôle of a Christian fool.

Bridoye comes at a particular crisis in the *Tiers Livre*. We find him placed between two madmen: between Panurge, driven mad by his encounter with Trouillogan, and Triboullet, the court fool, soon to give the most significant of all the answers to Panurge's questions. The strange case of Bridoye is not a matter of mere digression or even of artistically delightful padding. With the episode of Bridoye, Rabelais changes the terms of scholarly and Christian reference: the wise, as prophetically interpreted by Pantagruel towards the end of the symposium, failed to free Panurge from the snares of perplexity into which his self-loving obstinacy had brought him. The theology of decision which Renaissance Christians read into their Roman law when the matter to be decided was so perplexing that there was 'no other way', takes us into the realm both of Roman law and of Christian folly. Further reflexions by the heroes on the case of Bridoye lead us by rapid stages to the more obvious Christian folly of Triboullet, a real live fool in the royal court of France, known as such to probably all of Rabelais's readers. Bridoye's rôle is not to foretell Panurge's fate in marriage but to remind the learned Christian reader that both sound law and sound evangelical theology indicate that the only way out of truly perplexing dilemmas lies in submission to the divine will. Epistemon is there to remind us that this is not an easy way out: that Bridoye is a case apart, not an example to be followed in all decisions of life; judgments by lot are not to be lightly undertaken; they are quite exceptional means, reserved for matters of great complexity and obscurity – for matters which are *ambiguës, intrinquées, perplexes et obscures*. As Johannes Oldendorpius – a considerable legal authority of the time – wrote about lots as a means of decision, they should not be used 'as daily food, but as a condiment'. They are an 'ultimate help' in cases of 'necessity'. He refers readers to *Causa 26, question 2, chapter 1*, where the matter is 'beautifully treated'.

The final word on Bridoye, as distinct from on Christian folly, follows hard upon the account of the *casus perplexus* of the woman who had murdered her second husband, the murderer of her own son. This final word was given to Pantagruel in the first edition of the *Tiers Livre* but is later transferred to Epistemon. The conjectural quality of the argument makes it more appropriate to the wise but not inerrant Epistemon than to the sage that Pantagruel has become. Pantagruel is now so heroic in stature that his stoical 'grasping impressions' make him never at a loss for certainty in his judgments. In such circumstances, even at the cost of a little confusion, Rabelais apparently felt artistically justified in switching to Epistemon a major speech which begins with a confession of fallibility. The speaker felt obliged to 'confess' in his opening words, that he had no 'categorical' answer to the problems posed by Bridoye's long run of correct judgments (*TL*, *TLF* XLIV, 42f.).

At all events Pantagruel, later Epistemon, conjecturally explains Bridoye's success in terms of that Christian foolishness which is the antithesis of worldly wisdom: the heavenly intelligences doubtless recognised Bridoye's simplicity and purity of motive; they knew he was aware of the pitfalls and antinomies hidden within the law, a domain in which the Devil's agents are particularly busy turning (like Panurge, or like Cepola who was attacked in *Pantagruel*) black into white. Rabelais, interpreting his Vulgate literally, reads such a warning into the text of that great folly chapter which is the twelfth of St Paul's Second Epistle to the Corinthians: 'For Satan himself is transformed into an angel of light. Therefore it is no great thing if his ministers also be transformed *as ministers of justice*.' The Devil, in other words, works through those evil men who subvert the justice they are professionally supposed to serve. Their crime is all the greater for their masking of evil in the apparent light of righteousness. Rabelais uses this text twice in the *Tiers Livre*. Under such conditions, including the risk of Satanic deception, a simple and a good man like Bridoye may turn directly to God for advice – to God whom the scriptures call the Just Judge; he may invoke the help of heavenly grace, recognising his perplexity for what it is and seeking to *reconnoitre* the will of God. All this in accord with the interpretation of Roman law in Renaissance times.

The *Tiers Livre* is an intellectually committed book, taking sides in many of the quarrels of the day. This explains an oddity in Rabelais's advocacy of Christian folly.

Bridoye, early in his defence, cited a major *causa* of Gratian's *Decretum*: 26, *quaestio 2, canon 2, Sors*. Yet when Pantagruel (later Epistemon) comes to allude to an important saying of St Augustine's best known from its being cited in precisely this *causa*, he attributes it to 'the Talmudists' not to canon law: 'Comme disent les Talmudistes . . .' The words of these 'Talmudists' are a direct transcription of words of St Augustine: 'in lots there is contained no evil; only by lots, in human anxiety and doubt, is the will of God made manifest' (*TL, TLF* XLIV, 70f. and notes). St Augustine's remark was made with reference to the fifteenth verse of Psalm 30 (31): *Thou art my God. My lots are in thy hand.* As this is a mistranslation of the Hebrew (found already in the Septuagint), and as the word rendered *lots* in fact means 'occasions', it is most unlikely that the Hebrewless and virtually Greekless saint had any Jewish source for his remark. The words which are attributed to the 'Talmudists' are not even indirectly talmudistical. Rabelais is using the word as a term of mild abuse. He evidently wants to have the best of both worlds. He exploits his knowledge of canon law to support the scriptural ideal of Christian folly; yet he succeeds in belittling those whose expertise lies mainly or exclusively within that field. To defend lots as an indication of the divine will he quotes from *Causa 26, quaestio 2,* and, without over-honouring them, from its specialist glossators. This has the effect of likening – not canon law itself, but some of its glosses – to the Jewish Mishnah, suggesting that, just as the Mishnah is a system of laws intended to supplement the Pentateuch, so canon law, as traditionally glossed by reactionary lawyers, often seeks to bind the consciences of Christians with un-scriptural additions to the light yoke of Christ's religion. Such students of canon law, we are made to feel, are simply talmudists, a new form of judaïcising legalists. Most Jewish terms, when applied to Christians in this way, are felt to be pejorative. But such an amused suggestion of judaïcising tendencies within Christianity is not necessarily anti-Jewish; it does not presuppose any hostility to Hebrew learning and is certainly not, in any modern sense, antisemitic. Calling certain canon lawyers *talmudistes* is in keeping with the spirit of the *Tiers Livre,* which is soon to show itself deeply hostile to traditional interpretations of parts of the canon law. Even when citing canonist glossators to support his case, he tends to belittle them.

The episode of Bridoye ends with a sharp attack on Tribonian, the ancient jurisconsult who compiled the *Pandects* for the emperor Justinian (*TL, TLF* XLIV, 81f.). This serves as a reminder that Roman law, however majestic, was itself a partly tainted source, though nowhere like as tainted as canon law. Had some of Rabelais's earlier enthusiasm for the Roman law been damped down? I do not think that his respect for Roman law was fundamentally diminished; but, in the context of the *Tiers Livre* and its profound awareness of human uncertainty, even Roman law is not a pure and infallible source of certain knowledge. Rabelais is going no further than Budé and many others who both admired the Pandects yet affected to despise Tribonian, their 'architect', as a dishonest compiler. Rabelais clearly shared Budé's belief that Tribonian had deliberately made a bad job of editing and compiling the *Pandects*, cutting his material up into gobbets in order to weaken the force of law and to tie the hands of judges. Montaigne agrees with both of them.

24. Triboullet and legal madness

The terms in which Rabelais writes of Tribonian are so vitriolic, and the passage from Bridoye to the court fool Triboullet is so swiftly accomplished, that one might think that the law is now to be left behind and folly discussed in a purely comic or a purely theological manner. But nothing can be further from the truth. Rabelais's conception of Christian folly no doubt owes something to Erasmus's *Praise of Folly*; but it owes far more to Roman law as expounded by Budé and humanists generally, as well as to Erasmus's technical theological writings.

Panurge has had six days to bounce back from his melancholy stupor, but he is in no ways cured (*TL* XLV, beginning). He cannot recognise good Christian folly when he sees it. According to Pantagruel, there is 'no other way' out of his perplexity, so his unwillingness to take counsel from Triboullet leaves him well and truly past helping. As one would expect from the self-loving, superstitious booby he has become, he accuses all and sundry of the evil folly he is blinded by. Panurge offers Triboullet gifts and then, quite inappropriately, expounds his dilemma *en parolles rhetoriques et eleguantes*. Triboullet interrupts him, thumps him between the shoulders, gives him back an empty bottle, bonks him on the nose with a pig's bladder and makes no reply except, 'Par Dieu, Dieu, fol enraigé, guare moine, cornemuse de Buzançay;' ('By God, God; fool enraged; beware of the monk; bagpipe of Buzançay'). These disjointed utterances are taken by Pantagruel to be the fullest reply of all, confirming what all the other prognostications had said and suggesting that Panurge will be cuckolded by a monk – a detail not given by any other of the means of divination consulted. Triboullet, the Christian fool, uses the name of God twice in his first three words – an artistic indication of his divine inspiration, as telling as Panurge's tendency to talk of the Devil or to babble about folly and lunacy. In his reply to Triboullet, Panurge makes rambling references to *follie*, to *maniacques* and *enraigez*, as well as making no less than seven allusions to a fool or fools (*fol, folz*) not forgetting the place name *Fou* (*TL*, *TLF* XLVI, 33–44). At one single bound the bare page which describes Panurge's consultations with Triboullet takes us back to the full problems of the hypothesis. We are not now concerned with Bridoye's method of resolving legal perplexities, nor with the symposium of the learned theologian, doctor and philosopher, all making their contributions to the general thesis of matrimony and cuckoldom. We are back fairly and squarely to Panurge's problem; and this is the end of the road for him.

Panurge is like a Bourbon who has learned nothing and forgotten nothing: it is no idle detail that he should stupidly address the simple-minded idiot Triboullet (who was playing with his toy sword) with words which were 'rhetorical and elegant'. Panurge cannot detach himself from windy rhetoric nor speak with the simplicity appropriate to a genuine fool such as Triboullet. Nor does he appreciate the true worth of Triboullet's inspired utterance; and so, as often before, he accuses others, in his self-love, of precisely the fault which is dominating him now. By refusing to recognise, as Pantagruel does, the signs of inspiration in Triboullet's apparent foolishness, Panurge reveals himself yet again to be a fool of a very different kind:

That's good, I must say. What a fine resolution of the problem! He is a fool all right; that cannot be denied; but more foolish is he who brought him to me; and I, most foolish who communicated my thoughts to him! (*TL, TLF* XLV, 36f.).

Pantagruel – by whose counsel Triboullet was consulted – holds him in high regard, from the first time that he is mentioned in the *Tiers Livre*. He now defends Triboullet as a truly inspired fool. To do so, he uses Roman law as interpreted magisterially by Budé in his *Annotations on the Pandects*. The occasion for Pantagruel to expound Roman law on the question of folly is provided by the curious way Triboullet moved his head. The court fool, when he gave his reply to Panurge, jerked and wagged his head about; he was *branslant bien fort la teste* (XLV, 26). This motion is not to be confused with the state that Panurge was reduced to by his melancholy madness – *dodelinant de la teste* (XXXVIII, 4); on the contrary, it is to be contrasted with it. For the movement of the head that Triboullet made was actual, legal proof that his madness was a divine prophetic folly. Pantagruel presents it as such.

All legal systems need criteria for distinguishing the sane from the insane; some, such as Christian systems of justice, also need criteria for distinguishing between good madness, divinely inspired, and all other forms of insanity: diabolical, congenital or pathological. Most European systems of law, until quite recent centuries, had such criteria. Legal humanists centred their discussions of these matters on a passage of the first law of the twenty-first book of the Pandects. This passage was known by the words of its incipit: *If a slave among the fanatics should not always jerk his head and yet speak prophetically*. . . . It tells of a slave who claimed to be insane, consorted with 'fanatics', but did not jerk his head. An ancient jurisconsult variously known as Julianus and Vivianus decided authoritatively that the slave was sane, despite the fact that he consorted with the divinely inspired prophetic fools of the temple – the *fanatici*, – on the ground that divinely inspired prophets *must* jerk their heads; such head movements are the outward and visible sign of their inspiration. Pantagruel attaches great importance to Triboullet's head-shaking; it is for him what it was for Budé and for Roman law: a sign-proof of his being a fool inspired prophetically by God (Budé, *Opera* III, 251). His head-jerking is in keeping with his first utterance: *Par Dieu, Dieu*. The testimony of Roman law is supported by 'the teachings of the ancient philosophers, the ceremonies of the Magi and the observations of jurisconsults'. The physical cause of the jerking of the head is the sudden ingress of the prophetic spirit, which overloads the brain of the chosen vessel (*TL*, *TLF* XLV, 40f.). This notion had long since been made accessible to literary men by Quintilian. As he wrote (XI, 72) 'to toss the head about (*caput jactare*) and to roll it about until the hair flies out, are the signs of the true fanatic'.

By linking his legal sources with both ancient philosophers and Magi, Rabelais is calling for support on the tradition of the *prisca theologia*. The appearance of the Magi in this list serves to emphasise that many believed that the visit of the Magi to the infant Christ served to baptize good magic. (In Florence, incidentally, there was an influential religious brotherhood called the Confraternity of the Magi; Ficino belonged to it.) Rabelais's interests from the earliest days found a place for hidden, secret or kabbalistic knowledge. There is no reason to believe that he doubted the efficiency of good magic, however much he may laugh at a naïf attachment to it or disapprove of tendencies to make it a rival to Christian revelation. In *Pantagruel* he had sported quite sympathetically with secret magic lore in the episode of Thaumaste; in the *Tiers Livre*, with its different terms of reference and its different audience, the sporting gives way to a basically serious concern with such arcane knowledge as can discreetly be placed beside the purer sources of Roman law. The *Tiers Livre* is dedicated to the 'abstracted, enraptured and ecstatic spirit' of Margaret of Navarre. At this time the Queen of Navarre was moving more and more into mystic paths, preferring above all the *Pimander* of Hermes Trismegistus. Rabelais could be sure of a sympathetic hearing from his powerful patroness when expounding his theology of Christian folly and the partly secret wisdom by which it was justified, in terms which found an important place for the Gospel and also for the ancient philosophers and the Magi. But everything, at this point, takes second place to Roman law as Guillaume Budé expounded it.

Panurge, too, is a fool, as Pantagruel insists on Triboullet's authority. But he is a *fol enragé*, a raging lunatic. For the first time in the whole book – just when we are about to say farewell to this madman and his obsessive perplexity – Pantagruel states openly and without prompting what he really thinks of Panurge and his problems. Triboullet is right; he says that Panurge is a fool:

And what a fool? A *raging fool*, who seek to bind and enslave yourself in marriage in your old age (*TL* XLVI, beginning).

(Doubtless the flea he wore in his ear signified just such an enslavement.) Pantagruel goes on to assert 'on his honour' that Panurge will be cuckolded – by a monk. There is no suggestion that the monk will be Frère Jean; yet the final disgrace of Panurge – not simply to be cuckolded but to be 'infamously and scandalously' cuckolded, so that his conjugal bed shall be subject to the contamination of 'monkish incest' – is most appropriate. It not only brings back to mind all the tales of monastic lecherousness that Frère Jean confirmed in *Gargantua* and which he briefly reminds us of in the *Tiers Livre*; it also paves the way, by the use of harsh, non-comic, technical terms such as *incesté* and *contaminé*, for a final onslaught on the meddlesome sexual morality of the religious orders two chapters later.

The terms in which Pantagruel engages his honour are those of a gentleman at home in a court dominated by Francis I, whose favourite oath was *Foy de gentilhomme*. But Panurge rejects his noble master's verdict. He is still *au rebours*. As once he babbled on about devils, so he now babbles on about fools, attempting to avoid the imputations of madness and lunatic folly applied to him personally, by talking drivel about all men being fools in fact. So they may be; but not fools like him.

As for the empty bottle which Triboullet returned to Panurge, Pantagruel thinks it may mean that Panurge's wife will be a drunkard; Panurge takes it to be an invitation to visit the never-never-land of the holy Bottle, *La Bouteille* (*TL* XLVII). The heroes agree to set off in search of the Dive Bouteille and to seek her answer. Thus the book ends, so far as Panurge and his dilemma are overtly concerned. The advice that Panurge was offered was cogent and mutually consistent. Yet his wise Prince fails to convince him; he remains unconvinced when confronted with the unanimous advice of men of integrity, most of them, in various ways, expounding ideas which derive from revealed wisdom or revealed knowledge. No wisdom, classical, Hebraic or specifically Christian, can penetrate through the devilish barrier erected by blind *philautia*. As a last resort, Christian wisdom gave way to the revelations of Christian folly. All to no avail. Nothing suggests that the Holy Bottle will be any more successful.

As an ending to Panurge's search for certainty, the plan to visit the Holy Bottle – a vague quest, perhaps in some ways in indulgent parody of the quest for the Holy Grail – is in the comic tradition. Panurge remains unchanged in his ignorance and lunacy; he has not bored us by his perverse ingenuity, so that, while we condemn him totally, he remains dear to us since he has amused us. As for Pantagruel, he is unchanged in his charity and wisdom. The reader of the *Tiers Livre* has no more to believe that there will actually be a sequel telling of a journey to the Holy Bottle, than the reader of *Pantagruel* had to believe the comic outline of future adventures given banteringly at the end of the first book. Indeed, the reader thinks less of a sequel than of later versions of *Pantagruel*, for the heroes' journey will take them through the land of the Lanterns whose language, *Lanternois*, Panurge speaks in the *Tiers Livre* (*TL* XLVII, end). He does in the second edition of *Pantagruel* too, although the newly invented tongue is not identified as *Lanternois* before 1542 – that is, four years before the *Tiers Livre* was published. Rabelais borrowed the idea of a *pays des Lanternes* and of their language from the weakish imitation of his Chronicles published under various names, including that of *La Navigation du Compagnon à la Bouteille* and *Les Navigations de Panurge, disciple de Pantagruel*. This little work probably dates from 1537; several editions appeared before the *Tiers Livre* burst on the literary world in 1546. Instead of indignantly repudiating this pale imitation, Rabelais brings it into the orbit of his own imaginary world by sending Panurge off on an authentic quest for *La Bouteille*. But the invented language of the Lanterns existed in Rabelais's works long before he, or anyone else, thought of identifying it with *Lanternois*. In ways such as these Rabelais increased the links between his various books as the years went by (*Pant.*, *EC* 78–80, and notes).

25. Unsponsored marriage

Of all the surprises Rabelais reserves for his readers, the end of the *Tiers Livre* is among the greatest. Gargantua, fleetingly resurrected earlier in the book in order to make a couple of important but brief interventions, suddenly moves on to the centre of the stage, delivering a major tirade against clandestine marriages, in the sense of marriages undertaken without parental consent. One can see the relevance of this tirade to the artistic structure of the *Tiers Livre*. Panurge, the excitable learned booby, the man from nowhere, has to make personal decisions which are inevitably the decisions of a man without family and without roots; Pantagruel, the ideal prince, the wise man, the ideal son, the Christian sage marked by philosophical apathy, by Christian scepticism and indifference, has duties to many people, not least to a wise and kingly father. Pantagruel is completely indifferent towards wedlock. He awaits the advice of his father the king before he even starts to think about such an external matter as marriage. It is taken for granted that, as a prince destined to succeed his father to the throne, he should marry and continue the dynasty. It is philosophically right that Pantagruel should nobly hand over all such matters – including the choice of a wife – to the decision of his father; it will also be found to be both morally and legally right, in the eyes of the giants. This fact helps to explain why Gargantua was brought back from the land of the Faeries, to be presented as the noble, just and debonnaire monarch of whatever land the *Tiers Livre* is actually set in, waiting in the wings to urge his son, at the right moment, to enter into that fertile wedlock appropriate to the heir of a Christian monarchy.

The projected marriage of Pantagruel is firmly placed in a context of legal and religious polemic. The giants champion a conception of matrimony which derives from Roman law; it was sharply at variance with canon law as traditionally interpreted, but not, Catholic humanists alleged, with canon law itself, properly understood.

Chapter XLVIII of the *Tiers Livre* consists of two diatribes against unsponsored marriages: a brief one from Pantagruel; one, fully developed, from his father Gargantua. Father and son are in complete agreement: marriages made without parental consent are – or ought to be – illegal the world over. Pantagruel speaks with clarity and fervour. His father suggests that he should get married:

Father most debonnaire (replied Pantagruel), I have given no thought to that yet: in such a matter I was entirely relying upon your gracious will and fatherly command. I would rather pray God to be found stone dead at your feet, in your displeasure, than to be found alive, married without your pleasure. I have never heard that by any law – be it sacred, profane or barbarian – have children been allowed to marry without the consent, wish and promotion of their fathers, mothers and close relations. All legislators have removed this liberty from the children and reserved it for the parents.

At first, this seems a very curious thing to say. Where marriage was concerned, canon law was dominant throughout catholic Europe. When it clashed with civil law, it successfully claimed precedence. As traditionally interpreted, canon law did not require the consent of the parents. Children, once past the state of puberty, could get married without telling anyone – parent, friend or priest. They simply had to exchange two sets of undertakings in the form of a civil-law *stipulation*: 'Will you marry me?' – 'I will'. 'Do you marry me?' – 'I do'. (These stipulations, known as *verba de futuro* and *verba de praesenti*, are still found imbedded in the English marriage service.) Once exchanged, it sufficed for the couple to lie together: they were then man and wife. The Church disliked such marriages undertaken without parental consent; in order to make marriage a more public act, the Church encouraged these vows to be exchanged in the presence of a priest – before the Church door, like the much-wed wife of Bath, or before a monk in his cell, like Romeo and Juliet. But the absence of a priest or other witness did not in any way weaken the marriage bond thus established.

How then can Pantagruel make his astonishing claim that no law – sacred, profane or barbarian – has ever sanctioned such a thing? His royal father, far from correcting him for his ignorance, congratulates him on it.

He is pleased that his princely son does not know of the abuses so widespread 'on the continent'. There, children are encouraged to marry each other by monastic hypocrites, who will later have their immoral pickings from the girl. Such 'moles' as these monks should be slaughtered out of hand. These alleged marriages without parental consent should be classed as rape, whether the girls concerned agreed to them or not. The harsh punishments meted out to the aiders and abettors of rape should be applied to all concerned. And if the State fails to give satisfaction, noblemen should be able to take matters into their own hands. There is Old Testament precedent for this (*TL, TLF* XLVIII, 106–50 and notes).

At first reading, Rabelais seems to be siding with those schismatic reformers who totally rejected the canon law of the Roman Church. (One of the first actions of the City Council of Zurich, after the Zwinglian reformation in the 1520s, was to place marriage under civil jurisdiction and to permit divorce.) A reading of contemporary controversy makes this an impossible conclusion. Rabelais is writing as a Gallican, interpreting a crux of canon law in the light of Roman (civil) law. This becomes clearer if one reads such treatises as Gentian Hervet's *Oration to the Council* [of Trent]. *In which it is urged that marriages which are undertaken by Filiifamilias without the Consent of those in whose Power they are, should from Henceforth not be Held to be Lawful* (1556). This Oration was intended for the ears of the Tridentine fathers assembled at Bologna in 1548, but was not in fact delivered. More extreme – and closer to Rabelais – are Charles du Moulin and Jean de Coras – who both wrote later against unsponsored marriages, using the same terms as are found in the *Tiers Livre*. Bucer, who hoped to persuade Edward VI of England to outlaw these marriages, also used the same terms (*TL, TLF* XLVIII, 34f. and notes). A slightly less passionate but equally categorical statement of the contemporary position as found amongst some humanist lawyers in Rabelais's France is a treatise by André Pulvaeus, who was a distinguished member of the Paris Parlement. It is entitled, *Concerning Marriages, Which are not to be Contracted Without the Consent of the Parents* (Paris 1557).

These authors cite each other. The less extreme such as Hervet are pressed into service by the more extreme such as Coras and Du Moulin. What these predominantly Gallican humanist lawyers wished to do was to re-establish in France the Roman concept of *patria potestas*. (In Roman law, this *patria potestas* in fact belonged to the head of the family – who might well be the grandfather, not the father, of those who wished to marry. In the propaganda of Rabelais's time this was ignored: the consent required was that of the parents – or of those *proches parents* who acted as guardians.)

The technical arguments used by Hervet, Pulvaeus, Coras, du Moulin and others need not detain us here. But we need to know that they reached the same conclusion as Rabelais, not by denying the right of the Church to have a system of canon law to regulate marriage, nor by rejecting the actual texts of canon law. What they did was to claim that the canon laws – good and valid in themselves – had been long misunderstood and misinterpreted by the experts. This enabled them to assert, like Rabelais, that no law, sacred or profane, actually authorised the wanton marriages current at the time. It is this frontal attack on certain canon lawyers, not on the canon law itself, which explains why Rabelais can sneer at experts in the canon law, calling them *talmudistes* (*TL*, *TLF* XLIV, 71), while citing canon law itself with respect. In 1552, in the very Gallican *Quart Livre* (LVIII), he goes out of his way, when citing a text of Gratian's *Decretum*, to refer to this collection of canon laws as *les saincts decrets*, with marked respect.

By classifying marriages undertaken without parental consent as rape, Rabelais was challenging the weight attached to a basic decretal of an early Pope, Lucius III, who had refused to accept that a girl who had given her consent to an irregular marriage had in fact been raped. This decretal is regularly cited by lawyers, both civil and canon. Instead, Rabelais preferred Roman law, which made the girl's consent irrelevant, if the parental consent was withheld. In such circumstances it was rape *sive volentibus, sive nolentibus virginibus* – whether the girls consented or not.

Hervet had discovered a way of getting round Lucius III's decision. Henry II was not deaf to this propaganda. In 1566, he issued the famous edict against clandestine marriages. The terms in which it is drawn up are redolent of the assumptions of Roman law; they closely recall the language of Rabelais. But the edict itself was a damp squib, since it did not deny the validity of these clandestine marriages; it simply expressed great displeasure at them and enabled parents to disinherit children who contracted such a union. Etienne Pasquier, the learned legal authority, member of the Paris Parlement and historian of note, was deeply disappointed. Writing to two professors of law at Orleans he regretted that Henry II had not taken a more resolute step, summoning together the whole Gallican church and having it declare null and void 'all marriages of children' based on *verba de praesenti* 'without the authority and consent of the fathers and mothers' (*Oeuvres*, Amsterdam 1723, II, 49f.).

It is in such Gallican company that Rabelais should be placed, when we judge his propaganda against clandestine marriages in the *Tiers Livre*. He is so successful a writer of diatribes that he may take us in. Today most would reject any such claims as Rabelais and the humanist lawyers made. Most, even if unthinkingly, strongly support the belief (which we owe more to the Roman Church than to the Roman State) that children, having reached the age of discretion, should marry whom they please, not those whom their parents want them to. To judge from the evidence available, most of Rabelais's contemporaries thought so too. In England – which could have changed matters at will by act of Parliament – canon-law style marriages remained valid until the Marriage Act (26 George II c.33) of 1753 – that is, for two centuries after Henry II's edict! As for France, Royal governments multiplied their condemnations of clandestine marriages, but could never bring themselves to declare them invalid. Trent had said they were valid and eventually, even in Gallican France, Tridentine views prevailed.

Two points are worth noting in these attacks on unsponsored marriages in the *Tiers Livre*. First, Rabelais shows no sympathy at all for love-matches. All the skilful writing which goes into chapter XLVIII is designed to arouse sorrow for the parents of wilful children; at no point is any feeling expressed for the children themselves. This is typical of writing on this subject.

Yet if one were to think that the existing state of easy love-matches was in essence entirely preferable to those based on Roman law as Rabelais interpreted it, one might note that, no matter how much violence he used, a man, once betrothed, was *never* guilty of rape against the woman, especially if (but not provided that) *verba de praesenti* had been exchanged (J. Viguerius, *De Raptu*, in *Institutiones*, 1565, chap.VIII, § 5, p.90).

The second point is less typical; Rabelais makes the real enemies of sober, lawful wedlock to be the 'moles' – the monks, who viciously meddle with matters which are (in a latinate phrase) 'diametrically opposed' to their estate as professed celibates. He darkly hints that if these moles think they can lay down the law to noble laymen – whom they tithe so enthusiastically – then those same laymen may well decide that it is high time for them to control the 'ceremonies and sacrifices' of these lazy, ignorant, vicious brethren. That was no idle threat when Europe in general was earnestly debating whether the monastic game was worth the candle, and when England had shown how easily monasteries could be dissolved.

The authoritarian approach of Rabelais in matters of marriage is at one with that adopted by many authors of his time. A Gallican like Pasquier thinks no differently. But by making the monks particularly blameworthy, Rabelais may well be showing more than a little sympathy for the 'Lutheran' Bucer, whose Latin and French treatises on *The Kingdom of God* were addressed to Edward VI. It was easy enough to slip from royalist Gallicanism to an approval of certain Anglican attitudes. Bucer's attacks on unsponsored marriages (II, xviii) closely resemble Rabelais's own; and, of course, like Rabelais, Bucer had no time for the monks. But Rabelais does not go so far as the Lutherans did. They made all the 'priestly rabble' of Rome – both secular and monastic – fall under the same condemnation. Rabelais restricts such attacks to the monks: the secular clergy emerge unscathed (*TL, TLF* XLVIII, 41, note).

In artistic terms, Pantagruel's forthright assertions and Gargantua's diatribe counterbalance Panurge's rhetorical and dialectical nonsense at the beginning of the book. Here is rhetoric used cogently and morally, not making black seem white but showing up black and white for what they are. But we need to recall that a diatribe, by the conventions of the *genre*, did not weaken the case being made out by carefully listing the exceptions.

Rabelais, in this chapter XLVIII of the *Tiers Livre*, is extreme enough as it is. To read him out of context is to risk making him appear so extreme that other ideas he expresses make no sense! In fact he shows himself to be, already in the *Tiers Livre* of 1546, what he will be even more clearly in the *Quart Livre* of 1552: a forthright Gallican with no time at all for what the Council of Trent came to stand for, nor for the traditional interpretations of Church law. The Council of Trent eventually replied in kind. In the 24th Session (1563) it reasserted the validity (albeit the irregularity) of marriages contracted by *filiifamilias* without parental consent. And, of course, Rabelais was put on the Index.

26. *Pantagruelion*

Gargantua's diatribe against the canon lawyers' doctrine of matrimony would have formed a fitting end of the *Tiers Livre* if the book had been exclusively concerned with projected marriages. In fact Rabelais adds two long chapters (XLVI and XLVII) which he later breaks down into four (XLIX to LII). For the *Tiers Livre* is a book concerned to show how man in his perplexities may either profit from revealed wisdom and counsel – including those of good scholars, wise men and wise fools – or else, under the diabolical influences of self-love, use the God-given power of speech and the elaborate sister arts of rhetoric and dialectic to pervert or hide the truth.

Rabelais never discusses such matters, delighting to show good and bad rhetoric in action. Dialectical skill likewise – though he increasingly seems to detach himself from all logic, seeking in dialectical studies (as did Valla, at times, and many others) theories of language rather than methods of argument.

But elegant speech and ingenious argumentation can be a source of amusement. So the very last section of the *Tiers Livre*, the eulogy of Pantagruelion, shows what you can do with language. It can be used seriously; it can also be amusingly used to make a silk purse out of a sow's ear. Rabelais shows this by again choosing to end his new book with an enigma, this time in prose. The enigma takes a mysterious plant, named *Pantagruelion* by Rabelais, and praises it in an elaborate game. Gradually we realise that this extraordinary and semi-miraculous plant is none other than hemp – or more correctly, because of confusions dating back to classical times, than hemp, flax and that kind of asbestos which was once thought to be a plant (*Linum asbestinum*). All three were confusedly treated as the same plant in scientific treatises, though scholars such as Budé established distinctions between them.

Rabelais's ingenuity is delightfully copious and comic. We might even be over-impressed with his erudition, unless we realise that a great deal of the factual content of his rhetorical game comes straight out of Charles Estienne's useful little Latin book, first published in 1545, entitled *Concerning the Latin and Greek Names of Trees, Fruits, Herbs, Fish and Birds*. Other borrowings which help Rabelais's elaboration are made from classical writers such as Ovid, Servius (the glossist of Virgil) and Plutarch, as well as from more recent writers such as Polydore Vergil (the author of *Concerning the Inventors of Things*, a book crammed with information) and the scholarly compiler, Ravisius Textor. But the basis of his rhetorical spoof is Pliny, who eulogised flax as a 'natural miracle' in his great work of *Natural History*, still highly honoured in the Renaissance. Commentators on Pliny, as well as his devoted followers generally, were impressed by the thousand and one uses to which flax-hemp-asbestos could be put. Such a modest, indeed, humble plant vastly influences the whole life of man. Having passed through some of the many uses that Pantagruelion can be put to, ranging from hanging robbers with hempen ropes to letting in light through oiled linen windows, Rabelais makes a sustained imitation and adaptation of Pliny's famous rhetorical elaboration of the great sea journeys rendered possible by flaxen sails. The source in Pliny was so well-known, and Rabelais's adaptation of it to the new geographical horizons of the Renaissance so close, that any tardy spirit would have found in this part of the eulogy of Pantagruelion the *mot de l'énigme*. Most of the original readers, *sçavans et studieux* as they were, can confidently be expected to have pierced the fairly transparent jesting mystery a good deal earlier.

Rabelais gives to his comic eulogy an artistic fulness which enables it to balance aesthetically Panurge's wayward praise of debts. In this way the beginning and end of the *Tiers Livre* are dominated by examples of encomiums. Rabelais also gives to his praise of Pantagruelion a Lucianesque flavour. He specifically calls attention to it with a jest, referring to the *Tiers Livre* as *ceste tant véritable histoire* (*TL* LI, beginning). These words directly recall the title of Lucian's *True History*.

It is this Lucianesque flavour which partly explains the gay, open-ended optimism of the end of the praise of Pantagruelion proper. The Olympian gods were terrified by the possible uses Pantagruelion could be put to. Pantagruel's herb caused them to have new and irksome thoughts, evoking memories of the Aloïdes – the giants who had piled Mount Pelion on Mount Ossa in order to storm the heavens.

He will be soon married; he will have children by his wife. We cannot contravene this destiny, for it has passed through the hands and spindles of the fatal sisters, daughters of Necessity. By his children, perhaps, will be discovered another herb of similar power, by means of which humans will be able to visit the sources of the hail, the floodgates of the rains and the factory of the thunder; they will be able to invade the regions of the moon, enter the territory of the celestial signs and take up lodging there, some with the Golden Eagle, some with the Sheep, others with the Crown, the Harp, the Silver Lion, sitting down at table with us and taking our goddesses to wife, which are the only ways of being deified (*TL*, *TLF* LI, 159f.).

They decided to discuss it all at a special council meeting.

Rabelais's sources of this Lucianesque passage include Servius's glosses on Virgil's fourth Eclogue – from the same lines which supplied him with a quotation to mock Panurge in the episode of the Homeric and Virgilian lots. But the principal source is Pliny. Those many Renaissance scholars who followed Pliny all stress the myriad uses of the one plant 'hemp-and-flax'. One went so far as to write that there are so many uses to which flax can be put, 'that I think it impossible for any man to describe them all in due order'. – He ought to have studied his *Tiers Livre*, where Rabelais takes up the challenge by running through the many uses of this 'miraculous' plant and drawing many a laugh from it! (*TL*, *TLF* LI, 136, notes).

The light-hearted enigmatic eulogy of Pantagruelion is noteworthy for its optimism. The pessimism is all on the side of the silly Lucianesque gods. In this respect Rabelais breaks fundamentally from his Pliny and his disciples.

Pliny was renowned for his pessimism, for his nostalgic love of a simpler past and for his tendency to look upon human ingenuity as a threat to the gods. He execrated the man who invented the use of flaxen sails. Polydore Vergil follows him: 'There are a thousand uses for flax, but especially in the making of sails, which is worthy of execration, as being for the misfortune of Man.' For Rabelais, on the contrary, the plant hemp-flax-asbestos is a great boon, not least for making long sea-journeys possible. In a strikingly independent way, Rabelais sees the new geographical discoveries not from an exclusively European-centred point of view, but as a way of permitting Taprobana (Ceylon) to see Lapland, and Phebol in the Arabian Gulf to see Thelema. Artistically he makes the multifarious uses of Pantagruelion into a source of amused optimism. Indeed *Pantagruelion* may be even replaced by a new plant *inventée* (discovered) by Pantagruel's children: such a plant would set all Lucian's gods and goddesses a-buzzing. The new plant could even lead to the 'deification' of mankind, as men sit at table with the gods of the classical pantheon and marry their goddesses. Is there any suggestion here that Rabelais really believes in human progress – a rare notion in the Renaissance but not an unknown one? And does Rabelais really put forward seriously the belief that man can obtain to a divine status through an ingenious use of the modest fruits of the earth? Of course not – at least where this second question is concerned.

The eulogy of Pantagruelion is a learned joke based upon Pliny's *Natural History*. Rabelais, a more than competent botanist, knew his Pliny and often drew upon him. But he was not overawed by his authority. In each of the four Chronicles Pliny appears in contexts where we are made to see that he so intermingles truth and error that unaided human reason cannot be sure which is which. In *Pantagruel* IV and *Gargantua* III the unlikely births mentioned in the seventh book of Pliny's *Natural History* are interwoven in the tales. *Gargantua* V takes this up again; before that chapter ends we are shown how only revelation can lead us through such a maze (see pp.134f.). In this part of the *Tiers Livre* Pliny is exploited more for amusement than for wisdom or pure erudition. And in the *Quart Livre*, when questions of truth and error are squarely faced, it is precisely in the context of Pliny's assertions about the mysterous properties of the elder-tree that Rabelais chooses to place the climax of his comic scepticism (see below, pp.448f.).

The description of Pantagruelion is an example of a sustained eulogy, showing what human ingenuity can do with words, once rhetorical skill is divorced from mundane fact. What Rabelais thought of human progress as an element in the divine scheme for mankind is made clear in a few amusingly scathing chapters towards the end of the *Quart Livre*. As for man being capable of self-deification, while Rabelais delights in playing with such an idea in terms of Lucian's unimpressive pagan Pantheon and the two methods of deification noted by pagan commentators on Virgil, in sober reality he never fails to see the gulf separating man as creature from his Creator.

The eulogy of Pantagruelion may be best seen as an adaptation to the needs of the *Tiers Livre* of an original fable of Celio Calcagnini, an author who exerted a major influence as Rabelais's concept of myth, fable and apologue. Calcagnini was a humanist of note, especially influential among Frenchmen from being a subject of the duke of Ferrara whose duchess, Renée of France, was of the French royal family, being the daughter of Louis XII and Anne of Britanny. Ferrara was a city sought by evangelicals because of the support afforded them by a French duchess whose liberal theology led her to protect many men who were in trouble for their religious beliefs in France. Marot and Calvin were counted among them. Rabelais can be presumed to have met Calcagnini in his visits to Italy; one of the reasons which Marot gave for wanting to remain in Ferrara was to study under this great scholar. The sustained indebtedness of Rabelais towards several works to be found in Calcagnini's *Opera* of 1544 is evident in the *Quart Livre*. Here, in the episode of Pantagruelion, the debt is not certain but very probable.

The fable of Calcagnini's which Rabelais seems to have in mind is entitled *Linelaeon*, an enigmatic name forged out of *linum* (flax). It is dedicated to Duke Ercole d'Este of Ferrara. In it Calcagnini tells how Nature, in order to help mankind, hid great and unsuspected powers within the same modest plant that Rabelais chose to praise. Since Pliny, the chief miraculous power of hemp-asbestos-flax is always its being used as sails to capture the winds, so bringing distant shores together. For Calcagnini it is Penia (Want) who disclosed to mankind this and the other multifarious hidden qualities of the humble plant. In the *Quart Livre* too Penia will play an analogous rôle, in the episode of Messer Gaster. In Calcagnini's fable, Machaon, the son of Aesculapius, made a draught from this plant which enabled Hercules to live in Heaven as a god – *immortale cum immortalibus aevum deget* (Calcagnini, *Opera* 1544, p.398).

Rabelais's tongue-in-cheek eulogy of Pantagruelion has much in common with this fable of *Linelaeon*. Both praise the modest hemp-flax-asbestos as a thing of great utility to mankind; both play with notions of deification in a classical, not a Christian, context. Both are doing more than simply telling a story. In Calcagnini the sense of the fable seems to be that man, abetted by Nature, can by intelligent industry raise himself up to greater heights, using the gifts which Nature prodigally and wisely bestows on him. In such ways, man becomes more fully and more richly human, once he has learned to read the hidden secrets which Nature wishes him to discover for himself under the driving force of human need. In Rabelais there are important suggestions of the same meaning; but that does not, I think, exhaust the artistic or philosophical importance of the episode of Pantagruelion.

Coming as it does at the end of the book, the eulogy of Pantagruelion counterbalances the windy eulogy of debts which Panurge makes at the beginning. Panurge took the divine concept of love and ingeniously debased it for his own self-loving purposes: at the end of the *Tiers Livre*, the narrator balances this with a sustained eulogy of a modest plant chosen to bear the great name of Pantagruel. Man's ingenuity can put it to a thousand and one uses. And man's ingenious rhetoric can praise it in ways which seem to make it divine. Better to use one's words to extol the semi-miraculous powers of an humble plant than to cheapen great concepts by twisting them into a defence of the indefensible. And better still, no doubt, in default of inspired authority, is to distrust the suasive powers of all words, until one has firmly grasped the realities which underlie them.

27. *The end of the* Tiers Livre: *Christian scepticism triumphant*

The last paragraph of the *Tiers Livre* gives us a barely disguised, elegant, and classically erudite praise of *Linum asbestinum* under the name of *Pantagruelion asbestin*. The last few lines recall to mind the Abbey of Thelema, now under the aegis of Pantagruel, and seem to anticipate the *Quart Livre* by alluding to the arsenal of Thalasse, the sea-port from which the heroes set sail in the early stages of the next book.

The *Tiers Livre* closes with an eight-line poem which draws its allusions from the second of Virgil's *Georgics*: 'Not all lands', as Virgil wrote, 'can bring forth all plants.' France can be proud of her modest Pantagruelion as ever India was of her ebony.

A suitable ending for a humanistic book. But a truly enigmatic one. We are no doubt meant to be both amused and enlightened. The amusement comes from our delight in breaking the clues to the meaning of the enigma and in our admiring of Rabelais's skill in copiously developing his theme; our enlightenment consists in our seeing with our own eyes what rhetoric can do. It suffices to hide the name of the most humble of plants adaptable to multifarious uses, for it to become an object of an equivocal mixture of comedy and of awe. With skill you can even make flax into a source of worry, at least for the comic old gods and goddesses whom Lucian taught the Renaissance to laugh at with renewed and happy laughter.

The *Tiers Livre*, citing in its prologue Lucian's example of Ptolemy's failing to please his Egyptians, promised us a mixture of dialogue and comedy. That we certainly have had in copious measure. This book, playing with ideas, playing with legal concepts, playing too with words which humanists including lawyers saw as the symbols of things, is a watershed in literature. Nothing at once so complex, so learned and so comic had ever been written in the French language. Nothing like it has been done in French since. Apparently no other literature, ancient or modern, really has anything exactly like it either. In Europe, the reading public was soon to change so much that this peculiar admixture of complexity, learning and comedy ceased to be possible. For that reason it deserves to be studied, as well as simply enjoyed for the very real immediate pleasure it gives; it deserves to be read in detail as well as read in the bath. The learning that it juggles with is obsolete at best; old, rusty and forgotten at worst. But not so the wisdom. The great philosophical and moral commonplaces – those of scripture, of the ancient world – remain as valid now as they were then. No more, no less. At the time that Rabelais wrote, these commonplaces, these basic religious, moral and philosophical certainties, were buttressed by great authority, both inspired pagan and Judaeo-Christian, as impressive as it was in essentials unquestioned. What could men, with their sleazy, self-interested powers of speech and their diabolical errors, do to shake the confidence which a Christian sceptic like Rabelais could place in such revealed wisdom! There is a kind of laughter which arises when confident men and women see silly pretentious fools vainly trying to upset their certainties and deviating from their unquestioned norms. That is the kind of laughter which comes to the fore in many parts of the *Tiers Livre*. Men and women do seem to laugh best when they are most assured, most certain of themselves and of their ideas. Hatred, on the other hand, goes with uncertainty and faltering lack of assurance. As assuredly as Socrates before him and Molière's Cléanthe after him, Pantagruel knows how to tell right from wrong. With this assurance he reached the height of philosophy as Seneca saw it (*Epistulae* LXXXI, 7): Socrates, he writes, called all philosophy back to moral behaviour and asserted that the highest wisdom consisted in distinguishing good from evil – *bona malaque distinguere*. 'Follow these things', he adds, 'if I have any authority with you, so that you may be happy, and let some men think you are a fool.' Pantagruel found his answers in inspired writers, inspired sages and inspired fools. His world is one where God and God-given qualities reign supreme. Merely human knowledge can never shake such certainty, any more than purely human means could ever reach it either. The pretensions of man or devil to do otherwise are worthy of our hearty laughter. Christian scepticism, as Montaigne was to discover, is a powerful ally of orthodoxy, when held by men of a particular cast of mind.

Rabelais's native comic sense was given body and moral direction by Plato's conception of comedy as 'boyish jesting malice'. He builds up an entire book about a silly friend who fails to know himself, so sinking into madness as the thongs of perplexity bind him tighter and tighter in their snare. But that man is not hated. The philosophical laughter of the *Tiers Livre* seems a peculiarly fitting one for a wise Christian fool to write and for others to enjoy, especially if they know their Roman and their canon law.

7

The Quart Livre *of 1548*

1. A rushed, unfinished book

The *Tiers Livre*, by the profundity of its comedy and the careful complexity
of its writing, suggests a work long in maturing, long in composing. The
Quart Livre of 1548 is by contrast a rushed job. The sometimes slipshod
nature of the writing, the slapdash structure of the book as a whole, the
inconsistencies it contains, all suggest haste; the circumstances of the
publication, while puzzling, seem only consonant with speed and a degree
of improvisation.

The reception of the *Tiers Livre* by hostile men in the Sorbonne acting
through the Paris Parlement apparently obliged Rabelais to leave France
for the free imperial city of Metz. We are still not sure whether this
removal to Metz was a flight from danger; it may have been a discreet
combination of quiet diplomatic work abroad in the du Bellay interest
with a prudent withdrawal from the jurisdiction of his enemies. It is
ironical that Rabelais should have found himself obliged to live outside the
proudly fortified frontiers of France which he had so enthusiastically
praised in the prologue to his last book.

One can understand why his old enemies set about censoring the *Tiers
Livre*. From their point of view it was a dangerous and heretical book. They
did not like the propaganda against monks and clandestine marriage. Even
more serious was the mocking treatment Rabelais reserved for the
traditional doctrine of contrition: behind Rabelais's laughter lurks a
contempt for the whole of this dogma as developed by the scholastic
theologians (*TL, TLF* XXIII). The Sorbonne would have doubtless
considered Rabelais's attitude to be purely and simply Lutheran. Apart
from Guillaume Postel nobody seems to have commented upon the
scepticism of Rabelais. But a generation later, the only French author,
apart from historians, that Montaigne picked out for praise, in his chapter
Des livres, was Rabelais. He at least would have savoured the scepticism.

Was it in Metz that Rabelais composed the greater part of his slim new
book? Plattard suggested that the opening chapter of the 1548 *Quart Livre*
was written at the same time as the final chapters of the *Tiers Livre* in 1546.

On the whole, I would put it somewhat later. The evidence seems to suggest that the 1548 *Quart Livre* was written in Metz – some of it, indeed, soon after the publication of the *Tiers Livre*, but not all of it. Lucien Romier, in an important historical study, drew attention to certain phrases in the comic episode of the *Moutons de Panurge* which must refer to the new sessions of the Council of Trent in 1546, and to French royalist hostility to the whole concept of the council. That would suggest that Rabelais was writing these pages not long afterwards.[1] In the version of the *Moutons de Panurge* published in 1548, reference is made to the 'chapter general of the Lanternes' due to be held 'towards the end of next July'. *Lanternes* is a word of many meanings, here suggestive of silliness and, no doubt, of obscurantism. Rabelais is alluding mockingly to the sixth session of the Council which was originally scheduled to meet in Trent on 29 July 1546. It is clear from the evidence of both versions of the *Quart Livre* that Rabelais intended to have his say about this allegedly ecumenical Council, whose catholicity he was prepared to reject out of hand. In this we can see Rabelais mirroring the views of a powerful, but not always dominant, faction in the French court. In writing and publishing his laughter-provoking propaganda he was certainly not fighting a lonely battle. One of the reasons why the snarls of his enemies and the thunderings of the censors could not effectively stop him from being published and read, even in Paris where their writ was supposed to run, was the solidity of the support he now received. Rabelais, as a protégé of the du Bellays, was inevitably associated with the Montmorency faction, which was generally opposed to the political and ecclesiastical policies of the Guises and of the Cardinal de Tournon. Tournon, as a convinced ultramontane, as in the last resort a convinced papist, was in natural opposition to the policies of the du Bellays. Rabelais had fallen foul of him on at least one occasion. When, in the second prologue to the *Quart Livre* (1552) he jests about the Trojans, 'from whom the noble French are descended', he may be laughing covertly at the cardinal, who proudly traced his family name of Tournon back to Turnus, the Trojan hero. At the period when the first version of the *Quart Livre* appeared, towards the end of the reign of Francis I, his influence was great, though subject to sudden eclipses. The declining years of Francis's life were not ones in which the king was for long periods disposed towards the eirenic, tolerant policies of the du Bellays. On the whole it was a rival party which was in power, exerting fitful influence on the ailing monarch. But the Montmorency faction was apparently the party of the future, having won the ear of the dauphin Henry, soon destined, as Henry II, to

---

[1] The *editio princeps* of the 1548 *Quart Livre* is reprinted in its entirety by R. Marichal in *ER* IX, 1971. The introduction is very useful and raises some of the points discussed here. Cf. Plattard in *RER* X (1910), p.124f. The 1548 prologue is also to be found at the end of the *TLF, Quart Livre*.

succeed his father. A man like Rabelais, supported by statesmen allied to such interests, could not easily be silenced by the theologians of the University of Paris, as long as his patrons remained loyal to him. Moreover, the University of Paris found itself strangely half-allied with factions which contained many of its traditional enemies; for while the Sorbonne was suspicious of the monarchist extremists, who would have subordinated both Church and state to royal authority, they shared with many powerful statesmen a fundamentally Gallican hostility to the increasing powers and pretensions of the bishops of Rome and the papal curia. In defending the tottering privileges of the Gallican Church, university theologians sometimes found themselves with strange bed-fellows: precisely those monarchists who were eroding their liberties from another angle.

In Metz Rabelais was in a city where Cardinal du Bellay's agents were very much at home. When news reached him of the death of King Francis on 31 March 1547, he must have varied between fear and hope. The blanket privilege which Francis had granted him on 19 September 1545 remained valid: but would Henry II afford him the same protection, based on the same appreciation of his art and his value as a propagandist?

In fact Cardinal du Bellay and his household flourished under Henry; even before the death of Francis I, Henry was sympathetic towards the German policies of Rabelais's cardinal, secretly negotiating with the Elector of Saxony, John Frederick, without his royal father's knowledge. As soon as he succeeded to the throne, he freed his court from the dominant influence of the Cardinal de Tournon; Montmorency, a statesman well disposed towards Jean du Bellay, became his principal counsellor. If the accounts we have are reliable the breach with the policies of Francis was open, wilful and immediate – public knowledge within minutes of the old king's death. It was with the full support of his new monarch that Cardinal Jean left for Rome; he arrived there on 27 September 1547. In Rome, du Bellay was charged with the oversight of French interests, both religious and political.

When the cardinal, whose health was far from good, summoned Rabelais to join him is not known. Rabelais may even have made the journey with him; we simply do not know. But it seems reasonable to suppose that Rabelais passed through Lyons later, some time between the summer of 1547 and early 1548, leaving an incomplete manuscript of his new book with Pierre de Tours, the successor to François Juste. There are reasons, which do not amount to proof, to suggest that Rabelais gave his printer the manuscript about the middle of August 1547. On the other hand, the oddly unfinished nature of the 1548 *Quart Livre* is such that other explanations may be the right ones. However puzzling Rabelais's movements were at this time, even more curious was this new book, which appeared under the name of 'M. François Rabelais, Docteur en Medicine, & Calloier des Isles Hieres'. It bears no printer's name, being simply published 'A Lyon, Lan cinq cens quarante & huict'. It fills – more or less – a little 16mo volume; the 48 leaves it contains in its three gatherings are more than enough for what the editor had available to put into print. By padding out as much as possible with stock-in-trade woodcuts and a free use of empty spaces, ornaments and *culs-de-lampe* (tapering tailpieces), the printer managed to stretch his text over forty-seven of the pages. But even then the last one remained blank. In other words, he printed all he had to hand, and that was not enough. This doubtless goes far to explain why the 1548 *Quart Livre* ends so strangely: in the middle of a sentence. It would have been reasonable enough for Rabelais or his printer to finish the book with chapter x: the great storm episode ends there in the first version of the *Quart Livre*, making a not unacceptable conclusion to a book not striking for its consistencies. But that would have entailed leaving no less than three pages blank. So the printer printed the beginning of chapter xi, finishing in the middle of a sentence and adding, perhaps off his own bat, two concluding formulas. The words *Vray est que*, the beginning of a new sentence, are followed by *quia*, 'because,' and *plus n'en dict*, the words with which barristers ended their pleas in court.

The most reasonable assumption seems to be that Rabelais had started a new leaf in his manuscript after *Vray est que*; that the editor had access to the sheets up to and including those words, but no more. He was determined to use every word he had from Rabelais's pen, in an attempt to fill out his pages. We can only make informed guesses to explain how this situation could come about. Rabelais may have been in a hurry and failed to give adequate instructions to his printer on how to finish off his new little book. It is obvious that he had nothing to do with the correction of the proofs: the kind of error which slipped by make that certain. He was probably already far from Lyons, either in Rome or on his way there. Yet odd doubts remain: is it natural for an author to be so slipshod and indifferent when his last book has been the subject of the authoritative censorship of Sorbonne and Parlement?

Why Rabelais should have wanted to rush his book into print in so unlicked a state can again only be surmised. He was short of money, certainly. But it is by no means certain that his printers ever paid him for his manuscripts. Was he anxious to get out a book pleasing to his new monarch? In that case why does the 1548 *Quart Livre* appear without dedication or privilege? Francis had granted him a privilege not only for the *Tiers Livre* but for the 'livres et œuvres consequens des faictz heroïcques de Pantagruel, commençans au troisiesme volume'. Such words would legally cover the 1548 *Quart Livre*; why did he not reprint them?

It might be supposed that Rabelais had no part at all in the publication of the 1548 *Quart Livre*; that his printer had pulled a fast one, recklessly publishing that part of the author's manuscript which had legally or illegally come into his hands. In some ways this is a tempting idea: it is true that Rabelais never disowned the book – how could he, the manuscript was his? – yet he never again published anything with Pierre de Tours, in spite of his being the successor to François Juste and the publisher of two 1548 editions of the *Quart Livre*. But this explanation runs up against the snag that the 1548 *Quart Livre* has a prologue specifically written for it. It is on the modest scale appropriate to the new book; its authenticity has never been in doubt; nor indeed can it reasonably be so, since it in part derives from the very books Rabelais can be seen consulting in both the *Tiers Livre* and the opening pages of the *Quart Livre*. In addition, its preoccupations correspond to what we know of Rabelais's circumstances in real life. The 1548 prologue perhaps makes best sense if it was written, not after the rest of the book was completed, which seems to have been the case for his first three prologues, but during the period spent in Metz, contemporaneously with the first version of the first chapter.

Nevertheless there is a sharp contrast between the 1548 prologue, with its bitterness and its aggressive sense of grievance, and the largely uncontroversial chapters which follow it. Any mildly attentive reader is probably struck as well by the rough-hewn, unfinished state of the text. This feeling that one is reading a first draft not a finished work is quite independent of the fact that Rabelais did fundamentally recast the book in 1552, simply discarding the first prologue altogether, keeping a few of its ideas for a dedicatory letter to Cardinal de Châtillon. The feeling derives from the 1548 *Quart Livre* itself, from its inconsistencies and its non-sequiturs.

Yet the 1548 *Quart Livre* does not deserve its neglect. It is not the greatest of Rabelais's writings but it is an interesting book, bearing unmistakable signs of the master's hand. Perhaps the worst fate that can befall a good book has befallen this version of the *Quart Livre*. It is normally called the 'partial' *Quart Livre*, a title which manages to suggest that the 1552 *Quart Livre* was somehow already in Rabelais's mind, and perhaps even largely written, when the 'truncated' *Quart Livre* appeared. In addition it is hard for most readers to get hold of; it is rarely ever read for its own sake but for the light it can throw on its great successor; it is considered so unimportant that most collected editions of Rabelais do not bother to give us the text of it, at best banishing the 1548 prologue to the rag-bag of authentic and doubtful pieces appended to the *Cinquiesme Livre*. Most readers have to piece the original text of the *Quart Livre* together from often cryptic variants. To do this properly needs an eagle eye. A brief laconic line in tiny print saying '*X-Y: manque*' is misleading in itself (since the passage concerned is not 'missing' in 1548: it was added later to a text in itself complete in 1548); it is also easy to overlook. The first version of the *Quart Livre* was so fundamentally corrected, re-written and expanded that one really needs both texts side by side to appreciate fully the changes and improvements Rabelais made to his first rushed, but interesting, version.

2. *The 1548 prologue*

The 1548 prologue is about midway in length between that of *Gargantua* and the spacious artistry of the prologue to the *Tiers Livre*. It starts off with the same formula as the *Tiers Livre*: 'Beuveurs tresillustres, & vous goutteurs tresprecieux', but we look in vain for the name of the speaker. We are simply presented with the 'Prologue du/Quart Livre/Pantagruel'. There is no way of knowing whether the narrator is supposed to be Alcofrybas, or 'l'autheur', or 'M. L'abstracteur', or indeed Rabelais himself.

The circumstances apparently underlying the comic stance in the 1548 prologue seem appropriate to a Rabelais writing more closely in character than in his previous prologues. The speaker alludes to the 'ambassador' sent towards his 'Paternity'. If Father Rabelais were in Metz when those words were written, as I think he was, to refer to a messenger, perhaps from Jean du Bellay, as an ambassador would be comically appropriate, since Metz was not a French city but an Imperial one. As for the allusion to his 'paternity', Rabelais had taken to reminding his readers of his priestly status. For the 1546 *Tiers Livre* he coined a new pseudonym, *Caloïer des Isles Hyeres*: what connexion he had with the Iles Hières off the French Mediterranean coast is not known; but 'caloïer' ('handsome old man', 'venerable') is a well-known title given to Greek monks, and, loosely to Orthodox priests in general. Doubtless Rabelais had similar associations as those of Byron in *Childe Harold*: 'Here dwells the caloyer, nor rude is he, Nor niggard of his cheer.' It also suggests more than a little sympathy for Orthodox Catholicity over the Roman variety. Allusions to caloyers and to his Paternity both serve to remind readers that the author was in holy orders as a priest. But he was not a monk. Brother Rabelais has been left far behind. Another reminder of Father Rabelais's priesthood can be seen in the prologue's professionally dismissive attitude towards both old and liturgically new breviaries. (The Sorbonne did not like the new breviaries either, and had censored them.) But the breviary that the comic author of the prologue had been sent is in fact a small wine-cabinet in disguise! Such things did exist. Had Rabelais actually been sent one? Perhaps; a private allusion in the prologue to 'an old uncle' does turn out to be a reference to a real man, Rabelais's great-uncle the 'Seigneur de Sainct-George, nommé Frapin'. Other allusions in the 1548 prologue are so private that they have so far remained unexplained.

Artistically the prologue to the 1548 *Quart Livre* is constructed about a deformation of the ancient Roman praetorial legal formula: *do, dico, addico* ('I grant, I declare, I give judgment'). This fact is unexpectedly interesting, as it shows us what Rabelais was reading during the composition of the *Tiers Livre* and what he was recalling, somewhat inaccurately, during his writing of this *Quart Livre*. In the *Tiers Livre* Rabelais alluded to the ancient monarch Faunus, son of Picus, who on account of his prophetic powers was called by the ignorant mob 'Fatuel' (*TL*, *TLF* XXXVII, 38). He returned to the subject in the following chapter à propos of the Quirinal Festival in Rome (17 February), which he identified with the Feast of Fools. In his jest, the 'Dieu Fatuel' is made the husband of the goddess Fatua ('la dive Fatue'). The source of all this lightly borne but somewhat rarified and fundamentally serious erudition is a gloss of the fifteenth-century Italian scholar Antonius Constantius Fanensius on the *Fasti* of Ovid. This gloss and edition, as supplemented by Pietro Marsi, was a standard work, opening up to the humanists of the fifteenth and sixteenth centuries a mass of learning. Rabelais follows his source so closely that we can be certain that he had his text open before him when writing the *Tiers Livre*.[2]

When he came to write the *Quart Livre* Rabelais remembered what he had read in the glosses of Fanensius and Marsi, but in such a way as to suggest that he no longer actually had his annotated Ovid with him. In the 1548 prologue he wrote, referring to the 'Ambassador' sent to see him:

The summary of his proposition I resume in three words, which are of such great importance that formerly, among the Romans, the Praetor replied with these three words to all pleas expounded in judgment; with these three words he decided all controversies, all complaints, lawsuits and differences; and those days were said to be unfortunate [*malheureux*] and impropitious [*néfaste*] on which the Praetor did not use these three words: propitious and fortunate [*fastes et heureux*] the days on which he did use them: *You give; you say, you adjudicate* [*vous donnez, vous dictes, vous adjugez*] (*ER* IX, 152; *QL* A 2v°).

The insistence on there being three words (*trois motz*), coupled with the use of the terms *fastes* and *néfastes*, shows that Rabelais is alluding to the *Fasti* of Ovid (I,47), which indeed he closely paraphrases:

> *Ille nefastus erit per quem tria verba silentur:*
> *Fastus erit per quem lege licebit agi.*

(The day is of ill omen on which the Three Words are silent; that day is of good omen on which it is right to transact legal matters.)

The Fanensius–Marsi gloss explains that the three words the praetor had to pronounce, when mystically authorised to do so by the omens, were *do*,

---

[2] Ovid, *Fasti*, 1489 (Bodley, Auct. N. infra 1.26); f. lx v°, col 2; s.v. *Idibus agrestis fumant altaria Fauni.*

dico, addico: do ('I grant'), when giving the power to cite someone before the courts; *dico* ('I pronounce'), when bestowing the privilege to pronounce sentence, and finally *addico* ('I am propitious', 'I award' or 'I adjudicate'), a rare verb confined to augural and judicial terminology.[3] Rabelais builds his entire prologue about these three words: but did his memory let him down, leading him to cite them in the second person plural not the first person singular: *Vous donnez, vous dictes, vous adjugez?* This does seem to be what happened, despite *do, dico, addico* being so memorable a jingle.

The same partially correct recollection of the glosses on the *Fasti* explains his allusion, in the opening words of chapter I of the *Quart Livre*, to the *Vestalia*, the feast of Vesta and the Vestal Virgins:

In the month of July, on the day of the Vestal feasts, that very day on which Brutus conquered Spain and subjugated the Spaniards – on which also the avaricious Crassus was defeated by the Parthians . . . [and so on].

The learned glossists of the *Fasti*, Fanensius and Marsi, as well as explaining the nature of the *Vestalia* point out that the news of the defeat of Crassus by the Parthians reached Rome on the day of the Feast of the Vestals, when Brutus was surnamed *Callaecus* because of his victory over the *gens callaïcus*, a people of western Spain. Rabelais wrongly makes the Vestalia the day on which Crassus was defeated, not the day on which the news of the disaster reached Rome.[4] His calling of Crassus *l'avaricieux* is derived not from his humanist edition of Ovid but from Plutarch's *Lives* (543C). Similarly Plutarch's *Moralia* are used to condemn his hypocritical censoring enemies in the prologue (*QL* 291; *Moralia* 1128B). This combination of Ovid and his interpreters with Plutarch later gives rise to one of the most beautifully written chapters of the 1552 *Quart Livre*. Ovid and Plutarch are major influences on Rabelais at this time.

These details help, I think, to grasp what Rabelais's original plan for his *Quart Livre* might have been. The *Quart Livre* seems first to have been conceived as a mock-heroic tale unexpectedly evoking in the midst of its laughter memories of Homer and of Virgil. Rabelais makes Pantagruel and his fleet set off for the *dive Bouteille* – not yet hebraicised into the *dive Bacbuc* – on the feast of Vesta: as Fanensius points out in his gloss on Ovid's phrase *Vesta fave*, the Vestalia were held in especial respect because 'not a few writers' say that Aeneas arrived in Italy from Troy on that very day. In other words, Pantagruel and his heroes set out on their mock-epic voyage on the same day that the pious Aeneas finished his heroic journey and reached the future site of Rome. We might reasonably assume that the

[3] *Fasti*: 1489 edition, fol. a 8 r°; 1527 Alexander Paganini edition, p. 16 r°. (I have used these two editions for convenience sake.)

[4] *Fasti*: 1489, a 3 r°; 1527, ccxxvii r°.

Quart Livre of 1548 was first thought of in humanist vein, as a comic epic, drawing upon rare erudition to make some of its finer points.

Parts of the *Tiers Livre* as well as the prologue and chapter I of the 1548 *Quart Livre*, were written with the same glosses on Ovid's *Fasti* in mind. But then the ways part: the opening chapters of both versions of the *Quart Livre* are among the least erudite ones of Rabelais's entire writing. That does not mean that they evoke any less laughter!

On the cover of the drinking-set 'breviary' that Rabelais was given was a picture of an epic battle of the birds, between the magpies and the jays. The theme was well known before Rabelais took it up. Rabelais relates it for the sheer pleasure of the story, spicing it with mock-heroic comedy and classical adage or apophthegm.

Three sections of the 1548 prologue are introduced by the three praetorial words. The sections of the prologue built about *do* and *dico* are gay, uncomplicated and uncontroversial. We find an evangelical evocation of God's power and an invitation to do nothing without first praising his most holy name. We also find a subtle mistranslation of a well-known line from that 'ancient Pantagruelist' Horace, with which Rabelais proudly, and in very truth, claims that his writings pleased his monarch. Horace wrote (*Ep.* I. 17. 35): *Principibus placuisse viris non ultima laus est.* (To win favour with *principes* – the foremost men – is not the lowest glory.) Rabelais translates this into French verse, maintaining that it is no vulgar praise to be able to please 'princes':

> *Ce n'est, dict-il, louange populaire*
> *Aux princes avoir peu complaire* (QL, TLF 289; 100).

Horace doubtless merits the title of Pantagruelist on account of his ode, *Nunc est bibendum* ('Now is it right to drink!') Whatever else Pantagruelists are, they are certainly lovers of good wine.

It is Rabelais's proud boast, to be repeated in a serious context later, that his writings offend neither God nor king. But he feels forced to admit that the readers of the *Tiers Livre* did not find enough straight-forward laughter in it. That seems to be the sense of his defensive remarks about the quality and quantity of the 'wine' to be found in his last book:

You say that the wine of the *Tiers Livre* was to your taste and is good. It is true that there was only a little of it, and that the common saying does not please you: 'little and good.' (*QL*, TLF 289; 101f.).

Making the opening chapters of the *Quart Livre* examples of uncomplicated comedy and farce was probably Rabelais's reaction to criticism that the *Tiers Livre* was too intellectual to be copiously funny for unlearned men.

It is possible to feel that Rabelais is addressing someone specific – perhaps Jean du Bellay or the Cardinal de Châtillon – when he adds:

Moreover you invite me to continue the pantagrueline history, urging the usefulness and fruit received by the reading of it among good people.

On the other hand this sentence, recalling the claims made in Francis I's privilege, that Rabelais's Chronicles are 'useful and sweet' in an Horatian sense (mixing, that is, artistic excellence with moral teaching), make all the more baffling the omission of this valuable seal of approval from the new *Quart Livre*.

It is not really until the section introduced by the deformation of the third of the three words, *addico* (*Vous adjugez quoy?*), that Rabelais's bitterness spills over into terms reminiscent of the attacks on the Sorbonne added to the *Pantagruel* of 1534. Since those attacks were discreetly expunged from the 1542 *Pantagruel*, the only authorised work of Rabelais's actually in print which stirred up old memories by attacking hypocritical enemies in bitter serio-comic hyperbole was the new *Quart Livre*! The discretion of 1542 is thrown to the winds. The text of *Pantagruel* which duly appeared in 1542, stripped of its indiscretions, found it was rivalled by a pirated edition of the old unexpurgated text, printed by Etienne Dolet, a former friend, noted for his irascibility and indiscretion. Yet the new prologue recalls the aggressiveness and hostility of Dolet's unauthorised *Pantagruel*. The 1548 prologue has more in common with the tone of Dolet's *Pantagruel* than with the chastened text Rabelais officially approved of. Once more he holds up to hatred, ridicule and contempt those who censor his books – books they secretly enjoy but wish to deny to others. They are, in a string of colourfully aggressive words, for the most part already found in *Pantagruel* or the *Pantagrueline Prognostication*, 'caphards, cagots, matagotz, botineurs, papelards, burgotz, patespelues, porteurs de rogatons, chat-temittes'. These hypocrites hide behind the fair and ancient name of Cato the Censor, but they are really servants of the Devil. Once more Rabelais reminds his readers what *diabolos* means in Greek, insisting how great a detestation God has for calumny and slander, since the Devil takes his name from this hateful vice. With a sustained borrowing for Plutarch's treatise *On the Unnoticed Life* he compares these so-called censors to two ancient gluttons who used to spit into the best dishes at banquets in order to put other guests off. These censors are madmen. Some of them are lepers; some are buggers; others leprous buggers. Yet Rabelais, as a good doctor who knows how Galen advised a physician virtually to court his patients, even going so far as to tell him to clean his nails, is aiming to cure the sick with his books, so reaching a public wider than those he can treat person-ally. The sick can find in his books pleasure and joyful ways of passing the time, without offending God, the king or anyone else. It is possible that Rabelais is to be taken literally: the pain and suffering of a Cardinal Jean du Bellay and of many lesser men may well have been eased by the pleasure they found in reading these Chronicles. But Rabelais so frequently uses his books as a means of spreading a sound and attractive Christian philosophy based on Christian liberty that the sick he aims to cure may be more in need of spiritual aid than purely physical medicaments.

When one reads the 1548 *Quart Livre* after this brief but well constructed prologue it is hard to avoid a feeling of some disappointment, even if one studiously keeps the 1552 *Quart Livre* from dominating one's reactions by inviting constant comparisons. On internal evidence alone, we feel we are reading an unrevised early draft. In chapter I we are told that the voyage to the Indies was accomplished in less than four months – 'without shipwreck, without danger, without loss of their men, in great serenity'. Evidently when those words were written the very idea of the storm which constitutes so important an element in the story had yet to be conceived. Rather sheepishly Rabelais put the record straight in 1552 by adding the words, 'except for one day off the island of the Macraeons'. By any standard this is an inadequate correction of a major error. In 1548 the style is often flat, even at times dull. The corrections that Rabelais made in 1552 are universally happy ones. For example, in 1548 we are told how Frère Jean swore by Saint Benedict's holy barrel that he would immediately know the truth. The words fall flat and lifelessly on the page:

Frere Jean des Entommeures dist: Par la sacrée botte sainct Benoist, j'en sçauroy presentement la verité.

In 1552 the same words are effectively rearranged, and the word *sacrée* is replaced by the learned form *sacre*. The effect is much more satisfactory:

Par la sacre botte de sainct Benoist: dist Frere Jan, presentement j'en sçauray la verité' (*QL*, *TLF* 94 and variant).

In 1552 typically Rabelaisian turns of phrase (e.g., the provincialism *on moys*) replace duller standard forms such as *du moys*; three such changes occur in the first three clauses of the first sentence of chapter I. An appropriately archaic savour is introduced with a hundred and one major or minor changes. Not all the changes are aimed at increasing the olde-worlde flavour: a few even go in the opposite direction. Rabelais's concern is to improve his style in every sense; taken together, they show that he was not at all satisfied with the style of the first version of the *Quart Livre*. What is likely to escape the reader who cannot make a sustained comparison of the two versions of the *Quart Livre* is how much of the comedy and gaiety is lacking in 1548. It is tempting simply to assume that the 1548 version contains most of the 1552 one, up to the truncated sentence, *Vray est que*. But this is far from being the case. Whole episodes are added later, yet to be conceived and written no doubt. The readers of 1548 could not enjoy the exchange of letters between Gargantua and his son, nor could they laugh their fill at the complex farce of the *Nopces de Basché*. As for the episodes which do appear, such as the *Moutons de Panurge*, they are yet to be enriched with some of the finest writing from Rabelais's pen. Probably the only part of the 1548 *Quart Livre* that can really stand on its feet, free from comparison with the 1552 version, is the episode of the Storm. In 1552 it will become much more profoundly comic: but already in 1548 it bears the marks of artistic genius and has a compact comic completeness of its own.

3. *The Storm*

The Storm arises after the heroes had met a boat-load of monks on their way to the Council of Nitwits, bent on sieving through the articles of religion so as to exclude the new heretics. (1548 *QL* VIII, 1f.). The Council of Trent was being removed on papal insistence from Trent to Bologna. French hostility to it was increasing. Imperial pressure made any attempt to hold effective sessions in Bologna impossible and the Council was eventually recalled in Trent as before. The du Bellays, with no little support from Imperial diplomatists as well, had hoped to include representatives of the 'new heretics' in the Council debates; in this way the council would not only have become more truly ecumenical, but could conceivably have healed the schisms of the sixteenth century, instead of prolonging them indefinitely into the future. The episode of the Storm is an afterthought which breaks right away from the planned serenity of the heroes' journey to the Dive Bouteille. That it does so – and that Rabelais rushed it into print – suggests that his patrons may have made it known that a few shafts aimed at the council would not come amiss. This storm changes the whole nature of the 1548 *Quart Livre*. Prologue apart, the story contained, until then, hardly any controversial matter. The mockery of the cult of sentimental alliances between monks and nuns is innocent enough. It attacks neither the religious orders as such nor the sentimental alliances themselves on theological or evangelical grounds. The *Isle des Alliances* merely suggests, with much linguistic agility, that so-called spiritual alliances between individual monks and nuns are likely to be as grossly physical as the connexions of an axe-head with its shaft. Apart from such uncomplicated and undangerous humour, there is nothing, literally nothing, in the *Quart Livre* of 1548 to merit the hostile interest of Magistri Nostri or anyone else – until Rabelais dragged his cloak in the prologue, added the Storm and gratuitously brought in an allusion to the great council in the *Moutons de Panurge*. But the prologue and the Storm go far to remind us that Rabelais was no passive bystander: he was bitterly involved in religious controversy. Why the *Quart Livre* was rushed out in 1548 now seems much easier to explain, however tentatively. Had Jean du Bellay called upon Rabelais to advance the policies that he held dear, attacking especially the Council of Trent for being dominated by hated monks, who were accused of wanting to anathematise schismatics rather than to bring them back into the fold? Hostility to Trent would not in itself have been unwelcome, even to those theologians in the Sorbonne whose concern for the liberties of the Gallican Church made them deeply suspicious of a Council dominated by Italians and by an ambitious Curia. But Rabelais, throwing to the winds all chance of a temporary pact with his old enemies, does not dismiss Trent simply because it was papal-dominated or in the hands of a crowd of Italian clerics: his hostility is based on its being dominated by professed religious, including the Jesuits beloved by the Cardinal de Tournon. Most Gallicans disliked Jesuits, who were notorious for their corpse-like obedience to the Holy See and little concerned with the liberties of the Gallican Church. But to attack the whole monastic fraternity was bold, and certainly not destined to win friends among the Sorbonagres. Rabelais mocks the Council for wanting to exclude heretics; many in the Sorbonne heartily approved of doing just that!

In this they were opposed to both official French and Imperial policy. There was a widespread desire, especially in Germany, to include Protestant theologians in the deliberations at Trent. The efforts did not finally fail until 1549 or 1550, when it became clear that decisions already reached by the Council could not be reopened by the Protestants, a condition they could not accept. The establishment of doctrinal understandings with the Lutherans was a life-long concern of Cardinal Jean du Bellay and increasingly appealing to the Cardinal de Châtillon. They were in favour of Protestants being invited to the debates of the Council.

Rabelais's intervention in the affairs of Trent is almost entirely restricted, in 1548, to the episode of the Storm. In both form and matter his satirical comedy goes back to ideas expounded in the first two Chronicles of the series. Whenever Rabelais sets himself the task of opening the way to reconciliation with the Lutherans, he bases his propaganda partly on the problem of free will. Erasmus, with considerable perspicacity, had identified this as the real bone of contention in his crucial book *De libero arbitrio* (1524). Rabelais, a consistent partisan of a synergistic theology, seeks compromise by adopting terms not unpleasing to followers of Melanchthon. He laughs at traditional superstition in his own Church, suggesting that it is not only ignorant and silly but fatalistic and passive; at the same time he puts forward a theology of man's cooperation with God which moderate Lutherans ought to have been able to accept, as well as evangelicals generally.

The Storm of 1548 brings up to date the propaganda aims of the attack on Seuillé in *Gargantua*. It may have links with Pantagruel's prayer in the first Chronicle of all, though they become clearer in the later version.

The Storm is vastly enjoyable in itself. But the laughter is not gratuitous. We are given a moral. The moral lies in the contrast between the wordy, sanctimonious and superficially Catholic inactivity of the fearful Panurge, and the superficially blasphemous, practical activity of Frère Jean. No other character counts. One of the pleasurable artistic surprises of the *Quart Livre* of 1548 is the re-emergence of Frère Jean as a major comic character. This return to prominence of 'the monk' is not something which should be taken for granted: after dominating part of the second half of *Gargantua*, he slipped into the background of the *Tiers Livre*, a minor character playing a minor rôle. When Rabelais does bring him back into the foreground during the late-conceived episode of the Storm, it is in order to make, all over again, many of the theological points which he had made through him in the tale of the raid on the monastery at Seuillé. In case we do not realise this on our own, Rabelais points out that parallel through Frère Jean's own mouth.

In *Gargantua* the story of the attack on Seuillé was used to defend a synergistic doctrine which left room for man to exercise his free will, and to aid himself. Passiveness was equated with superstition: activity atoned for coarseness. The true Christian, as Rabelais sees him, never puts his trust in his own unaided powers; nor does he ever fall into the blasphemous notion of the *caphards*, that God helps those who help themselves. His task is to work together with God, neither thinking he can do it all himself nor, at the other extreme, leaving it all to a God who has to be bribed and cajoled with pious words and phrases used as magic charms. The monks of Seuillé and Picrochole's invading soldiers are the forerunners of the new Panurge of 1548. The monks did nothing effective to save their abbey, just as Panurge does nothing to save the ship; Picrochole's soldiers only turn to prayer on their death bed, relying on traditional concepts and superstitious formulas. Both in *Gargantua* and in the *Quart Livre* Frère Jean throws error into sharp relief by effective comic contrast. The prayers of the monks were condemned as a mockery of God – as meaningless sanctimonious jargon at best; blasphemous hypocrisy at worst. The prayers of Picrochole's silly dying soldiers were presented as laughable:

Some died without speaking; the others cried in a loud voice: 'Confession! Confession! *Confiteor! Miserere! In manus!*' (*Garg.*, TLF xxv, 142).

The formula which they end with, *In manus*, constitutes the opening phrase of Christ's last words on the Cross: 'Into thy hands I commend my spirit.' The words themselves are neither holy nor comic. They may be one or the other, depending on how they are used. The soldiers are more concerned to confess themselves to priests than to make their peace directly with their God. Like many other evangelicals, Rabelais had no time at all for auricular confession. The holy dying he admired was Ramina-grobis's in the *Tiers Livre* or that of Erasmus's sage in the *Colloquies* which was his probable model.

Panurge takes this one stage further. He hopes that God, hearing such pious words in his mouth, will not take back his spirit into his hands, but make him the subject of a special miracle!

God and the blessed Virgin be with us. Holos, holas! I'm drowning. Bebebebous, bebe, bous. *In manus.* True God, send me a dolphin to take me safely ashore, like a pretty little Amphion . . . (*ER* IX, F 3r°. In 1552, *QL* XXII, 52, *Amphion* is corrected to *Arion*).

Panurge also reminds readers of the pretentious mouthings of the Ecolier Limousin in *Pantagruel*, who abandoned his stupidly ornate Latinised French when he was frightened, returning to his yokelish local dialect. Panurge too slips back into his vulgar native jargon under the influence of fear. In his case his natural speech turns out to be uneducated Parisian. During the 1548 Storm Panurge fearfully evokes the name of Jesus twenty-seven times; on each occasion he used the Parisian 'cockney' form of Jesus, *Jarus* (a deformation caused by the confusion of *s* with *r* and the consequent lowering of *e* to *a*). Theologically and artistically we can see what Rabelais was up to: not least he was concerned to show that piety does not lie in sanctimonious words and formulas used as magic spells, any more than impiety lies in complex oaths designed to encourage effort. Rabelais seems to have found the word *Jarus* particularly comic. The amusement it causes is analogous to that which Englishmen find in the *Bejaysus* of the stage Irishman. But just as pressure from on high apparently obliged him to remove *Jarus* from the second version of *Gargantua*, so too all these twenty-seven *Jaruses* have to go in 1552, being replaced by the amusing but anodyne *zalas* (a popular deformation of *hélas*).

Panurge's 'prayers' during the Storm are all self-interested; his religious zeal is a temporary phenomenon, aimed at deceiving God himself. He even tries to get Frère Jean to act the prudent hypocrite: 'Let us not curse, my father and friend – not just now: tomorrow as much as you like!' Under the influence of fear and wrong theology he corrects his naturally vigorous language: so a 'bloody wave' is piously changed – *mea culpa, Deus* – into the equivalent of 'that holy wave that thou hast made'. In his fear, he does absolutely nothing to help save the ship; his best encouragement to those who strive to save their vessel is, 'Let us get out of danger, I pray you'. At this time of all times he wants to make his confession – to Frère Jean – not in order to purge his soul before he dies but in the hope that God, hearing his verbal piety, will save him, even if all the others perish.

To use a formula such as *In manus* can be a sign of resignation to the divine will, an imitation of Christ as the exemplar of the Christian life and of the Christian's acceptance of suffering and death. But in Panurge's case it is nothing of the sort. His prayers are sub-Christian and magical; they are a means of averting danger – at no cost to himself in suffering or effort; they are not a sign that he has placed his lot into the hands of God, while striving to carry out the divine will, at whatever cost to himself.

Frère Jean's ingeniously baroque curses are not held up as an ideal – they are comic too, but comic in a different way. Theologically they are wrong; but they are more than compensated for by the monk's fundamentally sound efforts to save the ship; that is, to add his human efforts to the power of God. But no one thinks that the ship was actually saved by the efforts of Frère Jean or of any other man or group of men. As Pantagruel declares at the end of the crisis of the Storm: 'Nobody here has died. The Saviour God be eternally praised for that' (1548 *QL*, *ER* IX, 173, F 4v°).

Rabelais's sense of the comic indifference of Frère Jean's colourful swearing may at first seem incompatible with the suggestions found in the *Tiers Livre* that speech is the mirror of the soul; that Panurge's 'talking of the devil', like Triboullet's stuttering evocation of 'Dieu, Dieu' in his inspired prophesying, tell us much about their spiritual states. But in fact there is no incompatibility. Panurge's so-called prayers do mirror his spiritual state; it is one of spiritual blindness, deriving from fear and from a complete misunderstanding of the true nature of God and the true nature of prayer. Frère Jean's green and vigorous oaths reveal, too, that he is right only in part: on the vital question of the need to work together with God through a dedicated striving to further his will by active virtue, he is correct. For the rest he remains what he was in *Gargantua*: 'a true monk, if ever there was one, since the monkish world began to monk about with monkery.' As far as the moral is concerned, he is not the hero of the Storm; Pantagruel and Epistemon are. This transpires when the Storm ends, like the fable it is, with a moral explanation (*ER* IX, 173, F 6v° f.).

Panurge is revealed in the Storm as a man of empty words, of useless, irrelevant and impertinent erudition. He is not simply a benighted fool, he is a 'sage-fol', an erudite idiot, a *morosophos*.

The desire to make a will – *faire testament* – at the height of the Storm reveals Panurge not simply as a stupid man but as a laughably romantic one as well. Wills, as the Bible stresses, are only validated by the death of the testator (Hebrews 9, 16f.). If he does die, what is the use of a will which goes down with the ship? Panurge's reply is a romantic rhapsody: *his* will and testament will be washed ashore as Ulysses was; a king's daughter will find it as she walks the shore in the cool of the evening; as happened in all the classical examples he cites, this royal lady will execute his will and build him a cenotaph. With such mad dreams he idles away his time while the others strive to stop the boat from going under. . . .

In 1548 Pantagruel is in the background; he plays no part in the actual storm, except quietly to hold the mast. But it behoves him as hero to give the full moral to this parable, though not before Frère Jean has drawn the parallel with Seuillé:

'I give myself to the Devil' (said Frère Jean) – 'God be with us.' (Panurge was saying, between his teeth) – 'if the vineyard at Seuillé had not been lost, if I had done no more than chant *Contra hostium insidias*, as the other monkish devils did, without succouring the vines against the pillagers from Lerné.' (1548 QL x; *ER* IX, 173, F 4v°; *QL, TLF* XXI, 54 *var.*).

Pantagruel, in a meaningful passage, shows that while his Christianity has a marked stoic tinge, it is removed from that kind of classical stoicism which is incompatible with Christian realism about human nature. Fear in itself is not condemned; what is condemned is a spineless fear which leads to inactivity.

These points are made by reference to Aeneas; this helps to recall that part of the artistic charm of the Storm lies in its being a moral farce mixed with a comic epic. Rabelais's Storm is, in his own inimitable way, a retelling of the mighty tempest which terrified the heroes in the first book of the Aeneid, with echoes too of the storm in Homer which terrified Odysseus. Aeneas, groaning with heroic fear at the height of Virgil's storm, cried: 'O thrice and four times blessed were they who could find death in the sight of their fathers, beneath the lofty walls of Troy.' Pantagruel quotes this, to justify fear of drowning even on the part of epic heroes. But Panurge is a wrong-headed and comic parody of such heroic fear:

'O thrice and four times blessed are they who plant cabbages! O Fatal Sisters, why did you not spin my thread as a planter of cabbages!'

The unheroic nature of Panurge's funk is conveyed to us through laughter. His fear is the ready fear of the proverbially unheroic German-speaking mercenaries. He squeals out, '*Tout est frelore, Bigoth!*' – an echo of the ready cry of the Lansquenets, who scream that all is lost before the battle has really begun: *Alles verloren bei Goth!* His boobyish terror is revealed to all, not only by his exclusive concern with his own safety but also by his repeated *Bous, bous, bous* and *Hu, hu, has.* Within a wider context, the classical references with which the Storm is strewn keep the mock-heroic savour fresh. The fear of Aeneas, the source of much commentating from Servius onwards, is the peg on which Pantagruel hangs the moral of the parable. The reason why the ancients rightly feared death by drowning was in fact based on erroneous theories of the nature of the soul:

Now if there is anything at all in the world to be feared, after offending God, I do not say it is death. I do not want to join the dispute of Socrates and the Academics, maintaining that death is not evil in itself, that death, in itself, is not to be feared. I say that this kind of death by shipwreck is to be feared, or else nothing is. For, in accord with Homer's judgment, it is a grievous, abhorrent and unnatural thing, to die in the sea. [. . .] The reason, given by the Pythagoreans, is because the soul is the element of fire and of fiery substance, so when a man died in the sea, the contrary element, it seemed to them – although the contrary is true – that the soul was entirely quenched (1548 *QL* x; *ER* IX, 173, F 4v°).

That the great classical heroes could show their fear in ways which were frowned on in later centuries was known and understood; that Aeneas, as Ulysses before him (*Odyssey* v, 312), should especially fear drowning, was regularly explained by the commentators in the same terms as Rabelais uses (whilst carefully not accepting them). For the ancients the drowned man not only lay unburied: his fiery soul itself might be extinguished by the raging seas.[5]

The classical references, which serve to show up Panurge's fear for the unheroic terror that it is, are rarely absent from our minds in this episode. Rabelais draws on several sources he had to hand. With his Plutarch before him, Rabelais tells us that the Argives called the star Castor by the name of Mixarchagevas – it is appropriately enough the classically learned Epistemon who treats us to this rare piece of knowledge. But even Rabelais's learned readers may have been puzzled by Epistemon's sighting the harbour and seeing the fire on *un Obeliscolischive* (as the 1548 *Quart Livre* puts it). Even the corrected version, *un Obeliscolychnie* must have foxed many readers: *obeliskoluchnion*, 'a soldier's lantern attached to an iron staunchion', is·not the commonest of Greek words! Perhaps it is enough that we smile indulgently at the bravely active Epistemon's gratuitous learning and recognise the generally classical flavour of the terms for what it is. On the other hand humanist readers would have recognised the scathing quality of Pantagruel's reference to Panurge, when the danger is over, the crisis of

---

[5] Cf. Servius on *Aeneid* I. 93, s.v. *Ingemit* (line before *Terque quaterque beati*): 'He groaned, not on account of death, but on account of the kind of death. For, according to Homer, it is a grievous thing to perish by shipwreck. For the fiery soul is apparently extinguished.' This was the basis of much later comment and development. For example Beroaldus insists on Aeneas's fear – not of death, but of an ignoble kind of death. Christopher Landino also stresses the hero's fear: he points out that Cicero (*Tusc.* II. 23, 55) concedes a man's right to groan (*ingemiscere*). But 'wailing (*ejulatus*) is not even allowed to a woman'. The dominance of 'wailings' in Panurge's fear shows him to be suffering from a more than womanish fear.

the storm is passed, but much remains to be done. Panurge now claims to have no fear – to be the only one who really gets things done! But Pantagruel asks: 'Who is that *Ucalegon* down there, who is yelling so and is so discomforted?' Ucalegon (regularly derived from *ouk alegōn*, 'the one who has no cares'), was the name of a Trojan in Homer and Virgil. The name also appears in Juvenal. As Josse Bade points out in a word list drawn up to elucidate Budé's widely read treatise, *On Coinage*, Ucalegon is applied to a man who acts as though he has no cares – once the danger is over (1548 *QL* X; *QL*, *TLF* XXII, 62; cf. Budé, *Opera* II, last page, v°).

As befits a parable told in a classical vein, it befalls the humanist Epistemon to explain the moral in terms which are only afterwards adapted to their Christian inner meaning. His terms are worth weighing carefully, since they probably explain why this part of the *Quart Livre* was so quickly written and published.

I consider that if, truly, to die is – as it is – a matter of fatal and inevitable necessity, to die in such a time or in such and such a fashion is partly in the will of the Gods, partly in our own free will.

The terms used are quite precise: 'est part en la volunté des Dieux, part en nostre arbitre propre.' He goes on:

Wherefore we must implore, invoke, pray, beseech and supplicate them. But we must not make that our only end, our only aim. On our own part we must similarly bestir ourselves and help them to the means and the remedy. If I am not speaking according to the decrees of the *matheologians*, they will pardon me; I am talking by book and authority (1548 *QL* X; *TLF* XXIII, 22 *var.*).

We are being given a lesson on the need for man to work together with God. What Epistemon asserts is essentially what Frère Jean gave as the theological meaning of his striving to save the abbey of Seuillé: passive prayers are not enough (especially when routine and superstitious); man must 'help' God to remedy wrongs – in other words man must make himself into an instrument of God's will; man must so act to further God's purposes that he too shares in what theologians called 'the dignity of causality'. The theme of life as a ship battling through a storm was so current in writings defending free will that we can be sure that this aspect of the parable was not hard to recognise, at least after the moral of the fable is given at the end.

The aggressively evangelical savour of the passage is particularly marked in the last sentence translated above: 'Si je n'en parle selon les decrets des matheologiens, ilz me pardonneront: j'en parle par livre et authorité.' The word *matheologiens* is an erudite satirical pun, current among

readers of Erasmus's *Commentaries on the New Testament*, through which it
reached a wide public. It is a portmanteau word, made up from *theologos,*
theologian, and *mataiologos*, 'idle babbler', a word known to students of St
Paul, as it appears in the Epistle to Titus (1, 10). In the English Bible it is
rendered by 'vain talker'. The corresponding noun, *mataiologia*, 'vain, empty
talk', found in the first epistle to Timothy (1, 6), is rendered in the Vulgate
as *vaniloquium* and in English as 'vain jangling'. So 'matheologians' are men
trifling with pure vanities while they claim to study the eternal truths of
God himself. Erasmus in his Annotations scathingly and memorably
showed how the term *matheologus* applies far too often to the scholastic
theologus, whose concern should be with the highest truths. But here the
attack is directed not against scholastics as such – Rabelais has trounced
them often enough – but against the theologians of the Council of Trent,
already laughed at as the 'chapter general of the Lanterns'. It is the duty of
'Catholic' (ecumenical) councils to issue *decrees*. In 1548, for a loyal
Frenchman like Rabelais to push aside 'les decrées des matheologiens' is to
make light of the canonical decrees on free will recently authorised by the
Council. In 1548 the French king deigned to explain to the assembled
luminaries of Trent why he had forbidden his bishops to attend their
'assembly'. But, curiously, the decrees of the Council of Trent on free
will, reached after debates in 1546 and published in the decrees of the sixth
session (dated 13 January 1547), are not fundamentally opposed to the
synergistic theology which Rabelais espoused. He learned of this in
time for the 1551 *Quart Livre* to be fundamentally rewritten at this
point.

The *livre & authorité* which Epistemon invokes are of course the Bible. But
the reader is puzzled: not until 1552 does Rabelais tell us unequivocally
what he means, with chapter and verse.

This view of man's relationship with God, for all its classical flavour,
would not have displeased Franciscans. It was part of their teaching.[6] Nor
are the terms displeasing to a wider traditional Catholic orthodoxy – nor
indeed to those Melanchthonian and Bucerian synergists in whom Jean du
Bellay placed his hopes of a reconciliation with the Lutherans. The episode
in fact states a notion of free will which would appeal to just those moderate Lutherans whom moderate Catholics believed ready to be reconciled
with a fully Catholic Church through a truly ecumenical Council. If only
the fathers of Trent would get down to discussions with them! Rabelais is
an adept at killing two birds with one stone: Panurge's timorous inactivity
and foolish attempts to bribe God with verbiage deal a blow at an

---

[6] St Bonaventure asserted that the good of human justice lies partly (*ex parte*) with divine
grace, which starts and increases a meritorious action, but also in part (*ex parte*) with free
will, which has to 'work together' – *coadjuvare* – with grace, 'because we are God's helpers'
(*eo quod adjutores Dei sumus*) (*Opera*, Quaracchi, ix, p.197 col.1).

essentially Catholic form of superstition; but Epistemon's synergistic summary is open to both a traditionally Catholic and a Melanchthonian interpretation, while excluding Calvinistic predestination as seen from hostile points of view. For many Catholics, the followers of Calvin, by claiming to have already reformed the one and only Church, had placed themselves beyond the pale. For these same moderate Catholics, even Luther – but above all Melanchthon, Bucer and their like – were men fundamentally orthodox, needing to be reconciled with Catholicity through essentially minor concessions made by a Church prepared to listen to them and to reform herself. Not so Calvin. Genevan theologians were not ones to mistake Rabelais's satire of Catholic error for hidden Calvinistic sympathies. They increasingly turned their hostile pens against him. In 1542 Rabelais had already made a retort in his own way, by interpolating in *Pantagruel* an allusion to the Calvinistic (not the Catholic) doctrine of the predestination of the elect, a doctrine which left no place at all for human endeavour, or for man's cooperation with God, where predestination is concerned. The terms he used are scathing ones: Calvin and his like are *prestinateurs*, a word which suggests that their theology is a mere sleight-of-hand, a prestidigitation. They are 'impostors' and seducers of men (*Pant.*, *EC*, prol., 47). In 1552 his hostility will become open, public and final.

There is so much in the *Quart Livre* as it first appeared which, at the cost of little trimming here and there, could have been made quite acceptable to the theologians of Trent and the Sorbonne that it is difficult to avoid the conclusion that Rabelais was seeking a quarrel. Put another way, reconciliation with allegedly heretical synergists itself entailed a mocking of the extremists of the other wing of the Church. At a private level Rabelais was smarting under the condemnation of the *Tiers Livre*. But Rabelais was not a private man. No doubt he and his patrons saw that a certain type of anti-Tridentine propaganda could play into the hands of the dreaded *caphards* of Paris. It was not enough to laugh at the Catholic pretensions of the Council of Trent on grounds which would have been pleasing to the particular form of Gallicanism favoured in the Sorbonne. His positive propaganda in favour of a synergistic conception of free will restates, in a masterly episode inserted at the last minute, precisely the same theological points that he had made in *Gargantua*, when reconciliation with schismatics was again the preoccupation and hope of the patrons he was pleased to serve. Even when rushed, the old master could bring to the service of truth, as his party saw it, a comic art of such lasting value that it remains alive long after the 'mere propaganda' of the period has sunk beneath the piles of dust. That he chose – twice – to use Frère Jean as the main vehicle for conveying these ideas contributes greatly to their lasting fascination and our enduring delight.

4. *Hostile reactions*

The hostile tone of the *Quart Livre* had the effect one could reasonably predict: Rabelais incensed his enemies. The monk Gabriel Dupuyherbault, a long-established admirer of just those theologians whom Rabelais had mocked in his earlier Chronicles, paid off old scores by inserting a violent attack on Rabelais in his *Theotimus, Or, Concerning the Removal of Bad Books Which Many are unable to Read with their Faith and Piety Intact* (1549). One of Dupuyherbault's wishes was that he could banish Rabelais to Geneva. If he had had his way not only the books would have been burned there: Rabelais might well have met his end on the same pyre as his Chronicles.

From now on, the positions that Rabelais adopts are fundamentally irreconcilable with the theology of the *Eglise réformée*, however 'Lutheran' they might smell to his enemies in the Sorbonne. This obvious fact is not lost on Calvin. But Calvin is not the whole of the Reformation. The people Rabelais moved among were no papists; they were essentially Gallicans who were in various degrees attracted to the theology of moderate Reformers such as Melanchthon and Bucer, sometimes viewing with real sympathy the Anglican schism, while often hoping it to be a temporary one. Although Rabelais was no Reformer in the sense that that word has acquired, he lived among patrons who hoped to purify their Church in ways which opened up the possibility of reconciliation with those Christians who were separated from the old religion by errors which were not all on one side.

The man who was soon to take Rabelais under his direct protection was Odet de Châtillon, one of the most civilised and attractive of the cardinals of France. The decisions of the Council of Trent drove him to find peace of mind in England. How this could be is shown by the full *Quart Livre* which Rabelais wrote and published under his effective patronage.

Considerations such as these are important. Other matters are equally so for understanding and appreciating the *Quart Livres* of 1548 and of 1552.

The first is the extraordinary fact that Rabelais chose to base the successor to his philosophical *Tiers Livre* on an anonymous booklet, of slender literary merit, normally known today as the *Disciple de Pantagruel*. This little book goes under several names in the sixteenth century: *Panurge disciple de Pentagruel* (before 1538?); *Le Disciple de Pantagruel* (1538); *Les Navigations de Panurge disciple de Pantagruel* (1543); *Bringuenarilles cousin germain de Fessepinte* (1544); *La Navigation du compagnon à la Bouteille* (1545). . . .

Why did Rabelais turn to the slight little *Disciple de Pantagruel* for inspiration? As Dolet had tried to pass it off as an authentic work, did he want to show what he could really do on such a theme? Or did even Rabelais want help and guidance in bringing his comedy back to a more accessible level after the erudite heights of the *Tiers Livre*? He certainly cashed in on the success of a book much slighter than his own Chronicles, just as he had exploited the success of the *Grandes Cronicques* at the outset of his literary career as author of *Pantagruel* and *Gargantua*.

Other aspects of the 1548 *Quart Livre* are worth our attention too. There is for example the visit to the *Isle de Chéli* (chap. v). This island has a Hebrew name meaning Peace. In itself that would be an interesting fact and no more. But the 1552 *Quart Livre* uses many more Hebrew names, changing the *Dive Bouteille* into the *Dive Bacbuc*. This suggests that the hebraïcising tendencies of the 1552 *Quart Livre* were not a completely new departure, but something already in germ in 1548. The fact that an island in the later version has a Hebrew name is not in itself proof that it was not already written or conceived in 1548.

On this island Frère Jean returns to amiable monastic coarseness, in reaction to the courtliness of King Panigon and his entourage. The monk strongly disapproves of the new mode of prancing about the ladies with fussy attentions, a fashion which contemporary Frenchmen attributed to mainly Italian influences, with Spanish contributions:

Kiss the hand of your Majesty [*majesté*], of your excellency; may you be most welcome; *pish, pish, tut, tut* . . .

In 1552 the Italianate flavour is more unmistakable:

Kiss the hand of your honour [de votre mercy], of your *majestà*; may you be . . . *pish, pish, tut, tut!* 'Bren!' – that's shit in Rouen – all this squitting and pissing about . . . (QL, TLF x, 37 and *var.*).

We can hardly expect Frère Jean to be gallant to the ladies. But it is interesting that at about this time a secretary of the du Bellay's, François de Billon, was writing his *Fort inexpugnable de l'honneur du sexe femenin*, which he published in 1555. In it he made Rabelais a leading anti-feminist, largely on the strength of Dr Rondibilis's contribution in the *Tiers Livre*. Rabelais would, of course, have known Billon. It is difficult to avoid the feeling that he was twitting him and his like in this visit to Panigon on the *Isle de Chéli*.

5. Panurge's servile fear

One other matter needs to retain our attention before we leave the *Quart Livre* of 1548: Panurge's fear. In the *Tiers Livre* Panurge's dominant qualities were those arising from a blind and diabolical self-love, from *philautia*. In the 1548 *Quart Livre* Panurge is above all a character given over to ignoble and inhibiting fear. The 1552 *Quart Livre* emphasises this. The Storm is re-written and expanded in such a way as to bring this out. Other episodes are added, in which Panurge is fear personified. Rabelais was not arbitrarily changing Panurge's character by making him a prey to fear. Mediaeval and Renaissance morality saw the kind of fear which dominates Panurge as the natural companion to self-love. Panurge does not suffer from the kind of fear that Epistemon can rightly experience: a fear which does not stop him from striving to save the ship. Nor is it the heroic fear of Aeneas, a fear which allowed for groans but not for funk and panic. Panurge's fear is technically known as servile fear, *timor servilis*. Such a fear 'proceeds from, and has its origins in, love of self'.[7] In the *Quart Livre* Panurge is true to character, moving further down the slope of self-love into that servile fear which inhibits even him from spinning his crafty and self-deluding webs of semi-intellectual argument. His words convey his fear not by means of rational discourse but by the connotations of his babblings and his ramblings. The most meaningful of all his sounds are purely animal in nature – splutterings, blubberings and weepings.

The *Quart Livre* of 1552 is partly based on literary and moral conceptions such as these. They contribute much to the comic philosophy of that remarkable book.

[7] Cf. Joannes Viguerius: *Institutiones Ad Christianam Theologiam, Sacrarum Literarum, universaliumque Conciliorum authoritate* . . . , Antwerp 1565, fol. 130v°: *De timore servili*. (Luther held that self-love was evil *per se*. The traditional doctrine is that that kind of self-love is an evil which makes the self into the ultimate good – as Panurge does. Luther wrote off any contrition arising from servile fear as pure hypocrisy.)

8

The Sciomachie *of 1549*

1. Du Bellay's mock battle

Although Rabelais's movements are not clear in the years separating the *Tiers Livre* from the final version of the *Quart Livre*, he was certainly in Rome with Cardinal Jean du Bellay during a crucial period of French national and religious history. In the late 1540s and at the outset of the 1550s the tensions between the French court and the Holy See were such that a break between them seemed inevitable. But not all of Rabelais's time or that of his cardinal was spent on high and complex diplomacy. A minor work of Rabelais's, *La Sciomachie et festins faits à Rome*, appeared in 1549, printed by Jean de Tournes for Sebastian Gryphius. The full title informs the reader of an imposing entertainment, a mock-battle (*sciomachie*) which was organised in the palace of my lord the Cardinal du Bellay in honour of the birth of my Lord of Orleans. The young prince whose birth was so expensively and elaborately celebrated by the loyal cardinal in Rome was Louis of Orleans, the short-lived second son of King Henry II. The printed version of the *Sciomachie* curiously leaves a blank for the prince's name to be inserted, presumably by hand. On no copy that I have seen has the blank been filled in. This may mean that the type was set up before the baby's name was known. He was christened on 19 May 1549.

The *Sciomachie* is artistically quite ambitious and quite carefully written. It is presented to the reader as being based on a letter written by 'M François Rabelais docteur en medicine' to the Cardinal de Guise. Other accounts of the festivities survive. One of them, simply signed A.B., is so close to Rabelais's relation that they must in some way be connected. (These texts are being edited for the *TLF* – Droz, Geneva – by Dr R. Cooper.)

For Rabelais this work was evidently simply a *pièce de circonstance*. He did not include it in any collected edition; he does not allude to it elsewhere. It is, nevertheless, a work of considerable interest. It forms, in one important way, a bridge between some of Rabelais's concerns in the *Tiers Livre* and in the 1552 *Quart Livre*; it affirms his loyalties and tells us quite a lot about the magical beliefs that were in the air and which he was far from espousing.

The account of the *Sciomachie* seems designed to show how loyal and devoted Jean du Bellay was, pouring out his wealth and his energies to the greater glory of France, the honour of her monarch – and (not least) – to the glory of Catherine de' Medici, the power beside the throne whose influence sometimes far outstripped that of her royal husband. The fact that the account was addressed to the head of the rival faction, the Guises, is not without a certain irony.

2. *Miracles – or homing pigeons?*

For readers today the most arresting aspect of the *Sciomachie* is probably the belief enunciated at the outset, that news of the birth of the young prince had reached Rome the very day the event occurred in France, at the castle of Saint Germain-en-Laye. On the evening of the day of the birth (3 February 1549) news of it was abroad, we are told, among the Roman bankers – the acknowledged source of hard international information. This was not, according to Rabelais, a matter of mere vague rumour or of intelligent guessing: the day, the hour and the place of the prince's birth were known with complete accuracy.

Before looking at Rabelais's reactions to this strange occurrence, it is well to recall that he was not alone in believing in such apparently miraculous transfers of news over such great distances that no known solely human agency could apparently be involved. Natalis Comes in his influential *Mythologiae* (III, 17) tells how news of Francis I's battles for Milan against the forces of Charles V reached Paris the same day. Early in the following century, Gabriel Naudé (who was well-informed about these matters) referred to such allegedly miraculous transfers of news in his *Apologie pour les grands hommes soupçonnez de Magie*: 'Noël des Comtes [Natalis Comes] wrote that, during the time of Francis I and Charles V, they knew at Paris, the same night, what had happened that day in the castle of Milan.' But Gabriel Naudé refused to believe this: for him it was a pure fable made up by those who wanted to add a reputation for magic powers to the established reputation for feats of arms enjoyed by these great princes. This he saw as a blatant imitation of the reputations of such ancient captains as Ninus and Zoroaster, Pyrrhus and Croesus, Nectanebus and Philip of Macedonia (Naudé, *Apologie*, ed. 1712, p.156).

The scepticism is Naudé's, but the basic judgment is a shrewd one. Such beliefs as Rabelais helped to spread were part and parcel of a Renaissance royalist mystique, which frequently associated superior spiritual powers with monarchy. These tendencies, already present in the reign of Francis I, could only be even more welcome in the court of Henry II, dominated as it was by Catherine de' Medici.

There is not the slightest reason to believe that Rabelais had invented these 'fables'. Not only does he accept the fact that news of the prince's birth was strangely conveyed to Rome, but he supplies other instances: how news of the defeat of King Francis at Pavia similarly reached Paris in 1525: how accounts of the fatal duel between Jarnac and Chastaigneraye, on 10 July 1547, had similarly travelled long distances by unknown means.

What is interesting is Rabelais's reaction to these apparently well-attested facts. It tells us much about the way his mind worked – and explains some important additions to the *Quart Livre* in 1552.

Rabelais refuses to find such occurrences prodigious or astonishing, although they might seem to be so:

Which is a prodigious and wonderful thing: not however where I am concerned . . .

He can cite news of ancient battles lost and won, the outcome of which was soon known five hundred leagues away. He acknowledges that such evidence leads Platonic philosophers to attribute divine powers to those tutelary gods which we call guardian angels. Rabelais's explanation of the phenomenon is not developed in the *Sciomachie* since, he says, that would take him beyond the proper proportion of a letter.

What then are Rabelais's views? Does he believe that the news travelled to Rome by the intermediary of guardian angels? I think not, though some scholars do take his words to mean just that. There is a certain vagueness about Rabelais's statements which leaves room for hesitation. His acceptance of a generally platonising Christianity – and hence of guardian angels – is evident from his books; but that is not the point at issue.

To understand what Rabelais means, we must look for help to other of his writings. His interest in the possibility of news travelling quickly over great distances dates from before the *Sciomachie* and continues after it. In the light of what we read in the *Tiers Livre* we can understand the fascination he must have felt when he heard accounts of the apparently miraculous communication of young Louis's birth to the bankers of Rome. For, in the *Tiers Livre*, Pantagruel defends consulting even such an uncompromising source of knowledge as the comic Sibyl of Panzoust, on the grounds that man should always be open to instruction. In doing this, he even corrects the wisely classical Epistemon:

What harm is done always to know, always to learn, even if it be from sot or a pot; or [in a set of three punning words meaning fool by implication] from an oil-pot, a mitten or a slipper – from a *guedoufle*, a *moufle*, a *pantoufle*? (*TL*, *TLF* xvi, 28).

The justification he gives for this opinion is based on an anecdote related by Lucian in his account of the *Stupid Orator*: Alexander the Great, having vanquished Darius, wished he could learn how things stood in his far-off kingdom. But when a poor merchant from Sidon said he could not only get news of his victory to Macedonia in five days but also bring news to Alexander from Egypt and Macedonia in the same period, he refused to listen. Afterwards he bitterly regretted his impatience. Pantagruel insists that Alexander ought to have listened. Nature has made our ears for ever open, so as to remind us of the need constantly to be ready to learn. The man who appeared before Alexander might in fact have been 'an angel, that is to say a messenger from God, sent like Raphael to Toby' (*TL*, *TLF* XVI, 31–70).

In the *Quart Livre* of 1552 Rabelais returned to the problem, in a major episode interpolated into the early chapters of the original version. It is convenient to consider it here. These new pages were presumably written after the 1548 *Quart Livre* and certainly before 28 January 1552 (new style), the date of the *achevé d'imprimer* of the new *Quart Livre*. In other words they were almost certainly written in 1549, 1550, or 1551; that is, at a period when the strange transfer of news which he wrote of in the *Sciomachie* was fresh in his mind.

Chapter III of the 1552 *Quart Livre* tells how Pantagruel, already far away at sea, received a letter from his distant father; it goes on to discuss ways of quickly hearing news from afar. It is entitled, *Comment Pantagruel receupt letres de son pere et de l'estrange maniere de sçavoir nouvelles bien soubdain des pays estrangiers et loingtains*. The correspondence between the *Sciomachie* and the new *Quart Livre* could hardly be closer.

The means of rapid long-distance communication which Rabelais reveals seems, anachronistically, something of a let-down. It consists in using homing-pigeons, birds which Rabelais dignifies by using the Arabic or Hebrew name of *gozal*. Perhaps he was specifically thinking of Barbary pigeons. Homing-pigeons were known to the ancients, being mentioned for example by Pliny. But in modern Europe the idea of employing these birds seems to date from the very time that Rabelais was writing. He was, in other words, on to something both ancient and new: an irresistible combination for a humanist (*QL*, *EC* III, 17, note).

Did Rabelais incline to believe that the news of the young prince's birth had been conveyed rapidly and secretly to the Roman bankers by relays of homing-pigeons? I think he did. We are told that among the uses which Gargantua and Pantagruel put *their* homing-pigeons to was the conveying of news of the 'happy or unfortunate lying-in at child-birth of a queen or great lady' (*QL*, *TLF* III, 51).

In the Renaissance an apparently prodigious event may be variously explained by the intervention of a messenger from God, by the powers of guardian angels or by the re-discovered means of homing-pigeons. That Rabelais favoured homing-pigeons in the 1552 *Quart Livre* – and probably in the *Sciomachie* – does not imply that he did not believe in guardian angels or other messengers from God. Both find their place in his Chronicles.

9

The Quart Livre *of 1552*

On 28 January 1552 (new style) the Parisian printer Michel Fezandat completed work on what is essentially the Fourth Book as we now know it: *Le Quart Livre des faictz et dictz Heroiques du bon Pantagruel.* A little over a year later, in April 1553, Rabelais died, to be buried in St Paul's Church, Paris.

When he wrote the final version of the *Quart Livre,* Rabelais was apparently about seventy years old. We are entitled to suspect that he considered it to be his *ultima linea rerum.* Some scholars believe the *Isle Sonante,* published under his name some nine years after his death, to be authentic; others think that the *Cinquiesme Livre,* published two years later still, in 1564, is either authentic or else based on lost manuscript notes. But there is to my mind a wholeness and completeness about the new *Quart Livre* which makes it a fitting climax, and a most satisfying end, to the series of Chronicles which started their life so successfully in the long hot days of 1531 or 1532.

Circumstances had worked in Rabelais's favour since the appearance of his first *Quart Livre.* He now enjoyed the support of Cardinal Odet de Châtillon. And this time, Rabelais was apparently there to see his book through the press. The new *Quart Livre* is unique in having a Liminary Epistle. It is addressed to Odet de Châtillon and bears the same date as the *achevé d'imprimer:* 'De Paris, ce 28 de janvier, 1552.'

The Liminary Epistle takes up a number of the themes of the abandoned prologue to the first *Quart Livre* of 1548. In it Rabelais also claims the direct support of Châtillon and of Henry II. This assertion of royal approval leads one to look closely at the new privilege. It is a blanket one covering all his books, both those already written, which he may revise and correct, and those which are to come. The title-page of the *Quart Livre* proudly bears in bold type the words: *Auec privilege du Roy.* Nevertheless the Sorbonne proceeded to censor the book and, on 1 March 1552, the Paris Parlement ordered it to be withdrawn from sale. Or so it seems. But Rabelais had a keen eye on the good opinion of his king. The *Quart Livre* exists in two states: in the second state, part of the gathering signed B was specially reprinted in order to insert the words *grand, victorieux, & triumphant* before the reference to Henry II. If this alludes to his triumphant entry into Metz on 18 April 1552, then the Parlement's interdiction in March, which in any case would not have applied throughout France, must have been either short-lived or ineffectual: there would have been no point in preparing new leaves for a book which could not be sold. What actually happened was that the Parlement did not dare to condemn Rabelais or his printer on their own authority. Having heard the printer Fezandat, the Court ordered an inventory of the unsold copies to be made, and forbade any more copies to be sold, 'until the aforesaid Court shall have heard more fully the will of the king on this matter'. This was on 8 April, 1552 (Heulhard, *Rabelais*, 1891, p.337). The wishes of the king were apparently that the *Quart Livre* should be put back on sale. Nevertheless all other editions of the *Quart Livre* were either published *sine loco* or else well away from Paris.

In none of Rabelais's writings is the national and international politico-religious climate so important for explaining how he could be so outspoken, and for helping us to understand the import of what he wrote. Yet the propaganda import of the book is only one strand among many. No work, not even *Pantagruel*, contains so many pages given over to sheer unadulterated amusement. And yet, among all this happy laughter, Rabelais's religious philosophy comes into its own, expressed in comic terms far surpassing the exigencies of immediate propaganda. In some ways the new *Quart Livre* resembles the *Tiers Livre*: it shows a sustained concern with humanist learning and Christian humanist values. But in other ways it represents a partial return to styles more reminiscent of *Pantagruel* and *Gargantua*. The *Tiers Livre* is a dense book, closely and complicatedly constructed and making considerable calls on the specialised knowledge of educated men: the *Quart Livre* paints its pictures with broader strokes. While itself drawing heavily on book-knowledge, especially from Plutarch – who was still largely an inaccessible author, being only partly available in translation – it makes fewer demands on the erudition of the contemporary reader himself. This time Rabelais digests the knowledge: the reader of the sixteenth century could have come to him with rather less erudition of his own. As for its form, it has a much more loosely conceived structure than the *Tiers Livre*, as one might expect from a story consisting of a series of visits to unknown islands. Both Lucian and the *Disciple de Pantagruel* contributed to this conception of the new book as a journey interrupted by amusing ports of call.

With the new spacious prologue to the *Quart Livre* all sense of distance between Rabelais the man and Rabelais the masked author is dropped. The Liminary Epistle ends duly signed 'Vostre treshumble et tresobeissant serviteur, Franc. RABELAIS, medicin'. Immediately after, follows the *Prologue de l'autheur M François Rabelais*. We are no longer beguiled by M. Alcofrybas with or without the Nasier; there is no more *Abstracteur de*

Quinte Essence, no more *Caloïer des Isles Hieres.* Rabelais keeps alive the fiction that he is an amiably bumbling, absent-minded-professor type of figure, but writes fully in his own name. His comic complicity as a storyteller is revealed by other techniques: 'M. l'Abstracteur' appears briefly in the tale as a character; an occasional use of *we* instead of *they* involves the author in the fictional voyage, just as a similar switching of pronouns involves St Luke in the Acts of the Apostles – though the parallel is doubtless accidental. Reality interpenetrates the fiction in strangely moving ways: for example Epistemon is said to have been present at the prodigious death of Guillaume du Bellay, the Seigneur de Langey; he vouches for the truth of the account by alluding to the presence of several doctors: 'Gabriel medicin de Savillan, Rabelays, Cahuau, Massuau, Maiorici. . . .' (QL XXVI-XXVII).

The new *Quart Livre* came off the presses on 28 January. So it is in essentials a 1551 book; much of its matter is relevant to the state of France and the Church in that year. But the privilege was granted 'to our dear and well-beloved Maître François Rabelais, doctor of Medicine' on 6 August 1550. That may suggest that Rabelais was already working on the new book a year or two before it was published. The privilege covered all his writings in Greek, Latin, French and Tuscan, as well as future volumes of his chronicles. It was bestowed by the king of France, signed by Du Thier, 'le Cardinal de Chastillon présent'. It was granted both for copyright reasons claimed by Rabelais and for 'other good considerations moving Us thereto'. These 'other good considerations' influencing the king included no doubt a shrewd awareness of Rabelais's value as a monarchico-Gallican propagandist. He was an author who was not to be easily silenced by pettifogging lawyers in Parlement or by censoring theologians in the Sorbonne. When royal policies were at stake and the power of the Roman pontiff was being seriously questioned by the Frenchmen of authority, Rabelais had a major part to play in influencing opinion.

The Cardinal de Châtillon was a prince of the Church, the son of the sister of Montmorency, the constable of France. The Cardinal de Bellay was long known for his devotion to Montmorency. He probably facilitated Rabelais's entry into the magic circle of those protected by Odet de Châtillon who, as well as being an enlightened protector of the arts, was a man who thrived in the company of liberal Christian humanists. His eventual flight to England in December 1564 and his public acceptance of the Anglican schism led to his being classified as frivolous and irreligious by many of his former French brethren, though some such as Ronsard continued to love and admire him. A Roman cardinal passing over to Anglican lands the very year after the Council of Trent had made its last reform, concluded its last deliberation, launched its last anathema! The fury and sneers of many of those who once sought his protection are humanly understandable. What is odd is that such verdicts are still commonly met even today. Yet a merely frivolous and pleasure-loving cardinal, as highly-placed as he was, could have remained happily and untroubled in France with his vast beneficed income, his influence and his mistress. His marriage to the woman the English jocularly knew as *Madame la Cardinale* and his flight to England can best be seen as the decision of a man whose religious convictions cut him off from the kind of church being consolidated by the decrees of the matheologians of the Council of Trent. *Gallia Purpurata* – that old history of Frenchmen raised to the purple of the cardinalate – sums him up as 'a deserter and fugitive from the Catholic Church, who was converted to the Anglican swamps infected with the mud of heresy, so that he could more freely live in feasting'. To serve such a man in the 1550s – not of course the caricature in *Gallia Purpurata* – must have been a liberating experience for Rabelais. If ever there was a time when the French Church was close to being reformed in ways which would have pleased a man like Châtillon, it was in 1551. In late 1551 or early 1552 it would have taken a bold man to be certain that Gallicanism was not to reach an autocephalous, schismatic solution *à l'anglicane*. Rabelais found himself able to spread himself, able to make his joyful laughter at ecclesiastical error reach the highest targets in Europe. The early years of Henry II's reign were marked by an increasing hostility to the papal see, culminating in the Gallican Crisis of 1551. During this period powerful forces were driving the French monarch towards a break with the papacy every bit as definitive as the Anglican schism. Plans were discussed to create a French patriarch, to reject the Roman obedience, to stop the flood of French money pouring into Rome, to reform the Gallican Church by a national council, while rejecting the Catholic pretensions of the Council of Trent.

Rabelais's epistle dedicatory to Odet de Châtillon shows him enthusiastically devoted to the cardinal's interests: indeed, without support he would have given up writing altogether. But the 'good news' of the privilege obtained by Odet de Châtillon was given him by the cardinal himself, apparently during a visit to Jean du Bellay in the 'rustic paradise' of St Maur. It was from that same prelate that Rabelais learned how the bishop of Mâcon had read his chronicles to Francis I, and that his late king had found them free from the taint of heresy. Odet de Châtillon's support enabled him to continue to rejoice the sick with his 'merry tomfooleries' – his *joyeuses folastries* – 'giving no offence to God or the king'. He was also enabled to ignore his 'devilish calumniators', who so little deserved the priestly title of father that they gave him a stone when he asked for a loaf, a serpent when he asked for bread. The grounds on which he was accused of heresy were frivolous – based, Rabelais unconvincingly alleged, on a misprint, which turned *asme* (soul) into *asne* (donkey). Misprint or not, the grounds are indeed frivolous, and if that was all that his enemies could really have mustered against him, he would have been safe enough from their fulminations.[1] Rabelais asserts that he was a far better Christian than his critics. With searing indignation he protested that if in his own life, writings, speech or thoughts he had found a single spark of heresy, he would have emulated the phoenix, gathering wood for his own pyre. Such expressions are not merely decorative in an age when the burning of heretics had become almost commonplace. But Rabelais was no longer on the defensive about his art or his thought. He had no need to be.

Odet de Châtillon was a new Gallic Hercules meriting the title of the ancient hero, *Alexikakos*, the Warder-off of evil. This was adroit and powerful praise; the myth of the Gallic Hercules, who drew men to himself by the charm of his speech, was dear to the heart of French humanists; it was also deeply pleasing to the cardinal, who placed Hercules among his forebears. Ronsard later dedicated his *Hercule chrestien* to him, out of a similar respect for the mythical ancestral cult associated with his name. Rabelais used the term *alexikakos* once before only; in his letter to Erasmus, to whom he applied the terms of 'most loving father, honour of your country, the *alexikakos* defender of literature and the most unconquered fighter for truth'. *Alexikakos* was, it seems, a term he reserved for the very great. Here, in his longest scriptural quotation ever, Rabelais amplifies it, applying to Châtillon the praise showered on Moses in Ecclesiasticus XLV: 'A man beloved of God and men . . . God glorified him in the sight of kings;. . . in his faith and his goodness he sanctified him and chose him above all men. . . . Through men he wished his voice to be heard: and to those which were in darkness his law of life-giving knowledge to be proclaimed.' Calvin, when he read such words from Rabelais's pen, was scandalised. But by 1552 no love was lost between those two (*QL*, *TLF*, *Ep. lim.*, 158).

Protected by such a powerful prelate and statesman, Rabelais boasts that he can write, at last, without fear: *hors toute intimidation*. We should be wise to weigh these words and the circumstances in which they were written, before taking them with naïf literalness: it might be the ultimate form of flattery to insist that what one writes at the behest of a great patron is precisely what one always yearned to write. But on closer examination the *Quart Livre* does indeed bear the imprint of personal conviction, of a

---

[1] In the *Tiers Livre* (XXII, 89 and XXIII, 8) Panurge twice deforms *asme* into *asne*. The joke is based on attenuated gingerbread oaths such as Golly! or Gosh! for God! The passage concerned is one where Rabelais uses Panurge's superstitious horror at Raminagrobis's holy way of dying as a means of mocking those traditional doctrines of contrition rejected by Evangelicals, as well as laughing at the Sorbonagres and the monks. It is one of the most outspokenly evangelical episodes of the *Tiers Livre*. Rabelais affects to believe that the censors could only find him censurable here by concentrating on trivialities.

Christian-humanist's comic vision turned upon the events and pretensions of the world of his day.

There is nothing the remotest bit secretive or impersonal about this last book. And in no prologue is Rabelais so much at pains to present himself to the reader in his professional rôle – not simply as lawyer, priest or theologian, but first and foremost as doctor of medicine.

If ever a book in an age of stakes and torturings, inquisitors and censors, gave the appearance of being the ultimate fearless statement of Christian truth as one man saw it, that book is the *Quart Livre* of 1552. Yet it is also spacious enough, in its three-hundred-and-twenty-odd pages in humanist type, to give Rabelais room for purely artistic and aesthetic concerns, to explore, in pages of pure delight, many questions, not least the nature of comedy and its relationship to heroic goodness.

Rabelais was now able under Châtillon's protection to write a book which combined something of the relaxed laughter of *Pantagruel* and of *Gargantua* with a new profundity which owes much to his continued classical reading. The hero Pantagruel moves even higher up the scale of perfection to become an inspired sage such as Socrates was. Renewed readings of Plato and of Lucian, a deeper acquaintance with Plutarch, a further reading of Erasmus, a cutting through of theological complexities to those two commandments of Christ on which hang all the law and the prophets, combine with a real and practical concern to change the nature of the Church by bringing her back to evangelical truth, enriched with the manna of inspired ancient learning. The Christianity of Rabelais, recognisably syncretistic at least since *Gargantua* and the *Pantagrueline Prognostication* for 1535, now spreads its wings. The riches of Greece and Rome are poured into the treasure-house of Christian myth and wisdom. The *philosophia Christi* of Erasmus and the Gospel is pointed and refined with the thoughts and writings of the ancient sages. And Christian scepticism plays a major rôle, opening the way for the triumph of revelation.

Classical-Christian syncretism is no invention of Rabelais's: it permeates the thought and art of the Renaissance at all levels of human endeavour. But Rabelais makes it widely accessible by writing in French and succeeds in presenting Christianity, attractively, as the divinely ordered fulfilment of the ancient Greek and Jewish worlds, not as a coarse rejection of their values. The therapeutic laughter of Dr Rabelais not merely sugars the pill of his erudition: it is of the essence of the *Quart Livre*. For while some chapters are strangers to laughter, no book of Rabelais's contains more laughter within its covers; nor in any of his other books does humanist Christianity so successfully point the philosophical nature of the laughter aroused.

2. The 1552 prologue

The prologue of 1552 completely abandons the themes of 1548 – some of which find their place in the epistle to Châtillon. It is a masterpiece of comic writing, a sort of happy sermon showing how ancient wisdom, Jewish as well as Graeco-Latin, can be successfully merged into the Christian values of a Renaissance man. At the outset it invokes the jesting Lenten greeting, *Bien et beau s'en va Quaresme*, reminding us that the new *Quart Livre* was available before Shrovetide 1552. So much of the laughter of the *Quart Livre* has a timeless depth about it that we may be tempted to forget that the book appeared in time for Carnival, when once more pale Quaresmeprenant was to win his annual victory over his jolly enemy. The battle between Carnival and Lent forms a major backcloth to episodes in the *Quart Livre*; many of the original readers must have found the presence of these chapters in this book entirely expected and *à propos*. Even those austerer Christians who would not read a happy book in Lent – were they really numerous? – could have enjoyed the *Quart Livre* on Simnel Sunday (*Mi-Carême*) or put it aside until the happy day of Easter. Not that the readership that Rabelais was apparently aiming at would have felt the reading of Pantagrueline chronicles to be inconsistent with religious observances.

The *Tiers Livre* had presented readers with a wise Pantagruel, one fully able to rise above the buffets of *choses fortuites*, yet one singularly devoid of laughter and gaiety. Virtually none of the laughter in the *Tiers Livre* is directly provoked by Pantagruel. Before the end the *Quart Livre* partially restores to Pantagruel his gaiety of spirit. As for Pantagruelism, it is now much happier again, being defined as a certain gaiety of spirit pickled in a contempt for fortuitous things (prol., 16). But there are moments when Rabelais shows a sharp awareness that laughter is a troublesome characteristic to give to a Christian humanist hero. Never again will Pantagruel be as indifferent to the moral implications of humour as he was at times in the previous books. Indeed his religious concern may suddenly douse our laughter like a shower of cold water when we least expect it. His philosophy is an increasingly gentle one, with plenty of scope for tolerant amusement but with no place at all for the belly-laughs of that far-off 'bon Pantagruel' who laughed at everything with gay abandon.

The *Quart Livre* prologue first quietly introduces its syncretistic concerns by discussing health: Rabelais keeps himself in good health so as not to merit the 'scathing satire'of Christ in St Luke's Gospel: 'Physician, heal thyself.'[2] This is juxtaposed to Galen's concern to keep himself in good

[2] *QL*, prol., 15f.: 'I am, by means of a little Pantagruelism (you understand that it is a certain gaiety of spirit, pickled in contempt for matters fortuitous) hale and hearty; ready to drink, if you want to. Do you ask me why, good folks? The answer is irrefragable: such is

health, lest he should deserve the mockery of Euripides as reported by Plutarch: 'He cures others while he himself abounds in sores.' There was nothing new in placing Christ's words and those of Euripides in happy harmony like this. Erasmus, who twice alludes to Euripides's proverb in the *Adages*, on the second occasion compares its sense to Christ's remark in St Luke (*Adagia* IV, 4, 32: *Aliorum medicus*). But Rabelais, for all his evident desire to show Christ fulfilling, not rejecting, the ancient world, does not let Christ's unique superiority suffer from comparisons such as these. In the *Almanach pour l'an 1535* we were invited to follow the advice of 'Plato, or better, *la doctrine Evangelique*' at the moment when the language became specifically and densely Christian. So too here; we are left no loophole for doubting the full divinity of Christ. In St Luke's account of Christ's 'satirical and mocking' remark, 'Physician, heal thyself', Christ is referred to simply as 'Jesus'. For Rabelais on the other hand, Christ, as for so many Christians throughout the ages, is the true possessor of the ancient title of Jupiter, *Deus Optimus Maximus*; he is the 'tresbon tresgrand Dieu' whom Rabelais obeys and whose Gospel he reveres. The divinity of Jesus could not be more effectively underlined.

The divine status of Christ is thus put beyond doubt. Yet both here and in the Liminary Epistle to Châtillon we can see that, even when alluding to the inspired and revered text of the Gospel and the Bible generally, Rabelais's memory was letting him down over important detail. He was after all an old man. In his letter to Châtillon he mistakenly attributed the Book Ecclesiasticus to King Solomon instead of to Jesus son of Sirach.[3] Similarly here, the context of Christ's remark is distorted. According to Rabelais, Christ-as-God addressed these words, 'with terrible sarcasm', to a 'doctor neglectful of his own health'. He did not: Christ put these words into his enemies' mouth, to use against himself. Doubtless, if Rabelais had lived long after this book was published, such errors would not have remained uncorrected. These slips of memory do not only apply to Biblical details: a few lines later he is virtually attributing to the obscure Ariphron of Sicyon words he certainly never wrote.

The Rabelais who presents himself to the reader in the 1552 prologue is

---

the will of the most-good, most-great God, to whom I consent [*onquel je acquiesce*: an echo of I Timothy 6, 3, Vulgate], whom I obey; [*auquel je obtempere*: cf. Hebrews 5, 9, Vulgate], of whom I revere the sacrosanct word of good news, that is, the Gospel [see below, p.430], in which it is said (Luke 4) in horrible sarcasm and bloody derision to the doctor negligent of his own health: Physician, heal thyself.' (The biblical nature of the language is not normally noticed. This greatly impoverishes the ideas being expressed.)

[3] Some early commentators did attribute Ecclesiasticus to Solomon; I doubt if that explains Rabelais's error. Just beforehand, he refers to Moses as 'the great *prophet* and captain of Israel', yet Moses is normally specifically distinguished from 'the prophets' on the basis of such texts as Luke 16, 31 ('Moses and the Prophets').

above all a humanist, evangelical doctor. He is also a man interested, as always, in law. Rabelais passes from this quiet syncretising of St Luke and Euripides into the full syncretic richness of the rest of the new prologue by means of allusions to the law.

Tiraqueau, who, thinly disguised as Trinquamelle, occupied a place of honour in the *Tiers Livre*, is suddenly alluded to as the 'just, learned and debonnaire' author of a new treatise commenting on an axiom of customary law: *Le Mort saisit le vif*. This axiom has, in law, a quite technical sense: a man is seized of the property he inherits as soon as the testator dies. Rabelais uses it playfully as a means of developing the theme of Plato's *bios abiōtos*, of the life that is not worth living. A life without health is such a *bios abiōtos*, a life to be avoided; health is to be seized hold of. If your health has 'escaped', then treat it as a runaway slave, whom ancient legislators allowed his master to recapture, wherever he might have fled (*QL*, prol., 56–82).

It is from this point onwards that the syncretistic intentions of the prologue become most evident. Rabelais juxtaposes the ancient ideal of the golden mean and the Christian notion of humility in a context of faith: God will hear our prayers since they are made in firm faith; he will grant us our request, seeing that it is a modest one, that is, one marked by *mediocritas*.

The eulogy of the golden mean in the 1552 prologue is an extension of the syncretism of Greek and Christian ideas into the domain of faith. Centuries of moral philosophy had made the golden mean of Aristotle's *Nicomachean Ethics* totally at home within Christian moral thinking; but this is another matter: now, the actual prayers of a Christian are also made subject to the flexible limitations of this classical ideal. Such syncretism seems so startling to many readers of Rabelais, that it is prudent to study his text closely, placing it against what other Renaissance Christians wrote on the same subject about the same time. *Mediocritas* for Rabelais was but another form of the Christian virtue of humility. Prayers made in firm faith man can confidently expect to be listened to by God, and answered – provided that what we ask is 'moderate' in its nature. It is no good praying to be richer than Croesus nor to be treated as a second Elijah. Rabelais contends that no man's prayers were ever left unanswered in the Bible, when what he prayed for was within the bounds of the golden mean. This is quite a surprising assertion, showing how fundamentally the approach of a Christian humanist to the scriptures could be conditioned by an enthusiastic respect for classical norms (*QL*, prol., 83f.).

The central core of Rabelais's colourful exposition of these ideas consists in an extremely funny Lucianesque re-telling of Aesop's fable of the woodcutter and the axe. This fable is shown to have an inner moral sense identical with that of episodes in both the New Testament and the Old. The New Testament furnishes the example of the little runt Zachaeus who had to shin up a tree to catch a glimpse of Christ – a moderate wish, open to anyone. Not only did he see his *tresbon Dieu*, but in addition he was honoured beyond his modest expectations. The Old Testament supplies an example evidently chosen because it concerns an axe and so is placeable beside Aesop's fable. In this strange tale, a 'son of a prophet' – a genuine prophet that is – lost his axe-head in the waters of Jordan. He was endowed with firm faith and confidence; his wish to have his axe back was a modest one, within the boundaries of the mean. And get it back he did, miraculously, not by asking for some unheard of miracle, but by showing faith conjoined with moderation, as well as by rejecting the easy earthbound wisdom of devilish censors. But what if he had prayed to become like Elijah, Abraham, Job, Samson, Absalom. Would his prayer have been answered then? . . . *C'est une question.* . . .

That Rabelais should turn to Aesop for his moral fable is understandable: Montaigne will do much the same in the last pages of his book. But the fable is told as only an admirer of Lucian could tell it. The gawky woodcutter Couillatris is a French yokel, with a suitably coarse name; the very tool he has lost, an axe, is open to gross puns, since *coignée* also meant a well-swived woman. Jupiter in this fable is as laughably irascible as Lucian's *Jupiter confuted*; he is also at times not unlike the Panurge of the *Tiers Livre*, for he is a god who can cry out saying, *J'en suys en grande perplexité!* (prol., 174). All this is told in a spirit of comic parable, by which religious insights are provided by unexpected means. Jupiter for all his confusion does succeed in dealing with the great problems of the day, including the question of Parma which was further embittering relationships between the Vatican and France. Comic suggestions are also made on how to put an end to the squabbles between Ramus and Galland who were disturbing the University of Paris with their quarrels over the authority of Aristotle – which Ramus held to be less impressive than many of his fellow professors thought proper – and over the new method of dialectic with which Ramus proposed to replace both that of Aristotle himself and those which derived from him. In 1543 Ramus's enemies had succeeded in getting his books banned while he himself was restricted to teaching philosophy – eloquence being specifically excluded. But in 1551 Ramus could boast that Henry II, 'a Gallic Hercules', had restored to him the right of professing both eloquence and philosophy. Pierre Galland, an old opponent of his, returned to the attack. Rabelais's reactions to this noisy academic quarrel of 1551 was to turn them both into gargoyles. Ramus and Galland are both called Pierre. They deserve to be 'petrified' like Pierre du Coignet – a mediaeval jurisconsult after whom was nicknamed a statue in Notre-Dame (*QL*, prol., *EC* 166; *TLF* 225). Rabelais's friend Antoine du Saix tells us that silly nurses frightened children with his name (*L'Esperon de Discipline*, Paris 1532, sig. D2r°). The tone Rabelais adopts is precisely right in a book characterised by so marked a Carnival spirit. Behind the laughter we can note that Rabelais, a life-long enemy of academic pretentiousness, has no intention of falling into a new scholasticism, having successfully freed himself from the old mediaeval one of his youth.

However busy Jupiter is, he has to find time for Couillatris: it is destined that he should; the poor peasant's axe was as vital to him as the much-contested duchy of Milan was to a French king.

The tale of Couillatris and his axe has both moral and theological meanings. It concerns free will and predestination. Jupiter establishes a general rule for losers of axes such as Couillatris: all will be given a free but limited choice; all will be rewarded or punished according to their free decision (prol., 343f.). Couillatris is the only one who chooses aright and so the only one who is rewarded; the predatory local squires, who sell their lands so as to buy axes in order to lose them, all end up with their heads chopped off. As is theologically appropriate, the wood-cutter does not choose his own axe out of entirely disinterested moral motives (prol., 350f.). But nevertheless he is in the right in a way none of the others is. He uses his free will, and does so, not in hope of cheating Jupiter, but of recovering his own lost axe: a moderate prayer. Couillatris does choose his own axe, not the golden or silver ones which were sent both to test his honesty and, it seems, to leave room for his free will to work within a context of predestined fate. His prayer is answered, we are told, because he had 'opté et soubhaité mediocrité en matiere de coignée'. The smile aroused by the ambiguity of the word *coignée* is in keeping with the tone of the whole parabolic fable as Rabelais tells it; but it does not deflect us or Rabelais from the points being made. The author returns twice to the basic theme, on each occasion pointing the moral and theological inner senses of his fable:

That is what happens to those who, in simplicity, desire and choose things which are *médiocre* (QL, TLF, prol., 457f.).

The fullest treatment is reserved, as is right in a parable, for the end. It is then that we see that the golden mean is in fact a way of approaching the central Christian virtue of humility:

Desire, therefore, mediocrity; then she, and better still, will come to you, while you, meanwhile, duly toil and labour. 'Yes', you say, 'but God could just as soon have given me seventy-eight thousand as the thirteenth part of a penny. For he is all-powerful. A million in gold is as little to him as a penny!' Hay, hay, hay! And who has taught *you* to argue and talk about the power and predestination of God, wretched people? Peace; *st, st, st*: humble yourselves before his holy face and admit your imperfections (QL, TLF, prol., 484f.).

The tone here is delightfully mixed. The colloquial turns of speech are intermingled with quite latinate words, as well as with the *st, st, st*, which both Terence and Cicero use to call for silence.

Here Rabelais returns to his well-tried theme of the need for man to act as well as pray. For Rabelais, passive prayer is not a substitute for possible human endeavour. But the linking of the mean with Christian humility, while new in Rabelais, was certainly not new to the Renaissance. It is instructive to note that Calvin, who safeguards his concept of divine predestination by placing elsewhere than Rabelais does the point at which discussion of God's power and predestination must stop, nevertheless uses language close to Rabelais's. In presence of the mystery of God's predestination man must be modest, he says:

So, learn theefore to humble yourselves, so confess your ignorance, and learn how to pray to God (Calvin: *Sermons de l'Ascension* III).

And in his commentary on Acts 1, 7 he insists that man, even in his theological inquiries, must remain within 'the true moderation between two extremes . . . As I say, you must safeguard mediocrity'. But of course where Calvin saw the golden mean of *his* doctrine Rabelais saw hypocrisy and error. The similarity of language and concept is nevertheless close. In the same spirit Erasmus, in his commentary on the adage *Ne quid nimis* (*Nothing to excess*), believes that an excess of anything at all leads to sin – with the sole exception of the love we owe to God. Aristotle, he thought, taught this also, though he substituted Wisdom for God. In ways such as these the classical world and the Christian met in fruitful harmony (*Adagia* I, 6, 96).

The moderate prayer that Rabelais justifies throughout this prologue is a prayer for good health. He was an old evangelical physician nearing his death, living at least part of the time taken to write the *Quart Livre* in the household of the seriously ill Jean du Bellay. The preoccupation with health is not difficult to explain. The prayer for health is one made with firm faith, just as little old Zachaeus's was; and if it please God in his goodness, health we shall all obtain, since we ask for nothing more. In this way the mean of antiquity and the humility of the Christian merge into each other, in the general context of firm faith and confidence. But the golden mean that true humility respects applies to the prayers of man: it does not apply to God's response, which often may be strange and miraculous.[4]

---

[4] The son of the prophet who lost his axe (*QL*, 102f.; II (IV) Kings 2, 11f.) asked for something quite modest: the return of his axe. What he got when, in firm faith, he cast the handle of the lost axehead into the water, was not one miracle but two: 'Suddenly there

3. The opening chapters

A tale which consists of a sea journey interrupted by visits to numerous imaginary islands is easy to expand. Rabelais could have simply taken up his 1548 *Quart Livre* as it stood, continuing it by adding more lands to visit. This he does not do; he does add several new islands, but the old *Quart Livre* is subjected also to detailed revision. A great many new pages are interpolated; the vigorously written Storm and the preceding chapters are fundamentally re-cast.

The effects of the rewriting and expansion of the chapters preceding the Storm are many. By making the heroes stop first at a new port of call, the Isle de Medamothi (Nowhere), the humanist terms of reference of the story are enhanced from the outset of chapter II. The journey becomes jestingly parallel to the more famous journey of Hythloday to a more famous Nowhere, *Utopia*. Those who knew their Plutarch would also have recognised the allusion to *On Isis and Osiris* (360A), one of his treatises dealing with mystical religion which Rabelais had open before him whilst writing large parts of the 1552 *Quart Livre*. It was in the Land of Nowhere, (*tēs mēdamothi gēs*), that Plutarch placed the Panchoans and Triphullians, fictional people whom the atheist Euhemerus had claimed as his authority for his rejected contention that the ancient gods and goddesses were merely men and women, deified by superstitious gratitude. Rabelais makes no allusion to such matters, contenting himself with borrowing the name and a few remote details – for example the pilot was dressed 'in the fashion of the Isiaci, the priests of Anubis in Egypt' – that is, in white linen garments. Plutarch brought that back to Rabelais's mind at the beginning of his treatise (*QL*, *TLF* II, 68; Plutarch, 352CD).

Although Medamothi is presented as being 'no less big than Canada', it is classical terms which dominate this island, encircled by marble towers and classically named light-houses (*phare*, from *pharos*, was a neologism, needing a detailed explanation in the *Briefve Declaration* appended to some copies of the book). The King of Medamothi is named Philophanes (a name made up from Greek roots, perhaps meaning 'Lover of appearances'); the name of his brother is Philotheamon ('Fond of seeing', 'Fond of shows or spectacles', an authentic Greek word this time).

All this has the effect of increasing the humanist comedy. Rabelais has

---

appeared two miracles: the iron rose in the water and fitted itself to the handle.' This way of maximising the miraculous response of God by breaking down the event into component parts is reminiscent of Peter Martyr's commentary: *Melachim, id est Regum libri duo Posteriores cum Commentariis*, Zurich 1566, p.246. Martyr makes it a triple miracle: 1. the axehead floated to the surface; 2. it inserted itself in the handle; 3. the wood kept the axe afloat. He stresses that the loss of the axe-head was providential; that God is the author of nature and so above its limitations; that the miracle has relevance 'today amongst the faithful'.

his heroes buying paintings of such things as Plato's ideas and Epicurus's atoms. (Later on in the book the allusion to Plato's ideas takes on a new meaning.) Paradoxically, the feeling of contemporary realism is not entirely lost. The purchasers of the *Quart Livre* were a public by now able to read many accounts of voyages of discovery; the *Quart Livre* does not so much parody these accounts as use them as a model for a whimsical and fantastic voyage which often has something in common with the world of Jacques Cartier and of the boyhood of Sir Francis Drake as well as the world of Odysseus, Aeneas or Lucian's heroes. There are other times of course where the world of the *Quart Livre* does become closer to that of the great classical epics amusingly treated; others when it has links with the world of Sir John Mandeville, the *Disciple de Pantagruel* or with Lucian.

Certainly the introduction of the letters exchanged between Gargantua and Pantagruel introduces qualities quite unsuspected in the version of 1548 (*QL* III and IV). The dignified formality of the style of the letters winds the heroes even higher above the heads of ordinary mortals: they are Renaissance humanist princes endowed with all the virtues of the ideal philosophical monarch. Their disinterested quest for knowledge, not mere gain, gives them qualities which Plutarch had helped Renaissance men to admire, even when they normally behaved differently.[5] The kingly grandeur of the giants gives importance to the idea of using homing-pigeons as a means of swift communication; if it works for Gargantua and Pantagruel in fiction, why should it not work for Henry II in real life? That a theme important in the *Sciomachie* with its sound journalistic qualities should appear again as a major addition to the *Quart Livre* a few years later helps to remind us how far Rabelais had gone in intermingling the real and the fanciful in his latest Chronicle. There is plenty of laughter in the 1552 *Quart Livre* but plenty of seriousness too.

Rabelais's reputation rests largely on his ability to make us laugh in a particular kind of way. That is a fair judgment, though an incomplete one. The *Quart Livre* of 1548 had its laughable incidents, but nothing like those of the earlier chapters of the new *Quart Livre* in quality or quantity, or in the unexpected intermingling of seriousness and humour. The episode of the *Moutons de Panurge* becomes much longer in 1552; now totally removed from its source in Folengo, Rabelais develops it in accordance with his own

---

[5] The heroes are no tradesmen; their search is for disinterested knowledge. This was noted by God during the Storm (*QL* xxv, 52): 'Pantagruel replied that the high Saviour had taken notice of the *simplicité et syncere affection* of his people – [the same qualities which marked out Bridoye for divine grace] – who were not sailing for gain or traffic or merchandise' but for knowledge. Amyot's translation of *On the Decline of Oracles* is close in wording to Rabelais: cf. *QL* xxv, 50f.; Plutarch, *Oeuvres*, trans. Amyot, I, p.337A.

predilection for the French farce and its techniques which occupied so great a part in the comedy of the *Tiers Livre*. Whole paragraphs are added, set out as a play and clearly conceived dramatically in the same way as Panurge's confrontation with Trouillogan (*QL* VI, 31–63). Panurge, who once only in 1548 muttered *Patience* to himself in face of the merchant's flood of words and insults, now adopts it as a comic refrain, which becomes laughable through repetition. Rabelais had also newly acquired a taste for the made-up word, often onomatopoeic. We are treated to a flood of *rr, rrr, rrr's* and *bê, bê, bê's*, whilst a routine verb such as *biscoter* used erotically becomes much more colourfully *sacsacbezevezinemasser*.

In these and other ways the story of the *Moutons de Panurge* becomes funnier and funnier. The fatuous merchant deserves what he gets – deserves it, that is, in the overflowing measure with which farces punish the foolish. In this episode Panurge, after being the butt of the comedy throughout all the *Tiers Livre*, is allowed his moment of glory. The author, with renewed and polished comic artistry, places him back into the amoral world of laughter in which we first met this *impostor* in *Pantagruel*. Rabelais has again switched the rôles of his characters about. The merchant Dindenault in the new *Quart Livre* has more than a little to remind us of the silly Panurge of the *Tiers Livre* (cf. *QL, TLF* VII, 78f. with *TL, TLF* XXV, 52f.). As for Panurge himself, he now leaps back over the *Tiers Livre* – and the silence, where he is concerned, of *Gargantua* – to become once more the kind of successful trickster he was twenty years before. Panurge's revenge on the merchant is of the same farcical nature as his erstwhile vengeance on the lady of Paris.

But there are two major differences. Although in both farces the story is told in such a way as to make us the accomplices of Panurge as well as of the naïf storyteller, Pantagruel is no longer the natural foil to Panurge. This change is deliberate. In 1548, after the narrator innocently tells us that the quarrel between Panurge and the merchant was entirely settled, Panurge at once confides in Pantagruel and Frère Jean that he is going to revive the squabble: they will find it all a pleasant pastime, as good as a play. In 1552 Pantagruel is quietly replaced by Epistemon. The harsh vengeance which the farce reserves for fatuousness and silliness is thus detached from any possible connexion with the heroic princely giant (*QL*, VI).

The second difference between the comic vengeance wreaked against the lady of Paris and the merchant Dindenault is that the lady is not maimed and does not die, whereas Dindenault is comically drowned together with his sheep. This is not a minor difference! The additions brought to these chapters in 1552 make it reasonable to suppose that Rabelais was intrigued by the comedy of cruelty. The whole new episode of the *Noces de Basché* is based upon just such atrocious comic cruelty, cruelty of ever increasing intensity (*QL* XII-XIV). This new episode alludes to

a real-life abuse – the tendency of minor legal officials to insult recipients
of summonses, thus provoking assaults. But the satirical implications, left
undeveloped, are negligible. Satire is sacrificed to pure laughter: and the
laughter derives from the 'cruel' punishment copiously reserved for the
fatuous Chicanous. It would have been easy in the realistic setting – Basché
is a real place – to make the comedy realist. Instead we meet the funny
Chicanous who enjoy their beatings and who, in comic terms, deserve them.
Only at the very end do moral considerations come to the fore (QL
XVI).

There was plenty of comic cruelty in *Gargantua* during the laughable
episode of the Picrocholine War. The deaths and wounds of the marauding
soldiers were only serious when realism unexpectedly broke through; the
rest of the time Frère Jean can bash about his enemies with all the gay
abandon of heroes in comic strips. Is there a connexion to be made between
a taste for comic cruelty and the cruelties of times such as Rabelais's and
our own, when beatings up, killings and maimings abound and are ever
present in the public mind? If so, is there a connexion between the physical
horrors of Renaissance wars, Renaissance justice, Renaissance medicine,
and the 'cruel' world of Rabelais's laughter? The comic cruelties certainly
had their ghastly counterparts in real life. But the real world of sixteenth-
or twentieth-century savagery inspires sorrow and pity; the world of
Rabelais's Chronicles, and of cruel comedy today, does not and should not:
either we laugh or else the jesters miss their mark entirely.

To take a comic hero's prowesses seriously – to feel for the soldiers
killed and maimed by his sword, his butt-end of a cross or his potent fists,
would be stupid and laughable. So too would it be if the maimed,
dismembered and dying Chicanous called forth our pity, not our amusement. Anyway, the Chicanous positively *like* to be beaten to death.

By treating subjects in these chapters of the *Quart Livre* in such a way as
not to permit the real world to intervene until the moment comes for moral
comment, Rabelais allows the theme of comic cruelty to flower,
unimpeded by irrelevant moral worries or by any contact with pity, an
emotion which successfully puts a stop to so much laughter. The starting
point of this episode, the alleged desire of the serjeants-at-law to be beaten
up, so that they can bring profitable actions for assault and battery, is
merged with the old custom of young men giving each other memorable
punch-ups at weddings. These exchanges of blows seem to have been
rather like the habit of beating schoolboys at the bounds. It was widely
believed that such beatings helped people, especially children, to
remember important events: a rough-house at a wedding was a good way
of remembering that this particular girl was out of circulation.

From the outset Rabelais's serjeants-at-law are a race apart: they are
non-human Chicanous, puppets adept at chicanery. Chicanous are not real

people at all; the first to come was 'old, fat and red': the second 'young, tall and thin' – the kind of Laurel-and-Hardy alliance which easily depersonalises both the companions. As for the third Chicanous and his associates, he was silly enough to start the whole process off by regretting that the world was going to the dogs, that old customs were dying out! He is the first to rain his blows upon his hosts, for old time's sake; they reply in such a way that these legal puppets are smashed to pieces before our eyes. In comic terms, the Chicanous brought it all upon themselves.

The entire episode of the *Noces de Basché* is stagey. In addition it contains the 'cruel' episode of the parish priest Tappecoue who refused to lend his robes for that archetypal *impostor* Villon to use in a play (*QL* XIII). The priest, of course is punished; he is set upon: his fancy sandals catch in his stirrups; when his mule gets home, all that is left of him is just the one foot entangled in the leather straps. The fate reserved for Tappecoue is, in comic terms, the one reserved for Hippolytus in high tragedy. Yet we laugh. Only by a joyful misuse of terms can it or the *Noces de Basché* be called a *tragicque farce*. We are given in the character Oudart (who bashes his enemies with an iron gauntlet hidden beneath his surplice) a character straight out of a lawyers' farce: a character named *Maistre Oudard de Main Garnie* appears in Guillaume Coquillart's legal romp, *Le Plaidoyé d'entre la Simple et la Rusée*. We are also reminded, with what seems to be the first recorded use of the word in French, of the joys of the *Carneval* as celebrated dramatically in Avignon (*QL, EC* XIV, 29, note). Rabelais's newly discovered amusement at comic sounds is given full dramatic play: made-up words as well as long *hho, hho, hho's* and onomatopoeias such as *brrrourrourrs* abound; a shattered serjeant's attempt to speak become a mere *mon, mon, vrelon, von, von* – understandably since he has little left to speak with but a jawless tongue!

This comedy of cruelty, never more successfully brought before French readers than in these pages, is eventually made the subject of two moral reflexions. The first is Frère Jean's reply to Panurge's defence of his wily treatment, and subsequent drowning, of the merchant Dindenault and his sheep. Panurge defends his actions by saying:

No man ever did me an ill turn, without repenting of it – in this world or the next. I'm not that daft.

The terms are comic, as is underlined by the words 'in this world or the next': *en ce monde ou en l'autre*. Panurge has no influence over the fate of men in the next world. We are led to recall his slick, wilful ignorance in the *Tiers Livre*, when he attempted to wriggle out of old Seneca's contention – cited by Pantagruel with approval – that what you do to others will be done back to you.

– 'Do you mean that', (asked Panurge), 'without exception?'
– 'Without exception, he says', replied Pantagruel.
– 'Ho, ho!' (said Panurge), 'by the little devil! He means in this world or the next' (*en ce monde ou en l'autre*) (*TL, TLF* IX, 44f.).

But Frère Jean makes a reply in 1552 which adds a serious note:

'You are damning yourself', said Frère Jean, 'like an old devil. It is written *Mihi vindictam, etc.*, That's breviary stuff' (*QL, TLF* VIII, end).

We might dismiss this as an obscure joke, though there is nothing obscure about the text which Frère Jean cites: 'Dearly beloved, avenge not yourselves, but rather give place unto wrath; for it is written, *Vengeance is mine*; *I will repay*, saith the Lord' (Romans 12, 19). It is harder still to dismiss Pantagruel's quiet reply to the casual knocks and slaughters in the farces of the *Noces de Basché*:

This narration would seem a joyful one, were we not obliged to have continually before our eyes the fear of God (*QL* XV, 1; cf. Psalm 36, 1; Romans 3, 18).

Why has this former accomplice of Panurge, this former gigantic foil to his merry pranks, been made into so wet a blanket? At this stage of the book one might almost think that Rabelais has turned his hero into one of those *Agelastes*, those 'non-laughing' enemies whom he had trounced in his *Epistre liminaire*.

It seems that Rabelais was artistically aware of an increasing tension caused by the interpenetration of his two worlds: the farcical world of merry bashings, painless wounds and funny dyings, and the real world with its pitiful pain and its ghastly suffering.

For all his rejection of monasticism, as it was or as it was seen to be by so many dissatisfied monks of the sixteenth century, Rabelais had received a sound monastic education. His humanist education overlay it: it did not entirely expunge it, for in real life there was no Dr Seraphin Calobarsy to do that with his hellebore. Monastic thinkers had for centuries been suspicious of laughter: they often saw it as a quite unsatisfactory response to a world laden with sin and suffering. And Christ, who is known to have wept, is not known to have laughed. In this the new Pantagruel of the 1552 *Quart Livre* is at times close to being an imitator of Christ. For his tears are open and copious: his laughter only a memory of earlier days. Pantagruel is often joyful in the *Quart Livre*, especially in the final chapters; but he only laughs once – in the final page of all. And his laughter is then both 'cruel' and unavoidable.

There is in Rabelais's maturer conception of Pantagruelism a strong element of that *contemptus mundi* which forms an important part of the monastic ideal in Mediaeval and Renaissance times.[6] It seems at least probable that Rabelais, precisely because of his sound theology and his unparalleled sense of the comic, was aware that an indulgence in laughter has to be purchased at a theological price. Artistically he resolves such tensions by cutting Pantagruel off completely from the comic world of which he once formed an essential part. But a sense of amusement and humour he does retain.

The tensions which Rabelais was aware of must have struck even comparatively insensitive monks. The bodily coarseness of traditional monastic jesting is legendary, while the spiritual striving after monastic ideals is impressive and in part directly aimed at taming the body. Perhaps that is why the sharpest clash between laughter and Pantagruelian seriousness occurs later, between Pantagruel and Frère Jean. The monk, at home among the Papimanes, takes the name of God in vain: he is at once criticised in some of the harshest language to be found in any of Rabelais's books:

'When', said Pantagruel, 'you tell us such tales, remember to bring a basin. I nearly vomited. Using the holy name of God in matters so vile and abominable. Fy, I say, fy. If such words are in use within your monkery, leave them there; do not transport them outside the cloisters' (*QL*, L 36).

The Latinism 'to bring a basin' ('apporter un bassin'; *pelvim dare*) emphasises the indignation. The adage applies, as Erasmus points out, when something is so annoying and disgusting that it can no longer be tolerated (*Adagia* III, 1, 68). Frère Jean plays only a minor rôle in the *Quart Livre*, after this sharp condemnation. Lovers of Frère Jean – and I am one – must be pleased that it comes late in the story, near the end of the visit to the Papimanes. It leaves him ample scope for laughter-raising earlier in the book. But there is in Pantagruel's curt criticism of Frère Jean something akin to King Hal's harsh rejection of Falstaff. Until the rôles of all the characters are confirmed in the final chapter, Frère Jean retreats into the background, a minor and an episodic character no longer on the centre of the stage. He becomes a somewhat shadowy figure, not infrequently introduced to remind us briefly of monastic coarseness and lechery rather than to make us laugh uninhibitedly, though he can still do that too.

We are prepared for this new condemnatory role of Pantagruel by his reaction to Panurge's treatment of Dindenault. From then on, his aptitude for lofty disapproval continues throughout the book. Confronted with the vast banquets of the belly-worshippers – for whom fasting means not

[6] Cf. *TL* (*TLF*) II, 36: 'For all the goods that the Heavens cover and which the Earth contains in all its dimensions: height, depth, longitude and latitude, are not worthy of disturbing our emotions or troubling our senses and our spirits.'

abstinence but doing without meat and putting up with oysters or caviare –
Pantagruel actually got angry – *se fascha* (*QL* LX, 2). To appreciate what a
revolution is represented by these words, we need to recall how his
character was described in the *Tiers Livre*: he was a stoical Christian sage,
who was never 'indignant, angry or sad' – *indigné, fasché ne marry* (*TL, TLF*
II, 29.) Now he can be all three. His condemnations become abrupt and
definitive. Asked whether he wished to land at the island of the Ganabin,
he replied sharply '*Non*', without a further word of explanation (*QL* LXVI,
9).

For laughter to remain joyful in the *Quart Livre* it needs, it seems, the
world of fantasy. While Chicanous remain Chicanous, not only can the
servants of the Seigneur de Basché knock them about, but so too can Frère
Jean, to their delight as well as to his and to ours. In such a world of fantasy
even the sober Pantagruel can see this as a comic extension of rights
established by the venerable Roman laws of the Twelve Tables of semi-
legendary ancient times (*QL* XVI, 24). But when Epistemon brings the
Chicanous out of the world of fantasy into a world of reality, moral issues
suddenly become urgent. In the real world, it was not the wretched
Chicanous who deserved the bashings and the beatings; it was the prior
who sent them off with their provocative summonses against the Seigneur de
Basché (*QL* XVI). This 'fat Prior', Jacques Le Roy, was prior of the abbey of
Saint-Louand in Rabelais's home territory of Chinon. Long before the
Quart Livre he was plaguing with summonses the real Seigneur de Basché, a
loyal servant of the crown who fought against Pope Julius II in Italy. In real
life Epistemon would have spared the Chicanous, making the blows rain
down on the bald pate of the prior who had sent them off to torment their
betters. Pope Julius II died in 1513. The *Noces de Basché* stir up old resent-
ments against Jacques Le Roy, still prior of Saint-Louand in 1552. If
Rabelais were seventy-odd in 1552, the events of some forty years before
may have seemed close enough to him, in that greener memory older men
have for times gone by. In the *Quart Livre*, cruelty only seems acceptable
when transmuted into a source of laughter. In *Gargantua* Rabelais could
both incite laughter against Janotus de Bragmardo *and* invite his King to
burn the very real principal and fellows of the Collège de Montaigu. In the
Quart Livre, even the punishment which the prior of Saint-Louand is said so
richly to deserve is, in the last resort, talked of in the terms of comedy not
of real pain.

In Gargantua, laughter was accepted as being the property of man. So a
good doctor may seek to make his patients laugh. In the *Quart Livre* Rabelais
is aware that it is a *human* property, having no connexion with the divine.
Laughter can cloud man's awareness of the holy fear of God, which the
wise man has for ever before his eyes. A wise man can be uneasy when he
laughs at even comic vengeance; for vengeance is reserved to God alone.

Nevertheless, the Pantagruel of chapter XVI does not have the last word on the subject. The *Quart Livre* still has plenty of laughs in store. Pantagruel's reservations over laughter do form a new and important element in the *Quart Livre*: they do not in themselves constitute the *altior sensus* of the book as a whole. Yet it is not a minor matter that the once impassive sage is no longer a tolerant giant, amused by the frailty of others; he can now get angry. Frère Jean can still make jokes about a Sorbonne professor who liked to whip his students (*QL* XXI, 67); but for Pantagruel, a papist school master who wanted to give his children a memorable beating is a source of deep-felt anger and indignation.

4. The Storm

The *Noces de Basché* over, we are treated to an erudite re-writing of the seventh chapter of the 1548 *Quart Livre* devoted to the island of Tohu-Bohu (the Hebrew Chaos) and to Bringuenarilles, the gigantic eater of windmills borrowed from the *Disciple de Pantagruel*. The learned banter finds a place for private memories of far-off Montpellier days, for praise of the warlike ancient French and for yet another anagram of Rabelais's name, *Bacabery l'aisné* (*Rabelais cy en ba*, no doubt: *QL*, *EC* XVII, 81, note). Nothing in it prepares us for the fundamental re-writing of the Storm episode which is to follow, and which is arguably one of the most delightful parables ever written.

The 1548 Storm was a classical affair: its terms of reference were classical in that the moral of the fable could be effectively summed up with quotations from Livy and Sallust. As many a classical fable does, it speaks not of God but of the gods, and so needs both interpretation and adaptation if it is to apply to a Christian world. The 1552 Storm is Christian in its actual terms, while being even more successful a mock-heroic classical Storm as well.

The Storm is still preceded by the boat-load of monks sailing to the Council of Chesil (Nitwits), though now the Jesuits are promoted to second place in the list of dishonour and the Benedictines are left out altogether (*QL* XVIII, beginning). This singling out of the Jesuits may well be a shaft aimed at the Cardinal de Tournon, their protector in France. Perhaps the dropping of the Benedictines was out of respect for Rabelais's old order; more likely there were reasons based on the likes and dislikes of his patrons. Modern historians believe that it was the combined influence of Tournon and the Jesuits which, in 1552, resolved the Gallican crisis in a papist manner, clearly different from anything the author of the *Quart Livre* could have wished. Panurge's errors are heavily underlined: filled with an excess of joy, he sees the shipload of monks as a prognostic of long days of good fortune – just before the Storm is about to break. His 1548 prayers to Castor and Pollux are now replaced by invocations addressed to all the blessed saints, male and female; his prayer to God is unnecessarily supplemented by an allusion to the blessed, worthy and holy Virgin. Here we can recognise techniques already employed in *Gargantua*. By the time the first chapter devoted to the Storm is over, we have got the full measure of Panurge; a few lines added in 1552 complete the picture:

By my faith, I'm well and truly frightened! Bou bou, bou bou, bous. I'm madly messing myself out of fear. Bou bou, bou bou! *Otto, to, to, to, to, ti! Otto, to, to, to, to, to, ti!* Bou bou bou, ou ou ou, bou bou, bous bous! I'm drowning, I'm drowning, I'm dying. Good people, I'm drowning (QL XVIII, end).

The *bou bous* and so on show Panurge a prey to that unheroic, worse than effeminate, self-loving, servile fear which has become his dominant recurring characteristic. In this he is especially in contrast with Frère Jean. The mock-heroic savour of the episode is enhanced when Panurge lifts from Greek drama the standard tragic exclamation of pain and grief, *ottototoi*. He uses its lengthened forms, as found in Sophocles, where we have *ototototototoi totoi* and in Euripides where we find *otototototototoi*. Even Panurge's blubberings are appropriately erudite! His fearful syllables join the other sounds, meaningless or meaningful, strewn thickly across the pages of the *Quart Livre*. Later on, sounds such as these move into the forefront of our attention. Meanwhile we simply enjoy them. But we cannot ignore that Panurge's ingenious rhetoric is now a thing of the past. Only fitfully is he now a spinner of words. Nowhere in the *Quart Livre* is he shown up as the plausible windbag of the *Tiers Livre*, to be contrasted with the clipped, solid wisdom of Pantagruel or the more discursive reasoning powers of Epistemon. Under stress, Panurge's language now takes on the qualities of direct, animal-like sound; it has become a direct expression of basic unheroic emotions, not of even erroneous intellectual processes. His words are at one with his actions when he messes his trousers or otherwise shows fear.

Fecal humour and the condemnation which accompanies it in Rabelais have a comeback in 1552, after being absent from the *Tiers Livre* and the *Quart Livre* of 1548. In ways that the *Tiers Livre* did not, the *Quart Livre*, in its final version, draws upon several of the comic techniques of *Pantagruel* and *Gargantua*. The laughter is not based on a preference for the earlier type of comic devices at the expense of those of the *Tiers Livre*, but on a blending of them all into a fresh and powerful mixture.

In the 1548 Storm, the dramatic contrast excluded Pantagruel. The new ending to the first Storm chapter has the effect of throwing Panurge into relief not only against the monk but also against Pantagruel, who now, at the outset of chapter XIX, gives the Storm an explicit Christian flavour totally absent from the dramatic parable of 1548:

Pantagruel, *after having previously implored the aid of the great Saviour God and made public prayer in fervent devotion*, by the advice of the pilot held the mast strong and firm (QL XIX, 1).

The term that Rabelais uses for Saviour God – *Dieu Servateur* – is based on the classical Latin term *Servator* rather than on the Christian Latin *Salvator*. Renaissance scholars often preferred the word *Servator*, since it kept the idea of salvation but also added the idea of protection dominant in the classical word.

As Panurge's comic Parisian *Jaruses* go out – all of them – Christian tragedy sweeps in, finding its place, not by driving away the mock-heroic pseudo-tragedy and pseudo-epic of Panurge, but by adding a new and totally unexpected depth. The moral comedy of the 1548 Storm was a two-character affair: Panurge's mealy-mouthed pseudo-piety and comic fear was in constant contrast with Frère Jean's florid curses and his brave devotion to active virtue. Now Pantagruel moves in at the outset of the Storm and at its crisis. The Storm itself becomes funnier and funnier, as Rabelais interpolates words, phrases and whole sentences designed to increase our laughter at Panurge's expense or to encourage our happy siding with Frère Jean's activity. The comedy of the 1552 Storm with its noise, its movement and its dramatic dialogue is seldom, if ever, gratuitous. Everything moves towards a higher moral sense. Even jests which might seem at first to be quite gratuitous, such as Frère Jean's capping of Panurge's last word *Hérodote* with the outrageous pun *il radote*, normally have effects other than the pure raising of laughter (QL xx, 18). In this case it takes us back to the echo chapter (IX) of the *Tiers Livre*, where Panurge's rôle was anything but firm and noble, and it prepares the way for later laughter and later wisdom.

Other reminders of the *Tiers Livre*, here and elsewhere, keep all the new Panurge's moral defects before us, while additions to the text show him blubbering, increasingly superstitious, stupidly curious about useless and irrelevant detail, and, of course, good for anything but constructive activity. Perhaps his most revealing reaction is to desire to have a whip-round to raise funds to send somebody off on a pilgrimage in the midst of a storm! It is useless now; pointless at best; and revocable at will, once the danger is over (QL xx, 76f.).

But the new Storm does much more than simply underline with renewed laughter the moral message of the old one. In 1548 Frère Jean's efforts, with those of Epistemon and the crew, come close to actually saving the ship. In 1552 two new characters emerge in the Storm: Pantagruel and God.

In 1552 the ship meets the crisis of the tempest with all sails down, the rudder unhooked and nothing more that man can do. As the captain gives the order to run before the Storm at the mercy of wind and weather,

Pantagruel shows the implications of this in fervent prayer:

'Have we reached that point?' said Pantagruel. 'May the good Saviour God be our aid' (*QL* xx, 70).

The captain orders each and every man to think of his soul, to pray, to seek help only from a miracle (*QL* xx, 74f.). Panurge's worries about his will provide a diversion, which ends in three layers of prayer (*QL* xxi).

Pantagruel's prayer is exemplary, calling upon the anguished cry of the disciples to Jesus during the great tempest on the lake: 'Lord save us, we perish.' Even more tragically, he calls upon Christ's example in the Garden of Gethsemane: 'Thy will be done.' By contrasting God's will not with man's *will* but with his emotions (his *affections*), Rabelais associates Christ's prayer with the moral insight of Stoicism – a Stoicism duly baptized, as it is throughout the *Quart Livre*.

Then was heard a pious exclamation from Pantagruel, saying in a loud voice, 'Lord God, save us. We perish. Yet may it not happen according to our emotions, but may thy holy will be done' (*QL* xxi, 44).

Panurge's prayer is a counter-example, blubbering, selfish, bribingly superstitious with his unresigned magical use of Christ's words, 'Into thy hands I commend my spirit'. Pleonastically he invokes not God alone but God and the Blessed Virgin. His self-loving slavish fear is also diametrically opposed to Stoic apathy in all its forms.

'God', said Panurge, 'and the Blessed Virgin be with us. Holos, holas! I am drowning. Bebebebebous, bebe, bous, bous. *In manus*. True God, send me some dolphin or other to bear me safely ashore like a good little Arion. I'll sound my harp well – if the handle's not come off!' (*QL* xxi, 48).

Frère Jean's prayer is a muddy one, as we should expect from this good-hearted ignorant monk:

'I give myself to all the Devils,' said Frère Jean – ('God be with us,' Panurge kept saying through his teeth) – 'If I come down there I'll prove to you that your balls are hanging from the arse of a cocky, cuckold-horned, cowardly calf. Mgnan, mgnan, mgnan. Come over here and help us, you great blubbering calf – by the thirty million devils who are leaping about in your body! Are you going to come over, you sea-calf you? Fy? How ugly he is, the cry-baby!'
– 'You never say anything else!'
– 'Come on then, old thirst-raiser! Forward march! Let me pluck you against the grain: *Blessed is the man that hath not walked, etc.*, – I know all this by heart' (*QL* xxi, 54f; punctuation changed as suggested in a private letter from the late Professor Watanabé Kazuo of Tokyo).

The active monk curses emptily; he mocks Panurge continually, but eventually pulls out his old thirst-raiser (his breviary) and intones the first psalm. He is on the right side of the great divide separating Pantagruel from Panurge.

The same genius for sudden changes of tone, which leave tragedy in perfect harmony with comedy, is seen in the way God works his miracle. The sails are down, the ship is at the mercy of the elements, the prayers are made. Frère Jean, jocularly attributing to St Nicolas a punning rewriting of a verse of Horace, alludes, by associations of ideas, to the famous *Tempestas* (Tempête), a former principal of the notorious Collège de Montaigu: if college fellows who beat wretched students are damned, he must be even now whipping the dog turning Ixion's wheel. If such fellows are saved, then he must be way above . . . the skies. Only, instead of the word *skies*, the chapter ends with Frère Jean's sentence incomplete. And the next chapter begins with the shout not of *Heaven!* but of *Earth!*

It is Pantagruel who cries out that land is in sight:

'*Terre, terre, s'escria Pantagruel, je voy terre*' (QL XII, 1).

At once all the characters except Panurge get back to work, in a spirit of joyful gratitude. Even Frère Jean remembers to give thanks to God this time (QL XXII, 21). The heroes' requests were scriptural, modest, unselfish. And they are answered. Panurge's prayers, in which he begged to be treated like a new Arion brought exceptionally ashore on the back of a dolphin, are not. They are fearful attempts to make ignoble emotions take precedence over the will of God.

The miracle of God has been quietly worked, without a word of explanation or description. The *Quart Livre* is not a book for those who need everything to be spelled out for them. That is part of its inner meaning. As one would expect, now that the storm has been elaborated, both tragically and comically, with the aid of scriptural words of the crucified Christ, the Christian flavour of the episode is now dominant in terms of its meaning. But this element does not squeeze out others. Both the classical and the nautical flavours are enhanced by copious borrowings from the ancient languages and a variety of modern sea-faring dialects. Many of the words which Rabelais uses are so rare that few could have understood them all. That does not matter; taken together they provide a general impression of stormy chaos and of the fury of the tempestuous elements.

5. Theological implications of the Storm

After the worst is over, the good characters show their relief through laughter.

The Christian explicitness of the episode is further increased by the striking out of the reference to the classical belief about fiery souls perishing in water, and by a fundamental recasting of Epistemon's moral conclusion (*QL* XXII, 75f.) At the crucial points 'the gods' give way to God; matters of life and death are no longer 'partly in the will of the gods, partly in our own free will'. They are entirely in the hands of God: *en la saincte volunté de Dieu*. What Epistemon now says is theologically most precise:

I consider that if, truly, to die is – as it is – a matter of fatal and inevitable necessity, to die at such and such a time or in such and such a fashion is in the holy will of God. Wherefore, we must ceaselessly implore, invoke, beseech and supplicate him. But that must not be our target or our limit; on our part, we too have to strive and, as the holy ambassador says, be cooperators with him (*QL* XXIII, 27f.).

The sneer at the 'matheologians and their decrees' is abandoned; a vague reference to 'the book and authority' is replaced by an important proof-text of scripture. The Christian God does not want passive worshippers. He intends that man should bestir himself. Such a contention is clinched with words taken from God's 'ambassador' Saint Paul, *le sainct Envoyé*. The title of ambassador is not lightly used. It was affected by evangelicals to remind Christians that even the apostles were bearers of their Master's good news, not their own.

In I Corinthians 3, 9, St Paul states that men must be 'workers together' with God' (*theou sunergoi*). Rabelais renders these words, very carefully, as *cooperateurs avecques luy*. This is the vital text with which to crown the parable of the Storm.

Rabelais returns to his long established synergistic preoccupations. In *Pantagruel* (*TLF* XIX, 68; *EC* XXIX, 59) – in the one particular domain of faith, where God's own honour is concerned – God needs *nul coadjuteur sinon . . .* in other domains he does. The word *coadjuteur* echoes the Vulgate reading of I Corinthians 3, 9: *Dei sumus adjutores*, 'We are God's helpers'. It was good enough for *Pantagruel* in the 1530s. But times had changed. Now Rabelais, with the best of scholarship behind him, does not talk of men being God's 'helpers' but 'cooperators'. This word echoes the Latin translations of Erasmus and Lefèvre d'Etaples, both of whom saw that *cooperatores* was a better rendering of the original Greek. The word cooperator also had the great advantage of avoiding any suggestion that an all-powerful God needs help; he requires man to cooperate – which is another matter. This synergistic theology of the 1552 Storm shows Rabelais loyal to his own teachings in *Gargantua*, as Frère Jean emphasises. Already in 1548 Frère Jean had established the parallel between the Storm and the attack on Seuillé. This parallel is now shifted to a place of greater emphasis, after Epistemon's exposition (*QL* XXXIII, 38). The Panurge who is now con-

demned is not simply the timorous booby of the Storm but the cocky do-
nothing Ucalegon. This is in keeping with other changes. Major additions
to the Storm emphasise that Panurge's verbal piety, all his vows and
promises, were quite without effect and never really meant anything at all.
The closing words of the episode leave us in no doubt about this; Eusthenes
cites a Lombardy proverb to emphasise the point: *Passato el periculo, gabato el
santo.* Panurge has proved this is true: once the peril was over this cardboard
saint had disappeared (xxiv, end).

The reasons for Rabelais's rewriting of the episode were not confined to
art for art's sake. The meaning of the whole Storm is changed, both in its
depth and in its complexity. In both cases the enemy is Calvin *and* the
Sorbonne. Somewhat to his surprise, no doubt, Rabelais had had time to
discover that the 1548 canons of the Council of Trent did not all deserve to
be laughed at as mere decrees of matheologians! In 1548, Calvin lost no
time in rejecting the Council of Trent's deliberations on salvation,
publishing the official decrees 'with a remedy against the poison'. For him
the papists were simply up to their old tricks, talking as though the power
were God's alone, but in fact keeping a place for man in the economy of
salvation. The Council's decrees, he says, simply contain the same old
'common doctrine of their Sorbonnistes': 'namely, that we are justified
partly by God's grace, partly by our own works.' Such words recall
Rabelais's doctrine in the first Storm.[7]

In fact the virtual identity of words hides a theological gulf. The *works*
which the Sorbonne championed were mainly theological, indeed peni-
tential ones. Such works included attending mass or fulfilling Church
obligations. By shortening the period man must spend in purgatory, they
contribute towards salvation. In many ways, man had to do more than rely
on Christ's saving action. For Rabelais in synergistic mood man's 'working
together with God' has nothing to do with theological works thus
conceived. What God wants from man is active virtue. The superstition of
Panurge in the Storm is unmistakably papist not Calvinist. Whilst
defending man's cooperation with God against Calvin, Rabelais laughs
whole-heartedly at the kind of superstitious, merely verbal, cooperation

---

[7] J. Calvin, *Les Actes du Concile de Trente: Auec le remede contre la poison*, s.l., 1548; pp.158f. (on
the sixth session of the Council, celebrated 13 January 1547 and devoted to the doctrine of
justification, as well as to the reform of abuses). Calvin protests against the doctrine that the
salvation of the elect by Christ requires man both freely to acquiesce in God's grace *and* to
'cooperate' with it, in such a way as not to be 'idle' (*oisif*). On p.180 Calvin gives the antidote
to such a 'poisonous' theology: this definition (he writes) contains nothing more than 'la
doctrine commune de leurs Sorbonistes: assavoir que nous sommes justifiez en partie par la
grace de Dieu, en partie par noz œuvres'. This doctrine he holds to be not much better than
that of the heretic Pelagius. Calvin goes too far in condemning Trent of Pelagianism; but
many who did try and defend traditional doctrines in the controversies of the sixteenth
century did unwittingly fall into semi-Pelagianism.

which he associated with the doctrines of the hypocrites of the University of Paris.

The phrase that Rabelais cites in 1552 would seem to decide the matter in his favour in an age which accepted the inerrancy of Scripture, since St Paul did indeed use the word *sunergoi*, '*labourers together*', on two occasions (I Corinthians 3, 9 and II Corinthians 6, 1). The first of these two texts is the vital one, since Saint Paul specifically talks of working together *with God*. Especially during the 1550s, but also much earlier, this text was currently used in Catholic circles – Gallican as well as papist – as a sort of slogan designed to give scriptural authority to a synergistic theology of salvation. But Calvin had little difficulty in showing that the text had for centuries been taken to mean something quite different, at least to the Western Church. It was not a question, he asserted, of man working together with God as a meritorious agent, but of God using man as a gardener uses a spade. Calvin overstates his case; but he was on fairly solid ground. Nevertheless Rabelais's exploitation of I Corinthians 3, 9 as an authority proving the reality of free will and its duty to cooperate with grace was important enough for Calvin to make a special interpolation into the 1559 edition of his *Christian Institutes*, attacking the synergistic theology expounded in the *Quart Livre*. Whether he had Rabelais specifically in mind is not certain but probable. He attacks and mocks those who try to defend 'their free will' on the grounds that St Paul called men 'cooperators with God'. The cap certainly fitted Rabelais very snugly. But Calvin, who at first called this a 'papist' error, later considered it to be the error of 'some people'.[8] Doubtless he realised that Catholic synergists such as Rabelais were, in this matter, at one with the followers of Melanchthon.[9]

---

[8] J. Calvin, *Institution chrestienne . . . Augmentée . . .* , Geneva 1560, p.137, §17: (II, 5, 17). 'The allegation made by some [*aucuns* – in former editions, *les papistes*] is no less daft: namely that saint Paul calls men *cooperateurs avec Dieu*. For it is very widely known that that only applies to the doctors of the Church, whom God uses, and puts to work, for the spiritual building which is the work of him alone. And so ministers are not called his companions, as though they had some power [*vertu*] of their own, but because God works through them, after having first made them suitable for this.'

[9] Calvin's preface to the French translation of Melanchthon's *Common-places* (*La Somme de Theologie*, 1546) is remarkably conciliatory. Nevertheless, Melanchthon's insistence on the need for man to do good works became increasingly unacceptable to many Lutheran purists, as well as to all Calvinists, despite the fact that the 'good works' Melanchthon required from man are scriptural ones: the spreading of the Gospel, the bearing of afflictions, right conduct towards one's neighbours, and so on (pp.599f., on Philippians 2, a predestination crux). Against Luther, and on the side of Erasmus, Melanchthon refused to allow the phrase 'I will harden Pharaoh's heart' (Exodus 4, 21) to be used as a proof-text clinching the argument in favour of the enslaved will. For Melanchthon as for Erasmus, *indurabo cor ejus* signifies permission: 'as though God said, "I will permit it to be hardened".' Similarly in the Lord's Prayer, *Lead us not into temptation* means, 'Do not permit that we be so led' (*Somme*, p.603).

It would be silly to assert that Rabelais in 1552 was simply still defending the policies of the late Guillaume du Bellay dating from the 1530s. But it is worth recalling that at the time that Langey was, with his episcopal brother's enthusiastic support, first seeking closer ties with Melanchthon, he made an unexpected and sustained appearance as one of the inter-locutors in Bishop Sadolet's dialogue-commentary on the *Epistle to the Romans* (1536), a work which did not endear the bishop to the Sorbonne – or to Rome, where it was felt that the rôle given to man's cooperation with grace was too great: if not Pelagian, then at least semi-Pelagian. Whether Rabelais, Sadolet, Jean du Bellay or Langey actually slipped into heresy in the 1530s is not an easy matter to decide. I do not think they did. But if they did, it was not by being excessively inclined towards a Lutheran enslaved will. All were defenders of free will, inclining if at all towards semi-Pelagianism on this point rather than towards Lutheranism. Sadolet's famous commentary associated the name of Guillaume du Bellay, Seigneur de Langey, with a liberal theology for which he remained widely-known in intellectual circles. While being a consistent proponent of synergism, Rabelais was also a consistent supporter of both the diplomatic policies of his patrons towards the German Lutherans and of their publicly stated liberal theology. Their natural allies were Melanchthonians not Lutheran extremists. Both Melanchthon and Rabelais would have appreciated Sadolet's doctrine that, in all our right doings, there is need of a minimal but very real *cooperatio* with God (*Commentarii*, 1536, p.134).

As far as the actual words *cooperateurs avec luy* are concerned, Rabelais seems to be using the same synergistic battle-cry as the Sorbonne itself in the 1550s!

The school in which Rabelais first learned his lasting devotion to Christian synergism was not particularly humanistic; not particularly prone to boldness or heresy. The words with which he claims to clinch matters in both 1548 and 1552, including the Vulgate version of St Paul's text, are ones he would have met as a novice. St Bonaventura supplies them. St Bonaventura was one of the luminaries of the Franciscan order: a scholarly Franciscan friar such as Rabelais, who successfully studied for the priesthood from within this order, would inevitably have made a prolonged and detailed acquaintance with his works. For Bonaventura as for Rabelais the justification of man depends 'in part' (*ex parte*) on divine grace for its beginning and for its increase, but also 'in part' (again, *ex parte*) on the hard work of man's free will; *eo quod adjutores Dei sumus*: 'Since we are God's helpers' (see above, pp.97f., 312 n.6).

Greek philology, when added to Franciscan theology, led Rabelais to see, as the years passed, that terms such as helper (*coadjutor*) and to help (*coadjuvare*) are best avoided. But he had learned his theology well at Fontenay-le-Comte. At basis his conception of man's 'working together' with God did not change. He did not see man as a puppet in the hands of God; nor did he see God as a super-puppet to be activated by pious formulas, however holy the formulas may appear. Man has a responsibility towards God: that of working with God towards his chosen ends; failure to recognise this exposes you to Rabelais's theological and moral laughter.

With rare comic artistry Rabelais brings his readers to laugh at both the extreme theologies ranged either side of his conception of Christian synergism. Calvin's doctrine of total predestination is like Panurge's peculiarly Catholic and, in essentials, magical manipulations of God: both see the Almighty not as a divine Person to be worked with but as a power who can be safely left, or brought, to do all the hard work himself. Or so Rabelais would have us believe. Fairness to the complexities of his adversaries' theologies is not a feature of Rabelais's writings. No wonder that Rome and Geneva, so snarlingly opposed in most things, were united in their hostility to him.

The man Rabelais so much admired, Erasmus, was the author of another famous Renaissance Storm: the *Naufragium* (Shipwreck) of the *Colloquies*. Rabelais was probably influenced by it, though not in the direction of synergistic propaganda. A good way for a modern reader to compare and contrast Erasmus's wit with Rabelais's comedy is to read the two Storms together. Neither endeared their authors to their enemies in either camp.

6. *The island of the Macraeons*

The Storm with its bustle, its dramatic farcical action, its cascade of words and its new interest in onomatopoeia and emotionally revealing sounds, its seductive mixture of classical learning and Christian laughter, its telling juxtaposition of tragedy and comedy leads abruptly and unexpectedly to the calm discussions which dominate the visit to the island of the Macraeons. These Macraeons live on an island which is an embodiment of the great ruined cultures of antiquity. The remains of temples, obelisks, pyramids and sepulchres symbolise this. So do the numerous inscriptions in Egyptian hieroglyphs, as well as in Greek, Arabic, Moorish, Slavonic and other tongues. The only surprising aspect of this humanist respect for the wisdom and beauty of the ancient world is the inclusion of 'Slavonic and so on' on the list. It suggests an unusually wide sympathy for the past, giving pride of place to Egypt and Greece, but even embracing the virtually unknown ancient cultures of middle and eastern Europe. The omission of Latin is odd; perhaps Latin did not seem sufficiently exotic to deserve special mention. More likely, Latin is taken for granted (QL xxv, 27f.).

The Macraeons themselves speak classical Greek (QL xxv, 46). Their name derives from *makraiōn*, 'vieillart, homme qui a des ans beaucoup'. They seem to be conceived as venerable ancients in touch with Greek culture and its sources both mystical and spiritual. But they share their island with ageing demi-gods who dwell in the woods and groves. I suspect that these were the original *Macraeons*, the *Longaevi*, as Martianus Capella calls Pans, fauns, faeries of the water-springs, satyrs, silvans, nymphs, *fatui* and *fatuae*, those mysterious 'long-livers' who dance through the woods, groves, glades, lakes, streams and rivers. Clearly the Macraeons live closely with them and know their ways (cf. *De Nuptiis Mercurii et Philologiae*, 1866, II, 167; p.74).

That these island-dwellers should be sages drinking from the fount of ancient Greek is appropriate, since the starting point of Rabelais's discussions in these chapters is the *Moralia* of Plutarch. Anyone wishing to understand and enjoy these chapters fully would be well advised to read the treatise *On the Decline of Oracles* either in the original or in Amyot's translation. It is quite short. It forms the framework of this episode and supplies other important matter to the *Quart Livre*. With Plutarch's text firmly in mind, we can better appreciate what Rabelais is doing: taking the best of ancient mystic wisdom and christianising it. The visit to the island of the Macraeons is Rabelais's own 'transition from Hellenism to Christianity', to borrow the title of Budé's book. It is as openly, clearly and sustainedly syncretistic as the new prologue of 1552. It shows how ideas and episodes in Plutarch can be so understood as to throw light on aspects of Christian history and Christian theology. At the time that Rabelais was writing, Plutarch's theological treatises were even more impressive, even more mysteriously meaningful, than they seemed to later generations, whose knowledge of Greek was more easily acquired. Amyot and Mont-aigne are more attracted to Plutarch's moral reflexions and to his urbane unpedantic style: Rabelais, on the contrary, is more strongly attracted to the light he throws on ancient religion and ancient mystical wisdom, as pro-legomena to Christian revelation. For Rabelais, Plutarch shares with many other of the great men of the past, Hermes Trismegistus and Plato among them, religious and spiritual insights which, when properly adapted and unveiled, strengthen, confirm and enrich the Christian revelation.

There are reasons for believing that the original conception of this episode also arose out of Rabelais's reading of Plutarch in conjunction with the Marsi edition of Ovid's *Fasti*. In other words it may have been conceived about the same time as the end of the *Tiers Livre* and the prologue to the 1548 *Quart Livre*. But if that is so, Rabelais probably did not publish it without revising and expanding it. We may note that the Holy Bottle is called *Bacbuc*, not *La Dive Bouteille* (QL XXVI, 55). This suggests revision, but it does not prove a late date of composition. The *Isle des Macraeons* would have been a good pendant to the first Storm as well as to the second. In the first Storm we were told of the ancient belief that fiery souls could die, in the sense of being totally quenched in the hostile element of water. The

Macraeons take up the theme of fiery souls which are dissipated by death. This time the ancient belief is not simply denied; it is so changed as to confirm Christian doctrine.

The venerable *Macrobe*, as the office of the chief magistrate of the Macraeons was called, explains to Pantagruel the cause of the Storm they have just weathered: when one of the heroes or daemons who live on their island dies, strange lamentations are heard in the woods, while plagues, darkness and tempests abound. Such a death must have occurred, foretold indeed three days beforehand by a comet (QL XXVI, 9f.).

The essence of this explanation is taken verbatim from *On the Decline of Oracles* (419Eff.). Rabelais adapts Plutarch's idea to his own needs by supplying the allusion to the comet, which is not a minor piece of embroidery tacked on to a classical tale, but the means of linking together the deaths of daemons and heroes, the death of Langey and the death of Christ.

Pantagruel's reply to the Macrobe's ancient lore reveals a new depth in Rabelais's use of Plutarch. In the *Tiers Livre* (XXIV, 97) it was Panurge who superstitiously drew upon Plutarch's account of the strange Ogygian Isles lying five days' sailing to the westward of England and inhabited by soothsayers and prophets. Epistemon dismissed his ramblings as mere fabulous nonsense. Yet what Pantagruel draws out of Plutarch may seem no less fabulous today, not least since it may concern the same Ogygian Islands. But as behoves a Christian humanist reading Plutarch or any other pagan sage, Rabelais knew that his hero must not swallow him whole, in an uncritical manner, as Panurge did. Ancient wisdom has to be unveiled, its *altior sensus* carefully sought out, the wheat separated from the chaff and its truths adapted to a higher revelation. The Macrobe's statements are confirmed by Pantagruel – confirmed, we may note, by Rabelais putting into his mouth the very next words in Plutarch's treatise. The extinction of an heroic soul is there compared to a candle guttering out. As Pantagruel sums it up: just as a candle shines brightly, but fills the air with stench when it is snuffed out, so too does the bright soul of a good daemon or hero bring troubles when it dies (QL XXVI, 23f.; *De defectu oraculorum* 419F).

Rabelais follows Plutarch closely: so closely that his christianising of the theme is thrown into sharp relief if his text and Plutarch's original are juxtaposed. In Plutarch the souls of daemons and heroes die in the sense that they are extinguished like a candle-flame. This is emphasised by some of the words he uses: *phthora*: 'corruption', 'decay', 'destruction', and *sbesis*: 'quenching', 'putting out'. The whole point of this part of the discussion in *On the Decline of Oracles* is to advance the disputed opinion that daemons and heroes have existences which are, in absolute terms, finite; that their souls can and do come to a complete end in the dissolution of death, snuffed out like candles. Such a notion of the death of a soul has no place whatever in Christian psychology. Rabelais quietly adapts the words of his original, so making the deaths of daemons and heroes analogous to those of human beings. The Renaissance overwhelmingly conceived of death in the centuries-old way as the separation of body and soul. In keeping with this doctrine Pantagruel states that the souls of heroes – *âmes nobles et insignes* – shine forth like a candle-flame, 'during all the time that they inhabit their bodies' (QL XXVI, 30). Their death is no extinction of a spiritual or 'animal' flame but the soul's 'departure' from the body, *une discession* (XXVI, 33). The word *discession* is a latinisation of the Old French word *decession*. Rabelais brings it closer to *discessio*, which in Latin means both a departure and a 'separation' of married couples in divorce. The choice of word is a happy one: Christian writers regularly liken the union of body and soul in a living man to a marriage, and their sundering in death to a divorce. Rabelais rejects the classical notion of the 'death' (that is, the quenching) of the soul, accepting that of a *discession*, of its departure in the great divorce of death. This is no accident of translation, no slipshod confounding of ancient and Christian categories through semantic confusion: it is part of a sustained christianising of Plutarch's pagan insights. If the soul was of the substance of fire, it could be quenched. Rabelais carefully dissociates himself from such a belief. This is a dominant characteristic of the episode of the Macraeons, where it is a central theme.

Of course, in the context of Rabelais's fully Christian psychology, Plutarch's analogy of the candle-flame no longer fits so snugly as it did in *On the Decline of Oracles*.

The old Macrobe, speaking in ancient Greek, does assert that the souls of heroes and daemons die 'finally' – *finablement*. His classification of souls into those of demi-gods, daemons and human beings is probably that of Hesiod as cited in this treatise by Plutarch (415B). There is a fourth category, the souls of 'gods', inappropriate for Christians, except insofar as it includes the manhood of Christ.

Frère Jean is not much of a theologian. Unaccustomed though he is to thinking theologically, he is just a little worried by all this talk of souls 'dying' – but he will follow wherever Pantagruel leads!

'These Heroes and Demi-gods you have spoken of – can they come to an end (*finir*) in death? [He thought, 'God forgive him' that they were 'immortal like fair angels'.] But this most reverend Macrobe says they die *finally*' (QL, TLF XXVII, 73f.).

Pantagruel does not counter this belief until Rabelais makes yet another borrowing from these same pages of *On the Decline of Oracles*. The wise giant points out that the Stoics did not believe that all souls 'died finally'; they believed that they were all absorbed into the world-soul after a long life, the duration of which (possibly 9,720 years) was based upon mystical mathematical calculations (*QL, TLF* XXVII, 79f.; *De defectu oraculorum* 415A-D).

These considerations afford Pantagruel the opportunity of making an unambiguous declaration of orthodoxy. Christian dogmatics had only recently felt the need to assert, as a matter of faith, the doctrine of the immortality of the soul. For long centuries it had largely been taken for granted. Pantagruel's profession of orthodoxy strongly recalls, in context, the language of the bull *Apostolici Regiminis* (1513) of Pope Leo X:

'I believe', said Pantagruel, 'that all intellective souls – *toutes âmes intellectives* – are exempt from the scissors of Atropos. All are immortal: *Anges, Daemons* and *Humaines*' (*QL* XXVII, 99f.).

This disposes of both the erroneous opinions found in Plutarch's treatise: souls are not mortal; neither are they basically merely One, being reabsorbed at death into the world-soul. In his own inimitable way, Rabelais is showing his loyalty to the definitions and anathemas of *Apostolici Regiminis*, which includes the words:

We condemn and reprove all who assert that the intellective soul is mortal, or one amongst all men. (*Damnamus et reprobamus omnes asserentes animam intellectivam mortalem esse, aut unicam in cunctis hominibus.*)

7. The death of Pan

If Rabelais is genuinely and convincingly to derive support for Christian doctrine by an unveiling of truths embedded in Plutarch, then he has to face the history of the death of Pan. Plutarch relates this strange event just before the matter which supplied the Macrobe with the explanation of the storm in terms of heroic souls guttering out like candle-flames. It was related precisely in order to prove that even divine or semi-divine beings such as Pan was *do* eventually come to an end in death.

The death of Pan now preoccupies Rabelais for an entire chapter – one of the best written, and most profound, to come from his pen (*QL* XXVIII; *De defectu oraculorum*, 419Bf.).

There has been great confusion over this episode. It has been treated as though the death of Pan were not presented by Plutarch as an historical fact. And generations of students of the *Quart Livre* have been baldly told that Rabelais's interpretation of the event is the same as that of Eusebius Pamphilus, who died as bishop of Caesarea in 340; this is simply not true.

Neither Plutarch nor Rabelais – nor any of their contemporaries – ever present the account of the death of Pan as myth, poetry or fiction. It is treated as a real, important historical event, presented as such by Plutarch in order to lend weight to an opinion which Rabelais does *not* hold: namely that daemonic and heroic souls die 'finally'. Rabelais in his telling of this history introduces it with an *however*, a *toutesfois* (XXVII, 102), for it is an event which, if Plutarch's interpretation were correct, would refute Pantagruel's belief in the immortality of all intellective souls, the souls, that is, of all angels, daemons and human beings. Pantagruel's wise and inspired interpretation of the real sense of the death of Pan is then introduced by a second *toutesfois* (XXVIII, 45), for he is supplying an exegesis which not only confirms his own belief in the immortality of such souls, but corrects Plutarch's interpretation and leads straight on to a powerfully emotive allusion to Christ, the crucified Pan of Christian belief.

To link Plutarch's account of the death of Pan with the living or dying Christ would not in itself have troubled Rabelais's literate contemporaries. Some of the best humanists had done so nearly a century before, not to mention bishop Eusebius Pamphilus in *The Preparation for the Gospel*. Eusebius's book was unknown to the mediaeval western world. Its rediscovery was one of the more exciting enrichments of the Renaissance. It was translated into Latin – not very well – and printed in 1470 by the Byzantine refugee, George of Trebizond; after several reprintings, it was again translated and printed by Tramezzino in 1550 – just before the *Quart Livre*. Eusebius believed that the Pan whose death concerned Plutarch was not a pagan hero. It does not occur to him to interpret him as the Christian God. He was a devil, cast out by Christ during his earthly ministry. Other devils spread the news of this to their fellow spirits by using captain Thamous as an intermediary (*Praeparatio Evangelica*, Oxford 1903, I, 267f.).

What might have impressed and surprised contemporary readers of the 1552 *Quart Livre* was Rabelais's introducing a mystically conceived account of the death of Guillaume du Bellay, Seigneur de Langey, into these chapters. The death of this great statesman deeply concerned Rabelais: twice in his novels he alludes to it (*TL* XXI, 46; *QL* XXVII, 51); one of his lost Latin books was designed as a eulogy of this patron's wise diplomacy. A public protestation of awed respect for Langey was an act of loyalty to the memory of a statesman whose charm and greatness seem beyond dispute. Written in his brother's household, it was a tribute to him too.

Pantagruel treats his death as the death of a hero, using that classical word to mean a great man, far above the general level of mankind (*QL* XXVII, title and text). In this sense, the hero has something in common with the saint. In Plutarch's treatise the word hero, *hērōs*, almost certainly means a demi-god; Rabelais knows this and puts the words *Heroes et Semidieux* into Frère Jean's mouth (*QL* XXVII, 73). In fact, of course, not for a moment is Langey allowed to be in any way divine. The multiple sense of the word hero in classical and Christian Greek made it easy for Rabelais to apply Plutarch's notions, suitably adapted, not only to a race of semi-divine creatures intermediary between God and man, but to great men like Langey. There was ample classical precedent for this sense; moreover in the humanist Latin of the fifteenth and sixteenth centuries the word *heros* was often pressed into service with a Christian connotation.

The high religious esteem in which Rabelais was prepared to hold famous men in whom the Lord had manifested his glory is shown by his applying 'Solomon's' praise of Moses in Ecclesiasticus to the Cardinal de Châtillon. Guillaume du Bellay was apparently in the same category of greatness. Rabelais weaves an account of his achievements and his heroic death into the fabric of these chapters. Nothing reveals more cogently his basic seriousness in parts of the *Quart Livre* than what he has to say here.

A man totally dependent on the patronage and protection of Cardinal Jean du Bellay and Cardinal Odet de Châtillon does not jest destructively or ambiguously about the death of Langey. The *Quart Livre* is probably the last word of an author whose view of the world and whose art could not be confined within the limits of comedy, even though it rarely lacks a comic tincture. The kind of classical-Christian syncretism dear to many Renaissance humanists he takes out of the study, the lecture-room, the learned artist's studio, and brings to the attention of intelligent men other than scholars. Rabelais is putting within reach of his French readers rare erudition, not easily accessible even to the Latin-educated.

Langey's death was a distressing one; but it was no merely human accident: it was a God-willed event. His death was preceded by portents – and by signs against the whole order of nature. Rabelais uses a standard classification of such divine warnings into *prodiges*, *portentes* and *monstres*. Such events, and others like them, he calls *precedens signes formez contre tout ordre de nature*. This last phrase emphasises that we are dealing with real, God-sent miracles – not simply because Rabelais frequently uses the word *signe* in this sense (following the New Testament), but because traditional doctrine emphasised that a real miracle was not merely an event 'against nature' – diabolical agencies can apparently produce such things – but an event *against the whole order of nature*, to use the words of Rabelais and of Thomas Aquinas (*ST* I, Qu. XC art.4).

The strange state of the heavens before Langey's death took the form of supernatural *feus de joie* serving a double function. The heavens were rejoicing at God's command, before the anticipated arrival of Langey; at the same time, mankind was being warned that such a venerable 'soul' was about to leave the body. The sense of these words is made clear: the death of Langey was, in accordance with standard Christian belief, a 'departure' of his soul from his body. Sixteen real people, including a 'doctor Rabelays', vouch for the truth of these events (*QL* XXVII, 25, 49f.). Rabelais's terms, despite the sustained influence of Plutarch, leave no room whatsoever for doubt; such souls are not extinguished: they leave 'their body and the earth'. As for Langey's soul, when that great man died, it 'departed' from its body (*QL* XXVII, 49, 55).

The presence of the account of Langey's heroic death contributes much to the serious historical savour of these chapters. The christianising of Plutarch makes *On the Decline of Oracles* and its discussions relevant to great events in Rabelais's time. And the history of Pan is adapted and interpreted in such a way as to lead to deep reflexions on the death of Christ.

Faced with the account of the death of Pan in Plutarch, a modern reader need not believe it. We have learned to refuse to accept a great deal of what an author tells us, however cogently it is expressed, however authoritatively it is presented, however little evidence we have for doing so. If even the greatest, most intelligent and most honest of past authors tell us things which do not conform to our view of the world, then we reject their testimony. Rabelais's age could not so easily reject accounts of well-authenticated events vouched for by great authors; neither could the generation of Montaigne, if they took his warnings seriously. For Rabelais the problem was not one of deciding whether Plutarch had simply made up this story or had been gullibly deceived. Plutarch was neither credulous nor a liar. But he was not of course infallible: when he put forward views at variance with Renaissance scholarship and experience or contrary to attested Christian truths, then he was wrong or partly so. The basic problem for Rabelais was how to interpret the well-authenticated event of Pan's death, while respecting all known truths. The death of Pan was not simply another example of a great author veiling the truth in fable; it was a true historical event, veiled from men's eyes by higher powers than man, for hidden purposes of their own.

On the Decline of Oracles tells us that a captain Thamous was sailing from Egypt when a strange and terrible voice thrice ordered him to take his ship to Palodes, a port in the Epirus. There he was to cry aloud: 'The Great Pan is dead.' He decided to do so only if his ship were to be unnaturally stayed off Palodes. It was. When he cried out 'The Great Pan is dead', lamentations were heard as of many voices sorrowing. And many frightening events occurred.

Tiberius Caesar was told by his scholars that the being who had died was Pan, son of Mercury and Penelope: a hero, then, with a divine father and a human mother. If these counsellors, as interpreted by Plutarch, were right, then an intellective soul, despite Pantagruel's assertion, had actually died, in the sense that the soul had dispersed like a guttering candle-flame. That is why Plutarch relates the event, to prove this precise point (*De defectu oraculorum* 419B-D; *QL* XXVIII).

Pantagruel has a powerful answer ready. This Pan was in fact Christ. Rabelais prepares the ground carefully for his hero's Christian interpretation of this mysterious event. In Plutarch's account, the voice ordered Thamous to cry out 'The Great Pan is dead'. In Rabelais the words are changed to 'Pan the great *God* is dead' (*QL* XXVIII, 20). Curiously,

Guillaume Postel, Rabelais's former friend and present enemy, did the same in a different context, introducing the word *god* into his account of the Pan's death when citing from memory and removed from his relevant books. Pantagruel's interpretation is not identical to Postel's, a man whose sanity he doubted – with good reason. But even an enemy may influence us, and one cannot rule out a possible influence here. Postel in fact makes a mistake, confusing Pan, the shepherd god or demi-god of Plutarch's account, with the other god Pan, meaning ALL. In Postel the daemons ordered Thamous to proclaim that the 'god ALL' had died. A far cry from Pantagruel's interpretation (G. Postel, *De Orbis Concordia*, 1545 (?), I, vii, p.50). By Rabelais's time Plutarch's history was known to the Latin-educated through other intermediaries besides Eusebius Pamphilus or Guillaume Postel. There is an interesting development of the theme in the *Prelude to Christian Philosophy* by Guillaume Bigot who was, like Rabelais, associated with the Du Bellays. Guillaume Bigot published his *Prelude* in 1549; he also dismissed any suggestion that Plutarch's dying Pan was the son of Mercury and Penelope. Bigot interprets that Pan, son of Mercury, as merely a great man superstitiously deified by posterity; that particular Pan had died long before these events.

According to Bigot the death of Pan related in Plutarch was a deliberately obscure message by which evil demons spread to others the bad news of Christ's triumphant death. In essentials he follows Eusebius, but brings him up to date. These devils alluded to Christ under the name of Pan lest more open testimony should encourage men to believe in the Son of God, their divine enemy. The wailings that greeting Thamous's declaration at Palodes were the lamentations of minor evil spirits, distressed by the victory of Christ, which they tried to hide from the knowledge of the Greeks, whilst using them as messengers to bring the bad news to their fellow evil spirits (Bigot, *Christianae Philosophiae Praeludium*, 1549, 442f.).

There were many attempts to reinterpret Plutarch's account because, although Eusebius's Christian interpretation of the death of Pan lent great authority to the event as such, it failed to satisfy the demands of Renaissance theology. Theological developments in the millennium and more separating Eusebius from Rabelais made his interpretation quite untenable by informed Christians. They knew that daemons cannot die. As Cardinal Caesar Baronius puts it, that fact has been convincingly proved – *exploratissimum est*. Devils were indeed cast out by Christ in great numbers. But they did not die: no evil spirits were killed by Christ (*Annales Ecclesiastici*, 1601, col.237f., §§129–130).

It seems it was a group of Italian humanists in the fifteenth century who first grasped the possibility of the account in Plutarch being an account of the actions of good daemons, who were making known to each other, suitably veiled, the news of the Crucifixion. Their account – the earliest I have found – appears in the annotated editions of Ovid's *Fasti* written by Antonius Constantius Fanensius and Paolo Marsi. As we have seen already, more than once, Rabelais was drawing on this text when writing the *Tiers Livre*, and on this text *and* Plutarch when writing the *Quart Livre* in both its versions. Here he is drawing upon the glosses on *Fasti* I, 397 (*Panes et in venerem satirorum prona juventus*).

The relevant gloss dealing with the death of Pan is arrestingly brought to our attention in the marginal titles of at least one edition of the *Fasti* (Venice 1520): the Fauns, we are told, knew of Christ's Passion: *Faunos cognovisse passionem domini nostri Jesu Christi*. And it was precisely the scholarly knowledge about Fauns and their attendant creatures to be found in this particular gloss that supplied one of Rabelais's important treatments of the fauns and *fatui* in the *Tiers Livre* (XXXVIII, 36f.).

Marsi was able to claim that other 'most holy men of our religion' supported his interpretation of Pan as Christ. Though he does not name them, it is certain that they include Ermolao Barbaro, who was translating *On the Decline of Oracles* into Latin at Marsi's request.

These 'most holy men of our religion' believed that the thrice-repeated command of the mysterious voice was heard by Thamous on the night following the Crucifixion. It was a superhuman voice, choosing to refer enigmatically to Christ as Pan, since Pan can mean ALL and the God who had died was the God of All Nature. Rabelais accepts this interpretation, but goes much farther.

The idea of the name Pan containing a supplementary allusion to the good classical shepherd-god Pan apparently did not appeal to Marsi and his circle, or did not occur to them. But by Rabelais's day, in contexts other than that of Plutarch's death of Pan, Christ was increasingly represented in poetry as Pan the classical shepherd. The theme appears for example in François Habert's *Songe de Pantagruel*, as well as in poems which may or may not be by Clément Marot and in a delightful *Noël* by the dashing Nicolas Denisot. The theme was to flourish, in poetry at least, until Milton's *On the Morning of Christ's Nativity*. And from very early days humanists had been able to admire Politian's beautiful hymn to Pan as the Christian God, written in Greek and so invested with a particular prestige (*Epigrammi Greci*, ed. Anthos Ardizzoni, Florence 1951, IX).

Scholars are naturally interested in the antecedents of Rabelais's account, which are important for the history of thought. Earlier interpretations can show how far Rabelais was being original, without striking out on interestingly idiosyncratic interpretations of his own. His forerunners, as far as we know, are important but few in number. Those that adopt the interpretation after him are legion, including Bishop Huet and Pascal, one of whose most tantalising *pensées* simply reads 'La mort de Pan'. Yet it is probably true that Rabelais's own scholarship, drawing heavily as it does on fifteenth-century Italian humanist sources, was beginning to look old-fashioned to some at least of a new generation of scholars. André Turnèbe's Latin translation of *On the Decline of Oracles* appeared in 1556. It passes over the death of Pan with a mere geographical footnote. In the dedicatory letter to Cardinal Charles of Lorraine he attacks the stupid and superstitious regard for divination in his day: all forms of divination not approved of in scripture are either false or the work of devils. We Christians who have been divinely instructed – *divinitus edocti* – know far more religious truth than Plutarch ever did. Turnèbe is clearly dissociating himself from the kind of mystic interpretation that appealed to Rabelais. He may be alluding to Rabelais quite specifically. I think he was.

Rabelais had both predecessors and followers in the matter of the death of Pan. But none of them comes within hailing distance of his artistry. That is what one would expect: they were mainly scholars not artists. None of them comes anywhere near his religious profundity and his sense of engagement. Pantagruel's exegesis has a movingly personal quality quite unknown before the *Quart Livre*. The 'great Saviour of the faithful' who lay veiled behind the name of Pan is not conceived of as a distant figure, dying in a far-off world and time, having no immediate connexions with Rabelais's own. The men who crucified him were the 'Pontifes, docteurs, prebstres et moines de la loi Mosaïcque'. We are made to feel that Christ is still being crucified by unworthy successors to these men under the new law in the Church:

However, I would interpret it as concerning that great Saviour (*Servateur*) of the faithful, who was ignominiously put to death in Judaea through the envy and wickedness of the Pontiffs, doctors, priests and monks of the Mosaic law. And this interpretation does not seem to me to be an inconsistent one: for he can rightly be called Pan in the Greek language, seeing that he is our ALL: all that we are, all that we live, all that we have, all that we hope, is him, in him, from him. He is the good Pan, the great pastor, who, as the passionate shepherd Corydon attests, not only holds his sheep in love and affection but his shepherds too. At his death there were plaints, sighs, terrors and lamentations in all the fabric of the universe – the heavens, the earth, the sea, and hell. The time agrees with my interpretation, for this *tresbon, tresgrand Pan*, our unique Saviour, died near Jerusalem, during the reign in Rome of Tiberius Caesar.

The Pan-Christ is not for Pantagruel an impersonal ALL, a symbol for the universe or even the God of all things: he is a God in so intimate a personal relationship with men, as to be not simply ALL, but 'our ALL': *le nostre Tout, tout ce que sommes, tout ce que vivons, tout ce que avons*. He is the Christ as preached by St Paul in Athens, with the help of a quotation from Aratus, the Stoic poet (Acts 17, 28: 'For in him we live and move and have our being'). This Christ-Pan is our All in that '. . . *tout ce que esperons est luy, en luy, de luy, par luy;*' he is, in other words, that Pauline Christ of Romans 11, 36: 'For of him, and through him, and in him, are all things.' (These texts were held to refute specific pre-Christian errors in Aristotle, the Stoics and the Epicureans.) To these texts are conjoined allusions to the hope that Christians must have in and through the Lord. Pantagruel is making it abundantly clear that the Pan whose death was so mysteriously announced to Thamous was no Stoic abstraction, no mere symbol representing classical pantheism. He was God himself, that 'great shepherd of the sheep', whom the ancient world only had fleeting and largely erroneous glimpses of beneath the name of Pan, the god of shepherds.

In a book like the *Quart Livre* of 1552, so consistently syncretistic, the impact of this account of God-veiled-as-Pan is considerable. Pantagruel believes that good daemons had so communicated to each other the tragic news of Christ's death that the Greek and Latin world was able to know of the good news, though in part only, and under a veil. The very person of Christ is conceived of in a manner which made him more accessible to wise and good ancients. With a deliberate confusion of adjectives, Christ is referred to not as the *great* Pan and the *good* shepherd, but as the *good* Pan and the *great* shepherd. By not exploiting the more obvious allusion to the good shepherd of John 10, 14, and by preferring to evoke memories of our Lord Jesus Christ 'that *great* shepherd' of the sheep of Hebrews 13, 20, Pantagruel takes over for Christ Pan's adjective *great*, leaving him free to attribute to the shepherd-god Pan Christ's adjective *good*. This makes the transition from the Christ as veiled by good daemons to the Christ as revealed to Christians in the Gospel more easy to grasp.[10]

Rabelais, while determined to safeguard the uniqueness of the Christian revelation in its fullness, is concerned as well to baptize as far as possible what was best in the ancient world. This is apparent from the complex interweaving of Christian and pagan terms and allusions. After enriching Pantagruel's exegesis with echoes of Hebrews, Acts, Ephesians and Romans, Rabelais makes him see veiled Christian truth in Virgil's second eclogue (verse 33), in which the passionate shepherd Corydon tells how Pan takes care of both the sheep and the shepherds, *Pan curat oves oviumque magistros* (QL XXVIII, 55). Rabelais takes this in a Christian sense, meaning, I think, that Christ loves both the laity and the priesthood. It is a curious text to cite. To see the *fourth* eclogue as a veiled prophetic allusion to the Nativity was quite usual. But I know of no one except Rabelais who applied to Christ this line from the second eclogue. I think I can explain

---

[10] QL XXVIII, 45: 'celluy *grand* Servateur des fideles'; 54: 'C'est le *bon* Pan, le *grand* pasteur'. Cf. Hebrews 13, 20 (Vulgate), where Christ is the *pastor magnus ovium*. Christ as good shepherd (the *pastor bonus* of John 10, 14) also underlies this episode, but at times less specifically than the *pastor magnus*.

what happened: the explanation reinforces the suggestion made elsewhere that Rabelais's memory was failing.

There is an interesting gloss on this verse in Cristoforo Landino's influential edition of Virgil (British Library, IB, 42176, fol. 6v°). In this gloss Landino says that Pan can be a symbol for ALL 'as Eusebius notes in *The Preparation for the Gospel*'; but he adds that what Eusebius wrote about the death of Pan 'is a different matter and does *not* apply to this text'. Rabelais apparently remembered Landino's associating of the dying Pan with the verse of Virgil's but did not remember his disclaimer. Nevertheless traditional classical commentaries on *Pan curat oves* did sometimes interpret the god as Jupiter conceived pantheistically. That may seem a far cry from Rabelais, as indeed it is: Rabelais's Pan is no pantheistic deity. On the other hand it may be relevant that the true godhead of Pan revealed in Christ is finally underlined by Pantagruel with Jupiter's ancient title *Optimus Maximus*. Christians had long since appropriated it for the true God; we saw Rabelais applying it to the scriptural Christ in the prologue. Behind the dying Pan of Plutarch must be seen *cestuy tresbon tresgrand Pan*, the *Optimus Maximus* who, truly understood, is *nostre unicque Servateur* (QL XXVIII, 60).

The adjective *unicque* is theologically aggressive in Rabelais's day when applied to the Saviour. It probably is here. It excludes, and is meant to exclude, all creatures, however great, from the scheme of the salvation worked by the Triune God. In the economy of God's salvation there is, in the last analysis, no place for the saints, for man's good works – however desirable and indeed essential in themselves – for angels, daemons or even for the Blessed Virgin. There is only one Saviour: Christ. The adjective *unicque* stamps out any possible confounding of Christ with actual pagan Pan or Pans. *Pan* is an appropriate name for good daemons to use amongst themselves, meaningfully veiling the name of Christ the Saviour; but in no sense were any of the pagan Pans real gods, anticipating the saving work of Christ. The adjective *unicque* declares that the salvation worked by Christ was achieved once, only once, and once for all, by Christ alone.

Pantagruel's interpretation is refreshing, ingenious and theologically mature. There is only one *theos*, one divine Person whom Renaissance Christians can accept as dying: Christ in his Manhood, of a reasonable soul and human flesh consisting. As for *daemones*, fauns, angels and the like, they are not gods but creatures, be they good or bad. They are nevertheless immortal, since they have intellective souls within their non-fleshly bodies. We men are the only known creatures to be endowed with an intellective soul who are able to die. And a human being's death is not the dispersing of his soul: it is its severance from the body, until Christ achieves his final victory over death at the the the end of the world, when the trumpet shall sound and our corruptible shall put on incorruption (Cf. *Pant.*, *EC* VIII, 21; above, pp.64f.).

'Heroes' such as Langey can die because, despite the hyperbole, they are but men, and so have souls which will, by death, be divorced from their bodies.

8. *'Tears like ostrich-eggs'*

It is an important aspect of Pantagruel's unique ability to penetrate through to the inner kernel of truth in this supernaturally veiled death of Pan that the key to the right understanding of it all should lie in a proper understanding of the *name* chosen by the good supernatural powers to convey to each other the cosmic tragedy of the death of the Son of God. How important this is does not appear in its fullness until later.

In these chapters Rabelais makes Pantagruel recall the death of Langey and the death of Christ. In the light of such great events, we would not wonder at the giant's tears, pouring down his face 'like ostrich-eggs', were it not for the fact that he had been made so impassive in the *Tiers Livre* that his tears seem almost as unique as the Saviour whose death provoked them. One is led to feel that Pantagruel is adding his tears to the angelic lamentations which filled the universe at the death of Christ.

That his tears should be 'as big as ostrich-eggs' worries some readers. They find the comparison too frivolous. But Rabelais delights in such rapid changes of mood. Anyway, he may be alluding – though I doubt it – to the 'ostrich-like mourning', the *luctus quasi struthionum*, of the prophet Micah (1,8). Or perhaps there is an echo of the traditional association of ostrich-eggs with divine grace operating in the minds of the pious; they were used symbolically with this sense by some emblematists.[11] Or it may simply be that Pantagruel as a giant needs to be provided with tears of unusual size, outstandingly large in their genre as an ostrich's eggs are in theirs.

A little while later, we saw the tears pour from his eyes, as big as ostrich eggs. I give myself to God, if I am telling a single word of a lie.

The unexpected comparison, the sudden reminder of Pantagruel's size, the fleetingly flippant tone adopted by the unheralded narrator – the *Je* in the last sentence – raise a smile of relief after the dense seriousness of these chapters. The giant exemplar of a quasi-stoic perfection with sceptical and

---

[11] For the ostrich as symbol of the pious man, forgetting earthly things for heavenly things, like an ostrich entrusting her eggs to the sands, cf. Guillaume le Clere's *Bestiaire*; he is indebted to a version of the Latin *Physiologus*. Cf. also Henkel and Schone, *Emblemata*, 1967, 807.

cynical overtones, weeping! . . . We have come a long way from the jolly giant of the first Chronicle who laughed and guffawed at everything. But we have also been made to see that Pantagruel's vaunted apathy was specifically limited to all the dimensions of *this* world, not the next. For Pantagruel to weep now, the tragedy must be greater than anything contained in the height, depth, longitude and latitude of this world, if he is to remain true to himself as presented to the reader in the *Tiers Livre*. Such an event was the Crucifixion.

A Christian Stoic's stoicism is no protection against that. Neither is a Christian Sceptic's scepticism or a Christian Cynic's cynicism.

But while we are aware, as rarely before, of Pantagruel's greatness and goodness, Rabelais is also at pains to take us quickly back to the happier world of the narrator of *Pantagruel*, no doubt partly so as to forestall the type of criticism made against an erudite and over-serious *Tiers Livre*. The account of the death of Pan ends with a rapid change of tone, as Rabelais's unheralded storyteller draws us away from the sadness of the weeping hero to his companions' joy, which was greater than usual. The opening sentence of the next chapter plunges us without preamble or preparation into this contrasting joy and contentment. We are told of the *joyeux convoy*, of the Macraeons, *plus que contents et satisfaictz*, and of *nos gens plus joyeulx que de coustume*. All the words stress happiness and wholesomeness: *refaictes et reparées*; *victuailles refraischiz*; *serain et delicieux*; *grande alaigresse*. Only a consummate artist could succeed in boldly snatching us away like this from Pantagruel's cosmic grief, leaving us with the feeling that even those who could not penetrate the mystery of the death of Pan were in fact lightened and quickened by the joy of the spirit. The change of mood conforms to Christian doctrine; diabolical deceptions start with joy and end with sadness; divine insights move from sadness into joy and contentment (cf. *TL* XIV, end).

The narrator breaks the spell by using an inverse adaptation of a standard technique found in *Pantagruel*: the storyteller protests the truth of what is being written about, at the very point where verisimilitude is farthest to seek. The teller of this tale of Pan will give himself to God if he is telling a lie: *Je me donne à Dieu, si j'en mens d'un seul mot* (QL XXVIII, end). The formula is a comic one: we expect, *je me donne au diable*. It is yet another variety of the standard jests found elsewhere: 'You are cheating here, drinkers, and do not believe that what I am telling you is the actual truth'; or, 'stop cheating here, and believe that there is nothing so true as the Gospel' (QL XXXVIII, 1, and end). These phrases have their counterparts in *Pantagruel* and *Gargantua* as well, though not in the *Tiers Livre*.

But at the end of the *Isle des Macraeons* the function of the formula is very different. Protestations of actual literal truth normally tumble from Rabelais's pen when the invention is more outrageous. Here the narrator protests that he is telling the truth, precisely when the truth is unambiguously present to the inspired Pantagruel but not to the insights of lesser mortals.

9. Strange words and strange meanings

The *Quart Livre* is entering a new phase, a phase of artistically skilful challenges and surprises. From now on we shall be surprised more than once when some of Rabelais's main characters say what we least expect them to. Pantagruel will sometimes say things which seem more at home in Frère Jean's mouth if taken literally; Panurge will say things which also, if taken literally, would make him a total convert to the evangelical wisdom of Pantagruel! It is by such means that Rabelais will lead us right up to the frontiers of knowledge, outlining for us, with the aid of laughter and of myth, the limits of truth and certainty as he saw them. In its simplest but very challenging form, how do we *know* that the death of Pan is a true account of angelic reactions to the Passion?

The point at issue can more clearly be seen by jumping ahead to chapter LII. There, Homenaz, the cruel, credulous, maudlin old bishop of the Papimanes, has his leg outrageously pulled by the merry companions of Pantagruel. Homenaz believed that the Decretals – laws based on papal authority alone – were uniquely inspired, more normative than the Gospel itself. Pantagruel's men spin him a series of tall stories, claiming to tell of miracles worked by pages torn from decretaline volumes: when Frère Jean wiped his behind on one, he got the piles; a chemist who made cornets out of them to wrap up his drugs spoilt their medical qualities; similarly, some girls who pressed their newly-laundered wimples inside a weighty tome of the Decretals found them all besmirched. At each account Homenaz cries, *miracle! Divine vengeance!* When he is particularly impressed, he orders drinks all round.

We know he is being mocked. Some of the characters defend the 'truth' of their stories by threatening to 'give themselves to the Devils' or to 'disown the Devil' if they are telling a lie. Nobody in fact doubts that the silly old Bishop is being laughed at. Yet we are never given a word of explanation. How then do we *know* that the tales are not true?

On the basis of the end of the death of Pan alone, it would be overbold to claim to solve the problem which Rabelais poses in the *Quart Livre*, but we can state it. Readers are aware that, in the account of the death of Pan, Rabelais has pressed great and awesome authors into service; aware also that he has again introduced into his books an account of the death of Guillaume du Bellay, the admired and beloved brother of his patron the bishop of Paris; aware that Rabelais has attributed to Pantagruel special insight into what lay behind the name of Pan; aware as well of Pantagruel's emotive use of key evangelical texts and of his copious tears. The reader knows that what he has just read represents a special and profound statement of the kind of syncretistic religious truth which appealed to Renaissance platonising Christians such as Rabelais. If he did not feel this, if he were not aware of all that made Pantagruel's interpretation of Pan the right one, then the flippant remarks of the narrator might seem to demolish the whole edifice of mystical thought that Pantagruel has just built up for us. If it does not, what are the criteria by which we judge it to be true?

In the *Tiers Livre*, or in the earlier chapters of the 1552 *Quart Livre*, it might be enough to say that we know it to be true because Pantagruel is the mouthpiece of the truth. Indeed up till now Pantagruel is, in the *Tiers Livre* and the *Quart Livre*, not infallible, but a Christian version of the Stoic sage whose 'grasping impressions' of the truth make him right whenever he does choose to speak out. But in the rest of the *Quart Livre* even that proof will be more than momentarily shaken, as Pantagruel's charity, his courteousness, his *Pantagruelism* in fact, lead him to make polite remarks which seem the contrary to the truth as we would expect him to hold it.

How then can we find out the truth? How *do* we know that, in the *Quart Livre*, Pantagruel's account of the death of Pan is a cosmic tragedy worthy of the tears of a Christian sage, while other events, where the storyteller insists that he *is* speaking the truth, are clearly comic inventions of a fertile literary brain? The question: 'How do we know what this means?' is one which Rabelais will ask us many times before he gives the answer.

Pantagruel's rôle is changing yet again. The amoral and boisterous giant of the earlier Chronicles is now little more than a memory; the ideal of the philosopher-king, first met in *Gargantua*, remains valid but does not explain all the profundity of the new Pantagruel; he is still the good prince towering above his companions more by moral worth and wisdom than by mere size; yet we are allowed again, as we never were in the *Tiers Livre*, to have glimpses of his physical size as he steadies the mast in the Storm, sheds his mighty tears or blasts off at a Papimaniac schoolteacher who wants to beat his charges. His rôle as a foil to Panurge is largely played out: Panurge's dominant characteristic is now his cowardice; in this Frère Jean and his valour are more than an ample contrast with him.

Pantagruel is now a character more mysterious, more deeply and mystically perspicacious, capable of seeing the Platonic reality lying beyond the flux and movement of the world of appearances. He declined to laugh at the *Basché* farces, not on moral or sociological grounds, but because the fear of God should constantly be before man's eyes: in this he plays a lonely rôle as a man standing apart from all the others. In the Storm we see him isolated by his very grandeur and by the majesty of his scriptural appeals to God. On the *Isle des Macraeons* he weeps as his mystical insight leads him to see through the veil of the the name *Pan* to the suffering godhead lying behind it. And he weeps alone.

Up to this point of the *Quart Livre* Pantagruel's loneliness and isolation emphasise his inerrant rightness, even though they make him into a cold and distant character. But much of this will change. Some of these characteristics will be deepened and enhanced; others will be played down. Above all, before the book ends, joy and gaiety will flood back into his character like an irresistible tide sweeping into a complex estuary.

Pantagruel can, and will, continue to be a pointer to the truth, but in a more complicated way. We, the readers, have to interpret what he says. Just as we have to use our critical acumen if we are not to be taken in by the companions' tall stories as Homenaz was, so we have to measure Pantagruel's words and silences against that prince's obligation to be courteous or polite. May he not be sarcastic or ironical? How can we find the truth lying behind the words which form the speech of man?

10. *Quaresmeprenant and the Andouilles*

With the appearance in Rabelais of Quaresmeprenant in person, the next chapters take us back in spirit to the Shrovetide revelling so much a feature of the first two Chronicles. Rabelais needs only a few lines to pass from tears to joy, to have his merry companions happily sailing out of harbour and sighting the island where dwell the *Tapinois*, the 'scrupulous bigots'. Quaresmeprenant, the incarnation of the onset of Lent, reigns there as king. Before the chapter is over we meet the Andouilles, the ancient meaty enemies of Quaresmeprenant who live on the *Isle Farouche*.

Readers of 1552 who did not know their Rabelais, if there were any, may well have expected chapters given over to pure uninhibited laughter. The theme of the annual battle between Carnival and Lent was an old one, though in mediaeval times Carnival was known to French literature as *Charnage* ('Flesh'). The theme was still a fresh and lively one in the Renaissance, giving rise to literary works, paintings and to entertainments designed to please town and sophisticated court alike as Lent approached. There was no difficulty in recognising the Andouilles as allies of Carnival: meat and sausages generally symbolised Carnival, just as fish symbolised Lent. The figures in the foreground of Brueghel's *Carnival and Lent* fight with weapons respectively decked with sausages and fish.

But although the *Quart Livre* appeared in time to be read during the Shrovetide of 1552, Rabelais does not in fact present us with yet another re-enactment of the annual battle between Carnival and Lent, a battle leading inevitably to the defeat of Carnival as pale Lent dominates the liturgical year. What he does is to turn this spirit of revelry into deeper and more controversial channels. In the *Quart Livre* Quaresmeprenant does not fight

Carnival or anyone else. He is, above all, presented as a gross and unnatural figure, the obvious enemy of all that is beautiful and good. Only with heavy irony can he be called 'a good catholic of great devotion' (*QL* XXIX, 21). Some of the words used to describe him recall expressions first found in the *Pantagrueline Prognostication*.[12] He has monkish characteristics and a double tonsure. His family ties are with the Ichthyophagi, the Fish-eaters, a people of ancient legend made popular as a symbol for Lenten cranks by Erasmus in one of the most delightful of his *Colloquies*. Panurge – but only Panurge – lapses into superstitious fear at the sight of him. His habits fly in the face of proverbial wisdom just as young Gargantua's did. He was a strange case. 'He worked doing nothing: did nothing when he worked; he corybantiated asleep: slept corybantiating.' So he was both lethargic and mad. This insistence on his 'corybantiating' makes him as mad as the old noisy Corybantes, the yelling, prancing worshippers of Cybele to whom Erasmus devoted an adage (III, 7, 39) *Corybantiari*, the commentary on which is much indebted to Lucian. Rabelais gathers together several adages at this point in order to show up the oddness of Quaresmeprenant. 'He fished in the air'; 'he hunted in the depths of the sea'; 'he feared nothing but his shadow' (cf. Erasmus, *Adagia* I, 4, 74 and 5, 65). As well as classical adages, what seem to be more popular proverbs are pressed into service to show up the oddness of Quaresmeprenant: 'he bathed above the high steeples, and dried himself in pools and streams. . . .' In every way he is silly and unnatural, as well as superstitiously given over to the writing of prognostications and almanacs (*QL* XXXII, 45–62).

Lent in Renaissance France was not even remotely like it is today. It was not a question of a minority of the population willingly giving up sweets or tobacco. The Church's ordinances concerning the eating of fish and the banning of flesh were backed up by legal sanctions potentially of great rigour. The victory of Lent, intended to be the victory of Christian charity and self-discipline, was often seen as the victory of gloom, hypocrisy and wilful asceticism, imposed, above all, with full rigour, primarily on the poor, who could neither afford to purchase exemptions nor find the money to buy the many kinds of expensive and delicious food which passed as Lenten fare among the rich. For the kind of Catholic whom Erasmus called Judaïcisers from their insistence on the letter rather than the spirit of the law, you could keep Lent by eating caviare: break it by eating the meanest of meats.

There are already strong suggestions in Rabelais's earlier Chronicles that he had no time for Lent as practised in the Church of the day. He

---

[12] *QL* XXIX, 14f.: Quaresmeprenant is described as 'un grand preneur de taulpes, un grand boteleur de foin'; cf. *Pant. Prov.* V, 20 and 46, where the same expressions appear.

shared with Erasmus a deep hostility to the legal enforcement of Lenten disciplines and to any asceticism practised as an end itself or as a means of acquiring proud religious merit. In the *Tiers Livre*, Pantagruel uses his father's authority and etymological punning to make the point. Gargantua often said that the writings of fasting hermits, of *jeusneurs*, were tasteless and jejune. They were in fact, like their bodies, redolent of bad saliva. The play on words, *de maulvaise salive*, arises from *saliva*, in Latin, meaning both spittle and flavour. Both excessive eating and excessive fasting, we are told, impede the grasping of spiritual reality and the contemplation of heavenly things. The golden mean is an ideal which applies to eating and drinking as much as to everything else (*TL*, *TLF* XIII, 82f., 140f.).

In the *Quart Livre* Rabelais presents his ideas mainly through fable, myth or literary forms analogous to them. This is true of the 1552 *Quart Livre* in a way it never was of any of the others. The prologue is dominated by the fable of the woodcutter and the axe; the Storm has all the characteristics of a dramatic fable, including a moral at the end; Quaresmeprenant and the Andouilles, as later the Papefigues and the Papimanes, partake of this quality, which triumphs above all, perhaps, in the episode of Messere Gaster. We are here confronted with a change of artistic and philosophical purpose; Rabelais makes us specifically aware of it. In the *Pantagrueline Prognostication* for 1533 the title *Mythologies Gallicques* was applied to a funny book which was probably entirely fanciful (*Au liseur*, 15). In the *Tiers Livre* Rabelais's interest in classical mythology takes on a new depth: we find him scouring the Marsi edition of the *Fasti* for rare mythological erudition; in the *Tiers Livre* too we come across the rare word *Mythologues* (LI, 70). In the *Quart Livre* (LXV, 49) these scholars become the *saiges Mythologiens*. But more important still is the first sentence of Rabelais's dedicatory letter to Odet de Châtillon. There he applies the term *myth* to his own works:

You are duly aware, most illustrious prince, by how many great persons I have been – and am – daily stipulated, besought and importuned to continue the Pantagruelical mythologies (*QL.*, *Ep.Lim.*, 1).

The term *mythologies Pantagrueliques* invests Rabelais's works with a new dignity. Whoever compiled the *Briefve Declaration* felt he had to explain the word *mythologies* as '*fabuleuses narrations. C'est un dicton Grecque*'. It is a weak definition. In Greek, *muthos* includes not only myths and legends but fables such as those of Aesop: its Latin equivalent was often *fabula* in most of its senses. It is the wider sense which applied to the 1552 *Quart Livre*.

The author who guided Rabelais into this fruitful direction was Celio Calcagnini – the scholar whose *Fable entitled Linelaeon* has close affinities with the Praise of Pantagruelion.

The influence of Calcagnini on the *Quart Livre* is definite, though never openly acknowledged. Rabelais borrows from him at some length in the chapters devoted to Quaresmeprenant and the Andouilles, taking over the idea and much of the detail of his own myth of Physis and Antiphysie (of Nature and Antinature), which he then uses in ways which leave Calcagnini far behind. The starting-point of the two-and-a-half chapters devoted to describing the deformed anatomy of Quaresmeprenant by means of grotesque analogies may well have been Calcagnini's remark about Antiphysie: 'If I tell you of his shape, I will make my readers laugh' (Calcagnini, *Opera Aliquot*, Basle 1544, p.622).

Calcagnini's rôle seems to have been to encourage Rabelais to dare to follow his Platonism to its logical artistic conclusion, by expressing and explaining his thought in myths as powerful and as profound as those of Plato himself, but marked by his own sense of the human comedy.

Quaresmeprenant is not merely a figure of fun. He has a frightening, monstrous side to him. But he does arouse laughter through his ugliness, while the description of his way of life recalls aspects of Gargantua's misspent childhood: as a poor wretched sort of fool he too goes against all proverbial wisdom, both traditionally French and classical.

The fable of Physis and Antiphysie is a platonising myth, setting the goodness and beauty of Nature against the evil and ugliness of Antinature. Rabelais calls it a fable to be found *parmy les apologues antiques*, though ancient myth and fable do not, rather strangely, have much to say about a personalised Nature, let alone a personalised Antinature. His direct source, from which he actually translates the greater part of his myth with skilful rearrangements and adaptations, is a literary invention of Calcagnini's entitled, *A Fable called 'The Giants'*. Its Platonic assumptions make it fit snugly into Rabelais's philosophy: it helps us to see that Quaresmeprenant is as unnatural as Antiphysie; that both they and their allies are not only laughable but evil, capable of spawning creatures as ugly and as evil as they are themselves.

Physis, for ever fertile, brought forth beauty and harmony without copulation. Antiphysie, not to be outdone, copulated with the Tellumon, the Roman god of the generative powers of the earth; the children she brought forth were Amodunt and Discord. In both Calcagnini and Rabelais the name *Amodunt* is puzzling, but represents ugliness, the opposite of beauty.

By means of this myth Rabelais successfully implies, without actually saying so, that Quaresmeprenant, in all his deformity, is another child of Antiphysie, an ugly and discordant parody of true religion. In fact by the time we come towards the end of the episode we are tempted to conclude that the enemies of Nature are simply the papist or Sorbonicole hypocrites with monastic undertones who once besieged Thelema with their ugly presences: the *Matagotz, Cagotz et Papelars*. But there is salt in the tail. The secret 'bacon-suckers' who are spawned by Antiphysie and whose name reminds one of the pope, the *Papelars*, are followed by three groups of evil-doers, the first and the last identified by distortions of their leaders' names: *les maniacles Pistoletz, les demoniacles Calvins, imposteurs de Geneve; les enraigez Putherbes*. These are assaults on men who had attacked Rabelais in print: the maniacal *Pistoletz* are followers of the mad Guillaume Postel, who considered Rabelais to be an arch-enemy of the Gospel; the 'diabolical *Calvins*' are followers of the French reformer of Geneva who had condemned Rabelais in his treatise *On Scandals*; the 'raging' *Putherbes* are 'stinking weeds', devotees of the Sorbonagre Gabriel Dupuyherbault, who wanted to have Rabelais's novels banned as blasphemous. Such men as these, although apparently opposed to each other, are all ugly and discordant off-spring of Antinature, at one with 'Briffaulx, Caphars, Chattemittes, Canibales' and other monsters, 'deformed and twisted in despite of Nature' (*QL* XXXII, end).

The point made is a good one: the extremes of error as Rabelais saw them meet in ugliness and disharmony. Geneva and Rome could and did gang up to burn Michael Servetus; Geneva, as described unsympathetically by Joachim du Bellay in the *Regrets* (Sonnet 136), does seem like a land where the theoretically banished Quaresmeprenant reigns forever supreme, despite the formal rejection of Lent by the Calvinists. And if the contemporary censors of Paris and Geneva agreed on anything, it was that Rabelais's works should be totally and permanently suppressed.

11. Hunting the whale

Quaresmeprenant is deprived of his annual right to go out and do battle with Carnival. He has to manage without the usual annual victory, which normally, but not always, falls to him in fiction, painting, masque, mummery or Carnival – the monstrous spirit of Lent does not depart in sombre triumph but is tossed into the ragbag kept for the botched children of Unnaturalness.

Quaresmeprenant is separated from all contact with his traditional enemy by two chapters devoted to a whale hunt. Tall stories about whales are common from the times of Lucian or of the Exeter Book to the *Disciple de Pantagruel*. As often as not the sailors mistake the whale for an island. Rabelais's whale hunt is basically more realistic than most – despite Pantagruel's superhuman accuracy with the bow, which enables him to turn over the pages of Frère Jean's breviary with his arrows without tearing a leaf. Here for the first time in the *Quart Livre* Pantagruel becomes human enough to crack a joke, making in fact an etymological pun parallel to Frère Jean's *Hérodote – il radote* in the Storm. Pantagruel's pun is *Perséus – Persé jus par moy sera* (XXXIII, 29–31). The technique is that of the *Echo* chapter in the *Tiers Livre*, especially as in both cases the word on which the pun is made is the last word of a sentence spoken by Panurge. But once again there is more to it than that, though Rabelais has not yet chosen to tell us what he is up to.

In this whale hunt we have a story told with gusto, apparently for its own sake; but artistically and theologically it balances and complements the lesson of the Storm. Panurge's fear and Frère Jean's energetic activity are equally emphasised, though more succinctly. The link with the Storm, evident enough in itself, is emphasised when Pantagruel light-heartedly harks back to Frère Jean's contention that Panurge was fated to be hanged, not drowned (QL XXXIII, 33; XXIV, 31). But, for all the easy laughter, erudition is there as well – for example, Panurge is urged to fear not whales but heaven-seeking fiery horses, for their element is the air – the element in which he will find his death by hanging; Pantagruel refers to these fiery steeds as '*celebres chevaulx du Soleil flammivomes*'. This is an echo of a phrase of the first-century poet Corippus (I, 338): *flammivomis raptatus equis* ('snatched away by flame-vomitting horses'). Only the learned could appreciate such jokes.

Pantagruel is now much more human. He is the centre of the action. If the whale is Leviathan, as Panurge timorously thinks, then he is a Leviathan whom man, unaided, can tame and bring low. Panurge, like so many mediaeval writers before him, thinks that the whale is connected with the Devil; Pantagruel's prowesses show that he is a creature to be hunted and no more.

The episode is in some ways reminiscent of the style and preoccupations of Rabelais's earlier works. This may partly be attributable to the influence of the *Disciple de Pantagruel* from which he made several borrowings and which encouraged a simpler style of narration. But one is struck by the fertility of Rabelais's invention when contrasted with the modest achievement of that unpretentious little work which dared to use his characters. The chapter ends with a rather out-of-place allusion to the Chicanous. It is possible that a first draft of the hunting of the whale was once intended to follow more closely after the farce of the Chicanous earlier in the book.

12. L'Isle Farouche

To cut up the whale the heroes land on the Isle Farouche where the Andouilles live. There is no prior hint of how the episode will develop: whether the Andouilles as allies of Carnival will triumph, or whether they will be found ugly and evil in their own way.

In fact we are presented with an episode of comic delight, one in which the spirit of Carnival really does dominate, in which indulgent parodies of the wars of mediaeval romance and the comic battles of the Shrovetide enemies, fought out with kitchen knives and pots and pans, mingle with mock-heroic echoes of Greek epic to produce a war funnier even than those of *Pantagruel* and *Gargantua*. Homer's heroes used the Trojan Horse; so Rabelais's heroes use a Trojan Pig – these Chitterlings (Andouilles) are pork-sausages, after all, and *Porcus Trojanus* (*Trojan Pig*) is a classical adage well-enough known to be listed by Erasmus. It was applied in times of Roman decadence to large animals stuffed with dainty meats. Erasmus links it with the Trojan Horse, with Saturnalias and oversumptuous banquets (IV, 10, 70).

Just as writing about Lent and its allies produced in Rabelais sour and unpleasant associations with vicious ugliness, the very idea of writing about the erstwhile allies of Carnival encouraged thoughts of joy and laughter. Wrong-headed the Andouilles may well be, but they are not deformed and monstrous in all their parts as was Quaresmeprenant. They are creatures once capable of being allies of the Pantagruelists themselves.

When we try to imagine what they look like, we find they are sometimes thought of as sausages, sometimes as furry animals, sometimes as human. Their occasional humanity and their dominant sausage-shape are easy enough to understand. Their furriness needs a word of explanation. Rabelais does not hide his indebtedness to the *Disciple de Pantagruel*, taking over the names of some of his islands from it and making its giant Bringuenarilles, the eater of windmills, into a major figure. But apart from the obvious debts, some aspects of the episode of the Andouilles are difficult to understand without a knowledge of this little book. When the heroes arrive on that Fierce Island which is the Isle Farouche, they find the Andouilles living there. In the *Disciple* there are two separate islands, the Isle Farouche and the Isle des Andouilles: the inhabitants of the Isle Farouche are described as being 'hairy like rats'. Rabelais runs these two lots of islanders together, making the anti-Lenten Sausages, the Andouilles, dwell on an island whose name is suggestive of prickly bravery. In our imagination, the Andouilles may well be, first and foremost, sausage-shaped Chitterlings. But Rabelais at times still thinks of them in terms of the hairy dwellers on the original Isle Farouche. When Pantagruel first descried them climbing trees (XXXV, 24), he mistook them for furry creatures (squirrels, weasels, minks or ermines). In at least one of the editions of the *Disciple*, a woodcut of a squirrel is printed as a decoration in the pages which tell the story of the Andouilles and their river of mustard. It is not in any way an illustration of the story, but Rabelais seems to have taken it as such. Rabelais's original conception of the dwellers on the Isle Farouche seems to have been of squirrel-like creatures; they become semi-humanised sausages; and when the fun-and-games are over, their queen, despite a name happily suggestive of a phallic form, turns out to have a beautiful, nubile daughter.

The return to earlier narrative styles, refined by years of experience, is marked. Yet the fun-and-games do not lead us to identify with the Andouilles: they are not Carnival himself but devotees of Carnival, actual worshippers of Carnival who have got on to the wrong track (*QL* XLII, 44). Renaissance writers and readers were constantly aware of man's potentiality for idolatry, making gods out of creatures of all sorts, from popes to bellies or from a beloved woman to a beloved self. A theme running through the *Quart Livre* is the pure folly of such idolatry.

The symbols he had created delighted Rabelais enough for him to allow them to take off on a gay life of their own, but they begin, unmistakably, as symbols for those German-speaking Protestants whom the du Bellays strove to bring back into a reformed Catholic Church.

The satirical sense of the episode, which was of great contemporary importance, is pointed for us by Rabelais with a delightful and meaningful play on words, which shows that what he has a mind to satirise is the Council of Trent. Addressing Xenomanes and referring to Quaresmeprenant and the Andouilles, Pantagruel says:

'Yea, fair friend, if you can see any honourable way by which we can reconcile them, give me your advice' (*QL* XXXV, 40).

The verb Rabelais uses is *reconcilier*.

Xenomanes replies that he had tried to *reconcile* them some four years before (in 1547 or 1548, that is) and had indeed succeeded in making them less bitter enemies. But Quaresmeprenant would not include either the Puddings or the Mountain-dwelling Sausages, their *confoederez*, in the peace-treaty. As for the Andouilles, they insisted on complete discretionary control over both Fort Herring-Barrel and Salt-Meat Castle.

Despite disagreements, enmities were toned down by these negotiations, until *la dénonciation* – the official condemnatory declaration – *du concile national de Chesil*. After that, things became so bad that, in the last words of the chapter, 'more easily would you have been able the cats and the rats, the hounds and the hares, to reconcile': 'Plus toust auriez vous les chatz et ratz, les chiens et lievres ensemble *reconciliez*.' With this play on the words *concile* and *reconcilier* Rabelais is making an important point: an ecumenical council, a *concilium*, should not divide Christians, but *reconcile* them. Rabelais's perspicacity is remarkable: the Council of Trent was indeed destined to divide Christians into sheep and goats for at least four hundred years.

Plays on the words *concilium* were not confined to Rabelais (Postel has a relevant one: 'would it had never been called a *concilium*, since from thence has come such *dissilium* (disunity)': *De Nativitate Mediatoris Ultima*, s.l.n.d., p.7). Rabelais is utterly outspoken. The Council of Trent is, for him, the

Concile national de Chésil, with the *ch* of *chesil* pronounced as a *k*. It is, then a merely *national* council – the adjective being aimed at denying its universality, its catholicity; it is a local council of *nitwits*, for *kesil* in Hebrew means fool.[13] This goes further than the disrespectful name he gave the Council in 1548, the *chapitre général des Lanternes*, and its mockery is more ambitiously damning.

Four years before 1552 takes us to 1548; the year in which Xenomanes tried his reconciliation was the one in which Charles V imposed the Leipzig *Interim* on his factious subjects. At that date, the du Bellays' agents, as ever, seem to have been striving for religious tolerance and understanding. Lutherans whom the du Bellays admired or hoped to get along with – Melanchthon, Bugenhagen, Major, Camerarius – all supported this *Interim*. Promulgated on 22 December 1548 in Imperial German lands, it imposed by law an interim solution to religious disputes, enforcing a show of mutual tolerance on religious groups until a true Catholic Council should find a just and lasting settlement. For this to be achieved it was vital that Protestants should attend the Sessions of the Council of Trent, taking a full part in the discussions and decision-making. The attempt to open Trent to the Protestants fell through in 1552. Manoeuvres against the whole attempt were complex, prolonged and eventually successful in squashing the whole idea. The royalist Gallicans did not like Trent anyway: but if there were to be a Catholic council they wanted Lutherans and others to be present too.

Trent was not destined to move towards reconciliation. Christendom remained divided, its divisions cemented by exclusive definitions and a multitude of harsh anathemas. Rabelais lays responsibility for this on the Council of Nitwits itself; so too, later, did Paolo Sarpi in his famous *History of the Council of Trent*. As for the French monarchy, in 1551 it was on the verge of breaking with the papacy, partly over Trent. In 1551 Henry II was on the point of summoning a rival Gallican council to reform the Gallican Church, making her autocephalous under a French patriarch. Four months before the *Quart Livre* was published, Bishop Amyot attempted (1 September 1551) to read an official letter from Henry II, explaining why he had forbidden his French clergy to attend. As the preamble addressed the dignitaries not as a *Concilium* but as a mere *Conventus* (Assembly), there was uproar. The clergy in council declined to take note of any correspondence – be it from the king of France in person – which was not addressed to it as a lawful and Catholic Council.

This was the backcloth against which Rabelais makes his puppets act out their mock-heroic battle: a battle not between Carnival and Lent but

[13] My friend and colleague Raphael Lowe tells me that *kesil* is one of several words in Proverbs and elsewhere meaning fool. Its derivation suggests stupidity arising from reliance on one's own brawn.

between the Pantagruelists and Carnival's wayward allies, the Andouilles, fierce, treacherous Christian Sausages excluded from Trent! The Shrovetide spirit takes over completely: we are lifted away from the bitter schemings and entrenched hatreds of the real world. We can almost forget the politics of Church and State. The password of the Pantagruelists is *Mardi Gras*, since (as Gymnaste reminded the Andouilles) they are on the side of 'Mardigras, your old confederate'. The twice-used term *confoedéré* doubtless refers to the allies of the Swiss federation. As for Frère Jean's battling scullions, their password is *Nabuzardan*, the name of a leader of Nebuchadnezzar's army, who cared more for food than war and for cooks than scholars. Or so he is depicted in mediaeval legend and Renaissance scholarly moralising.[14]

The revival of the indulgent parodies of the mediaeval romances last seen in *Gargantua* is most successful: '*C'estoit pitié. . . . Et dict le conte. . . .*' The slaughter is made even less worrying than comic slaughter is in Rabelais, as one might expect in a battle where a mighty sword is no Excalibur but a two-handed blade yclept *Baise-mon-cul*, and where, in mock-heroic vein, the slaughter recalls, in the midst of laughter, battles in Caesar's wars. The original tale of the battle against the Andouilles in the *Disciple de Pantagruel* has the dead Andouilles cut up into slices and put aside to provision the ship. In the *Quart Livre* that will not do at all. The slaughtered and wounded Andouilles are cured by the monstrous pig whom they worship; it drips twenty-seven barrels of mustard on to the battlefield (mustard being good for Andouilles and their like). As Phallus (*Niphleseth*), the Queen of Sausages, tells the heroes, mustard is their balm from heaven, their Holy Grail.[15]

At a satirical level, the war between Pantagruel's men and the Andouilles is a war between parties who ought to be allies, friends even. The war was attributable to misunderstandings rather than to fundamental disagreements.

Queen Niphleseth's daughter is the *Infanta* Niphleseth (*QL* XLII, 28): her title inevitably suggests that the Andouilles are peoples subject to the

---

[14] Cf. *Dyalogus Linguæ et Ventris*, s.l.n.d., (Berne, Cantonal Library, at Inc., IV. 42(4); sig. a3 r°.): 'Nabuzardan cared more for eating than fighting; he greatly loved his cooks, just as nowadays there are many great men who take more joy in – and pay out more money for – a cook rather than a scholar. O evil times! O sordid manners!' The last page says that the book was printed for Claudius Jaumar, bookseller to the University of Paris.

[15] *QL* XLII, 50: The queen replied that mustard was their *Sangreal* and *Baume celeste*. Dr Lowe tells me that the name *Niphleseth* is a corruption of *Miphletseth* found only in I Kings 15,13 (and the parallel passage, II Chronicles 15,16), where it refers to 'a horror', a disapproved cult-object. In Hebrew the root suggests some visually frightening object; but the Vulgate renders it by *simulacrum Priapi*. (AV: 'an idol in a grove': Moffat and RSV, 'an obscene object'). Jewish tradition interpreted this 'horror' as a dildo used by Queen Maachah, mother of king Asa. How much of this Rabelais knew is not certain.

Spanish monarchy, that is, in practice, to the Holy Roman Empire. These *confoederez* include, however, German Swiss as well as German-speaking Lutheran subjects of Charles V (*QL* XXXVIII, 20). The criticism laid against them is a fairly light one contained in the Greek inscription hanging round their Holy Pig's neck: *HUS ATHĒNAN*, 'A Pig teaching Minerva' (XLI, 65). This adage, well-known as usual from Erasmus's collection (I, 1, 40), condemns the ignorant who would presume to instruct the wise. The Protestant Andouilles actually think they can give lessons to the wise and Catholic Pantagruel and his men, teaching their grandmother (as it were) to suck eggs. . . . The Andouilles are not right but merry; Quaresme-prenant is wrong *and* repulsive.

13. Linguistic comedy and linguistic wisdom

Within this gay and delightful fantasy a new element appears. It is connected with proper names but extends to language generally. Our attention is drawn to it by what Rabelais wrote in Chapter XXXVII which is significantly entitled: *How Pantagruel sent to fetch captains Riflandouille ('Killer of Andouilles') and Tailleboudin ('Slicer of Puddings'); with a notable discourse on the proper names of places and persons.* It shows Rabelais's fertile mind sporting with intellectual matter which also deeply impressed him.

Readers have already noted Rabelais's delight in playing about with proper names. Sometimes, it seemed, the aim was purely comic; at others, a satirical intention was present.

Chapter XXXVII combines the sense of amusement with a sense of awe and wonder. The chapter is primarily devoted to examples of great men who, in classical times, were given apparently supernatural, prophetic advice through the names of people or places: Octavian Augustus who saw a good augury in meeting a Greek called Fortunate driving an ass named Victory; young Vespasian, unexpectedly coming across a slave called Royal; and so on.

At first sight this may seem an extension of Rabelais's general preoccupation with divination, dominant in parts of the *Tiers Livre*. It is certainly that as well, revealing as it does a marked sympathy for a neo-Pythagorean belief in names as a means of prognostication or of acquiring special knowledge. We might reflect though, that if proper names have, or may have, such power, they are to that extent an apparent exception to Pantagruel's neo-Aristotelianism about language, according to which words have senses according to arbitrary imposition and convention. But the exception is only apparent (*TL* XIX, 38f.).

To understand what Rabelais is doing we must pay attention to the linguistic assumptions of his day. This entails reading some fairly austere volumes. But it is worth the effort.

Rabelais's main starting-point is a work of Calcagnini's. Editions of the *Quart Livre* leave readers with the impression that Rabelais gathered the matter of this chapter from several sources. This is misleading. *All* the erudition comes from a few pages of Celio Calcagnini's *Dialogue called 'Equitatio'*. In this dialogue Rabelais found *all* his examples of names of places, people or animals which proved to be prophetically meaningful. In Calcagnini these examples are used to show that the ancient Greeks attributed great power to proper names: from an informed study of names one might receive prophetic advice; erudite Pythagorean techniques might reveal something real about the people whose names they were. Such knowledge of names can even tell us whether a man was wounded, or infirm, on the left side or the right. This is not treated as some sort of exploded classical superstition by either Calcagnini or by Rabelais, though the fact that Calcagnini was expressing his ideas in a dialogue makes him less committed. For Rabelais the matter is of sufficient importance for reality to break through the fiction. He alludes to a real man of genuine importance in his time: to his legal friend the Seigneur du Douhet, who is eulogised for possessing just such a neo-Pythagorean ability to draw unexpected knowledge from a study of proper names. Douhet – *le tant bon, tant vertueux, tant docte et equitable president Briend Valée* – could tell from the syllables of a man or woman's name whether that person was lame, blind or hunchbacked on the left side or the right (*QL* XXXVII, 58f.).

Pantagruel sees this as confirmation of what Plato wrote in the *Cratylus*. This should warn us that Rabelais came to the *Cratylus* with certain presuppositions in mind. After expounding several examples drawn straight from Calcagnini, Pantagruel invited his companions to go and read Plato: 'Voyez le *Cratyle* du divin Platon' (*QL* XXXVII, 44). In other words, the learning which Rabelais takes from Calcagnini at this point is to be treated as a gloss on the *Cratylus*. We are not invited, as we might expect, to read Calcagnini, the unacknowledged primary source, but the work of Plato's which Pantagruel takes to be behind Calcagnini's own onomastic assumptions. Rhizotome replies: 'By my thirst, I want to read it: I often hear you citing it.' In the best available edition of the *Quart Livre* it is said that Pantagruel never cites the *Cratylus* on any other occasion, and that Rabelais never exploited it anywhere in his writings. These statements are wrong, very wrong. What Rabelais got out of his *Cratylus*, and what he read into it, explains a great deal of the sporting with proper names in all four chronicles, as well as the refreshingly new amusement with names and sounds that characterises the *Quart Livre* of 1552. Rabelais also uses the *Cratylus* to expound his dearest artistic and philosophical ideas. Later in the *Quart Livre*, the *Cratylus* makes a major contribution to Rabelais's myth-creation at its most ambitious, in which funny sounds play a deeper rôle.

Cratylic assumptions have a major part in the *Quart Livre* whenever Rabelais is dealing with both language and knowledge.

The *Cratylus* is a complex work. Modern scholars differ widely over its meaning. Renaissance scholars interpreted it in ways different again from us, not least because this dialogue had influenced Patristic authorities, as well as a whole string of philosophers. These in turn influenced them.

The number of Renaissance scholars able to read the *Cratylus* at first hand must have been few. Apart from its appearing in Ficino's massive *Opera Omnia* of Plato, the *Cratylus* survives in a markedly small number of copies: the British Library possesses only three.[16] Where Plato in general was concerned, Renaissance scholars were often ill at ease with Socrates's irony and playfulness, tending to take all his jests with total seriousness. Rabelais is quite remarkable for his independent use of the *Cratylus*, in that he refuses to be overawed by Socrates, despite his great admiration for him.

Rabelais's linguistic theories have been touched on several times in this study. They now need to be looked at in greater detail.

The terms and concepts which Rabelais uses are ancient ones, going back to Plato, Aristotle and the Alexandrine Greeks. From the thirteenth century onwards these terms were current amongst Western European philosophers and linguisticians. Words, it was held, derive their meanings from 'arbitrary' decisions on the part of a lexical creator. He 'imposes' his senses upon symbols; these symbols, with these senses, are then accepted 'by convention'. Francis Bacon still thinks in these terms, as did many philosophers until quite recent times (see above, pp.87f.).

These theories which Pantagruel championed unambiguously in the *Tiers Livre* do not mean that each person makes up his own language for himself. Pantagruel follows the standard view that words were created by an act of the intelligence; their acceptance is a matter of their being approved as conventional signs by the people who share the same language.

Although Rabelais does not specifically explain his linguistic assumtions before the *Tiers Livre*, they are, as expressed there, so standard and elementary that we may confidently assume that they were pre-supposed in *Pantagruel* and *Gargantua*. To understand what Rabelais is doing in the *Tiers Livre* and the *Quart Livre*, which both show a much more self-conscious awareness of language than the first two Chronicles do, it is essential to rediscover the linguistic assumptions of his time: to try to pull him towards fashionable modern theories is misleading in the extreme, not so much because some recent linguistic theories are obscure or opaque – truth sometimes is – but because they are often applied with an historical

[16] These are all amateurishly bound together in a nineteenth-century school exercise-book; the editions are T. Martinus, Louvain 1523; E. Gormontius, Paris 1527; I. Bene-natum, Paris 1573. There are no copies listed in the catalogue of the B.N., the Cambridge Libraries or the National Library of Scotland. There were other editions.

ignorance which amounts to an indifference to, or contempt for, the thought and art of the past.

The standard text-book on meaning and language from which Pantagruel's doctrine of language derives is that part of Aristotle's *Organon* known in mediaeval and Renaissance times as *Perihermeneias* (often written thus, as one word) or as *De interpretatione*. This short treatise *On Interpretation* was not the preserve of a handful of linguistic specialists. For century after century it had been studied by those who had to deal with language professionally. Its theories were of fundamental interest to students of the law as well as to theologians and philosophers.

The unique importance of *On Interpretation* did not lie exclusively in the towering authority of Aristotle, in its shortness or indeed in its almost elementary clarity. Great names of scholarship were connected with it: Boethius had done it into Latin; Aquinas had commented upon it; Ammonius Hermaeus's explanations and comments became inextricably associated with it; Porphyry's treatise *On the Five Words* was in some ways an extension of it. These were the kind of authors being read in Rabelais's circle in those early days spent at Fontenay-le-Comte. This transpires from a simple reading of Bouchard's *Tēs gunaikeias phutlēs, adversus Andream Tiraquellum.*

The best way for a modern student to enter into the world of Rabelais's linguistic assumptions is to read the opening pages of Aristotle's *On Interpretation.* Then, if his Latin is good enough, to read the commentaries of Ammonius Hermaeus and Aquinas, following this up with those of two Renaissance scholars, Rosario and Nifo. These are the principal sources used here.[17] In his commentary on Aristotle's *Perihermeneias* Ammonius draws upon Plato, especially on the *Cratylus.* He is at some pains to reconcile his two authorities. So, at least from Ammonius's time onwards (that is, from the second half of the fifth century) anyone who knew Greek and who read *On Interpretation* would have been reminded in the glosses of an apparent clash of opinion between Aristotle and Plato, and of the manner in which this clash could be resolved. From the late thirteenth

[17] I have normally used Renaissance editions of these works. For modern critical texts consult the Loeb edition for Aristotle, *The Organon* I, and *On Interpretation* (pp.114ff.); Ammonius, *Commentaire sur le Peri Hermeneias d'Aristote: traduction de Guillaume de Moerbeke. Édition critique et étude sur l'utilisation du commentaire dans l'œuvre de Saint Thomas,* by G. Verbeke, Centre de Wulf-Mansion: *Corpus Latinum Commentariorum in Aristotelem Graecorum* II, Louvain and Paris 1961; Laurentius Minio-Paluello: *Aristoteles Latinus* II, 1–2: *De Interpretatione vel Periermentas. Translatio Boethii. Specimina translationum recentiorum* (in *Corpus Philosophorum Medii Aevi*), Bruges-Paris 1965. Of basic importance is Thomas Aquinas's *Commentary on the Peri Hermeneias* (cf. J. Isaac: *Le Peri Hermeneias en Occident de Boèce à Saint Thomas,* Bibliothèque Thomiste, XXIX, Paris 1953; for early editions, cf. Minio-Paluello, *op. cit.* XXXV). For an English version see *Aristotle On Interpretation . . .* ed. J. T. Oesterle, Milwaukee 1962.

century onwards – since the completion of William of Moerbeke's Latin translation in 1268 – Ammonius's commentary became so widely known that its ideas were the standard ones even in the West. Quite routine writers, of no depth or originality, know it and cite it. In its new Latin garb, Ammonius and his commentary became commonplace amongst even those scholastic philosophers and dialecticians whom the humanists most despised. Renaissance scholars were not so much breaking new ground as going back to better and surer texts, when they read their Aristotle in the light of the new learning. Rabelais, not untypically, enriches his knowledge of Aristotle and of the Latin Ammonius with an acquaintance (direct or indirect) with the Greek originals and with the Plato of the *Cratylus* – in this case, certainly, his knowledge was first-hand, though his interpretation of Plato was conditioned by prior assumptions. This direct knowledge of the *Cratylus* is by no means to be taken for granted. In the West, the *Cratylus* was unknown at first hand from late classical times until the fifteenth century. But some idea of what it contained was kept alive, above all by Ammonius's commentary. Aquinas knew it from that source.

Aristotle holds the opinion expressed by Pantagruel in the *Tiers Livre*; Plato in the *Cratylus* apparently holds the contrary view defended by Pantagruel in the *Quart Livre*. A reading of Ammonius helps us to see how Rabelais could reconcile Aristotle and Plato. Indeed it does far more: it guides us towards a fuller understanding of Rabelais's meaning and art. Rabelais makes the same associations of ideas in the *Tiers Livre* and the *Quart Livre* as Ammonius does in his commentary – a sure sign that, as one would expect, he knew his Aristotle *On Interpretation*, and knew it moreover in its traditional context.

Pantagruel insisted that *les voix ne signifient naturellement, mais à plaisir*. The word *voix* translates the Latin *voces*: 'sounds that are uttered by the voice.' In practice this blanket definition was the subject of an important clarification in Ammonius's commentary. Aristotle, very simply, divided significant verbal utterances into *nouns* (which included adjectives) and *verbs*. In both cases their meanings are derived from imposition and convention. But he does briefly distinguish between those human sounds, the meanings of which differ from one language-group to another, and certain other sounds which do have a natural meaning. These sounds are 'unlettered noises such as beasts make'. The term he uses for these 'unlettered vocal utterances' is *agrammatoi psophoi*. In Latin these words are normally translated by some such term as *voces illiteratae*. So *voces* (verbal utterances) may be of two kinds: 'significant and literate ones' – the meaningful words used by men – and 'significant and illiterate ones' – such as the barking of dogs (Ammonius, trans. Moerbeke, ed. Verbeke, p.58f.). The point is that human beings may also make sounds analogous to those of a dog barking. This is a major limitation to the general statement that *voces* signify *per placitum* (that 'human utterances' signify by 'arbitrary institution' and convention alone).

Aquinas picks this up. After insisting that no noun exists 'naturally', he draws attention to Aristotle's reservation concerning 'unlettered sounds such as those of the brutes'. Since he did not know the original Greek text, the distinctions that he makes are Latin-based. The crucial distinction is between *voces* (*les voix* of Pantagruel) and *soni*, mere noises. He explains that Aristotle talks of sounds (*soni*) rather than *vocal sounds* (*voces*) at this point, partly because some animals, those without lungs, cannot make noises which can be classified as *voces*. Such animals signify proper passions by some kind of non-vocal sound which does signify naturally. This distinction between *voces* and *soni* is nearly always borne in mind, even by those many writers who occasionally confound the words themselves.

It is this distinction between sounds akin to the noises made by beasts, which do have a natural meaning, and the conventional literate sounds of human language which do not, that is fruitfully exploited by Rabelais, first to arouse laughter and then to point to deeper meanings.

Ammonius explains that Aristotle's phrase excluding the 'illiterate noises made by beasts' can and should be extended to cover a wide range of both animal and human noises. *Voces*, 'vocal sounds' in Aristotle's technical sense of nouns and verbs, must have their meaning imposed on them *ex instituto* – that is, by Pantagruel's *institutions arbitraires*. It is because of this that they differ from one language group to another. But animal sounds, those *soni* for which Ammonius and others are sometimes prepared to use the word *voces illiteratae*, are *not* in fact vocal utterances in the stricter sense at all. An example of such sounds which signify naturally and so do not differ from one culture to another or, if they do, can be recognised by all men for what they are, is a dog barking at a stranger. Ammonius in his Latin guise uses the same technical terms as Rabelais – naturally so, as their theories of language coincide: dogs do not bark *ex instituto* (because of *institutions arbitraires*) nor *ex convenientia* (because of *convenences des peuples*); they do so naturally, and so their barking has a natural meaning.

The important point made by Ammonius is that this kind of sound – *voces* is the term used here, but it will be corrected later on – may be found in human beings too. Men, irrespective of their language, emit them under the stress of great emotional disturbances (*perturbationes*). Such sounds include groans, laughter, the noises made by mutes as well as the sounds made by children before they have learned to talk. In fact these human sounds correspond to illiterate noises made by animals, both when men are profoundly agitated and when they are quite contented.

The rôle of meaningful sounds – *voces* which have become nouns or verbs by human institution and convention – is to signify things conceived by the mind (*animi conceptiones*). Greeks, Indians, Egyptians and so on decide which of these sounds mean what. But groans, laughter and the verbal utterances of babies or animals are quite different. Their rôle is not to signify things conceived by the mind at all but disturbances of the mind (*perturbationes animi*), as well as emotions (*affectiones*). And they, from the outset, qualify the statement that words do not signify naturally: such sounds do (Aquinas, *Comm. in Peri Hermeneias* I, 4, 41ff.; Ammonius, ed. Verbeke, 43ff.).

If this seems rather rarified and removed from Rabelais, one might note that it is in the *Quart Livre* that these 'sounds such as animals make' chiefly appear. The mute witness of the Chicanous with his jaws bashed in says *Mon, mon, mon, vrelon, von, von*, 'like a monkey' (QL XV, 59); the sheep of the merchant Dindenault – in 1552 – go *bês, bês, bês, (o la belle voix!)* (QL VI, 50). Panurge in the Storm cries, *Bous, bous, bous, paisch, hu, hu, hu, ha, ha, ha, ha, ha* – and we know that we are witnessing not an expression of the noble conceptions of his mind but the animal-like natural outpourings of significant, unlettered sounds which, in all languages, reveal the perturbations of his soul and his base emotions. Even those who do not know their Greek know what emotion is shown by Panurge's *Bou, bou, bou, bou. Otto to to to to ti, Otto to to to to to ti. . . .*

And so on.

It might be objected that, as these sounds can be written down, they come into Aristotle's definition of a noun, which excluded only sounds such as beasts make 'which are not expressed in letters' (*agrammatoi*). But Ammonius had long since countered that error. Indeed, if it had not been scotched, it would have obliged linguistic philosophers to accept animal noises and their human counterparts as the same thing as the meaningful verbal utterances of the various distinct languages! A confusion of categories of this sort would have confounded distinctions of great importance. Such a conclusion for Ammonius would be quite absurd. Comedians for example imitate frogs when they enunciate their cries (*brece ce cex, coax, coax*), pigs (*coi, coi*), or birds, and many other imitations of animal cries.

Such noises can be written down. But these sounds, despite their being imitable by men, cannot, and must not, be thought of as the *voces litteratae* as, that is, the meaningful verbal utterances of these animals. They are *voces illiteratae*, or *soni*. If we were to confound such distinctions, we would have to make other sounds which comedians can imitate into meaningful verbal utterances too: the whinnying of a mare, for example, the squeaking of wheels, or the hundred and one sounds made by inanimate objects. Sounds such as these are found later in the *Quart Livre*, where they are used with a profound comic intention. When Pantagruel says that vocal utterances (*voix*) signify by imposition and convention he is talking, quite normally, of *voces litteratae*. In the *Quart Livre* of 1552 these are contrasted with the emotionally revealing sounds of the fearful Panurge or the 'thawing sounds' of later chapters (cf. Ammonius, ed. Verbeke, 46.; Aquinas, *Comm. in Peri Hermeneias* I, 4, 18; etc.).

This is apparently taking us away from Rabelais's acceptance of the mysterious significance of at least some proper names. It might even seem to be taking us away from the *Cratylus*. This is not so. Before returning to the matter of chapter XXXVII, one might note that the fact of Rabelais's reading his *Cratylus* in the light of Ammonius or Aristotle does not mean that he did not read it at first hand at all. One example of sound which is akin to animal noises, and which therefore signifies naturally, is the merchant Dindenault's taunting of Panurge with a series of well-rolled r's: 'Mais, *rr, rrr, rrrr, rrrrr*' (QL VII, 16). And he meaningfully adds: *Vous n'entendez ce languaige* – a sentence which I would end with a question-mark, not a full stop. According to Socrates in the *Cratylus* (428B), *r* is a sound particularly appropriate for all sorts of movement. I think it is used in that sense here. If Diogenes's aggressive sounds towards the end of the prologue to the *Tiers Livre* should be read as *Grr, grrr, grrrrr* (and not *Gzz, gzzz, gzzzzzz*) – it is not clear from the original editions how it should be read – then that would be another example. The sound of the letter *r* has a special place in Latin. It is what Persius, in his first satire, calls the *litera canina*, the dog's letter, on account of its snarling noise. These sounds of Diogenes, appearing in what was probably the last page of the *Tiers Livre* to be written suggest that the comic potentialities of Ammonius's distinctions were already in Rabelais's mind before the *Quart Livre* was begun.

But Plato was a defender of the theory that words are the 'images' of things. How the question of animal-like natural sounds links up with the *Cratylus* and meaningful proper names is to be found, yet again, in Ammonius's commentary on Aristotle's treatise. Both animal noises and meaningful names are, unless properly understood, incompatible with Aristotle's definition of language, accepted by nearly everyone, including Pantagruel. Properly understood, the views of Plato in the *Cratylus* were thought to be totally in agreement with those of Aristotle. Ammonius had discovered how to harmonise the apparently incompatible opinions of the two great philosophers. Agostino Nifo, in a remarkably independent edition of Aristotle's *On Interpretation*, published at least seven times between 1507 and 1560, sums up the standard opinions like this: the Greeks have hesitations about language and meaning, since Aristotle holds 'that the meaning of nouns is not natural', while 'Plato and Socrates in the *Cratylus* hold that words derive from Nature herself. And so they hold contrary views – which seems a remote possibility to the Greeks.' Nifo then explains how the apparent clash was traditionally resolved:

Some (as Ammonius writes) hold that nouns are purely and simply a matter of human decision, (*institutum*). They have nothing to do with Nature at all.

Hermogenes was of this opinion, and so was the discreet Diodorus.

Others say that nouns come from Nature directly (*simpliciter*), insofar as they are likenesses of things. This was the opinion held by Cratylus [the man] and by Heraclitus of Ephesus. Ammonius maintained that nouns were in fact natural in respect to their etymology. He wanted all names to have been imposed in the light of an appropriateness found in the thing named: *lapis* (a stone), for example, as though meaning *laedens pedem* (hurting the foot); *petra* (a rock), as though *pede trita* (worn down by the foot). But as far as the actual meaning is concerned, words arise out of human decision (*institutum*) (Aristotle, *De interpretatione*, ed. Niphus, 1555, 4r°).

The examples given by Nifo are his own; they are loyal to the traditional theories but are not taken from the text he is resuming.

Nifo is not impressed with such an attempt at harmonisation, but several centuries of thinkers had been. Ammonius was believed to have upheld Aristotle's assertion that words do not have natural meanings, while at the same time vindicating Plato's assertion that words may have a real connexion with the things they signify. This harmonisation is really quite ingenious, though doubtless unconvincing enough today. Aristotle's opinion that there is no natural language is accepted: words do not have any natural connexion with the things they signify. On the other hand, the wise word-maker may have chosen so wisely the sounds on which he imposed his meanings, that the etymologies of his words may comport clues to their meaning, and so may have links with the things they signify, which are discoverable by a use of human intelligence. If one then goes on to allow the word-maker to have been sometimes inspired, words may have no natural sense, yet have a supernatural one.

Rabelais accepts these linguistic assumptions in his writings and puts them to constant use, for both comic and serious effect. The way in which names may be mystically revealing is treated at some length; the possibility that words may be the vehicles of revealed truth is one of the beliefs advanced in the closing chapters of the *Quart Livre*. And in the antepenultimate chapter, Pantagruel attaches profound importance to the fact that the Amycleans gave Bacchus the name of *Psilax*, meaning 'winged'. He emphasises that this was an example of *propre et convenante denomination*, of the bestowing of a name which did reveal the properties of the god and which was appropriate to his nature (*QL* LXV, 81f.).

Ideas such as these had entered the Christian conscience from Origen onwards. Origen is influenced by them in his book *Against Celsus*. The assertion of Ambrosiaster that 'the name of everything reveals its true origin and nature' became attached to St Augustine; Clement of Alexandria was a fervent etymologist: Jerome, partly under the influence of Philo and Origen, was convinced of the power of Hebrew names (cf. H. de Lubac, *Exégèse Médiévale*, Paris 1961, II, 1, 32–3).

The sixteenth-century Renaissance in France was a rediscovery of those authors as well as the rediscovery of classical antiquity. The apparent clash of opinion between *On Interpretation* and the *Cratylus* is a constant source of comment and explanation amongst students of language; and virtually always Ammonius is the key to the solution. One did not have to read the commentaries themselves to know this, but doubtless most scholars did. Humanists would quite naturally have turned also towards such studies as Laurentius Laurentianus's *In Librum Aristotelis de Elecutione* (Venice 1550) which was honoured with a preface by Pietro Crinito.

The same assumption that Aristotle and Plato really agree over theories of language was shared by numerous Renaissance writers besides Rabelais. Spiritus Martinus Cuneus, for example, in his *Dialogus de Entelechia* published in Paris in 1543 (*BL* 3832-aaa-19) insists that 'disputes about names are in no wise to be despised, since (as Aristotle says) names are the symbols and signs of things'; many quarrels arise out of a misunderstanding of names, even when people are really in agreement about the things themselves, as 'Cicero said about the Stoics and Peripatetics; [. . .] Plato in the *Cratylus* taught that there was a remarkable power in names; sometimes those who despise names go astray badly over the things themselves; [. . .] in choosing names we must choose those which are most apt, most appropriate.' What makes the matter all the more attractive to Rabelais's contemporaries – and I think to us today – was that this orthodoxy was under attack in Rabelais's time, obliging him to stand up and be counted. The nature of language and of meaning was in the air throughout the lifetime of Rabelais. Nifo is one, important, authority amongst many.[18]

Nifo's account of Ammonius's thought is too brief to do him justice, though scrupulously fair. For Ammonius, both the word *Nature* and the word *Imposition* have more than one meaning: when you have recognised the ones which applied to Aristotle's and to Plato's theories you realise that they were saying complementary things.

Cratylus and Heraclitus did indeed believe that Nature created words, he writes. Others believed that men with a special gift for naming things were endowed with the ability to choose names genuinely corresponding to the nature of the things to be named. It is here that we meet Rabelais's significant proper names as conceived in the *Quart Livre* under the direct influence of Calcagnini and the *Cratylus*. The names cited by Ammonius include prudent princes called Archidamus, Archisilaus, Agesilaus, Basil.

---

[18] A useful way into this quarrel is to read Mario Nizolio (*De veris principiis et vera ratione philosophandi contra pseudophilosophos*), in the edition of Quirinus Breen (*Edizione Nazionale dei Classici del Pensiero Italiano*: serie III, Rome 1956). In III, 9, especially p.101, Nizolio (an opponent of Celio Calgagnini) refuses to accept the validity of Ammonius's attempts to harmonise the *Cratylus* and Aristotle.

Ammonius does not consider such names to be stupid or fanciful, any more than the names latinised by Rosario in his translation of Ammonius as Fortunatus, Felix or Prosper. Such names are an 'image' of the person properly named – not equivalent to an image reflected in water, as the out-and-out naturalists asserted, but analogous to a portrait made by an artist. This became a standard assertion (Ammonius, ed. Verbeke, 66–7; 1559 edition of Rosario's version, p.226).

This notion of the natural connexions that may be found within proper names, despite their being the subject of arbitrary imposition, is a fruitful one and an ingenious one. It corresponds to a deep human need – most of us name our children with care and with some attention to both the meanings of the names and our hopes for our offspring. The theory has the advantage of accounting for the cases which do not work; bad people with good names were named by people lacking the onomastic gift. The fact that we are dealing with a gift opens the way for all sorts of divine influences to be at work. And since the imposition of names can be wilfully arbitrary, it also opens up the way to the kind of jesting with names which Rabelais delights in.

In chapter XXVII of the *Quart Livre* Rabelais alludes to the *Cratylus* both in the light of Ammonius and in the light of Calcagnini's *Dialogue called 'Equitatio'*. This dialogue is concerned with the prophetic powers of proper names, not of ordinary nouns, but the theory applies in principle to all words. Rabelais would not extend it to all nouns and verbs; but it is clear from his writings that he would extend it to many.

The theories of Aristotle and of Plato, whether harmonised by Ammonius or not, apply to all languages, civilised or barbarian. Jews and Christians, holding religious beliefs which postulate a Creation, sometimes made a special exception for Hebrew. After all, 'Out of the ground the Lord God formed every beast of the field and every fowl of the air; and brought them unto the man to see what he would call them: and whatsoever the man called every living creature that was the name thereof' (Genesis 2, 19). Such a belief can be exploited either in an Aristotelian or a Platonic way, or else in the light of Ammonius's harmonisation. The confusion of human speech in the Tower of Babel arose out of a definite intention on the part of God (Genesis 11). It suggests a divine purpose in language, both at the Creation and ever since. Since Plato remained vague about who his word-creator was, it could be God, an angel, Adam. Since the confusion of the Tower of Babel was divinely ordained, it was consonant with all languages having potential links with natural meanings – since they are not products of pure chance, they may have meanings hidden behind linguistic veils. By and large Renaissance thinkers found little difficulty in believing that the names given to things at the Creation by God and by Adam may well have real natural connexions with the things signified. But this did not imply a gullible propensity for swallowing each and every etymology claiming to show the real or natural meaning of any words in any language.

It was an established assumption that statements in the *Cratylus* about real natural connexions between names and things applied especially, but not exclusively, to proper names. The exchange of letters mentioned earlier between Erasmus and Agostino Steucho in 1531 is of interest here. It is a pointer to how far Erasmus would go in this matter, at the period when Rabelais was conscious of all that he owed to him. Erasmus's letter was public knowledge; Steucho's also. Erasmus criticises Steucho for being over-ingenious in his search for etymologies; he does not deny that the *Cratylus* may guide us towards insights into the true, natural meanings of proper names in scripture, but he is cautious. Above all he condemns, on sound ancient authority, those who seek the inner, natural meanings of the words found in one language by etymological fantasies based on another language altogether: i.e. by explaining the meaning of Hebrew names by reference to Greek; Greek names by reference to Latin (*Erasmi Epistolae* IX, 204f.).

Such questions were even more in the air when Rabelais wrote the *Tiers Livre* and the *Quart Livre*. They give a new richness to his juggling with language. They also explain jests in the two earlier Chronicles.

First, we may note that Rabelais did not believe all proper names to have natural connexions with the persons they are applied to. The naming of Pantagruel and Gargantua in the earlier Chronicles are good examples of the kind of fun that can be squeezed out of ignorant attempts to explain the senses of proper-names in one language by means of allusions to words taken from others. *Pantagruel* and *Gargantua* are close enough in time to Erasmus's quarrel with Steucho for us to see what is possibly a direct influence at work, especially as the general terms of reference are Old Testament in both cases.

Similarly in the *Tiers Livre* Rabelais, by 'arbitrary institution', takes the name *Raminagrobis*, which means a hypocrite, and paradoxically applies it to the good, pious and totally non-hypocritical, prophetic evangelical poet. The paradoxical comedy arises from the tension we feel when Rabelais imposes this name arbitrarily, in such a way as to fly in the face of convention which alone fixes the meaning of words once created.

Over and over again he gets his comic effects by showing what happens to words when used outside the confines in which convention has rightly placed them. A striking example of this is the list of sixty-one verbs in the prologue to the *Tiers Livre*, which tell us how Diogenes trundled his barrel about, up hill and down dale. The verbs are not used with their conventional meanings; their juxtaposition in a skilfully arranged list drains them of these meanings, endowing them with the qualities of 'unlettered sounds', sounds which enable us to hear and to feel the various movements of the barrel.

In this mood Rabelais calls the venerable legal authority of the *Tiers Livre* by the name of Bauble (*Trinquamelle*), sporting with the Latin name (*Tiraquellus*) of his famous and powerful friend Tiraqueau. By so doing he creates a comic tension between the august character in his book and a silly name arbitrarily imposed upon him. All this is good, clean, harmless, inoffensive jesting – unless it is held that there is a necessary connexion, or even a probably etymological one, between the name of the great Tiraqueau and mere baubles. With assumptions such as that friendships became enmities! But Rabelais, by laughing in this way at the ease with which verbal utterances can either have new arbitrary meanings imposed upon them or else, on the contrary, be so used as to turn them into 'naturally meaningful', comic 'unlettered sounds', is not demolishing theories he holds dear. For Rabelais ideas (like pennies) have two sides: the seriousness of an idea does not stop it from having a comic side as well. That some names and words are the vehicles of inspired meanings is a vital part of his philosophy.

If Rabelais had been told that philosophical jokes such as are implied by the names of Raminagrobis, Trinquamelle, Bridoye and so on suggest that he was being Aristotelian about language at the expense of Plato, he might well have been amused. He would have referred the critics to Ammonius. No work on language is of more basic importance. Moreover, when writing the *Tiers Livre*, where this kind of jesting with words, including proper names, occurs many times, Rabelais was apparently reading Plato's *Letters*. He refers to one of them in the episode of Dr Rondibilis. In the seventh letter (342–3), whatever may be said in the *Cratylus*, Plato asserts that words do *not* have fixed meanings; what, he asks, is to stop us calling *straight* what is in fact *circular*? The meaning will be no more and no less fixed after you have switched the words round like this. Plato is not suggesting that anyone can with impunity use the word straight to mean circular, while everybody else accepts the conventional meaning. To do that would be mad, or comic.

Rabelais can call a good man Raminagrobis because, in so doing, he does not change the man; he arbitrarily changes the meaning of the word. But as he is breaking the undoubted meaning of the term as fixed by convention, the effect is both paradoxical and comic. If the conventional meaning of *hypocrite* were to be lost, then Raminagrobis would be a name like any other in a work of fiction: arbitrary, not necessarily meaningful or allusive.

In the *Quart Livre* the ideas which Rabelais and others drew from the *Cratylus* do not replace such theories of language and the jests which can be based on them: they complement them. At a comic level Rabelais gets amusement from the alleged etymologies which French-speakers can read into classical names: *Hérodote: il radote; Perséus; persé jus*. As Erasmus pointed out, you cannot quote the *Cratylus* to justify this kind of nonsense. Insofar as some Church fathers did this sort of thing they were censurable – Rabelais would add, laughable too. When Rabelais seriously claims to find the natural meanings lurking behind the names of things, he sticks to the language concerned: *Philautie et amour de soy vous deçoit*. It is the French term which is seriously explained with French words, not the Greek; it is *amour de soy*, 'love of self', which 'deceives you' – *vous deçoit*.

There is doubtless an element of satire in Rabelais's jokes of the *Hérodote – il radote* type. Theologians were inclined to use such ignorant pseudo-etymologies in their preaching. To go by Madame Pernelle's account in *Le Tartuffe* (I, 1, 160–1), they still did so a century or more later, enabling Molière to have a good laugh at their expense. Her favourite preacher believed that *Salons* were a new *Tour de Babilonne*: 'Car chacun y *babille*, et tout le long de *l'aune . . .*'

That Rabelais is concerned with proper names in part of the *Quart Livre* is emphasised by the 150-odd French surnames he gathered together for his cooks in chapter 42: the amusement comes from the fact that these names do have etymologies appropriate to cooks who are hiding in a Trojan Pig and about to belabour the hosts of the Andouilles with pots and pans. If these names are authentic French surnames, the comic effect is greater than if they had simply been created for the occasion. This undemanding jesting with names is a counterweight to the serious classical examples of significant proper names taken from Calcagnini. We should remember that Pantagruel's insight into the true nature of the dying Pan arose out of etymological reflexions based upon the Greek meanings of the Greek name that good daemons chose to call Christ by.

Here the influence of the *Cratylus* (408D) may be a direct one, for Socrates unwraps the 'true sense', the etymology, of the name of the god Pan by reference both to *Pan* as he who does *all* things and to the double-natured goat-god *Pan*. If Rabelais were to have followed Plato here it would not be hard to understand why. In terms which cannot fail to evoke Christian echoes, Pan is called 'either the *logos* or the *logos*'s brother'. By *logos* here Plato doubtless meant 'speech'. But it could be taken to mean the Word. Budé was of the opinion that 'nobody can doubt' that Plato, when writing of the *logos*, was sometimes 'talking of the Son of God'; but he found it appropriate, like Socrates, to veil such revealed truth until the fullness of time revealed it in Christ. (Budé, *Opera* IV, 243). When names can be as meaningful as that, anything can happen.

What Rabelais is chiefly concerned with in chapter XXVII of the *Quart Livre* is the light which may be thrown upon some words, especially proper-names, by an informed awareness of their mysteriously apt etymologies, when the names concerned have been imposed by inspired name-givers. Can it merely be chance that it is to Rhizotome that

Pantagruel recommends the reading of the *Cratylus*? He is a minor character appearing once only in *Gargantua* and once only in the *Tiers Livre*. Why was he of all people picked out for the advice to go and read the *Cratylus*?

Etymology, as the classical world understood it and passed it on to later ages, was the science of so analysing a word as to discover its true meaning. (*Etumos* means true, sure, real; hence the *Etumon* was the true, sure, real meaning of a word in the light of its 'etymology'.) The etymologist, as we prefer to put it, goes back to a word's roots. Rhizotome's name seems curiously appropriate. It is a light gallicising of the Greek word for a botanist, *rhizotomos*: 'a man who cuts (and gathers) roots.'

As the *Quart Livre* draws towards its close, it becomes clearer that Rabelais believed certain words, in more than one language, were profoundly and 'etymologically' meaningful. The languages to which this applies certainly include Greek, Latin and French. But any Renaissance theorist is likely to accord a special place to Hebrew. Does this explain Rabelais's renewed interest in Hebrew names in the *Quart Livre*?

Rabelais's interest in Hebrew was manifest in *Pantagruel*. But after that, until 1552, Hebrew takes a back seat however honoured theoretically. In 1552 it bursts into sustained prominence – in nearly every case in proper names.

In the *Tiers Livre* and the 1548 *Quart Livre* the Never-Never-Land goal of the heroes' quest is the *Dive Bouteille*. In 1552 this is changed into the *Dive Bacbuc*. Even today Hebrew speakers who have never heard of the *Cratylus* have pointed out to me how appropriately named a bottle is in their tongue, since *bacbuc* seems to imitate the sound of a liquid poured through the neck of a bottle. Some readers of the *Quart Livre* were given this 'etymology' by way of explanation in the *Briefve Declaration*. But *bacbuc* is a rare word: not one that you would expect a casual hebraicist to know.[19]

A good example of Rabelais's jestingly making a Hebrew name specially appropriate is his calling the Queen of the Andouilles by the phallic name of Niphleseth; for the serpent who tempted Eve was arguably sausage-shaped – like the Andouilles and their Queen. An opinion had, indeed, been put forward for debate by the German magus Henry Cornelius Agrippa, who suggested that the 'serpent' which tempted Eve in paradise was actually Adam's penis (*QL* XXXVIII, 13).

[19] In all questions of Hebrew names I am indebted to the patient erudition of Dr Raphael Lowe: 1. *Baqbūq* is a rare word; Rabelais may have found it in I Kings 14,3 or Jeremiah 19,1 or 10. Or he may have found it in explanations of the strange proper name *Bakhbukia* (*Baqbuqya*: 'God's Bottle') in Nehemiah 11,17; 12, 9 and 25. 2. *Belīmāh* occurs in Job 26,7 where it oddly, but probably, means *without-what?* (God suspends the earth on *without-what?*, i.e. nothing). 3. *Chaneph* (*hāneph*) is a noun-adjective which in a few contexts means [a] hypocrital [person]. In Isaiah 32,6 there occurs, uniquely, the abstract noun meaning, approximately, hypocrisy; but the form is *Choneph* (*hōneph*) with an ō not an ā.

There were no Hebrew proper names at all in Rabelais before 1552, except real ones like Rabbi Kimhi and one name of an island in 1548. In 1552 they abound, most of them explained in the *Briefve Declaration d'aucunes dictons plus obscures* added to some copies of the *Quart Livre*. We have *Belima* (Nothing) in Hebrew – as well as *Medamothi* (Nowhere) in Greek. We have *Thohu et Bohu* ('Hebrieu: deserte et non cultivée'); *Ruach* ('vent ou esprit, Hebr.'); *Ganabin* (thieves); *Chaneph* (hypocrisy), and many more. The penultimate word of the entire book is one with which many psalms end: *Sela* ('certainement; Hebr.'). This time, exceptionally, it is not a proper name. Similarly when Rabelais wishes to lend added dignity to his suggestion that the use of homing-pigeons could revolutionise communications, he calls them by the name *gozal* ('en hebrieu: pigeon, colombe'). And I suspect it was meant not only as a good joke but as a deep and cutting wound to call Trent the Council of *Chesil*, of fools.

When attempting to understand both the fun and the philosophy of the *Quart Livre*, it is advisable to look closely at the Hebrew names which mark the various stages of the voyage.

Rabelais's linguistic terms of reference are essentially eclectic. The differing linguistic emphases in the *Tiers Livre* and the *Quart Livre* do not mean that Rabelais had made Pantagruel inconsistent in so central a matter. This can only seem to be so if Aristotle's *On Interpretation* and Plato's *Cratylus* are wrenched from the intellectual context in which he read them. Rabelais is neither Aristotelian nor Platonic exclusively: on linguistic matters he is essentially Ammonian, in that Ammonius supplied the bridge which linked Aristotle's and Plato's linguistic theories together. The *Quart Livre*, in its jests and its philosophy, is an extension of the *Tiers Livre* and a complement to it. Rabelais did not feel the slightest need to repudiate, change, re-write, or recast anything. The *Tiers Livre* is not discreetly modified; nothing is stricken out; there is no recantation of Aristotelian linguistics in the *Quart Livre*. In many ways Pantagruel's neo-Pythagorean reading of the *Cratylus* where proper names are concerned is as much at home in the divinatory *Tiers Livre* as in the questing *Quart Livre*. As for the Aristotelian theory according to which names are given arbitrarily and then consecrated by convention, nothing in the *Quart Livre* goes against it – provided that we know our Ammonius. Rabelais is far from accepting Pontus de Tyard's later, anti-Aristotelian, hebraïcising Platonism, which is so marked a feature of *On the Right Imposition of Names*.

Pontus de Tyard does think the ideas that he finds in the *Cratylus* are incompatible with Aristotle's. And indeed they are. But Pontus de Tyard also believes that you can find the inner sense of a French word by going back to Hebrew roots. He considered Rabelais to be the prince of buffoons, a new Gallic Lucian. This led him to assert that the name of Rabelais – despite its being a surname not a personal name – was no accident of fortune but one intended to be especially meaningful. He derived *Rabelais* from two Hebrew words, *Rab* and *lez*, meaning 'The Prince of Mockers'. Pontus de Tyard was a good Hebrew scholar but, for those who thought like Rabelais, a bad linguistician! It was allegedly Cratylic silliness like this which stirred Erasmus to protest, Rabelais to arouse laughter and Molière's audience to find Madame Pernelle's priest just as silly as she was.[20]

The intellectual and artistic stimulus which Rabelais derived from the *Cratylus*, read against the standard background dominated by Aristotle and Ammonius, increased his zest for sporting with words, for punning amusingly, satirically or meaningfully at various levels of seriousness. The *Cratylus* also reinforced his taste for Pythagorean verbal mysticism and onomastic divination: in this case his interpretation of Plato was clearly influenced by both Ammonius and Calcagnini. His reading of the *Cratylus* in context may have encouraged him to take up Hebrew again; unless, that is, a renewed taste for Hebrew led him to new reflexions on the origin of language. Hebrew studies and the kind of interest he shows in language often go hand in hand at the time he wrote.

This fresh sensitivity to the theory of language leads to both comic and straightforwardly serious episodes in the *Tiers Livre* and the *Quart Livre*, in keeping with that Heraclitean tension so frequently noticeable in his writings.

Almost to a man Renaissance thinkers knew of the *Cratylus* at second hand before they read it for themselves. They might first have read about it in Aquinas, in Ammonius, or in a great many lesser writers. To these influences one must add, in the case of Rabelais, Plutarch's treatise *On Isis and Osiris*. There Rabelais could read etymological explanations of the names of these deities, drawn from the *Cratylus* and backed up with other examples and sources. Plutarch adopts a linguistic position close to that of Ammonius, assuming that etymologies can, and sometimes do, explain the true essence of things named. Such an authority as Plutarch could only have increased Rabelais's attraction towards the theory. But Plato is cited as saying that these etymologically meaningful names were given by the 'men of ancient times'. (In his translation of Plutarch Xylander uses the word *Veteres*.) Plutarch saw no clash between names being both naturally

[20] Pontus de Tyard, *De Recta Nominum Impositione*, Paris 1603, p.27. Tyard is an out-and-out Platonist. From page 1 he makes it plain that he does not accept any harmonising of Plato and Aristotle: he accepts the Platonic contention that meanings were originally imposed under the leadership of nature, not by frivolous human decision. Aristotle's opinion is stated, but contrasted with the authority of Plato 'who was called by Panaetius divine, most holy, most wise and the Homer of the philosophers' (p.2). On the authority of the *Cratylus*, of the 'pious' Socrates and the 'pious' Plato, as well as the 'supreme Prophet Moses' and the 'express words of Philo', the first 'imposers of names' are said to be God and Adam (1–4).

meaningful on occasions and yet, like the others, being arbitrarily imposed by men of ancient times (375D). Neither does Rabelais.

When Rabelais does specifically mention the *Cratylus* by name in 1552, it is not to quote it or to allude to a particular passage. If all the evidence we had were the invitation to read 'the *Cratylus* of the divine Plato' in order to justify onomastic divination we might indeed be tempted to assume that he never read it, simply citing its authority for ideas exclusively lifted from Ammonius and Calcagnini. This can be shown to be wrong. But nobody in the French Renaissance can be assumed to have read any work of Plato's without at least a glance at Ficino's Latin version and the commentaries accompanying it. The commentary on the *Cratylus* is an influential one. Insofar as Rabelais differs from the views expressed in it – and he differs in emphasis – then we may assume it was in full knowledge of what he was doing.

It is not a minor matter that Rabelais, despite these reservations and despite assumptions to the contrary, did know his *Cratylus* in the original Greek. Influenced though he was by others, by venerable commentators and by humanist intermediaries, he also made a very original and idiosyncratic use of his Greek *Cratylus* at a climax of the *Quart Livre*. In fact the *Cratylus* as he interpreted it is integrated into the central core of his philosophy, giving it its own peculiar place in a system in which Heraclitean philosophy, Aristotelian linguistics and Platonic notions about the nature of knowledge all find themselves in exciting harmony with Christian revelation.

Rabelais does not simply raid the stores of other men's ideas like a marauding squirrel stealing nuts. He selects, simplifies, sees new relevancies, new connexions, new implications, His authors are normally inwardly digested as well as being read, marked and learned.

Prompted by Aristotle and Ammonius, Rabelais exploited to high comic ends the gulf separating Panurge's brute noises, revealing passions and perturbations, from true verbal signs which, when properly used, conventionally signify conceptions of the mind.

He was also fruitfully aware of the ways in which what are virtually brute noises can masquerade as true verbal signs or symbols. Most of Panurge's utterances during his frequent bouts of fear in the *Quart Livre* include both brute noises, such as *bou bou bous*, and paragraphs of verbal ramblings which also convey perturbations of the mind rather than rational thought. Fear as Panurge experiences it is pathological, a brute-emotion produced by *philautia*. His language is proof of this. Epistemon's fear was no less intense than Panurge's, but it was a higher, not a servile fear, and controlled by the mind: both his action and his silences reveal this, before he himself spells it out in philosophico-theological terms.

Mutatis mutandis the same considerations often apply to Frère Jean. Much of his blasphemy is only a matter of mere sound. Panurge, who is foolish but not unlettered, saw this (*QL* xx, 3f.). For him, Frère Jean's cursing and blinding during the Storm was equivalent to the relief a man feels, when chopping wood, if a bystander shouts *Han* as he makes his stroke. This attitude towards exclamations encouraging effort, which are sharply to be distinguished from those caused by 'womanish fear', is a standard one. It is normally derived from Cicero who, in the *Tusculan Disputations* (II. xxiii. 55) deals with this question with considerable clarity and precision (cf. also his *De Finibus* v. xi. 31–2): there is no shame in uttering groans and grunts when training or fighting; it helps to make the blows strike home. Such is the actual force of Frère Jean's shouts and oaths. As for Panurge's fearful outpourings, they correspond to the wailings of Philoctetus, the Greek hero whom Cicero sharply condemns for giving himself over to fear and lamentations.

But Rabelais does not allow all of Frère Jean's blasphemies to be lightly excused. When he is striving to save his abbey or his ship, much may be overlooked and understood. Not so, when such spiritual coarseness is manifested in moments of calm or safe repose. When Frère Jean does cold-bloodedly tell a tale involving a blasphemous use of the name of God, then he is roundly told off for it by Pantagruel (*QL* L, 29f.).

All this is most relevant to the understanding of Rabelais's meaning and an appreciation of his art: yet if it were all he had got out of the *Cratylus*, I for one would have felt somewhat disappointed.

The *Cratylus*, however we interpret it, is concerned with the possibility of man acquiring real knowledge. Socrates is at times light-hearted in the *Cratylus*, even using slightly pejorative terms to explain his thought. But we are left in no doubt that without the Platonic teaching about 'ideas' (or 'forms') no real knowledge is open to man in the words he employs.

In the *Cratylus* Socrates is shown as deeply disturbed by Heraclitus's doctrine that all is in a state of flux. If language shares this quality, then the verbal signs we use to mean things, the things we mean by them, as well as we ourselves, are changing so constantly that no lasting certainty is possible about anything at all. Even if a less extreme Heraclitean position is held, Plato believes that man can have no knowledge whatsoever about things which are in a constant state of flux: about such things one can only have opinions. This contrast between knowledge and mere opinion is a vital one.[21]

Today we tend to give pride of place to empirical knowledge arising out

[21] Useful help on these matters can be found in Bertrand Russell's *History of Western Philosophy* (London 1947, pp.171f.) as well as from studies such as Henry Jackson's excellent, and short, *Plato's Cratylus* ('Praelections delivered before the University of Cambridge, 25, 26 and 27 January 1906), and F. M. Cornford's *Plato's Theory of Knowledge: The 'Theaetetus' and the 'Sophist' of Plato with a Running Commentary*, London 1935. I follow them closely.

of perception. But precisely this assumption is demolished by Plato in the first half of the *Theaetetus*. For Plato no real knowledge can be gained from perceptions, since knowledge is a matter of concepts, and concepts are matters for the mind not the senses. Fighting against the prevailing Heraclitean orthodoxy, Plato felt the need for language to contain at least some words which must be fixed in meaning, if not for ever at least for a long time. Without such a pre-requisite, no assertion can ever be held to be true or false. This curiously brings Socrates closer to the Heraclitean Cratylus, who holds that, when things are properly named, they have names corresponding to their true natures.

But, granted such a language, words will still be dealing with mere opinion not truth, if the world is subject to constant flux, while words themselves can only refer to particular things. However many beautiful things one can name, for example, that does not amount to the knowledge a philosopher may have of beauty itself. Unless we are prepared to accept that there are entities which we can have knowledge of, and which are not subjected to Heraclitean flux, then knowledge of anything at all is impossible.

It was considerations such as these which led Plato to his doctrine of ideas. The ideas are stable, unchanging and permanent, where all else save God is transitory. If words can somehow partake of this stability, encapsulating in themselves some small part of the changelessness of the celestial ideas, then they become possible sources of knowledge.

The snag is how to relate something as slight and as passing as human speech to these majestic unchanging ideas. Yet a way must be found of breaking out of the confines of the purely transitory into the durable domain of the ideas, if ever man is to escape from mere opinion into the realm of true knowledge.

It was here that Cratylus and his Heraclitean linguistics were felt to be so attractive. Individual things which share a common name (all tables for example) can only be known if one knows their essence; the name itself, if properly imposed by the name-giver, may be an instrument enabling men to discern their essence. This being so, a man may learn through names something of the ideal forms; this constitutes knowledge.

Socrates is in fact tentative, though this tentativeness by no means transpires in all the various translations of the *Cratylus* that I have consulted. Socrates acknowledges that words and their etymologies *may* lead to a knowledge of the truth; but they may not.

This aspect of the *Cratylus* Rabelais did see – more clearly in fact than some of his contemporaries. He takes up a markedly independent position in the matter, keeping us waiting till chapter LV before he has his very challenging say. There are good reasons for his keeping us waiting like this: not least Rabelais is going to sow confusion before he grants enlightenment. Some of the certainties he has built up artistically in our minds are deliberately confounded. It is as though clear, sharp reflexions in a still pond were to be troubled by a purposeful stirring of the waters. We need time to become aware of this and to make the necessary adjustments.

Meanwhile to the jesting with names Rabelais increasingly adds jesting with ideas. We leave the Andouilles with our ears ringing, not with the earlier puns (*Riflandouilles rifloit Andouilles; Tailleboudin tailloit Boudins*), but with happy talk about the Flying Pig of the Andouilles being *L'Idée* of Mardigras, their tutelary god. New sources of humour such as this unexpectedly bind pairs of episodes together. The Papimanes not only worship the pope: they cherish, above their high altar, an *Idée de celluy Dieu de bien en terre* – it consists of a pretty poor picture.

Such jesting is not destructive of the actual theory of Platonic ideas: it serves among other things to keep alive in the readers' minds the memory of these ideas, until Rabelais returns to them later at a mythological climax to the *Quart Livre*.

14. The inhabitants of Ruach

Quaresmeprenant and the Andouilles did not form a balanced pair of rivals. Rabelais and his hero are presented as champions of the golden mean, but these two figures were not equidistant from the balanced centre. The Andouilles, for all their errors and treachery, are less wrong and they are much more amusing; but Antiphysie produces just such births as a reader of the *Cratylus* would expect: monstrous and impious – like Quaresmeprenant.

We find a similar lopsidedness in the twin episodes of the defeated Papefigues, who used not to care a fig for the pope, and the victorious Papimanes, who rave over him. We soon see where Rabelais's condemnation sits more squarely. But we do not meet either of this new pair of rivals until we pass through the Island of Ruach (QL XLIII f.).

The interest of this brief episode is considerable. With it returns, after a long absence, the scatological humour last met in *Gargantua*, some seventeen or eighteen years earlier. If ever proof were needed that Rabelais's scatology is not a concession to the alleged tastes of the vulgar populace this episode supplies it. The humour is learned at several levels.

The name of the island presupposes some knowledge of Hebrew. Only later states of the *Quart Livre* explain the term in the *Briefve Declaration*: 'Ruach, vent ou esprit. Hebr.' The original readers were supposed to know this unaided. Is this a joke at the expense of the notion that a Hebrew name necessarily tells us something basic and true about the person or thing named? From the name alone how are we to tell whether these islanders are spiritual or merely windy? We soon discover that they are 'windbags', living greedily on choice winds. When they die, as becomes creatures who live by stuffing themselves with wind, they fart their souls away. The expression is of course arresting: 'And the men die farting; the women, fizzling. So their soul leaves by their arses' (*QL* XLIII, 50).

Again we hear of souls leaving the body in death. In this case, we are not dealing with the death of a Seigneur de Langey or a Christ-Pan, but of gross Epicurean pigs. We weep for the former; we laugh at the latter.

At one level we are being treated to a sustained medical joke. We have allusions to Hippocrates's treatise *On flatulence* and to Scyron, Rabelais's venerable academic sponsor for his doctorate of medicine (as distinct from his M.B.). These chapters are full of stagey medical jokes based on pills, purgations, clysters and cuppings. The last word in the episode – revealing as often – is *Medicins*, as we are told how Bringuenarilles, the giant windmill-eater, died from following their advice. It was on the advice of his doctors that Bringuenarilles started plaguing the islanders in the first place.

The medical humour is allied to semi-learned jokes based on a classical commonplace – *vento vivere*, 'to live on wind', that is, on next to nothing (*QL* XLIV, 5). Once more Erasmus lists it and explains it in the *Adages* (IV, 9, 3). Readers without a basic erudition would also miss the point of the remark: *Rien n'est beat de toutes pars* (Nothing is in all parts blessed), a line of Horace's *Odes* (II. 16. 27), which had become proverbial. Such knowledge was not rare: but the common people did not have it.

A link with earlier chapters is established by the visits of Bringuenarilles to Ruach. The original idea of this windmill-eating giant comes straight out of the *Disciple de Pantagruel*. It is a simple tale there, with not the slightest hint at medical learning or philosophical humour. But when we meet Bringuenarilles in chapter XVII of the *Quart Livre* the humour is already specifically medical. Can it be a coincidence that he dies after a surfeit of just such pots and pans as Frère Jean presses into service against Quaresmeprenant? (*QL* XVII). When his doctors advise him to visit Ruach to purge himself annually with windmill-pills, the dwellers on Ruach try to avert his visits with special Rogationtides, as well as by celebrating three or four Lents a year (*QL* XLIV, 37). It all fits together. The Ruachites are in some ways followers of Quaresmeprenant, delighting no doubt in the pre-Lenten excesses.

Philosophically these gross islanders (whose name recalls both Baisecul and Humevesne) are simple, harmless Epicureans. As Pantagruel remarks: 'If you accept the opinion of Epicurus saying that sovereign good consists in pleasure (I mean pleasure which is facile, not difficult) then I repute you to be very happy' (XLIV, 3). These folk are not atheists: for them a good tasty wind is a 'bon et grand vent de Dieu' – a kind of 'heavenly manna'.

The Andouilles held mustard in religious respect, as their Holy Grail and a heaven-sent balm: 'leur Sangreal et Baume celeste'; in this following chapter, the king of the Windbags has a special wind which used to belong to Ulysses, 'lequel il guardoit religieusement comme un aultre Sangreal'. Decidedly, both Andouilles and Ruachites have their eyes fixed permanently on lower things; even their Holy Grails are terrestrial and unspiritual. If the Ruachites were right in their easy Epicureanism, then the soul appropriate to them would indeed be one which left the body through its grossest orifice. One cannot see what the higher qualities and functions of a human soul would have to do on their isle.

That the coarse and flatulent Epicurean inhabitants of Ruach are laughably wrong about this world and the next, we know (if we know it at all) from the account of them that we have. We do not learn it from Pantagruel: he says nothing that savours of condemnation, if we take his words literally.

Rabelais is deliberately shaking our certainties. For, even according to Pantagruel, these wind-breaking Ruachites are living the good life, *if* simple Epicureanism were the true philosophy. So if we see that Ruachites are wrong, it is because we have been brought to realise that scatological humour in Rabelais is always partly condemnatory. Explicit guidance on this we get later on in the book. But this time, if we look to Pantagruel for guidance, we do not get it. He smiles down benignly on Ruachites Papefigues and Papimanes, almost alike.

Pantagruel, in other words, has ceased for the while to be overtly normative with his pregnant silences, his grasping impressions of the truth, his resonant condemnations or judgments. In the *Tiers Livre* his authoritative declarations had something of the force of an Old Testament prophet and the Stoic sage, bathed, both, in the light of Christian truth. Even in the first half of the *Quart Livre*, Pantagruel is more eloquent in his actions and his silences than in his judgments. In the remainder of the *Quart Livre* his rôle is even more unexpected: he leaves us floating in the air, wondering how to take what he says. Far from condemning the Ruachites, Pantagruel seems the epitome of amoral politeness: 'Pantagruel praised their polity and way of life.' Subsequent developments show that this disturbing tolerance is no accident; it is not an isolated phenomenon. Islanders of all sorts and conditions are praised; alms are distributed with calm indifference to merit; words are used by one character which are unmistakably more at home in the mouth of another.

This troubling of our certainties is part of the essential nature of the *Quart Livre*. Heraclitean flux and changeableness will not be fully felt unless it also affects Pantagruel. He has already changed unrecognisably since 1532; further change is required if he is to fulfil a new function in 1552. What he says now often has to be interpreted: it cannot always be taken literally. Only fitfully is he given his former quasi-infallibility; and that he now has in a new form, starker and more abrupt. At other times he often has quite ordinary things to say, words lacking in the authority to be drawn from scripture or antiquity. His ordinary polite reactions to the people he visits have the form of words which, taken literally, do not fit in with what we otherwise know to be true of him.

By daring to shift Pantagruel's character yet again, Rabelais makes possible a new climax to his book in philosophical uncertainty.

There are a hundred and one ways in which we can, if we so wish, explain Pantagruel's gentle lack of verbal censoriousness in many places where we would expect to find it. He is a courteous prince; politeness is *de rigueur*; he is touched by Pantagruelism, that refusal to take things in bad part when they can be taken in good; Epistemon in the *Tiers Livre* similarly interpreted the words of the dying Raminagrobis in ways which are naïf and wrong (*TL* XXII, 63); much of what Pantagruel now says may be sarcastic, ironical. But as the book unrolls towards its ambitious close we are confronted with basic problems of meaning and basic problems of truth. Words do not always mean what they say – Pantagruel's no less than anyone else's. Pantagruel's character, fixed and sure in the *Tiers Livre*, has now changed into something different. In the *Tiers Livre* Pantagruel was a hero of striking 'apathy', a man who, hearing nonsense or stupidity, 'ne feut en soy aulcunement indigné, fasché ne marry'. In the *Quart Livre* he does show indignation; we see him sad and frequently *fasché*. These changes are too consistent to be minor or accidental. Rabelais has broken the mould in which Pantagruel had formerly been cast. If Pantagruel were now to be always unambiguously right as he was in the *Tiers Livre*, always transparently and literally clear in what he says, there would be no philosophical tension in the *Quart Livre*. Rabelais carefully forces his audience to read between the lines. We are given far less overt guidance. A major miracle saves the heroes during the Storm; it is not related or described: it takes place during a jest (*QL* XXI, end; XXII, beginning). Pantagruel does not boom out his interpretation of the death of Pan; he does so quietly and is left weeping alone while the others rejoice.

He is now both more human and, at times, more divinely inspired than he ever was in the *Tiers Livre*. As befits a more complex character, what he says is less straightforward.

How we know what we know is a problem Rabelais is about to tackle – once he has led us to feel sorry for the Papefigues and to laugh heartily at the Papimanes. Until Rabelais explains himself, we must be content with laughter, half-statements and hints.

But he has not really left us up in the air where the Ruachites are concerned. We wonder why Pantagruel's condemnation is so conditional a one, depending on gross Epicureanism not being the true philosophy for man. But the very fact of our laughter at the expense of these fat pleasure-seekers, who cram themselves with wind and then fart their souls away in death, is enough to show they are wrong.

Rabelais's readers had a further hint, from a source of laughter which now escapes even readers alerted to the learned nature of his jests. Appropriately, the humour depends upon a proper name. Rabelais's mentor and supervisor appears unexpectedly in this tale; we are told how the inhabitants of the Isle Ruach used to make a medicinal broth out of one of the winds. A blown-up little Ruachite remarks:

If only I could have a bladder of the good wind of Languegoth called Cercius! The noble doctor Scurron, passing through this country one day, told us it is so strong that it can blow over laden carts. What a lot of good it would do to my oedipodic leg (QL xlɪɪɪ, 22f.).

The allusion to Dr Scyron seems hostile, though it may not be so. The play on his name is entirely appropriate to this anal-centred Epicurean island. *Sucrra* is the Latin for a jester or a buffoon; *Scyron* is one of the names of the north-west wind among the Athenians; it was also the name of an Epicurean philosopher mentioned by Cicero. And finally, there is a learned pun; I owe the explanation to a remark of Rabelais's friend Bouchard, who says that the French 'call *scyron* what the Greeks called hemmoroids'. The joke in Rabelais depends on the word *haimorroides* meaning both a kind of shell-fish and piles. Dr Scyron, Dr Piles, was an appropriate doctor for these inflated Epicureans.[22]

These grossly stuffed Ruachites are conceived in terms of sixteenth-century luxury and pleasure-seeking. They are not overwhelmed by a mountain of consumer goods. Pleasure-seeking in the hungry centuries before our own in Europe was a matter of eating and drinking copiously. That transpires even more clearly in the episode of Messere Gaster. These Ruachites eat, drink and are merry; when tomorrow they die, their tainted soul is an appropriate one for them to have, and its departure through the anus is comically the right way for it to go.

15. The Papefigues and the Papimanes

The Papefigues call forth our pity not our laughter. Such amusement as there is is introduced from without, with the tales of how the amateur devils were thwarted by peasant shrewdness. Sorrow for the wretched state of the island, first laid waste by the Papimanes and now ruled by

[22] For Sciron the Epicurean philosopher, see Cicero, *Academica* ɪɪ, 23, 106. For Bouchard, see *Tēs gunaikeias phutlēs*, p.58 r°: ' . . . vide simile nonnihil in maribus nasci quod Scyron appellant: Graeci *Hemorrhoidas* vocant.' I enjoyed discussing these matters with Robert Ireland of the Classics Departments in University College London; he helped me a lot.

them, is clearly evoked. We are given no picture of heretics brought back to the true and loving Church; of lost sheep brought back to the fold; of the father's loving forgiveness for the returning prodigal son. What the Papefigues once stood for has been smashed, replaced by superstitious priests controlling peasants in the midst of ruins. These victorious priests are like the 'fathers' condemned in the Liminary Epistle, who give you a stone when you ask for bread.

The episode is made an excuse for evangelical, not ecclesiastical or pro-papal, comment. Students, we are told, now have their bibles: it is all the harder to lead them to perdition. As the wretched little devil realises, no more undergraduate souls will be devoured unless the *caphards* stamp out all this reading of St Paul by means of burnings and repression generally (*QL* XLVI, 71f.).

The only persons to gain anything from the massacre of the Gaillardetz (as the Papefigues were formerly called) were the devils and the priests. The kindly treatment Rabelais reserves for the Papefigues is closely linked to the time in which the *Quart Livre* was prepared for publication: 1551, the year, as we saw, in which anti-papalist Gallican fervour reached its crisis. But it also has links with the earlier policies of the Seigneur de Langey. This chapter seems to have been in part a last tribute to an admired hero and a bold sneer at his avowed enemies.

It is probable that behind the once-jolly Gaillardetz, now Papefigues, lie the Vaudois Protestants massacred at Mérindol and Cabrières in 1545. The bloody fierceness of the suppression of these simple people, after prolonged manoeuvring by lay and clerical politicians hostile to the du Bellays' aspirations, shocked a public already hardened to religious and political intolerance.

The massacre of 1545 had marked the triumph of policies of the du Bellays' rival, the Cardinal de Tournon. He sought to stamp out heresy and to compel Catholic conformism by main force. This set him in marked opposition to both Jean and Guillaume du Bellay whose policy was one of enlightened charity and, within a wider catholicism, of eirenic tolerance. In part this came out of hard-headed calculations of the French interest. But exclusively cynical interpretations of the motives of statesmen of the past are not always right; for Crespin, in his movingly committed, protestant *Histoire des Martyrs*, the Catholic Guillaume du Bellay (Langey) was the hero of this sad affair. While he was royal lieutenant in the Piedmont, Langey was ordered to inquire into the injustices and the already real persecutions of the king's subjects in the area of Mérindol. His delegates gave a most favourable account of the Vaudois immigrants, who for two hundred years had brought wealth and industry to a depopulated part of France. It is true that they do not use holy water; do not cross themselves when at prayer. But they are pious and tolerate no blasphemy.

In 1543 the Vaudois were reassured when they were told that they would
not be required to make formal recantations of error, 'seeing that everyone
knows that they do not live according to the ordinances of the Church,
and that they hold the pope in no more esteem than any other man'
(Crespin, 1619 edition, p.145f.).

Langey did all within his power to protect the Vaudois: supporting the
man on the spot, Président Chassané, intervening at court, reporting well
on the Vaudois and their way of life. But those who wanted to stamp out
the Vaudois heretics were powerfully led. At the head was the Cardinal de
Tournon. Together with the bishop of Aix-en-Provence he wanted
persecution and suppression. The king was believed to be unfavourable
towards the idea of persecution. But it was felt that he would be brought
round: meanwhile, to massacre the Vaudois was to please the Cardinal de
Tournon.

It is doubtless significant that the sad Papefigues were once called
Gaillardetz, a name suggestive of jolliness and good-fellowship with a dose
of extravagance. There may be other allusions behind the name which
remain unexplained. At all events, the little devils who go off to visit the
nuns at the amusingly named convent at Dryfart, *Pettesec*, hope to tempt
them to the '*guaillard* peché de luxure'.

The Papefigues are like Vaudois heretics in apparently having their own
Rabiz – 'rabbis', ministers of religion (*QL* XLV, 7).

The episode is noteworthy for its unexplained irony. Rabelais seems to
be challenging us to say how we recognise the irony to be what it is. The
Papefigues acquired their name when their representatives cocked a snook
(*fit la figue*) at the papal portrait carried in procession by the Papimanes.
For this, we are told, they deserved sharp punishment. Their descendants
ever since have suffered hail, tempest, plague, famine and all manner of ill,
'as eternal punishment of the sins of their ancestors and parents'. Taken at
its face value, this is history as written by bishop Homenaz of Papimanie
(cf. *QL* XLV, 47f. and LI, 69f.).

The tongue is firmly in the cheek. But Pantagruel makes no comment,
simply leaving 18,000 golden Royals in the alms box for the fabric fund 'in
contemplation of the poverty of the people and the calamitous state of the
place'. The 'misère et calamité du peuple' had been stressed at the outset.
We are left, once more, to draw our own conclusions. There is no
underlining of the irony. The peasant of Papefiguière plunges into holy
water up to the nose, having first made confession and taken his
communion 'comme bon catholicque'. All the unslaughtered Gaillardetz
are now 'good Catholics' no doubt. Yet the term 'catholic' is far from
naturally pejorative for Rabelais, though it is twice used sarcastically in
this book, once of Quaresmeprenant (XXX, 21) and now of a forcibly
converted labourer (XLVII, 17). Evangelicals and Gallicans, as well as

schismatics and heretics, were acutely aware that 'papists' claimed a monopoly of catholicism!

The Papefigues were punished for not venerating the papal portrait – it was the *louable coustume* to carry it round on feast days. Again we laugh. Yet in *Gargantua* the words *coustume des bons Christians* are used straightforwardly, to praise infant baptism in the early Church (*QL* XLV, 10; *Garg.* VI, 16).

The very lack of emphasis on Rabelais's part, coupled with Pantagruel's lack of condemnation, seem to invite us to ask ourselves: how *do* we know that in one case the words are serious; in the other, ironical?

In the case of the Papimanes the irony and the amused satire are even more strikingly present, without Rabelais taking time off to tell us coldly and literally what he is doing. Yet these Papimanes we recognise as being the antithesis of the Gospel, to which they are as opposed in their own way as Antiphysie was to Physis.

The basic framework of the comedy of the Papimanes is a simple one: papist lawyers had for decades been claiming that the powers of a reigning pope were such that he was *quasi Deus in terris*: 'as though God on earth.' In one famous document they forgot the *quasi*! This became a favourite taunt, not only from Protestants and schismatics but from the many Catholics who were shocked by the pretensions of the papal curia and the papalist lawyers. The phrase *quasi Deus in terris* is found repeatedly in sermons, propaganda and satirical writings. For comic propaganda purposes Rabelais affects to believe that these papist Catholics were idolaters, actually worshipping the true God in heaven less enthusiastically than their little god in Rome. Words such as *adorer*, used for the veneration of a new pope, and claims, far from universally accepted, for *ex cathedra* infallibility, justified these sneers up to a point; yet of course at no time did popes or their servants actually claim godhead for the Vicar of Christ. Rabelais's uproarious episode derives from his imagining an island, far from Rome, where the simple people have made the pope into their earthly god. It is all very laughable. But in the context of 1551–2, all very scathing as well.

The religion of Christ may be summed up in the two commandments on which hang all the Law and the Prophets:

Thou shalt love the Lord thy God with all thy heart, and with all thy soul, and with all thy might.

This is the first and great commandment. And the second, like unto it, is this: Thou shalt love thy neighbour as thyself.

The Papimanes break both of them. God the Father revealed himself to Moses at the burning bush as pure Being: I AM THAT I AM – in Latin, 'I am he who is'; in the Septuagint version, 'I alone am the Being-one',

I alone truly exist. Nothing on earth can hope to rival such a claim: hence its appearance at the outset of the episode of the Papimanes, for the simple-minded Papimanes do believe they have a God-on-earth to place beside God as Being. Yet this papal God-òn-earth actually has a humanity which Rabelais can stress in amusing terms: being no Popess Joan he has ample male genitals; he also has an arse which his devotees can kiss. And kiss it they will if they ever get the chance (*QL* XLVIII, 1–61).

It is soon clear that Rabelais is going beyond the immediate needs of royalist Gallican propaganda, even in 1551–2, when the French were close to a reformation *à l'anglicane*. During the time that the du Bellays were in London in the 1530s after the Anglican schism was effected, they would have heard some refer courteously to the pope as Bishop of Rome, while others, such as Thomas Cromwell, called him The Idol. Rabelais sides, as it were, with Cromwell and those who thought like him. The pope, for the Papimanes at least, *is* an idol; their worship of him is idolatry.

They have a wrong god, so break the first and great commandment. They also break the second. Their bishop is a blood-and-thunder bishop, rejoicing in bloody repression, imprisonments, tortures and spectacular deaths (*QL* LIII). According to his version of Christ's commandments, 'thou shalt love thy neighbour as thyself: provided he be not an heretic' (*QL* LI, 70–83).

These errors arise out of their scriptures, which are not the Bible but papal law: the decretals. Decretals are collections of papal rescripts promulgated on papal authority alone, in reply to questions addressed to the Holy See. Some of the most notorious, as far as Protestants and Gallicans are concerned, were forged, and already known to be so. All Protestants and non-Roman Catholics, as well as many Gallicans and conciliarists, questioned or rejected the authority of decretals, the true as well as the false.

Decretals are sharply distinguished from *decrees* (papal ordinances enacted with the advice of the cardinalate) and *canons* (ecclesiastical laws enacted by ecumenical councils or synods). *Canons* are also often called *decrees*(but never, of course, *decretals*). Homenaz makes a real gaffe, worthy of the farcical spirit which informs these chapters, when he slips into praising *decretistes* not *decretalistes* (*QL* LIII, 45).

Rabelais in both the *Tiers Livre* and the *Quart Livre* shows some real knowledge of the decrees compiled by Gratian in the twelfth century, though he is at times sharply critical, as over their baleful influence on marriage when wrongly interpreted. But on the question of the decretals he is scathing. As reformers had sung before him, it was when the decrees took on wings (*aeles*) so becoming *decretales*, that papal abuses multiplied (*QL* LIII, end).

In attacking the decretals head-on Rabelais was making a move popular in the circles in which he lived; popular too at the highest level at court, when Cardinal de Châtillon and others were pushing Henry II towards a final break with Rome. What Rabelais was doing with laughter in French, Charles du Moulin was doing in effective and unsmiling Latin in his *Commentary on the Edict of Henry the Second . . . against the Abuses of the Roman Curia*, 1552. This powerful little Latin book has an important dedicatory letter written in French for Henry's and others' benefit. The title-page boasts a royal Privilege for nine years. Of the three Scriptural quotations on the same page, two stress the religious man's confidence in truth including *Magna est veritas, et prevalet* (I Esdras 4, 35): Great is truth and it shall prevail.

If Rabelais had limited himself to attacking and mocking the decretaline basis for those aspects of papal authoritarianism which royalist Gallicans loathed, his list would have already been quite long. But he goes much farther. Royalist Gallicans rejected the claims of popes to make and unmake kings; they saw the great sums of money going from France to Rome as a totally unjustifiable abuse, filling the coffers of the enemy of France.

Rabelais's principal comic device at this point (*QL* LI) is to put a laughable praise of the decretals in Bishop Homenaz's mouth, as he harangues his guests during a banquet. All the jests still strike home: they must have done so even more in 1552. It suffices to invert Homenaz's eulogy to arrive at the truth. The Bible is being perverted and driven out by decretaline law; kings and princes are being held to be subject to papal authority; monasteries flourish; torturing and killing heretics is all the rage; universities confound the Bible in their coats-of-arms with a book of decretals. The laughter increases as Rabelais, with a genius that has never been equalled, puts his power to evoke laughter at the service of his religion. He even makes the terrible reality of torture and slow death comic. It is a method of propaganda at least as effective as the diatribe, not least when written for a public which knew its theology. Rabelais, before he finishes with his silly bishop, condemns the Papimanes against clear theological norms. Homenaz sees the decretals as the sure way to success, in this world and the next. He sees in the decretals alone the source of the authority of the pope over Heaven, Earth, and Purgatory, and preaches this to his guests with tipsy fervour and maudlin sentimentality. Any idea that the pope has power over Hell or Purgatory is effectively dismissed through laughter. So too are the religious orders – all dependent upon mere decretaline law, apparently. All this is enhanced by the clerical unctuousness of Homenaz's language. Homenaz goes so far as to make the decretals into rivals of both Pantagruelism and of St Paul who was caught up in ecstasy to the third heaven (II Corinthians 12) – for it is by studying the decretals alone that we, the faithful, find:

an assured contempt for all fortuitous and earthly things; ecstatic elevation of your spirits – yea, unto the third heaven; certain contentedness in all your emotions (*QL* LI, end; prol., 16f.).

The liturgical hocus-pocus leading to the unveiling of the papal portrait kept in honour above the high altar leads our laughter into different channels. This is no portrait of an individual pope: the portrait is the Platonic idea of the quintessence of popery: 'C'est l'Idée de celluy Dieu de bien en terre, la venue duquel attendons' (*QL* L, 13).

The individual pope is not even for the Papimanes a reflexion of the divine universal who is God. The rôles are reversed. God himself is less important than the ideal form of popery, the earthly rival of his godhead which stretches forth its claims to Heaven, Hell and the dubious world of Purgatory. Such a pope is antichrist, if he indeed made such claims for himself. In the *Quart Livre* the claims are made for the pope by the Papimanes, but not by the pope on his own behalf.

One might have expected Pantagruel to have stood sadly aside or to have thundered against idolatry. In fact he restricts his overt condemnations, which are very sharp, to two occasions only. Once he intervenes to stop the local dominie from giving his boys a sound and memorable whipping in order to impress upon them the importance of Pantagruel's visit; the second is when he condemns Frère Jean for taking the name of God in vain (*QL* XLVIII, 79f.; L, 35f.).

The very forcefulness with which these condemnations are made emphasises Pantagruel's failure to condemn the Papimanes themselves in any explicit form of words. This in itself would not create any tension, comic, philosophical or other. We do not doubt that the Papimanes are a laughable perversion of the Christian religion. But we have been schooled by the *Tiers Livre* to expect Pantagruel, at some stage, to say so. He says no such thing. Quite the reverse. The doubt we feel about his final remarks is carefully and artistically contrived. The episode of the Papimanes revolves around the question of what constitutes a good Christian. Rabelais draws our attention to it quite discreetly. For Frère Jean, who is particularly at home in the boozy, sensuous atmosphere of bishop Homenaz's banquet, his episcopal host is a man who speaks 'en bons termes, et en bon Christian'. As for Homenaz, he believes that the decretals alone, to the exclusion of all other learning, constitute the 'perfaicte institution du vray Christian'. We are amused but not surprised when he begs his captive congregation at the banquet, with dripping clerical unction, not to believe, think, say or do anything whatsoever, save what is to be found in the holy decretals, 'si voulez estre dictz et reputez vrays Christians' (*QL* XLIX, 8; LI, 53; LIII, 25). So *vray christian* joins *bon catholicque* as a term which can, ironically, mean the reverse of its literal sense. . . . So far the irony, though unexplained, is steeped in laughter. Yet when we have laughed our fill at Homenaz and his sentimental tears, we are astonished to hear Pantagruel say that he will take the pears he has been given by the Papimanes and graft them on to his trees in Touraine; he will then call them *poires de bon Christian*: 'For never saw I Christians better than are these good Papimanes.' Frère Jean caps this with the hope that Homenaz will lend him a couple of cartloads of the local girls, on whom he will graft a new race of children: *enfans de bon Christian* (*QL* LIV, 26–39).

As the heroes depart, Pantagruel, at his most liberal, gives money (again for the fabric fund), as well as a gift of cloth to Homenaz to thank him for showing him the portrait of the papal Idea. He also leaves money as dowries for the girls who served at table dressed up like choristers (*QL* LIII, end).

Pantagruel's remarks have to be explained – explained, indeed, away. This is easy enough to do. Human ingenuity can think of a multitude of ways in which a man's words can bear meanings other than those of their face-value. What is not in doubt – not least in 1551 when written, and 1552 when published – is that these chapters hold the Papimanes up to ridicule against scriptural standards and norms. In the full flood of Gallican enthusiasm, Rabelais holds up the papist opponents of his king and patrons to public mockery, against the standards of the Gospel they are supposed to preach and to live by. The comedy is still accessible, even in an age when the scriptural norms are less widely recognised or accepted; the laughter rolls off the pages, across the centuries, precisely because we know *grosso modo* what Rabelais is talking about and have been brought by his art to sympathise with the normative wisdom against which the folly of the Papimanes is judged. A modern reader may be vague about the extent of the far-reaching Gallican crisis of 1551–2; vague about the origin of the formula *quasi Deus in terris*; vague about the degree to which the cloying sensuousness of Homenaz's banquet would have evoked comparisons in French minds with the goings-on in the courts of popes Paul III or Julius III; vague about the wide tolerance allowed to Catholic thinkers before the Council of Trent sealed its last definition and dotted the i's on its last anathema in 1563: but he would have to be totally ignorant of the irreducibly basic tenets of evangelical religion before he failed to see the Papimanes as a comic perversion of Christ's own teaching and as an explicitly idolatrous compromising of God the Father's great and awful revelation of himself as uniquely true Being to Moses at the burning bush. Rabelais also shows that Homenaz flouts the basic and best wisdom of the ancient world; the bishop believes that his decretals are every bit as heaven-sent as the *know thyself* of Delphi (*QL* XLIX, 12f.).

It is precisely this certainty about the Papimanes which constitutes the challenge when Pantagruel has his say about them and about the pears he names *poires de bon Christian*. A few students who have read Rabelais with me have been puzzled at this point, wondering whether Rabelais could actually be laughing at Christianity itself; and if he were to be doing so, wondering how to square this fact with the strong protestations of orthodoxy in his letter to Odet de Châtillon, the Gallican cardinal, or with his open veneration for the godhead of Christ and the Gospel in the prologue, and in so many chapters of the *Quart Livre*.

The farce of the Papimanes ends without more than a hint of how such a problem is to be resolved. The answer lies in the chapters immediately following, chapters devoted to showing how difficult it is to reach the truth by means of words.

The hint lies in Pantagruel's action as a name-giver. He has just 'arbitrarily imposed' a name on those 'good Christian pears' for which Touraine was famous. One explanation would be that he has named these pears by antiphrasis – a standard but puzzling etymological possibility, by which the true root of a name can be sought in the opposite to its meaning. Another is that *poyre* in old French meant 'to fart'. Were these *poyres de bons Christians* not pears at all, but broken wind? Were they papist Ruachites?

Rabelais may appear to be holding contradictory views: names such as those which gave rise to Pantagruel's citing of the *Cratylus* or to his interpretation of the death of Pan seem to have important mystical and natural relationships with the persons named; on the other hand, names such as that bestowed on the 'good Christian pears' seem to depend on the arbitrary whim of a name-giver with a taste for antiphrasis or recondite humour.

In fact by holding both opinions in a state of tension Rabelais is close to the Socrates of the *Cratylus*. Moreover Socrates and the *Cratylus* lie behind the episode of the thawing words about to follow. This episode helps to supply answers to the questions which Rabelais has raised, and resolutions to our doubts and hesitations as readers. The answer to our doubts about the condemnation of the Papimanes lies in the fact that words are imprecise and confusing things. Actions speak louder than they do. And one unmistakable action is the action of laughter. Another is the bodily grossness of a fatuously complacent bishop whose fluent nonsense produces diarrhoea in others, whilst he himself 'farts, fizzles, laughs, slobbers and sweats' at his own weak jokes (QL LIII, 93f.; LI 65f.). One hint of how we are to take Pantagruel's gracious magnanimity in these episodes we will miss if we do not know our Plutarch. The Papimanes are unsophisticated rustics. Poor old Homenaz admits this, once the girls have got him out of his maudlin fit: 'Since it pleases God to be so, we are simple folk. And we call figs figs, plums plums, and pears pears.' The last phrase is an adaptation of a Greek idiom, 'to call a spade a spade' – the source of our own expression. Philip of Macedonia applied it to his countrymen, 'who were rough and countrified people, used to calling a spade a spade'. He advised his son

Alexander to treat such simple people with indulgence, whilst he was yet a prince. By acquiring the goodwill of their leaders – the good and the bad – he would later be able to use them fittingly, to his own royal purposes (QL LIV, 22; Plutarch 178B – Amyot's translation, first edition, 191F; Erasmus, *Adagia* II, 3, 5: *Ficus ficus, ligonem ligonem vocat*).

This is all very well, no doubt. But we need to *know* that we are right to reject Homenaz's unctuous, churchy blandishments, and his complacent cruelty, against the standards of revelation. The following episode does tell us this, in its own inimitable way.

16. *The thawing words*

The tale of the frozen sounds which thaw out in the hearing of Pantagruel and his companions occupies chapters LV and LVI. It is a major episode. Rabelais prepared the ground for it thoroughly. But once more his ideas have become obscure, not least because his allusions and terms of reference have become obscure also.

It is worth some time and trouble to try and understand these *Parolles dégelées*. The chapters given over to them are partly of interest because they contain remarks about words made by a master of the craft of using them; more important, they contain the reflexions of a great comic philosopher, written in the final stages of his life, on what constitutes truth for men in the world as it is.

It might be wise for anyone reading this study to refresh his memory of chapters LV and LVI. That will allow us to deal more effectively with detail, without trying to tell Rabelais's story for him and without making excessively long summaries or paraphrases.

We jump from the Papimanes to the thawing words in half-a-dozen lines. They tell us how the heroes spent their time in pleasant eating and drinking, accompanied by civilised conversation (QL LV, 1-7).

This civilised conversation deserves a comment. The phrase which Rabelais uses is: *divisans et faisans beaulx et cours discours*. Here is Platonic etymology in action. The suggestion that all 'fair discourse' is naturally brief, not long-winded, is contained in the rime *cours: discours*. To this is added the discreet suggestion that the word *diviser* ('to exchange conversation') had supplied the first syllable of the word *discours*. In its context this etymology has all the marks of being a serious one, explaining a French word by French associations, not by hopping about from one language to another. And it is, of course, quite distinct from the fustian silliness of punning rebuses, based upon 'inept, tasteless, rustic and barbarous homonymies', which the ignorant confused with hieroglyphic emblems in *Gargantua*. It is also distinct from the more ingenious comic homonymies by which Rabelais so successfully provokes the amused laughter of the attentive reader. Sporting with laughable etymologies whilst, in the same books, reverently seeking true and revealing ones, is yet another variant of Rabelais's delight in presenting, often at one and the same time, both the serious and the comic faces of a question, a dogma or a dearly held conviction. Making *discours* derive from *diviser* and *cours* (the plural of *court*, 'short') is the mystical antithesis of the sort of laughable nonsense we find scattered throughout the Chronicles; it is in keeping with the kind of etymology expounded by Socrates in the *Cratylus* and elsewhere. Fair discourse, it is suggested, has its true meaning rooted in both these words. Civilised conversation is an exchange of brief remarks, not an exercise in monologue or suasive rhetoric. Homenaz has just shown us how hollow these latter things may be.

Analogous points are made later in the same chapter, when we are told how Orpheus's lyre, struck by the moving winds (*les vents mouvens*), harmoniously 'accorded its chords' to the singing of his severed head. This is not so much poetry as etymology put to work suggestively (*QL* LV, 83–5).

Tales of frozen sounds thawing out were not unknown to Rabelais's readers. A travellers' tale of such sounds, situated in Muscovy, finds its place in Castiglione's *Courtier*. (Rabelais alludes to this book in the *Tiers Livre* in such a way as to show that he expected his readers to be familiar with it.) In addition, seamen coming home from distant journeys to strange new lands told similar tales (*QL* LV, 72).

In ancient times, Plutarch (79A) used the theme metaphorically: Antiphanes (he tells us) compared Plato's teachings to frozen words which only thawed out as one grew older in wisdom. The idea is taken up by Calcagnini in an elegant little fable to be found in the same volume which inspired or influenced other parts of the *Quart Livre*. Addison treats the subject in *The Tatler* for Thursday 23 November, 1710.[23]

All the earlier uses of the theme of thawing words can be assumed to have been known to Rabelais; but neither separately nor in combination do they explain his meanings in these chapters. To understand these pages more fully we must refer again to chapter XIX of the *Tiers Livre*. That was where Rabelais last put into Pantagruel's mouth his theory of language.

To go back to that chapter is not an arbitrary act. The thawing words are an extension and modification of the ideas expressed there. Both episodes partly derive from the same legal source: from glosses on Book 45 of the Roman *Digest* which is entitled, *On the Obligations of Words*. Rabelais was especially intrigued by the first law of this legal title. It states that, 'A

---

[23] Useful note in *The Tatler*, vol. IV, London 1797, pp.424f. Cf. Calcagnini, *Opera*, p.638; Castiglione, *Libro del Corteggiano* II, §1v (*Opere*, ed. Cordié, Milan 1960); *La Letteratura Italiana* 30, pp.155–6). The story in Baron Munchhausen to which the note in *The Tatler* refers appears to be a later interpolation, not found in versions available to Rabelais.

deaf mute who understands from the movements of lips is *not* allowed to stipulate'. This was challenged by jurisconsults, despite its being defended by Bartolo of Sassoferrato. It was a well-known legal bone of contention.

This section of the *Digest* is concerned with signs other than verbal ones. Rabelais showed in both *Pantagruel* and the *Tiers Livre* that non-verbal signs are quite capable of conveying meanings. Nazdecabre, the deaf-mute of the *Tiers Livre*, is directly linked by Rabelais with this first law of Book 45 of the *Digest*, and, as such, has a special meaning for those who know their Roman law.

At the beginning of chapter XIX of the *Tiers Livre*, Pantagruel first keeps silent, probably under the partial influence of Plutarch's ideas in his treatise *On Garrulousness*. Having noted that Panurge was seduced by the Devil, Rabelais draws on Plutarch's treatise to make a further point: the most certain oracles of antiquity were held to be not those which were expressed in words (*parolles*) but those which were expressed in signs. Or so Pantagruel had read. This preference for signs over words was because classical oracles gave excessively clipped verbal replies and because words (*mots*) are full of 'amphibologies, equivocations and obscurities'. Such was the opinion, we are told, of 'the good Heraclitus'. And indeed in *On Garrulousness* Heraclitus is shown as conveying his opinions by sign and gesture rather than by speech (*TL* XIX, 1f.).

When Rabelais revised the *Tiers Livre* in 1552, just after the publication of the full *Quart Livre*, he added the words in italics in the following sentence dealing with oracles: those prognostications 'which were expounded *by gestures* and by signs (*par gestes et par signes*) were considered the most true and certain' (*TL* XIX, 14). The additional words are not an example of idle padding. Rabelais is at pains to make us classify gestures with signs; for such they are. This will enable him to apply to gestures – dominant in parts of his chronicles since *Pantagruel* – the linguistic, legal and philosophical theories applied to signs. It will also allow him to apply to other signs analogous theories traditionally applied to gestures.

Already in the first version Rabelais had gone beyond the strict warrant of the legal text which Pantagruel cited to support his contention (Bartolo's gloss devoted to explaining the sense and implications of the law *On the Obligations of Words*). There we find Rabelais's own example of an Italian deaf mute, immortalised in legal history. This man, Nello de Gabrielis, could lip-read: that was evidently a rare and somewhat mysterious accomplishment. Twice the gloss states that Nello could understand what people said by watching their lip-movements (*motus labiorum*). Pantagruel, on the other hand, claims that Nello could understand a man talking at the sight of his *gestures* and the movement of his lips (*à la veue de ses gestes et mouvement des baulevres*). The interpolation of the words *par gestes* earlier in the chapter prepares the way for this extension of the legal text. In law the word gesture (*gestum*) has a precise meaning, namely a matter (*res*) treated without words (*sine verbis*).[24]

If we are to avoid the trap of falling into semeiological error, it is important to realise that by sign Rabelais often means gesture, especially when talking of human beings. In *Pantagruel*, the *Tiers Livre* and the *Quart Livre*, episodes making us laugh at certain kinds of language or bringing us to doubt its efficacy lead on to physical gestures thought of as signs. In *Pantagruel*, the Babel of Panurge's languages leads to Thaumaste's gestures – gestures which are called signs and intertwined with allusions to texts, real and imaginary, classical or Biblical, dealing with *semeia, signa*: 'signs'. Pantagruel's reflexions on the obliqueness of classical oracles lead to Nazdecabre's signs, specifically corrected to 'gestures' by implication. In the *Tiers Livre* (XIX, 73f.) the point which has just been made seriously is made again comically. Sister Fessue's bottom makes 'signs' indicative of the pleasure she was finding in illicit love-making; nobody is taken in by her claims that the bouncings of her bottom were (given her vow of silence in the dormitory) equivalent to verbal cries for help! As Panurge says – rightly for he is erudite despite his silliness – in matters of love, signs (*signes*) are more attractive, efficacious and valid than words (*parolles*). Repeatedly in *Pantagruel*, *Gargantua*, and the *Tiers Livre* deceptive or deliberately ambiguous use of words is contrasted with concrete gestures.

The *Quart Livre*, in the episode of the thawing words and Messere Gaster,

---

[24] *Lexicon Juridicum. Hoc est juris civilis et canonici in schola atque foro usitatarum vocum Penus*, Cologne 1615, s.v. *gestum*. Cf. Bartolus on *Digest* (Basle 1562 edition, v. 423f.) *D. XLV. titulus I, De verborum obligationibus, Lex I, §7 (Mutus et surdus, qui intelligit ad motus laboriorum, non potest stipulari)*: 'I ask, what if there is a deaf mute who can understand by seeing the movement of lips, such as Nellus Gabrielis de Eugubio, who, because of his great perspicacity, even though he cannot hear, does understand from their lip movements everything that people say, however secretly. . . . ' It would seem that he was entitled to make legal stipulations, since he did understand what was said. Bartolo disagrees: 'I believe the contrary, since the law requires that men should understand through the sense of hearing and the sound of the voice (as in *l.i, in fin, ʒ tit.i.*) and not by the movement of the lips or by other gestures (*seu alio nutu*); for what is the difference between the movement of the lips, or of fingers or of shoulders, in which there is motion? None, certainly.' The *Additiones* show that this judgment was widely challenged. The points raised in these challenges are directly relevant to the chapters consecrated to the thawing words. This makes the links between *TL* XIX and the *QL* even closer (see below, pp.432f.). (Alciati does attempt to temper Bartolo's judgment, but is forced to accept that, where stipulations are concerned, words and words only are a legal requirement: no gestures of any kind will do instead (Alciati, *Opera* 1560, III, 290 r°; *De Verborum Significatione*, 247). The judgment of Bartolo is supported by Johannes de Imola who also knew Nellus de Gabrielibus (as he calls him): despite his skill at reading lip movements he could not stipulate: 'it is required that one hears the sound of the voice; it does not suffice that one should perceive by signs (*signa*), as you can see in the same *l. § si quis ita.*' But contracts other than stipulations càn be made. (There is a full discussion of the position of deaf mutes in Roman Law in Andreas Barbatia's *Commentaria in titulum De Verborum Obligationibus*, Bologna 1497 (*BL*, at *IC*, 29202, leaf [9]f.).

continues this process with massive comic precision. Messere Gaster's signs are not human gestures: he is not sufficiently anthropomorphic for that; but they will prove to be physical, certain, natural and unambiguous. The *Quart Livre* is a climactic book, explaining so many matters which the earliest books simply laughed at or passed over lightly.

Rabelais showed in *Pantagruel* that signs (gestures, that is) may be divided into two categories. First there are those which signify naturally, being understood from one culture to another: such are to cock a snook; to suggest sexual intercourse by thrusting the index-finger on one hand in and out of a ring made by the index-finger and thumb of the other; to show disapproval by pointing to one's anus and then to another person; to indicate stench and rejection by pinching one's nose and pointing at someone. In contrast to these, there are signs of the second category: signs the meaning of which have been learnedly and wisely imposed. Such signs include certain physical gestures used by initiates but are not limited to them. When these signs are verbal and consecrated by convention, they are language. When they are physical they include learned kabbalistic gestures and solid non-verbal signs such as Egyptian hieroglyphs and Renaissance emblems. Such signs are understood *only* by the initiated. And they *do* know. Nobody else can or does.

To mix up the categories is comic. Natural physical gestures can only be misunderstood by fools – including learned ones: hence the happy laughter at the expense of Thaumaste. Kabbalistic and hieroglyphic signs will be misunderstood by everybody, unless and until they are allowed into the secret of their conventional meanings: the silly non-initiate will even confound them with punning rebuses.

But these signs are all, in relationship to words, solid and concrete. Verbal signs are the 'lightest of things': *levissima res* (Erasmus, *Adagia* III, 1, 18). They can be twisted to mean anything. Most of them – because of the confusion of languages – are meaningless to most people anyway.

Except in certain legal contexts concerned with the right to stipulate, gestures and signs were not considered as essentially different from words, either spoken or written. All were symbols either naturally or by imposition. The comic potential of misunderstandings of signs, gestures and such-like symbols – verbal, hieroglyphical, emblematical, heraldic, kabbalistic, mimetic, natural – is a recurring preoccupation. It is laughable to think that one can understand them naturally in the cases where their meaning has in fact been imposed: funnier still to think one can impose meanings of one's own on to symbols which *do* signify naturally or supernaturally.[25]

---

[25] Cf. *Aristotle, On Interpretation* (with commentaries of Thomas Aquinas and Cajetan), ed. J. T. Oesterle, Wisconsin 1962, p.40: 'Then, he says, *by convention* is added because

In the *Tiers Livre* solid physical gestures and other non-audible signs are above all contrasted with words, since words are ambiguous shifting things. There *is* no natural language; Pantagruel refused to give credence to the one and only example usually cited to defend such a notion – Herodotus's account of an experiment arranged by King Psammeticus. The king claimed to have proved that the natural language of mankind was Phrygian. It was Panurge who cited it not Pantagruel. Pantagruel dismissed it on transparently Aristotelian grounds. It was in this context of the ambiguity of spoken oracles that we were told about the deaf-mute Nello de Gabrielis, regaled with an account of Nazdecabre's gestures and brought to laugh at Sister Fessue's interpretation of the alleged meaning of *her* gestures as she bumped her bottom about during forbidden pleasures.

Rabelais could not have chosen a more striking way of defending his Ammonian linguistics than by rejecting the validity of the experiment of Psammeticus. The story of the isolation at birth of two poor boys, subjects of Psammeticus, who eventually said *bekos* ('bread', in Phrygian), is re-told by Polydore Vergil in the third chapter of the first book of his compendium, *On the Inventors of Things*. What is in Polydore Vergil became standard knowledge among educated men. Since this chapter specifically deals with 'The origin of the variety of languages' it is very much to the forefront of most discussions on the nature of words and language generally. Louis Le Roy defends the miraculous origin of language with this example alone.[26]

The episode of the *Parolles dégelées* and the chapters which follow take up again these themes of words, signs and their meaning – or lack of it. These chapters are complex ones, but understandable when put back into the

---

nothing is by nature a name, etc.' Here Aristotle explains the third part of the definition. The reason it is said that the name signifies by convention, he says, is that no name exists naturally. For it is a name because it signifies: it does not signify naturally, however, but by institution. This he adds when he says, *but it is a name when it is made into a sign,* i.e., when it is imposed to signify. For that which signifies naturally is not *made* a sign, but *is* a sign, naturally.' Aquinas then goes on to treat 'unlettered sounds' such as animals make.

[26] Louys Le Roy, dict Regius: *De la Vicissitude ou Varieté des choses*, Paris 1579, Livre 2, sig. d. 4f.: 'Now, while speech (*la parolle*) is natural to men, yet they only talk artificially, by hearing others talk, first mothers and nurses, then the crowd (*le commun vulgaire*). Wherefore, of necessity, those who imposed names on to things, since there was nobody from whom they could have taken them, must have learned them miraculously in a language where the nature and truth of things accorded with their origins and etymologies: these one strives to find, up to the present day, in all languages, in the meanings of their vocables. The Jews give this honour to their language, that they judge it to be the first and oldest in the world.' Then follows the account of the Phrygian boys and King Psammeticus. Le Roy adds that 'Pythagoras attributed a sovereign wisdom to him who first imposed names on to things; and Plato in the *Cratylus* affirms that this was done by a superhuman power.' (The whole of this section would be worth quoting if space allowed.)

intellectual context in which Rabelais wrote. This intellectual context embraces Plutarch, Aristotle's *On Interpretation*, Plato's *Cratylus*, Ammonius Hermaeus, Celio Calcagnini and that great mass of commentaries on Roman law which formed the delight of so many Renaissance authors. And, as often, the Bible is cited with crucial importance.

Rabelais is now, with the *Parolles dégelées* and the following chapters, about to confront ambitiously the problem of the possibility of human knowledge within this transitory life. Some of his assumptions are Platonic.

Plato in the *Cratylus* is not primarily concerned with language as a means of communication between men. That view is Aristotelian and is accepted by some of the best legal authorities of the Renaissance: by Alciati for example in his treatise *On the Meaning of Words*. For Plato, on the other hand, language is above all a means of acquiring knowledge by putting the speaker into contact with reality: speaking is an action which puts one into relationship with things. It is this which makes the proper naming of things a possible source of knowledge. If words have natural meanings, then to know the word can be a way of knowing the thing (or, indeed, as Le Roy points out, of harnessing its powers in magical ways).

In the *Quart Livre* Rabelais is closer to this Platonic notion of language than he was in the *Tiers Livre*, although in both the books he is concerned to show how language can also be a barrier to understanding or reaching the truth.

As a follower of the Ammonian tradition Rabelais can have his cake and eat it. He can hold that there is no natural language and yet assert that wise name-givers gave some words senses in accord with the natural qualities of the thing signified. This means that words can sometimes put one into direct contact with truth itself, especially if one realises that the denial of a natural language does not exclude supernatural forces being at work.

But before looking more closely at that assumption it is necessary to remember that Rabelais, like Aristotle, made the meanings of words depend on both the arbitrary imposition of the word-creator *and* on the acceptance of the symbol by convention.

Lawyers in the humanist tradition were well aware that these two forces of imposition and convention did not always work in harness. The debased Latin of the glossists they despised was an example of a slack and ignorant convention replacing an earlier classical convention lost in the long night of gothic darkness.

Classical Latin and classical Greek were special cases in which words had long since been established in their true sense by ancient convention. The scorn felt by the French partisans of the Gallic method of legal study for the partisans of the Italian method is connected with this. Scholars of the Gallic method sought to recover the meanings of words in classical Latin and Greek by a study of the convention represented by good ancient usage in the best authors; scholars of the Italian method sought to interpret ancient words in accordance with bad later usage or even later impositions, so getting it all wrong. A good, linguistically Aristotelian jurisconsult such as Alciati is especially sceptical about recent Latin neologisms: they can be made to mean anything. Not so classical words.

What Pantagruel had called in Aristotelian terms *les convenences des peuples* is accepted by all schools of thought. Rabelais sees departures from these *convenences des peuples* as always potentially funny. But if language were a matter of convention and nothing more, then it could not possibly be a vehicle for providing men with informed insights into the ideal truths underlying its symbols.

Rabelais believes that language has precisely this capacity for revealing truth – not always but in many cases, including the case of many proper names of men and gods.

In the *Cratylus*, Hermogenes and Cratylus defend opposing views, not only about language but about the nature of the universe. Hermogenes is a follower of Parmenides, for whom all things are fixed, stable, potentially knowable. Cratylus is a follower of Heraclitus; for him all things are in a state of flux, unknowable in themselves yet knowable through their names, since true names correspond to things in a natural way.

Ficino's commentary christianises the *Cratylus* in accordance with his standard practice. It plunges us into Hebrew names and into his usual learned combination of kabbala and prisca theologia. God (we are told) first inscribed his divine law on the minds of men, writing only coming later. The Jews were fully aware of the real power inherent in names. As for the Platonics, 'a true name is nothing other than the power of the thing itself, first . . . conceived in a mind, then expressed as a word (*vox*), and finally signified by letters'. St Paul accepted this doctrine: the name of God was, for him, 'sharper than a two-edged sword'.

According to Ficino, Socrates approved of the doctrines of *both* sets of major protagonists in the *Cratylus*. The doctrines of Heraclitus and Cratylus are correct, but only where physical things are concerned: the doctrine of perpetual flux applies to this world of ours. On the other hand, the doctrines of Hermogenes and Parmenides are also true; they apply to the realm of metaphysics: in the celestial realm we do find permanence and stability. In the *Quart Livre* Rabelais accepts this interpretation, significantly modified.

But it is noteworthy that even a thorough-going Platonist like Ficino remains essentially Aristotelian in an Ammonian sense about language: in the last resort, the natural connexions of names with things (except in the case of the divine names) is a matter of wise imposition by a wise name-creator. To trust names is therefore potentially misleading: the name-giver might have given names which correspond, not to things as they really are but as he thought they were. That is a considerable concession. But then, Ficino held Ammonius in high regard (Plato, *Opera*, ed. Ficino, Lyons 1590, 769f.; Ficino, *Opera* II, ii, 1544–5).

To return to the *Cratylus* itself, Plato leaves everything undecided. Socrates would prefer to believe that, while sensible things are in a state of flux, there are nevertheless, in the mind of God, eternal, immutable ideas or forms, corresponding to the multifarious particular objects of this world. This doctrine is put forward with striking tentativeness.

The question being faced is one of universals. From the time of Socrates onwards it has struck the unphilosophical as silly. Yet it is a serious one.

Plato postulated that for each set of particular objects an idea or form existed in Heaven. These ideas were often thought of as existing in the mind of God. To know such an idea is indeed to know something.

Aristotle opposed what are essentially common-sense objections to Plato's theory of ideas, but he perspicaciously noted that the entire theory resulted directly from Plato's acceptance of the Heraclitean principle that everything in the world is in a state of flux.

Heraclitus is a name to be conjured with in Rabelais's writings. When questions of meaning or symbol are raised he is often to the forefront. One might have expected a fervent admirer of Socrates such as Rabelais to sneer at Heraclitus and to reject his opinions. But Ficino had shown that it was possible to accept the opinions of both Heraclitus and Hermogenes without challenging those of Socrates. Heraclitus and his doctrines certainly underlie Rabelais's beliefs in the later chapters of the *Quart Livre*. This is not entirely new. Rabelais from his early scholarly writings onwards regularly attributed to Heraclitus the metaphor normally attributed to Democritus, which placed truth at the bottom of a deep well. For the laughing Rabelais the tearful Heraclitus is rather surprisingly the *bon Heraclite*. A strong Heraclitean thread runs through all his Chronicles.

Ficino maintained that it was unthinkable that the human race should have been left without any divine instruction. In his *Commentary on the Cratylus* he asserted that such divine instruction must have been vouchsafed to men at the Creation or after the Flood. He believed that this divine enlightenment consisted in the truth which the inspired name-givers veiled in the etymologies of certain words. Noting that Socrates introduced his theory of ideas with the Greek verb which he translates into Latin as *somniare* ('to dream up'), he suggests that Socrates used this word because the mob and the Greek comic authors laughed at his theory of ideas. On the other hand, knowing ideas through the mind's activities *is* akin to dreaming, since the soul is coming into contact with higher entities outside this world. Ficino accepts that the ideas have a real and stable existence, but the soul comes into contact with them in circumstances which resemble dreams. As he understands the *Cratylus*, Socrates in his conclusion means 'that the knowledge of things is to be sought not from words but from ideas, notions of which, grafted on to us, are the first and true names of things'. It is presumably these first and true names which can lead us back to the ideas which gave them their existence.

Finally Socrates warns the young not to try to resolve difficult problems too quickly. They should take a long time over the process of learning, reaching maturity before they judge difficult matters.

This in brief is the background against which the thawing words acquire their fuller significance.

Ficino's commentary shows how differently the *Cratylus* was interpreted in the Renaissance from whatever we think it means today. The *Cratylus* was used to defend a bundle of concepts, some of which would have surprised Plato: the prime importance of Hebrew names, for example; of kabbalistic knowledge; of the mysterious nature of the name of God in all known languages.

Ficino defends the vital power of names properly imposed and the doctrine that not names but the ideas themselves are the source of truth. Rabelais saw all this from the distorting standpoint of Ammonius's interpretation of Aristotle. But he was not content to remain passive. There are sure signs in the *Quart Livre* of personal reflexion, of personal commitment. Whatever he owes to others, he also read the *Cratylus* for himself. Because of this he even dared to differ in emphasis from the divine Socrates.

17. *The words and sounds thaw out*

Pantagruel is the first to hear the thawing sounds. They are not in fact words (*parolles*) despite the title of chapter LV; they are *voix* and *sons*. This apparently establishes the distinction between meaningful verbal utterances (*voces*) and brute noises (*soni*), accepted by Ammonius after Aristotle. Rabelais also uses the word *voix*, a few sentences later, with the sense of human voices.

The repetition of words and concepts is an important aspect of these chapters. It points their meaning: the heroes drank in the air, 'pour entendre si *voix* ou *son aulcun*' were to be heard; 'Protestions *son aulcun* n'entendre'; 'Pantagruel continuoit affermant ouyr *voix diverses* en l'air, *tant de hommes comme de femmes*'; 'discernions les *voix*, jusques à entendre *motz entiers*'; 'entendons *voix* et *sons tant diverses, d'hommes, de femmes*, d'enfans, de chevaulx'. In this last example we have the standard division of aural signs into *voces* (*voix*, fully human verbal utterances) on the one hand, and on the other noises made by children, horses, or inanimate objects like squeaky wheels.

Voix and *sons* abound in these pages; but not so *parolles*. Rabelais uses the term *parolles* most sparingly. *Parolles* are now being distinguished not only from 'sounds' but from other human utterances represented by *voix*. Among all the sounds which abound in these pages, the word *parolles* found in the chapter-heading is applied only to words of Homer and Plato. We read of *parolles de Homere*; as for Plato's doctrine, it is likened to the frozen words which Plutarch wrote about, to *parolles . . . qui . . . gelent*.

In chapter LVI, the maelstrom of sound is even more pronounced, comic in its effect, profound in its implications.

Rabelais, the philosophical comic artist with words, is creating a myth to explain the relationship of some words to truth.

Panurge, on hearing the thawing sounds, wants to run away. His babbling attempts to justify his cowardice are akin to all his attempts to turn black into white from the *Tiers Livre* onwards. As in the praise of debts and debtors he twists words and great moral *exempla* out of context in order to apply them to his own immoral purposes: Brutus, defeated at 'Pharsalia' (or rather at Philippi), refused to seek safety in flight; alluding jocularly to the adage 'by the hands and by feet', the great Roman declared he would only run away 'by hands', that is, by stoically taking his own life. Panurge affects to believe that Brutus was a coward like himself, seeking to run away from danger! In his own opinion he differs from Brutus only in wishing to make his escape more maritime in flavour, not 'by hands and by feet' but (in the words of a parallel adage), *remis velisque* ('by oars and by sails') (*QL* LV, 29f.; Erasmus, *Adagia* I, 4, 15 and 18).

Such are the confusions one can spin out of words, when the Devil, fears and *philautia* muddle the mind. *Philautia*, as always, blinds a man to truth however cogent. Never has Panurge's brutish fear been more inappropriately displayed; he may well be in the presence of truth, yet all he wants to do is to run away. All our laughter at his expense during the Storm or the whale-hunt comes flooding back to mind. This foolish man is blind to truth.

We know that we are in the presence of truth, because Pantagruel tells us so in a myth. The source of this myth is a mysterious passage in Plutarch's *On the Decline of Oracles* (422A-E). To understand the full import of what Pantagruel says demands close analysis. To do this requires paying sustained attention to some of the words and expressions which he uses to render Plutarch's original Greek. His choice of words is the key which opens up to us the profound sense of his mystery.

Pantagruel calls upon his companions to pay attention: 'Mais entendons.' He then plunges into his philosophical myth:

I have read that a Philosopher called Petron was of the opinion that there were several worlds (*mondes*), all touching each other, in the form of an equilateral triangle; he said that in the hearth and centre of them was the Manor of Truth (the *Manoir de Verité*). And there dwell the Words (*Parolles*), Ideas (*Idées*), the Forms and Patterns (the *Exemplaires et protraictz*), of all things, past and future; and around them is the Age (the *Siècle*).

(This last clause is one which proves pregnant with meaning: *et autour d'icelles estre le Siècle.*) Pantagruel goes straight on to say:

And in certain years, by long intervals, part of them drops down upon mankind like catarrhs, and like the dew dropped down on the fleece of Gideon; part remains there, set aside for the future, until the end of the Age.

Again, the last phrase proves to be full of meaning: the words Rabelais uses are, *jusques à la consommation du Siècle* (QL LV, 51–62).

Rabelais, as a good Renaissance humanist, is 'veiling truth in fable'. Such men did not create their fictions so as to make their ideas immediately clear to all and sundry: the inner meaning must be looked for beneath the veil. The ultimate implications of the myth do not become finally clear until the episode of Messere Gaster which is to follow. But there are clues in plenty in the myth itself.

Rabelais's myth is an adaptation of the doctrine of the obscure Greek philosopher Petron, who is known only from Plutarch's account. In the treatise *On the Decline of Oracles* (422B-E), he appears not long after the history of the death of Pan. Plutarch wrote about Petron in order to show the real source of the teachings of a rather pretentious *guru*, met by his friend Cleombrotus on the far shores of the Red Sea.

Rabelais simplifies and condenses the account, making striking changes to it, in order to adapt it to his own mythic purposes. According to Plutarch's account of Petron's teachings, *Logoi*, Ideas and *Paradeigmata* (Patterns, or Models) dwell inside mystic celestial triangles surrounded by Eternity (*ho aiōn*), part of which flows into things which are in time (*ho chronos*). The central field of the celestial triangle wherein dwell the *logoi*, the ideas and the patterns is called the Plain of Truth (*kaleisthai de pedion alētheias*). This Plain of Truth inevitably calls to mind the Plain of Truth for which Plato in the *Phaedrus* (248B) uses the same words: *to alētheias pedion*. Plato believed that human souls seek the Plain of Truth in order to free themselves from the tyranny of opinion (*doxasma*). This was elementary Platonism, widely known.

In Plutarch there is a religious dimension to the myth: the Plain of Truth is the reality of which all the religious mysteries of men are but a dream; it is the beauty that philosophy seeks if she is not to waste her time on meaningless pursuits. This is not directly germane to Rabelais's myth and so is quietly discarded, in the sense that no specific reference is made to it. But it is not in fact forgotten. The following episodes show that the truth Rabelais is preoccupied with embraces the Christian revelation: indeed, it is primarily concerned with it.

Rabelais changed the name Plain of Truth to *Manoir de Verité*, partly to link it up with the death of Pan and its *Manoir des heroes*, even more in order to link this chapter to the next episode, which is concerned with Hesiod's *Manoir de Vertus* (which is not a plain but a high and fair plateau). It may also be relevant that Turnèbe, explaining this passage of Plutarch a few years later, refers indifferently to the 'plain', 'seat' or 'region' of truth.

Pantagruel alludes directly to Petron's philosophy, but most of Rabelais's original readers would not of course have compared what he says with what Plutarch wrote. For us today the clue is a great help. By comparing Rabelais's French with Plutarch's Greek we divert our minds towards important aspects of Rabelais's thought in these pages which might otherwise escape our adequate notice.

We might first of all mark the names that Pantagruel gives to these celestial dwellers in the seat of truth. For Pantagruel, *Parolles* as well as *Idées* and *Exemplaires-et-protraictz* dwell in the heavenly triangle. Yet *Parolles* is emphatically not the word we expect to find being used to translate Plutarch's wide-ranging term *logoi* in this context. For Rabelais this translation is vital: it alone links together Petron's doctrine and this part of the *Quart Livre* with its words: frozen, thawing, and now celestial. It is vital for his myth that the heavenly Plain of Truth should contain words as well as ideas. In Petron the *logoi* are probably reasons or causes. In Rabelais human speech may reflect not only celestial ideas and celestial patterns but even partake of the celestial words, however these words are to be explained. These words, unlike some earthly ones, are true by the very nature of their dwelling in the seat of truth.

The next most meaningful of Rabelais's departures from the original text are kept to the end. They show once more how his thought readily combined Platonism and Christianity in a syncretic union where Christian doctrine dominated. This is not least true of his creation of veiled myth and fable throughout the *Quart Livre*.

For Petron, the dwellers in the Plain of Truth are motionless. In this respect they conform to Platonic teaching. Round about them lies eternity. (The word Plutarch uses for eternity is *aiōn* ('aeon').) It is not from the immobile *logoi*, ideas or patterns that Petron's motion proceeds, but from the surrounding eternity. From thence a stream of time flows into things temporal.

Much of this Rabelais changes, christianising this part of *On the Decline of Oracles* as thoroughly as he had Christianised the history of the death of Pan.

What surrounds the dwellers in Rabelais's *Manoir de Verité* is named *le Siècle*: the word *Siècle* is regularly used to translate the Biblical and liturgical term *saeculum* ('age'; the period which stretches to the end of time). This translation will prove an important one.

What flows into things-temporal in Rabelais's myth is not *le Siècle* but part of the actual words, ideas and patterns themselves: *part d'icelles tomber sus les humains*. This 'part' is described as falling down on mankind in two striking comparisons: 'comme cattarrhes, et comme tomba la rouzée sus la toizon de Gedeon.'

The other parts of the *Parolles*, *Idées* and *Exemplaires* stay where they are. They do not drip down on mankind. But they do not last for ever. *Parolles, Idées, Exemplaires* last only *'jusques à la consommation du Siècle'*.

These are fundamental changes. With them Rabelais has succeeded in bringing his myth closer to the *Cratylus* while making it conform to the teachings of the Gospel. It is no longer an ancient myth of time and eternity; it is a myth of celestial words and ideas lasting to the end of the Christian epoch.

In Rabelais's re-writing of Petron, droppings from the Seat of Truth will fall down on man until *la consommation du Siècle*. This phrase is by no means an obvious one to use in a classical Greek context. By using this term (for which Plutarch gives no warrant) Rabelais places the myth within the context of Christian eschatology. And the phrase he uses does so more clearly than any other short formula could possibly do. There is only one source for the phrase *la consommation du Siècle*, from which it entered into Christian language and consciousness: Matthew's Gospel.

The words *la consommation du Siècle* are a direct translation of the term *consummatio saeculi*, by which the Latin Bible renders Saint Matthew's Greek phrase, the *sunteleia aiōnos*. This expression, traditionally rendered in English as 'the end of the world', means something like 'the consummation of the age' – the end of this 'world' which culminates in the final establishment of Christ's kingdom. In the Vulgate the expression which Rabelais takes over, the *consummatio saeculi*, appears five times – in each case in eschatological contexts, within Matthew's Gospel (13: 39, 40, 49; 24: 3; 28: 20). These words appear thrice in the parable of the sower (a parable concerned with the Judgment to follow hard upon the *consummatio saeculi*); once specifically and directly in relationship to Christ's Second Coming; fifth and lastly in the final words of the Gospel: Christ's promise to remain with the faithful 'until the end of the world'. We have in Rabelais a specific echo of the end of Matthew's Gospel: *jusques à la consommation du Siècle* directly translates, *usque ad consummationem saeculi*; *'even unto the end of the world'*.

The links with Plutarch's account are now tightly forged. Rabelais does this by so translating Plutarch as to bring him closer to Matthew. In all five texts where the Vulgate refers to the *consummatio saeculi* the Greek original uses the same word 'aeon' (*aiōn*) which Rabelais translated in Plutarch's case too as *le Siècle*. Plutarch uses this word for the eternity which surrounds the Plain of Truth. Xylander rendered this *aiōn* by *aeternitas*. But Rabelais, to prepare his readers for a Christian interpretation of Plutarch's myth, translates it by the Christian term. (The Biblical and liturgical word *aiōn* is regularly translated in Latin as *saeculum*. The English liturgical phrase, 'world without end' corresponds to the Latin *in omnia saecula saeculorum*.) By using this Biblical and liturgical word *siècle* to translate Plutarch's classical word *aiōn*, Rabelais brings Petron's myth into the field of meaning represented by the sense of the word as used by Matthew. It was by no means the obvious term to employ. Like Xylander, Amyot arouses no Christian associations in his translation: he uses the word *éternité*. But in Rabelais, distillations from the seat of truth itself fall down on to mankind across the surrounding aeon, and that, not for an unending classical eternity, but until the *sunteleia aiōnos*, the *consommation du Siècle*, the 'end of the world' – until, that is, the 'consummation of the age' which will mark Christ's Second Coming, the Judgment and the destruction of the world as it at present exists.

So much in so few words.

In a period of commonly shared culture such complex meanings could be quietly achieved. Rabelais does not have to shout and scream to show what he is doing: he can introduce Christian eschatology into Petron's myth by the effective device of rendering both Plutarch's *logoi* and his aeon by words which evoke Christian terms of reference, foreign to the world of Plato and Plutarch.[27] It was in ways such as this that many humanist evangelicals married the partial and veiled classical wisdom they so much admired to that clearer Christian revelation, by the light of which they lived. Rabelais's Christianity, like that of so many of the humanists whom he admired or lived among, including Erasmus, welcomed Plato and welcomed Plutarch. It could find ways of incorporating aspects of classical Epicureanism, Stoicism, Scepticism, or almost any eclectic mixture of classical thought. But over all was placed the philosophy of Christ.

18. *The 'catarrhes' of the* Cratylus

First Rabelais gives us the fundamentally adapted myth of Petron; next he adds Platonic terms of reference by echoing the *Cratylus*; his dominant Christian philosophy both guided the adaptation of the myth and led to its

---

[27] The Greek text of Plutarch available to Rabelais differs from that current today on one or two vital points. Especially noteworthy is the reading at 422c. Rabelais follows the reading, accepted also by Xylander, according to which the *aiōnos* (*siècle*) flows into the things which are 'in time', not into 'the worlds'. (A scribal confusion between *Chronos* and *Kosmos* is quite understandable.) Cf. Xylander, 422B: 'All those things are motionless (*immobilia haec omnia*); and about them lies Eternity (*aeternitas*), of which a part, as though flowing down, is borne into things temporal' – *aeternitatem, cujus quasi defluens quaedam portio feratur ad ea quae sunt in tempore*. The Loeb translates this passage as: 'and round them lies Eternity, whence time, like an ever-flowing stream, is conveyed to the worlds' – *epi tous kosmous*. Rabelais, by accepting the reading *epi tous chronous* makes the down-flowing from the Plain of Truth something which will cease at the end of time.

being placed within the meaningful limits of Christian eschatology. The consummation of the age will bring to an end the period during which words, ideas and patterns drip down upon human beings *comme catarrhes* (QL LV, 59).

Before looking more closely at the striking comparison, 'like catarrh', we may note the downward motion which Rabelais suggests in his myth. This is absent from Petron. Rabelais's universe is the same as the one we meet for example in Macrobius's *Commentary on the Dream of Scipio*. The world is seen as the ultimate recipient of the waste matter of the universe. The off-scourings, excrements and material rejects of the higher spheres sink down naturally on to our round world. There they stop: they can go no further. Downward motion stops with this world. This is a commonplace, clearly set out, for example, in Pompeo della Barba's *Discorsi sopra il Platonico et divino sogno di Scipione* (Venice 1553, p.34r°).

Such a cosmology was standard in Renaissance as in mediaeval times. There was no need to stress it; things were simply assumed to be so. Rabelais's comparison *comme catarrhes* is, on the contrary, neither standard nor routine; nor is it merely colourful. The words *comme catarrhes* are as energetic and meaningful as they are unexpected, if their source is not recognised. They reveal Rabelais as an Heraclitean, accepting the doctrine that everything in the universe is in a state of flux. Rabelais in some ways even goes beyond Socrates's doubts and hesitations in the *Cratylus*, plumping for a doctrine that the divine Socrates was troubled by, would like to have refuted but could not succeed in proving wrong.

The expression *comme catarrhes* is an echo of the end of the *Cratylus*, where it appears twice. The Greek word for catarrh, *katarrhoos*, is not common. Apart from one use taken from a medical work (Hippocrates's *Aphorisms*, no doubt representative of a wider medical currency), the examples cited by Liddell and Scott are all from Plato: one from the *Republic* and two from the end of the *Cratylus*, from the *locus classicus* being evoked here.

In his next to last speech in this dialogue, Socrates, still troubled by the thought that if everything is constantly changing we can know nothing, returns to the teachings of Heraclitus. He tries to counter them by stressing that if beauty and the good do exist in stable immobile heavenly ideas, forms and patterns, then some knowledge becomes possible. But supposing truth were to lie in the teachings of Heraclitus after all, which are held and taught by so many people? Socrates cannot resolve the dilemma. Yet can a man of sense renounce all hope of really knowing anything at all, except by relying entirely on the power of names and their etymologies? Is it wise to have recourse to words alone, entirely trusting in their authors? Must a man view the world as being like leaky earthen pots? Must he see all things as analogous to men suffering from catarrh (*hōsper hoi katarrhō nosountes anthrōpoi*) accepting, in fact, that everything is suffering from rheum and catarrh (*hupo rheumatos te kai katarrhou panta ta chrēmatā echesthai*)? Socrates hesitates. Perhaps so. Perhaps not.

Cratylus is impressed, adding nevertheless: 'I much prefer the doctrine of Heraclitus' – that is, the world of leaky pots and dripping catarrhs.

So did Rabelais in its Christian garb. In Pantagruel's account of Petron's myth the very dwellers in the seat of truth, the *Parolles*, the *Idées* and the *Exemplaires*, are destined to go partly leaking down on to mankind until the end of the world, falling on to mankind like a rain of catarrh. The assumption is, of course, that they were created for that end. At the *consummatio saeculi* their distillations will cease, when they themselves are 'reserved' for other things. By making even the dwellers in the seat of truth partake of the general flux of the world, Rabelais has most effectively christianised and de-platonised the central core of his myth. God alone (as we were reminded during the visit to the Papimanes) exists as ever unchanging unalterable essence.

Yet it is from the *Parolles*, the words, and the other dwellers within the seat of truth, that enlightenment falls down on to mankind, especially where prophecy is concerned. That these dwellers include *logoi* conceived of as *Parolles* remind us that one of the ways in which man can find revealed truth is by a study of words – including a careful study of their etymologies.

It would be a mistake to try to turn Rabelais into a neo-Cratylistic Heraclitean extremist, in the sense that he believed knowledge could proceed from etymology alone. Apart from anything else he wrenched his myth too far from Plutarch, Petron and Plato for this to be the case. But with Socrates, as the Renaissance interpreted the *Cratylus*, Rabelais does believe that, sometimes, words do contain truths enveloped in their etymologies – that is what makes the ignorant punning *rebuses* of *Gargantua* so funny in one context and so stupid in another. Words at their best are part of the general enlightenment of mankind, which drips down on to them within this shifting world of ours, bearing globules of truth. As for proper names, they may sometimes be endowed with prophetic force by special grace. When the proper names are those of gods, their meanings may be especially meaningful. One of the manners in which the old pagan gods survived was in this way. Christian writers often sought and found mystical truths veiled in their names or in their attributes.

Such ideas Renaissance men either found in the *Cratylus* or else read into it. If we turn to André Turnèbe's note on this part of his Latin translation of *On the Decline of Oracles* (Paris 1556) we can understand Rabelais better; it represents a thoroughly tenable contemporary view, not a private or idiosyncratic interpretation. The note was later reproduced by Johannes Camerarius in his *Two Books of Plutarch on the Nature and Effects of Daemons* (1576, p.98). Turnèbe's dedicatory letter to the Cardinal of Lorraine is not favourable to Rabelais's kind of divination. But his note on Petron's *Plain of Truth* is very apposite: our world is 'the region of the false and of opinion; hardly anything here is really sure; we know few things definitely and with certainty. In most matters we are either wrong or can only have opinions; but the other world can be perceived by reason and intelligence. In it are the ideas and patterns of things: that is, the region of truth and her seat.'

Turnèbe goes on to cite the relevant part of the *Phaedrus* and points out how close these doctrines are to Plato's.

Petron's myth and doctrine in their original form in Plutarch were taken as emphasising the contrast between the world of mankind, the domain of opinion, and the mystic world, the dwelling place of stable and unchanging *logoi*, ideas and patterns, where alone truth may be found and whence all earthly truth and justified certainty do proceed.

In the *Quart Livre* the myth has an analogous sense in its adapted form. It embodies the substance of themes found elsewhere in Rabelais: that this world is merely transitory, subject to change, generation and corruption, lasting only until Christ hands over his kingdom to the Father. Meanwhile the only knowledge that man has is a divine gift, a *manne celeste de bonne doctrine*, or perhaps a more individual gift of grace such as Bridoye's gift of prophecy or Pantagruel's gift of wisdom. In all cases knowledge and wisdom derive from the Father of Lights. Such revealed truth culminates in the Christian revelation but was not confined to it: the classical world and other ancient cultures had their share of it.

Considerations such as these take us back to the text of Rabelais, to those drippings down from on high which were not only 'like catarrhs' but also 'like the dew' which fell at God's behest on Gideon's fleece and not on the surrounding ground. Theologians of most persuasions were in general agreement over the *altior sensus* of Gideon's story. They accepted the allegorical interpretations adopted by Origen and Augustine: Gideon's fleece represents the elect, on whom descends the dew of the teachings of the word of God as set forth by prophets, apostles and Christ himself (cf., amongst many other examples, Lewis Lavater, a Zwinglian minister of Zurich, in *Liber Judicum, Homiliis CVII Expositus*, 1585, p.41; and the Jesuit Cosma Magalianus, *In Sacram Judicum Historiam Explanationes . . .*, 1626, II, xi, pp.597f.).

Chapter LV is dealing with grace and vouchsafed revelation to be found in certain words (*parolles*). Such revelations *may* sometimes be made through the inner meanings of names as well as by other means.

As for the *logoi* existing in heaven alongside the Platonic ideas and patterns, both the Old Testament and the New, as well as the Platonic philosopher Porphyry, seem to be behind Rabelais's interpretation of them as words (*parolles*).

Nothing in classical Greek thought justifies placing 'words' within the seat of truth. And nobody except Rabelais (as far as I can tell) had ever taken Petron's *logoi* to be words. But classical Greek texts look different when read with the meanings of Biblical Greek uppermost in mind.

To complete this chapter, Rabelais makes three further classical allusions: to Aristotle's eulogy of Homer's lively words; to the thawing of frozen words applied to Plato's teachings; to the song proceeding from Orpheus's severed head.

The eulogy of Homer's words is brief but striking. Pantagruel remembers hearing that Aristotle had said that Homer's words (*parolles*) were 'fluttering, flying and moving – and therefore animated', that is, endued with soul (*'voltigeantes, volantes, moventes, et par conséquent animées'*). To find Homer praised in a Heraclitean context is to be expected: Socrates lumped Homer and Heraclitus together on the question of the doctrine of flux (*Theaetetus* 122B). Rabelais is freely adapting here a judgment on Homer related by Plutarch, this time in the treatise *On the Oracles of the Pythian Goddess* (398A). There Aristotle is cited as saying that Homer was the only poet who used names (*onomata*) 'endowed with movement, because of their vigour'. Aristotle is not credited with saying that Homer's words were *animées* ('endowed with soul', 'with *psyche*'); but later on in the *Oracles of the Pythian Goddess* (404F) things which are animate are said to be 'endowed with movement'. Rabelais has glossed one part of the treatise with another: or, if he did not, an intermediary source did so for him.

In addition to these qualities of movement and 'animation' applied to Homer's words, Rabelais makes them *voltigeantes* and *volantes*. The second of these two epithets at least can only be an allusion to the epic phrase 'winged words' (*epea pteroenta*). This is frequently used by Homer rather than of him. It is once found in Hesiod. Rabelais may be following Erasmus (*Adagia* III, 1, 18: *Levissima res oratio*).

The sense would be: that the words of such as Homer who was privileged to be touched by the catarrh or dew dropping down from the seat of truth have souls, as it were, which soar up on wings from earth to heaven: an essentially Platonic notion. In this way man's upward striving is linked to the distillations of catarrhal dew.

Alciati, more cynically, thought that Homer's 'winged words' refer to the light things that mere words really are. That notion was in Rabelais's mind too: it comes to the fore in the following chapter.

In terms of the application of the myth, no hint is given about which poets or prophets are endowed with these winged words apart from Homer. It is no part of a myth like this to be over-explicit. But in his explanation of the real meaning of the death of Pan, Pantagruel cited a line of Virgil in a Christian sense (*QL* XXVIII, 54f.).

The second classical allusion, to Antiphanes's likening of Plato's doctrine to frozen words which only thaw out when his listeners grew old in wisdom, is already an apologue in Plutarch and Calcagnini. In terms of Rabelais's myth, words of wisdom from the philosophers are not to be supposed to be easy to understand. Rabelais, an old man, is warning us that a lifetime of thought and reflexion is necessary to understand the inspired words of the great thinkers. There may be an echo of the closing sentences of the *Cratylus* here too; if so, the echo is one of theme not of vocabulary.

Rabelais's final classical allusion is not to words as spoken but to words as sung, as well as to musical sounds. We are beautifully reminded of the lugubrious singing issuing from Orpheus's severed head as, with his lyre stirred to music by the wind, it was borne down the River Hebrus to the isle of Lesbos in the Pontine sea. The eventual poetic sources are the fourth book of Virgil's *Georgics* and Ovid's *Metamorphoses* (QL LV, 73f.).

Orpheus was so widely important a classical figure for Renaissance syncretists and mythologists that it is hard to be certain for which particular characteristic Rabelais chose to end this chapter with this striking allusion to him. Orpheus was a Greek David; the inspired singer who tamed beasts and the beast in man. The Orphic hymns, especially venerated by Renaissance Platonists, were interpreted as inspired revelations, individually vouchsafed to the good and pure Orpheus, by which he was inspired to sing of the one true God and of the Christian Trinity. This gave Orpheus the theologian a place of unique honour among those inspired ancient philosophers whose veiled knowledge of revealed Christian truths fascinated Renaissance platonising Christians. He is much to the fore in Ficino's commentary on the *Cratylus*.

At the very least, Rabelais is making a claim for song and music to join with inspired wisdom as beneficiaries of distillations from the seat of truth. The *Quart Livre* is striking for the place it gives to music. Nearly sixty composers are mentioned by name in the prologue.

The myth is now complete, so far as chapter LV is concerned.

Words, so often the noisy vehicles of mere opinion which triumphs in this world of ours, can exceptionally convey truth. Such truth as they convey derives from divine revelation: from catarrhal dew dripping down from the ideal words, forms and patterns dwelling in the seat of truth.

This seat of truth and the great entities which dwell therein are not themselves eternal nor exempt from change: their purpose will be fulfilled within time. The ideal words, forms and patterns are destined to enlighten mankind with vouchsafed revelations until the end of the age: the *consummatio saeculi* which will seal the fate of the world and all its inhabitants. Meanwhile, the words in which revealed truth is stated or sung have to be cherished, meditated upon and thawed out, if the message that lies within them is to be found.

Rabelais implies that amidst the flux and manifold changes of this transitory world some little verbalised truth is to be found, as and when it is revealed to man. Appropriately enough in a series of Chronicles marked by the cankered Muse of laughing satire, these revelations are seen not only in high Judaeo-Christian terms as welcome dew from heaven but in grosser Heraclitean terms as a rain of catarrh.

The word *catarrhe* in French was Greek enough to have some nobility. But the basic comparison is amusing, at least in part. The dignity of the word *catarrhe* was such as befits a learned word for an unheroic ailment; no more. Satirical writers take pleasure in deflating human pretentiousness by emphasising our bodily grossness. Catarrh is one of those physical byproducts like sweat, dribbling, urine and faeces which Rabelais uses to this effect; it had the additional advantage of being an ailment.

The uglies excluded from Thelema were (in a delightful pun) *catarrhez et mal nez* (*Garg.* L, 47). But in a sense all mankind and the world in which we live can be thought of in such snotty terms.

Rabelais's myth is concerned with revelation, which can introduce some truth and certainty into a world given over to mere opinion. The veil of his myth is not so thickly woven that we cannot see through it by the light of what has gone before and of what there is to follow.

That everything that man knows is a gift of grace is a theme met in Rabelais's Chronicles from the outset. The truths that Rabelais held dear in theology, law, medicine, philosophy, divination, poetry – all truths in fact – are not the fruits of human conquest but drop down from heaven like a spiritual manna. This applies to more fields of scholarship and learning than a modern might suspect. A Renaissance Christian humanist was not a blinkered man. He sought his wisdom from among the sacred writings of Egyptian hieroglyphs; from Greek philosophy; from the inspired medical knowledge of Hippocrates. Great classical precepts such as 'Know Thyself' were embraced within his concept of revelation. So too were adages and proverbs, which were imbued with a dark mysterious power which made it not surprising that they bore traces of truth within them. As for Roman law, it was thoroughly christianised. The *Pandects* are headed with an invocation of the name of Christ; its first law places jurisprudence in the context of both human and divine affairs. As Bridoye and Pantagruel showed in the *Tiers Livre*, law's final appeal was to Fortune and the *Justus Judex* who is God. The terms which Pantagruel uses in his myth also apply most appositely to prophecy.

Naturally, a Christian humanist such as Rabelais gave pride of place among all revelations to what is called in the prologue to the *Quart Livre*, the 'sacrosaincte *parolle* de bonnes nouvelles, c'est l'evangile'. Rabelais owed that very expression of praise for the Gospel to the Gospel (Acts 15, 7: '*ton logon tou euangeliou* – the *word* of the Gospel'); to the whole tenor of his age he owed his veneration of Socrates as a vehicle of 'divine' knowledge, endowed with 'superhuman' understanding. And so, in vary-ing degrees, for all the truth which formed the lasting heritage of the ancient world, Jewish, Egyptian, Greek, Latin. . . .[28]

The wise man picks his way through the complexities of this world by seeking the marks of revealed truth. But such truths are often expressed in words. And words, as every book of Rabelais has shown, can be either vehicles of lofty philosophical or religious truths or else, at the other extreme, light, trivial, empty, noisy things. They can also be devilish snares, catching the unwary and making black seem white.

The *Tiers Livre* was impregnated with grace and revelation. The wise Pantagruel owed his wisdom to it. In this he was no different from the inspired Bridoye and Triboullet, the heaven-touched fool. The *Quart Livre* carries this one stage further. This world is a world of flux and change. Nobody remains fixed and unchangeable: not even Pantagruel. In the *Tiers Livre* Pantagruel's authority lay, we now see, not within his human self, but in the revealed authoritative force of the wisdom he drew upon and in the gift of wisdom he had received from God. In the *Quart Livre* (where, until towards the end, Pantagruel says very little), even *his* words, like any other man's, can at times be vague, unclear or deformed by the requirements of politeness, irony, or what you will. The authority of what a man says or writes depends on the extent to which his words partake of the revealed truth. Pantagruel's do not do so all the time. Not now. When Pantagruel cites the Gospel in the agony of the Storm, he is exemplary. When he praises the Papimanes in words having no intrinsic authority he is not – at least, not at a literal level. As the *Quart Livre* progresses he becomes more authoritatively correct when he is most directly inspired; such inspiration is increasingly a matter of right decision on his part: of a 'yes' or 'no', inflexibly decided under inspired guidance (*QL* XLVI, 7f.).

But truth clothed in words can be misused by self-loving man and ingenious devil. In Rabelais's Chronicles the only way open to man to distinguish truth from error and to avoid being misled by slippery rhetoric and perverse argumentation is to hold on to truth supernaturally revealed. Without it the black may indeed seem white; the white, black.

We know – or we should know – that Panurge is wrong in his praise of

[28] Words are often associated with the divine in Scripture; cf. Psalm 50 (51),4: God will be justified 'in his *logoi*' (cf. Romans 3,4). Rabelais's *logoi* dwell in the manor of *alētheia* (truth): cf. Revelations 19,9 (where both notions appear). But such *logoi* are not divine (Revelations 21,5; 19,10 and context). By placing his *logoi* within created time, Rabelais has made it possible (even obligatory) to interpret them in the light of Biblical Greek; he has also made it impossible to interpret them as an allusion to Christ himself, the supreme *Logos*. In the following chapters reference is made to the Ten Commandments (the *deka logoi* as Deuteronomy 10,4 calls them). Any – or none – of these associations may be evoked by Rabelais's word *Parolles*. But insofar as he is evoking scriptural *logoi* he is more certainly thinking of the '*logos* of the Gospel' (*QL*, prol., 22).

debts and debtors, just as he is wrong, say, in his defence of cowardice; his misuse of venerated sayings and authoritative wisdom cannot be hidden by his web of verbosity. We know – or should know – with greater clarity still, that the Papimanes are wrong, since they go against the imperatives of the greatest verbal revelation of them all.

If we do not know the truths which a Renaissance evangelical humanist might believe to be revealed – and if we cannot put ourselves imaginatively in his place – then we shall simply prove the rightness of what Rabelais affirms, being unable to distinguish truth from falsehood. Modern common-sense alone will not help us much to understand his works. The conventions of the satirical eulogy did not lie, for example, in a weakening of the form of the eulogy but in misusing the matter. The *declamatio*, so favoured by Renaissance authors and so influential on Rabelais's writings, deliberately mixes strong arguments and weak ones, the serious and the comic, the true and the false, and it does this without losing sight of its ultimately serious intention.[29] Unless one knows where revealed authority lies, one gets lost in the cloud of words.

19. Noise

Chapter LV shows through myth how some human words share in the truth, thanks to distillations from on high.

The traditional reading of Aristotle's *On Interpretation* sometimes expanded the two categories into which speech was classified – verbal utterances with imposed meanings; animal-like noises with natural ones – into several others. This was made easy by the explanation given by the third century scholar Porphyry – the *philosophe argut* of the *Tiers Livre* XVIII, 142 – whose ideas were incorporated in the glosses and whose treatises, for some Renaissance dialecticians, were intimately bound up with Aristotle's. Porphyry explained Aristotle's need to define at the outset the terms latinised as *nomen* and *verbum*, because the ancients believed that verbal utterances signified forms and ideas as well as mental conceptions, sense perceptions, sensations, or things which exist. A scholar such as Nifo was uneasy about this assertion, but it was widely known (Aristotle, *Peri Hermeneias*, ed. W. A. Niphus, Venice 1555, p.12). Inspired words in Rabelais came into the first category. They alone are called *Parolles*.

But the time has come for Rabelais to have a good philosophical laugh at other categories of sound, both *voces* and *soni*.

In both the *Tiers Livre* and the *Quart Livre* the comedy of man's situation and of the questions posed by Rabelais does not only, or even at times

---

[29] Cf. H. C. Agrippa: *Apologia adversus calumnias propter Declamationem de Vanitate scientiarum et Excellentia Verbi Dei sibi per aliquos Lovanienses Theologistas intentatas*, 1533, ch. 42.

primarily, arise out of men misunderstanding each other. It sometimes arises from the often silly efforts of men to battle through a mass of verbalised pseudo-knowledge, interlarded with truths and half-truths, to such wisdom as has been vouchsafed them in this world.

Verbalised truth is especially hard to acquire. (One only has to recall the enlightened ingenuity required of an Erasmus, a Pantagruel or a Gargantua to get at the kernel of truth lying within the apparently fatuous or immoral gnomic sayings of ancient sages cited in the *Tiers Livre* XXXV.) Even in its most authoritative form, Holy Writ, it was conveyed in words – vehicles of thought capable of being misused, misunderstood, perverted by self-love or devilishness. The Bible as cited by Pantagruel is a different thing indeed from the Bible as cited by Panurge.

In the *Tiers Livre* Pantagruel with his normative wisdom and his massive classical and Christian lore could guide our footsteps and show up Panurge's folly for what it was. But all did not revolve around Pantagruel alone. Another way to reach certainty was the simple trust of Bridoye; yet another way to escape from the 'amphibologies, equivocques et obscuritez des motz' was seen to lie in the use of gestures and of signs – gestures in fact rather than signs, in chapter XIX where the question was raised.

Chapter LVI of the *Quart Livre* takes up this theme afresh. Rabelais is about to tell us, from chapter LVII conwards, about the signs which govern most of human life – all that part of human life not bathed in the light of verbalised revelation. But before he does so he has his last joyful Ammonian fling at the laughable clatter and chatter of words and sounds; for, in this life, inspired words have to take their place beside noises of all sorts.

Chapter LVI is a laughing, funny, farcical chapter, forming a diptych with the serious mythology of chapter LV. We are made to find certain types of words and sounds comic. But not in the void. This chapter is linked with both the *Tiers Livre* and the previous chapter by certain shared assumptions and preoccupations. They also have a source in common: it is still the first title of Book 45 of the New Digest: *On the Obligations of Words*. This is the context in which Rabelais places his laughable noises. The joke is as much a legal one as a linguistic one.

It was a knotty legal problem how far one had to have exclusive resort to words in circumstances where gestures can also be significant. Many jurisconsults could not accept Bartolo of Sassoferrato's refusal to permit a skilled deaf-mute such as Nello de Gabrielis to make legal stipulations by signs, even though the signs were perfectly understandable. In order to maintain the stricter view that words – and words only – made stipulations valid, it was necessary to interpret in exclusively audible terms some of the common synaesthesias found in all languages. There were prolonged disagreements involving some of the great names of late mediaeval and Renaissance glossists over, for example, how far it was permissible to say one had heard something (*se audivisse*) in circumstances where another person would say he had seen it (*se vidisse*). These quarrels were often attached by gloss or reference to just that part of the *Digest* to which Rabelais alluded in the *Tiers Livre*. And they turn up in glosses on Canon Law as well.

To show how even scripture allowed such synaesthesias, legal authorities quoted Revelations 1,12, *Conversus sum ut viderem vocem* ('I turned round to see the voice'). They also cited the great example of Exodus 20, 18; there the people of Israel, fearfully watching while Moses went up into the mountain to receive the divine law, *videbat voces* ('saw the voices'). This cryptic phrase of Exodus is cited by both Roman and canon lawyers in their glosses. These are the very bases which Rabelais takes for his jokes in chapter LVI, as a simple reading of the texts will show. The relevance of all this to the philosophy of the *Quart Livre* is that *voces*, in linguistic parlance, means human utterances on which meanings have been imposed; and that such *voces* can be interspersed with sounds which have a natural meaning. Rabelais sets about playing with various other meanings of *voces*, making them things that can be felt, heard and seen. It is Panurge who alludes to the legal chestnut: 'I remember having read that the people, beside the mountain on which Moses received the law of the Jews, saw the voices with their senses' – *voyoit les voix sensiblement*.[30]

Rabelais's pilot in the *Quart Livre* brings the myth back to earth and to the dimensions of a travellers' tale. The thawing words are said to be the frozen remains of the sounds of a recent battle. Pantagruel and his companions handle them, cast them on the deck, thaw them out. This, together with Panurge's tarnished authority, stops us from taking the

---

[30] *QL* LVI, 10f., and 38f. Compare this with the *Additiones* to Bartolus in *Ad lib. XLV Digest* (Basle 1562) v, fol. 423, *sub litera e* (on *De verborum obligationibus*, *lex* 1 § 7). Against Bartolo's refusal to allow a deaf mute to stipulate by signs we find a meaty gloss which includes a reference to the fact that some say *se audivisse* where others say *se vidisse*. After technical references to interpretations by Baldus and Alexander Tartagno on texts of the Digest, we find a defence of Revelations 1,12 (*Conversus sum ut viderem vocem*) and of the reading of Exodus 29 (*Cunctus autem populus videbat voces*). As for canon law, cf. *Decretum Gratiani*, with glosses of Hugo, Johannes Theutonicus, etc, Paris 1550 (*BL*, at 1600/196), fol. 257, col. 2; gloss on *que noverunt & viderentur*: 'that is, they perceived by any bodily sense. For *visus* (sight) is taken widely, as in the expression *Taste and see* [a reference to Psalm 33,9]; and in Exodus we find *Videbant voces* (they saw the voices), that is, they *heard* them.' So if one hears fornication (as distinct from seeing it) one can nevertheless testify to it: 'For it suffices that it should be known by some means or other (*Decretum: 22, question 5: Hoc videtur*). Even if someone is dumb, as long as he can hear and write he can properly testify (as *Codex, qui testa. fa. pos. discretis*).' Similarly a blind person can testify if he can hear: 'It is no objection to say that a blind person may be deceived by a verbal utterance (*vox*) (as in *27, question 1, Nec aliqua*), since we can also be deceived by sight (*31, question 1, quomodo*), and by touch (*34, question 2, in lectum*).'

allusion to Exodus as a serious theological point, even if we fail to spot the legal nature of the jesting. If Pantagruel had made this remark earlier, one might have been tempted to discover deeper implications in the curious phrase 'the people *saw* the voices'. They would have been easy enough to find. St Ambrose could supply quite a few: *voces* refers to the inner sense of the words 'seen' spiritually; in the New Testament St John did see the word incarnate (I John 1, 1–2), and so on (cf. A. Lippomanus, *Catena in Exodus*, 1550, p.192v°).

But such ingenuity would be misplaced. Not because the voices that the people saw were (it seems to modern scholarship) lightning flashes accompanied, by thunder; nor because Rabelais may not have accepted Ambrose's metaphorical interpretations of these texts. To look for the meaning in such authors would be wrong because the context is wrong. Where *seeing* words is concerned we are in the context of legal humour. Not only did the people of Israel 'see the voices', but so does Rabelais's fictional narrator: '*Et y veidz des parolles bien picquantes.*' Taking the verb *to see* literally when talking about 'seeing words' would have evoked standard amusing associations for lawyers. To check this one only has to consult Albericus and his legal *Lexicon*. Under *verbum* one reads: 'A word cannot be seen but heard' ('*Verbum videri non potest, sed audiri*'). The legal authority for this is *Speculator*, that is Guillaume Durand, author of the frequently reprinted *Mirror of the Law* (*Speculum Juris*). Similarly, again on the authority of *Speculator*, we read under *vox* this rather astonishing entry: 'A *vox* (verbal utterance) or word cannot be seen but heard, despite Aristotle's saying that some verbal utterances are white, others black.' Aristotle's 'saying' is an obtuse literal reading of an allusion to black and white words in his book of *Topics*. *Speculator* makes this statement when dealing with the circumstances in which a deaf or blind man may testify. He takes exception to a blind man saying that he 'saw' something when all he had done was to hear the words. Renaissance editions of Guillaume Durand often quietly point out what Aristotle meant (*Speculator*, lib. I, partic. 4, §7, *de teste*). By black and white words Aristotle means clear or unclear words, sharp or weighty ones. Such associations enable Rabelais to have a gay time with 'coloured' words. He starts with *motz de gueule*, 'gullet words' (words to do with eating); by a pun these words become not *gullet* but *gules* (the heraldic word for red). And so quickly we pass through words of other heraldic colours, sinople, azure, and sable – all meaningless – until we come to *motz dorez*, the 'golden words' associated with the name of Cato (*QL* LVI, 19f.).

We soon realise that this chapter is to be mainly given over to playing about like this with 'words'. There are classical puns, accessible through Erasmus's *Adages; donner parolles*: to mislead each other as lovers do (*QL* LVI, 31; *Adagia* I, 5, 49); *vendre parolles*: to sell words as lawyers, poets or makers of empty promises do (*Adagia* II, 6, 100). Even *parolles* can be abused.

Several of the jests depend on taking adjectives literally: 'sharp' words and 'bloody' words can be seen. *Prendre au mot*, interpreted literally, means to steal somebody's word; with an allusion to Rabelais's favourite farce of Maistre Pathelin, *vendre à son mot* ('at the agreed price') again gives rise to puns and laughter.

The cascade of puns is shimmering and entirely delightful. We are shown through laughter what slippery things sounds are. The sounds which thaw out in the arctic summer are not all made by humans, nor are they all 'words'. They include both words and cries (*parolles et crys*) of men and women, the shock of arms, the clatter of armour and caparisons, the whinnying of horses and other frightful noises of battle.

The noises prove, when thawed out, to be of the two sorts into which Ammonius classified them in his extended definition after Aristotle. They are conventionally meaningful verbal utterances and *agrammatoi psophoi*, unlettered sounds such as animals make. As we have seen, such 'unlettered sounds' were taken to include not only childish noises and direct expressions of emotions but the cries (vocal and non-vocal) of beasts themselves, as well as the noises made by inanimate objects – the rumbling of carts, the sound of the sea or the myriad other noises that men can imitate. This doctrine of Ammonius, clear enough in itself, was made the subject of influential commentaries, throughout the centuries. Rabelais, from all this welter of sound picks out two categories only as being genuinely and really meaningful: inspired *parolles* (which were treated above in chapter LV) and *agrammatoi psophoi*, unlettered sounds. All the rest of the noises – even human speech – is meaningful only to those admitted to the conventions to which they belong. So, some of the sounds are *motz*; but as they were in barbarous tongues, the travellers 'did not understand'. One *mot* when it melted turned out not to be a word after all but a sound: the discharge of a gun. Similarly, even several *parolles* are discovered to be, not words, but sounds akin to animal noises. These, by definition, are natural sounds, understandable across linguistic frontiers. And so we hear – and recognise for what it is – thin laughter, *hin, hin, hin, hin*, or the copious blubbering of *bou bou bou, bou bou bou, bou bou*. The various noises mingle in a new Babel, where only unlettered sounds are universally meaningful. Barbarous unknown words jostle with onomatopoeics. Some of these we have already met, especially in the mouth of Panurge. Others are new: *trac* and *trr, trr, trr, trrr, trrrrr*. And there is the strangely disturbing yet laughable *on, on, on, on, on, ouououon*.

In these chapters, with all their joy, Rabelais is, as often, getting his greatest effects by juxtaposition. He is contrasting brief learned *discours* and, more explicitly, those winged, inspired words endowed with real meaning from being touched by the catarrhal dew of heaven-dwelling truth, with the confusing din by which a man may be surrounded.

Apart from the 'unlettered sounds' the din means nothing in and of itself.

It is as if Rabelais were at pains to explain the comedy arising from Panurge's taste for spouting incomprehensible foreign languages since his appearance in *Pantagruel*. But his ambitions go farther. When we leave the barbarous tongues and the significant brute sounds to return to the French language, the conventions of which are known to readers of the *Quart Livre*, then the play on words leads to quarrels and offence: 'Panurge somewhat annoyed Frère Jean'; so 'Frère Jean threatened to make him sorry for it'.

Rhetoric, when venal, comes in for harsh treatment too: twice Demosthenes is mentioned: once in chapter LV, 6; again in chapter LVI, 36. This archetypal word-spinner is twice picked out for belittling treatment: he was a man who sold his silence for hard cash; a man capable of being as cowardly as Panurge.

Pantagruelists are never short of 'gullet words' in their stricter sense of words to do with food. But, as Frère Jean recalls, a man may be caught by his words as surely as a bull by his horns (LVI, 66). This legal axiom was associated especially with Durand's *Speculator* (lib. I Partic. 4, 9: end), the authority to which the reader is referred by Albericus's *Lexicon*. In Rabelais it is first met in the *Tiers Livre* (XXXVI, 130f.). In the *Quart Livre* it serves to bring back to mind the Pyrrhonism of Trouillogan (the regius professor and the philosopher of the new-style sceptical school), for Gargantua cited this axiom in the *Tiers Livre* in order to make an amused but favourable judgment on contemporary scepticism. Scepticism of a sort seems to have been in vogue. In this, as in so much else, law played its part. The *Speculator* points out that the Pharisees tried to catch Christ 'in his *words*' (Mark 12, 3; Luke 20, 20). And for a discussion of the implications of this, he refers the reader to the beginning of *De verborum obligationibus* in the Institutes.

Mere uninspired words may be noisy, ambiguous or even meaningless; they can nevertheless spread error and dissension. The maxim, 'Bulls are caught by their horns: men are caught by their words', in Frère Jean's mouth is a means of taunting Panurge: when Panurge is married he will seize him by his cuckold's horns, like the calf that he was reproached with being during the Storm.

Words used this way can lead to anything. This time Panurge gets the better of Frère Jean in the end, by not using words at all. He replies with a sign, making a gesture the meaning of which is unmistakable: 'Panurge feist le babou, en signe de dérision.' To answer Frère Jean's verbal insult Panurge *feit le babou*: that is, he kept flipping his lower lip against his upper one with his finger. In this episode, the only *word* mentioned after this is the *mot de la dive Bouteille*, the word of that Holy Bottle that the book will end without ever reaching.

Chapters LV and LVI form a pair, whose value depends upon their being viewed together. Chapter LV gives man hope: there is pleasure in discourse; pleasure in singing and music; truth to be found in human language when touched by revelation. Time and patience are needed to thaw out these revelations for the use of man. But not all sounds thaw out so meaningfully. Chapter LVI completes the diptych: apart from that, there is Babel. The babble of tongues nobody knows; confusions, misunderstandings, the threatening sounds of Gog and Magog, bantering, quarrels, rhetoric, amphibologies, equivocations, obscurities. The only noises which have an absolutely natural meaning, understood by all, are sounds akin to those made by brute beasts. They at least mean something, if only laughter, fear, the whinnying of a horse, the bang of a gun.

The appearance at this juncture of Gog and Magog, learnedly Germanicised as 'Goth, Magoth' (LVI, 4) may be more than a happy joke, despite the warlike noises of this chapter being the sounds of airy battles between Herodotus's one-eyed Arimaspians and the 'cloud-walking' Nephelibates. For, in Revelations 20, 8, Gog and Magog are to be set fighting by Satan, who 'gathers them together to do battle'. This confusion precedes the triumph of Christ's kingdom.

Perhaps one should not read too much into the mention of Gog and Magog – in mediaeval times they often simply stood for vague, barbarous nations. They may do so here. It is safer to fix our gaze for a while on the *amphibologies, equivocques et obscuritez des mots* which Pantagruel complains of in chapter XIX of the *Tiers Livre* – the chapter so intimately connected by source and concept to this episode of the thawing words. For Bridoye had found his way out of the wordy snares, the 'antinomies and contradictions of the law', by simple trust in divine guidance (*TL* XLIV). In the *Quart Livre* the guidance afforded by revelation is amply honoured. But in addition to such verbalised wisdom man has signs to guide him: signs with meanings that no-one can challenge.

Amid the welter of confusing sound a natural sign or gesture stands out as particularly meaningful.

The scholar in Rabelais would have been encouraged towards such attitudes by his studies of the law, not only because his main starting-point was the opening pages of Book 45 of the *Digest*, *On the Obligations of Words*. As Tiraqueau points out in *De legibus connubialibus* (Glossa 7, §17), one of the ways a man may sometimes give his consent in law is by 'nods or *evident* signs'. As for words, sources as basic as Albericus's *Lexicon* put the legal tyro on his guard against them, comparing them to fog or clouds, contrasting them with concrete things or subordinating them to active morality. Perhaps this is why Rabelais's battle of noise is fought by Nephelibates, 'walkers in the clouds'. As Albericus's editor stresses: 'For the illuminating of truth, the assistance of words is not required. We should not be concerned to make words flourish but morality. . . . And note that words are compared to winds, to clouds, to pelting rain.'[31]

20. *Messere Gaster*

Messere Gaster, the 'Signor Belly' who dominates the next island to be visited, exemplifies the meaning of this diptych in action. We are to be shown the vital importance of signs in the life of man. We are told how these signs must be controlled by other ones. We are shown also how the limits of these signs are fixed by truth and wisdom revealed to man in inspired words. And we see how scatology, by recalling man to his bodily squalor, is a sign which works with Christian revelation to keep man in his place.

That Messere Gaster works through signs we know: 'He talks only by signs. But his signs are obeyed by everyone, more quickly than the edicts of the praetors or the commands of kings' (*QL* LVIII, 46f.). This aspect of the belly's imperious nature is approved of by Pantagruel six chapters later, when the wise giant consents to answer his companions' doubts and questions. This he will do, not with long roundabout wordy speeches, but by signs:

The reply will be promptly expounded to you, not by long circumlocutions and discourse of words: the hungry stomach has no ears [an Erasmian adage II, 8, 84]; he hears absolutely nothing. By signs, gestures and actions will you be satisfied . . . (*QL* LXIII, 75f.).

The words that Rabelais uses to describe the 'signs, gestures and actions' by which we shall have a satisfactory resolution of our problems are *signes, gestes et effectz*.

And just as, in the *Tiers Livre*, Nazdecabre, the deaf mute's, gestures or signs were introduced with an allusion to Heraclitus and his preference for sign over speech, so here we are given an account of the famous use of signs by Tarquin, who 'par signes respondit à son filz Sex'. To lighten this rather gruesome example of the use of meaningful signs by the proud Tarquin, Rabelais introduces a parenthesis to show Frère Jean, as a true monk, immediately reacting to the stimulus of another sort of sign: the bell which Pantagruel accidentally struck (LXIII, 81). It sends a true monk like Frère Jean dashing off to the kitchen.

In the above quotation Rabelais puts together *signes*, *gestes* and *effectz*. Each word is important. The significance of the alliance of sign with

---

[31] See Albericus's *Lexicon*, s.v. *vox, verbum, signum, mutus, surdus*, etc. Later editions are preferable: they contain additions.

gesture has already been commented upon. By adding *effectz* to the list Rabelais opens his gates on to a far wider field of meaning, throwing a sudden new light, retrospectively, on to all his Chronicles. We now see that under the general heading of signs Rabelais specifically includes *actions.* A prime meaning of *effect* in French and *effectus* in Latin was precisely *action.* As such, *effet* was constantly being contrasted with *paroles.* Corneille was working a standard theme when he wrote that anyone who pays attention to actions – *effets* – can ignore mere words:

> *Et qui songe aux effets néglige les paroles* (Pompée II, 4).

Albericus has a rubric s.v. *verba:* 'Are we to take more notice of *words* or *actions (verba* or *effectus)*?' The answer is unhesitating: actions speak louder than words: an ignorant priest's barbarous Latin, for example, is unimportant: his good morality is very important.

By linking *effectz* with *signes* and *gestes,* Rabelais shows that his bundle of concepts is widely inclusive. Signs, gestures and actions are diverse facets of the same complex notion. Signs and gestures can themselves be subjected to the same classification as words, in so far as some are naturally significant, some are significant in accordance with imposed, conventional meaning. Not so *effectz,* actions; for not only do they speak louder than words, but they speak more certainly. (A true Christian is recognised by what he does, not merely by what he says. So is a philosopher.)

In the episode of Messere Gaster we move into the context of signs, gestures and effective actions the meanings of which cannot be doubted. In the course of Rabelais's Chronicles, many, many things have come under these headings. To these, sometimes ambiguous, signs and gestures – ambiguous because not all have meanings known to other than the initiate – are joined the clearer signs which are actions. Frère Jean's saving of the abbey and his toiling to save the ship were both *effectz:* effective signs and gestures, to be contrasted with the misleading battological wordiness of his fellow monks at Seuilly or the parallel, superficially pious, verbosity of the frightened Panurge during the storm. In these cases pious words were belied by cowardly deeds, while selfless deeds belied coarse and super-ficially blasphemous words.

It is an easy matter to gather together from Renaissance texts many examples of *effectz* being allied with *parolles* or contrasted with them. In Montaigne it is a commonplace. In English too the association was absolutely routine, a phrase such as *in effect* formerly meaning 'in fact, in reality, opposed to *in show* or *in words*'. It might at first sight seem less easy to understand how Rabelais could link together in one complex semantic field sign, gesture and action. But on second thoughts the semantic linkage is clear enough: a good man's actions are both a manifestation of his professed convictions and a token of his real beliefs. In the case of a good, brave and sincere man, his deeds are symptomatic of his beliefs. This sense is specifically attested in Renaissance English where one of the obsolete meanings of *effect* was 'an outward manifestation, sign, token, symptom' (*NED*). (Cf. also Huguet, *Langue du XVIᵉs.*, s.v. *effet*).

Words can be easily twisted and deformed. They can be misunderstood or made deliberately misleading. Actions are far more certain.

Messere Gaster argues by signs in this sense. The belly's signs are pangs of hunger; his ultimate argument, starvation unto death. Such signs are unambiguous: *effectz* which speak louder than *parolles*.

Because of the very unambiguity of the belly's signs, he acts as the supreme driving-force in human society. He is, in an established term, the *Magister Artium*, the 'Master of Arts'. Although Rabelais is probably the first author to apply the term to the belly in modern times, the title, as satirically applied to the belly, goes back to classical Latin literature. Greek literature has parallel usages. The need to grow and raise food, to store it, protect it, distribute it, led not only to agriculture but to all the manifold complexities of human society: this is an idea Rabelais could read in his Plutarch, and probably did, though he takes it much further. There is no end to Messere Gaster's ingenuity. Give him a magnet, and he will invent a means of using its negative poles to repel cannonballs. . . .

The satirical, cynical tone of the opening chapters devoted to Messere Gaster is striking. It recalls – and rightly recalls – the great Cynical diatribes of classical times. In the last resort Messere Gaster does it 'all for the guts', *Tout pour la trippe!* Diogenes the Cynic would have understood that. Diogenes was a hero for the Stoics too, and so could preside over the partly Stoic *Tiers Livre*; but he still retains something of his dog-like view of the world and passed this on to Pantagruelism. It is as a Christian Cynic that Rabelais returns complaisantly to the refrain, *Et tout pour la trippe!*

Messere Gaster was not the only candidate for the title of *Magister Artium*. Erasmus in the *Praise of Folly* gave this rôle to Folly herself – and was accused of heresy for doing so by the irascible Sutor of the Sorbonne, since God was the author of the arts! Erasmus soon made short shrift of him (*Ep.* VI, p.305). Ficino developed at some length the claim of love to play that rôle. His *Commentary on Plato's Symposium* contains a chapter headed, *That Love is the Magister Artium and the Governor*. A contemporary reader who could follow Rabelais at all seriously would have seen the joke of the belly, not love, being held to be Master of Arts and the *Gouverneur* of his island! Ficino, in order to defend his paradox that love was the driving-force in all creation, had to jumble together all sorts of love: *philautia* as well as *eros* and *agape*. His animals kill and eat each other out of love for themselves! Such a concept does seem to deserve Rabelais's refrain: *Et tout pour la trippe*. . . .

Another candidate for the title of *Magister Artium* was put forward in an oration delivered in Paris in October 1551 by Nicolaus Charton, an extreme partisan of the new-fangled dialectic of Ramus and the rhetoric of Omer Talon. It is tempting to see Rabelais mocking such things too, in a book where Ramus and his quarrels are laughed at in the prologue. According to Charton it is dialectic which is the *omnium artium domina et gubernatrix*, being the 'parent and procreatrix of arts'. But Ficinian Platonism and its *Magister artium Amor* seem stronger candidates for satirical mockery; anyway, one may not exclude the other.

Like Erasmus, Rabelais could distinguish sharply between some aspects of authentic Platonism and certain idiosyncratic developments of Ficinian Platonism, which they both reject. In Rabelais, love is put firmly where Plato put him; he is the offspring of Poros (Plenty) and Penia (Want), whose task was to mediate between heaven and earth, 'comme atteste Platon *in Symposio*'. That is quite unlike the love of Ficino's *Commentary* in its fullest development. Even as mediator between heaven and earth, love is the subject of only passing reference in this episode.

When Panurge developed his praise of debts and debtors he misused Platonic and Ficinian arguments to defend his indefensible case. This could mean that Rabelais was already mildly jesting at Ficino's concept of a so-called Platonic love which kept the macrocosm, the microcosm and their parts in harmony. It need not be so: Panurge misuses many good arguments. But in the *Quart Livre* the conclusion seems inescapable: Platonic love as Ficino conceived it was good for a laugh. Love as Plato himself conceived it is another matter: love is a link between heaven and earth; it is not a dominant element in the actual life of creation and in man's collective endeavours here on earth.

Satire of Ficino is an element in these chapters, but it is incidental to the main theme. That Messere Gaster is the driving-force in man is an idea with a very respectable classical antecedence. Rabelais had only to change a word or two here and there to tap a very rich ore of proverbial material. That is why any departures from the classical commonplaces take on some considerable importance.

When describing love as the offspring of Penia and a latinised Porus (*Poros*) Rabelais went beyond Plato and Plutarch, where the myth also appears, making Penia also the mother of the nine Muses. That is quite unclassical; and this time Calcagnini, despite his frequent allusions to Penia, is not an influence.[32] The claim is an arresting one, widely extending

---

[32] *QL* LVII, 30f. Cf. Plato, *Symposium*, 203B,E. Calcagnini treats of Poros and Penia several times (*Opera*, pp.244, 610, 916, etc.). Cf. Plutarch, *De Iside et Osiride* 374c. Readers of Plutarch, Erasmus, Calcagnini and Rabelais will note that the same commonplaces may be found in them all. This is important: Rabelais's authorities were reinforcing each other. For example Rabelais goes on to talk of Harpocras, god of Silence, surnamed *astomos*

the scope of this Cynical verdict on human activity and industry. By making Penia produce the Muses, Rabelais allies her to Gaster, who produces the arts. In all fields of human endeavour the driving-force is fear of want, of hunger, of starvation. In fact Penia and Gaster are really one and the same figure behind their comic masks. Messere Gaster is basically a renaming of the Penia of classical proverbs, fused with classical *limos* (hunger) and touched by greed. The wisdom that Rabelais is pressing into service was condensed into adages and literary commonplaces. Most are not far to seek: they are in Erasmus's collection.

Once again Rabelais is putting powerful new wine into old bottles. He is adapting to his own purposes several classical proverbial truths as expounded by Erasmus. The most influential of these is *Want produces Wisdom* where Want is *Penia*, the 'inventor of many arts'. Erasmus takes us through texts of Virgil, Theocritus, Aristophanes and so on, all of which give this arrestingly vital rôle to Want. The two most strikingly apposite authors are Ps–Theocritus and Aristophanes, both of whom make Penia into the Master of Arts. The beginning of a poem of Ps–Theocritus (XXI, *Alieis*) is particularly striking, being Erasmus's own starting-point:

Want, Diophantos, is the only Master of Arts, the only Teacher of labour . . .

In Aristophanes's *Ploutos* (510f.) Penia praises herself at some length: she alone ensures that humans work hard; without her there would be neither art nor industry. Rabelais's allusions suggest that he was indeed also turning to his Greek comedians and tragedians, though not always at first hand.

In most of the classical authors whom Rabelais found explained by Erasmus, hunger, like his own Messere Gaster, is personified. The starting-point of Messere Gaster is Erasmus's explanation of *Want produces Wisdom*. To this basic adage, Rabelais joins others, notably *Hunger teaches many things* – where it is Hunger who is named the Master of Arts – and *A hungry man is not to be disturbed*, which is more than once in evidence in these closing pages of the *Quart Livre*. Rabelais also makes use of many more adages, including *The Belly has no ears*, *There is no contradicting Hunger* and *Saguntine hunger*. Not only the adages as such but Erasmus's essays on them are put to good account. Formative and important are two other adages: *Gasteres, that is, Ventres* and *Manduces*.[33]

(mouthless). Apart from more obvious sources this is also in Calcagnini, p.916; cf. QL LVII, 42f.)

[33] To establish Rabelais's debt to Erasmus and the *Adagia* it suffices to read *Paupertas sapientiam sortita est* (I, 5, 22) – the major source – as well as *Fames multa docet* (IV, 2, 48); *Famelicus non interpellandus* (III, 8, 12); *Venter auribus caret* (II, 8, 84) – which includes *Contra famem etenim nulla contradictio est*; *Vulpi esurienti somnus obrepit* (II, 6, 55); *Decempes umbra* (III, 4,

Rabelais, with striking and paradoxical originality, links Messere Gaster, conceived in terms of want and hunger, with Hesiod's famous myth of the Seat of Virtue (*Works and Days* 289): to reach virtue man must toil and sweat up a rocky slope. Hesiod's powerful myth was destined to become a favourite one with Renaissance poets. Rabelais gives it his own forceful twist by making want and hunger the driving-forces which gave man the force to struggle onwards and upwards to virtue. Once he has done so, Hesiod's fertile plateau of virtue stretches out delightfully before him. In this way earth has its *Manoir des Vertus*, while heaven has its *Manoir de Vérité*, dropping its enlightenment on to men (*QL* LVII, 21; LV, 55; cf. the *Manoir des heroes* of *QL* XXVI).

Rabelais takes care to use the Greek word for Virtue. This is the *Manoir de areté (c'est vertus)*. The effect is to recall that virtue in Greek (*aretē*) – like *virtus* in Latin – often bears a sense closer to active excellence than to the rather passive associations of the word in English or French.

Although the tone is bantering, the case made out is a harsh one, born of a realism about hunger arising both from personal experience and from classical wisdom, which united to stress the peremptoriness of the belly's demands.

Messere Gaster only talks by signs. But all the world obeys his signs more promptly than the edicts of praetors or the commands of kings. He brooks no delay, no lingering over his summons. You say that when the lion roars all the beasts quake – so far, that is, as his voice can be heard. It is written. It is true. I have seen it. I can certify to you that at the command of Messere Gaster the sky trembles, the whole earth moves. His order has been given: do it – or die (*QL* LVII, 45f.).

The *Quart Livre* is a comic book, so the terror evoked by Gaster is not incompatible with jests about 'the belly always going before'; but in no wise does this soften the blows. Sir Belly's orders must be met. He is a governor whom even kings and parliaments obey.

Yet he is no tyrant. He drives men not to gluttony but to civilised polities: he urges them to invent their arts, their sciences, the civilised products of their muses, the moral strivings of their natural virtue. Is Gaster then a god, if he is higher than kings and mighty potentates?

Having praised Messere Gaster in this striking way, Rabelais then proceeds to reduce him to his real level. A power so great as Gaster could be taken for a god, even though he seeks no such doubtful honour. Rabelais topples him from such an idolatrous height in several ways. To do so he calls canon law into play, as well as the Gospel and his classical authors.

Belly-worshippers are classified into two categories. The first consists

---

70); *Molestus interpellator Venter* (III, 10, 9); *Saguntina fames* (I, 9, 67), *Gasteres i.e. Ventres* (II, 8, 78); *Manduces* (IV, 8, 32); *Eurycles* (IV, 1, 39); *Ventre pleno, melior consultatio* (III, 7, 44). The list could be prolonged; the debt to Erasmus is a major one.

of ventriloquists – a word which then meant, not tedious comedians with talking dolls, but people possessed of spirits dwelling inside their belly and claiming to prophesy. A famous one was described by a widely read Italian scholar, Richerius Rhodiginus, in the *Ancient Readings* (v, 10). This ventriloquist – a local woman, Jacoba Rhodigina – was frequently heard by Rabelais in Ferrara (*QL* LVIII, 19f.). Rabelais draws upon Richerius Rhodiginus's account to tell us about her. Her spirit, called Cincinnatulus, was an *esprit immonde* (a foul fiend), an *esprit maling* (a devil). If we find these tales of lying belly-devils strange, we are the odd men out. They appear in Plutarch who condemns them in the same treatise which Rabelais drew on for the death of Pan and other parts of the *Quart Livre*. They figure in important glosses on canon law. Both the classical world and the Christian knew cases where prophesying spirits inhabited the regions of the belly.[34] What Rabelais and Richerius heard issuing from Jacoba's belly I do not claim to know. But Rabelais tells us that what he heard was the lying, deceiving voice of an *esprit immonde* (LVIII, 23), an *esprit maling* (LVIII, 30). These are truly diabolical persons, met in both *Gargantua* and the *Tiers Livre*.

The second category of gastrolaters are monks; and it seems this time that Rabelais lumps all the religious orders together. Divided by vestments, they are united in gluttony and idleness. In *Gargantua* he had mocked the *ocieux moynes*. These belly-idolaters are *all* idle (*tous ocieux*). Like the monks condemned in the far-off days of 1534 and 1535, these monks are *masquez, desguizez*: hypocrites in fact (*QL* LVIII, 40f.).

Rabelais applies to them the harsh words, 'a useless weight and load to the earth' (*'poys et charge inutile de la Terre'*) which he attributes forgetfully to Hesiod – they come in fact from Homer. Before him many others, including Budé, had made similar uses of Homer's words. The full force of the condemnations lies in their associations with a well-known attack in Lucian on lay-abouts and parasites, with whom evangelicals identified the hated monks of their own day.[35]

Curiously enough Rabelais was reminded of these devilish and greedy monks by the same text of Plutarch which had made him think of ventriloquists: *On the Decline of Oracles* (435B). There Euripides's Cyclops 'sacrifices to no god but himself – and to his belly, the greatest God of them

---

[34] Cf. Plutarch, *De defectu oraculorum*, 414E, for a sharp rejection of 'ventriloquists', which probably explains why they are brought into these chapters. See also Alciati (*Opera* II, 343): *Parergo juris*, cap. VII: 'In what ways the belly is interpreted by jurisconsults and ancient authorities.' He refers to *26. qu. 3* of Gratian, as Richerius Rhodiginus and Rabelais do (*QL* LVIII, 11–12).

[35] Cf. Homer, *Iliad* XVIII, 104; *QL* LVIII, 45. The intermediary is Lucian (*Icaromennipus* 29) where the expression is used against false philosophers. Cf. Budé's harsh attack on lazy, uneducated priests (*De asse*: in *Opera* II, p.279) and his slashing attack on them in the *Annotationes in Pandectas* (*Opera* III, 63f.). Where Budé attacks idle priests, generally, Rabelais restricts the attack to idle monks.

all'. Rabelais cites this at the end of the chapter (LVIII, 66f.); but not before he makes a long and authoritative condemnation of gastrolatry drawn directly from the Epistle to the Philippians 3, 18. Once again we find in Rabelais what is often found in Erasmus: Plutarch in easy harness with the highest authority of all: the New Testament.

They all took Gaster for their great God, adored him as God, sacrificed to him as to their God almighty, and recognised no other God but him; they served him, loved him above all things, honoured him as their God. You would have said that the holy Ambassador had written specifically of them in Philippians 3: 'There are many, of whom I have told you often (and now tell you even weeping), enemies of the cross of Christ, whose end will be death, whose God is their belly.'

All those who, like the monks, make gods of their bellies stand condemned. The repetition of the word God is striking. It reminds readers that these idolators of the Belly are breaking the first of the ten *logoi* revealed at Sinai: 'Thou shalt have none other gods before me.' This is completed by the New Testament, with a long, clear and authoritative quotation from St Paul, the Holy Ambassador of God. And then a final blow is delivered by the elegant Plutarch.

A third way in which Rabelais dethrones Gaster and his worshippers is by drawing attention to the body's excrement. We watch as these idolaters pile rich dish upon rich dish, varying their habits only by substituting caviare, sardines or salted salmon for equally rich meats on fast-days (*QL* LIX; LX). The calmly philosophical Pantagruel of the *Tiers Livre* is angry now: *il se fascha*. But even this is not as crushing a condemnation of these monkish idolaters as was a well-known saying of Antigonus I, which Rabelais found in Plutarch, Erasmus and Calcagnini. Called a god by the poet Hermodotus, Antigonus rejoined that such a claim would be denied by his *lasanophoros*, the servant whose task it was to empty his chamber-pot. Messere Gaster – who does not want to be worshipped – draws the same lesson for these monkish *Matagotz* whom we last met besetting Thelema:

Thus Gaster referred these Matagotz to his lavatory seat, to see, consider, philosophise, and contemplate on what godhead they found in this faecal matter.

The wisdom which Rabelais so colourfully expresses here (*QL* LXI, 89f.), one could also read in Plutarch (*On Isis and Osiris* 360D), in Calcagnini (*Opera*, p.235) and in the *Apophthegmata* of Erasmus (IV, 203; Antigonus, vii). But Rabelais blends this classical wisdom with Christianity more successfully than any other author I know. To worship the belly is to join in a wicked *farce*, worthy of both St Paul's tears and our laughter. And since the word *farce* in French can mean not only the comic play but force-meat stuffing, it is meet and right that the *issue de cette farce* should be stinking excrement (*QL* LX, 3). This recalls to us the sign by which Epistemon condemned the bishop of the Papimanes. Fed up with his farce, this learned companion of Pantagruel was seized with a violent access of diarrhoea (*QL* LI, 65).

Throughout Rabelais's novels farcical stuffing and the ensuing excrement play this moral rôle. Man is reminded of his grossest humanity when he needs such a reminder. Error and hypocrisy are revealed for what they are, especially when a man or boy delights in excrement at the expense of his higher spirituality. Men and women are more than their backsides might suggest. But they are not gods. When men are tempted to treat themselves or others as divine, they are reminded of their arses. Similar points can be made by having characters break wind: Rabelais's Ruachites are self-condemned by such grossness. So too was Cincinnatulus, Jacoba Rhodigina's devil; he always lied about the future, since he knew nothing about it, replying to questions with a *un gros pet* (*QL* LVIII, 38).

Such considerations introduce laughter into the means by which Rabelais condemns idolatry. This laughter is allied to a sustained concern to keep satirical considerations before the reader who knows his Latin satirists, at first or second hand.

At the outset the 'sentence of the Satirist' is alluded to, 'who said that Messere Gaster was Master of all Arts' (*QL* LVII, 29). This is an allusion to the *Magister Artium Venter* of the choliambic poem which serves as a prologue to the *Satires* of Persius. Persius tells us that it was only that Master of Arts, the belly, who taught him to sing his verses – just as he teaches crows and parrots to talk. This is alluded to a few lines later (76f.). The dreadful cannibalism of the besieged Vascones recalls a line of Juvenal; later, when Diogenes's quip is cited ('that the rich man should eat when he is hungry: the poor man should eat when he can'), we are reminded of Juvenal's silly rich women who, even when ill, would eat only when their *Petosiris* (a kind of *Old Moore's Almanac*) let them (*QL* LXIV, 46f.; Juvenal, *Satires* VI, 581).

Latin satire is bitter, and easily given over to hate. Rabelais (partly thanks to Lucian) had learned to marry satire to laughter, to great effect. All this worship of Gaster (like the worship of the pope) really *is* a 'farce'. As a god Gaster is but a figure of Carnival, a bugaboo with 'eyes bigger than his belly'. For this Rabelais turned to Erasmus's adage *Manduces*, which is a description of the Manducus of old, a ridiculous masked Carnival figure, with big teeth kept artificially chewing. It was employed in Roman processions and comedies to create merriment.

Such grotesque figures evoked memories of Juvenal's satires, Plautus's comedies and Carnival processions in Lyons, where the modern French descendant of Manducus seems to have been a masked figure of fun called Maschecroutte (*QL* LIX, 7f.; Erasmus, *Adagia* IV, 8, 32).

This is the kind of figure Messere Gaster is, if considered as a god. Yet the gluttonous monks show by their actions (by their *minoys* and,

unmistakably, by their *gestes*) that they really do worship him with their
excessive eating and drinking and their Bacchic songs. It is not until these
monkish 'devils' withdraw – *ces diables Gastrolatres retirez* – that Messere
Gaster finally takes up again his honourable part as noble Master of Arts;
but no god (*QL* LXI, 1).

Within the realm of Nature there is bread in plenty for the belly to be
satisfied. But the belly's driving force does not always lead to good.
Rabelais is very aware of the technical advances that mankind has made
under the belly's orders: windmills, new means of transport, finer towns
and even control of the weather. Nevertheless there is no tendency in
Rabelais to think of this, in nineteenth-century terms, as 'progress'. For the
devil is at work here too, using this force to conquer Nature by Art –
inventing diabolical field artillery, capable of killing more men than were
ever killed by thunderbolts (*QL* LXI, 69f.).

21. Questions unanswered

Alone of the major episodes Messere Gaster does not end in a clear and
definite fashion. His last chapter, LXII, merges almost imperceptibly into
the final chapters of the book. The belly invents an ingenious anti-
projectile system by means of a magnet – still a mysterious object – and
then disappears from view as Rabelais lists a number of strange facts
vouched for by great classical authorities. The two principal authorities
cited are Pliny – whom Rabelais is not inclined to swallow whole – and
Plutarch, who supplies many strange details, especially from his *Table-Talk*.
Of these two authorities, only Plutarch is cited by name (*QL* LXI, 15), since
he had proved by experiment one of the stranger facts alleged (*Symposiaca*
II, vii; 641B). Rabelais teases his readers: they should not be so difficult to
convince in the future! (*QL* LXII, 14).

Renaissance scholarship could not check many of the strange facts
alleged by ancient authors. It was not enough to reject them simply because
they did seem strange and unlikely: it was precisely for their strangeness
and unlikeliness that they had been cited in the first place!

Pliny was an author many were prepared to criticise in the Renaissance.
Plutarch, much less so. By jumbling their strange facts together, Rabelais
greatly increases his readers' hesitations: Renaissance scholarship neither
allowed men to swallow these alleged facts uncritically, nor to reject them
out of hand. The implications are: how can one know whether such things
are possible or not? Plutarch experimented with a species of thistle called
eryngion, putting it in the mouth of one of a group of stampeding nanny-
goats. When he did so, all the herd came to a halt. Do you believe it or do
you not? The little fish called *echineis* (the *remora*) was widely believed in
Antiquity to have the power to stop a ship in mid-ocean; another plant

cures arrow-wounds in deer and makes the arrows fall out. Do you believe it or do you not? A glance at, say, Dr Rondelet's *History of Sea fishes* or Dr Laurent Joubert's *Erreurs Populaires* will soon disabuse any modern who might think it was easy or obvious to decide to disbelieve such stories. On the whole, learned opinion veered towards credulity in such paradoxical matters.

Plutarch is in Rabelais's mind throughout these pages. And Plutarch is less concerned to get people to believe the strange facts he alleges – he believes them himself without difficulty; what he is concerned to do is to discuss their causes, in a civilised manner over a glass of wine. He warns his readers how easy it is to jump to conclusions, foolishly jumbling together incompatible so-called causes. One of the passages in which he does this (*Table-Talk* II, vii; 641BF) is one of Rabelais's sources (QL LXII, 55, 81 etc.).

This tells us much about these closing pages of the *Quart Livre*. More than once Rabelais has shown his sceptical, Pyrrhonian bent. But Christian scepticism is as good an ally for belief as it is for disbelief. It leaves us in suspense about all matters untouched by revelation.

The strange facts alleged by Pliny or by Plutarch may be true or not. But even if the story or alleged fact was not believed to be literally true, the problem did not end there. Renaissance man had another worry: if the fact is not literally true (or even if it is), should he not be looking for an inner, deeper sense? Rabelais gives a good example, taken from Calcagnini, *Opera*, 1544, p.29. The elder-tree is said to make better flutes when grown in areas where the cock is not heard to crow. Theophrastus said this was because crowing harmed the wood; others say the wild elder (found far from human habitation and so where no cocks are kept) naturally produces better wood; still others search for an inner spiritual meaning – *plus haultement, non scelon la letre* – interpreting Pliny's statement in terms of Pythagorean allegory. For the last group the sense is indeed profound: avoid trivial and vulgar music, seek heavenly, divine, angelic music, hidden music from afar, from regions where 'no cock is heard' (LXII, 90f.).

Rabelais leaves you to take your choice. So does Calcagnini.

Irresistibly one is taken back to the prologue of *Gargantua* where one is invited to seek – and not to seek too ingeniously – the *altiores sensus* of Rabelais's own Pythagorean symbols. Despite the leg-pulling in the prologue and the playful allusions there to Pythagorean symbolism, the case of *Gargantua* seems straightforward enough: it is not a Chronicle simply telling a story; it does have its say about religion, politics and 'domestic economy'. But can or should one accept every claim made for a work to be yet another example of *symboles Pythagoricques*? And even in the case of *Gargantua*, where do you stop? (*Garg.*, TLF, prol., 55–86; QL LXII, 104f.).

A man who made as much use of Erasmus's adages as Rabelais did, not least in the last few pages, would long since have been acquainted with his lengthy, basic and important essay on *Pythagorean Symbols*, forming part of the commentary on the second adage of Book One (*Friendship: Equality; A friend is another self*). The point Rabelais is making is not whether it is right to seek the heavenly, divine and angelic music – that is a precept for good living, right enough – but whether such a meaning really is to be found in Pliny's saying about the wood of the elder-tree grown where no cock is heard. How can one know?

As for earthly music, Rabelais is prepared to enjoy it even when it *is* trivial, provided that first-rate musicians compose the music. That much is clear from the new prologue, 303f.

But to the questions raised by the elder-tree and so on, Rabelais gives no explicit answer. Similarly Pantagruel gives no answer to the vain and idle questions asked by the drowsy companions, as they lie half-dozing, becalmed off the Isle of Chaneph, where Hypocrisy lives, or perhaps the Flatterers (QL LXIII).

22. *Pantagruel's answer: the Christian Bacchus*

Pantagruel promises to reply to all these questions, but not with words. He intends, as we saw, to avoid the indirect wandering pathways of speech, giving his answers by effective signs. There is no point in talking to a hungry man: the belly has no ears and it is time to eat (QL LXIII, 72f.; Erasmus, *Adagia* II, 8, 84).

At this point Erasmus again supplies several adages and apophthegms, as well as much varied erudition. Particularly relevant is the adage 'Deliberation is better on a full belly' (III, 7, 44). These adages all help to associate these pages and those which follow with Messere Gaster. The interconnexions are close and meaningful. The companions may be becalmed off a different island, but we have not finished with Messere Gaster yet: he has more to teach us.

We are prepared to be amused: Pantagruel promised to reply to the questions; yet the heading to the next chapter, LXIV, stresses that he did *not* do so. Comedy is to the fore: Aristophanes and Plautus are mentioned, as well as the happy Diogenes of the prologue to the *Tiers Livre*. As for satire, Juvenal, unnamed, is present through the allusion to the Petosiris almanac.

Pantagruel's answer to all the idle questions – an answer made indirectly *par signes, gestes et effectz* – turns out to be a civilised banquet, enjoyed by all the friends. The wind springs up during this happy meal, before the pudding is even brought in; the companions then sing canticles to God (LXIV, 53f.).

These Christian friends recall the practice of Gargantua once his education had been reformed by Ponocrates. Pantagruelists do not mumble routine graces or routine thanksgivings; God is praised at table with great bursts of spiritual song: 'Whereupon they sang divers canticles in praise of the highest God of heaven.'

Idle questions have been answered, or left unanswered and time has been joyfully spent. Behind this confidence in the power of food eaten happily together lie bookish memories of Plutarch and Erasmus, but it is also a lasting and major element in Rabelais's philosophy. The belly is not to be crammed with food: but neither is it to be starved by fasting. The wise and spiritual man does not avoid the excesses of the Gastrolatres by falling into the ascetic excesses of thin, gaunt, jejune, lonely, fasting hermits. The body is actually lightened by food: so the fasting man, depriving himself of food, is more terrestrial than the man who has eaten and drunk, not less:

For, as the body is more heavy dead than alive, so too is the fasting man more earth-bound and heavy than when he has drunk and eaten. [. . .] Do you not know that, in days of yore, the Amyclaeans revered and adored above all Gods the noble father Bacchus, and called him *psila* by an act of proper and appropriate naming? In the Doric tongue, *psila* signifies 'wings'. For, as birds lightly fly high in the air with the help of their wings, so, too, with the help of Bacchus (that is, of good wine, dainty and delicious) the spirits of men are raised high, their bodies manifestly lightened, and that which was earth-bound in them made supple (*QL* LXVI, 75f.).

The *Quart Livre* is nearly at an end. These words are worth a closer scrutiny. They serve to help make yet another diptych. The rejection of fasting takes up a theme treated at some length in the *Tiers Livre*.

The fasting that concerns Rabelais now is not merely the farcical fasting of belly-worshippers who substitute caviare for beef during Lent or on Fridays. The somewhat bitter laughter at that sort of fasting has produced its own rejection through mockery. The fasting that Rabelais is rejecting now is real fasting when taken too far: attempts to discipline the body, and to liberate the spirit, by depriving the belly of food or strictly limiting its intake.

Rabelais rejects extreme and rigorous fasting for the same reasons as he rejects over-eating: it is not consonant with the golden mean. The *Tiers Livre* made these points partly on medical grounds, partly on grounds of etymology.

The reasons were given in convincing medical detail, after which Pantagruel related how the hungry body, far from releasing the spirit, draws it down to earth like a hawk which strives to soar aloft but is tugged back by its string to the gauntlet. The body is the host of the spirit. If the body is not moderately content, then the spirit is preoccupied with it, not with those spiritual goods to which it would otherwise aspire. Fasting is not to be rejected in all circumstances: in accordance with the precepts of the *medium per participationem*, fasting is a corrective to preceding gluttony. But apart from that one single circumstance, nothing good is said about it (*TL* XIII, 88f.).

In the *Quart Livre* the medical detail is taken for granted, but the undesirability of hermits and such is not forgotten. The hypocritical monkish inhabitants of the Isle de Chaneph are all male or female ascetics, living on alms 'like the hermit of Lormont' near Bordeaux. As for the truths that can be garnered from a proper understanding of etymology, they sweep into the forefront in an area where Platonic etymology was often believed to be most sound: in the names of gods.

In the *Quart Livre* the powers of wine are sung in truly philosophical and spiritual terms: to call Bacchus the god of wine *Psila* (or rather, *Psilax*, winged) as the Amyclaeans did was not an example of stupid or irresponsible imposition but an act of proper and appropriate naming, of *propre et convenente denomination* (LXV, 80f.). The eventual authority for this is Pausanias who, in his *Description of Greece* (III. 19. 6) told how the Amyclaeans gave the surname *Psilax* to Dionysus (Bacchus), adding the comment: 'Quite rightly I think; for *psila* is Doric for wings, and wine uplifts men and lightens their spirit no less than wings do birds.' Wine is, then, the corporeal equivalent of Homer's words in Rabelais's version of Petron's myth: a winged thing, helping man to cast off his earthiness, to 'raise his spirits aloft', to 'lighten his body'. The figure of Bacchus can now be placed beside the figure of Orpheus, with whose twanging lyre and whose disembodied song the first chapter of the thawing words ended (*QL* LV, 74f.).

Many Renaissance authors have made us feel at home with Christian Sceptics, Christian Stoics, Christian Epicureans. But a word or two needs to be said about Bacchic Christians, in case Rabelais is taken as being in favour of an orgiastic Christianity in which nunnish maenads run rutting through forests. Rabelais was not advocating a tipsy Christianity, in which blear-eyed wineskins are inspired to prophesy ecstatically in dithyrambs. The temptation to interpret Rabelais that way is greatest among those who accept the authenticity of the posthumous *Cinquiesme Livre*, for that book does venture some way into such territory, with the heroes prophesying rhythmically in the presence of the Dive Bouteille. But, authentic or not, the *Cinquiesme Livre* dates from 1564 and Rabelais died in 1553.

The kind of wisdom represented by Bacchus Psilax is not to be confounded with Bacchic orgies or Dionysiac extremes. The only specific reference to Bacchic orgiastic singing in the four Chronicles published by Rabelais himself is pejorative. It is found within the episode of Messere Gaster (*QL* LIX, 1f.). There the hated idolaters of the belly sing Bacchic songs to their ridiculous god Manducus.

This figure of Manducus is borrowed from Pompeius Festus, but not directly. Rabelais calls him *Manduce*: that is the form in which he appears in Erasmus (*Adagia* IV, 8, 32, *Manduces*).

In the *Quart Livre* Manducus is described at some length; he is likened to a monstrous comic figure, Maschecroutte, borne through the streets of Lyons during carnival processions. As for his teeth, they were clacked together by means of a cord attached to a pole – just as the dragon's did which Rabelais had seen carried through the streets of Metz. The dragon, Graulli, was proverbially killed by Saint Clement: its monstrous effigy, with moving jaws into which gifts were thrown, was carried through the streets of Metz on St Mark's day (25 April) and at Rogationtide. Pierre Gras, in the *Dictionnaire du Patois Forézien* (Lyons 1863) states that 'Mâche-croûte' was a carnival figure, formerly paraded through the streets of Lyons; it was the equivalent 'of today's Mardi Gras which we have all seen tossed into the Rhône'.

Rabelais tells us that Manducus, this carnival bugaboo, 'was an effigy, ridiculous, hideous and frightening to little children'. He was probably thinking of Erasmus's comparison of the *manduces* to the *mormolukia* of the Greeks: little monsters used by nurses to frighten children into being quiet. The association of ideas was a good one. Antoine du Saix (*L'esperon de Discipline* II, 1532, sig. D2r°) cites *Maschecrotte* amongst such scarey figures used by foolish women to frighten children.

The carnival aspect of Manducus is emphasised comically by the accoutrements carried by the servants of the chanting Gastrolastres. As these belly-worshippers approached, the storyteller 'saw that they were followed by a large number of fat varlets, laden with baskets, paniers, packs, pots and boilers'.

Within such a comic, carnival setting we might have expected the Gastrolastres to get off lightly. They do not because, comic or not, they are idolaters. And we condemn them in a way which the *Quart Livre* has by now made authoritative: by what they do, by the *minoys et les gestes* of these lazy, big-throated idolaters (*QL* LIX, 1f.). Under the guidance of Manducus they sing orgiastic songs – 'I know not what dithyrambs, crapaelocomes and epaenons' – as they open their baskets, pots and bottles and pour food and drink down their throats in vast quantities. So carnival, too, becomes an idol.

These dithyrambs – drunken songs addressed to Bacchus – and the rambling drunken babblings known as crapaelocomes, put us firmly back into a classical Bacchic context. The laughter provoked by their comic stuffing – their *farce* – is a bitter, moral laughter. Pantagruel was angered by this priestly rabble (*ceste villenaille de sacrificateurs*) and by their countless sacrifices (*QL* LX, 1). It is at the close of this chapter that we are reminded of Antigonus I's wise saying. The 'issue of this farce' is faeces. What divinity is there in that?

This rejection of Bacchic orgies is vital for the understanding of

Rabelais's religion, not least when he expresses it in quasi-Bacchic terms. The most striking example of his doing so (though not the first by any means) is to be found in the prologue to the *Tiers Livre*.

Wait a while for me to have a little drink from this bottle: it is my true and only Helicon; it is my caballine Fountain; it is my unique Enthusiasm. Here, drinking I deliberate, I discourse, I resolve and make conclusions. After the epilogue I laugh, I write, I compose, I drink. Ennius wrote drinking, drank writing; Aeschylus (if you trust Plutarch in his Table-Talk) composed drinking, drank composing; Homer never wrote fasting; Cato never wrote anything, except after having had a drink – so that you cannot tell me that I live without the example of the most highly praised and the best esteemed of men. It is good, and quite cool enough – as you might say, about the beginning of the second degree; for which God, the good God *Sabaoth* (that is, of hosts) be for ever praised. If you fellows also have one big or two little drinks on the quiet, I find nothing wrong in that, provided that you praise God just a little bit (*TL*, prol., 73f.).

Here we do have wine praised for its power to inspire. The context is both Christian and classical, juxtaposing the Lord of Hosts and learning drawn from Erasmus's essays on two important adages: *He is no dithyrambic poet if he drinks water* and *You will achieve nothing good if you drink but water* (*Adagia* IV, 3, 58; II, 6, 6.).

How these Bacchic adages are reconciled with Christian moderation is best seen from the emblem books, where they are associated with such sayings as *Wine fosters the mind* and *Wine sharpens the intellect*. Scholarly emblematic writers such as Alciati associated Bacchus with Pallas, the goddess of wisdom; with Concordia, the goddess of harmony; or with Apollo, the god of medicine and poetry. Later in the Renaissance, Adrian Junius, in his learned *Emblemata*, cites the same texts as Rabelais does in both the *Tiers Livre* and the *Quart Livre*; he gives Bacchus wings, associating him with the winged horse Pegasus. He stresses that his Bacchus signifies the spiritually quickening power of wine taken moderately. Claude Mignault, the author of a dense and authoritative commentary on Alciati, does not give Bacchus wings, since the emblems he discusses do not do so; but his erudition covers the same ground as Rabelais, drawing on the same examples. His moral point is identical, praising the spiritually lightening and quickening powers of wine, taken in moderation, amongst friends at table.[36] Such a practice is normally explained by reference to the heroes of Homer and Virgil. A major source of the idea is Plutarch's *Table-Talk*: the opening chapter (612C) discusses the question, 'Should we philosophise

[36] Consult especially: 1. Adrianus Junius, *Emblemata*, Antwerp, Plantin, 1565, emblem 34, p.40; the long scholarly note covers all Rabelais's erudition; 2. Claude Mignault's commentaries on Alciati's emblems (*Emblemata*, Lyons 1614; on emblems XCIX, p.348f.). These authors almost certainly drew directly on Rabelais and help to explain him.

over a drink?' Plutarch is such a marked influence on Rabelais in the *Quart Livre*, that it is reasonable that he should help to explain why, towards the end of an epic journey, the heroes resolve their problems over a joyful banquet.

It is in contexts such as these that Bacchus Psilax takes on his fuller force. Rabelais's sustained respect for Bacchus and the liberating powers of wine is expounded with the hyperbole found in his classical sources and repeated by Renaissance authors, including the humanist scholars. But Bacchus truly understood is the power of wine, drunk amongst friends in happy moderation. Bacchus has power to raise aloft the soaring spirits of men. He is no mad god of drunken, earth-bound squalor; he symbolises that spiritually liberating power of joyful wine, which classical and Christian man drank as a conscious act of wise and ennobling humanity, encouraging eloquence and the quest of truth.

23. *Actions speak louder than words*

Bacchus Psilax, duly tamed by mythographer, poet, fabulist, emblematist and scholar, is a source of joy and spiritual elevation for Renaissance Christians. But the devilish Gastrolastres are another matter altogether. Make Manducus or Master Belly into gods, and they are dreadful figures behind their funny faces; for then they become all-devouring idols, worshipped by wicked men.

What Rabelais delights in is a platonising banquet, the civilised joy in good company at table, lightened by good wine which sweeps the spirits heavenwards, away from the dross of the physical world. Such devotees of Bacchus Psilax sing no orgiastic dithyrambs to idols; they sing canticles to God in the highest (*QL* LXIV, 64).

Why! Good food and wine can turn even Panurge momentarily – and so far as verbiage is concerned – into a second Pantagruel! His words can ape the Christian peace of mind of Pantagruelism:

Without fear of correction, we ought indeed to praise the good God, our Creator, Saviour and Preserver, who, with this good bread, this good fresh wine, these good viands, has cured us of such perturbations of body and soul, not to mention the pleasure and sensuous delight we have in drinking and eating (*QL* LXV, 30f.).

If words were actions we would be impressed. But we know our Panurge by now. Can those 'perturbations of body and soul' which have dominated his character throughout this book be really cured? Are we to have no more accesses of fear, no more physical and spiritual faeces? Of course not.

The few remaining pages of the *Quart Livre* are largely devoted to showing how superficial and shallow his pious verbiage is.

If the *Quart Livre* had ended with Panurge's borrowing of Pantagruel's style of speech and philosophy, we would have been left with a booby and a coward apparently reformed – if we could trust in words. The last two chapters of all define and confirm anew the personalities of the three main characters, Pantagruel, Frère Jean and Panurge, fixing them afresh in the rôles they have been allotted during this long and complex voyage of comic discovery.

This final definition of the characters is precipitated by the arrival of the travellers off the Island of Ganabin (Thieves and Robbers). The principal geographical feature of the place is a mountain called Antiparnassus. This island contains an impudent imitation of the double-headed mountain of Greece, inhabited by false and rival Muses. In relation to the real Parnassus of the real Muses it plays a rôle analogous to Antiphysie in relation to Physis: the Muses inspire men to beget truth in beauty; so the Anti-Muses of Anti-Parnassus must beget lies in ugliness (QL LXVI).

The decision to salute the false Muses with a blank cannonade brings on the self-loving Panurge's final attack of servile fear and leads to his final isolation, an object of laughter, disapproval and disgust.

There are indications that a first draft of these pages may have existed in 1548. There is a joke about 'blond English souls' and the Isle of Horses (QL LXVII, 20): it is an allusion to successful French attacks on the English garrison occupying the Isle of Inchkeith, near Edinburgh, in 1548. But if this were so, the chapters must have been fundamentally recast, to make a fitting end to the far more ambitious book of 1552.

The Isle de Ganabin is an Antiparnassus which recalls, we are told, the Thracian town of Poneropolis (QL LXVI, 20). Plutarch mentions this *Poneropolis*, this 'City of Bad Men', in a treatise Rabelais exploited for the *Tiers Livre*: *On Curiosity*. There the inhabitants are likened to critics with a taste for ugly things, collecting defective verses of Homer and generally preferring the maimed and the deformed to the beautiful. In so Platonic an author as Rabelais, the implied condemnation is severe and fundamental (Plutarch 920B).

Panurge talks of the Isle de Ganabin as being like the Channel Islands, then no gentle tax-haven but poor, wild, lawless places. In the *Tiers Livre* Panurge showed some bookish knowledge of the waters and seas off Saint Malo, alluding to Plutarch's Ogygian Islands, where Saturn was said to dwell in chains. These associations with his boundless superstition help to explain his fear – and no doubt, the other characters' general hostility to the place, since, however unreasonable Panurge's fears may be, they derive in part from the august Plutarch (*TL* XXIV, 96).

Panurge, in a final access of fright, begs his fellows not to land. Frère Jean, ever madly brave, wants to dash valiantly ashore. Pantagruel, under inspiration, refuses to land:

I feel, said Pantagruel, an urgent withdrawal in my soul, as if it were a voice heard from afar, which tells me that we must not disembark. Each and every time that I have felt such a motion in my spirit, I have found myself fortunate, when rejecting and abandoning the direction from which it drew me back; on the contrary, I have found myself unfortunate, when following the direction from which it repelled me. And never had I reason to repent me of it (*QL* LXVI, 53f.).

Epistemon explains that it is 'like the daemon of Socrates, so famous amongst the followers of Plato'.

In retrospect, this seems the inevitable and logical conclusion: Pantagruel is a new Christian Socrates, a man inspired by a good daemon. The *Quart Livre*, no less firmly than the earlier Chronicles, places ultimate certainty in divine guidance.

Pantagruel's inspiration is not something new, something that will guide him only from now on. Socrates was already an ideal figure in *Gargantua* and the 1535 Almanac. In a sense Pantagruel has been a new Socrates since the opening stages of the *Tiers Livre*, guided by his *esprit munde* whilst Panurge was led astray by his *esprit immunde*. But with this fully Socratic ending the *Quart Livre* joins two other Renaissance books – the *Praise of Folly* and the *Essays* – in being drawn, irresistibly and with artistic inevitability, to the man whom Erasmus, Rabelais and Montaigne believed to be the greatest philosopher of them all.

Pantagruel is a sage. As a man inspired he is not infallible, but he is never wrong when he does adjudicate. He is a man who, in the human marriage of body and soul, is weighted more towards the soul and to things spiritual.

Frère Jean and Panurge are similarly confirmed in their characters. Both exist more in body than in soul. Both are far from exemplary. But Frère Jean is a man of bravery and activity, whereas Panurge is a man of fear and trembling, of bodily and spiritual perturbations, of craven inactivity and empty verbiage. Their words, in both cases, though in different ways, are at variance with their actions. Since we have just heard Panurge mouthing words representing ideas which, if truly held in balanced wisdom, would have made him into a reformed man, the establishing of his rôle of comic reject is made in powerful and convincing ways, all of which Rabelais would have classified as signs.

There is first the evidence of his speech: not of his carefully contrived argumentation and rhetoric, but of his babblings under the impetus of fear. He again lapses into Parisian cockney as he did in the storm; expressions like *men amy* and *men pere* remind us both of his terror during the storm and of the exploded pretentiousness of the silly *Ecolier Limousin*. Our happy laughter at this is accompanied by laughter more troubled in its nature, as we see Panurge's unwitting preoccupation with the Devil and matters diabolical. In his very last speeches of all Panurge mentions the Devil or devils nine times; *diableteau*, once; hell, thrice; damned souls, once;

phantastic visions – the speciality of hallucinating devils – once. God gets no mention, until he appears in an oath in the last burst of bravado. The technique is the one Rabelais used in the *Tiers Livre*, where Panurge talked of the Devil while Pantagruel and Triboullet talked of God. At this climax, to Panurge's cries of 'Je me donne au Diable', or, 'Au diable soyt le Diable', Pantagruel calmly answers: 'Allez, allez, de par Dieu . . .' (*QL* LXVII, 114 to end).

Frère Jean's language knows of the Devil too! It always has done so. But there is a fundamental difference. Frère Jean's oaths are full-blooded and, insofar as they can be taken literally, explicitly condemned in canon law.[37] But they do not in fact suggest diabolical possession. At the end of the *Quart Livre* this is partly a question of degree – he mentions the Devil only once; 'millions of devils' twice; hell, not at all. At other times Frère Jean can out-swear Panurge. But his colourful language is an aid to further effort, not the empty, pious-sounding substitute for it which Panurge affects in moments of danger, nor an impediment to any effort at all. Humorously regrettable as Frère Jean's language is, his actions 'work together' with the general purposes of God. The strongest evidence in Frère Jean's favour (apart from the fact that we laugh with him not at him) lies in his *gestes et effetz*: in his bravery, his effective action.

Rabelais makes this point during the last verbal confrontation of Panurge and Frère Jean *des Entommeures*, reminding us of the monk's bravery by recalling to us his full name – and what that name means. Panurge is terrified of landing on the Island of Ganabin:

'The Devil may have his share,' said Panurge. 'This devil of a monk here, this monkish mad devil, is afraid of nothing. He'll hazard anything, like all the devils, and care nothing for the others. He thinks everybody is a monk like he is.'

'Go, you green leper', (replied Frère Jean) 'to all the millions of Devils, and may they anatomise your brain and make it into mincemeat [*entommeures*]. This devil of a fool is so cowardly and bad that he's always shitting himself out of bloody fear [*male raige de paour*]. If empty fear leaves you so consternated, then stay on board with the baggage! Or else go and hide under Proserpine's skirt, by all the millions of Devils' (*QL* LXVI, 38–50).

Monks who sing responses diligently but do nothing to work together with God are much more blameworthy than a coarse monk like Frère Jean, whose language is all blasphemous expletive but whose whole activity is as a sign or symbol of brave synergism. Frère Jean is on the right side in the final

---

[37] During the Storm (1552 version) Frère Jean is given an extremely colourful oath to swear (*QL* XX, 22): *Teste Dieu plene de reliques*. In canon law (*22, quest. 1. Si quis*) a man in orders risked being unfrocked if he swore 'by God's hair or God's head'. A layman would, for the same offence, be anathematised. 'God's head full of relics' clearly comes into this category.

symbolism. Panurge was so frightened by the dummy cannonade fired to salute the Anti-Muses that he hid away in a locker. He eventually emerged covered with crumbs, lacerated by Rodilardus, the ship's cat, trembling like a monkey and stinking of dung, having copiously messed himself in his funk. This fecal sign of cowardice is emphasised by the context: it follows two scatological stories which laughingly remind readers of the curious connexions linking fear and faeces, by which a good fright can be as laxative as an aperient.

When Panurge reappears, the visible epitome of the comic butt and the laughable reject, he at first talks fair. His *words* are quite courteous and saintly; he begs Frère Jean 'devoutly' to have 'compassion upon him'. But actions speak louder than words, and not least the action of the bowels. Panurge is summed up by Frère Jean with a sign, a gesture of transparent meaning:

Pinching his nose with his left hand, Frère Jean pointed out to Pantagruel, with the index finger of his right, the shirt of Panurge (*QL* LXVII, 8f., 27f., 107f.).

Pantagruel, for the first time since many a day, laughs; and laughs *at* somebody. He simply 'could not help it'. Rabelais's choice of words at this stage shows that he wished to insist once more on the cruelty of comedy. Pantagruel laughed at Panurge because he was in a sorry state, not in spite of it. Panurge, emerging befouled and ignoble from his locker, had asked for compassion. But he gets none – as long as the laughter lasts. His penultimate outburst, full of the Devil, is contrasted with Pantagruel's very last words ever: words remarkable for their cleanliness and godliness. We hear the authentic voice of the man whose *nous* or *mens* is dominated by *l'esprit munde*, the clean spirit, the pure spirit. To Panurge befouled, such a man talks of God, of bathing, of being clean, of white linen, of fresh vestments, of confidence regained. These last words of his need to be savoured:

'Allez,' dist Pantagruel, 'allez de par Dieu, vous estuver, vous nettoyer, vous asceurer, prendre chemise blanche, et vous revestir' (*QL* LXVII, 121–2).

But Panurge is dominated by *l'esprit maling*, the Devil who, in the *Quart Livre* (LVIII, 23) is finally given his commonest New Testament title: *l'esprit immonde*, the *pneuma akatharton*, the *spiritus immundus*, the '*unclean* spirit'. The Greek word for unclean in St Paul as in Plato suggests both physical and moral impurity: unclean thoughts and unclean lives; ugliness and dirtiness as associates of evil.

The moral and physical squalor which repels others is a source of perverse delight for Panurge. Pantagruel is a man bathed in the light of revelation; a man inspired; a man on the side of *Physis* and of whatsoever things are true, whatsoever things are to be revered, or are lovely, gracious, virtuous. Panurge is a man who, despite his fears, would really be at home in that *Poneropolis* which is Antiparnassus, a man who himself deserves the epithet *poneros*: bad, sick, wicked, diabolical; a man who delights in the foul, the dirty, the ugly, the unclean.

Panurge is now where Gargantua was years ago, before he learned cleanliness, godliness and a wider *humanitas* at the hands of Ponocrates. The contrast between Panurge's squalor and Pantagruel's right-thinking purity is absolute. The characteristics once locked together under the one name of Gargantua, as he passed from befouled ignorance to clean enlightenment, are now separated for ever. The higher qualities of man, both spiritual and physical, are enshrined in Pantagruel, the wise man who joyfully and truly profits from the twin stimuli of distillations falling down on mankind from the *Manoir de Vérité* and of manly moral strivings symbolised by the *Manoir de Areté (c'est vertus)*. He is a man who, inspired by the clean spirit and a Socratic daemon, lives life gratefully within its due confines of humanity at its highest, lightened by winged words and winged wine.

As for Frère Jean, he shows that, for those who cannot reach such heights, there is still the way of a grubbier active virtue under God – such activity being an effective sign, more than atoning for language which is blasphemous only in form, though reprehensible indeed if it passes beyond the limit.

As for Panurge, his archetypal *philautia* has produced a servile fear of correspondingly epic proportions; as a result of craven cowardice he is stinking and befouled from head to foot, his shirt an object of vile disgust. Yet, in spite of the rejection signified by his ignoble squalor, Pantagruel's laughter and Frère Jean's gesture, Panurge is not hammered into the ground. He is, after all, a funny fool. A man who can find sixteen ways of naming shit, some of them very erudite, is neither reformed nor definitively cleansed (*QL* LXVII, 129–131). Words for Panurge are still a way of hiding, twisting and avoiding truth, not of reaching it. He has at his disposition a veritable Roget's *Thesaurus* of terms copiously naming human excrement. Yet, in the end, this basic odoriferous sign of the corruptibility and humanity of our vile bodies is not called by any of them. Panurge claims that *his* dung is saffron – Irish saffron, the best there is. The Romans characterised *philautia* with just such a proverb: *Suus cuique crepitus bene olet*; 'Everybody likes the smell of his own wind' (*QL* LXVII, 129f.; Erasmus, *Adagia* III, 4, 2).

The adage is used by Erasmus as yet another warning against self-love, that root of all evil which corrupts man's judgment of each and every thing. Rabelais does the same in a more effective way.

Not for the first time, a disgraced and beaten Panurge glories in the grossest, foulest, ugliest aspects of our common humanity. One of the surest *signs* in all four Chronicles is the stinking ordure with which he is finally besmirched.

And yet, as befits a character in comedy, Panurge is bloody but unbowed. As a rule comic characters do not change in any fundamental way. Panurge remains the butt of our laughter unto the end. He is neither reformed, nor broken up and cast aside. He is set apart for condemnation and mockery, but he is not crushed with brutal finality, nor sent off like Gargantua's old tutor to drink himself to a comic death.

When we have tired of our play and thrust down the lids on our favourite jack-in-the-boxes we compress their springs for another jump if ever we feel like making them go through their tricks again. So too with Panurge. We are pleased that he has some jump left in him, for he has made us laugh.

Chronology

1409
(First) Council of Pisa

1414–18
Council of Constance

1431–39
Council of Basle

1438
1 July: Proclamation of Pragmatic Sanctions of Bourges

1463
Death of Villon

1469 (?)
Birth of Erasmus (or, 1466, 1467 . . .)

1471
Accession of Pope Sixtus I (1471–84)

1483
Birth of Rabelais (?)
30 August: Death of Louis XI; Charles VIII succeeds to throne of France
10 November: Birth of Luther

1484

12 August: Death of Pope Sixtus I. Succeeded by Innocent VIII (1484–92)

1492

25 July: Death of Innocent VIII

3 August: Columbus sails from Palos, sighting San Salvador on 12 October

11 August: Alexander VI elected pope (1492–1503)

1494

July: Sebastian Brant's *Narrenschiff (Ship of Fools)*. (First Latin edition, 1497)

(Alternative date for Rabelais's birth. Not well supported)

1498

8 April: Death of Charles VIII; succeeded by Louis XII

1500

July: First edition of Erasmus's *Adagia* (not authorised)

1500–10

During these years Rabelais apparently studied law, perhaps at Bourges, Angers or Poitiers

1503

18 August: Death of Pope Alexander VI; succeeded by Pius III (22 September; died 18 October)

1 November: Julius II elected pope (1503–13)

1506

Future Emperor Charles V, on death of father, Philip the Fair, inherits Low Countries and Franche-Comté

1509

10 July: Birth of Calvin

1510

Gallican Council of Tours called by Louis XII on advice of Philip Decius

1510–1526

Rabelais, previously at La Baumette (?), is priested; moves to Fontenay-le-Comte; remains there until 1526

1511

Erasmus publishes *Praise of Folly*

(Second) Council of Pisa (*Conciliabulum* of Pisa)

1512

Lateran Council (closes March 1517)

1513

20–1 February: Death of Pope Julius II; succeeded, 11 March, by Leo X (1513–21)

Tiraqueau publishes *De legibus connubialibus*

1514

Expanded edition of *Praise of Folly* (much more satirical)

1515

31 December 1514 (night): Death of Louis XII

1 January: Francis I becomes King of France

13 September: Battle of Marignan

1516

More's *Utopia* published in Paris

13 August: future Charles V becomes King of Spain; succeeds also to domains of Austrian Hapsburgs (including Alsace); also ruler of Naples, Sicily and vast territories in New World

Treaty of Noyon assures Francis I of Milan, despite Charles's accession as King of Sicily

18 August: Bull declaring Concordat between Leo X and Francis I. Increases Francis I's powers at expense of liberties of Gallican Church. Disturbances in University Quarter of Paris (1516–18)

'Perpetual peace' with Swiss Confederation

1517

March: Reuchlin's *De arte cabbalistica*

16 March: Closure of Lateran Council

31 October: Luther posts up his 95 theses against indulgences

1519

Charles V elected Holy Roman Emperor, despite rivalry of Francis I (influence of Jakob Fugger, the banker). The Imperial emblem (two pillars with the device *Plus oultre*) becomes ever more widely known

1520

Rabelais a Franciscan at Fontenay-le-Comte, writes his first (lost) letter to G. Budé

1521

4 March: Second letter of Rabelais to Budé

12 April: Budé's reply

Luther outlawed in Holy Roman Empire

15 November: French lose Milan

1 December: Death of Pope Leo X; succeeded (9 January 1522) by Hadrian VI (1522–23)

1522

Jean de la Barre charged, as *bailli-juge*, with University discipline in Paris

Amaury Bouchard publishes *Tēs gunaikeias phutlēs* against Tiraqueau

1523

14 September: Death of Pope Hadrian VI

19 November: Clement VII elected Pope (1523–34)

1523–24

Rabelais and Pierre Amy in trouble for studying Greek; Rabelais has already translated first book of Herodotus into Latin. Pierre Amy flees his convent; Rabelais becomes Benedictine. About this time Rabelais translates a work or works of Lucian into Latin

1524-26

Rabelais, based at Benedictine house at Saint-Pierre-de-Maillezais, works for, and travels with, bishop Geoffroy d'Estissac

1524

September–October: Erasmus's *De libero arbitrio*, against Luther

October: French reverses in Piedmont

30 November: Second edition of Tiraqueau's *De legibus connubialibus*

1525

Rabelais in Lyons (?). Death of Pierre Amy in Basle

24 February: Defeat of French at Pavia, partly attributable to cowardly flight of certain leaders, including the husband of the King's sister Margaret (Charles IV, Duke of Alençon). About 10,000 French troops killed. Francis I taken prisoner

December: Luther replies to Erasmus with *De servo arbitrio*

8 December: Paris Parlement forbids all *farces*, *momeries* and *sottises* during Twelfth-night revels in the colleges of the University of Paris next term

1526

14 January: Peace of Madrid. Francis I released from captivity in Spain; royal children held hostage pending final peace settlement

Milan ceded to Charles V

Francis I undertakes to marry Eleonore of Austria, sister of Charles V

1526-30

Rabelais leaves Poitou. Studies medicine in Paris (?)
Living irregularly (as secular priest or layman?)
Two children, François and Junie, perhaps date from this period

1527

Margaret of Angoulême, duchess of Alençon (sister of Francis I), widowed, marries Henry II d'Albret, king of client kingdom of Navarre

1528

Late summer: beginning of over five years of drought in parts of France

1529

5 August: Peace of Cambrai ('Paix des Dames', Louisa of Savoy, Margaret of Angoulême and Margaret of Austria). Francis I renounces claims to territories in Italy and to suzerainty over Artois and Flanders. Royal children to be released against ransom of 2,000,000 crowns

(Drought continues throughout 1529).

1530

Foundation of *lecteurs royaux* to profess Hebrew, Greek and Latin. Hostility of Sorbonne

20 March: Francis I marries Eleonore of Austria (by proxy, in Madrid); French ceremony, 7 July

1 July: Royal children released from captivity, making formal entry into Bayonne, 2 July

17 September: Rabelais signs matriculation list at Montpellier

1 November (or 1 December): Rabelais, bachelor of medicine

(Drought continues throughout 1530 in parts of France)

1530–32

From September (?) 1530 to June (?) 1532, Rabelais in Montpellier

1531

17 April–24 June (Quasimodo to St John's Day): Rabelais lectures at Montpellier on *Aphorisms* of Hippocrates and Galen's *Ars Parva*

February: Quarrels of jurisdiction in University of Paris; theologians wish to require Artiens to provide public orators; they resist

17 May: Paris Parlement controls the powers of the Sorbonne to censor books, perhaps because of excesses dating from early March

(The prolonged drought fills Lyons with starving people; exceptional measures taken to deal with problem)

15 September: Parlement further restrains rights of Sorbonne to censor books without due permission first obtained

October: French alliance with Schmalkalden League (Treaty of Saalfeld)

[During 1531, Erasmus publishes first complete Greek edition of Aristotle; Vivès publishes *De Disciplinis*]

(Drought continues throughout 1531 in parts of France)

1532

Twelfth-night revels (or earlier?): Rabelais, in Montpellier, acts in *Farce of Man who Married a Dumb Wife*. Meanwhile, in Paris, a student farce mocked Béda as a 'monster'.

Lenten sermons in Paris by Girard Roussel and Michel d'Arande. (Rabelais practising medicine in Midi, including Narbonne; by June, established in Lyons. Remains there until 1534, with perhaps, a visit to Chinonais?)

10 May: Canons of Notre-Dame confirmed in their rights as official Visitors to Béda's Collège de Montaigu

3 June: Rabelais dedicates Manardi's *Epistolae Medicinales* to Tiraqueau (Lyons, Sebastian Gryphius)

15 July: Rabelais dedicates *Hippocratis ac Galeni Libri Aliquot* to bishop Geoffroy d'Estissac (Lyons, Sebastian Gryphius)

Summer (?): *Grandes et inestimables Cronicques* on sale in Lyons

First edition of *Pantagruel* printed (?) and sold by Claude Nourry at Lyons

4 September: Rabelais dedicates *Lucii Cuspidii Testamentum* to Amaury Bouchard (Lyons, Sebastian Gryphius)

1 November: Rabelais appointed physician to Hôtel-Dieu, Lyons

30 November: Rabelais writes to Erasmus; frequenting his friend Hilaire Bertolph and his family

Autumn? Winter? *Pantagrueline Prognostication* for 1533 (François Juste, Lyons)

4 December: Holy Sindon at Chambéry miraculously saved from destruction by fire

(Drought continues throughout 1532, worse than before in parts of France)

1533

6 February: Permission to wear masks in street of Paris during Shrovetide; elaborate revels (Margaret of Navarre, Henri de Navarre, Dauphin)

Lent (2 March–13 April): Evangelical sermons in Louvre (Girard Roussel, Michel d'Arande . . .)

('Anti-lutheran' demonstrations and sermons orchestrated by the Sorbonne; Margaret of Navarre and Jean du Bellay accused from the pulpit of being lukewarm over repression of heresy)

May: Possible attempts by Sorbonne to censor *Miroir de l'âme pécheresse* of Margaret of Navarre

8 May: Girard Roussel put under house arrest at Margaret of Navarre's; his orthodoxy to be inquired into

26 May: Béda, Picart and Leclerc exiled twenty leagues from Paris. Posters (*placards*) criticising royal action found displayed in Paris. Reprisals

26 June: Sorbonne sends delegation begging return of exiled theologians; refused

1 July: Sorbonne authorises Nicolas Bouchart and Louis Theobald to supplicate Francis I on behalf of Béda. (Unsuccessful)

27 October: Some doctors of theology deny censoring of *Miroir de l'âme pécheresse*

3 November: Bishop of Senlis appears before assembled Faculties of University of Paris to condemn their censoring of *Miroir*. The charge is denied

8 November: All members of Faculties required to sign denial of any attempt to censor *Miroir*; this done, 1 December

About this time (?) Rabelais published augmented 1533 *Pantagruel* and the *Pantagrueline Prognostication* for 1534

October: Francis I meets Clement VII in Marseilles

10 December: Francis orders vigorous measures against heresy. Jean du Bellay's powers compromised during absence in England. Fears of persecution

24 December: Montmorency ordered to recall Béda to preach against the *Confession de foy de Maistre Noël Béda*

(Drought continues throughout 1533; climax of hot dry weather in parts of France. Plague, endemic in Europe, spreads; amongst those killed in Lyons are Hilaire Bertolph, the friend of Erasmus, together with his wife and all their children)

1534

(Early in 1534, the great drought, lasting from late 1528, broken)

9 January: Béda protests against Hebrew teachings of the *Lecteurs royaux*. Legal action broken off. (The lectures were advertised by posters (*billets*) in Paris)

15 January: Rabelais leaves for Rome with bishop Jean du Bellay. (Did he entrust manuscript of *Gargantua* to François Juste in Lyons? Does *Gargantua* date from January 1534?) Rabelais arrives in Rome, 2 February. Leaves in March

February–March: Béda re-arrested

1 April: Girard Roussel, vindicated, preaches in Louvre. Disturbances. Did he preach throughout the summer? (Other evangelical preachers noted)

14 April: Rabelais in Lyons with Jean du Bellay (who arrives in Paris, 18 May). Rabelais's movements unknown (14 April–1 August). Was he revising *Pantagruel*; adapting *Pantagrueline Prognostication* for 1535? Could *Gargantua*, if not already published, now be in hand? (Cf. January; November–December 1534; 1535)

1 August: Rabelais takes up office again as physician in Hôtel-Dieu, Lyons

22 August: Barbarossa drives Moulley Hassan from Tunis

31 August: Rabelais dedicates Marliani's *Typographia Romae* to Jean du Bellay (S. Gryphius, Lyons)

25 September: death of Pope Clement VII

(October: another possible date for *Gargantua*)

13 October: Pope Paul III elected (1534–49)

17–18 October: *Affaire des Placards*. Some repression follows

19 October: Procession of Holy Sacrament as act of national expiation

21 November: University discusses possibility of sending delegation for Béda's release

November–December? Publication of *Almanach pour l'an 1535* and expanded *Pantagrueline Prognostication* for 1535, critical of suppression of evangelicals. *Gargantua* – if not already published?

1535

Death of Rabelais's father, Antoine Rabelais, if not earlier

Rabelais's son Théodule born about this time(?)

(*Pantagruel* published by Saincte-Lucie in Lyons, '1535'; probably later in year)

13 January: *Affaire du 13 janvier*: rash repeat of *Placards* of 17/18 October 1534. Violent repressions. Many flee. All printing forbidden; restored (when?) by influence of Budé and the du Bellays

21 January: Great national act of expiation led by Francis I; du Bellays remain in favour. Heretics burned

February (or earlier): Widespread rumours that Charles V is to invade Tunis. Could *Gargantua* refer to this? If so, it is later than normally thought

– Rabelais abandons post in Hôtel-Dieu, Lyons. Definitively replaced, 5 March. (Rabelais in Maillezais? Grenoble?)

12 February: Guillaume du Bellay publishes 'Francis I's' letter to German states (dated 1 February)

Last Sunday in February (or a little later?): Béda's *amende honorable* before Notre-Dame; exiled to Mont-Saint-Michel

21 May: Jean du Bellay named cardinal

14 June: Charles V storms Goletta

22 June: John Fisher beheaded

23 June: Francis I invites Melanchthon to Paris (negotiations going on at least since early 1534). Jean and Guillaume du Bellay also write to Melanchthon

6 July: Thomas More beheaded

15 July: Jean du Bellay (and Rabelais?) leave for Rome

16 July: Edict of Coucy; prisoners released; religious exiles may return if heresy abjured

20 July: Charles V captures Tunis

31 July: Jean du Bellay and Rabelais arrive in Rome; pass through Ferrara; (meet Marot?). (Second edition of *Gargantua*, dated 1535, left with printers in Lyons?)

1535-36

10 December 1535–17 January 1536: Rabelais arranges papal absolution for his 'apostasy'. (Part of manoeuvre to turn him into a secular priest)

1536

11 February: Rabelais installed in Jean du Bellay's Benedictine abbey at Saint-Maur-les-Fossés; it is secularised, and Rabelais with it

February–April: French occupy Piedmont

March: Calvin's *Institutes*

31 May: Edict of Lyons suspends measures against moderate reformers; two years of comparative tolerance follow

12 July: Erasmus dies in Basle

21 July: Jean du Bellay appointed lieutenant-governor of Paris

17 August: Rabelais's name figures among canons of Saint-Maur

July–September: Charles V invades Provence. Ends in disaster

1537

8 January: Béda dies in exile (Mont-Saint-Michel)

(During this year, *Gargantua* and *Pantagruel* republished in Lyons by François Juste and in Paris by D. Janot)

February: Rabelais at banquet in Paris with Etienne Dolet, Budé, Marot, Danès, Macrin . . .

3 April: Rabelais, in Montpellier, from *bachelier* becomes *licencié* of Medicine (stage on way to doctorate)

22 May: Rabelais becomes Doctor of Medicine

June–September: Rabelais in Lyons?

10 August (1537?): Intercepted letter causes him difficulties with Cardinal de Tournon

End of August: Guillaume du Bellay passes through Lyons on way to govern Piedmont

18 October 1537 (St Luke's day) – 14 April 1538 (Palm Saturday): Rabelais lecturing at Montpellier on Hippocrates's *Prognostics*

1538

June–July: partial reconciliation of Francis I and Charles V; (June: Truce of Nice; July: interview of Aigues-Mortes. – Rabelais present: then goes to Lyons)

10 December: stiffening of French attitudes to 'heresy'; increased influence of Cardinal de Tournon: new edict supersedes tolerance of Edicts of Coucy and Lyons (1535)

1538–40

Rabelais in Lyons? Visit to Bordeaux (??). (Théodule Rabelais could date from this period)

1539

1 February: Treaty of Toledo (Charles V – Francis I)

24 June: Fresh stern measures decreed against heresy in France

(Summer: Rabelais in Montpellier)

1540

Rabelais's children François and Junie relieved of stigma of illegitimacy by papal curia

1 June: Edict of Fontainebleau. Parlement specifically charged with fighting heresy; Sorbonne has power only by delegation. From 6 June, judicial suppression of heresy leads to executions

10 December 1540 – Rabelais back in France (via Chambéry)

1540–42

Rabelais sometimes in Piedmont (Turin etc.) with Guillaume du Bellay

1541

May–November: Rabelais in Turin, returning to France in November (Guillaume du Bellay reports on Piedmont)

October: failure of Charles V's expedition against Algiers

1542

1 March: Rabelais at Château de Saint-Ayl (near Orleans) with Etienne Lorens (?)

April: Rabelais passes through Lyons en route for Turin with Guillaume du Bellay. (Does revised, expurgated, *Gargantua* and *Pantagruel*, printed by François Juste, date from this period?) Etienne Dolet brings out unrevised text. Pierre de Tours, successor to François Juste, protests

12 May: Rabelais arrives in Turin with Guillaume du Bellay

July: war breaks out between Charles V and Francis I

10 November: Guillaume du Bellay, ill, includes Rabelais amongst the beneficiaries of his will

December: Guillaume du Bellay, and Rabelais, leave Turin for France

1543

9 January: Guillaume du Bellay dies near Roanne (at Saint-Symphorien-de-Laye)

30 January–4 February: Rabelais, with Etienne Lorens, accompany body of Guillaume du Bellay to Le Mans

2 March: *Gargantua* and *Pantagruel* figure on list of censorable books drawn up by Sorbonne for Paris Parlement

5 March: Rabelais present (with Ronsard . . .) at burial of Guillaume du Bellay (Cathedral of Le Mans)

10 March: Sorbonne draws up normative statement of Catholic faith; (published 10 July with Royal approval)

30 May: Bishop Geoffroy d'Etissac (Rabelais's first patron) dies

1544

19 August: revised Sorbonne list of censorable books (including additions since 23 April 1543) sent to printers. Rabelais figures in it

18 September: Treaty of Crépy; Charles V and Francis I decide on concerted repression of heresy

December: on royal authority, twelve theologians, in Melun, proceed with systematic censoring of books

1545

8 January: François Bribart, secretary of Jean du Bellay, burned

5 April: five commissioners of Parlement charged with eradication of heresy in French provinces

18 April: Massacre of Vaudois (Cabrières, Mérindol)

28 June: Catalogue of censored books (after two years of delays) published by criers in Paris

1 July: Parlement requires Sorbonne to provide two theologians and two *Artiens* to visit bookshops, forbidding sale of books not approved by *visa*. (Private possession of such books forbidden)

19 September: Francis I provides royal *Privilège* for *Tiers Livre de Pantagruel* (signed by Delauney)

13 December: Council of Trent (scheduled to meet 15 March) finally assembles: only 34 delegates present

1546

(Before Easter: *Tiers Livre* printed by Christian Wechel (Paris). At least 3 other printings)

6 January: Tiraqueau obtains *Privilege* for third edition of *De legibus connubialibus*. All references to Rabelais left out

18 February: Luther dies

(About this time, Rabelais discreetly goes to Metz, perhaps on behalf of Jean du Bellay, perhaps out of prudence)

24 July: Council of Trent scheduled to meet in Bologna. (Put off)

3 August: Etienne Dolet burned, Place Maubert, Paris

August: Jean du Bellay named bishop of Le Mans

31 December: Expanded catalogue of books censored since 13 May 1544 published; it includes the *Tiers Livre*

1547

13 January: 6th session of Council of Trent: canons on justification, reformation . . .

28 January: Death of Henry VIII; Edward VI succeeds to throne with (31 January) Somerset as Lord Protector

11 March: Majority at Trent in favour of transfer of Council to Bologna. (Protestants hostile; so, too, are many Gallicans)

31 March/1 April: Death of Francis I. Succeeded by Henry II who immediately favours Montmorency against sterner orthodoxy of Cardinal de Tournon

21 April: 9th session of Council (at Bologna) prorogued

24 June: (Last?) payment to Rabelais in Metz? (Could be forgery)

27 July: After coronation of Henry II at Rheims, Jean du Bellay leaves for Rome

(Summer (?) Rabelais travels from Metz to Rome. Leaves 'partial' *Quart Livre* with Pierre de Tours in Lyons (?). Remains in Italy until 1549)

15 September: Jean du Bellay passes through Bologna (Council)

27 September: Jean du Bellay arrives in Rome (via Turin, Ferrara, Bologna). Could Rabelais be with him?

1548

18 June 1548: Rabelais cashes a bankers' order in Rome

May 1548: Ausberg Interim (chalice conceded to German laity, pending decisions by Council)

(During this year, two printings of 'partial' *Quart Livre*, P. de Tours, Lyons)

1549

3 February: Birth of Louis of Orleans, second son of Henry II

14 March: The festivities in Rome, described by Rabelais in *Sciomachie*

19 May: Christening of Louis of Orleans. (Does *Sciomachie*, where Christian name is left blank, date before this?)

13 September: Paul III prorogues Council in Bologna

22 September: Jean du Bellay leaves Rome (with Rabelais?) for France

10 November: death of Paul III

1550

8 February: Julius III elected Pope (1550–55)

August–October: Rabelais at Saint-Maur with Jean du Bellay (convalescent). Meets Cardinal Odet de Châtillon, who assures him of royal favour and his support

6 August: Royal *Privilège* for all Rabelais's works, granted in presence of Cardinal Odet de Châtillon

24 October: Death of baby Louis of Orleans

1551

January: Rabelais given two benefices: Meudon; Saint-Christophe-du-Jambet (Sarthe). He does not reside

11 October: 13th session of Council at Trent (on Eucharist)

25 November: 14th session of Council of Trent (penance; auricular confession – subjects of Rabelaisian amusement in *Quart Livre* of 1552)

1552

28 January: *Quart Livre* of 1552 printed by Fezandat in Paris; date of Liminary Epistle to Odet de Châtillon. (Fezandat also publishes revised *Tiers Livre*)

1 March: Paris Parlement condemns new *Quart Livre* at request of Sorbonne

8 April: Parlement forbids sale of *Quart Livre* pending royal decision

18 April: Triumphant entry of Henry II into Metz. (Fezandat reprints a signature of *Quart Livre* to refer to this or to German victories generally)

October: (Untrue) rumour that Rabelais is in prison

1553

9 January: Rabelais resigns his two benefices

9 April (?): Death of Rabelais. He is buried in St Paul's Church, Paris

1555

Death of Julius III (March). Succeeded by Paul IV (1555–59)

1556

Abdication of Charles V

1559

10 July: Henry II killed in tournament. Succeeded by Francis II

1560

2 February: Death of Francis II; Regency of Catherine de' Medici, Charles IX on throne

29 November: Reconvocation of Council of Trent

1561

Colloque de Poissy

1562

17 January: Edict of Saint-Germain formally recognises rights of protestants in France

March: Massacre of protestants at Vassy; start of wars of religion

(*L'Isle Sonante* dates from this year)

1563

Assassination of François de Guise

Peace of Amboise (end of first Huguenot War)

1564

4 May: Death of Calvin

(Publication of *Cinquiesme et dernier livre de Pantagruel*)

December: Cardinal de Châtillon flies to England

End of Council of Trent. Proclamation of *Index Librorum Prohibitorum* (including Rabelais's works among authors of the first class). (Decrees of Council *not* registered in France)

*

This chronology is mainly based, where Rabelais is concerned, on the *Chronologie* in the *Edition Critique*, (*Gargantua* p.cxxviii ff.), completed by that of V-L. Saulnier in his *Pantagruel* (*Club de Meilleur Livre*, Paris 1962). Of considerable value is the precise information in R. Marichal's introduction to the *Quart Livre de 1548* (*ER* IX, p.131f.) and his preface to *ER* XI.

Bibliography

1. The number of books devoted to Rabelais is large; the number of articles – some of them more important than the books – is very large. It would take a life-time of scholarly *otium* to read and judge them all. I have cut this list to a minimum, apologising to those many scholars whose work is not mentioned. The serious student will get on to such books and articles quickly enough, if he is keen: for other readers a large detailed bibliography is a work of supererogation.

A recent student guide to Rabelais is J. Larmat's *Rabelais* in the series *Connaissance des Lettres*, Paris 1973 (useful bibliography). A sound introduction is, still, P. Villey's study of Rabelais in *Marot et Rabelais*, Paris 1923, reprinted 1967.

More useful, in many ways, than books and articles on Rabelais himself are the wide-ranging studies of Renaissance problems by Dame Frances A. Yates or Professor D. P. Walker. Particularly useful is D. R. Kelley's *Foundations of Modern Historical Scholarship: Language, Law and History in the French Renaissance,* New York 1970.

2. Useful bibliographies are to be found in the various texts of Rabelais published in the *TLF* ('*Textes Littéraires Français*', Droz, Geneva): *Pantagruel,* ed. V. L. Saulnier; *Gargantua,* ed. R. M. Calder and M. A. Screech; *Le Tiers Livre,* ed. M. A. Screech; *Le Quart Livre* ed. R. Marichal; *La Pantagrueline Prognostication* (and the *Almanacs* for 1533, 1535, etc.), by M. A. Screech (with assistance). The bibliographies in those volumes cover not only the texts themselves but questions of biography, bibliography, language, religion, interpretation. To keep up to date, the reader should consult the standard bibliographies of French literature (listed for example in the *TLF Gargantua,* pp.441f.). A flourishing review, the *Etudes Rabelaisiennes* ('*ER*') appears frequently, containing both articles and whole books. These studies are often most helpful; to which may be added the numerous volumes of the *Travaux d'Humanisme et Renaissance* ('*THR*'), also published by Droz, Geneva.

3. Studies mentioned under the following headings are often of wider interest than their placing might suggest. The following works will help readers to find their way into some questions of Rabelais's scholarship: all contain bibliographies or footnotes which may lead the reader to many more studies of importance.

(a) CHAPTER ONE: HUMANIST COMEDY

— — On questions related to the Carnival element in literature, see *Les Plaisants Devis*, Paris 1834 (Bodley, Douce 7.359); F. J. E. Raby, *A History of Secular Latin*

Poetry in the Middle Ages, Oxford 1934, second edition, corrected, 1957 (1967); Joël Lefebvre, *Les Fols et La Folie: Etude sur les genres du comique et la création littéraire en Allemagne pendant la Renaissance*, Paris 1968 (very useful indeed); M. Baktine, *L'Oeuvre de François Rabelais et la culture populaire au moyen âge et sous la Renaissance*, Paris 1970; English translation, *Rabelais and his Work*, Massachusetts' Institute of Technology 1969 (written when the author was cut off from western studies – useful if treated with caution: Russian text, Moscow 1965). Cf. also *ER* XIII, 93f., on Court revels of 1533; N. Z. Davis, *Society and Culture in Early Modern France*, 1975, 97ff., for study of 'misrule'.

— — On questions of syncretism, see all works dealing with Rabelais's religious thought – for example my own study, *The Rabelaisian Marriage: Aspects of Rabelais's Religion, Ethics and Comic Philosophy*, London 1958 or *L'Evangélisme de Rabelais*, *ER* II.

— — On the influence of Lucian, etc., D. G. Coleman, *Rabelais: A Critical Study of Prose Fiction*, Cambridge 1971 (a very different Rabelais from the one presented here).

— — On Renaissance laughter, 'Some Renaissance attitudes to laughter', by M. A. Screech and R. M. Calder, in *Humanism in France*, Manchester 1970, pp.216–28. Also useful: E. Gilson, *Les Idées et les Lettres*, Paris 1932.

— — On the Adages of Erasmus: M. Mann Phillips, *The Adages of Erasmus*, Cambridge 1964 (also in paperback, abridged).

— — On Rabelais's language: The linguistic notes in the *Edition Critique*; L. Sainéan, *La Langue de Rabelais*, Paris 1922–3; P. Rickard, *La Langue Française du XVI's. Etude suivie de textes*, Cambridge 1968. F. Rigolot, *Les Languages de Rabelais*, Geneva 1972. The editions of Rabelais's works in the *TLF* series contain glossaries; useful explanations also in the Garnier edition (ed. Jourda) and the Pléiade edition (ed. Boulenger and Scheler).

— — For a highly personal philosophical view see M. de Diéguez, *Rabelais par lui-même*, Paris 1960. For another, less controversial, interpretation, see B. C. Bowen, *The Age of Bluff: Paradox and Ambiguity in Rabelais and Montaigne*, Illinois 1972.

— — On the popular literature which Rabelais was inspired by, consult M. Françon, *Les Croniques admirables du puissant roy Gargantua*, Rochecorbon 1956. J. Lewis is nearing completion of a University of London thesis on this subject (texts and study), which promises well.

— — On the 'mediaevalism' of Rabelais, consult J. Larmat, *Le Moyen-Age dans le 'Gargantua' de Rabelais*, Paris 1973.

(b) CHAPTER TWO: RABELAIS BEFORE PANTAGRUEL. The standard life of Rabelais is still J. Plattard's *Vie de Rabelais*, Paris-Brussels 1928. Consult also his *L'Adolescence de Rabelais et Poitou*, Paris 1923, and his *François Rabelais*, Paris 1932. Useful complements and precisions in articles by R. Marichal (which are always worth reading from this point of view) and in A. J. Krailsheimer, *Rabelais and the Franciscans*, Oxford 1963 – useful section on the death of Pan.

(c) CHAPTER THREE: PANTAGRUEL. More recent studies include G. Defaux, *Pantagruel et les Sophistes; Contribution à l'Histoire de l'Humanisme Chrétien au XVI's.*, The Hague 1973. Useful details in Lefranc's preface to *Edition Critique* – applies also to other volumes in the series, for other works of Rabelais.

(d) CHAPTER FOUR: ALMANACH POUR L'AN 1533. Details in *TLF* edition (1974). Also, C. Ginzberg, *Il Nicodemismo: Simulazione e dissimulazione religiosa nell'Europa del'500*, Turin 1970, especially pp.29ff. For scholarly precision on the vocabulary, consult F. Baldinger, *Beitrage zum Glossar der Pantagrueline Prognostication (Ag. Screech, TLF, 215, 1974)* in *ER* XIII, pp.183ff.

(e) CHAPTER FIVE: GARGANTUA. The studies of G. Defaux raise many questions. Important are the articles dealing with the episode of the *Cloches de Nostre-Dame* ('Le Prince, Rabelais, Les Cloches et l'Enigme: les dates de composition et de publication du *Gargantua*', in *Revue de l'Université d'Ottawa*, July–September, 1972, vol. 42, no. 3, pp.408f.; 'Rabelais et les cloches de Nostre-Dame', in *ER* IX, 1971, pp.1f.) R. Marichal strongly supports this interpretation (*ER* XI, 1974, preface; q.v. for other relevant studies). A very useful study (covering the end of *Gargantua*) is D. P. Walker's 'Esoteric symbolism', in *Studies in Honor of J. Hutton*, 1975. A study which students might miss, as it is not in the 'obvious' reviews is H. D. Saffrey's, ' "Cy n'entrez pas, Hypocrites": Thélème, une nouvelle Academie?', in *Revue des Sciences Philosophiques et Théologiques*, LV, no. 4, October 1971, pp.593f. For the *Affaire des Placards* and the *Affaire du 13 janvier* consult G. Berthoud, *Antoine Marcourt, Réformateur et Pamphlétaire*, THR 129, Geneva 1973.

(f) CHAPTER SIX: LE TIERS LIVRE. Useful is R. Antonioli's *Rabelais et la Médicine*, *ER* XII, Geneva 1976. Judging from an excellent talk given in the Warburg Institute, with which I found myself largely in agreement, also most useful will be J. Céard's *La Nature et les Prodiges*, now printing, Droz, Geneva (*THR* 158). On Renaissance scepticism, with many references, there is Ch. B. Schmitt's 'The recovery and assimilation of ancient scepticism in the Renaissance', in *La Rivista Critica di Storia della Filosofia* IV, 1972, pp.363f. On divine, charismatic, Platonico-Christian prophetic folly, see Screech, *Ecstasy and the Praise of Folly*, London 1980.

(g) CHAPTER SEVEN: THE QUART LIVRE OF 1548. Indispensable is R. Marichal, 'Rabelais et les censures de la Sorbonne', with facsimile of text, in *ER* IX, 1971, pp. 135f.; also J. Plattard's edition of the *Quart Livre Partielle*.

(h) CHAPTER EIGHT: THE SCIOMACHIE OF 1549. R. Cooper is now preparing an edition and study of this work for Droz, Geneva. Meanwhile, consult his Oxford Ph.D. thesis, *Rabelais and Italy: with special reference to the du Bellay household*, type-script, 1975, which gives text, study and very useful notes.

(i) CHAPTER NINE: THE QUART LIVRE OF 1552. R. Marichal, 'Quart Livre: Commentaires', in *ER* V, 1964, pp.65f.

— — On the role of Bacchus, see T. C. Cave, 'The triumph of Bacchus and its interpretation in the French Renaissance' (à propos of Ronsard's *Hinne de Bacus*, but of wider interest), in *Humanism in France*, Manchester 1970, pp.249f.; and, for a more directly relevant view, F. M. Weinberg, *The Wine and the Will: Rabelais's Bacchic Christianity*, Detroit 1972. (For the theme of the winged Bacchus see *Journal of Warburg and Courtauld Institutes*, 1980.)

—— For aspects of Rabelais's debt to Plato, see F. Rigolot, 'Cratylisme et Pantagruelisme: Rabelais et le statut du signe', in *ER* XIII, 1976, pp.115f.

—— On Orpheus and on the Prisca Theologia generally, consult D. P. Walker, *The Ancient Theology: Studies in Christian Platonism from the Fifteenth to the Eighteenth Century*, London 1972.

—— On certain questions of discourse and knowledge, see F. Bacon, *'The Advancement of Learning' and 'The New Atlantis'*, ed. A. Johnston, Oxford 1974; L Jardine, *Francis Bacon: Discovery and the Art of Discourse*, Cambridge 1974, and her valuable article, 'The place of dialectic teaching in sixteenth-century Cambridge', in *Studies in the Renaissance* XXI, 1974, pp.31f.

—— For the Gallican crisis of 1551, consult L. Romier, 'La crise Gallicane de 1551', in *Revue Historique* 108 and 109 (essential reading).

Index

Index of Biblical Passages

General Index

This index is intended to supplement the table of contents. It does not contain entries for Rabelais's life, Chronicles or characters. For such matters the reader is referred to the various headings of the table.